The UTAH GUIDE

THIRD EDITION

ALLAN KENT POWELL

Fulcrum Publishing
Golden, Colorado

The information in *The Utah Guide, Third Edition,* is accurate as of January 2003. However, prices, hours of operation, addresses, phone numbers, websites, and other items change rapidly. If something in the book is incorrect, please write to the author in care of Fulcrum Publishing, 16100 Table Mountain Parkway, Suite 300, Golden, Colorado 80403; fulcrum@fulcrum-books.com.

The Utah Guide provides many safety tips about weather and travel, but good decision-making and sound judgment are the responsibility of the individual. Neither the publisher nor the author assumes any liability for injury that may arise from the use of this book.

ISBN 1-55591-114-5
ISSN 1543-365X

Printed in the United States of America
0 9 8 7 6 5 4 3 2 1

Project manager: Daniel Forrest-Bank
Editorial: Kris Fulsaas, Alison Auch
Design: Trina Stahl
Photograph signatures design: Nancy Duncan-Cashman
Photograph of Topaz Japanese Relocation Camp in World War II (page 12, second photo signature), courtesy of the Utah State Historical Society.
Maps: Fulcrum Publishing; Salt Lake City map by Marge Mueller, Gray Mouse Graphics
Cover photograph: Indian paintbrush, Arches National Park, Utah, copyright © Tom Till.

Fulcrum Publishing
16100 Table Mountain Parkway, Suite 300
Golden, Colorado 80403
(800) 992-2908 • (303) 277-1623
www.fulcrum-books.com

Contents

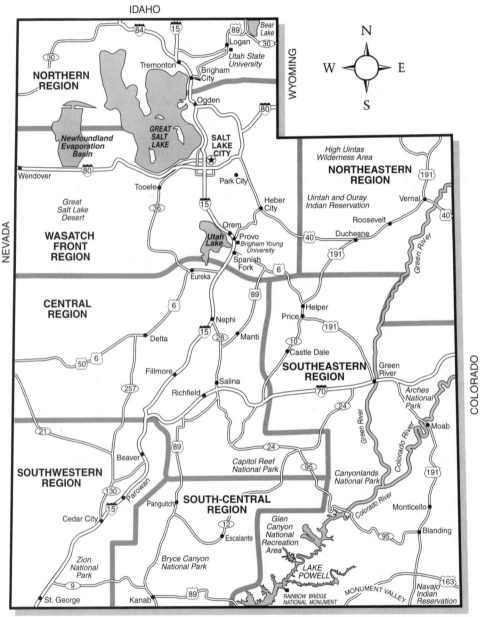

Acknowledgments

My parents, Leland and Luella Powell, instilled in me a deep love for Utah. Both contributed in important ways to my view of Utah and its people. My father, who spent many years traveling the state, knew it as well as anyone of his generation and is my bridge between the past and the present. My mother helped me see that people are at the heart of any endeavor.

This guidebook is really a Powell family production. My wife, Brenda, has been an enthusiastic supporter, adventuresome and good-natured travel companion and unabashed promoter of *The Utah Guide*. Our three children, Lee, Liesel and Adrianna, and their respective spouses, Julie, Spencer and Lance, have also had a hand in the project, providing their own perspectives of what is important and worth including in the book. Having the opportunity to involve them made the project all the more rewarding and worthwhile. I appreciate their enthusiasm, their help and their patience.

Bob Baron and the staff at Fulcrum Publishing deserve special thanks. I appreciate Bob asking me to write *The Utah Guide*; I especially appreciate his good advice to simply have fun researching and writing the guidebook. Daniel Forrest-Bank has been a knowledgeable, professional, supportive and easy-to-work-with project manager. Kris Fulsaas did an outstanding job as copy editor, offering valuable suggestions for new information to be included and effective ways to organize and present the material.

It is impossible to list the hundreds of people who have provided information, read chapters, shared secrets about their favorite places and guided me as I learned more about this special state. I am indebted especially to regional and local travel directors; to staffs of the National Park Service, U.S. Forest Service and Bureau of Land Management; to city, county and state employees throughout Utah; and to the owners, managers and staffs of the hundreds of businesses and facilities who made my work in compiling this guidebook so easy and enjoyable. To each of you, I extend my heartfelt thanks.

Introduction

This Is Utah

In 1846, a year before the first Mormon pioneers arrived in Utah, a visitor from Switzerland en route to California named Heinrich Lienhard stopped at the Great Salt Lake after a laborious and difficult wagon journey through the Rocky Mountains. In one of the first written descriptions of the land now known as Utah, the 24-year-old Lienhard captured the essence of what is still the Utah experience for visitors and residents alike: "The clear, sky-blue water, the warm sunny air, the nearby high mountains … made an unusually friendly impression. I could have whistled and sung the entire day."

More than 150 years after Lienhard's visit to Utah, this place and its 2 million people still make a good impression. The scenery is as beautiful and varied as you will find anywhere. As the 15 million annual visitors to Utah will attest, it offers something for everyone. Within a few hours' drive, you can find 12,000-foot mountain ranges with alpine forests, meadows, lakes, streams, ski slopes and hiking trails. Monuments of stone cut and shaped by the forces of nature have been left in the galleries of an outdoor museum laid out over thousands of square miles of deserts, plateaus and canyons. The Wasatch Front mountain range, which includes the greater Salt Lake City area, offers a wealth of cultural, educational and recreational opportunities.

For the last several years, much of my spare time has been spent researching, writing and revising this guidebook. In working on this task, I have tried to describe and explain things as if I were writing for my personal friends. By looking at Utah with an eye to sharing it with others, I have seen it in even more varied and exciting ways than in the past. My love and appreciation for Utah have grown in ways I had not anticipated when the project was first proposed. I have met hundreds of people who also love the state and love to share it with others.

The third edition of *The Utah Guide* includes several major changes from previous editions. Major revisions have been made in describing new places to eat and to stay. For the first time, color photographs are included inside the book, and the number of photographs has been greatly increased. The updated maps, including a new map of Salt Lake City (see page xvi), provide better reference to the hundreds of places mentioned in the guide and easier directions on how to get to them. Websites are also included; readers will find a wealth of information at these websites that is impossible to include within the printed pages of any book.

New recreation opportunities have developed, especially with the developments surrounding Utah's newest national monument—the Grand Staircase–Escalante National Monument. New museums have opened and others have relocated to larger facilities. Heritage tourism has expanded throughout the rural areas of the state to enhance travelers' experience. The 2002 Salt Lake City Winter Olympics has left a legacy of great winter sport facilities and a worldwide recognition of Utahns' friendliness, competence and volunteer spirit.

Whether you are a longtime resident or are preparing to spend your first day in Utah, you will find that history, scenery, activities and people are the basic ingredients of your Utah experience. I hope this book helps add a measure of enjoyment and understanding to that experience.

History

The human habitation of what is now called Utah stretches back at least 12,000 years to a people archaeologists call the Paleo-Indians, which included the Clovis and Folsom cultures. These people, who appeared after North America's last ice age, were essentially hunters of large game. As the Paleo-Indians began to gather plants and seeds to supplement their diet, they moved into what is known as the Archaic stage, a period that lasted from about 7,000 to 1,500 years ago. Two cultures, the Anasazi and the Fremont, began to plant corn and squash crops and to raise animals, such as turkeys, for food. They left behind an abundant treasure of rock art, artifacts and structures. The Anasazi culture existed in southern and southeastern Utah from 2,000 until 700 years ago. The Fremont culture was roughly contemporaneous, beginning about 1,500 years ago and located to the north and west of the Anasazi. Like the Anasazi, the Fremont culture disappeared about A.D. 1300, although it is uncertain whether the Fremont people were absorbed by the Ute and Shoshoni Indians who wandered into what is now the state of Utah in search of game. The Anasazi moved southeast into the area that is now New Mexico and Arizona, as an apparent combination of long-term drought and incoming Navajo and Ute Indians forced them to leave.

The first known European to enter what is now Utah was Juan Maria Antonio de Rivera, a Spaniard who journeyed northwest from Abiquiu, New Mexico, and reached the Colorado River at present-day Moab in the fall of 1765. Eleven years later, in 1776, an expedition led by two Franciscan friars, Francisco Atanasio Dominguez and Silvestre Velez de Escalante, left Santa Fe, New Mexico, in search of an overland route to Monterey, California. Forced to swing far to the north because of the impassable canyons of northern New Mexico and southern Utah, the group entered Utah from Colorado near the present route of US Hwy. 40 and continued westward to Utah Valley, where they encountered friendly Ute Indians who seemed anxious for them to return and establish a Catholic mission. Early snows blocked the route to California, and the expedition returned to Santa Fe after an arduous journey through the rugged canyons of southern Utah. The expedition left a fascinating diary of its travels that has provided historians and anthropologists with a wealth of information.

Traders traveled into Utah from New Mexico until well into the next century. In the early 1800s, Utah became the focus of fur trappers. From New Mexico, men who reached Santa Fe after the Mexican Revolution in 1820, including Etienne Provost and Antoine Robidoux, brought both a French-Canadian and a Mexican influence. From Canada, Peter Skene Ogden represented the British Hudson's Bay Company in search of pelts. The beaver population was already declining by the time American trappers such as Jedediah Smith, William Ashley and James Bridger, coming from St. Louis, Missouri, could claim Utah for American interests. Trappers of all three countries met in Utah in 1825, leaving a legacy of adventure tales and place names that still stir the imagination.

The Mormon pioneers reached the Salt Lake Valley on July 24, 1847. Their arrival followed a remarkable series of events that began in western New York State in 1820, when Joseph Smith, caught up in the fervor of religious revivals that swept the region, prayed for guidance about which church he should join. According to Smith, God and his son, Jesus Christ, appeared to him, telling the young boy not to join any existing church; instead, through him, the pristine Church of Christ would be restored. In subsequent visitations, he was instructed where to find inscribed golden plates that provided an account of early Christians in the Americas and recounted a visit by Jesus Christ to the American continent following his crucifixion and resurrection. The new scripture was translated by Joseph Smith and published as the Book of Mormon in 1830. That year Joseph Smith also established the Church of Jesus Christ of Latter-day Saints, which was based on the Bible, the Book of Mormon and the doctrine that Joseph Smith and subsequent leaders of the church were prophets chosen by God to provide ongoing revelations for the church. The nickname "Mormons" was quickly applied to members of the church, and while it is not an official name, it is recognized and used by Mormons and non-Mormons alike. "LDS" is also a popular short form for the Church of Jesus Christ of Latter-day Saints.

Under Smith's charismatic leadership and an aggressive missionary program, the church grew rapidly and moved from its New York location first to Kirtland, Ohio, then Missouri. Conflicts developed with neighbors in each location, and Mormons were forced to leave Missouri. Then, after Joseph Smith was assassinated by a mob in Nauvoo, Illinois, in 1844, Brigham Young organized the exodus that brought Mormons to Utah in 1847.

Young had a vision of the region as a beehive of industry and activity, thus explaining Utah's nickname as the Beehive State. The Mormon leader used the beehive image in his choice of the word "Deseret" as the name for the provisional state. "Deseret" is a Book of Mormon word that means "honeybee." You will see the bee, the beehive and the word "Deseret" used on highway road signs and historic markers; even the name of Salt Lake City's baseball team, the Stingers, traces its roots back to the pioneer symbol. The word "Deseret" is still used in names and titles in everything from newspapers to banks and livestock companies.

One of the attractions of Utah was that it was not inhabited by other Americans, and under Brigham Young's leadership, more than 300 settlements were made throughout Utah and much of Idaho, Wyoming, Arizona and Nevada. A number of these settlements, such as Nephi, Lehi, Manti and Moroni, took their names from places and individuals in the Book of Mormon. Others, such as Brigham City, Heber City and St. George are named for early Mormon leaders. These settlements were populated by an influx of Mormon converts from the East, Great Britain and the Scandinavian countries, as well as through the practice of polygamy instituted by Joseph Smith in Illinois. Young's dream of statehood for Deseret, which would have included all of Utah and Nevada, southwestern Wyoming, western Colorado, northwestern New Mexico, the northern two-thirds of Arizona and southern

California, including San Diego, did not come to pass. Politicians in Washington, D.C., burst the bubble of the unrealistic dream and created the Utah Territory as part of the Compromise of 1850. The name "Deseret" was dropped, but the boundaries of the Utah Territory, a name taken from the Ute Indians, still included all of Utah, most of Nevada, western Colorado and southwestern Wyoming. By 1868 Utah was reduced to its present size.

Abhorrence of polygamy and the conviction that the Mormon authoritarian system clashed with the American ideals of democracy led to nearly a half century of conflict and contention between Mormons and both mainstream America and the federal government. A federal army was sent to Utah in 1857 and 1861, and federal laws were passed that greatly curtailed the activities and businesses of the Mormon church. Utah was denied statehood until 1896. Statehood came after the church agreed in 1890 to abandon the practice of polygamy (although not all residents of Utah did so—an underground polygamy movement continues) and to disband its church-directed political party in favor of participation with the national political parties.

Mormons, who saw all Native Americans (including the Shoshoni, Utes, Paiutes, Goshutes and Navajo in Utah) as descendants of the ancient people who left the Book of Mormon, undertook measures to convert and control the area's Native Americans. Despite generally good relations, conflicts broke out in the 1850s and 1860s. The first, known as the Walker War, occurred in 1853–1854 and is named for the Ute leader Wakara or "Walker." As Mormons moved onto Indian hunting lands and disrupted traditional trading practices, Wakara and his followers retaliated with raids on Mormon settlements, resulting in the deaths of about 20 settlers and many more Indians. A second war, known as the Black Hawk War, began in 1865 and lasted until 1868. A much longer and more extensive war, the conflict led to the abandonment of many Mormon settlements in Utah, the construction of forts for protection, raids on Mormon villages and the pursuit of Black Hawk and his followers across the mountains and deserts of much of southern and central Utah. At the conclusion of the war, all Utes were forced to relocate to the Uintah Reservation in eastern Utah, which they still inhabit. Also during the 1860s the Shoshoni and Navajo suffered greatly at the hands of American soldiers. In January 1863 Col. Patrick Connor led a force of 200 soldiers north from Ft. Douglas in Salt Lake City to the junction of Beaver Creek and Bear River in Cache Valley. Here, in an early morning attack on a Shoshoni village, they killed more than 250 Shoshoni, including nearly a hundred women and children. The battle turned into a massacre after the Indians ran out of ammunition and could no longer defend themselves. At the same time, in the southeastern corner of the territory in what would become known as the Four Corners area, Gen. James Carlton hired Kit Carson to round up the Navajos and relocate them to a new reservation at Ft. Sumner in eastern New Mexico. Using scorched-earth tactics to destroy flocks, orchards, fields and homes, they captured more than 8,000 Navajos and forced them to make the "Long Walk" to Bosque Redondo. However, some Navajos escaped Carson and his men by moving north across the San Juan River into the canyons and mountains of southeastern Utah. In 1868 those held at Bosque Redondo were allowed to return to their homeland, although at least 3,000 had perished during the ordeal. The Indian wars eventually led to the placement of Utah Indians on reservations by the U.S. government.

Other individuals and forces also had a significant impact on Utah. Prospectors discovered rich mineral deposits, and mining boomtowns sprang up all over the state. The completion of the transcontinental railroad at Promontory Summit on May 10, 1869, not only had a tremendous impact on Utah but on the rest of the nation as well. That same year Maj. John Wesley Powell made his first voyage down the Green and Colorado Rivers and initiated an era of

water reclamation and recreation that continues to this day, crowned with the creation of Lake Powell and Flaming Gorge Reservoir in the 1960s. By the turn of the last century, the railroads, coal mines and copper mines of Utah were drawing non-Mormon immigrants from southern and eastern Europe, creating a much more diverse population.

With the removal of polygamy from church doctrine and the granting of statehood, Utah seemed to abandon its peculiar course and to become more integrated with the rest of the United States. Utahns rushed off to fight in the Spanish-American War and World War I; they feared that communists and their agents were deceiving fellow citizens; Utahns consumed illegal alcohol during the Prohibition Era; and they suffered as much as the rest of the country during the Great Depression.

World War II brought about the expansion of military installations in Utah and left a defense industry that continues to be an important part of the state's economy. A large area of the western part of the state is restricted to public access because of its use by the military. An even larger area of Utah would have been off-limits if the MX project proposed in the late 1970s had been built; it would have deployed more than 200 missiles that could have been moved secretly into 4,600 shelters on a circular railroad track, in a sort of gigantic shell game. The postwar period experienced a boom in recreation and tourism, which continues to focus on the ski industry and travel to Utah's national parks and monuments, historic sites, wilderness areas and wild rivers.

Utah entered a new era in 1995 with the selection of Salt Lake City to host the 2002 Winter Olympic Games. The effort to land the Games had begun decades earlier, after the first Winter Olympic Games were held in 1924 in Chamonix, France. Just five years after, in 1929, the Utah Ski Club submitted a bid for the 1932 Games, which went to Lake Placid, New York.

Utah's first serious effort came much later, for the 1972 Olympics, which were won by

Sapporo, Japan, over Salt Lake City as well as Banff, Canada, and Lahti, Finland. In 1976 the Winter Games were awarded to neighboring Colorado, but the offer was rescinded when voters refused to use public money for the Games. Salt Lake City offered to pick up the spurned bid, but instead the Games went to Innsbruck, Austria. In 1992 and 1994 Salt Lake City lost out to Anchorage, Alaska, as the United States' choice to bid for the Games, but for 1998 Salt Lake City was back in the running and local officials were convinced that the long-sought bid would be given to Utah. Instead, it went to Nagano, Japan. The loss may have come because the 1996 Summer Olympic Games were awarded to another U.S. city—Atlanta. But others argued forcefully that Nagano had been more adept at wining and dining the International Olympic Committee (IOC).

Learning their lesson from the Nagano and previous defeats, Salt Lake Olympic Committee (SLOC) organizers Tom Welch and Dave Johnson, knowing that Salt Lake City was the odds-on favorite to win the 2002 bid, made sure that whatever the IOC members wanted, or were suspected of wanting, was provided. Scholarships, ski trips, shopping sprees, surgery, rifles, jobs, attractive real estate deals, donations to political campaigns and much more were all part of the price that SLOC organizers were willing to pay for the Games. In late 1998 news of the "bribes" was leaked to the media and soon the "Salt Lake Olympic Bid Scandal" made headlines around the world. Welch and Johnson were forced to resign and indicted by federal authorities. The IOC was forced to reorganize and face revelations that their conduct seemed to violate the basic principles of the Olympic Games. The scandal threatened to cast a dark shadow over the 2002 Games. However, as time moved on and revelations surfaced about similar practices by other cities to win Olympic bids, the scandal lost its sting. In 2001 a federal judge dismissed the charges against Welch and Johnson, and in the aftermath of the terrorist attack on September 11, 2001, the Winter Games offered a way to recapture part of the world's lost innocence and optimism by joining together in the celebration of sports. During and in the aftermath of the Olympics, Utah won high praise for the excellent organization and conduct of the games, but above all for the enthusiasm, hospitality and friendliness of the thousands of volunteers who welcomed the world to Utah.

Today Utah remains an interesting and diverse state. It is still the headquarters for the worldwide Church of Jesus Christ of Latter-day Saints, and the Mormon religion does affect much of what happens in Utah and the attitudes that shape key decisions. But Utah has also tied its future to high-tech industry and recreation and tourism, and the legacy of the 2002 Winter Olympic Games is expected to shape the next decades in ways that Utah's pioneers could hardly have imagined.

Suggested Reading

Dean L. May's *Utah: A People's History* (University of Utah Press, 1987) is a well-written, nicely illustrated 200-page history of Utah that provides an excellent overview of the state's history from prehistoric times to the 1980s. A more recent and more comprehensive volume is Thomas G. Alexander's *Utah: The Right Place,* published in 1995 as part of Utah's Statehood Centennial Commemoration. Edward Geary's *Goodbye to Poplar Haven* and *The Proper Edge of the Sky* (University of Utah Press, 1985 and 1992) are two remarkable books that get to the heart of the Utah experience. The first is a collection of stories from his and my small hometown of Huntington; the second examines, through history, travel narrative and personal essay, Utah's high plateau country. *The Story of the Latter-day Saints* (Deseret Books, 1992), by Mormon historians James B. Allen and Glen M. Leonard, is the most comprehensive one-volume chronological history of the LDS church. For detailed histories of each of Utah's 29 counties, consider the volumes of the Utah Centennial County History Series published by the Utah State Historical Society.

Geography and Geology

Utah's 84,916 square miles make it the 11th-largest state in the United States. The state has one of the largest elevation differentials in the nation—Beaver Dam Wash, in the extreme southwestern corner of the state, is the lowest point at 2,350 feet and Kings Peak, in the northeastern part of the state, is the highest at 13,528 feet. Kings Peak is one of 24 peaks in the Uinta Mountains with an elevation greater than 13,000 feet. Although the Uintas are Utah's highest mountains—and there are three other mountain ranges with peaks over 12,000 feet: the La Sals, Deep Creeks and Tushars—it is the Wasatch Mountains where all the world-famous ski resorts are located. The tallest mountain in the Wasatch Range is Mt. Nebo, at 11,877 feet.

Three major physiographic provinces are found within the state. The Rocky Mountain province is the smallest and consists of the Wasatch and Uinta Mountains. The Great Basin includes most of the western half of the state. Named by John C. Frémont in the 1840s, the Great Basin has no outlet to the sea, and much of the Utah portion was beneath the waters of ancient Lake Bonneville, which covered roughly the western two-thirds of Utah until about 12,000 years ago. The eastern half and extreme southern part of Utah is on the Colorado Plateau. All the rivers and streams on the Colorado Plateau eventually drain into the Colorado River, which makes its way to the Gulf of California and thence to the Pacific Ocean. The Colorado Plateau has some of the most spectacular scenery in the world. Five national parks, four national monuments, Lake Powell, the Glen Canyon National Recreation Area (including Lake Powell), several wilderness areas, wild and scenic rivers, the northern portion of the Navajo Indian Reservation and smaller Indian reservations are located within Utah's Plateau country.

The geologic history of Utah can be summed up in four words: diverse, complex, spectacular and ongoing. Geologists have identified more than 600 rock units, which they have consolidated into eight phases, to tell Utah's geological story.

The first phase (3,000 million to 1,000 million years ago), the basement for Utah's geologic structure, saw the formation of metamorphic rocks by extreme heat and pressure.

During the second phase (1,000 million to 360 million years ago), warm, shallow-water conditions deposited thick accumulations of sediments. These gray limestone rocks contain many fossils, such as trilobites, that record the habitat and life in these seas.

During the third phase (360 million to 250 million years ago), sedimentary rocks continued to be deposited at varying thicknesses. This phase also saw the sinking of the Paradox Basin in the Four Corners area and the uplift of the Uncompahgre Highland north of the Basin. Contemporary with the Paradox Basin was the Oquirrh Basin, in which shallow sea deposits formed layers of sandstone, shale and limestone as much as 3 miles thick.

During the fourth phase (250 million to 100 million years ago), warm seas and extensive sand dunes filled deserts that developed during Sahara-like conditions. These deposits became the colorful conglomerates, shales and sandstones found in southern Utah's national parks. Rocks of this phase also contain dinosaur remains and uranium deposits.

The fifth phase (100 million to 60 million years ago) occurred when the North American continental plate collided with the Pacific oceanic plate, just off present-day California. The impact caused reverberations in the earth's crust and produced the series of mountain ranges that stretch across the Great Basin like an accordion. To the east, extensive swamps were covered over time by sedimentary rocks that hardened to produce Utah's rich coal deposits.

During the sixth phase (60 million to 37 million years ago), the uplifts that created the Uinta Mountains, San Rafael Swell, Waterpocket Fold and Circle Cliffs anticline occurred, as a result of the creation of the Rocky Mountains.

The seventh phase (37 million to 15 million years ago) was a period of tremendous volcanic activity, the evidence of which is most visible in the high areas of central and southwestern Utah. Some of the heated rock was not spewn from the ground but congealed with mineral-bearing fluids to form the ore-bearing rock that was extracted at Alta, Park City and Bingham Canyon. In southeastern Utah the Henry, Blue and La Sal Mountains were formed.

The eighth and last phase (15 million years ago to the present) saw most of the western North American continent lifted to its present elevation and tremendous erosion forces unleashed that carved the spectacular canyons of the Colorado Plateau. In many of the mountain ranges, glaciers cut canyons such as Little Cottonwood Canyon, in which the ski resorts of Alta and Snowbird are located. In the western half of Utah the mountain ranges appeared like chains of islands amid Lake Bonneville, which, at its crest approximately 25,000 years ago, stretched over more than 20,000 square miles and reached a depth of more than 1,000 feet. About 15,000 years ago, the lake spilled over into the Snake River. The remnant of the lake evaporated, leaving Utah's geological marvel, the Great Salt Lake.

Suggested Reading

These books offer more information on the geology and geography of *Utah: Geologic History of Utah* (Brigham Young University Press, 1988) by Lehi F. Hintze; *Geology of Utah* (Utah Museum of Natural History, 1986) by William Lee Stokes; *Roadside Geology of Utah* (Mountain Press Publishing, 1990) by Halka Chronic; and *Utah Atlas* (Brigham Young University Press, 1981) by Wayne Walquist et al.

Flora and Fauna

Utah's deserts, benchlands, mountains and the marshlands around Great Salt Lake provide a diverse habitat for a wide range of plant and animal life. Mountain wildflowers are especially beautiful in the late spring and early summer, with some lasting until fall when the autumn leaves make scenic drives and mountain hikes an unforgettable experience.

Wildlife observation areas have been noted in the Seeing and Doing sections throughout this book. Deer, elk and moose are found throughout the state and are often seen from the road—and too often, especially at night, can become traffic hazards and fatalities when struck by oncoming trucks and cars. Bears and mountain lions or cougars prowl the mountains and backcountry. Free-roaming buffalo herds can be found on Antelope Island in Great Salt Lake and in the Henry Mountain area in south-central Utah. Hawks and eagles soar majestically over the mountains and deserts of the state, and the marshlands around Great Salt Lake are home to several refuges frequented by more than 200 species of migrating and nonmigrating birds.

The state bird, the California seagull, is an odd choice for a landlocked state. However, the bird won the eternal respect of Utahns when huge flocks of them flew to the rescue of Mormon pioneers shortly after the settlers arrived in the Salt Lake Valley. After crops were planted and showed signs of promise, hordes of crickets swarmed out of the mountains and began devouring the crops. As if by a miracle, the seagulls descended from the skies to gorge themselves on the crickets and thus saved the precious crops. Mormon crickets and swarms of grass-hoppers still make their appearance in a few parts of the state from time to time, but no miracle of the seagulls has been repeated in these more recent occurrences.

The reservoirs, lakes, and streams of Utah are well stocked with trout, and kokanee salmon can be found at some locations. Flaming Gorge Reservoir is home to the largest trophy-sized lake trout. Bear Lake is known for the Bonneville cisco, a 7-inch-long fish that spawns in late January. Lake Powell is popular for bass fishing.

The Utah Division of Wildlife Resources is the wildlife authority for the state. It has a number of programs to promote the protection and enjoyment of wildlife and works closely with other state and federal agencies. The division has an extensive education program. Call or write the **Utah Division of Wildlife Resources, 1596 W. North Temple, Salt Lake City, UT 84116; 801-596-8660.**

Suggested Reading

Utah Wildlife Viewing Guide (Falcon Press, 1990) by Jim Cole, a wildlife biologist with the Wasatch-Cache National Forest, is a handy and inexpensive guide to some of the best and most easily accessible wildlife viewing sites in Utah.

Climate

The mountains and deserts are responsible for a wonderful variety in Utah's climate. You can be skiing in a snowstorm in the mountains above Salt Lake City and the next hour be on the first tee at one of the valley golf courses in a light sweater, ready for a pleasant round of golf. Generally the ski season runs mid-Nov.–Apr., although the ski season often ends before the snow does! The Utah Department of Transportation keeps the roads to the ski areas plowed and sanded, but there are usually several days during the year when the roads are closed due to avalanches or avalanche danger. Because automobile travel throughout Utah usually involves going over high mountain passes, it is always a good idea to check on road conditions; **801-964-6000.**

Utah weather patterns are tricky, and snowstorms do not always cover the entire state. Often while northern Utah is being covered by snow out of the Pacific Northwest, southern Utah is enjoying sunny skies. Occasionally storms will move in from southern California to inundate the southern part of the state while the northern half remains dry.

Utah temperatures are quite mild, especially compared to the cold extremes in Wyoming and Montana to the north or the searing summer heat in Arizona to the south and Nevada to the west. Areas of the state do get very hot, however,

especially the St. George area, the Mojave Desert, the southern Utah canyons and the deserts of the Great Basin. In the Salt Lake Valley, winter daytime temperatures are usually between 20° F and 45° F, with nighttime temperatures dropping into the single digits and below zero for some nights but usually in the teens and twenties. In the summer, temperatures reach above 100° F, but the humidity is usually very low, making the heat much more tolerable than in moister climates. Summer evening temperatures are usually in the 60s and 70s. The St. George area within the Mojave Desert in extreme southwestern Utah is known for its mild winter temperatures and is a favorite destination of "snowbirds." The summer temperatures, however, can soar well above 100° F, making air-conditioned buildings and cars a must.

During the summer months, afternoon thunderstorms can develop quite unexpectedly, especially over the mountains, so be prepared. The thin mountain air causes temperatures to cool off considerably at night, so if you are going to be in the mountains after dark, be sure to have a coat or warm sweater. Whether hiking the mountain trails or boating on the many reservoirs in the summer, skiing the well-groomed slopes in the winter or sightseeing in the state and national parks, you will get plenty of exposure to sun, so be prepared with hats, sunscreen and lots of drinking water.

For state weather information, visit "The Weather Channel" website; **www.weather. com/weather/us/cities/UT.**

Suggested Reading

Dan Pope and Clayton Brough, weathermen for Salt Lake City's Channel 4, have edited a popular volume, *Utah's Weather and Climate* (Publishers Press, 1996), which includes chapters on major weather events from 1847 to 1996, monthly climatic data for more than 50 Utah locations and daily climatic data for Salt Lake City and St. George.

Visitor Information

General Information

In Salt Lake City, visit the Utah Travel Council, located in historic Council Hall, across the street from the State Capitol. You may also write or call for information; **Utah Travel Council, Council Hall/Capitol Hill, Salt Lake City, UT 84114-7420; 801-538-1030; www.utah. com.** One of the council's best publications is its annual "Utah Travel Guide," which is available at no cost. The council also sponsors welcome centers on Interstate 15 near the Utah-Arizona border outside St. George; in northern Utah on I-15 near Brigham City; along I-70 at Thompson near the Colorado-Utah border; near Echo Junction on I-80; and in Vernal on US Hwy. 40. Multi-agency visitor centers are located in Ogden, Hanksville, Moab, Monticello and Escalante. In Salt Lake City the **Visitors and Convention Bureau** in the Salt Palace complex on **W. Temple and 100 S.** is an excellent source of information. The bureau also operates a center at the Salt Lake International Airport.

Most counties and major communities have travel and tourism offices. These have been noted in the Services section at the end of each chapter. A number have established useful websites, which are also indicated. Most offices are part of a network of nine travel regions funded with local room taxes and some money from the Utah Travel Council. Each region has its own travel office with full-time staff and is an excellent source of information for its particular area. The nine regions are:

1. **Bridgerland, 160 N. Main, Logan, UT 84321; 1-800-882-4433; 435-752-2161.**

2. **Canyonlands, Moab Information Center**, corner of Center and Main Sts., **Moab, UT 84532; 1-800-635-6622; 435-259-8825;** and **San Juan County Tourism Office, 117 S. Main, P.O. Box 490, Monticello, UT 84535; 1-800-574-4386; 435-587-3235.**

3. **Castle Country, 625 E. 100 N., P.O. Box 1037, Price, UT 84501; 1-800-842-0789; 435-637-3009.**

4. **Color Country, 906 N. 1400 W., P.O. Box 1550, St. George, UT 84771-1550, 1-800-233-8824; 435-628-4171 .**

5. **Dinosaurland, 25 E. Main, Vernal, UT 84078; 1-800-477-5558; 435-789-6932.**

6. **Golden Spike Empire, 2501 Wall Ave., Ogden, UT 84401; 1-800-255-8824; 801-627-8288.**

7. **Great Salt Lake Country, 180 S. West Temple, Salt Lake City, UT 84101-1493; 801-521-2822.**

8. **Mountainland, 2545 N. Canyon Rd., Provo, UT 84604; 801-377-2262.**

9. **Panoramaland, 4 S. Main, P.O. Box 71, Nephi, UT 84648; 1-800-748-4361; 435-623-5203.**

Suggested Reading

John W. Van Cott's *Utah Place Names* (University of Utah Press, 1990) is a handy paperback arranged alphabetically with brief explanations for the names of several thousand place names throughout the state.

Tips for Visitors

The Mormons

If you like to experience different cultures, Utah is a good place to visit. For many outsiders, Utah and Mormons are often considered synonymous. While the majority of Utahns are members of the Church of Jesus Christ of Latter-day Saints, there is, however, a rich diversity of other religions and ethnic groups. This is especially true along Utah's Wasatch Front, the urban corridor that lies generally between the west slope of the Wasatch Mountains and the eastern side of Great Salt Lake. But to understand the Mormon culture and its people, here are a few facts to keep in mind.

• Mormons practiced polygamy for nearly a half century, from the early 1840s until the

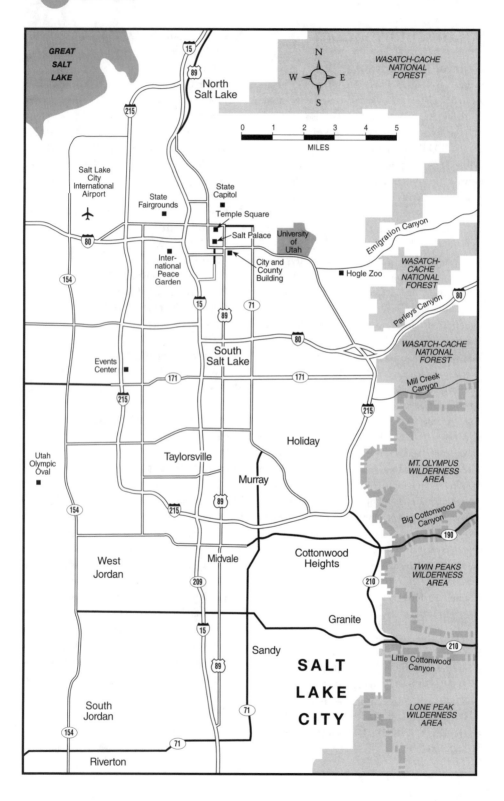

leader of the Mormon faith issued the "Manifesto" in 1890, which ended any new "plural marriages," as they were called. From 1890 to the present, there have been followers of the Mormon faith who did not accept this. These people practice polygamy, and consequently they are not considered members of the official church.

- While some religious groups claim that Mormons are not Christian, members of the Church of Jesus Christ of Latter-day Saints do identify themselves as Christian. Mormons accept the Bible, both the Old and New Testaments, as scripture. Their modern-day scripture, the *Book of Mormon*, carries the subtitle "Another Testament of Christ" and recounts the teachings and ministry of Jesus Christ on the American continent between 600 B.C. and A.D. 400.

- Most Mormons do not use tobacco, alcohol, coffee or tea (although herbal tea is acceptable). The consumption of caffeinated soft drinks is left to individual choice; however, you will not find them for purchase on the Brigham Young University campus and in church-operated cafeterias or facilities.

- Mormons are encouraged to tell others about their faith. Some of the more zealous will take the opportunity to inform you of the church and its doctrine, but this is more the exception than the rule. Most missionary work is done by full-time missionaries who leave their homes for up to two years for this endeavor. Young men leave at age 19, young women at 21, and more and more retired couples are going as missionaries during their golden years. Missionaries are assigned to a specific location; many learn a foreign language and pay their own expenses. While most missionaries serve proselytizing missions, some also serve in many ways on what are perhaps best described as "humanitarian missions."

- The Mormon Sabbath is on Sun. Most members attend a 3-hour block of meetings that begin at 9 or 10 A.M., although they may begin as late as 3 or 4 P.M. if several congregations (called "wards") share the same church building. All visitors are welcome at these meetings.

- Members of the Mormon faith range from those who are antagonistic or apathetic to those who are sometimes called "cultural Mormons"—that is, those who remain Mormons because of tradition and family—to those who are totally committed to those who are the most extreme and are sometimes considered zealots or "iron-rods" by the rest.

- All places of worship are open to the public except for dedicated temples. Temples are considered sacred places that only worthy members of the faith can enter with a "recommend" obtained each year from their local church leaders. However, when new temples are constructed and before they are formally dedicated, the public is invited to an open house that includes a tour inside the temple.

- Mormons give strong emphasis to the family. Having children is encouraged, and Mormons believe that families can be together forever. Marriages performed in Mormon temples are considered binding not only for this life but also for eternity.

- According to principles of the Mormon faith, each member is to pay 10 percent of his or her income. Until after World War I, most LDS church members paid their 10 percent tithe in kind—that is, one out of every 10 eggs, one out of every 10 bushels of wheat, one out of every 10 calves that were born. To receive and disburse these tithes, tithing offices were constructed and tithing lots maintained in every Mormon village; these historic structures can be seen throughout Utah. Today tithes are usually monetary.

- Mormon doctrine does call for living a practical religion with openness and Christian behavior. In the last of the Thirteen Articles of Faith that founder Joseph Smith Jr. penned in 1841 as a summary of Mormon beliefs, he wrote: "We believe in being honest, true, chaste, benevolent, virtuous, and in doing good to all men. ... If there is anything virtuous, lovely, or of good report or praiseworthy, we seek after these things." More recently, in his 2001 Pioneer Day address church president Gordon B. Hinckley said, "I take this occasion to plead for a spirit of tolerance and neighborliness, of friendship and love toward those of other faiths. This city and state have now become the home of many people of great diversity in their backgrounds, beliefs, and religious persuasions. I plead with our people to welcome them, to befriend them, to mingle with them, to associate with them in the promulgation of good causes. We are all sons and daughters of God."

Suggested Reading

Leonard Arrington and Davis Bitton, in *The Mormon Experience: A History of the Latter-day Saints* (Alfred A. Knopf, 1979), look at three periods in Mormon history—the early church, the kingdom in the West and the modern church.

Drinking Laws

Contrary to popular belief (both inside and outside the state), alcoholic beverages are available in Utah. Prohibition was repealed in Utah in February 1933. In fact, Utah takes credit as the state that ended national prohibition, since it was the 36th and final state to ratify the 21st Amendment. Alcoholic beverages are served with meals in many restaurants and hotels; however, often they are not on the menu and you have to ask your server for the alcohol list. The server cannot volunteer the information. The maximum alcohol content for beer is 3.2 percent—the common percentage for most of the United States. Beer is readily available in grocery stores and quick-stop markets. Bottled liquor can be purchased only at state-operated liquor stores, easily identifiable by their gold-and-brown logos and letters and open daily except Sun. 8 A.M.–8 P.M. Mixed drinks are served in nonexclusive private clubs, but visitors are welcome at these clubs, with temporary memberships, usually for two weeks, available for a nominal fee. A common Utah practice is for a paying member to "sponsor" other guests, thereby avoiding the membership fee.

Driving

To drive in Utah, you need a national driver's license or an International Driver's Permit. Utah law requires that seat belts be worn. A right turn is permissible on a red light, after you come to a complete stop and traffic is clear. Statewide driving and road condition information is available by calling the Utah Travel Information Service number—**511**—or the Utah Department of Transportation Winter Driving Conditions number—**801-964-6000.**

Health and Safety

You should feel as safe in Utah as anywhere. However, use common sense. In urban areas, avoid being out alone late at night and take care to safeguard your possessions. Local campaigns against road rage have been launched and seem to be quite successful. Utahns pride themselves on being courteous drivers, but if you become a victim of road rage, don't antagonize or challenge the offender; take down the license number and get a full description of the vehicle and driver, identify your location and call 911.

You will likely be spending most of your time out-of-doors so take proper precautions to protect your health. Use sunscreen year-round. Sunburn has ruined many a promising ski vacation or week on the water. Drink plenty of water to prevent dehydration. Don't drink the water from streams, lakes and natural water sources unless it has been properly purified. The single-cell parasite *Giardia lamblia* is likely to be found in these water sources, and giardiasis's severe cramps and diarrhea are an awful price to pay for violating this unfortunate but necessary rule of the outdoors.

Dress in layers and stay warm. Temperatures can fluctuate greatly, especially in the mountains, so be prepared for cold weather, even in the summer. Take your time to adjust to Utah's higher elevations. Much of the state is a mile or higher in elevation, and in the mountains you are especially likely to notice the shortness of breath that turns to a persistent headache, nausea, dizziness or worse with the onset of altitude sickness.

Telephones

The entire state of Utah is served by two long-distance prefixes, 801 and 435. The latter area code was added in September 1997 and covers all of Utah except the Salt Lake, Provo, Davis County, and Ogden areas, which retain the 801 prefix. If you are calling from outside the state, you must use the prefix. Long-distance calls within the state also require using the 801 or 435 prefix before the number. For long-distance directory assistance outside and within Utah, call **1-801-555-1212** or **1-435-555-1212.** For emergency assistance dial **911.**

Time

Utah is on Mountain Standard Time, which is 2 hours earlier than Eastern Standard Time (New York) and 1 hour later than Pacific Standard Time (California). Utah is either 7 or 8 hours earlier than Western Europe, depending on the time of year.

Getting There

Since pioneer days, Salt Lake City has been known as the "Crossroads of the West." First it was wagons, then the railroad and later automobiles. Now it is airplanes. Air travelers to Utah can be in Salt Lake City from most parts of the United States in less than half a day. Six airlines, including Delta Airline's western hub, are located in the two main terminals at the **Salt Lake City International Airport; 801-355-4542.** Once you arrive at the airport, it is easy to get to downtown Salt Lake City, a short 10-minute drive 6 miles east on I-80, or to the nearby ski resorts, all within an hour's drive. From Salt Lake City, you can catch connecting flights to Cedar City and St. George, but most people rent a car in Salt Lake City and drive to their destinations in Utah and the surrounding states. Car rentals are also easily arranged at the

Salt Lake International Airport. Utah Authority Bus service, short-term parking and car rentals provide easy access to the airport from Salt Lake City.

Travelers to the canyons of southern Utah may want to consider flying into Las Vegas, Nevada. There are good air connections in Las Vegas, and from there it is only a 2-hour drive to St. George. Salt Lake City and Las Vegas are both located along Interstate 15, about 7 hours' driving time apart.

Limited train service is available on **Amtrak,** with a station located at **600 W. and 320 S.; 1-800-421-8420; 801-364-8562; www.amtrak.com.** The California Zephyr, which runs between Chicago, Denver, Salt Lake City, Reno and San Francisco, arrives daily. In addition to the Salt Lake City stop, the Zephyr also stops in Provo, Helper and Green River, Utah. Amtrak trains that serve Utah pass through some of the most memorable scenery in the world. Everyone should take the California Zephyr between Salt Lake City and Denver at least once.

Greyhound bus service is available to Logan, Ogden, Provo, Cedar City and St. George; more limited service is available to Brigham City, Roosevelt, Vernal, Wendover, Price, Green River and Salina. The Salt Lake City bus terminal is located in the downtown area, less than a block west of Temple Square, at **160 W. Temple; 801-355-9579; www.greyhound.com.**

Getting Around

Salt Lake City and most Utah cities and towns are laid out on a grid system. Main Street and Center Street are usually the primary intersecting streets. (In Salt Lake City, it's the four streets around the Mormon Temple, which are named West Temple, North Temple, South Temple and Main St.) Streets are numbered in sequence from the center point: 100 S., 200 S., 100 N., 200 N. and so on. If you are given an address such as 450 W. 300 S., it is easy to find your way—if you know where you are starting from.

You can survive in Salt Lake City and the adjacent ski resorts without your own vehicle by using public transportation or private limousine service to Park City. Otherwise, public transportation is pretty much nonexistent, making an automobile essential, especially if you plan to visit any of the national parks and monuments or travel outside the Salt Lake area. The major **car rental** agencies have counters at the Salt Lake City Airport, which are conveniently located in the parking terrace adjacent to the terminals. Depending on the time of year, sometimes you can get excellent weekend and weekly rates. During the winter, rentals come equipped with ski racks; four-wheel-drive vehicles are especially popular. Agencies at or near the airport include:

Advantage, 1-800-777-5500; 801-531-1199; www.arac.com

Alamo, 1-800-462-5266; 801-575-2212; www.goalamo.com

Avis, 1-800-331-1212; 801-575-2847; www.avis.com/local/slc

Dollar, 1-800-800-4000; 801-575-2580; www.dollar.com

Enterprise, 1-800-RENT-A-CAR; 801-534-1888; www.erac.com

Hertz, 1-800-654-3131; 801-575-2683; www.hertz.com

National, 1-800-227-7368; 801-575-2277; www.nationalcar.com

Payless, 801-596-2689; www.paylesssaltlakecity.com

Thrifty, 801-265-6677; www.thrifty.com

Information for Disabled Visitors

Each year Utah becomes more conscientious about providing better facilities, access and activities for those with disabilities. In March 2002, two weeks after the close of the 2002 Winter Olympics, Utah hosted the Paralympic Games. Athletes from around the world demonstrated amazing abilities in downhill skiing, cross-country skiing, the biathlon and sledge hockey to appreciative audiences. Parks, museums and other attractions have designated handicapped parking and wheelchair access to buildings. Excellent **disabled ski programs** have been established at **Snowbird, Alta** and **Park City.** River guide outfits are expanding their float trips to accommodate people with disabilities. Mountain trails at **Snowbird** and **Brighton** have been made wheelchair accessible, as have a number of trails in Utah's national parks. Campgrounds in national and state parks are improving their handicapped facilities. Handicapped fishing areas have been established at Brighton's **Silver Lake** and at **Payson Lake.**

Utah has made a concerted effort to comply with all provisions of the Americans with Disabilities Act passed by Congress in 1992. Persons with disabilities may receive helpful information from the **Utah Association of Community Services; 801-328-4580; www. uacs.org.**

How the Book Is Organized

The Utah Guide is arranged into seven geographic regions: Northern, Wasatch Front, Northeastern, Central, Southwestern, South-Central and Southeastern. Maps at the beginning of each region locate that region in the context of the rest of the state. Within the seven regions are 35 chapters or "destinations," including cities, areas and national parks. Each chapter begins with the necessary background and history, plus how to get there. These are followed by Major Attractions, Festivals and Events, Outdoor Activities, Seeing and Doing, Where to Stay, Where to Eat and Services. Website information is provided throughout the book; the index at the back of the book is as comprehensive as possible and should be of considerable help. The following is a look at the principal subject areas covered in each chapter:

Festivals and Events

Utahns celebrate all of the major national holidays and a few of their own. The most important state holiday is Pioneer Day, celebrated annually on July 24, which commemorates the arrival of the first Mormon pioneers in Utah. Celebrations and activities are held in many communities throughout the state, but the largest is in Salt Lake City with the Days of '47 parade, rodeo, fireworks, races and other activities. Communities have their own special celebrations, and most of these are indicated in the appropriate chapters. For an events calendar that is updated weekly, contact the **Utah Travel Council, Council Hall/Capitol Hill, Salt Lake City, UT 84114-7420; 1-800-200-1160; 801-538-1030; www.utah.com/events.**

Outdoor Activities

The possibilities for outdoor activities in Utah are almost endless. Bicycling, hiking and backpacking, skiing, snowmobiling, river floating, golfing, tennis, fishing and horseback riding are some of the most popular. Activities are given in alphabetical order throughout the book.

BIKING

Mountain biking has taken Utah by storm, and at least two locations—**Moab** with its unique slickrock and **Brian Head** with its high mountain trails—have developed national and international reputations. Fat-tire festivals are held in numerous locations during the summer months. Many local travel offices have published biking guides to their areas. Local bike shops are a good source for rentals, repairs, equipment and information about other possibilities.

Suggested Reading

See Greg Bromka's *Mountain Biking Utah* (Falcon Press, 1998). For the Moab area, check out Lee Bridgers's *Mountain Bike America Moab* (Beachway Press, 2000) and David Crowell's *Mountain Biking Moab* (Falcon, 1997). In addition, **Bicycle Utah** maintains a website and provides useful information about biking in Utah; **www.bicycleutah.com.**

FISHING

A favorite pastime of Utahns, fishing in Utah ranks as high as anywhere in the West and includes well-stocked lakes and reservoirs and rapid-flowing trout streams. You can purchase one-day, seven-day and annual fishing licenses online. Contact the **Utah Division of Wildlife Resources, 1596 W. North Temple, Salt Lake City, UT 84114; 801-596-8660; www.wildlife.utah.gov.**

Suggested Reading

There are several good books on fishing in Utah, including two by Hartt Wixom, the dean of Utah anglers: *Fishing and Hunting Guide to Utah* (University of Utah Press, 1999) and *Personalized Fishing Guide to Utah* (Bonneville Books, 2001). Others include Brett Prettyman's *Fishing in Utah* (Falcon, 2001) and James B. Demoux's *Fly Fisher's Guide to Utah* (Wilderness Adventures Press, 2001).

GOLF

There are nearly 100 golf courses in Utah, and new ones are under construction all the time. Most of Utah's courses are municipal- or county-owned, and greens fees are reasonable. There are a number of fine courses in the Salt Lake and Park City areas. The St. George area, with its several courses, is a golfer's mecca during the winter when snow closes Utah's other courses and the warm St. George winters draw thousands. The **Utah Travel Council** offers a free annual "Utah Golf Directory" upon request or on its website; **www.utah.com/golf.** The Utah Golf Association publishes *Fairways* four times a year, with news about tournaments, courses and the Utah golf scene. For more information about golf in Utah, contact the **Utah Golf Association, 110 E. Eaglewood Dr., North Salt Lake, UT 84054; 801-299-8421; www.fairwaysmag.com.**

HIKING AND BACKPACKING

Whether you are a lifelong resident or this is your first day in Utah, you can't spend your time better than on Utah's unforgettable hiking trails. Less traveled than the national park trails are those in the national forests and on Bureau of Land Management (BLM) land. If you want to sever contact with the outside world for a few days, there are more than a dozen designated wilderness areas, from the Paria Canyon and Pine Valley Mountain areas in the south to the Mt. Naomi and Wellsville Mountain areas in the north. There are also a number of wilderness study areas that are open to backpackers. Hikers and backpackers as well as all visitors to the outdoors should practice the "Leave No Trace" ethics outlined below in the Camping section under Where to Stay. In addition to these practices, also keep in mind a few commonsense rules:

- Carry plenty of water and snack foods, even on short hikes.
- Be prepared for changing weather. Carry a windbreaker, rain gear, sweater or jacket and an emergency Mylar-type blanket.
- Carry maps of the area, a flashlight, waterproof matches, a first-aid kit, sunscreen and a knife.
- If a storm comes in, seek shelter in lower areas off mountain- and butte tops, which are prone to lightning strikes.
- Maintain a safe distance when observing or photographing wildlife, and don't approach animals or try to feed them.
- Horses have the right-of-way on the trail. Step off the trail when you meet them, and remain quiet until they have passed.
- Let someone know where you are going and when you expect to return.

Suggested Reading

There are a number of hiking guides, and most regional travel offices have prepared hiking guides to their areas. Three books that cover the entire state include J. David Day, *Utah's Favorite Hiking Trails* (Rincon Publishing Company, 1998), Dave Hall, *Hiking Utah* (Falcon Press, 1996) and Michael R. Weibel and Dan Miller, *High in Utah: A Hiking Guide to the Tallest Peaks in Each of the State's Twenty-nine Counties* (University of Utah Press, 1999). For hikes in the mountains around Salt Lake City, see John Veranth's *Hiking the Wasatch* (University of Utah Press, 1999).

HORSEBACK RIDING

Riding clubs, rodeos and horseback rides are a part of the cowboy tradition that still flourishes in the West. There are a number of riding stables and trail rides available throughout Utah, and this book tries to cover as many as possible. New stables are being established all the time, so check with local tourist officials. You can also request the *Outfitters and Guides* book from the **Utah Travel Council.** Published annually, it includes listings for horseback rides; **www.utah.com/guides.**

RIVER RAFTING

The eastern half of Utah is cut by three rivers—the **Colorado,** the **Green** and the **San Juan**—that provide excellent opportunities for river floats. The rapids don't get any bigger or more violent than through Cataract Canyon below the confluence of the Green and Colorado Rivers. There are plenty of outfitters in the Moab area to provide any kind of trip you can imagine. Flaming Gorge, Vernal and Green River are locations for float trips on the Green River, and you can retrace the route of the historic 1869 John Wesley Powell expedition. Bluff provides access to the San Juan River for an interesting float to Mexican Hat or beyond through the Goosenecks of the San Juan and on to Lake Powell. If you don't have time for a multi-day river adventure, there are day and half-day tours that introduce you to Utah's rivers and awaken a desire for more. Not all trips are through roaring rapids. Some are a nice leisurely float that gives you time to relax and enjoy Utah's canyon country from a whole new perspective. For literature about river trips, contact the **Utah Travel Council, Council Hall/Capitol Hill, Salt Lake City, UT 84114-7420; 1-800-200-1160; 801-538-1030; www.utah.com.**

Suggested Reading

A good source is Gary C. Nichols, *River Runners'*

Guide to Utah and Adjacent Areas (University of Utah Press, 2002).

ROCK CLIMBING

Rock climbers can be found throughout Utah, from Salt Lake's Little Cottonwood Canyon to the sandstone walls of the Moab area and as far south as Zion National Park.

Suggested Reading

Stewart M. Green's *Rock Climbing Utah* (Falcon Press, 1998) is recommended.

SKIING

Utah has an international reputation for some of the best powder skiing on earth. As moisture-laden clouds move eastward from the Pacific coast, part of the moisture is combed out of the clouds by the mountains over which they pass. As the snows reach the Utah mountains, they become light and powdery. The mountains of powder provide a challenge and an unequaled thrill: to ski through the waist-deep substance that is even lighter than feathers. The majority of Utah ski resorts, located in the **Park City** area and **Big** and **Little Cottonwood Canyons,** all east of Salt Lake City, are within an hour's drive from the Salt Lake City Airport. Skiing is big business in Utah, and the 2002 Winter Olympics have already marked Utah as one of the world's premier ski areas.

Suggested Reading

For a history of skiing in Utah, see Alan K. Engen, *For the Love of Skiing: A Visual History* (Gibbs Smith Publisher, 1998). An older and still excellent history is Alexis Kelner, *Skiing in Utah: A History* (self-published, 1980). The book is being revised and updated and should be available soon. In *Wasatch Tours* (Wasatch, 1976), Alexis Kelner and David Hanscom cover the cross-country and backcountry tour possibilities in the Salt Lake area canyons. The **Utah Travel Council (Council Hall/Capitol Hill, Salt Lake City, UT 84114-7420; 1-800-200-1160; 801-538-1030)** also publishes a free annual

"Winter Vacation Planner," which gives up-to-date information on Utah's ski areas. Additional information is available from **Ski Utah; 1-800-754-8824; 801-534-1907; www.skiutah. com.**

SNOWMOBILING

Snowmobiling is one of Utah's favorite winter pastimes, and trail systems can be found throughout most Utah mountains. The Utah Division of Parks and Recreation offers trail maps, *The Utah Snowmobile Directory* and other information about snowmobiling possibilities. Contact the **Utah Division of Parks and Recreation, 1636 W. North Temple, Ste. 116, Salt Lake City, UT 84116; 801-538-7220.** The **Utah Snowmobile Association** also provides information on upcoming events and activities; **www.snowut.com.**

Seeing and Doing

The Seeing and Doing section in each chapter covers a variety of activities, including cultural activities, museums, historic sites, ghost towns, scenic drives, wildlife, nightlife and shopping.

ARCHAEOLOGICAL SITES

You're never very far from archaeological sites in Utah. Most are from the Fremont and Anasazi cultures, which reached their high point in Utah about A.D. 1250. Government agencies, including the Utah Division of Parks and Recreation, the National Park Service, the Bureau of Land Management and the U.S. Forest Service have given archaeological resources a high priority at places like **Edge of the Cedars, Anasazi State Park, Fremont State Park, Grand Gulch, Hovenweep National Monument** and various locations in Utah's national parks. The rock paintings (pictographs) and chiseled inscriptions (petroglyphs) of the ancient inhabitants are of special interest, as Utah has some of the best preserved rock art in the world at places like **Barrier Canyon** in Canyonlands National Park, **Nine Mile Canyon** in the Price area and **Parowan Gap** near Cedar City. For more information about sites that are open to the public, contact the **Antiquities Office, Division of State History, 300 Rio Grande, Salt Lake City, UT 84101-1182; 801-533-3500.**

DINOSAURS

Children and adults alike have long been fascinated with dinosaurs, and Utah is dinosaur country. More dinosaur bones have been excavated in Utah than any other place in the United States, and you could plan a weeklong trip to visit the quarry sites and museums that interpret the 100-million-year-old bones. **Dinosaur National Monument** is the first place to start, along with a visit to the **Museum of Natural History** in Vernal. The **Cleveland-Lloyd Quarry Site** in Emery County is open to visitors in the summer, and nearby museums—in Price, the **College of Eastern Utah Prehistoric Museum,** and in Castle Dale, the **Museum of the San Rafael**—have dinosaur skeletons taken from the quarry. While at these places, ask about the Long Walk Site, which promises to add even more information about the prehistoric dinosaurs. You can also see dinosaur skeletons at the **Brigham Young University Physical Science Museum,** the University of Utah's **Museum of Natural History,** the **North American Museum of Ancient Life** at Thanksgiving Point in Lehi, and the **Dinosaur Museum** in Blanding. In Ogden, a **Dinosaur Park** has been established, with replicas of more than 100 dinosaurs.

HISTORIC SITES

A number of local historical societies have worked with their travel offices and the Utah State Historical Society to produce brochures and pamphlets that serve as guides to local historic sites. These are mentioned in the appropriate chapters. For specific questions about historic sites in the state, contact the **Utah Historic Preservation Office, Utah State Historical Society, 300 Rio Grande, Salt Lake City, UT 84101-1182; 801-533-3500.**

MUSEUMS

There are a variety of museums in Utah, but the most museum-oriented organization has been the **Daughters of Utah Pioneers** (DUP). Since its founding in 1901, the DUP has established an impressive museum on Salt Lake City's Capitol Hill, three blocks north of Temple Square, and dozens of local museums, often called "relic halls," throughout the towns and cities of the state. Many of these museums are included in this book, and they offer an interesting glimpse at the past and at the way Utahns interpret and cherish their past. You will also want to visit the **LDS Church Museum of Art and History,** located across the street west of Temple Square in Salt Lake City. Other museums range from a fine prehistoric museum in Price and an interesting mining and railroad museum in Helper to a superb Greek ethnic museum in Salt Lake City and museums of fine art and natural history at the University of Utah and Brigham Young University. For more information and a free booklet listing all of Utah's museums, contact the **Utah Office of Museum Services, 300 Rio Grande St., Salt Lake City, UT 84101 1-800-533-4235; www.utah.org/museum.**

PERFORMING ARTS

The Utah Travel Council as well as regional and local travel councils keep a calendar of events that includes concerts, theater, art festivals, folk festivals, and other cultural activities. The Utah Arts Council, established in 1899, was the first state arts agency in the nation, and it continues to support and encourage endeavors in all areas of the fine arts and folk arts. The Utah Arts Council is also known as the **Division of Fine Arts, 617 S. Temple, Salt Lake City, UT 84102; 801-533-5895.**

SCENIC DRIVES

Some 27 byways and 58 back roads have been given official designation. Most of these are described in the appropriate sections. If you notice one of the road signs designating a scenic byway, you can assume you are in for some spectacular sights. All of the scenic drives are suited to passenger cars unless otherwise noted. Off-highway routes requiring four-wheel-drive vehicles are included in the Outdoor Activities section under Four-Wheel-Drive Trips.

Suggested Reading

Utah Scenic Byways and Backways, a joint publication of local, state and federal agencies, has full-page sections with color photographs and descriptions of all the designated byways, as well as shorter descriptions of the backways throughout Utah. Ward J. Roylance's *Utah: A Guide to the State* (Utah Arts Council, 1982) is a revision of the original 1940 *Utah Writers' Project Guide* and includes 11 detailed driving tours that cover the entire state.

Where to Stay

Accommodations

The selection of places included is based on personal experience, local recommendations and availability. Since most people know what to expect at hotel and motel chains, these are generally not included unless they are the only accommodations available, or because the high demand for lodging merits listing a larger number of choices. If you would like a complete listing of all lodging facilities in a particular area, contact the county and regional travel offices, listed at the end of each chapter under Services. For toll-free reservation numbers for the chain hotels and motels, call **1-800-555-1212** and ask for the number of the specific chain.

Bed and breakfast inns are given high priority in this section because of the personal attention they provide and the unforgettable facilities they offer. If you've never stayed at one, treat yourself to this memorable experience. Contact the Utah Travel Council for information on the bed and breakfast directory it publishes annually. **Bed and Breakfast Inns of Utah (P.O. Box 3066, Park City, UT 84060; 435-645-8068)** can also provide up-to-date information about its members.

Only a couple of youth hostels can be found in Utah—in Salt Lake City and Moab—but an attempt has been made to include inexpensive lodging in each of the chapters. Prices vary depending on the season and room type. The following approximate price range, based on double occupancy, has been used throughout this guidebook:

$	less than $40
$$	$40–$80
$$$	$80–$120
$$$$	$120 and up

Camping

Perhaps because of Utah's pioneer heritage, there is a long tradition of camping in Utah. Camping opportunities range from backpacking into wilderness areas, to basic campground facilities in the national forests and national parks, to the most luxurious private RV parks. In the national forests, you can camp anywhere unless it is posted otherwise. In those national parks where camping is permitted, you may use only designated areas, with the exception of some backcountry primitive sites. Review the sections on the individual national parks and inquire about camping regulations at the various park headquarters. Most campgrounds on public and state land with such amenities as showers, rest rooms and drinking water charge fees for camping. For wilderness and backcountry camping, there is no charge. Without exception, all private campgrounds charge fees. Each Camping section lists both public and private campgrounds. **The Utah State Campground Owners Association** publishes an annual directory to Utah's private campgrounds and RV service centers. It is available free of charge at most visitor centers, or by writing to **USCOA, 9160 S. 300 W., Ste. 6, Sandy, UT 84070.**

Despite its rugged-looking mountains and scenic wonders, Utah is a very fragile area. The impact of more and more visitors and residents requires that everyone follow a few basic practices that will enhance the quality of the outdoor experience for others and help preserve the land for future generations. Remember to leave each campsite cleaner than you found it, and for back-country camping, be sure to practice minimum-impact camping techniques.

- Tread lightly when traveling and leave no trace of your camping. Drive and ride only on roads and trails where such travel is allowed; hike only on established trails, on rock or in washes. Camp at designated sites or, where allowed, at previously used sites. Avoid placing tents on top of vegetation. Unless signs indicate other-wise, leave gates open or closed as you find them.
- Pack out your trash and recycle it; clean up after less thoughtful visitors and dispose of human waste properly. Carry a small shovel or trowel to bury human waste 6 to 8 inches below the ground. Select a site well away from water sources. Pack out all toilet paper in a plastic bag with your other trash. Do not bury any trash.
- Camp at least 300 feet from isolated water sources to allow for wildlife access. Where possible, carry your own drinking water. Leave potholes undisturbed and wash well away from pools and springs (at least 100 feet), using biodegradable soap.
- Minimize your use of campfires by using a portable stove or self-contained charcoal fire for all your cooking. If you must have a camp-fire, keep it very small and avoid building new fire rings. Collect only dead and down wood and gather it from seldom-used areas well away from popular campsites. Do not build fires in alcoves or underneath cliff faces, and keep all cans, bottles, aluminum foil and other items that do not burn out of the fire ring. Burn the wood down to ashes, then douse with water. Don't smother a campfire with soil, and always make sure the fire is dead out before you leave.
- If you encounter wildlife, maintain your dis-tance and remain quiet. Teach children not to chase or pick up animals. Leave pets at home if possible—if not, keep them under control.

- Leave historic sites, Native American rock art, ruins and artifacts untouched for the future. Admire rock art from a distance and never touch it. Stay out of ruins, leave arti-facts in place and report violations.

Where to Eat

Listings for Where to Eat are determined by per-sonal experience and favorites, recommenda-tions by locals, an aversion to chain restaurants and availability. I have personally visited nearly every one of the restaurants listed in this guide. Those I was not able to visit but that had good local recommendations and those that met my fourth criteria of availability but without any-thing special to mention have been listed in the guide without much elaboration. I've tried to include restaurants to fit all budgets. Remember that changes in hours and ownership make it impossible to guarantee that all information is up-to-date, so use the material provided only as a guide.

Anyone who has traveled the backways of Utah knows that of the four factors mentioned above, availability is often the most important in choosing a restaurant. After a full day of travel and sight-seeing, you are happy just to find a place that is open and that will cook for you. For a second opinion, consult the *Zagat Survey* for Utah, **www.zagat.com,** which provides lists of restaurants under a number of categories such as Best Buys, Most Popular, Top Food, Top Views, Favored by Women, Favored by Men, Sleepers and Worth a Trip.

A general price guide, based on the price of an entrée per person, is provided under the fol-lowing system:

$	under $5
$$	$5–$10
$$$	$10–$20
$$$$	$20 and up

Here We Go

Now that you have an overview of Utah's natural and human history and an idea of how the guidebook is put together, just use it. I hope that you will use the book at least two ways. Keep it by your comfortable reading chair, as I do with my favorite guidebooks, and visit or revisit any of the 35 areas through the pages of the book. But hopefully there will be many occasions to throw the guidebook into your car or backpack and set off on your own adventures. May they all be as fun and rewarding as mine have been in creating *The Utah Guide*.

Northern Region

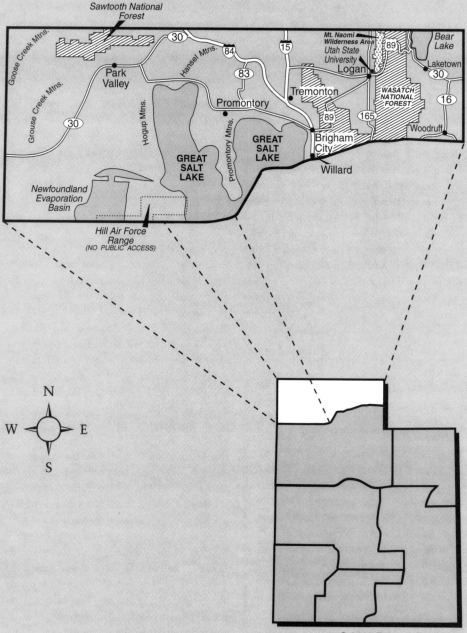

© 2003 Fulcrum Publishing

Bear Lake

Surrounded by mountains, Bear Lake—Utah's second-largest natural freshwater lake—is like a drop of turquoise. Geologists postulate that the lake was formed by earthquake action about 28,000 years ago. Until about 10,000 years ago, the Bear River ran into and out of the northern end of the lake. However, a series of upheavals that created the Bear River Plateau along the eastern side of the lake changed the course of the river to bypass the lake. Since then, the level of the lake has remained relatively constant, with the inflow from a half dozen small streams and precipitation equaling the outflow from evaporation and percolation. In addition, canals have been constructed to bring excess water into the lake from the Bear River and to discharge water through the lake when needed downstream.

The lake has 71,000 surface acres and 48 miles of shoreline; it is shared by both Utah and Idaho, as their borders divide the lake roughly in half. The deepest part of the lake is 208 feet near Cisco Beach on the east side of the lake. The western and northern ends of the lake are the most shallow. There are four rare species of fish found only in Bear Lake—the Bonneville cisco, Bear Lake whitefish, Bonneville whitefish and Bear Lake sculpin. Biologists believe that these fish are descended from species that lived in ancient Lake Bonneville. However, anglers usually seek the larger lake trout and the Bear Lake cutthroat. Since the establishment of Bear Lake State Park in the early 1960s, recreation at the lake has continued to expand. The Utah side has undergone more extensive development than the Idaho side, particularly along the western and southern shores, but the many interesting sights just across the Idaho border are also covered in this chapter.

History

Shoshoni Indian campsites dotted the shores of Bear Lake for many decades before Donald Mackenzie, a red-haired Scottish fur trapper for the North West Company of Canada, discovered the lake in 1819. He named it Black Bears Lake, which was later changed to Bear Lake. Fur trappers also called it Weaver's Lake, apparently for John Weber, who led a group of American trappers to the lake in 1824, or Sweet Lake, for its contrast to the Great Salt Lake located 70 miles to the southwest.

As the western fur trade developed during the 1820s, Bear Lake became a central location for the third and fourth annual fur trapper rendezvous, which were held at the southern end of Bear Lake in 1827 and 1828. Because of the lack of navigable rivers into the West, annual trading caravans made their way overland each year, bringing goods and equipment to a designated location where they would be exchanged for the beaver pelts taken by fur trappers during the previous year. Held for a couple of weeks during the month of July, the annual rendezvous was much more than a business convention. American trappers, Native Americans and others from

---

Getting There

Bear Lake is located 125 miles north of Salt Lake City and 40 miles northeast of Logan. Take Interstate 15 north from Salt Lake City for 56 miles and exit at Brigham City (Exit 364), then turn east onto US Hwy. 89, which skirts south of Brigham City, then heads northeast for 25 miles to Logan. Continue on Hwy. 89 for 40 miles, through Logan Canyon, to Garden City on the western side of Bear Lake. Here, Hwy. 89 continues north along the lake's west shore into Idaho; Hwy. 30 heads south from Garden City to Laketown on the south shore.

throughout the West came together to renew acquaintances, socialize, drink and catch up on events back East and throughout the world. Of the 16 rendezvous held between 1824 and 1840, the two held at the southern end of Bear Lake were among the most memorable. William Ashley, organizer of the Rocky Mountain Fur Company, sent west a group of 46 men with $22,500 worth of supplies and a cannon mounted on wheels, which became the first wheeled vehicle to cross the Rocky Mountains. While waiting for the caravan, 20 Blackfeet Indians killed a Snake Indian and his wife. The assembled Indians and some 300 trappers responded and killed several of the Blackfeet during a 6-hour fight. A few days after the battle, Jedediah Smith reached the rendezvous, having spent the past year traveling to California and returning across the Sierra Nevada and the Great Salt Lake Desert to reach Bear Lake on July 3.

Thirty-six years after the fur trappers broke camp at the conclusion of the 1828 rendezvous, Charles C. Rich built cabins on the western shore of the lake, at what is now Garden City. Early residents reported seeing on several occasions a huge creature swimming in the lake at speeds faster than a horse could run on land, and stories of the Bear Lake Monster have been told and retold ever since. Earlier, the Shoshoni Indians had also reported that a great beast lived in the lake that preyed on buffalo when they came to the edge of the lake to drink. The buffalo vanished in the 1830s and, according to the Indians, the monster did as well.

Beginning with the settlements in 1864 of Garden City and Laketown on the western shore of Bear Lake, Mormon settlers moved north to establish settlements across the state line in Idaho at Fish Haven, St. Charles, Paris and Montpelier—all within the Bear Lake Valley. At the same time, other settlers moved southeastward approximately 25 miles from Laketown into the Bear River Valley, where Randolph was founded in March 1870. Other Mormons moved into the Bear River Valley from more populated settlements near Salt Lake City to establish Woodruff, 10 miles south of Randolph, in 1871.

Festivals and Events

Raspberry Days

first week in Aug. Garden City is the place to be for fun-loving raspberry eaters in early August. Besides plain, simple and pure raspberries, you can try chocolate-covered raspberries, raspberry jam, raspberry honey, raspberry taffy and even raspberry fettuccine. In addition to the food, other events include a parade, games, entertainment, a craft fair and a rodeo. **1-800-448-BEAR.**

Outdoor Activities

Biking

Bear Lake Loop

You can circumnavigate Bear Lake in a fairly easy 45-mile loop that offers a spectacular view of the lake and the Bear Lake National Wildlife Refuge at the north end of the lake. Most riders begin at Garden City and ride south on Hwy. 30 to Laketown. Outside Laketown, watch for a country road that heads north around the eastern side of the lake—the road to Cisco Bay—and continue on this road around the lake until it joins US Hwy. 89 at St. Charles, Idaho. Follow Hwy. 89 south back to Garden City.

Bear Lake Summit to Meadowville

From the Bear Lake Summit to Meadowville is 15.5 miles; it is an easy to moderate ride. A loop ride from Garden City to Bear Lake Summit and Meadowville requires a leg-burning climb from Garden City to the Bear Lake Summit at 7,800 feet; most cyclists catch a ride on Hwy. 89 to the summit and begin the bike ride from there. Follow the dirt road south to Temple Canyon, where it heads northeast to Meadowville. If you are making a loop to Garden City, continue from Meadowville down to Hwy. 30 and ride north along the western side of the lake for about 8 miles to Garden City.

Bear Trail

This paved 4.2 mile bicycle/pedestrian path with magnificent views of Bear Lake connects Harbor Village near the Bear Lake Marina and Ideal Beach south of Garden City on Hwy. 30.

Boating / Diving / Waterskiing / Windsurfing

Boating, sailing, waterskiing, windsurfing, and scuba diving are all popular activities on Bear Lake. The Bear Lake Marina, on the west side of the lake a few miles west of Garden City, has an 80-foot-wide launching ramp and dock spaces for 350 boats. Rendezvous Beach at the south end of the lake, and First Point and Rainbow Cove on the east side of the lake, also have boat launching ramps. Motorboats, sailboats, canoes and wave runners are available for rent (reservations suggested) at **Bear Lake Marina, 435-946-2717; Rendezvous Beach, 435-946-2900; Garden City-Bear Lake Funtime, 435-946-3200 and Blue Water Beach, 435-946-8611.**

Fishing

When you talk about lake fishing in Utah, Bear Lake usually comes to mind first. Fifteen species of fish inhabit the lake, although the cutthroat trout is the only true native. Cutthroats up to 15 pounds have been taken; however, lake trout twice as large have been caught! Half a million cutthroat trout are planted in the lake each year. Rainbow trout, whitefish, and cisco are also popular to catch. Each year for a week or so in late January, the cisco run occurs as thousands of 7-inch-long Bonneville cisco come to the surface to spawn along the lake's eastern shore. Anglers scoop the fish up in nets through holes chopped in the ice or by wading in the icy water. Some claim the fish are good eating, while others use them only for bait. Ice fishing occurs during the winter along the western side of the lake, and protective "sheds on sleds" can be rented at the **Bear Lake Marina; 435-946-2717.**

Golf

Bear Lake Golf Course

This 9-hole golf course located at the south end of Bear Lake on the hills above the lake offers beautiful views of the southern end of Bear Lake Valley. It is considered one of the most difficult 9-hole courses in the state. The two par 5 holes are especially difficult—the 4th hole is nearly a semicircle with three lakes and a creek to negotiate; on the 9th hole, a steep incline intimidates with thoughts of your ball rolling right back down the hill past you to leave you with negative yardage on your drive. If you clear the hill with your drive, you have a nice roll downhill before negotiating a second hill as you approach the green. The 6th hole also can bring on a case of the jitters as you face a blind approach to the green, bordered by a grove of pines on the left and a lake on the right. **435-946-8742.**

Hiking

Limber Pine Trail

If you drive to Bear Lake via US Hwy. 89, or if you drive up the mountain west of Garden City for a panoramic view of Bear Lake, take time for the 1-mile round trip hike to Limber Pine. For years it was thought that the limber pine growing here was a single tree 25 feet in circumference and more than 2,000 years old. Closer study, however, indicates that the tree is actually five trees that have grown together; it is less than 600 years old. At the trailhead, located at the Bear Lake Summit approximately 5 miles west of Garden City, a free nature trail guide provides fascinating insight into the flora, fauna and geography of the area.

Seeing and Doing

Historic Sites

National Oregon Trail Center

Experience the Oregon Trail and travel back to 1849. Meet Peg Leg Smith at his trading post. Visit with pioneers in their wagon train encampment at the Clover Creek grazing area as they pause on their epic journey. Located in Montpelier, Idaho, at the junction of Hwys. 89 and 30. **208-847-3800; www.oregontrailcenter.org.**

Paris Tabernacle

Located 14 miles north of Bear Lake in Idaho, the 1889 Paris Tabernacle is a must for anyone traveling in the area. This magnificent building, constructed of local fieldstone, is the primary religious building in the Bear Lake Valley. It was designed by Don Carlos Young, a son of Brigham Young, with the stonecutting and carving carried out by Jacob Tueller and his three sons. The Tuellers were immigrant stonemasons from Switzerland who spent years working on the project. To reach the Tabernacle, drive north on US Hwy. 89 as it passes through the small southern Idaho town of Paris; you can't miss it on the east side of the highway. **1-800-448-2327; 208-945-2072.**

Performing Arts

Pickleville Playhouse

The name Pickleville raises a smile when most people hear it spoken, and that smile will continue if you enjoy the humor offered at the Pickleville Summer Theater. Late June–Labor Day, the Pickleville Playhouse Summer Theater presents an old-fashioned musical melodrama that is fun for all ages. A Western cookout featuring rib-eye steaks, beans, salad, rolls and brownies, with cowboys serenading while you eat, begins at 6:30 p.m.; the show starts at 8 p.m. The early residents of this community were so grateful to Charles C. Pickel, who supervised the improvement of the town's water supply, that they named their hamlet, located a couple of miles south of Garden City on Hwy. 30, Pickleville. Reservations are strongly recommended. **435-946-2918; 435-753-1944.**

Scenic Drives

Laketown Scenic Byway

The Laketown Scenic Byway is really an extension of the Logan Canyon Scenic Byway (see the Logan and Cache Valley chapter). It follows around the southwestern end of Bear Lake between Garden City and Laketown along state Hwy. 30. The 15-mile byway provides access to Rendezvous Beach and offers spectacular views of the lake and plenty of photo opportunities.

Tours

Minnetonka Cave

The cave was discovered in 1907 by Edward Arnell of St. Charles, Idaho, when he felt a draft coming from a small hole near a cliff. The reason the cave was named Minnetonka is not entirely clear, but old-timers indicate that it is an Indian word meaning "falling waters." The entrance was enlarged and steps installed as one of the federal government's New Deal projects in 1936. This nine-room, half-mile-long limestone cavern contains remarkable stalactites, stalagmites and banded travertine. The largest of the nine rooms is the 90-foot-high, 300-foot-diameter Ballroom. Ninety-minute tours of the cave depart every half hour. Visitors must be able to climb stairs since you go down and then back up a total of 896 stairs inside the cave. Be sure to take a warm jacket with you since the temperature inside the cave remains a constant 40° F. Open daily mid-June–Labor Day 10 a.m.–5:30 p.m. Located 10 miles up St. Charles Canyon, just across the Utah–Idaho border via Hwy. 89. **208-945-2407.**

Wildlife Viewing

Bear Lake National Wildlife Refuge

The 17,600-acre national wildlife refuge is located in the marsh and grasslands north of Bear Lake. There are observation sites where you can watch for the wide variety of birds— Canada geese, mallards, pintails, canvasback ducks, sandhill cranes, herons, egrets and white pelicans. **208-847-1757.**

Where to Stay

The Bluebird Inn—$$$$

Just a half mile across the Utah-Idaho border in Fish Haven, on a hill overlooking Bear Lake, this five-room bed and breakfast inn is owned by Dick and Jan Motta. Dick, a native of Fish Haven, had a distinguished college and NBA basketball coaching career. The rooms are all outfitted with fireplaces, king-size beds and private baths with double sinks, shower and separate tub. Three of the rooms—the Bear, Beehive and Honeymoon—have fine views of the lake. The Hummingbird Room, with two double beds, can accommodate four people. **423 Hwy. 89, Fish Haven, ID 83287; 1-800-797-6448; 208-945-2871; www.thebluebirdinn.com.**

Canyon Cove Inn—$$$

Some of the 33 units have three beds and some two bedrooms. Exercise room, Jacuzzi and heated indoor pool. **315 W. Logan Hwy., Garden City; 1-877-232-7525; 435-946-3565; www.canyoncove.com.**

Harbor Village Resort—$$$

Fifty one-bedroom condominiums and several two- and three-bedroom townhomes. Location just west of the state marina at **1900 Bear Lake Blvd., Garden City; 435-946-3448.**

Camping

PRIVATE
Bear Lake KOA Kamp

This 143-site campground has 100 full hookups, all the usual KOA amenities and five cabins. Open mid-May–Oct. Located on Hwy. 89 in Garden City, on the western side of Bear Lake. **435-946-3454.**

Bluewater Beach Campground

Offers 152 sites, 55 with full hookups. Toilets, showers, laundry, wheelchair-accessible facilities and group sites. Open mid-May–mid-Sept. Located about 1 mile south of Garden City on Hwy. 30. **2126 S. Bear Lake Blvd.; 435-946-3333.**

PUBLIC

Bear Lake State Park at **Rendezvous Beach,** with 138 sites (46 with full hookups), toilets, showers, laundry facilities and nearby boating and swimming opportunities, is a popular campground located at the southern end of the lake 2 miles west of Laketown on Hwy. 30. **1-800-322-3770; 435-946-3343.** An additional 15 trailer sites and 22 tentsites are available at the **Bear Lake Marina,** with showers, toilets, boating and swimming. Located 2 miles north of Garden City on US Hwy. 89. **435-946-2717.** On the eastern side of the lake at **Cisco Beach,** there are 100 primitive campsites. **Sunrise Campground** has 26 RV trailer and tentsites. Open mid-June–mid-Sept. Located in the Cache National Forest, 8.2 miles southwest of Garden City on US Hwy. 89. **435-755-3620 reservations.**

Where to Eat

Places to eat are not abundant around Bear Lake, especially if you get there in the off-season, which is anytime but summer.

LeBeau's Drive In—$

There is an ongoing debate about whether LeBeau's or the Quick 'N' Tasty (see next entry) have more fruit in their raspberry shakes. During the raspberry season, La Beau's gives you only fresh raspberries and ice cream in its shakes. While some may be able to live on raspberry shakes alone, LeBeau's special hamburger—topped with ham, cheese, onions, a special sauce and the usual pickles, lettuce and tomatoes—is a local favorite. Summer hours Mon.–Sat. 10:30 A.M.–10:30 P.M. **69 N. Bear Lake Blvd., Garden City; 435-946-8821.**

Quick 'N' Tasty Drive-In—$

This is another favorite Garden City drive-in. It features home-cut fries, family-grown beef burgers and raspberry shakes made from freshly picked berries from the berry patch just outside town. Summer hours Mon.–Sat. 10:30 A.M.–

10 P.M. **28 N. Bear Lake Blvd., Garden City; 435-946-2875.**

Services

Visitor Information

Cache Valley Tourist Council—160 N. Main St., Logan, UT 84321; 1-800-882-4433; 435-752-2161; www.tourcachevalley.com.

Logan and Cache Valley

Logan is one of Utah's most popular cities, where the lush green Cache Valley offers a welcome respite from the deserts and red rock of much of the state. Many people also feel that the Logan area combines the best of small-town, rural America with the intellectual and cultural atmosphere of a 20,000-student university. Much of the Cache Valley's 20th-century prosperity came from the 1888 decision to establish Utah's land grant agricultural college in Logan. Known today as Utah State University, the institution is the valley's largest single employer. Many Utah residents have attended school at Utah State University in Logan.

North of Logan, the Cache Valley encompasses many small towns, including North Logan, Hyde Park, Smithfield, Amalga, Richmond and Cove on its east side; Mendon, Clarkston and Trenton in the west; and Lewiston and Cornish near the Idaho border. South of Logan are the towns of River Heights, Providence, Millville, Nibley, Hyrum and Wellsville.

In the Wasatch Mountains immediately east of the valley is Naomi Peak, the highest point in the Bear River Range—9,980 feet. The Wellsville Mountains, in the southern end of Cache Valley, are said to be the steepest mountains in the United States. Within a couple of miles, the mountains rise nearly 5,000 feet over the communities of Wellsville and Mendon. The mountains are a designated wilderness area.

History

Like much of northern Utah, Logan and the surrounding Cache Valley were home to fur trappers in the 1820s, who wintered in what is now called Willow Valley. During the summer of 1826, a trapper was accidentally buried alive while excavating a cave in which to store or "cache" furs. The unlucky trapper's body was left buried; ever afterward, the valley was known as Cache Valley. That same year another fur trapper, Ephraim Logan, was killed by Indians and his body buried in the mountains east of Cache Valley, leading the canyon to be called Logan Canyon.

During the Mormon trek westward in 1847, Brigham Young met several fur trappers who advised the Mormon leader to forego the Salt Lake Valley because of the scarcity of timber and to settle in Cache Valley. Although Young opted for the Salt Lake Valley, Mormons began settling the Cache Valley in 1856, when Maughn's Fort, known today as Wellsville, was established in the southern end of the valley. Three years later, five additional settlements were established: Providence, Mendon, Logan, Richmond and Smithfield. Prosperity came to Logan with the arrival of the Utah Northern Railroad in 1873, which

---

Getting There

Logan is located 81 miles north of Salt Lake City and can be reached by taking Interstate 15 north for 56 miles to the Brigham City exit (Exit 364), then following US Hwy. 89 east-northeast for 25 miles through the Wasatch Mountains, by way of Wellsville (Sardine) Canyon into Cache Valley.

opened markets for the valley's grain and dairy products.

Logan has been something of a regional religious center for northern Utah and southern Idaho for more than a century since the construction of the Logan Temple, which began in 1877 and was completed in 1884. The Logan Temple is one of four historic temples constructed by the LDS church in Utah during the 19th century. The other three are located in St. George, Manti and Salt Lake City.

Major Attractions

Utah State University

Established in 1888 as Utah State Agricultural College, in 1957 the institution became known as Utah State University. Although the sports teams are known as the Aggies, and agricultural studies continue to be one of the school's leading areas of study, the university has a strong diversity of programs from the humanities to the sciences. The university's landmark building, "Old Main," dates from 1889 and sits on the brow of the hill overlooking Cache Valley. The university has a full schedule of concerts, programs and sporting activities. Don't miss USU's famous Traditional Aggie Ice Cream, which is available at the student union building or at the Food Science Building at the east end of the campus. **750 N. 1200 E.; 435-797-1158 event information; 435-797-0305 tickets; www.usu.edu.**

Festivals and Events

Cache Valley Cruise-In

weekend closest to July 4. One of the western United States' largest vintage, hot rod and collectible car shows. The cruise down Logan's Main St. draws a crowd of more than 35,000. **435-753-5825.**

Festival of the American West

last week of July–beginning of Aug. One of Utah's most popular summer festivals is held at the American West Heritage Center near Wellsville at the south end of Cache Valley. Artisans demonstrate traditional crafts, including woodcarving, leather carving, blacksmithing, wheelwrighting, quilting, Indian jewelry and beadwork. You will also find historic games and contests, reenactments and Dutch-oven food, buffalo stew, Mormon johnnycakes and Navajo tacos. (See the American West Heritage Center in the Museums section under Seeing and Doing.) **1-800-225-3378; 435-245-6050; www.americanwestcenter.org.**

Martin Harris Pageant

mid-Aug. Martin Harris is one of Mormondom's most important figures. In 1830 Harris, along with Oliver Cowdery and David Whitmer, gave their solemn witness that an angel of God showed them the golden plates from which Joseph Smith translated the Book of Mormon. After many years away from the church he helped found, Martin Harris journeyed to Utah to spend the last years of his life among the Mormons. The Martin Harris Pageant, sponsored by the Church of Jesus Christ of Latter-day Saints, depicts Harris's life and the early history of the Mormon church. No admission charge; however, because the pageant is popular, obtain tickets beforehand by writing the **Martin Harris Pageant, P.O. Box 151, Clarkston, UT 84305.**

Top of Utah Marathon

fourth Sat. in Sept. The 26.2-mile marathon begins at the Hardware Ranch in Blacksmith Fork Canyon at an elevation of 5,700 feet and for the first half of the race descends more than 1,000 feet in elevation through the canyon, bedecked in all its autumn leaf splendor, to Cache Valley. The course continues north through the towns of Nibley, Millville, Providence, River Heights and Logan, where there is a nice downhill finish. The race is limited to 2,200 runners. **435-797-2638; www.topofutah.com.**

Outdoor Activities

Biking

The mountains surrounding Cache Valley provide plenty of opportunities for mountain bikers. The "Bridgerland Mountain and Roadbike Trails" guide describes 23 routes, ranging from easy to moderate rides, from around Cache Valley to 50-mile-loop mountain rides to steep, technically demanding up-and-back climbs. The free guide is available at the **Cache Valley Tourist Council Office, 160 N. Main St., Logan; 1-800-882-4433; 435-752-2161.**

Green Canyon

Green Canyon is the location of the quarry that produced the granite used in the construction of the Logan Temple and Tabernacle, as well as numerous pioneer homes in and near Logan. The 12-mile up-and-back ride through Green Canyon is an easily accessible mountain ride along a well-maintained dirt-and-gravel road that is especially pretty in the spring and fall. Take 1900 N. to reach the trailhead, which begins about a mile east of 1600 E. in North Logan at the Cache National Forest boundary.

Little Pyrenees Loop

This moderate, rolling hill route gives you a good view of south Cache Valley. The 24-mile loop offers an excellent view of the farmland and communities along the east side of the valley, a close-up view of the towering Wellsville Mountains and an interesting ride alongside the marshes of the Little Bear River before the road crosses the Logan River just west of Logan. Head south out of Logan on Hwy. 165, past Providence, Millville and Nibley for about 7 miles to Hyrum. After turning west through Hyrum, the route passes around the northern end of Hyrum Reservoir and continues west to US Hwy. 89/91. After crossing the highway, turn north and follow Hwy. 23 through Wellsville and on to Mendon. Take 100 E. through Mendon and, just north of town, turn east for the last leg back into Logan at 600 S.

Richmond / Cornish Loop

To see the northern end of Cache Valley, take this 28-mile loop through beautiful farmland and the towns of Richmond, Cove, Lewiston, Cornish and Trenton. Start in Richmond, at the intersection of Hwy. 142 and US Hwy. 91. Head east to 3000 E., then turn north and follow the route as it moves up and down the hills for about 3 miles to 11800 N. Turn west and ride through Cove back to Hwy. 91, then follow the highway north to its intersection with state Hwy. 61. Turn west on Hwy. 61, passing through Lewiston and on to Cornish. In Cornish, turn south on Hwy. 23 and follow it back to its intersection with state Hwy. 142. Turn east and follow Hwy. 23 through Trenton and back to the starting point in Richmond.

Rentals

Sunrise Cyclery—138 N. 100 E.; 435-753-3294.

Boating / Waterskiing

Hyrum State Park

The most popular motorboat and waterskiing location in Cache Valley is Hyrum Reservoir, located 8 miles south of Logan, southwest of Hyrum on Hwy. 165.

Newton Reservoir

Located northwest of Logan, the Newton Reservoir was one of the first reservoirs constructed by Mormon pioneers in Utah. Today it is popular for waterskiing, and a barefoot waterski championship is held there in June. Take US Hwy. 91 north from Logan to Smithfield, turn west on Hwy. 218 and follow the road west to about 1 mile east of Newton to the turnoff to the reservoir.

Canoeing

Bear River

Although Utah is not noted for its canoeing opportunities, the Cache Valley area offers the best locations in a state known more for its deserts than its waterways. The Bear River can be navigated from below the Oneida Dam in Idaho across the border into Utah as far as Cutler Reservoir. With the exception of a 4-mile-long section of moderate whitewater below the Oneida Dam, the Bear River is placid, offering good opportunities for bird-watching.

For local canoers, the most popular stretch of the river is the 11-mile section between Trenton and Amalga, which is just west of Smithfield. Access to the river is still quite primitive, but boaters on this section can put in at the bridge across the Bear River on Hwy. 142 and take out at the bridge on Hwy. 218.

Rentals
Utah State University Outdoor Recreation—Open 10 A.M.–6 P.M. 1050 N. 950 E., USU campus, Logan; 435-797-3264.

Fishing

Blacksmith Fork River
An excellent fly-fishing stream, Blacksmith Fork River can be reached by following Hwy. 101 east out of Hyrum toward the Hardware Ranch Game Management Area.

Hyrum Reservoir
In addition to being a popular boating and waterskiing area, Hyrum Reservoir is also stocked with rainbow trout and bass. Located 8 miles south of Logan, southwest of Hyrum on Hwy. 165.

Logan River
One of the most popular fly-fishing streams in Utah, the Logan River in scenic Logan Canyon is stocked primarily with rainbow trout, but some cutthroat and brown trout are also found in the river. Follow US Hwy. 89 northeast out of Logan into the canyon.

Golf

Birch Creek Golf Course
As Cache Valley's oldest 18-hole public golf course, Birch Creek is popular with locals—the views of Cache Valley are spectacular. Located in Smithfield, 7 miles north of Logan. Take US Hwy. 91 north out of Logan to Center St. in Smithfield, then turn east for six blocks to reach the course. 435-683-6825.

Logan River Golf Course
Opened in 1993, the Logan River Golf Course offers a radical change from the more parklike, open and easier courses that the majority of Utah golfers are accustomed to. In a word, most duffers find this a fairly difficult course, with narrow fairways and small, difficult-to-hit greens. Through it all, you are surrounded by nearly century-old trees, the Logan River and a half dozen beautiful ponds. 550 W. 1000 S., Logan; 435-750-0123.

Sherwood Hills Golf Course
Situated in picturesque Wellsville Canyon and visible from US Hwy. 89/91, this 9-hole course is part of the Sherwood Hills Resort (see the Where to Stay section). While the course does not look very appealing from the highway, don't let that deceive you; most of the holes are hidden in the maples and quaking aspen. Uncrowded, with tee times usually easy to arrange, the resort and course are located 12 miles southwest of Logan. 435-245-6055.

Hiking
If you are an avid hiker and are going to spend any time in the Cache Valley area, you will want to pick up a copy of "Bridgerland Hiking Trails," a guide that describes 15 trails, is available at no cost from the Cache Valley Tourist Council, 160 N. Main St., Logan, UT 84321; 1-800-882-4433; 435-752-2161; www.tour-cachevalley.com; or the Logan Ranger District, Wasatch-Cache National Forest, 150 E. Hwy. 89; 435-755-3620. The trails range from short, easy rambles, like the Riverside Nature Trail described below, to strenuous climbs, like those in the Wellsville Mountains, that challenge the most fit of hikers.

High Creek Trail

Heading up into the mountains east from Richmond, the 12-mile round trip High Creek Trail climbs 2,600 feet, passing mountain wildflowers and waterfalls to reach snow-fed High Creek Lake at the base of Naomi Peak on Mt. Naomi. To reach the trailhead, drive north past Richmond on US Hwy. 91, then watch for a marked turnoff on the eastern side of the road about a mile past the Pepperidge Farm factory (where you might want to stock up on cookies for the hike—the factory thrift store is open at various hours Tues.–Sat.). Drive east for 5 miles to the end of the road.

Riverside Nature Trail

This easy 3-mile round trip trail follows the Logan River in Logan Canyon between Spring Hollow Campground and the Guinavah Campground–Picnic Area. The trail is a favorite of bird-watchers, and the Bridgerland Audubon Society in cooperation with the U.S. Forest Service has prepared an excellent brief guide to the flora and fauna along the trail. The brochure, "Riverside Nature Trail," is available at both trailheads and local tourist offices. To reach the lower trailhead, from the east side of Logan follow US Hwy. 89 up Logan Canyon for about 4 miles and watch for the Spring Hollow turnout, where parking and rest rooms are located across the river.

Tony Grove Lake Area Trails

Tony Grove Lake is one of the most popular areas in Logan Canyon. The Tony Grove turnoff off US Hwy. 89 is 19.2 miles east of Logan; it is another 7 miles over paved road to Tony Grove Lake. From the lake's day-use parking area at an elevation of 8,000 feet, you can take one of several trails ranging in length from just under 4 miles to 20 miles round trip.

Coldwater Spring Trail—It is 1.9 miles long and rises 700 feet along its course through spruce–fir forest and aspen groves to the spring. Side trails to Twin Creeks, Cottonwood Canyon, Smithfield Canyon, Green Canyon and Blind Hollow leave from the main trail.

White Pine Lake Trail—It is 3.4 miles one way and climbs to an elevation of 8,800 feet, then drops down off the ridge to 8,400 feet at White Pine Lake. This is an especially beautiful hike as it passes through stands of fir, spruce and aspen and meadows of wildflowers that are most colorful in July and Aug. White Pine is a beautiful glacial lake surrounded by cirque cliffs and high mountains.

Naomi Peak Trail—This is a steep climb with an elevation gain of nearly 2,000 feet in 2.9 miles that ends with a magnificent view of the surrounding mountains and Cache Valley below. You can continue north from Naomi Peak along the High Creek Trail to another glacial lake, High Creek Lake, surrounded by towering cliffs. High Creek parallels the trail and forms several waterfalls, especially along the last 2 miles to the lake. This is a 20-mile round trip hike from Tony Grove Lake.

Wellsville Mountain Trails

In the Wellsville Mountains in the southern end of Cache Valley, there are three trails that lead to the summits for a spectacular view of Cache Valley to the east and the Great Salt Lake and Bear River to the west.

Box Elder Peak Trail—A steep, 4-mile-long trail, with an elevation gain of 4,000 feet. The trailhead is south of Wellsville, off US Hwy. 89/91. Follow the highway south, past Wellsville, to the first big turn, then look for an unpaved road just north of the turn, which is the beginning of the trail. Plan at least 5 hours to make the 8-mile round trip.

Stewart Pass Trail—The 3-mile-long trail heads south for 0.75 mile toward Coldwater Lake; past the lake, it turns west for about 2 miles as it makes a steep climb past Hughes Peak to Stewart Pass. The trailhead is southwest of Mendon and is reached by turning west off the Mendon Main St., south of the stop sign, onto a gravel road. Drive along the gravel road for about 3.5 miles, until it ends near a watering trough, then look for the trailhead. Allow at least 3 hours to the summit and back.

Deep Canyon Trail—If you take the Stewart

Pass Trail to the summit of the Wellsville Mountains, you can continue northwest along the ridgeline for 1.75 miles past Mendon Peak and Scout Peak, then descend using the Deep Canyon Trail. The total hiking distance up the Stewart Pass Trail and back along the Deep Canyon Trail is approximately 8 miles, with the steep climb making it a strenuous undertaking requiring the better part of a day. The long-distance views and surprisingly thick foliage are a just reward. To make this loop, leave a car at the Deep Canyon trailhead, reached by driving west out of Mendon on 3rd N. for about 2 miles. Take plenty of water and protection against the winds and colder temperatures that can be expected along the ridgeline.

Wind Cave Trail

One of the most interesting features in Logan Canyon is Wind Cave, located in the China Wall Formation on the north slope of Logan Canyon. It is actually a series of three openings that resemble a triple arch. The largest opening is about 40 feet high. It is a strenuous 2-mile hike to the cave as the trail climbs nearly 1,000 feet. There are exposed cliffs near the cave. The parking area at the trailhead, which has space for a dozen or so cars, is located 5.3 miles up Logan Canyon from the Lady Bird rest stop. A sign indicates Wind Cave.

Horseback Riding

Beaver Creek

Bryan and Helen Lundahl operate a horseback riding facility in Logan Canyon, 25 miles northeast of the city and 0.25 mile east of the turnoff to the Beaver Mountain Ski Resort. Rides are from 1 to 2.5 hours, through the mountains covered with aspen, pine trees and wildflowers, past a beautiful mountain stream. Open summer Mon.–Sat. 10:30 A.M.–7:30 P.M. **435-753-1076.**

Skating

ICE
George S. Eccles Ice Center
Opened in early 2002 in time to see service as a practice arena for Olympic figure skaters, short

track racers and hockey teams, this state-of-the-art indoor ice arena is open for public skating. **2825 N. 200 E., North Logan; 435-787-2288.**

Merlin Olsen Park
When there is the right combination of snow and cold, Logan City Parks employees create a huge outdoor ice rink. Merlin Olsen Park is named for Cache Valley native and USU football All-American and NFL Hall of Famer Merlin Olsen, who is now best known as an actor. You can rent skates at the park, located south of Logan Temple. **300 E. Center; 435-716-9240.**

IN-LINE / SKATEBOARDING
Logan Skate Park
This 17,000-square-foot park features 8-foot bowls designed for all levels of skaters and boarders. Open daily from dawn to dusk. **451 S. 500 W.; 435-716-9250.**

Skiing

CROSS-COUNTRY
Cross-country skiing has become particularly popular with USU students and other residents of Cache Valley. Groomed ski tracks are located at the entrance of **Beaver Mountain Ski Resort** (see Downhill) and at **Sunrise Campground** on US Hwy. 89, overlooking Bear Lake, near the Logan Canyon summit. There is also a groomed track in Green Canyon a short distance from Logan. "Cache Tours" lists 30 cross-country ski areas in the Cache Valley area that are of interest to serious cross-country skiers. The "Bridgerland Winter Guide" lists eight of the most popular trails. Available at **Cache Valley Tourist Council, 160 N. Main St., Logan, UT 84321; 1-800-882-4433; 435-752-2161; www.tourcachevalley.com.**

Sherwood Hills Resort
This resort has more than 11 miles of groomed trails. Ski rentals are available. Located 12 miles southwest of Logan on US Hwy. 89/91. **435-245-5054.**

DOWNHILL
Beaver Mountain Ski Area
The only downhill ski area in northern Utah, Beaver Mountain has been family-operated since 1939. It has three double chairlifts to serve the 26 runs on 464 skiable acres. The longest lift is the 4,600-foot Harry's Dream (named for owner Harold Seeholzer), which climbs to an elevation of 8,800 feet and is within a few feet of the summit of Beaver Mountain. The capacity of all three chairlifts is 2,600 skiers an hour. With day passes the cheapest in the state, Beaver Mountain is popular with USU students. Sixty-five percent of its terrain is for beginning and intermediate skiers. Beaver Mountain averages 400 inches a year. There is a ski school, ski rental shop, and lodge with a cafeteria and short-order homestyle food. The resort is also a popular evening snow tubing location. Tubes are provided, and a paddle lift saves the strenuous climb back up the mountain. Located 30 miles northeast of Logan off US Hwy. 89. **435-753-0921 information and ticket prices; 435-753-4822 ski reports.**

Swimming
Logan Aquatic Center, an outdoor swimming complex, is open daily June–Aug., Mon.–Sat. noon–8 P.M., Sat.–Sun. 11 A.M.–6 P.M. **451 S. 500 W., Logan; 435-716-9250. Logan Municipal Pool** is an indoor pool that is open year-round. **114 E. 1000 N., Logan; 435-752-9323.**

Tennis
Community Recreation Center
Except for the 12 tennis courts on the USU campus, the Community Recreation Center is the best place for tennis. With four unlighted outdoor courts and two indoor courts available by the hour (fee charged in addition to admission to the Recreation Center), die-hard tennis players can be accommodated. You cannot reserve the outdoor courts, but the indoor courts can be booked. **195 S. 100 W., Logan; 435-752-3221.**

Seeing and Doing

Children and Families

Willow Park Zoo
If you are looking for an inexpensive—or free—outing for children, the Willow Park Zoo is worth an hour or two of your time. The zoo is located in a section of Logan's 15-acre Willow Park. Most of the animals are birds such as ducks, swans, wild turkeys, peacocks and bald eagles, but there are also pygmy goats, monkeys, two black bears and a family of wallabies. Open year-round, except Thanksgiving, Christmas and New Year's Day, 8 A.M.–dusk. **419 W. 700 S., Logan; 435-752-3060.**

Historic Sites
Logan has an abundance of historic homes and buildings. Available at no charge is the booklet "A Self-Guided Walking Tour of Logan's Historic Main Street" (available at the **Cache Valley Tourist Council (160 N. Main St., Logan, UT 84321; 1-800-882-4433; 435-752-2161; www.tourcachevalley.com),** which provides information on 14 Main St. buildings, most of which were constructed at the turn of the century. In addition to the Logan Tabernacle (see below), other buildings include the 1883 Cache County Courthouse, the oldest county building in Utah still being used for its original purpose; the 1908 St. John's Episcopal Church, the oldest non-Mormon church in Logan; the 1913 Lyric Theater; the 1923 Capitol Theater; and the J. R. Edwards Saloon where, in 1895, Joshua Paul, president of the Agricultural College, was struck over the head by Edwards when the president entered the saloon in an effort to keep his students from frequenting that den of iniquity.

Bear River Massacre Site
For more than a century, it was known as the Battle of Bear River. Historian Brigham D. Madsen, in his study *The Shoshoni Frontier and the Bear River Massacre* (University of Utah Press, 1985), has put the events of Jan. 29, 1863, into perspective and leaves little question that the deaths

of 250 to 350 Shoshoni (most of whom were women and children) were a massacre. More Native Americans were killed by whites in a single day at Bear River than even at the 1864 Sand Creek Massacre or in 1890 at Wounded Knee. Twenty-three soldiers, under the command of Col. Patrick Connor, stationed at Ft. Douglas in the Salt Lake Valley, died in the encounter. The massacre site is where Battle Creek joins the Bear River. Efforts are underway to interpret and preserve the site, which is a sacred location for members of the Northwestern Shoshoni. The site is located about 10 miles across the Utah–Idaho border. Follow US Hwy. 91 north to Preston and continue north toward Downey and Pocatello for approximately 3 miles. You will drop down off a bluff and cross the Bear River to its confluence with Battle Creek.

Logan Tabernacle

One Mormon building that non-Mormon visitors can enter is the historic Logan Tabernacle, which is used for community meetings and is open to LDS members and nonmembers alike. Construction commenced in 1864, but the building was not completed until 1891—partly because subsequent work on the Logan Temple took a higher priority. Built of gray granite trimmed in white, the Logan Tabernacle is one of the oldest remaining tabernacles in the Mormon West. The green space surrounding the building offers a parklike atmosphere in the heart of Logan. The building is open for tours. Located **between Center and 100 N. on Main St.**

Logan Temple

Mormon leaders had a good eye for the proper location of their most important religious buildings. The Logan Temple and the Manti Temple in Sanpete County (see the **Central Region**) are the most dramatically situated of the nine Mormon temples in Utah. Constructed on a hill overlooking downtown Logan, the temple can be seen from nearly every part of Cache Valley. Since its completion in 1884, the Gothic-style gray stone edifice, with its towers, buttresses and battlements, has seemed to preside over affairs

much like the castles and fortresses of medieval Europe. In 1979, amid great controversy from both within and outside the Mormon church, the interior was extensively remodeled and most of the historical interior was lost. But unless you are a Mormon yourself with proper credentials, you will not be allowed inside the temple to see it. Still, the exterior of the building is well worth a look, and the view of Cache Valley from Temple Hill is glorious. Located **between 200 and 300 N. and 200 and 300 E.**

Museums

American West Heritage Center

This fine facility looks to interpret a century of Western American history from the fur trade era of the 1820s to the typical Cache Valley farm of the 1910s. A major focus is the interpretation of the Northwestern Shoshoni Native Americans who occupied what is now the site of the Heritage Center and surrounding valleys for hundreds of years. Working with the Northwestern Shoshoni tribe, the center's staff have established an 1835 encampment as part of the center and are working toward the construction of an interpretive center that will not only present the Shoshoni experience from their perspective but preserve artifacts, documents and oral histories of tribal members as well. In addition to the Shoshone encampment, the other elements of the Center include the late 19th and early 20th century Jensen Historical Farm and a pioneer interpretive site. Other areas in the planning and development stages include a mountain man site patterned on a Hudson's Bay Company fort, a military encampment, a frontier village and a ranch.

You can visit the Shoshoni encampment, Jensen farm and military encampment during the summer and for special events and activities at times throughout the rest of the year. The major event—the Festival of the American West (see the Festivals and Events section) is held in late July and early Aug. Other events and activities include Baby Animal Day in the early spring, Fall Harvest Festival in Sept., Pumpkin Day in Oct. and Frontier Christmas in Dec.

The visitor center, located just west of US Hwy. 89/91 at the south end of Cache Valley, is the state welcome center for Northern Utah and offers tourist information, rest rooms, exhibits and a gift shop. The Welcome Center is open Memorial Day–Labor Day, Mon.–Sat. 9 A.M.–5 P.M., and the rest of the year, Mon.–Fri. 8 A.M.–5 P.M. **4025 S. Hwy. 89/91, Wellsville, UT 84339; 1-800-225-3378; 435-245-6050; www.americanwestcenter.org.**

Nora Eccles Harrison Museum of Art

This museum features permanent exhibits of the art museum's own collections, as well as new exhibits every six to eight weeks. Workshops and gallery talks are featured. Open Tues., Thurs. and Fri. 10:30 A.M.–4:30 P.M.; Wed. 10:30 A.M.–8 P.M.; Sat.–Sun. 2–5 P.M.; closed holidays. Admission is free. Located on the USU campus. **435-797-0163.**

Performing Arts

Old Lyric Theater Repertory Company

Housed in the historic Lyric Theater in downtown Logan, this theater company is operated by the USU Department of Theater Arts. During June, July and Aug., it offers a variety of comedies, drama and musicals in repertory. The 1913 building is also reported to house a friendly ghost who is a fan of Shakespeare. The ghost has been spotted at the edge of the balcony wearing a fool's cap and Elizabethan-era clothing, and laughing during rehearsals. **Old Lyric Theater Repertory Company, Theater Arts Dept., USU, 28 W. Center, Logan, UT 84322-4035; 435-797-1500.**

Utah Festival Opera Company

Thanks to Cache Valley native Michael Ballam, July and Aug. have become opera time in Logan as the Utah Festival Opera Company, which launched its first season in 1993, performs operas, light operettas and musicals in repertory. The company has an excellent facility, the restored Ellen Eccles Theatre (formerly the historic Capitol Theater, which was built in the early 1900s and is located at 43 S. Main); involvement from the USU music department; support of a large all-volunteer guild; and encouragement from the community. **59 S. 100 W., Logan, UT 84321; 435-750-0300.**

Scenic Drives

Cache Valley Historic Driving Tour

This fact-filled, self-guided driving tour begins at the towns of Wellsville and Hyrum in the south end of Cache Valley and extends for more than 50 miles to Banida and Oxford at the north end of the valley in Idaho. Shoshoni, mountain men, Mormon settlements and heritage sites are indicated. Pick up a copy of the tour at the **Cache Valley Tourism Office, 160 N. Main St., Logan, UT 84321; 1-800-882-4433; 435-752-2161; www.tourcachevalley.com.**

Hardware Ranch Rd. Backway

If you don't mind traveling on a single-lane dirt road, you can make a nice loop combining the Logan Canyon road with the Hardware Ranch Rd. Otherwise, the more commonly used route up Blacksmith Fork Canyon to Hardware Ranch is a worthwhile trip in itself. The route follows Hwy. 101 east from Hyrum for 18 miles to Hardware Ranch, a popular winter wildlife viewing area. The paved road to Hardware Ranch takes you past steep canyon walls into broad meadows. To combine the drive with a return via Logan Canyon, continue along the dirt Hardware Ranch Rd. that heads north from the ranch for approximately 25 miles to its junction with Hwy. 30 at the southern end of Bear Lake at Laketown. From there, head north to Garden City, then west on US Hwy. 89 to Logan.

Logan Canyon Scenic Byway

The 41-mile drive from Logan to Bear Lake through Logan Canyon is not only the most often used route to the resort area, but it is also one of the most scenic drives in the state. It is another favorite place to view autumn colors. The limestone cliffs in the lower end of the canyon, the swift-flowing Logan River and the groves of quaking aspen and pine trees show off Utah's mountains at their best. The ascent to the summit of Logan Canyon is a gradual 30 miles. Along the way, Logan Canyon offers several interesting stopping points:

The **Old Jardine Juniper** is located on a limestone ridge 1,500 feet above the road and can be reached by a steep 1.5-mile climb from Cottonwood Campground, located about 15 miles east of Logan. The juniper is the largest known Rocky Mountain "red cedar" and is estimated to be more than 3,000 years old. The tree, discovered in 1923, is 45 feet high and 27 feet in circumference.

Another historic event occurred in 1923 when an 11-foot **grizzly bear** known as Old Ephraim was killed. An 11-foot-high granite shaft marks the site. It is located 6 miles from the highway on an unpaved forest road along Temple Fork, which can be reached by heading southeast about a mile up US Hwy. 89 from Cottonwood Campground. The bear's skull, a relic owned by the Smithsonian Institution, is on display at Utah State University's Merrill Library.

Ricks Spring. This popular stop 16 miles up the canyon was long thought to be a spring that emerged from the cavern discovered by pioneer Thomas E. Ricks, but it is actually a diversion of the Logan River.

Tony Grove Lake is a beautiful body of water that is popular with anglers. It is located 5 miles off the highway, 20 miles up the canyon from Logan.

At the summit of Logan Canyon, an easy mile-long trail can be taken to the Limber Pine (see the **Bear Lake** chapter). A steep 11-mile descent over switchbacks takes you to Garden City in Rich County (see the **Bear Lake** chapter). Along the road are several pullouts, where you can stop and admire the breathtaking view of turquoise-colored Bear Lake that takes up most of the valley below.

Wellsville Canyon

The primary access to Cache Valley is via US Hwy. 89/91 from Brigham City. The 12-mile drive between Brigham City and Wellsville in the southern end of Cache Valley is picturesque year-round, but it's particularly beautiful in the fall.

Wildlife Viewing

Bird-watching

The Bear River meanders through Cache Valley, forming marshes and wetlands that offer a variety of locations for bird-watching. More than 250 species of birds have been sighted along the river. The most popular location, **Cutler Marsh,** also known as the Cutler Wetlands Maze, is located about 6 miles west of downtown Logan on 200 N. and approximately 4800 W. For more information check with the **Utah State University Outdoor Recreation Office, 435-797-3264,** or the **Cache Valley Tourist Council, 435-752-2161.**

Hardware Ranch

Originally homesteaded in 1868, Hardware Ranch is one of the most popular winter wildlife viewing locations in the state. Owned and operated by the Utah Division of Wildlife Resources since 1946, the ranch produces wild meadow hay used to feed more than 700 head of elk during the winter. Visitors ride sleighs across the snow into the meadows where hundreds of elk are fed. The elk have become very tame and, if not frightened, will come right up to eat hay off the sleigh. Some elk stay year-round and the visitor center/restaurant is open throughout the year. During the summer months, you can see newborn elk calves under the watchful eye of their mothers. In Oct., you are likely to hear the bull elks bugling their mating calls. You can take covered wagon and horseback overnight trips that include barbecue dinner, western games and a Dutch-oven breakfast. Hardware Ranch is an interesting spot all four seasons. Winter days are cold; temperatures with the windchill factor can drop well below 0° F, so dress accordingly. Take Hwy. 101 east out of Hyrum up Blacksmith Fork Canyon for 18 miles; the road can be snow-packed in the winter, but is usually well sanded. **435-753-6168.**

Where to Stay

Bed and Breakfasts and Inns

Anniversary Inn—$$$$

In this complex of five different buildings, there are 20 different suites and rooms with different themes such as King Arthur's Castle, Amazon Rain Forest and Jesse James Hideout—the most popular room, with its full-size pool table. Four suites are located in the classical Victorian-style home built in 1890 for Logan's first college-trained doctor, Oliver C. Ormsby. Later, Logan businessman and music teacher George W. Thatcher Jr. acquired the home in 1909. Within the Ormsby–Thatcher home are the Opera House as well as the inn's Presidential, European Honeymoon and Grand Bridal Suites. Most of the guests are honeymooners or couples celebrating a special anniversary. All of the rooms have jetted tubs and large-screen TVs with DVD players. A breakfast of fruit, ham and cheese croissants, cinnamon rolls and a yogurt parfait is served to each room. At night, guests are treated to sparkling cider and cheesecake. **169 E. Center St., Logan, UT 84321; 1-800-574-7605; 435-752-3443; www.anniversaryinn.com.**

Beaver Creek Lodge—$$$

Until recently there were no accommodations at the Beaver Mountain Ski Resort. Now Beaver Creek Lodge provides 10 cozy rooms outfitted with lodgepole bed frames and quilts. The jetted tubs will soothe your tired and sore ski muscles. Complimentary breakfast; dinners are available at a relatively modest cost. **435-753-1026.**

Logan House—$$$$

This well-maintained six-room bed and breakfast inn is located in a turn-of-the-20th-century brick Victorian home a block off Logan's Main St. If you like a sunny, cheerful room, opt for the upstairs guest room, which is bathed in sunlight through its south- and west-facing windows. A baby grand piano on the main floor and plenty of books, many of them classics, in bookshelves throughout the house indicate that music and lit-erature are important elements of the home's charm and tradition. **168 N. 100 E., Logan; 1-800-478-7459; 435-752-7727.**

Providence Inn—$$$ to $$$$

Housed in the 1871 Providence LDS church, this inn serves a dual function as a bed and breakfast and wedding reception inn. Owner Karl Seethaler insured the preservation of the church when he opened the bed and breakfast inn and reception center in 1995. Actually most of the inn is a 1926 Georgian-style addition to the original church, while the former chapel of the historic stone church serves for weddings and receptions. Some of the third-floor rooms are built in the upper gable of the original church; in the Pioneer Room, the original wooden church beams are part of the design, and in the Log Cabin Room, a section of the interior of the original rock wall is exposed. There's a tasteful and spacious Honeymoon Suite fit for any new couple. Each of the 14 rooms has a private bath and TV/VCR. There's a large and charming parlor area decorated with original paintings and antique dishes. Karl and his friendly staff make this a perfect place—it's not too large, it's not too small, it's just right. A full breakfast of french toast; blueberry pancakes; bacon, eggs and breakfast potatoes; or gourmet omelettes is served in the parlor, or you can have it brought to your suite. **10 S. Main St., Providence; 1-800-480-4943; 435-752-3432; www.providenceinn.com.**

Sherwood Hills—$$ to $$$

Eighty-five rooms and a restaurant, plus there is a golf course and cross-country skiing in the winter. Located off US Hwy. 89 in Sardine Canyon, approximately 12 miles south of Logan. **1-800-532-5066; 435-245-6424.**

University Inn—$$

Seventy-four rooms within walking distance of the college football stadium, basketball arena and library. Located in the center of the Utah State University campus, adjacent to the Student Center. **1-800-231-5634; 435-797-0016.**

Motels

Best Western Baugh Motel—$$
Heated pool; 77 rooms. **153 S. Main St., Logan; 1-800-462-4154; 435-752-5220.**

Best Western Weston Inn—$$
The heated indoor swimming pool is a favorite of children; 89 rooms. **250 N. Main St., Logan; 1-800-532-5055; 435-752-5700.**

Camping

PRIVATE
There are four small private campgrounds in the Logan vicinity. **Western Park Campground** has 13 sites with complete hookups; **350 W. 800 S., Logan; 435-752-6424.** The **Riverside RV Park and Campground** has 19 sites, 15 with complete hookups; **447 W. 1700 S., Logan; 435-245-4469.** Traveland RV Park has 45 sites with full hookups plus 10 tentsites, a general store and laundry facilities; **2020 S. Hwy. 89/91, Logan; 435-787-2020.** Phillips 66 has 13 sites with full hookups, a dump station, showers, a general store and laundry facilities; **1936 N. Main St., Logan; 435-753-1025.**

PUBLIC
Hyrum
Three Forest Service campgrounds within a distance of 3.5 miles in Blacksmith Fork Canyon along Hwy. 101 offer a total of 27 camping spots. **Pioneer Campground,** 9 miles from Hyrum, has 18 sites; **Friendship Campground,** 1.5 miles farther up the canyon, has 6 sites; and **Spring Campground,** another 2 miles up Hwy. 242, has 8 sites. Only Pioneer Campground has drinking water; it is the only campground where a fee is charged. **1-800-280-2267 reservations; 435-755-3620 Logan Ranger District.**

Logan Canyon
Within a 23-mile stretch along Hwy. 89 through Logan Canyon, there are 10 public campgrounds. All include both tent- and trailer sites, but there are no hookups. Most campgrounds have fewer than a dozen sites, although the Tony Grove Lake Campground and the Guinavah-Malibu Campground have 37 and 40 sites, respectively. Beginning with those closest to Logan, the campgrounds and their distances from Logan are **Bridger,** 10 sites, 5.8 miles; **Spring Hollow,** 12 sites, 6.5 miles; **Guinavah-Malibu,** 40 sites, 8 miles; **Preston Valley,** 3 sites, 10.7 miles; **Wood Camp,** 6 sites, 12.4 miles; **Lewis M. Turner,** 10 sites, 22.2 miles; **Red Banks,** 12 sites, 22.7 miles; and **Tony Grove Lake,** 37 sites, 28.7 miles. Fees are charged for most campgrounds; most have drinking water and rest rooms. **1-800-280-2267 reservations; 435-755-3620 Logan Ranger District.**

Where to Eat

Angie's Restaurant—$ to $$
This is Logan's favorite place for breakfast. Nearly a dozen different kinds of omelettes plus the usual waffles, pancakes and skillet breakfasts are served all day long. Scones and cinnamon rolls are made fresh daily. Lunch and dinner items include sandwiches, burgers, salads, pasta, chicken, steak and seafood. Open Sun.–Thurs. 5:30 A.M.–10 P.M., Fri.–Sat. 5:30 A.M.–11 P.M. **690 N. Main St., Logan; 435-752-9252.**

Bluebird—$$ to $$$
This restaurant has been on Logan's Main St. longer than anyone can remember, starting out as a soda fountain and ice cream and candy store in 1914, then expanding to include lunch items like sandwiches, soup and chili. The present building was constructed in the early 1920s, and some of the fixtures, including the marble soda fountain and rich wood fixtures, date from that era. Under the ownership of John Booth, the Bluebird continues to serve traditional American dishes such as roast beef, prime rib, sirloin steak, baked ham, roast turkey and fish. Open Mon.–Thurs. 11 A.M.–9 P.M.; Fri.–Sat. 11 A.M.–10 P.M.; Sun. noon–8 P.M. **19 N. Main St., Logan; 435-752-3155.**

Copper Mill—$$ to $$$

The Copper Mill specializes in prime beef. In addition, there are chicken dishes, plus halibut, scallops and shrimp. Open Mon.–Thurs. 11 A.M.–9:30 P.M. and Fri.–Sat. 11 A.M.–10:30 P.M. **55 N. Main St., Logan; 435-752-0647.**

Cottage Restaurant—$$ to $$$

Located behind the Baugh Motel in a more modern house, the Cottage Restaurant is open for breakfast, lunch and dinner. Menu items are mostly traditional American fare such as pork chops, chicken breast, liver and onions, trout, halibut, hot and cold sandwiches, salads and pasta. The dinner menu expands to include seafood and steaks. There are four dining areas, including a nice outside patio. The well-kept yard and lawn are especially inviting. **51 W. 200 S., Logan; 435-752-5260.**

Kate's Kitchen—$$ to $$$

If you've ever wondered what it would be like to eat in a human beehive, Kate's Kitchen comes as close to it as anything I have experienced. Named for the youngest child of Don Searles's six children, the restaurant is designed for those who want good food served family style in heaping bowls and plates where kids can come, make noise and laugh, and parents and grandparents don't have to worry about the mess. Family members work in the restaurant, and waiters and waitresses wear ever-changing funny hats to add to the festive atmosphere. In addition to an endless supply of rolls, salad, beverages and real mashed potatoes, you can select a main entrée of barbecued ribs, roasted chicken, pork tenderloin, pot roast or country-fried steak. Open Tues.–Sat. 4–10 P.M. **71 E. 1200 S., Logan; 435-752-5733.**

Services

Visitor Information

American West Heritage Visitor Center— 4025 S. Hwy. 89/91, Wellsville; 1-800-225-3378; 435-245-6050; www.americanwest center.org.

Cache Valley Tourist Council—160 N. Main St., Logan, UT 84321; 1-800-882-4433; 435-752-2161; www.tourcache-valley.com.

Brigham City and Promontory

For many Utahns, Brigham City means peaches, and it is unfortunate that, with the completion of Interstate 15, many visitors are unaware of the string of fruit stands along the 12-mile stretch of US Hwy. 89/91 that runs south from Brigham City through Perry and Willard. Located near the northeast end of Great Salt Lake, Brigham City has long been an access point for observing the rich variety of waterfowl that inhabit or visit the marshes where the Bear River reaches the lake. This area is home to many smaller towns, including Willard, Perry, Mantua, Corinne, Bear River City, Penrose, Thatcher, Honeyville, Elwood, Tremonton and Plymouth. Driving down Brigham City's Main St., you will pass under the "Welcome to Brigham" archway sign that has greeted visitors to the city since its construction in 1928; underneath the welcome the sign reads "Gateway— World's Greatest Game Bird Refuge," the Bear River Migratory Bird Refuge on Great Salt Lake.

Since the establishment of the Golden Spike National Historic Site in the 1960s, Brigham City has hosted thousands of railroad buffs who have made their pilgrimage from all over the world to Promontory Summit. Each year the driving of the last railroad spike is reenacted, and other events take place at the site. Brigham City continues its involvement in transportation on a grand scale: Morton-Thiokol, the area's largest employer of Brigham City's 17,000 or so residents, manufactures rockets and rocket motors, including motors for the *Challenger* spacecraft.

History

The prehistoric inhabitants of the region found that the marshes at the mouth of the Bear River where it enters Great Salt Lake offer a rich supply of food, and archaeologists have studied their lakeside camps with great interest. West of the lake, in places like Hogup Cave, archaeologists trace the Desert Archaic culture back 10,000 years.

Much more recently, in 1851, Mormon settlers moved to what they called Box Elder. The settlement was renamed Brigham City for Mormon leader Brigham Young in 1854, when he sent his trusted friend Lorenzo Snow to direct affairs. Snow encouraged Scandinavian immigrants to come to Brigham City and worked with them to establish the Brigham City Mercantile and Manufacturing Association, a cooperative that employed more than 500 people in a variety of economic endeavors, including a store, a woolen mill, a planing mill, a sheep herd, a dairy herd, a hat and cap factory and other ventures designed to make Brigham City completely self-sufficient. The Brigham City Cooperative encouraged Brigham Young to push for the establishment of other cooperatives throughout the state, under what was known as the United Order Movement.

The completion of the transcontinental railroad at Promontory, 30 miles west of Brigham City, on May 10, 1869, marked not only a new phase of American history, but a new era for Utah. A non-Mormon city named Corinne was established in 1869 on the Bear River just

---

Getting There

Brigham City is located about 60 miles north of Salt Lake City, off Interstate 15 at Exit 364.

---

5 miles west of Brigham City. The pretentious city of 1,500 people quickly overshadowed Brigham City. It pushed to become the western terminus for the Union Pacific Railroad and the eastern terminus for the Central Pacific Railroad and seemed destined, at least in the minds of Corinnethians, to become the new capital of Utah Territory. Merchants, speculators and camp followers moved into the town as the railroad was completed. Within a few years, though, the dreams vanished, people moved on and Corinne, despite its still-standing historic 1870 Methodist church, became another Mormon village.

By the turn of the 20th century, the cooperative movement had died. Brigham City moved placidly through the first half of the 20th century—until World War II led to the opening of Bushnell Military Hospital, where more than 13,000 wounded veterans of the battlefields were treated. In the postwar era, Brigham City's economy depended heavily on the defense industry.

Major Attractions

Golden Spike National Historic Site

Some say it was the most significant accomplishment of the 19th century: linking the Atlantic coast with the Pacific coast by rail. That event took place at Promontory Summit on May 10, 1869, as dignitaries and officials of the Central Pacific Railroad and the Union Pacific Railroad met to drive the last spike to join the two railroads. Four symbolic spikes—two gold, one silver and one a combination of iron, silver and gold—and a laurel rail were used in the ceremony. Then the actual last spike, an ordinary iron spike, was hammered home at 12:47 P.M., and the Union Pacific's "Engine No. 119" and the Central Pacific's "Jupiter" pulled forward. Men on both locomotives shook hands, marking the completion of the railroad.

The transcontinental railroad was built by Chinese laborers, the main workforce for the Central Pacific, and by the Irish and German immigrants, many veterans of the Civil War, employed by the

Union Pacific in constructing the line west from Omaha, Nebraska. Once the line reached Utah, Mormon workers augmented the efforts of both companies. Lucrative federal land grants and subsidies were awarded for each mile of track completed. Another incentive was the promise of Mormon trade to whichever company reached Ogden first. The competition caused miles of parallel grades to be constructed within Utah at a frenzied pace, until Congress acted to set the meeting point for the two railroads at Promontory. The Promontory route remained the primary transcontinental route until 1904, when the Lucin Cutoff, a trestle constructed across Great Salt Lake west from Ogden, was completed. Finally, in 1942, the original 123-mile-long Promontory track was salvaged for the war effort.

After World War II, local people began commemorating the driving of the golden spike with a ceremony and a reenactment of the event. In 1957 Congress set aside 7 acres at Promontory as a National Historic Site, later enlarged to 2,176 acres in 1965. That year a road was constructed to the site and plans were developed for a huge centennial celebration. A visitor center and working replicas of the original steam engines were built in 1980. The Golden Spike National Historic Site is now administered by the National Park Service.

Festivals and Events

Each year on the anniversary of the **driving of the last spike,** local actors dress up in period costumes and take on the roles of the participants at the first driving of the last spike. Based on historical documentation, the event is reenacted as accurately as possible on May 10 at 12:47 P.M. using the speeches of the day and two reconstructed steam engines. There is usually a large crowd for this event, so plan to come early. Be prepared for any kind of weather, from warm summer days to a wintry snowstorm.

Outdoor Activities

At the visitor center, pick up a booklet describing the **driving route** past the parallel grades built by the two companies, cuts and fills, rock culverts and other remnants of the original construction work. Numbered signs along the route correspond to interpretive information in the booklet. For a more extensive tour, requiring most of the day and a four-wheel-drive vehicle, see the Central Pacific Railroad Trail Backway in the Scenic Drives section.

At the eastern end of the driving tour, you can take the **Big Fill Hike,** an easy 0.75-mile walk down the railroad grade to the Big Fill and Big Trestle sites. Here, the difficult terrain forced the Central Pacific Railroad to spend two months building a massive fill 170 feet deep and 500 feet long to get across the deep ravine. The effort required 500 men and 250 teams of animals. The Union Pacific did not have two months to make a fill, so its workers constructed an elaborate but temporary wooden trestle, parallel to the Central Pacific's Big Fill.

There are two easy loop **bicycle tours** near the site. The East Grade Tour covers 3.5 miles and the longer West Grade Tour is 14 miles.

Getting There

Take Exit 368 from Interstate 15 and drive west on Hwy. 83 approximately 30 miles to the visitor center. The center provides an excellent orientation, with a 20-minute introductory slide presentation, films and talks given by Park Service rangers. Books on railroading and Utah history, maps, souvenirs and film are available for purchase. Inquire about times for the steam engine demonstrations. The visitor center is open daily 8 P.M.–6 P.M. in summer and 8 P.M.–4:30 P.M. the rest of the year. **Superintendent, Golden Spike National Historic Site, Box W, Brigham City, UT 84302; 435-471-2209; www.nps.gov/gosp.**

Festivals and Events

Peach Days Festival

weekend after Labor Day. Brigham City peaches and its Peach Days Festival are known throughout Utah as one of the state's oldest community celebrations. Held just at the conclusion of the peach harvest, the festival features a parade, a carnival, the Peach Queen pageant, an art show and bicycle and foot races. **435-723-3937.**

Outdoor Activities

Biking

Bear River Migratory Bird Refuge

One of the most enjoyable ways to see the Bear River refuge is on a bicycle, on the 12-mile gravel loop. For a longer ride, from Pioneer Park, at 800 W. Forrest St. in Brigham City, take Forrest St. west from Brigham City for 17 miles, then ride the refuge's loop. **Bear River Migratory Bird Refuge, 866 E. Main, Brigham City, UT 84302; 435-723-5887.**

East Box Elder County Loop

This 50-mile loop is relatively flat on paved roads. It begins in Pioneer Park in Brigham City and follows Hwy. 83 northwest to Corinne, then continues to the junction with Hwy. 102. Turn north and ride through Penrose and Thatcher and follow the highway as it turns east to Tremonton. East of Tremonton, turn south on Hwy. 84, which passes through Elwood and Bear River City before rejoining Hwy. 83 at Corinne. Follow Hwy. 83 east back into Brigham City.

East Promontory

A paved road that heads south along the eastern side of the Promontory Mountains and the western side of the Bear River arm of Great Salt Lake can be followed to Promontory Point, a round trip ride of 50 miles. As you ride, watch for pelicans and other birds. Take Hwy. 83 to the turnoff for Golden Spike National Historic Site, and a couple of miles past it, before the road starts up the mountain to Promontory Summit, take the paved road to the south.

Willard Peak Rd.

Willard Peak Rd. is a popular biking route for advanced riders. From Mantua on US Hwy. 89/91, it heads south to Willard Basin, then climbs 4,200 feet to Inspiration Point at 9,400 feet at the top of Willard Peak, 14 miles one way. The view of Great Salt Lake and the valley below from Inspiration Point is worth the journey.

Boating

Willard Bay State Park

From Interstate 15, it looks like a part of Great Salt Lake, but Willard Bay is a freshwater, human-made reservoir constructed between 1958 and 1964. Fed by waters from the Ogden and Weber Rivers, the 14-mile-long Arthur V. Watkins Dam separates the freshwater from the salt-laden waters of Great Salt Lake. Because of its easy access from Interstate 15 and its close proximity to Brigham City and the Ogden metropolitan area, Willard Bay hosts more than a half million boaters, water-skiers and sailboaters a year.

There are two marinas with boat-launching ramps. The **North Marina** has an excellent sandy beach, ideal for swimming. To reach it, head west from Willard on 300 N. St. (Exit 360 off I-15). The **South Marina** is primarily a day-use area for boaters and is less crowded than the North Marina. Reach it by taking Exit 354 off I-15 at Pleasant View, then head west 3 miles on 4000 N. St. **435-734-9494.**

Fishing

Mantua Reservoir

The 554-acre reservoir on the east side of the town of Mantua is well stocked with trout. Located just off US Hwy. 89, 4 miles north of Brigham City.

Willard Bay State Park

Willard Bay contains 16 different species of fish, including carp, and it is stocked with walleye, catfish and trout. For access, see Boating, above.

Golf

Belmont Springs Park Golf Course

Two partners purchased this land to grow tomatoes, but after they took up golf, they decided to build a golf course instead of a farm. They laid out the course themselves and opened it about 1975. You be the judge of how well they did, but if you like the challenge of hills and slopes that leave your ball 100 yards from where you thought it should be, this is the course for you. There is a swimming pool adjacent to the clubhouse, and RV camping is available nearby. Located 1 mile south of Plymouth, off I-15. **435-458-3200.**

Eagle Mountain Golf Course

This course, opened in 1989, is located on land that was part of the Bushnell Military Hospital during World War II. Later the hospital buildings were used for the Intermountain Indian School. Some of the structures are still standing, considered eyesores by some but historic sites by others. The golf course, which is not considered difficult, runs along US Hwy. 89/91 along the southern edge of Brigham City. **780 E. 700 S., Brigham City; 435-723-3212.**

Hot Springs

Belmont Springs

Located in a campground once used by Shoshoni Indians and astride the Salt Lake Cutoff, which pioneers used to travel northwest from Salt Lake City to join the California Trail near City of Rocks, Idaho, this historic site was first developed as a resort in the 1920s. After a couple of decades of disuse, it was redeveloped in the 1970s. There are six main springs from which 4,000 gallons flow every minute into the adjacent Malad River. Facilities include a swimming pool, three hot tubs and a well-maintained dressing room. Located 1 mile south of Plymouth, off I-15. **435-458-3200.**

Crystal Springs Resort

There are hot mineral baths, a freshwater swimming pool and water slides at this year-round water park. Open in summer daily 10 A.M.–

10 P.M.; in winter, Mon.–Thur. noon–9 P.M., Fri.–Sat. 10 A.M.–10 P.M., Sun. noon–7 P.M. Admission fee is charged, with additional charges for the water slide. Located in Honeyville, 10 miles north of Brigham City on Hwy. 69; also reached via Exit 375 off I-15. **801-279-8104.**

Swimming

Brigham City Swimming Pool

A brand-new state-of-the-art outdoor community swimming pool with slides, fountains and everything to delight all members of the family. Call for hours and activities. **800 W. Forest, Brigham City; 435-734-0991.**

Seeing and Doing

Historic Sites

Brigham City Depot

Constructed in 1906 by the Oregon Shortline, this stone railroad station once served as many as 15 trains a day and was the location at which patients en route to Bushnell Military Hospital during World War II arrived in Brigham City. The depot was last used for rail service by Amtrak between 1971 and 1977. The building is now being restored as a museum by the Golden Spike Association. If you want to visit a railroad station that has all the charm it had when constructed at the beginning of the 20th century, this one will surely fit the bill. **833 W. Forest, Brigham City; 435-723-7130; 435-723-2989.**

Brigham City Tabernacle

With its 16 brick buttresses and steeples, imposing front tower and varying colors of fieldstone, the Brigham City Tabernacle is one of the most picturesque neo-Gothic church buildings constructed by 19th-century Mormons. Originally built between 1865 and 1890, it burned down in 1896 and was rebuilt within a year with the addition of the 16 buttresses and towers. Open daily for tours May–Oct. 9 A.M.–9 P.M. **251 S. Main St., Brigham City; 435-723-5376.**

Corinne Methodist Church

Constructed in 1870, this noble brick building is the oldest Protestant church building in Utah. As Corinne prepared to challenge Salt Lake City for the right to be Utah's territorial capital, the building was expected to be the forerunner of many more magnificent Protestant and Catholic churches, but these dreams were never realized. A small Methodist congregation continued to use the building until 1957, when it was finally necessary to dispose of the building. By then Corinne was simply a small Mormon farming village. Mormons within the community stepped forward and organized the Corinne Historical Society to save the building and use it for a community museum. Under the direction of Deverle Wells and others, a successful fund-raising campaign has been undertaken and the building is well on its way to being restored to its original condition. Although the building is not open any regular hours, it is well worth a visit and chances are, someone will be working at the church or nearby. Located at **Colorado and 6th St.** Call Deverle Wells to make arrangements to visit the church; **435-744-2442.**

Willard Stone Houses

Situated on a narrow neck of land between the Wasatch Mountains and Great Salt Lake, Willard is one of the most beautiful communities in the entire state. Much of its beauty comes from the wonderful collection of 19th-century stone homes that have been preserved here. Willard was one of the first historic districts in Utah listed in the National Register of Historic Places. The houses were constructed during a 20-year period (1862–1883) by Shadrach Jones, a stonemason from Wales who came to Utah in 1854 at the age of 17. The houses—all located within a 12-block area—are said to reflect styles and construction methods of the stone houses in Wales. None of the homes are open for tours, but the owners are proud of their houses and don't mind picture taking. Of particular interest are the 1862 **Omer Call Home** at **95 S. 100 W.,** the first house built by Jones; the **John L. Edwards Home** at **55 S. 200 W.,** built of stone but stuccoed right after its construction; the house Jones constructed for himself and his wife, Mary Williams, in about 1872 at **101 W. 200 S.;** and the **Robert Bell Baird Home** at **195 W. Center St.,** the last house built by Jones before he left for Wales.

Museums

Brigham City Museum and Art Gallery

This unique combination of community museum and art gallery features regional and national art exhibits as well as Brigham City history. Under the able direction of curator Larry Douglass, it is well worth a visit. Admission is free. Open Tues.–Fri. 11 A.M.–6 P.M., Sat. 1–5 P.M. Located on the lower floor of the building at **24 N. 300 W., Brigham City; 435-723-6769.**

Scenic Drives

Central Pacific Railroad Trail Backway

If you want to experience part of the distance covered by the transcontinental railroad through the vastness of the West, you can continue west from the Golden Spike National Historic Site to Promontory, where the road bends to the northwest to get around the north end of Great Salt Lake. At the north end of the lake is Locomotive Springs National Waterfowl Management Area. You can also reach it by driving southwest from Snowville via Exit 7 off Interstate 84. From Locomotive Springs, follow the old Central Pacific Railroad Grade west along the northern extension of the Great Salt Lake Desert for 80 miles to Lucin near the Utah–Nevada border. About half of the road is maintained as a county road; the unmaintained portion requires a four-wheel-drive vehicle and is best traveled during dry weather. Take plenty of time to stop and view the rockwork and trestles that remain. You can return 80 miles to Snowville or Brigham City by driving 5 miles north from Lucin to Hwy. 30, but if you have time, continue north 20 miles to Grouse Creek, an isolated ranching community that time seems to have forgotten.

Willard Peak Rd. Backway

During this 14-mile drive south to Willard Basin

and up Willard Peak, the elevation gain is nearly a mile, from 4,200 feet in Mantua to 9,400 at Inspiration Point. The road winds through forests of aspen, spruce and fir; past Perry Reservoir; and close to terracing done by Civilian Conservation Corps crews during the 1930s. Plan at least 3 hours for the trip, with extra time for sight-seeing, hiking and picnicking. High-clearance vehicles are required for this drive. The road begins in Mantua off US Hwy. 89.

Wildlife Viewing

Bear River Migratory Bird Refuge

Situated at the crossroads of two of North America's major migratory waterfowl flyways, the 65,000-acre refuge at the mouth of the Bear River provides an excellent opportunity to view more than 200 species of birds. The dikes, dams and roads that comprised the historic refuge were largely destroyed by the rising waters of Great Salt Lake in the early 1980s, but the refuge is making a comeback. The 12-mile auto and bicycle tour loop is open daily from sunrise to sunset except Jan.–mid-March. All visitors must leave the refuge before dark. Located 15 miles west of Brigham City. For more information contact the **Refuge Manager, Bear River Migratory Bird Refuge, Brigham City, UT 84302; 435-723-5887.**

Willard Bay Harold S. Crane Waterfowl Management Area

Another excellent place to view the Great Salt Lake birds is at Willard Bay. During the high migratory periods in the spring and fall, a great variety of birds can be seen. The area is part of Willard Bay State Park, where bird lists, maps and the free *Nature Guide to Willard Bay* brochure are available. It is best reached from Interstate 15 by taking Exit 354, then turning west onto 4000 N. and driving to the South Marina of Willard Bay if you want to walk in; for vehicle access into the area, continue west on 4000 N. onto the gravel road. Managed by the **Utah Division of Wildlife Resources; 435-479-5143.**

Where to Stay

Motels

Crystal Inn—$$

All 51 rooms have microwaves and refrigerators; some rooms have whirlpools. Swimming pool and restaurant. **480 Westland Dr., Brigham City; 435-723-0440.**

Howard Johnson—$$

Year-round swimming pool and therapy pool; 44 units. Restaurant. **1167 S. Main St., Brigham City; 435-723-8511.**

Camping

PRIVATE
Brigham City KOA

This is a smaller KOA campground, with 50 sites, 25 with full hookups. Open Mar.–mid-Nov. Located in Perry, south of Brigham City, on US Hwy. 89. **435-723-5503.**

Crystal Springs Campground

Part of the Crystal Springs Resort in Honeyville, with 124 RV trailer sites, half with full hookups. Toilets, showers and swimming. Open year-round. **8215 N. Hwy. 69, Honeyville; 435-279-8104.**

Golden Spike RV Park

Equipped with 60 sites with full hookups, tent spaces, Laundromat, rest rooms, private showers, game room, playground, horseshoe and volleyball area, picnic area and hot tub. Open year-round. **1025 W. 975 S., Brigham City; 435-723-8858.**

PUBLIC
Box Elder Campground

There are 26 RV trailer sites and tentsites. Open mid-May–Sept. Fee charged. Located off US Hwy. 89, 3 miles north of Brigham City and 2 miles south of Mantua, just west of Mantua Reservoir. **435-625-5112.**

Willard Bay State Park

The **North Campground** has 62 campsites, wheelchair-accessible rest rooms, showers, group camping and group pavilions. From I-15 take Exit 360 and follow the signs west.

The **South Campground** has 30 sites. Located 2 miles off I-15 from Exit 354. Park headquarters is located at **900 W. 650 N., Willard; 435-734-9494.**

Where to Eat

Idle Isle Restaurant—$ to $$

The Idle Isle is one of my favorite historical restaurants in Utah. During World War II, a large percentage of the 13,000 patients at Bushnell Military Hospital just south of Brigham City were amputees. The Idle Isle Restaurant announced that as soon as any patient who was being outfitted with artificial legs could walk through the door on his own, he would be given a free steak dinner. Needless to say, that kind of offer encouraged many men in their recovery and rehabilitation. One of Utah's oldest continuously operating restaurants, the Idle Isle was established in 1921 by P. C. and Verabel Knudson, as an ice cream and candy store. It evolved into a full-service restaurant and survived the Great Depression, sometimes staying open as long as necessary to take in enough money to pay the daily bills. Although a modern sign graces the exterior, the interior is little changed from the 1920s. A marble-and-onyx fountain, handcrafted wooden booths, old-fashioned candy cases and coffee urns all give the feeling of stepping back a half century or more in time.

Dinners consist of a three-course meal, including homemade rolls with apricot preserves and pie for dessert. For lunch try a bowl of homemade soup along with rolls and preserves, or one of the daily specials such as corned beef and cabbage, mountain trout or roast turkey with sage dressing. Also try the chocolates made in the basement of the restaurant. **24 S. Main St., Brigham City; 435-734-9062.**

Maddox—$ to $$

This steak house in Perry on old Hwy. 89 just south of Brigham City is a northern Utah institu-

tion. Since 1949, several generations have made Maddox a destination for burgers and steaks. Founded by Irvin Maddox, who developed a legendary ability to judge cattle, the restaurant has a reputation for serving the very best beef at very reasonable prices. Irvin has passed that tradition on to his son Steve, and Maddox remains one of Utah's most popular restaurants.

One patron claims that "Maddox takes you back to the days before cholesterol." If you want to test that claim to the limit, order the 32-ounce porterhouse steak. If you don't want to go inside to the restaurant, an old-fashioned drive-up area is located on the northern end. Open Tues.–Sat. 11 A.M.–9:30 P.M. **1900 S. Hwy. 89, Perry; 1-800-544-5474; 435-723-8845.**

Ricardo's Mexican Restaurant—$ to $$

For years the two Brigham City eating institutions—Maddox and the Idle Isle—had little competition except from a couple of locally owned drive-ins and a number of fast-food chains. Then in 1992 Richard Velazquez, a native of Brooklyn, New York, and Miriam, who grew up in the outskirts of San Salvador in El Salvador, opened their Mexican restaurant and many locals found that eating in Brigham City had entered a new era. Ricardo's is not fancy and it is generally a three-person operation, with a single waitress teaming with Richard and Miriam to keep things going. The food is basic Mexican with some El Salvadoran improvements, thanks to Miriam. Everything is made from scratch, including the salsa and complimentary chips. Weekdays try the daily lunch special; otherwise the burritos are a good bet, as are the large chiles rellenos. Open Tues.–Thurs. 11 A.M.–8:30 P.M.; Fri. 11 A.M.–9 P.M.; Sat. noon–9 P.M. No credit cards. **131 S. Main St., Brigham City; 435-723-1811.**

Services

Visitor Information
Brigham City Area Chamber of Commerce Visitor Center—6 N. Main St., Brigham City, UT 84302; 435-723-3937.

Wasatch Front Region

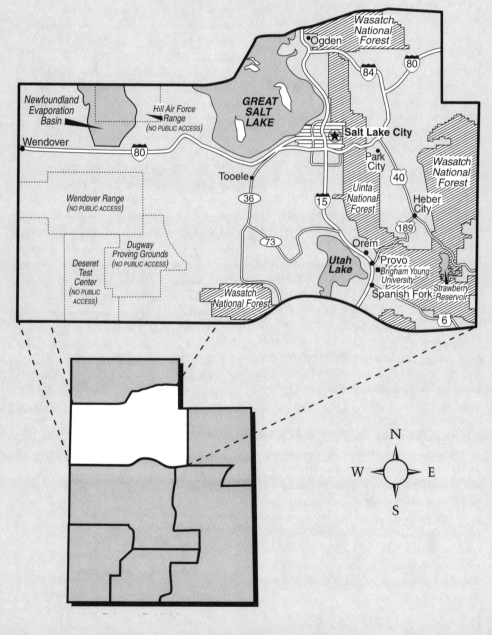

Ogden

The city of Ogden lies nestled beneath the towering peaks of Ben Lomond and Mt. Ogden, between the Wasatch Mountains and the east side of Great Salt Lake, at the junction of the Weber and Ogden Rivers. With a population of nearly 70,000, Ogden is one of Utah's largest cities and, throughout much of the state's history, has ranked second only to Salt Lake City in size. Ogden has been a railroad center since 1869. It is the only major Utah city located directly on the transcontinental railroad route and the closest connecting point to the railroad for Salt Lake City. Ogden also lies at or near the mouth of two major Wasatch Range canyons: Ogden and Weber Canyons. Ogden Canyon provides access to three ski resorts—Snowbasin, Nordic Valley and Powder Mountain; to Pineview Reservoir; and to the towns of Huntsville, Eden and Liberty in the Upper Ogden Valley. Weber Canyon—through which the transcontinental railroad was constructed in 1869, followed a century later by Interstate 84—is just south of Ogden and leads to the towns of Mountain Green and Morgan.

Ogden Defense Depot, Clearfield Naval Supply Depot and Hill Air Force Base were established in and just outside Ogden in the 1930s and 1940s. They have brought both economic prosperity and a considerable influx of military personnel and civilian defense employees and their families from throughout the country. Ogden is home to a regional office of the Internal Revenue Service and the U.S. Forest Service. Weber State University, which celebrated its centennial in 1989, has a student body of approximately 16,000. The university maintains a strong liberal arts and technology orientation and offers master's degree programs in education and accounting. With its majestic mountains, recreational opportunities and close access to Great Salt Lake, along with some of Utah's best museums and local festivals, the university and a cosmopolitan population, Ogden is an attractive destination for all visitors.

History

If you look at the area's place names, you understand what an important part the early American fur trade played in Ogden's history. Its first settler, Miles Goodyear, was a fur trapper. The city, canyon and river were named for Peter Skene Ogden, a fur trapper for the Hudson's Bay Company who arrived from the Northwest in 1825. John Henry Weber, a German-Danish immigrant who became a fur trapper, reached the Wasatch Mountains in 1824. He is immortalized throughout the area, in such places as Weber Canyon, Weber River, Weber County and Weber State University.

Weber Canyon was the site of one of the most famous events during the fur trapper era—an event that had international implications. Peter Skene Ogden had been sent into Utah to completely trap out beaver in the area in order to keep American trappers from pushing farther into the Hudson's Bay Company's domain, which covered present-day Oregon, Washington and British Columbia. Ogden and his men took a large number of beavers, but then they came into contact with a group of trappers in Weber Canyon led by Johnson Gardner (a subordinate of John Weber). Gardner proclaimed that the British trappers were trespassing on American soil (actually both groups were trespassing in Mexican Territory) and invited any of Ogden's men who wanted to to join the Americans. Many of Ogden's men did desert, taking with them their beaver pelts, even though most had been paid in advance by the Hudson's Bay Company for the beaver they would trap. Americans called

Getting There

Ogden is located 35 miles north of Salt Lake City, off Interstate 15.

the location in Weber Canyon the Mountain Green Trapper Confrontation Site, while Ogden bitterly marked the location on his map as "Deserter Point."

The failure of the overall Hudson's Bay strategy to keep Americans out of the Northwest was apparent in less than a decade. American missionaries journeyed to the Oregon Territory, forerunners of the American migration along the Oregon Trail during the 1840s. One who traveled west in 1836 with Oregon-bound missionaries Marcus and Narcissa Whitman was Miles Goodyear, a fur trapper who went on to establish Ft. Buenaventura on the Weber River to serve westward-bound emigrants. He finished his trading fort in 1846, the year before the Mormon immigration to Utah. In 1848 his holdings were purchased for $1,950 by James Brown, under the direction of Mormon leaders. Goodyear left for the goldfields of California, where he died in 1849. Originally named Brownsville, the name of the settlement was changed to Ogden by the Utah Territorial Legislature in 1850, in honor of Peter Skene Ogden, even though Ogden did not actually visit the location of his future namesake.

California-bound Swiss-German emigrant Heinrich Lienhard traveled through Weber Canyon and around the south end of Great Salt Lake during the summer of 1846, but did not visit Ft. Buenaventura; however, he did leave a record of his favorable impressions of the area: "If there had only been a single family of white people here, I probably would have remained. What a shame that this magnificent region was uninhabited." Lienhard would be surprised to see what changes have been wrought in the century and a half since he passed through the region. Within a year the Mormon vanguard would arrive in the area and establish a line of settlements along the east side of Great Salt Lake stretching from Bountiful to Ogden. With the completion of the transcontinental railroad in 1869, Ogden became known as the "Junction City" and has served as a key railroad transportation center ever since.

Major Attractions

Antelope Island State Park

If you were to ask the Utah Division of Parks and Recreation what has been its most frustrating park, they would surely say Antelope Island. At 26,000 acres, it is Utah's largest state park. More than a half million people visited Antelope Island in the 1970s, and it became one of Utah's most popular state parks. However, in the early 1980s the waters of Great Salt Lake started to rise, and the 7-mile causeway road connecting the island with the east shore of the lake was covered by water, along with many of the beaches and newly constructed facilities on the island. In 1987 Great Salt Lake reached 4,212 feet above sea level, its highest elevation since Mormon pioneers arrived. Since then, the waters have receded and the road across the causeway has been rebuilt to provide access to the variety of activities on the island.

Antelope Island was named by U.S. Army Capt. John C. Frémont in 1845, when the low level of the lake allowed him to ride across to the island, which he found to be inhabited by a herd of pronghorn antelope. By the 1870s the antelope were gone, and the island was used by Brigham Young and others to graze cattle and horses. Today you can still find a variety of wildlife. More than 350 species of birds have been identified in Great Salt Lake surrounding Antelope Island. Other animals include deer, pronghorn antelope, coyotes, badgers, bobcats, eagles, rabbits and buffalo. The present herd of buffalo was started in 1893, when William Glassman brought 12 buffalo from Nebraska to Utah and transported them to Antelope Island on a barge. The herd has grown to approximately 600 head. The free-roaming buffalo herd is one of the island's major attractions.

There is a paved road to the historic Garr Ranch House. Built of adobe by Fielding Garr in 1848 or 1849, the house is one of the oldest remaining pioneer buildings in Utah. Antelope Island is also the burial site for Mrs. George Frary. She and her six children accompanied

George Frary to the island in the early 1890s, where she died of a ruptured appendix in 1897 before her husband, fighting storm-driven waves, could return from the mainland with a doctor.

The island offers plenty of opportunities for hiking, biking, horseback riding, wildlife watching, sunbathing and swimming. A new visitors center on the northeast part of the island opened in 1996. **801-773-2941.**

Weber State University

Situated at the base of the mountains on the eastern rim of the valley on Ogden's eastern bench, Weber State University has been a vital part of Ogden's social and cultural life since Weber Academy was established in 1889. The university's **Dee Events Center (801-626-8500)** offers a regular schedule of programs and activities for the community. Adjacent to the Dee Events Center is the Ogden Ice Sheet, the location for the 2002 Winter Olympics curling competition. **801-626-6000; www.weber.edu.**

Festivals and Events

Hof Winterfest

third weekend in Jan. In cooperation with its German sister city, Hof, Ogden stages one of the best winter festivals in the entire state. The festival usually includes a delegation from Hof, and is held in the Weber County Fairgrounds. The authentic German musicians, dancers and singers, and plenty of bratwurst, Wiener schnitzel, *kartoffelsalat,* sauerkraut, *rotkohl* and beer will make you wonder if you've suddenly been set down in the Bavarian Alps. There are nonstop German brass bands, accordion-playing yodelers and dancing for all ages. Sat. morning activities begin with a 5- and 10-kilometer volkswalk. **801-388-0690.**

Taste of Ogden Festival

Memorial Day–last Mon. in May. Since 1994 Ogden has celebrated its ethnic diversity each Memorial Day with the Taste of Ogden Festival. Held on the grounds of the Ogden Munici-

pal Building on Grant Ave. and 25th St., the focus of the festival is music and food. You can watch belly dancers, a German polka band, classical Thai dancers, Native American dancers, African-American performers, Latino musicians and American cloggers. The diverse cuisine includes everything from Navajo tacos to Greek dolmathes, to Japanese, Thai and Tongan specialties. **801-479-6503.**

Ogden City Pioneer Days

mid-July–July 24. Commemorating the 1847 arrival in Utah of the first Mormon pioneers, Pioneer Days runs for six days. Outdoor western concerts, a craft fair, a children's parade, car shows and the Pioneer Days Rodeo are among the events. **801-629-8284.**

Outdoor Activities

Biking

Bicentennial Trail

As on the Northern Skyline Trail, which this trail intersects, you can reach the summit of Ben Lomond Peak. It is a steep, sometimes rocky, physically and technically challenging ride for advanced bikers. There are several springs along the ride and a beautiful cascading waterfall that comes out of Cold Springs. The out-and-back ride is about 14 miles. The trailhead is located at North Fork Park, which can be reached by following the signs from the town of Liberty, east of Ogden on Hwy. 162. If you want to make a loop ride of it, go up the Bicentennial Trail, take the Northern Skyline Trail back down, and then complete the loop by riding the North Ogden Canyon road down into Liberty.

Bonneville Shoreline

This ride is named for the ancient shoreline of Lake Bonneville, which the route follows along the east bench of Ogden. The 5-mile out-and-back ride is a favorite for novices and intermediate riders. The route begins at 22nd St. and Buchanan Dr.—about a mile east of Harrison Blvd. Most of the route follows along a regularly maintained dirt road. There is an impressive panoramic view of the metropolitan Ogden area throughout nearly all of the ride. There are a few uphill and downhill sections, but the maximum elevation gain is less than 500 feet in the first 2.5 miles. The turnaround point is at the Beus Canyon trailhead.

Huntsville / Monastery Route

This ride is highly recommended if you want to see and visit the sites of Ogden Valley. You can cover more than 20 miles by visiting the towns of Eden and Huntsville plus the Bluff swimming and picnic area at Pineview and the Trappist monastery east of Huntsville. Almost the entire out-and-back ride is over pavement and there are no mountains, only a few gentle rolling hills to climb. If you can get away for a summer weekday ride when there is less traffic, it is easy to imagine that you have journeyed to an isolated European valley with a special invitation to explore at a leisurely pace.

Unless you are staying at the Wolf Creek Resort or one of the Ogden Valley bed and breakfasts where you can take off right from your lodgings, start out from the North Arm trailhead on Hwy. 162 west of Eden. Ride east toward Eden, turn right on 5700 E. then left onto 1900 N. and follow it east to 7800 E., then turn left and ride south into Huntsville. You will see signs directing you to the monastery and Pineview Reservoir.

Ogden River Pkwy.

The paved parkway stretches for 3.1 miles along the Ogden River from Washington Blvd. to the mouth of Ogden Canyon. See the Running and Jogging section for details.

Pineview Reservoir Circle Tour

A pleasant ride around Pineview Reservoir in the upper Ogden Valley is a 15-mile loop that begins from Hwys. 39 and 162 and swings through the towns of Eden and Huntsville. If you want to extend the ride, you can continue northwest from Eden to Liberty or ride east of Huntsville to the Trappist Monastery (see Huntsville/Monastery Route, above).

Powder Mountain

The Powder Mountain ski area encourages mountain bikes with bike rentals and guided tours from the Powder Mountain Sports Shop. There is no charge for access to the ski area, but all bikers must adhere to proper biking etiquette, wear safety helmets and stay on established roads and trails. At this time there is no lift service for bikers, so be prepared for some strenuous climbing. Open daily 9 A.M.–4:30 P.M. Take Hwy. 39 east to the Pineview Dam, then turn left (north) onto Hwy. 162 and follow it north through Eden and Liberty to Powder Mountain. **801-745-3772; www.powder-mountain.com.**

Boating and Fishing

Ogden River

Trout and whitefish fishing is possible along the Ogden River, below the Pineview Reservoir, but the most popular trout fishing stream in the area is along the south fork of the Ogden River above Pineview Reservoir (both are along Hwy. 39). This is a very picturesque stream, as it flows through a narrow canyon of the Wasatch Mountains.

Pineview Reservoir

Located up Ogden Canyon, 12 miles east of the city on Hwy. 39, Pineview Reservoir is a popular boating and fishing spot. The reservoir is best known as a crappie and tiger muskellunge fishery. Bass, bluegill, perch and black bullhead are also common. Trout are sometimes found, though not in the same abundance as in other lakes.

Golf

El Monte Golf Course

Built in 1926, El Monte is one of Utah's oldest golf courses and one of two golf courses run by Ogden City. The course has a wonderful clubhouse, designed by local architect Eber F. Piers and built of stone quarried nearby. The course is located near the mouth of Ogden Canyon, and canyon winds are so blustery that early morning golfers are given an incentive of reduced green fees to play before 9 A.M. on weekdays. The course is a 9-hole par 35, with nice wide fairways, rolling terrain and a parklike setting. **1300 Valley Dr.; 801-629-8333.**

Round Valley Golf Course

Round Valley is a pleasant, uncrowded golf course not far from either Salt Lake City or Ogden. Located just east of Morgan, the 18-hole course is set on the south side of the Weber River. The modern clubhouse includes a snack bar. Pull carts, electric carts and golf clubs can be rented in the pro shop. Take the Morgan exit off Interstate 84 and follow State St. to 100 S. Watch for a sign on the east side of the street that says Round Valley. The usual golf course sign of a bouncing ball headed toward the flag has been placed on the west side of the street, but it is well hidden by the branches of an overhanging tree. Follow the road as it heads west and then swings north around a hill for a couple of miles into Round Valley. **1870 E. Round Valley Rd.; 801-829-3796.**

Valley View Golf Course

This beautiful course, opened in 1974, has been recognized by *Golf Digest* as one of the top 75 public golf courses in the United States. It is enjoyable for a number of reasons: the variety of holes where no two seem the same; the beautiful view of the mountains to the east and Great Salt Lake to the west; and the trees, which include pine, cottonwood, Russian olive, scrub oak and Lombardy poplar. The trees seem almost like participants in the game rather than obstacles. The front 9 are easier than the back 9, and good golfers have a possibility at birdies on the last 4 holes. Reached from US Hwy. 89, which runs along the base of the mountains between Ogden and Farmington. **2501 E. Gentile, Layton; 801-546-1630.**

Hiking

Weber Pathways (435-393-2304; www. weberpathways.org), a private, nonprofit organization dedicated to the promotion and preservation of open space and trails in the Ogden area, has prepared an excellent map and guide to 30 trails in the Ogden area. The guide is available at several locations in Ogden, including the visitor center at the Ogden Union Depot. The following trails are some favorites.

Indian Trail

This ancient trail took Indians above the bottom of Ogden Canyon and was especially useful in the spring, when the high waters of the Ogden River made it dangerous and nearly impossible to travel along the canyon bottom to reach the Upper Ogden Valley. Local volunteers and the U.S. Forest Service have labored to reestablish this trail and connect it with the Cold Water Canyon Trail farther up Ogden Canyon. Its close location to the city makes it a popular route with local hikers.

The trail is 10 miles round trip, although many hikers cover only a portion of the trail. For example, a 3.3-mile hike to the Coldwater Canyon Viewpoint requires about 2 hours one way and takes you past the highest point of the trail, where a small emergency shelter has been constructed. The trail climbs high along the mountains as it winds out of Ogden into Warm Water and Cold Water Canyons. There are places where the trail is very narrow. Exercise great caution because one misstep could send you on a long and dangerous slide down the slope. A brochure describing the trail is available at local information centers. Park at the western end of the trail (take 22nd St. as far east as you can and look for the parking area with the trail beginning at the northeast corner). The eastern terminus of the trail is in Ogden Canyon on Hwy. 39 at the Smokey Bear sign. There is a parking area and interpretive sign here as well.

Skyline Trail

The Skyline trailhead at the top of North Ogden Pass has north and south options. Heading **south,** you follow the Skyline Trail for 3 miles, then take a western branch, the Lewis Peak Trail, for 2.7 miles to an outstanding overlook that takes in the Ogden Valley from Willard on the north to Antelope Island on the south. The eastern branch continues another 4 miles to the trailhead near the Port Boat Ramp on the northwest side of Pineview Reservoir.

The **north option** is a 9-mile hike to Ben Lomond Peak. This is a more difficult hike, with an elevation gain of about 3,500 feet, but the trail offers spectacular views and the possibility of seeing mountain goats and other wildlife. Hwy. 39 up North Ogden Canyon provides access to the Skyline trailhead. From I-15 north of Ogden, take Exit 374 to reach Hwy. 39.

Snowbasin Ski Resort Trails

From the Snowbasin Ski Resort, several hiking trails offer a variety of possibilities, ranging from easy to difficult.

Green Pond Loop—Beginning about 30 yards behind the sign at the entrance to the upper parking lot, this is a 2-mile loop around Green Pond, an active beaver pond.

Maples Campground to Sardine Ridge Trail—This begins in the lower Snowbasin parking lot, heads north to the Maples Campground and continues north up to Sardine Ridge for a 3.1-mile round trip hike with a 700-foot elevation gain.

Mt. Ogden Trail—This strenuous and difficult 8-mile round trip hike up Mt. Ogden climbs more than 3,000 feet in elevation. It begins by following the ski lift service road west, between the ski school and ski patrol buildings.

Taylor Canyon Trail

Another trail with easy access from Ogden is the Taylor Canyon Trail, which climbs nearly 5,000 feet along its 4.5-mile-long precipitous route. There are spectacular views along the trail, which climbs up Malan's Peak to Malan's Basin, where there are opportunities for primitive overnight camping. The trailhead is at the eastern end of 27th St.

Wheeler Creek Trail

With easy access and beautiful scenery, the Wheeler Creek Trail is popular with Ogden-area hikers. The trail follows Wheeler Creek as it dances down a narrow canyon with hills covered by woods. There are pools and waterfalls along the route, and at the end of the 2.2-mile trail there is a spectacular view of the Snowbasin area. From here you can continue another 3 miles on a rugged single-track trail to the Maples Campground. This section parallels the Snowbasin Rd. above you. Whether you do the 4.4-mile round trip to the end of the old jeep trail or continue on to make the 10.4-mile trek to Maples Campground and back, you are in for a pleasant hike. The trailhead, well marked with a U.S. Forest Service sign, begins on the south side of Hwy. 39, the Ogden Canyon Rd., near the base of the Pineview Reservoir dam.

Running and Jogging

Ogden River Pkwy.

One of the most exciting developments in Ogden during the 1990s was the establishment of the Ogden River Pkwy. The result of the combined efforts of government, private corporations and countless hours of donated time by community groups, the parkway stretches for 3.1 miles along the Ogden River from Washington Blvd. to the mouth of Ogden Canyon. Taking the trail out and back is a 10-kilometer jog or hike. The trail passes through the MTC Learning Park, where part of the Utah State University Botanical Gardens have been relocated; goes by the Big D sports park, with a children's playground and baseball and soccer fields; skirts the north side of the El Monte Golf Course; and passes Ogden Dinosaur Park (see the Children and Families section under Seeing and Doing). The entire route is blacktopped and offers wheelchair access.

The next phase will extend the parkway another 2 miles west, from Washington Blvd. to the confluence of the Weber and Ogden Rivers. Later, a parkway will be established along the Weber River and, with the development of other trails on the eastern slope of the Wasatch Mountains, a 21-mile loop around and through Ogden will be available to recreationists.

Skiing

DOWNHILL

The three ski resorts in the Ogden area are usually uncrowded and a good alternative to the Salt Lake City and Park City resorts. **Snowbasin** with 1,800 skiable acres, and **Powder Mountain** with 1,600 skiable acres, are among Utah's five largest ski areas, behind Park City (2,200 acres; see the Park City chapter) and **Alta** and **Snowbird,** each with 2,000 acres (see the Salt Lake Area Canyons chapter).

Nordic Valley

Located at an elevation of only 5,500 feet, Nordic Valley usually receives less snow than the other Utah resorts and therefore opens later and closes earlier than other locations. Eighty percent of the 85 skiable acres served by two double chairlifts are beginner and intermediate runs, making this a good area for beginners and families (especially since lift tickets here are cheaper than at the other resorts). Open Mon.– Sat., night skiing 5 P.M.–10 P.M. Located southwest of Liberty, off Hwy. 162. **801-745-3511.**

Powder Mountain

The land on which this private ski resort is located has been in the Cobabe family since 1903, but it wasn't until 1972 that it opened for skiing. Dr. Alvin Cobabe, an Ogden family practitioner, was urged by friends not only to establish the ski area on the family land, but to take up skiing. Dr. Cobabe did that at the age of 54 when the resort was established. Powder Mountain remains a friendly, family-operated ski area with excellent powder skiing and very reasonable rates. As Dr. Cobabe explains, he never planned Powder Mountain to be a big glitzy resort; rather, he wanted a more personal, family-oriented experience.

The four chairlifts at Powder Mountain— one quad, one triple and two double (plus two surface lifts)—provide access to three mountains and a wide variety of skiing, from beginning slopes to powder bowls. Each of the three lifts, including the 6,000-foot-long Hidden Lake lift, offers beginner to expert runs down the mountain. This means that whatever your choice of slopes, you can still meet at the bottom of the lift to ride back to the top with friends and family.

Powder Mountain has a well-deserved reputation for good powder skiing. Some days the powder is so light you can hold it in your glove and blow it away with a gentle breath. Access to the backcountry powder skiing is provided by a snowcat. There is a 1,900-foot vertical drop on the Hidden Lake side (where a shuttle will pick you up on the highway road) and a 1,700-foot drop on the Timberline side.

The ski school serves skiers of all levels. There is a nice beginner ski package with a day-lift pass, ski rental and group lesson for a very reasonable price. An excellent women's program is available throughout the season. Powder Mountain is also a favorite area for snowboarders.

Lodging facilities are minimal, with a two- and three-bedroom suite with kitchens and five motel-type rooms with microwaves and small refrigerators. At the mouth of the canyon, the Wolf Creek Condos are popular lodging facilities with Powder Mountain skiers. Eating facilities include the Powder Keg Restaurant, Powder Mountain Lodge, Hidden Lake Lodge and Sundown Lodge.

Open for night skiing 4:30–10 P.M. on the Sundown Lift—known for its access to unbelievable sunsets. Most skiers drive up from the Ogden area through Ogden Canyon on Hwy. 39 to the Pineview Dam, then turn left (north) onto Hwy. 162 and follow it north through Eden and Liberty to Powder Mountain. Skiers coming from Salt Lake City (55 miles to the south) can take the Trappers Loop Rd. from Interstate 84, then head north through Huntsville and around the east side of Pineview Reservoir to Eden and Hwy. 162. **801-745-3772; www.powdermountain.com.**

Snowbasin Ski Resort

Snowbasin, opened in the 1940s, is one of Utah's oldest ski areas. During World War II, amputee patients from Bushnell Military Hospital were taught to ski here. Snowbasin gained worldwide recognition as the site of the men's and women's downhill ski races during the 2002 Winter

Olympic Games. A snow day lodge was constructed for the 2002 Olympics. The ski area has nine lifts—two gondolas, one high-speed quad, four triples, one double and one jib back tram—providing access to the 3,200 acres of skiable terrain on 53 designated runs and in several excellent powder bowls. The total uphill capacity is 15,500 skiers per hour. All lifts are open to snowboarders. A ski and rental shop can handle all equipment needs. Children and beginners ski packages are offered through the ski school.

Located east of Ogden 17 miles on the other side of Mt. Ogden. Take Hwy. 39 through Ogden Canyon to Hwy. 226 on the south shore of Pine-view Reservoir. From Salt Lake City, a 40-mile drive, take Interstate 84 up Weber Canyon, exit onto the Trapper's Loop Rd. (Hwy. 167) and take it to Huntsville and the intersection with Hwy. 39, then follow it back west to the junction with Hwy. 226. **1-888-437-5488; 801-620-1000; www.snowbasin.com.**

Swimming

Ogden has three public indoor swimming pools: **Ben Lomond Community Pool, 800 Jackson Ave.; 801-399-8690. Ogden Community Pool, 2875 Tyler Ave.; 801-625-1101. Marshall White Center Pool, 222 28th St.; 801-399-8346.**

Layton Surf and Swim

This outdoor public swimming pool is open only during the summer, but the Wild Wave Pool is open year-round. During the winter, the Wild Wave Pool is also used for water aerobics, school classes and school swim teams. During cold weather, a bubble is placed over the Wild Wave Pool, and it functions as an indoor swimming pool during the day, except 6 P.M.–9 P.M. when the wave machine churns up the water. Summer hours are noon–8 P.M. **465 N. 275 E., Layton; 801-546-8588.**

Tennis

There are six public tennis courts located at the entrance to **Mt. Ogden Golf Course, 3000 Taylor;** six courts at **Ben Lomond High School, 800 Jackson Ave.;** four in Liberty Park, at **22nd St. and Monroe St.;** and two courts each at **Bonneville Park,** at **Quincy and 2nd St.; Monroe Park,** at **30th St. and Monroe;** and the **Marshall White Center, 1220 23rd St.**

Seeing and Doing

Children and Families
Ogden Dinosaur Park

Opened in April 1993, the Dinosaur Park is located on several acres of land at the mouth of Ogden Canyon and contains replicas of more than 100 prehistoric dinosaurs. Well-placed information signs provide insights into the life and characteristics of the individual dinosaurs, which make this a positive educational experience. For adults, watching children look at the dinosaurs is more than worth the admission fee. **1544 Park Blvd.; 801-393-3466; www. dinosaurpark. org.**

Historic Sites

Eccles Historic District

The Eccles Historic District consists of 15 houses that were built during the first two decades of the 20th century for Ogden's wealthiest citizens. Most reflect the influence of Frank Lloyd Wright and his Prairie School style as expressed by local architects. One of the residents, Marriner Eccles, an Ogden native and prominent banker whose home is at 2541 Van Buren Ave., became a staunch supporter of Franklin D. Roosevelt's New Deal. He helped draft the Emergency Banking Act of 1933, which created the Federal Deposit Insurance Corporation (FDIC). He served as chair of the Federal Reserve Board of Governors from 1935 to 1952. The Ogden City Landmarks Commission has developed an attractive walking tour brochure that includes a summary of the development of the area, a map of the district and brief histories and sketches of the 15 houses. **Ogden City**

Landmarks Commission, 2549 Washington Blvd., Ogden, UT 84401; 801-629-8931.

Historic Downtown Ogden

The Ogden City Landmarks Commission has prepared an excellent walking tour guide that includes nine buildings in the downtown Ogden area. A photograph and brief description is included for each of the buildings. The oldest building is the **1845 Miles Goodyear Cabin** (see Ft. Buenaventura in the Museums section), built by the trapper two years before the Mormon pioneers arrived in Utah. The other 19th-century building is the **Episcopal Church of the Good Shepherd,** a carpenter Gothic–style church built in 1874–1875. Early 20th–century buildings include the **1906 Masonic Temple;** the old **Post Office,** a classical Revival–style federal building built between 1905 and 1909; the **1913 Eccles Building;** two 12-story **skyscrapers** built in 1927; the **First Security Bank;** the **Biglow** (now the Radisson) **Hotel;** and the **Ogden Municipal Building,** a wonderful art deco–style building constructed as a New Deal WPA project in 1939.

The guide also includes one of the state's real architectural treasures: the **1924 Egyptian Theater.** Designed by Utah architects Hodgson & McClenahan, the Egyptian Revival–style theater was built in 1924 and is one of the few surviving examples of this style of architecture, which was used primarily in movie theaters. The building is covered in Egyptian ornamentation, including two sculpted Egyptian deities seated on the roof and six sculpted pharaohs on the facade. The theater was constructed two years after the discovery of King Tut's tomb—an event that set off a nationwide craze in Egyptian decor. Used as a motion picture theater from 1924 until the mid-1980s, a long and finally successful struggle has preserved the theater as one of the historic gems in Ogden. Reopened in 1997, the theater is now used for theater and musical productions and showing films. It is a major part of the revitalization effort of downtown Ogden as it connects with the newly constructed David

Eccles Conference Center. **Ogden City Landmarks Commission, 2549 Washington Blvd., Ogden, UT 84401; 801-629-8931.**

Historic 25th St.

Imagine a time when the country's railroad stations bustled with the arrival and departure of America's traveling public—a time before air travel or cross-country automobile jaunts over an elaborate interstate highway system. In those days, transcontinental travel took several days. Ogden served as one of the nation's principal railroad centers and was the major connecting point on the transcontinental railroad route between Chicago and San Francisco. One of the most famous businesses on historic 25th St. was the **London Ice Cream Parlor,** operated by Belle London, an infamous madame. She served her famous cherry pie and ice cream in the main floor parlor and, in the small rooms on the second floor, delicacies of another sort. Local wags referred to the London Ice Cream Parlor as the place to get pie on the first floor and tarts on the second floor. Pick up the walking tour guide to 25th Street prepared by the **Ogden City Landmarks Commission, 2549 Washington Blvd., Ogden, UT 84401; 801-629-8931.**

Museums

Daughters of Utah Pioneers Museum and Miles Goodyear Cabin

Utah's oldest surviving cabin was constructed by fur trapper Miles Goodyear sometime between 1845 and 1846. Goodyear was born in 1817 in Hamden, Connecticut, orphaned at four, and bound out to families until he was 19. In 1836 he joined the Whitman-Spaulding Missionary Group bound for Oregon, but left the company at Ft. Hall on the Snake River and set out on his own. He became a mountain man, marrying Pomona, the daughter of Ute Chief Peeteetneet, in 1839. As the fur trade declined and westward emigration increased, Goodyear followed the example of other trappers like Jim Bridger and erected a fort for trade with the emigrants. After the arrival of the Mormons in 1847, Goodyear

▼ *Lake Powell*

▶ *Desert soil and rock formations in Canyonlands National Park*

▼ *Rafting, San Juan River*

1

▼ *Desert waterfall, Zion National Park*

▲ *Cactus flowers in Southwestern Utah*

▼ *Campers and hikers on historic Hole-in-the-Rock Trail*

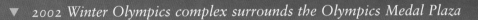

◀ *Olympic ski jumper visits with spectators at the Utah Olympic Winter Park*

2002 Winter Olympics fireworks
▼ *illuminate downtown Salt Lake City*

▼ The west shore of Bear Lake

▼ Boats at the Bear Lake Marina

▼ *Dr. Pierce's painted barn, south of Logan, west of Highway 89*

▼ *Homestead at American West Heritage Center near Wellsville*

▲ *Wellsville Mountains with buffalo in the south end of Cache Valley*

▼ *Along the Transcontinental Railroad Route west of the Golden Spike National Historic Site*

▲ *Trestle along the Transcontinental Railroad Route built in 1869*

▼ *Lot Powell Homestead located near the Altonah in the Uintah Basin*

Petroglyphs in Dinosaur National Monument ▶

◀ *Dinosaur bones in the rock inside visitor's center*

Split Mountain where the ▶ *Green River breaks through the mountain into the Uintah Basin in Dinosaur National Monument*

13

▼ *Fishing and boating on the Green River just below Flaming Gorge Dam*

▼ *Flaming Gorge Dam completed in 1963*

Flaming ▶
Gorge
Reservoir
with the
Cart Creek
Bridge in the
distance

sold them his cabin and animals and moved on to California, where he made a rich gold find on the Yuba River, but became ill and died in November 1849.

His cabin was moved to this site in 1928 and has been preserved by the Daughters of Utah Pioneers. The cabin is adjacent to the 1902 Relief Society Building, built for the women's organization of the LDS church and acquired by the Daughters of Utah Pioneers in 1926; it has been used as a pioneer museum ever since— with the exception of World War II, when it was requisitioned by the federal government to be used as Ogden's first day-care center for children of women working at the defense installations in and around Ogden. Open mid-May– mid-Sept. Mon.–Sat. 10 A.M.–5 P.M. **2148 Grant Ave.; 801-393-4460.**

Ft. Buenaventura

In 1846 Miles Goodyear named his outpost Ft. Buenaventura. Earlier travelers and mapmakers had speculated on the existence of a river that flowed west to the Pacific Ocean, which they called the Rio Buenaventura. Perhaps Goodyear believed in the mythical river, or he was using the Spanish word for "good fortune" or "good journey" to welcome the expected California- bound travelers.

After the Miles Goodyear Cabin was moved in 1928, the location of the original fort was preserved in historical documents and established as a state park in 1979. Following extensive archaeological study of the site, the fort was reconstructed, using wooden pegs and mortise- and-tenon joints instead of nails and cottonwood logs. The reconstruction of Ft. Buenaventura and refurbishing of the buildings involved consider- able research to make everything appear as authentic as possible. Bedsprings are of rope, blankets are of elk skins, the washable green milk paint used for chests was reproduced using the traditional ingredient of green pigment from clay and, as Goodyear did, corn is still planted in the garden.

Mountain men reenacters hold an annual rendezvous at the park and, throughout the year,

other activities and programs recall the days when Peter Skene Ogden, John Weber, Etienne Provost, Jim Bridger, Jedediah Smith and others camped along the banks of the Ogden and Weber Rivers as members of the elite fur trap- per fraternity. Guides in mountain man cos- tumes interpret the fort and the lifestyles of the mountain men as well as of the Native Ameri- cans of the region.

Open Mar.–Oct. 8 A.M.–dark. Admittance fee charged per vehicle. Take the Ogden 24th St. exit (Exit 347) off Interstate 15 and head east. Watch for the signs directing you to turn south off 24th St. onto A Ave., then almost immedi- ately make a left turn east off the bluff and fol- low the road south to the parking area. **Ft. Buenaventura State Park, 2450 A Ave., Ogden, UT 84401-2203; 801-621-4808.**

Hill Aero Space Museum

This is a must for any World War II buff or any- one interested in airplanes. Construction of Hill Field began in 1939, and the base played an important role during World War II when it employed more than 22,000 personnel as a cen- ter for maintenance and rehabilitation for com- bat aircraft. Today Hill Field is home to F-16 squadrons.

The main museum building contains small exhibits, a gift shop and a theater showing a video about Hill Field. The museum hangar houses a dozen aircraft including a P-51D Mus- tang, a B-17 Flying Fortress, a C-47 Douglas Skytrain, an F-84 Thunderstreak and a Lockheed Blackbird spy plane. One of the most recent additions is a P-38 fighter bomber that took three years and a half million dollars to restore once it was salvaged 50 years after crash landing on Buldir Island, Alaska, in 1945. Outside the museum building there is a collection of more than three dozen old aircraft. A restored World War II vintage Post Chapel has a stained glass window replicating the one placed by members of the U.S. Eighth Air Force in the Grafton- Underwood Chapel in England. The museum is free. Open Tues.–Fri. 9 A.M.–3 P.M.; Sat. 9 A.M.– 5 P.M.; Sun. 11 A.M.–5 P.M. Located just east of Interstate 15 at the Roy exit (Exit 341). **801-774-0956.**

Ogden Union Station

The Ogden Union Station was the center of activity in Ogden for nearly a century—from the time the first station was constructed shortly after the transcontinental railroad was established in 1869 until air travel finally replaced rail travel in the 1960s. As rail traffic increased substantially, an ornate Victorian station was constructed in 1889, but after it burned down in 1923, the present Spanish Colonial–style station was constructed. The 1924 Ogden Union Station is listed in the National Register of Historic Places. Visitors will find a variety of museums and shops housed in the station, something not to be missed when you are in Ogden.

Among the museums are the **Browning Firearms Museum,** with more than 100 models made by John M. Browning, considered the world's greatest gun inventor; the **Browning-Kimball Car Collection** with Packards, Pierce Arrows, Lincolns and Cadillacs on display; the **Utah State Railroad Museum** with a collection of historic locomotives, a model railroad and other railroad artifacts; and the **Natural History Museum,** with gems and minerals from the intermountain area on display.

The model railroad is the most popular attraction in the Wattis-Dumke Railroad Museum. The detailed diorama depicts the transcontinental route from Weber Canyon to the Sierra Mountains, with 12 trains running along the route. There is also a full-sized engine box where children of all ages can pretend they are locomotive engineers moving a mighty train down the track.

Open Mon.–Sat. 10 A.M.–6 P.M. year-round and during the summer also Sun. 1 P.M.–5 P.M. Admission fee charged. Located at the western end of 25th St. **2501 Wall Ave.; 801-629-8444.**

Other Sights

Holy Trinity Abbey

The alpine valley setting for the Holy Trinity Abbey near Huntsville makes you think that you are visiting a centuries-old monastery in Bavaria or Austria, even though the abbey was founded in only 1947. The buildings, grounds and the 30 or so Cistercian (often called Trappist) monks who live in the abbey convey a feeling of serenity, love and godliness that makes a visit rewarding to individuals of any faith. The monks live in 8-by-10-foot rooms in war-surplus Quonset huts. They support themselves by raising alfalfa hay and Angus cattle, and by selling their honey, cereal and peanut butter. The abbey consists of 1,878 acres of land, of which about 780 are under cultivation. There are approximately 500 head of cattle. When not working at their assigned tasks, the monks devote themselves to prayer and scriptural reading.

Visitors may attend the mass and chants held in the chapel, also a converted Quonset hut. For those in search of longer spiritual refreshment, the abbey also offers one- or two-day retreats to males of all faiths over the age of 20. While no tours are provided, a slide show describes life and work at the monastery. Items produced at the monastery can be purchased by visitors at the abbey's reception room, open Mon.–Sat. 8 A.M.–noon and 1–5 P.M. Located 4 miles southeast of Huntsville. Head east out of Huntsville on Hwy. 39 and follow the signs. **1250 S. 9500 E., Huntsville; 801-745-3784.**

Scenic Drives

Ogden River Scenic Byway

Sometimes known as the road over Monte Cristo, this scenic byway actually follows the Ogden River along Hwy. 39 east to Huntsville in the Ogden Valley, and then up the South Fork of the Ogden River through heavily wooded hills that are especially beautiful in the fall.

While the officially designated Scenic Byway ends 44 miles from Ogden at the eastern boundary of Cache National Forest, it is certainly worth continuing the drive down the canyon to Woodruff. A half day or an entire day could be spent driving over this byway, and then north to Bear Lake and back to Logan over the Logan Canyon Scenic Byway (see the Northern Region chapter). This route is especially recommended in the fall on a weekday, when there is less traffic.

Trapper's Loop Rd. Scenic Backway

This designated Scenic Backway follows what was probably the route of Peter Skene Ogden and his Hudson's Bay fur trappers as they moved south out of Ogden Valley across the mountains to the Weber River in May 1825. The drive across the 9-mile paved road from Mountain Green (reached from Exit 92 off I-84) north to Huntsville (on Hwy. 39) gets you thinking about which hills Ogden must have crossed and what ravines he followed before meeting up with Etienne Provost and Johnson Gardner along the Weber River. The all-weather route also offers a spectacular view of Mt. Ogden from the west side and provides access to the Weber County ski resorts of Snowbasin, Powder Mountain and Nordic Valley.

Weber Canyon

Interstate 84 through Weber Canyon reveals the east side of the Wasatch Mountains, the beautiful Morgan Valley and two interesting sites—one historical and the other natural. The Mountain Green Trapper's Confrontation took place in the vicinity of the Mountain Green Rest Stop on the westbound side of the interstate. At the rest stop, a monument to Peter Skene Ogden recalls the events of 1825, when American trappers challenged the British Hudson's Bay brigade under the leadership of Ogden.

Devil's Slide is one of the most unusual natural formations in Utah. Devil's Slide is an outthrust of a bed of quartzite, with two parallel reefs of Jurassic–era limestone 20 feet apart and 40 feet high stretching up the side of the mountain. The unusual formation is the result of the faster erosion by the softer soil and stone that covered the limestone. Devil's Slide is located just north of Interstate 84 at Exit 111, 7 miles north of Morgan.

Sports

Ogden Raptors

If you want to see professional baseball at its beginning level, the Ogden Raptors of the Pioneer League offers 35 home games between mid-June and the beginning of Sept. The Raptors are an affiliate of the Milwaukee Brewers. The new 3,000-seat Lindquist Field, located on 24th St. between Lincoln and Grant Ave., opened in 1997. **801-393-2400; www.ogden-raptors.com.**

Wildlife Viewing

Ogden Bay Waterfowl Management Area

This extensive 20,000-acre wetland area on the east side of Great Salt Lake is an excellent area for viewing such wetland birds as gulls, sandpipers, grebes, herons, ducks and geese. Hikers have access to the dike roads past vehicle gates year-round. A vehicle loop is also open. There are several ways to reach the area. Perhaps the easiest is to take Exit 341 (at Roy) off Interstate 15 and head west on Hwy. 97 to its end. Then turn north on Hwy. 108 for 0.1 mile, turn west onto Hwy. 98, which in Hooper becomes 5500 S., and continue west to 7500 W. Turn north to the management area headquarters.

Ogden Nature Center

Some might find it ironic that this 127-acre nature center has the Internal Revenue Service as its western neighbor and the army's Ogden Defense Depot as its eastern neighbor. The fact that the nature center lies between these two huge complexes makes it a real oasis in this urban setting. The area along Mill Creek was used as farmland until 1940, when it was acquired by the Ogden Defense Depot and used to store munitions until after World War II. In the 1970s the Defense Depot donated the property to Ogden City, with the provision that it be used for recreation purposes. The nonprofit Ogden Nature Center was set up in 1977 to administer the property and to help restore the area to a natural state. Ponds and marshlands have been established and thousands of trees planted. Bird species include great blue herons, snowy egrets, willets, Canada geese, wood ducks, red-winged blackbirds, meadowlarks and red-tailed hawks. Mammals include raccoons, muskrats, red foxes, porcupines and mule deer. Admission fee charged. **966 W. 12th St.; 801-621-7595.**

Where to Stay

Bed and Breakfasts and Lodges

Jackson Fork Inn—$$ to $$$

Have you ever wanted to sleep in a barn? Here's your chance. Jackson Fork Inn is an old dairy barn that has been converted into a restaurant and inn with eight rooms, each with a private bath; four rooms have hot tubs large enough to accommodate two adults. A self-serve continental breakfast is included, and dinner meals can be purchased in the evening. Located on Hwy. 39. **7345 E. 900 S., Huntsville, UT 84317; 800-255-0672; 801-745-0051; www.jacksonforkinn.com.**

Snowberry Inn—$$ to $$$

Located 15 minutes up Ogden Canyon, the Snowberry Inn overlooks Pineview Reservoir and is an excellent choice for both summer and winter stays. Boating, swimming, hiking and biking are primary activities in the summer, while close proximity to Ogden's three ski resorts makes this a good location for skiers. Wildlife watching is a popular year-round activity. Roger and Kim Arave offer five nonsmoking rooms, each with its own bath. A full homemade country breakfast and access to the hot tub are included. The inn is wheelchair accessible. **1315 N. Hwy. 158, Eden, UT 84310; 801-745-2634; www.snowberryinn.com.**

Hotels and Motels

Best Western High Country Inn—$$ to $$$

Heated pool, whirlpool, exercise room, tanning bed and free VCR; 110 rooms. Restaurant open 6 A.M.–10 P.M. **1335 W. 12th St.; 1-800-594-8979; 801-394-9474.**

Crowne Plaza Hotel—$$$

Located in the historic 1913 Eccles Building next to the David Eccles Conference Center and the Egyptian Theater on Washington Blvd., the Crowne Plaza opened in Jan. 2002 just in time for the 2002 Winter Olympics. There are 137 rooms, a private club and a restaurant. **2401 Washington Blvd.; 801-394-9400.**

Historic Radisson Suite Hotel—$$$

This is the former historic Ben Lomond Hotel, for many years the best hotel in Ogden. All 126 rooms have been renovated. Dining room and coffee shop open 6 A.M.–9:30 P.M. Located in the center of downtown Ogden. **2510 Washington Blvd.; 1-800-333-3333; 801-627-1900.**

Ogden Marriott Hotel—$$$

Heated indoor pool, whirlpool and exercise room; 287 rooms. Restaurant open 6 A.M.–11 P.M. **247 24th St.; 801-627-1190.**

Camping

PRIVATE
Century RV Park

Has 73 paved pull-through sites with full hookups. Also a heated pool, Laundromat and showers. Open year-round. Take Exit 346 off I-15. **1399 W. 2100 S.; 801-731-3800.**

PUBLIC

East of Huntsville along a 6-mile stretch of Hwy. 39 (see Ogden River Scenic Byway in the Scenic Drives section under Seeing and Doing), there is a series of 10 campgrounds on national forest-land that have a combined total of 261 RV trailer sites and nearly 350 tentsites. All have toilets and nearly all have drinking water. Open mid-May–late Sept. or late Oct. The largest, with 96 sites, is **Anderson Cove,** 2.5 miles southwest of Huntsville. The other nine are: **Jefferson Hunt,** 25 sites; **Hobble,** 9 sites; **Magpie,** 30 sites; **Botts,** 11 sites; **South Fork,** 32 sites; **Perception Park,** 24 sites; **Lower Meadows,** 15 sites; **Upper Meadows,** 9 sites; and **Willows,** 10 sites.

Where to Eat

Bavarian Chalet—$$ to $$$
Established in 1983, this is the most authentic German-style dinner restaurant in the state. In 1977 Wolfgang and Heidi Stadelmann visited southern Utah and fell in love with Lake Powell. Heidi, a native of Heidelberg, had graduated from the chef's school at Tegernsee in Bavaria, while Wolfgang, a native of Stuttgart, with a master's in business from the University of Munich, had worked nearly 10 years as the city manager of Fellbach, a town outside Stuttgart. It took them four years to immigrate to Utah, but after a year of traveling around the United States, they moved to Ogden and opened their restaurant. Their establishment has all the charm of a Bavarian inn, with all kinds of old-world collectibles throughout the restaurant. In fact their daughter, Claudia, operates a small but charming gift shop within the restaurant. The food is traditionally German—schnitzels, sauerbraten, sausage, fish and chicken, along with made-from-scratch *apfelstrudel* and *kasestrudel*. The Stadelmanns had special plates made to hold the Wiener schnitzel, jaeger schnitzel, bratwurst, knockwurst, sauerkraut, red cabbage, spätzle and vegetables. Open Tues.–Thurs. 5 P.M.–10 P.M., Fri.–Sat. 5 P.M.–11 P.M. Located in a complex of shops and businesses. Reservations recommended, especially on weekends. **4387 Harrison Blvd., Ogden; 801-479-7561.**

Cajun Skillet—$$ to $$$
There aren't many places in Utah where you can get authentic Cajun food, and that makes the Cajun Skillet a top choice of those who enjoy authentic New Orleans food. Thomas Jackson, owner and cook, grew up in Baton Rouge, Louisiana, and learned to cook from his grandparents. He claims that some of his recipes, including those for corn bread, jambalaya, gumbo, hush puppies, fried okra, plantation vegetable soup and sweet potato pie, go back to when his ancestors were slaves. After graduating

from culinary school he worked at a variety of places, eventually becoming a chef at the Hotel Utah until its closure in 1989. At the urging of friends, he opened the Cajun Skillet that same year. Thomas is from a family with 17 children; six of his brothers operate a 175-acre plantation 15 miles outside Baton Rouge, where they raise the catfish, frogs, turtles and alligators that Thomas has air-expressed to Utah for his customers. The daily fresh fish selections and special dishes, like alligator and frog's legs, are chalked on a large blackboard on the north wall in his restaurant. Open 9 A.M.–11 P.M., so you can also order Cajun-style breakfasts. Located across the street from the Ogden Municipal Building. **2250 Washington Blvd., Ogden; 801-393-7702.**

Gray Cliff Lodge—$$ to $$$
Located 5 miles up Ogden Canyon, the Gray Cliff Lodge makes for a nice evening getaway. Dinners include steaks, prime rib, lamb, chicken and fresh trout. Open Tues.–Fri. 5–10 P.M.; Sat. 5–11 P.M.; Sun. 10 A.M.–2 P.M. (brunch) and 3–8 P.M. **508 Ogden Canyon Rd.; 801-392-6775.**

La Ferrovia Ristorante—$$
About 10 years ago, sisters Giuseppina and Rita Lodice came to the United States from Naples, Italy. Along with their husbands and children, the sisters have worked to establish a good, inexpensive Italian restaurant in one of the restored buildings on Ogden's historic 25th St. They offer a good selection of pasta, calzones and soups made from authentic southern Italian recipes, as well as an excellent house dressing. All breads and pizza dough are made in the restaurant. If you have a favorite Italian dish that is not on the menu, you can call in advance and they will make it for you, providing they can obtain the correct ingredients. Daily specials, takeout service and a children's menu are available. Open Tues.–Thurs. 11 A.M.–9 P.M., Fri.–Sat. 11 A.M.–10 P.M. Located just south of the Ogden Park Hotel. **210 25th St., Ogden; 801-394-8628.**
Prairie Schooner Steak House—$$ to $$$

In keeping with its namesake, this restaurant offers dinner in covered wagons surrounded by what seems to be a beautiful outdoor prairie under the stars. Steaks, prime rib and a daily seafood special top the menu. Open Mon.–Thurs. 5–10 P.M., Fri.–Sat. 5–11 P.M., Sun. 4–9 P.M. **445 Park Blvd., Ogden; 801-392-2712.**

Roosters 25th St. Brewing Company—$ to $$

Ogden's oldest and best known microbrewery (some consider it the best microbrewery in the state, and locals voted it the best place to bring a first date) is located in a two-story red brick building built in 1892 and first occupied by the Kansas City Liquor Store. In subsequent years it became in turn a Chinese laundry, Salvation Army store and antique store before Roosters was opened in April 1995. Seating is available in three locations: the main floor, where you have a full view of the brewing vats; upstairs in a spacious hall-like area; or, in season, outside on the patio. In addition to such popular freshly brewed beers as Bees Knees Honey Wheat, Junction City Chocolate Stout and Golden Spike Ale, there is also a nonalcoholic homemade root beer—all brewed under the direction of award-winning brewmaster Steve Kirkland. There are plenty of food choices, ranging from tasty soups, sandwiches, fish, pasta and pizzas available by the slice, to beer-battered fish-and-chips, fish plates, buffalo wings and barbecue platters. Be sure to try the What-a-crock appetizer made of crab, artichoke and blended cheeses served hot with French bread for dipping. Open Mon.–Thurs. 11 A.M.–10 P.M.; Fri.–Sat. 11 A.M.–midnight; Sun. 10 A.M.–9 P.M. **253 25th St., Ogden; 801-627-6171.**

The Shooting Star Saloon—$

Even in the West there are few saloons that have lasted more than a century. Huntsville's Shooting Star Saloon, however, is one. Opened in 1879, the saloon has been a second home for generations of Huntsville residents and has earned fame as one of the most hospitable places anywhere. The food is good, too, even if there is only one item on the menu. The Star Burger is made with two quarter-pound beef patties topped with knockwurst, cheese, sautéed onions, tomato, lettuce and a special sauce—all served on a bun. This is one burger you will not forget. The Shooting Star is also one unforgettable place. Owners John and Heidi Posnien have taken great care to preserve as much of the ambience of the old saloon as possible. A combination of western saloon, English pub and German *kneipe* (Heidi after all is *"eine echte Berlinnerin"*), the saloon has charm and hospitality, and lives by the rule "Enjoy yourself, but don't impose on others." Open Mon.–Sat. noon–midnight, Sun. 2 P.M.–midnight. Customers must be 21 or older. **7350 E. 200 S., Huntsville; 801-745-2002.**

Timber Mine—$$ to $$$

This interesting restaurant, housed in a huge timber building, has been made to look like an old mine on the inside. Antiques and artifacts are on display, and individual booths are constructed like side rooms off the main passageway. The booths have individual dimmer lights, so you can eat in total darkness if you want. The fare includes steaks, prime rib and seafood. Open daily 5–10 P.M. in summer, 5:30–10 P.M. in winter. **1701 Park, Ogden; 801-393-2155.**

Services

Visitor Information

Multi-Agency Visitor Center—Golden Spike Travel Region and the Ogden and Weber Visitors Bureau are located in the historic Ogden Union Station. **2501 Wall Ave., Ogden, UT 84401; 1-800-ALL-UTAH; 801-627-8288; www.allutah.org.**

Transportation

Rental cars—Avis, 1-800-831-2847; 801-394-5984; Hertz, 1-800-654-3131; 801-621-6500; National, 1-800-227-7368; 801-393-8800; and Thrifty, 1-800-393-4324; 801-394-2765.

Taxis—Yellow Cab Co., 801-394-9411.

Utah Transit Authority (UTA)—Provides

regular bus transportation throughout the Ogden area and as far north as Brigham City. Express buses run on fairly regular schedules between Ogden and Salt Lake City. **801-627-3500.**

Salt Lake City and Environs

For more than a century and a half, Salt Lake City boosters have given their city the title "The Crossroads of the West." (See map of Salt Lake City on page xvi in the Introduction.) Located in the center of the Intermountain West, Salt Lake City links California and the West with the Great Plains, and the Desert Southwest with the Pacific Northwest. Included in the greater Salt Lake Valley are the communities of Centerville, Bountiful, West Valley City, Taylorsville, Kearns, Holliday, Murray, Midvale, West and South Jordan, Sandy, Riverton and Draper—all connected by a web of highways.

Salt Lake City also sits at the crossroads of the nation's national park system, the hub of a wheel with one Utah national park at the end of each of five spokes. Spokes also extend to national parks in Nevada, Colorado, Wyoming, Montana and Arizona, which include Grand Canyon National Park, Great Basin National Park, Mesa Verde National Park, Rocky Mountain National Park, Yellowstone National Park and Glacier National Park.

Salt Lake City is, however, much more than a place to pass through, as the term "crossroads" may suggest. Since it was founded by Mormon pioneers in 1847, it has been the world headquarters of the Church of Jesus Christ of Latter-day Saints. It is a city that has always known its destiny—to become a religious and spiritual center for people all over the world.

Mormon values have provided a solid foundation for the city and shaped its development in many ways; but Salt Lake City has not grown up in a Mormon vacuum. Many different groups play important roles in the collective life of the city. In addition to the old-world flavor brought by Mormon converts from Great Britain and western Europe, other ethnic groups—Irish-Catholic miners and German-Jewish merchants in the 19th century; Italian, Greek and Slavic laborers at the beginning of the 20th century; and, more recently, Southeast Asians, Southeast Pacific Islanders, Hispanics and African-Americans—contribute a richness and vitality.

Salt Lake City serves as the state capital. But long before the capitol was constructed in 1916, the city and the entire valley were laid out from Temple Square in the heart of the downtown area, using a grid street system based on Joseph Smith's plan for the City of Zion. The four streets on each side of the Temple are known as North Temple, West Temple, South Temple and Main Street, which is on the east side of the temple. Using the grid system, you can determine where you are in relation to Temple Square by counting the blocks in the address. For example, the University of Utah is located at 1400 E. and 200 S., which is 14 blocks east and two blocks south of Temple Square. The Wasatch Mountains are to the east, the lower Oquirrh Mountains are to the west, and downtown Salt Lake City is at the north end of the valley. As long as you can see the mountains, you should know in what direction you are headed. In the downtown area there are 6.75 blocks per mile; elsewhere in the valley the ratio is eight blocks to the mile. The population of the city is approximately 200,000 people, while another 700,000 people live in the valley outside the Salt Lake City limits. The valley is approximately 25 miles long from south to north and 20 miles across from east to west.

The settlement of Salt Lake City has often been compared with the Puritan settlement of Massachusetts two centuries earlier. Both Mormons and Puritans claimed to suffer from unresponsive governments and intolerant circumstances. Responding to God's direction, both fled their familiar homes for the wilderness, where they sought to establish a model society.

Even though today fewer than half the population of the city are active Mormons, the Mormon influence is strongly felt throughout the community and state. As with any community built on religion, tradition and history, these influences can be both positive and negative. The Mormon foundation, it is argued, helps build close families and good neighborhoods, promotes a positive work ethic, brings economic opportunity and contributes to a viable community life. On the other hand, Mormons have been criticized at times as being intolerant, clannish and too eager to force their views and lifestyle on others. But Mormons—like all Americans and citizens of the world—are becoming more tolerant. During the 2002 Salt Lake Winter Olympic Games, Utahns of all religious and political persuasions earned high praise from visitors from all over the world as warm, friendly and considerate hosts. Salt Lakers expect themselves to maintain this hard-earned and well-deserved reputation, so look for and expect the positive while enjoying the religious, social and political undercurrents that make Salt Lake City such an interesting place.

To understand Salt Lake City and its people, a visit to Temple Square is essential. But there is much more to the city than the religious and historic buildings associated with the Mormon faith. Take time to visit Great Salt Lake. It is a landmark that is still little understood and perhaps underappreciated by local residents. If you come to Salt Lake City in the winter, chances are you are coming to ski. Salt Lake City is one of the skiing capitals of the world because of Utah's majestic mountains, unsurpassed snow conditions, moderately priced lift passes, excellent ski schools, easy air access, close proximity of the airport to the ski resorts, fine accommodations at Snowbird, Alta, and Park City and its great success as the host city for the 2002 Winter Olympic Games.

But if you come in the summer or fall, the mountains are just as attractive to hikers and sight-seers. Enjoy the music and arts of the city. The Utah Symphony performances, free Temple Square concerts and performances of Ballet West, and other groups in the restored Capitol Theater are all opportunities for experiencing the cultural quality of Salt Lake City.

Getting There

Salt Lake City International Airport
is only 6 miles from downtown Salt Lake City via Interstate 80, and is served by nine major airlines and three regional carriers that offer more than 500 flights daily. Salt Lake City is a regional hub for Delta Airlines, which serves nearly 50 western destinations and connections to most major U.S. cities. The airport has a full range of car rentals, and overnight accommodations are just a few miles away.

Amtrak operates passenger trains out of Salt Lake City. The Amtrak office and station are located at **340 S. 600 W.; 1-800-872-7245; 801-364-8562.**
Salt Lake City is at the crossroads of Interstate 15, which runs south from Idaho through Utah, Arizona, Nevada and southern California, and Interstate 80, which runs west from Wyoming through Utah, Nevada and northern California.

History

Before the arrival of the Mormons, the Salt Lake Valley had been something of a neutral zone between the Ute Indian tribes living in Utah Valley to the south and the Shoshoni tribe to the north. Before them, the Fremont people had occupied the marshlands around Great Salt Lake. When Brigham Young and his band of 147 pioneers founded Salt Lake City in July 1847, the area was still Mexican Territory. However, with the end of the Mexican War and the signing of the Treaty of Guadalupe Hidalgo on February 2, 1848, a large area of the Southwest, including all of present-day Utah, was ceded to the United States.

Soon after the arrival of the first Mormon group, others quickly followed, as the Mormons completed their exodus from Illinois and Iowa. Converts to the faith also arrived, mostly from Great Britain, Denmark and Sweden. With Utah as the new Mormon homeland, Salt Lake City became the capital of a region of religious settlements, which ultimately expanded north across the Canadian border and south into Mexico. In directing the settlement of more than 300 town sites in the vast Intermountain West, Brigham Young earned the apt name "The Great Colonizer."

Although Mormons had sought a place of refuge in the wilderness, they were seldom alone. Two years after Salt Lake City was established, the great California gold rush was in full swing. Many '49ers stopped off in Salt Lake City to get supplies and exchange worn-out animals for those that would carry them on to California. A number of them spent the winter in Salt Lake City when it became impossible to complete their journey due to heavy snows.

The federal army arrived in 1857 and established a large camp 40 miles south of the city, at Camp Floyd. Although the camp was abandoned at the outbreak of the Civil War in 1861, California Volunteers were sent to Salt Lake City to keep the mail lines open and to keep an eye on the Mormons. These volunteers were veterans of the California goldfields and quickly took up prospecting in Utah's mountains, a practice discouraged by Brigham Young, who wanted to see the Mormons build up their farms and home industry rather than pursue the fickle promises of gold or silver mining. Discoveries were made in the mountains surrounding Salt Lake City, and mining operations were greatly enhanced with the completion of the transcontinental railroad in 1869.

Mining, the railroads, smelting, the military, politics and merchandising were all factors that brought non-Mormons to Salt Lake City, and they often came into conflict with the Mormon settlers. Following Mormon abandonment of polygamy and separatist politics, statehood was granted to Utah in 1896. Soon after, a public school system was established, and children from all religious backgrounds met on common ground. The communitarian ideas of Joseph Smith and Brigham Young were abandoned and capitalism fully embraced.

Salt Lake City has grown and prospered throughout the 20th century, but like much of the nation, suffered severely during the Great Depression, recovering during World War II when the defense industry grew. The postwar boom left its mark on a highly urbanized Salt Lake City and suburbanized Salt Lake Valley. Recreation, including the budding ski industry, became more important. New businesses moved into the city. The University of Utah built on its reputation as a research facility and leading medical facility. Technological and environmental issues continued to grow in importance. And people of ethnic and religious diversity worked together more effectively for the good of the community.

This cooperation was nowhere more evident than in the united effort to host the 2002 Salt Lake Winter Olympic Games. More than 60,000 people volunteered for the 25,000 unpaid positions needed to prepare for and host the Games. All kinds of people worked long hours as drivers, translators, hosts, venue technicians, security personnel, parking and transportation assistants, performers, snow removers and food handlers and in countless other assignments that stretched from 8- to 12-hour shifts night and day before and during the Olympics. Visitors described the athletics and the volunteers as being the heart and soul of the Olympic Games.

Politicians are pleased that the Games' financial balance sheet ended in the black and that the public money loaned to construct the venues was repaid in full at the end of the games. Many see the Olympics as a historical watershed, even comparing it with the impact on Utah of the completion of the transcontinental railroad in 1869 or the end of World War II in 1945. Most Salt Lakers hope and expect that the unity, good will and pride experienced during the Games will resonate as the hallmark of their city's character for decades to come. Today Salt Lake City is a very different city from the one envisioned by the original pioneers, but the seeds they planted have brought forth good fruit and, combined with the contributions of subsequent generations and new arrivals, have made Salt Lake City a special and unforgettable place.

Major Attractions

Temple Square

Each year Temple Square receives more visitors by far than any other attraction in Utah. Its location in the heart of downtown Salt Lake City makes it easy to get to, and there is plenty to do when you arrive. Temple Square is the Mormon Mecca, and while the religion does not require the faithful to make a pilgrimage to this particular temple, most do. In Mormon theology, the temple serves as the holy place in which sacred ordinances or rituals for individuals, ancestors and living families are performed. Among these are marriages, and you are likely to see young couples in wedding attire having their pictures taken on the temple steps following their marriage ceremony.

Because of the sacred nature of the temple, only members of the Mormon faith in good standing are permitted inside; however, visitors are welcome inside all the other buildings. Expect to be asked by guides if you would like a tour of the square and a brief explanation of the history and doctrine of the Church of Jesus Christ of Latter-day Saints. These tours are well worth the time because they not only provide basic information but allow you to meet a committed Mormon. Many of the guides are young missionaries who are part of the more than 60,000 members engaged full-time for two years seeking converts in almost every country in the world.

The Salt Lake Temple was one of the major reasons so many thousands of Mormon converts came to Utah from England and Europe during the century between 1850 and 1950, but with the construction of temples around the world, members are now encouraged to remain in their homelands to "build up the Kingdom" there

rather than emigrate to Utah.

The site for the Salt Lake Temple was selected by Brigham Young four days after the Mormons arrived in the Salt Lake Valley in July 1847. A 10-acre block was set aside for the temple, and construction began in 1853 after plans were prepared by Truman O. Angell, based on a sketch given him by Brigham Young. For various reasons, the temple was not completed until 1893, while three other temples were completed and in use in St. George, Manti and Logan. Meanwhile, temporary buildings were constructed and used. The famous tabernacle, for services and meetings open to everyone, was completed in 1867.

Temple Square itself has five buildings that you will want to visit: the **temple,** the **tabernacle,** the **Assembly Hall,** and the north and south **visitor centers.** In addition, there are several monuments on the square: one dedicated to Joseph Smith; another to the handcart pioneers; and yet another to the seagulls, which saved early Mormon crops from infestation by crickets. Just outside the square, to the east, is the **Brigham Young Monument,** erected in 1897 during the 50th anniversary of the Mormon arrival in Utah. In 2000 Main St. between N. and S. Temple on the east side of the Temple was closed to automobile traffic, and a pedestrian plaza area with a fountain and flowers was added, providing much better pedestrian access to the two historic blocks and a more open view of the east side of the Temple. Across the street, north of Temple Square, a new 21,000-seat assembly building opened in April 2000.

Plan also to extend your visit to the blocks to the east and west of Temple Square. On the east block is located the **Joseph Smith Memorial Building,** formerly the Hotel Utah; the **Church Administration Building;** the newer 26-story **Church Office Building;** the **Relief Society Building;** and **Brigham Young's Beehive House** and **Lion House.** The **Conference Center** is located on the block north of Temple Square. On the west block, facing Temple Square, are the **Family History Library,** where genealogists come from all over the world to do research; the **Museum of Church History and Art;** and the **Osmyn Deuel Log Cabin.**

Since you will need lunch if you are spending the entire day, consider **The Lion House Pantry** (see the Where to Eat section), the **Garden Restaurant** located on the top floor in the Joseph Smith Memorial Building (see Buildings in this section) or one of the food courts in the **Crossroads Mall** and **ZCMI Center,** located across the street, south of Temple Square. Depending on your schedule, you may want to arrange your visit around one of the following events. Call **801-240-3318** for information about upcoming concerts and special events.

Festivals and Events

LDS Church General Conference—Twice a year, the first weekend in Apr. and Oct., church leaders and members of the LDS church meet in the 21,000-seat Conference Center for the semiannual conference. Before the new center opened in 2000, the conference was held in the historic Salt Lake Tabernacle, which still seats overflow crowds, who can view broadcasts from the proceedings across the street. Sessions are held on Sat. and Sun. mornings and afternoons. No church services are held in the meeting houses throughout Utah and surrounding states, and members are encouraged to listen to or watch live broadcasts in their own homes. This is an especially busy time on Temple Square, and unless you come with the express purpose of attending the conference (which is possible, if you are willing to wait in long lines for the limited public seating that is available), these are two weekends during the year that the casual traveler may wish to avoid.

Mormon Tabernacle Choir Broadcast— Perhaps as famous as Temple Square itself is the Mormon Tabernacle Choir, which traces its beginnings back to 1849, when Brigham Young invited John Parry, the leader of a recently arrived group of Welsh converts, to organize a choir for the next general conference. This choir became the nucleus from which developed the Mormon Tabernacle Choir. Today members of the choir come from all walks of life to volunteer their time and talents. As worldwide ambassadors of the LDS church, the members are selected on the basis of character and musical competence. The choir made its first recording in 1910. Since then millions of records, tapes and compact discs have been sold. On July 15, 1929, the choir made its first radio broadcast of what is now the oldest continuous nationwide network broadcast in America.

The weekly broadcast is released worldwide to nearly 1,000 radio and television stations. The half-hour broadcast begins at 9:30 A.M. on Sun. To attend the live performance of the choir in the tabernacle, you must be seated by 9:15 A.M., so plan to arrive early. Babies and small children are not permitted in the tabernacle during the broadcast. In addition to the selections by the choir, a brief "Spoken Word" is given, which touches on universal Christian and humanitarian themes. After the program, remain at the east entrance of the Tabernacle for a few minutes to watch, and perhaps participate, as missionaries speaking languages from all over the world invite visitors to join them for a free tour of Temple Square.

Mormon Tabernacle Choir Rehearsal— The choir rehearses on most Thurs. evenings throughout the year, and the tabernacle is open to the public 8–9:30 P.M. You can come and go as you please. Try to visit Temple Square on a Thurs. evening for the rehearsal and return Sun. morning for the broadcast.

Mormon Tabernacle Organ Recitals— One of the world's magnificent organs, the Mormon Tabernacle Organ is outfitted with 11,623 pipes, which form a dramatic backdrop at the west end of the hall. They are accessible through the five ranks of keyboards and numerous stops at the organ console. Free half-hour organ recitals are offered every day of the year Mon.– Sat. at noon, and Sun. at 2 P.M. In addition, from Memorial Day to Labor Day, another recital is given Mon.–Sat. at 2 P.M.

Temple Square Christmas Lights— From the Fri. after Thanksgiving through New Year's Day, Temple Square is decorated with thousands of Christmas lights and a nativity scene. It seems as though every Utah family makes an evening visit to Temple Square during the Christmas season to see the lights. This is a special time on Temple Square, and if you have the opportunity, don't miss it.

Temple Square Concert Series—On most Fri. and Sat. evenings (and some weekdays as well) at 7:30, you can attend a free concert in the Assembly Hall or Salt Lake Tabernacle. There are a wide variety of instrumental and vocal performances throughout the year with choirs, chamber music and vocal and instrumental soloists.

Buildings

Assembly Hall—This Victorian Gothic–style chapel was designed by Obed Taylor and built on the southwest corner of Temple Square between 1877 and 1882. The spires, though lower, offer a nice balance to the larger temple located on the opposite corner of the square.

Beehive House, Lion House, Brigham Young's Office and **Eagle Gate**—This complex along South Temple is what remains of Brigham Young's estate. The earliest building, Brigham Young's small office, was built in 1852 and is located between the larger Beehive House and Lion House. The Beehive House, named for the beehive that adorns the roof as a symbol of activity and industry, was constructed of adobe between 1853 and 1854. Open for free guided tours Mon.–Sat. 9:30 A.M.–4:30 P.M., Sun. 10 A.M.–1 P.M. The Lion House, constructed the year after the Beehive House in 1855, housed some of Brigham Young's 56 wives, 16 of whom bore a total of 56 children. It's not open for tours, but you can see part of the house if you eat lunch in the **Lion House Pantry.** East of the houses, spanning State St., is the **Eagle Gate.** The gate has been enlarged several times since my great-grandfather, Ralph Ramsay, a handcart pioneer from the Durham area of England, carved the original eagle placed atop the gate in 1859. It can be seen in the **Pioneer Memorial Museum at 200 N. Main St.**

Church Administration Building—The gray granite Greek Revival–style Church Administration Building at **47 E. South Temple**—an address as famous to Mormons as 10 Downing St. is to the British—was completed in 1917 and houses the offices of the general authorities of the LDS church. The lobby has walls of polished marble. The building was constructed as an expression of both stability and respectability by early 20th-century church leaders. The building is not open to the public.

Church Office Building—Utah's tallest building, the 26-story Church Office Building was built between 1969 and 1972 and houses most of the auxiliary and departmental organizations of the Mormon church. The building is not without controversy, as some argue that it overshadows the historic temple too much, leaving the impression of a church more concerned about its bureaucracy than the spiritual needs of the members. Be that as it may, the building offers a wonderful view of the Salt Lake Valley from the top-floor observation deck, which is open to the public.

Conference Center—Opened in 2000, the 21,000-seat Conference Center auditorium is now the site of the semiannual church conferences formerly held in the historic Tabernacle. Other programs are also held in the auditorium, as well as in the 905-seat theater on the west side of the center. Check at the information desks for upcoming programs. The exterior of the center is constructed of granite taken from the same quarry in Little Cottonwood Canyon that provided the granite for the Salt Lake Temple. While the Center and its grounds extend horizontally along all of the block north of Temple Square, much of the building was built below ground level to insure that it did not overshadow the historic buildings across the street. Tours of the interior are offered every 10–15 minutes and last approximately a half hour. Enter the building at the southwest corner through doors 9, 10, 11 or 12 to join a guided tour.

Family History Library—While many people come to ski or to visit Utah's national parks, Salt Lake City has become a mecca for genealogists and those interested in tracing family history. The world's largest genealogical library is located in downtown Salt Lake City on the west side of Temple Square, at 35 N. West Temple. The LDS Family History Library is open to the public. On your first visit to the library, take a few minutes to view the video presentation. It will acquaint you with the five-story library's mission and resources. You will also be provided with the booklet "How Do I Start My Family History?" to help you get started.

Briefly, Mormons believe that all persons, whether living or dead, will have the opportunity to hear the full gospel of Jesus Christ and accept or reject Christ as their savior. Because certain "saving" ordinances (such as baptism) must be performed here on earth even for the deceased, Mormons have identified the names of dead ancestors and have acquired copies (often through a cooperative microfilm program) of church, civic and other records from around the world to help identify all those who have lived on the earth. Most of the records date from 1550 to 1930. These records are open to anyone for personal and scholarly use; genealogists and historians are able to use these records in the Family History Library, which would otherwise be very difficult to locate and obtain access to. Furthermore, trained staff are available on each floor to answer questions and assist in using the collected records. Inquire about the daily classes, which each month feature a different area of research. Open Mon. 7:30 A.M.–5 P.M., Tues.–Sat. 7:30 A.M.–10 P.M. **801-240-2331.**

Joseph Smith Memorial Building— Constructed as the Hotel Utah in 1911, this building was designed to provide visitors to the city with first-class accommodations, a function it performed admirably until August 1987 when it closed to undergo renovation. It now houses offices; banquet, reception and meeting rooms; a chapel; restaurants; and a 500-seat theater. The Grand Lobby, which was the most impressive feature of the old hotel, has been restored to its original elegance and is well worth a visit. During the Hotel Utah days, the **Roof Restaurant** was one of the most popular eating places in Utah for special occasions. It has been

reopened for dinner and features a gourmet buffet and a panoramic view of Temple Square below; open Mon.–Sat. 5–10 P.M. **801-539-1911.** The **Garden Restaurant** is located on the south end of the top floor and is more moderately priced; open Mon.–Sat. 11 A.M.–10 P.M. **801-539-3170.**

Museum of Church History and Art— Mormons have always had a sense of history. This has left Utah with a tremendous collection of diaries, artifacts and works of art, which have been used to great advantage by a professional museum staff in the Museum of Church History and Art. The 1983 museum includes a scale model of Salt Lake City in 1870, a covered wagon, an immigrant ship's bunk and exhibits focusing on events and developments in LDS church history from Utah and around the world. There is something for everyone in the museum, with free audio tours, multimedia programs, films, puppet shows and children's activities. Open Mon.–Fri. 9 A.M.–9 P.M.; Sat.–Sun. and holidays 10 A.M.–7 P.M. **45 N. West Temple; 801-240-3310.**

Relief Society Building—Occupying the southeast corner of the intersection of Main St. and West Temple, the Relief Society Building was built in 1956 and houses one of the most important institutions of the Mormon religion. The Women's Relief Society was organized in 1842 in Nauvoo, Illinois, under the direction of Joseph Smith, as a charitable, educational and religious sisterhood. Once in Utah, the Relief Society built its own halls and granaries, in which were stored wheat and grain that had been harvested by the women for distribution or sale for charitable purposes. This tradition is symbolized by the ornamental wheat stalks on the front of the Relief Society Building. The Relief Society had its own publication, and many of its early leaders, including Eliza R. Snow, were active in the women suffrage movement— women had the right to vote in Utah before it became a state in 1896. The Relief Society continues to be one of the foundations of the Mormon religion, as women look to the needs and welfare of both members and nonmembers in the neighborhoods and communities throughout Utah and other places.

Salt Lake Tabernacle—Built between 1864 and 1867, the Salt Lake Tabernacle is one of the most finely engineered, interesting architectural structures to be found anywhere. The tabernacle was constructed under the direction of Henry Grow, with later modifications to the interior made by temple architect Truman O. Angell. The long, low-arching dome rests on 44 sandstone pillars. A 10-foot-thick wooden arch rests on each of the 44 pillars. These arches are braced by latticelike cross members that were originally fastened with wooden pins and rawhide thongs. The lattice truss arch roof system displays a unique engineering system that has been documented as part of the Historic American Engineering Record. The tabernacle is 250 feet long and 150 feet wide, with a seating capacity of approximately 8,000, including both the floor and balcony areas. The original tabernacle organ contained 700 pipes, but it has since been expanded to more than 11,000—some as small as ⅜ inch and the largest 32 feet long. Be sure to attend one of the musical performances (see page 47) to experience the wonderful acoustics of this historic building. The acoustics are also demonstrated several times during the hour by one of the guides, who drops a pin on the pulpit that can be heard throughout the tabernacle.

Salt Lake Temple—The Salt Lake Temple, with its famous six spires, took 40 years to complete (1853–1893) and is a worldwide symbol of the Mormon faith. The east tower rises 210 feet from the ground with the 12.5-foot, gold-leaf-covered statue of the Angel Moroni (the compiler of the *Book of Mormon,* who returned to earth as an angel to pass the holy scripture on to Joseph Smith) standing atop the center tower. The temple is 186.5 feet long and 118 feet wide. The 167.5-foot-high walls were only 20 feet high when Brigham Young died in 1877. Although access to the interior of the building is restricted, visitors can marvel at the unique design and craftsmanship in this building, and especially its native granite, which was hauled by ox team from the quarry in Little Cottonwood

Canyon, about 15 miles to the southeast.

Tours

If you arrive at the Salt Lake City airport and find yourself with an hour and a half or more layover, you can take advantage of a courtesy van that will transport you to and from Temple Square and provide you with a guided tour of Salt Lake's number one visitor attraction. Vans depart on the hour and half hour from the airport and Temple Square. Check any luggage you have at the airport and just show your airline ticket indicating the connecting flights. The van leaves the airport from the loading area between Terminals One and Two. Offered daily 10 A.M.–7 P.M. **801-699-3503; 801-599-1676.**

Welfare Square/Humanitarian Center Tour—In addition to the free airport shuttle, there is a free shuttle from Temple Square to Welfare Square, where a guided tour is given of the LDS church's premier facility for giving employment to poor, disabled and elderly members while producing goods and items that can be used to help feed and clothe the needy. The square includes a dairy farm, cannery, grain elevator and repair and cleaning facility for used clothing, appliances and other items. Check at the visitor centers for information on bus and tour schedules. Usually 1-hour tours are offered Mon.–Fri. at 10 A.M., noon, and 2 P.M. **750 W. 800 S.; 801-240-2609.**

Visitor Centers

Located at the north and south entrances to Temple Square, the modern visitor centers offer a good introduction to the religion of the Latter-day Saints through pamphlets, displays, films and other media. Be sure to visit the north visitor center to see the wonderful replica of the Christus Statue by Danish sculptor Bertel Thorvaldsen. The south visitor center has an interesting exhibit on the construction of the Salt Lake Temple and a panoramic window facing north for an unobstructed view of the south side of the Temple. Open daily 9 A.M.–8:45 P.M. **801-240-2534.**

Great Salt Lake

Great Salt Lake is the largest water body between the Great Lakes and the Pacific Ocean. It is also the largest salt lake in the Western Hemisphere. The lake is a shallow remnant of ancient Lake Bonneville, a large, deep freshwater lake that occupied much of western Utah, but disappeared about 10,000 years ago at the end of the last ice age. Great Salt Lake is fed by several streams but has no outlet. As a result, the salt content of what was once freshwater has increased over the centuries due to evaporation. The Great Salt Lake is eight times saltier than the ocean and has had a salinity level as high as 27 percent—a level exceeded only by the Dead Sea.

Because its dimensions can change drastically as its water rises and falls, it is difficult to give an exact size of the lake. For example, in 1962 the lake elevation was 4,192 feet above sea level, giving it a surface area of 969 square miles. A 20-foot rise in elevation to 4,212 feet above sea level in the early 1980s allowed the lake to expand to a surface area of 2,300 square miles. At 4,200 feet above sea level, the lake is approximately 75 miles long and 50 miles wide. Each year 2 million tons of minerals are added to the lake through erosion and evaporation.

In early days, there were rumors of a school of whales living in the lake, but in reality only small brine shrimp and blue-green algae can survive in the lake, and a few insects, notably the brine fly, live around the lake. The brine flies are annoying but do not bite. Dead brine shrimp, algae and vegetation exposed by the ever-changing shoreline are the sources of the sometimes unpleasant odor around the lake, which, when the wind is blowing from the west, spreads across the Salt Lake Valley.

Great Salt Lake supports more than 200 different species of birds that use the lake and surrounding land for breeding, migrating and wintering.

The freshwater marshes around the lake were used by prehistoric inhabitants as an excellent source of food, including ducks and cattails.

As early as 1703, reports circulated in Europe about a large body of salt water west of the Mississippi. In 1776 the Dominguez-Escalante Expedition recorded accounts of the lake from the Ute Indians, although the explorers did not journey the 50 miles north from Utah Lake to see it for themselves. In the 1820s trappers visited the lake, including Jim Bridger, who may have been the first American to see the lake, and was convinced initially that it was an arm of the Pacific Ocean. U.S. Army Capt. John C. Frémont explored part of the lake in 1843. Four years later, Mormon pioneers arrived in the uninhabited region.

The Mormons initially called their city Great Salt Lake City, but in time it was shortened from four to three words. Shortly after their arrival, pioneers started to take advantage of the endless supply of salt. While there were a few places where the salt was pure enough for table use, most of it had to be boiled down, with four barrels of salt typically yielding one barrel of usable salt. Commercial salt production began in the 1850s and continues today.

Heinrich Lienhard, a Swiss-born, California-bound traveler, stopped at the south end of Great Salt Lake and recorded in his diary for August 9, 1846, the first known written description of swimming in the Great Salt Lake. "The morning was so delightfully warm and the absolutely clear water so inviting that we soon resolved to take a salt water bath. The beach glistened with the whitish-gray sand which covered it, and on the shore we could see the still-fresh tracks of a bear, notwithstanding which we soon had undressed and were going down into the salty water. We had, however, to go out not less than a half mile before the water reached our hips. Even here it was still so transparent that we could see the bottom as if there were no water whatever above it, yet so heavy that we could hardly tread upon the bottom with our feet; it was here quite a trick to stand even on tiptoe."

The lake became a popular recreation spot for early Utahns, and a number of bathing resorts were established along its shores. The largest and most famous was **Saltair,** which was built in 1893 atop 2,500 piles driven into the lake bed, about 0.75 mile from the shore. Saltair became known for its roller coaster, wonderful dance floor and buoyant waters. It closed in 1968 after the receding lake left it high and dry. The beautiful onion-domed pavilion was destroyed by fire two years later. A second Saltair was built, but this time the rising waters of the lake flooded the building. It remained closed until 1993, when it was reopened, 100 years after the original Saltair was built.

A few industries have been established along Great Salt Lake. Each year 400,000 tons of salt, used for everything from table salt to salting icy roads, is harvested from the lake. Also extracted are magnesium, used in structural metal; potash, used as fertilizer; and lithium, used as an alloy in steel.

Few Utahns really know the Great Salt Lake. To most of the million or so people who live within a half hour or less drive to its shores, it is as remote as the most isolated canyons of southern Utah, as distant as the ocean. Although the lake has been visited and admired for nearly two centuries, it remains largely undeveloped. Utahns accept the lake as it is; visitors often wonder why it is so difficult to visit and so unappreciated by locals. Perhaps the lake is just waiting for a younger generation to appreciate, understand and love it. As urban Utahns look for quality outdoor experiences close to home, the lake seems to beckon with open arms.

Seeing and Doing

Antelope Island—This 15-mile-long, 5.5-mile wide island near the lake's eastern shore is accessed from Ogden (see the Ogden chapter).

Farmington Bay Wildlife Management Area—Under the administration of the State Division of Wildlife Resources, Farmington Bay is less than a half hour's drive north from downtown Salt Lake City. The marsh was inundated by the Great Salt Lake in the 1980s, but after the lake receded, marshlands reestablished themselves and thousands of migrating and resident birds returned. Interpretive activities at the site include identification of and information about the birds, the relationship between the fresh-

water and salt water, and the management of a marsh system. There is an auto tour route you can drive. Open daily 8 A.M.–5 P.M. Take Interstate 15 north to Exit 325 and head west across the interstate on State St. to 650 W. Drive south to Glover Ln., then turn west and follow the signs to the Farmington Bay Wildlife Management Area. **801-451-7386.**

South End of the Lake—To reach the lake from downtown Salt Lake City, head west on Interstate 80 about 15 miles and take the Great Salt Lake State Park/Saltair exit (Exit 104). At the state park you can wade in the shallow waters, swim or go for a 20-minute speedboat tour of the lake. The modern Saltair Resort hosts concerts, dances and parties on most weekends. **801-355-5522.**

University of Utah

Utah's largest public institution of higher education, with approximately 27,000 full-time students, the University of Utah was originally established by Mormon pioneers as the University of Deseret in 1850. With the approach of statehood, the name of the institution was changed to the University of Utah in 1894. The federal government gave 60 acres from Ft. Douglas as a new campus site on the east bench of Salt Lake City. Classes opened at the new campus in October 1900, and the campus has now expanded to 1,400 acres. Utah's only medical school is located at the University of Utah. The medical center has received worldwide recognition, especially in the research and development of artificial organs.

Two popular museums on the campus are the **Museum of Fine Art** and the **Museum of Natural History** (see the Museum section). Other popular activities include football and basketball games (the men's basketball team made it to the NCAA Championship game in 1998, but lost a heartbreaking contest to the University of Kentucky), gymnastics meets featuring the **Lady Ute Gymnastic Team** (perennially one of the top two or three gymnastic programs in the nation), concerts at the University's **Jon Huntsman Special Events**

Center and theatrical productions at the **Pioneer Memorial Theatre, Kingsbury Hall** and **Babcock Theatre.** The University's football stadium was the site for the Opening and Closing Ceremonies for the 2002 Winter Olympics, and newly constructed student housing on the eastern edge of the campus was the Olympic Village for more than 2,500 athletics and officials. **801-581-7200; www.utah.edu.**

This Is the Place Heritage Park

Besides Temple Square, the most historic spot for Utah Mormons is at the mouth of Emigration Canyon, where Brigham Young and the first band of Mormon pioneers entered the Salt Lake Valley. This is the spot where, after a more than three-month wagon journey from Nebraska, the Mormon leader declared, "This is the place!" The site was commemorated with a small marker until 1947 when, during the centennial celebration, the striking **This Is the Place Monument** was erected. In 1960 the monument and surrounding grounds became a state park, and in 1970 planning for the "Old Deseret" village began, and the first building, the 1863 Brigham Young Forest Farm House, was moved to the site in 1975.

The park grounds are open year-round daily 8 A.M.–8 P.M. Admission fee charged. To reach the park head east on 800 S. to the entrance of the park at **2601 E. Sunnyside Ave.** (800 S. becomes Sunnyside Ave. at about 1400 E.). The park is located across Sunnyside Ave. north of Hogle Zoo. A visitor center includes a gift shop, exhibits and films. **801-582-1847; www.thisistheplace.org.**

This Is the Place Monument

Utah's largest human-made historical monument, at 60 feet high and 86 feet long, this monument was dedicated in 1947 to mark the centennial of the arrival of the first group of Mormon pioneers to the Salt Lake Valley. Historians have debated for years just how and where Brigham Young expressed his conviction that the valley was to be the new Mormon homeland. But if it wasn't on the brow of the ridge overlooking the valley and if the exact words were a not a prophetic proclamation, "This is the place!" they should have been. On top of the monument are the three principal Mormon leaders: Brigham Young in the center, flanked by Heber C. Kimball on his right and Wilford Woodruff on his left. On the lower platforms to the south are members of the 1776 Dominguez-Escalante Expedition, and to the north are fur trappers who entered the area in the 1820s. Bas-relief sculptures on the sides depict a variety of events from Utah's early history. The monument was designed by Mahonri M. Young, a grandson of Brigham Young, and is a wonderful visual aid to the early history of Utah.

Old Deseret Village

Old Deseret Village is a collection of more than two dozen buildings from the early Utah pioneer era, with more additions planned for the future. In the village, the buildings are spread out in a manner typical of Mormon villages, where there were often four houses located on the four corners of a block, with the rest of the space used for pastures, barns, corrals and gardens.

The first building located in the park, the **Brigham Young Forest Farm House,** was moved from its original location near 800 E. and 2400 S. in the valley in 1975. At the time of its construction in 1863, the farmhouse was about 4 miles outside the city limits on a 600-acre farm owned by Brigham Young, but on which he spent little time. It was occupied by some of his wives from time to time and provided dairy products for Young's large family. Its new setting at Old Deseret—on the outskirts of the village, separated from the other buildings in the village by orchards, pastures and corrals—maintains a sense of isolation, though on a much smaller scale. Nevertheless, the house seems more like a country manor house and provides an excellent opportunity to tell the story of 19th-century family life and the kind of organization needed to provide for a many-member family.

Among the reconstructed buildings are a blacksmith shop, a pioneer dugout house and the

Social Hall—a two-story Greek Revival–style building built with 2-foot-thick walls in downtown Salt Lake City in 1852–1853. The other buildings have been moved to the village from towns throughout Utah and locations in the Salt Lake Valley. They include adobe, log and frame buildings. The 1858 **Milo Andrus** house, a large frame structure, was used as the family residence and as an inn for travelers. In the village, it represents a pioneer general store. The oldest building is the 1847 **Levi E. Riter** cabin, which was originally located in the Old Pioneer Fort and was constructed shortly after the initial settlement.

The village is located on sloping hills, atypical of most Utah pioneer villages, so be prepared for a strenuous uphill hike along dusty roads, or take advantage of the horse-drawn wagons if you want to see all of the village. Throughout the year a number of special activities are planned at the village. As you might expect, Pioneer Day, July 24, is the most popular day of the entire year and there are plenty of activities to justify a visit even on such a crowded day. Independence Day, July 4, is also a popular day, when you can experience a 19th-century Fourth of July celebration. Other events include Pioneer Spring Days, Old Deseret Days, Pioneer Harvest Days, Pumpkin Harvest Days and the Christmas Candlelight Tour. Dates for these events vary, so check at the village for the exact days. Open daily 11 A.M.–5 P.M. Memorial Day–Labor Day, and on some weekends during the rest of the year.

Festivals and Events

First Night

Dec. 31–Jan. 1. Downtown Salt Lake City's First Night Celebration (New Year's Eve) is one of the most exciting and innovative events to come along in many years. Apparently the First Night idea originated in Boston in 1976 and has spread to many cities in North America. The first Salt Lake City First Night was held in 1994 and since then has grown to become the place where more Salt Lakers ring out the old and ring in the new year than any other location in the city. This is an event for the masses, and those who attend once will never be content to stay home to sleep into the new year or watch New Year's revelers on television.

First Night is a smorgasbord of activities held in more than a dozen downtown locations that include the Salt Lake Art Center, Capitol Theater, Salt Palace, Abravanel Hall, Hansen Planetarium, ZCMI Center, Crossroads Mall, Cathedral of the Madeleine and Salt Lake Tabernacle. Indeed, First Night is a wonderful opportunity to visit this treasure of buildings to watch thousands of exceptionally talented performers. Purchase a very reasonably priced button and pin it on your jacket for admittance to all of the activities.

This is an event for all ages. Special activities for children are set up at several locations and children under 10 are admitted free. Bring grandpa and grandma. If they tire of the crowds and the more modern venues, they will find a delightful variety of performers and groups in the spacious Salt Lake Tabernacle from 6 P.M. to shortly before midnight. There are food booths all up and down Main St., and shuttle buses provide transportation from parking areas outside the downtown area. The highlight of the evening comes at midnight with a huge fireworks display. **801-364-4885.**

St. Patrick's Day

usually third Sat. in Mar. If you're Irish, or just love St. Patrick's Day, you don't need to feel like an exile in Salt Lake City. Utah's Irish heritage goes back to the early hard-rock miners, many of them Irish-Catholic, who worked in the mines in the mountains surrounding Salt Lake City. The Hibernian Society of Utah has made St. Patrick's Day a fun-filled event that seems to mark the transition from winter to spring. On the Sat. before St. Patrick's Day, which is Mar. 17, there is the annual parade in downtown Salt Lake City with more than 150 bands, floats and family entries. One of Utah's best known Irish-born residents, Roma Downey, star of the television series *Touched by an Angel,* has served as

Grand Marshal of the parade—causing locals to quip that while the Pioneer Day parade of July 24th includes the Saints, the St. Patrick's Day parade was led by an angel.

Living Traditions Festival

third weekend in May. This celebration of Salt Lake City's folk and ethnic arts is a joint project of the Salt Lake City Arts Council and the Folk Arts Program of the Utah Arts Council. Music, dance, crafts and foods are the ingredients that make this Salt Lake City's most popular spring festival. Nearly 20 different ethnic groups have food booths offering everything from Native American to Palestinian to Vietnamese delicacies. The music and folk-dancing performances are even more diverse, with 40 different groups performing on two stages. The festival is held on the grounds of the historic Salt Lake City and County Building, which makes an ideal setting for the event. The stages are located on the south and the north sides of the massive building and are usually staggered just enough to allow festivalgoers to walk to the other side of the building for the performances. The groups change each year, although some have performed nearly every year since the first festival in 1986. The countries and cultures represented include the Philippines, Mexico, Ukraine, Vietnam, Korea, Germany, Serbia, Bosnia, Croatia, Tonga, Samoa, Switzerland, Peru, Argentina, India, Greece, Lebanon, Scotland, Thailand, Russia, England, Africa, the Basque area of France/ Spain and the Jewish culture. **801-533-5760.**

Gina Bachauer International Piano Competition and Festival

mid-June. For two weeks in mid-June, the Gina Bachauer International Piano Competition is held as pianists from around the world compete for thousands of dollars in prize money, a Steinway grand piano and recording and concert contracts that could, in the tradition of a Van Cliburn, skyrocket them into worldwide fame. If you are a classical music lover, this is a great opportunity to enjoy performances by pianists who will likely be the stars of tomorrow. The competition involves about 60 pianists selected from several hundred applicants. Four rounds of competition conclude with the finalists performing their favorite piano concerto movement with the Utah Symphony. **801-521-9200.**

Utah Arts Festival

end of June. Since its establishment in 1976, the Utah Arts Festival has become Utah's largest and longest-running gathering of artists. The festival has been held at different locations in the downtown area, and more recently on the State Fair Grounds at **10th W. and North Temple.** Efforts are underway to return the festival to downtown Salt Lake City. The five-day event begins on Wed. and runs through the last weekend in June. Exhibitions highlight the work of new and emerging artists as well as underexhibited artists. Festivalgoers will also enjoy the wide variety of entertainment provided by more than 50 musical groups, artistic demonstrations, an artists marketplace and food booths. The literary arts are also represented with a book fair and book signings by Utah authors. Separate children's programs are offered, with a special family admission designed to encourage parents to bring their children to the festival. The activities run from noon to midnight each day, except Sun., when the festival ends at 10 P.M. **801-322-2428.**

Days of '47

mid-July. Ask any Utah Mormon what, next to Christmas, is the state's most important holiday and chances are, he or she will say the 24th of July. This was the day that the vanguard of Mormon pioneers under the leadership of Brigham Young arrived in the Salt Lake Valley. Also known as **Pioneer Day,** the event has been celebrated in one way or another since 1848. It is a state holiday, and many Utah communities hold special celebrations. In Salt Lake City, the big event is the 24th of July Pioneer Parade, one of the largest and oldest in the United States. The parade includes approximately 200 floats and groups, and many parade goers make it a ritual to sleep out the night before along the parade route to secure a good viewing spot. This is not necessary, though, unless you want to join in the all-night festivities. It's usually possible to go down an hour or two before the parade and find a good spot.

Two other parades are held in connection with the Days of '47: a horse parade with more than 1,200 horses is held the week before the 24th, and a children's parade—reportedly the largest children's parade in the country with more than 4,000 children dressed mostly in pioneer costumes—is held the Sat. morning before Pioneer Day. Other activities on Pioneer Day include the 26.2-mile-long Deseret News Marathon and a 10K race. The marathon begins at 5:15 A.M. in the mountains above Salt Lake City and follows part of the original pioneer route down Emigration Canyon. The mountain course takes its toll on runners and is not one on which you should expect to set a personal best time. The last segment of the races follows the parade route, providing a large audience to watch and cheer on the runners.

Another morning option is the sunrise service at 7 A.M. in the Salt Lake Tabernacle, which features selections by the Mormon Tabernacle Choir and an address by one of the elders of the church. An eight-day World Champion Rodeo concludes on the evening of July 24. Firework displays all over the valley are an appropriate ending to the celebration. Salt Lake Convention and Visitors Bureau; **801-521-2822.**

Summerfest International Arts and Folk Festival

second week in Aug. Since 1989, the Bountiful/Davis Art Center has sponsored this festival that attracts dance groups and musicians from a dozen or more countries around the world. Throughout the week, performances are scheduled from Ogden on the north to Bountiful on the south. Each group performs for approximately 30 minutes during the day and 10 minutes in the evening. A highlight is the Parade of Nations down Bountiful's Main St. on Thurs. evening. Utah artists join in the festival with

booths and exhibits. Ethnic and American food is served. Admission to the parade and the opening ceremonies on Thurs. evening is free; otherwise, admission fee is charged. Performances are held in the **Bountiful Park (400 N. and 200 W.)** all day Fri.–Sat., noon–5 P.M. Sun. **801-292-0367.**

Utah State Fair

beginning of Sept. Sept. is fair month in Utah, with the Utah State Fair running for 10 days, usually from the first Fri. in the month through the next Sun. Judging by the crowds, it seems that every Utahn attends at least one day of the fair, and for many reasons. There is plenty to see and do with countless exhibits, contests, shows and demonstrations, livestock auctions, carnival rides, a rodeo, a horse show, music competition and live entertainment nightly. Wonderful turn-of-the-century fair buildings have been restored and are listed in the National Register of Historic Places. Located at **1000 W. and North Temple Sts. 801-538-8440.**

Greek Festival

first weekend after Labor Day. If you are in Salt Lake City the first weekend after Labor Day, don't miss the annual Greek Festival at the historic Holy Trinity Greek Orthodox Church. Begun in 1976, it has become one of the most popular of all festivals in Salt Lake City. The festival begins at 11 A.M. on Fri. and runs until Sun. evening. Almost the entire downtown community comes to the festival for lunch on Fri., so expect long lines about 11:30 A.M.–2 P.M. But the *dolmathes, fasolakia, pilafi, pastitsio, spanakopites, stifatho, souvlakia, gyros* and Greek chicken make any wait worthwhile. Even longer lines seem to form for honey-sweetened Greek pastries such as *baklava,* made from recipes brought by immigrant Greek women to Utah.

The Greek Orthodox community of the Salt Lake Valley spends nearly all year preparing for the festival, and almost as impressive as the food is the cheerful efficiency with which the well-trained volunteers carry out their assignments. In addition to the food, festival visitors can participate in traditional Greek dances, attend cooking demonstrations, listen to a Byzantine choir program, watch a slide presentation on the history of Greek immigration to Utah, visit the first Greek museum in the United States and tour the historic church at 300 S. and 300 W. **801-328-9681.**

Outdoor Activities

Golf

Recently *Golf Digest* ranked Salt Lake City as the number one golf city of big cities in the country. The ranking was based on the number, quality and cost of local golf courses. There are 14 public golf courses spread throughout the valley, along the Wasatch Mountain foothills and in Parleys Canyon. The golfing season usually begins in Mar. and concludes in late Oct. or early Nov., although for die-hard golfers, a good year is when they can claim to golf in every month of the year. The following are some favorite courses:

Bonneville Golf Course

Situated on the east bench of Salt Lake City, just south of the University of Utah, and amid one of the valley's most exclusive older residential areas, the Bonneville Golf Course has been a longtime favorite for many Salt Lake golfers. The course has a good combination of difficult and easy holes, with most locations offering a beautiful view of the valley. The course can be reached by turning south onto the first street (Connor St.) after crossing the intersection of Sunnyside Ave. and Foothill Dr. (approximately 850 S. and 2100 E.) as you head east on Sunnyside Ave. **954 Connor St.; 801-596-5041.**

Bountiful Golf Course

This beautifully landscaped, well-maintained course, located high up on the west slope of the mountains north of Salt Lake City, offers a spectacular view of the Davis County cities of Bountiful, Centerville, Farmington and Woodscross, snuggled between the expansive Great Salt Lake and the Wasatch Mountains. While the course is challenging, with plenty of oak brush and trees

to claim errant shots, the fairways seem to be wider and more inviting than those at other mountain courses in the state. With the mountain terrain as a factor, each hole is different. From Salt Lake City, drive north on Interstate 15 to the Woodscross exit (Exit 318), then head east through the intersection to Orchard Dr. Turn north and follow Orchard Dr. to 1800 S. Head east up the mountain, until just before you start into the canyon (Mueller Park), then turn south on Bountiful Blvd. to 2430 S. **801-298-6040.**

Forest Dale Golf Course

There are a lot of reasons to recommend the Forest Dale course, not the least of which is that it is the oldest existing golf course in Utah. Built in 1906, it was acquired by Salt Lake City in 1924 and has been open to the public ever since. One of the nice features of the course is the historic clubhouse that has been recently restored. On the south side of the interstate is the golf course, and on the north side is Fairmont Park. But even though the interstate parallels the left side of the first hole, it is located high above the golf course and generally screened by trees, so there is relatively little noise. The course was renovated in the mid-1980s; new tee areas and berms and mounds were added to give more contour to what was formerly a flat and level course. Located at **2375 S and 900 E. 801-483-5420.**

Mountain View Golf Course

Mountain View is a most appropriate name for this golf course. From anywhere on the course, you can look to the east and see the magnificent Wasatch Mountains 8 miles away. The view of the mountains is unsurpassed anywhere else in the Salt Lake Valley, and it is worth the price of the greens fees just to walk around the course gazing at the fortress of mountains across the valley. As a golf course, Mountain View is a flat, easy-to-play course, with few obstacles and wide fairways. For an urban course, noise is at a minimum here, which, along with the breathtaking view of the mountains and ease of play, makes this a favorite. Located at **2400 W. and 8660 S. 801-255-9211.**

Wingpointe Golf Course

This golf course caters to both local golfers and air travelers. If you have a couple hours' layover at the airport, walk or take a taxi there and either hit a bucket of balls or play 9 or 18 holes. The clubhouse is well stocked with rental clubs, but if you just want to hit a bucket of balls, the accommodating clubhouse personnel will loan you a club or two at no charge. The course is Scottish links–style with no trees but plenty of water. With automobile traffic on three sides and airplanes taking off overhead, Wingpointe is the noisiest course in the state, but it demands enough concentration that you tend to forget about the noise. Single players can usually join a group without much trouble, but if you are from out of town and you want to make a reservation, you can do it with a credit card using the Salt Lake City automated reservation system. Located at **3600 W. and 100 N.,** just off Interstate 80 and the north end of the Bangerter Hwy. as it enters the airport. **801-575-2345.**

Hiking

Ensign Peak Nature Park

On July 26, 1847, Brigham Young and eight other leaders of the recently arrived vanguard pioneer group climbed to the top of a peak that Joseph Smith had seen in a dream and described to Young and others before his death. With the aid of field glasses, the men surveyed the mountains, canyons, streams, valley and lake that lay before them. Wilford Woodruff recalled the Old Testament scripture (Isaiah 11:12) wherein the Lord would set up an ensign for the nations to which the outcasts of Israel and dispersed of Judah would be gathered. The name stuck, and Ensign Peak has been an important landmark ever since.

In July 1996 the Ensign Peak Nature Park was established with a half-mile-long dirt trail to the peak 400 feet above the parking area and 1,085 feet above the valley floor. It is a steep climb around the east side of the peak where the final ascent is made from the north, but the magnificent view is worth the effort. Downtown Salt Lake City and the Salt Lake Valley stretch out before you to the south, flanked by the Wasatch Mountains on the east and Oquirrh Mountains to the west. Turning to the west, you can see the Great Salt Lake with Antelope and Stansbury Islands clearly visible. A plaza at the trailhead contains several markers that outline the human and natural history. If the climb to the top of the peak is beyond your physical abilities, a short climb up the paved walkway to the Vista Overlook provides a fine view as well.

To reach the park, take State St. north and continue around the east side of the State Capitol and up the hill on E. Capitol St. for about 1.25 miles past the Capitol Building. Near the terminus of E. Capitol St., turn left (west) onto Ensign Vista Dr. and follow it to the park entrance marked by three large flag poles. Allow at least an hour for the hike up and back and to read the informative markers.

Ice Skating

Gallivan Utah Center Ice Rink

Located in the heart of downtown Salt Lake City between Main St. and State St. and 200 and 300 S., surrounded by some of Salt Lake City's tallest buildings, the Gallivan Plaza offers outdoor ice skating mid-Nov.–mid-Mar. Mon.–Fr. noon– 9 P.M., Sat. noon–11 P.M. Rentals are available. **801-535-6117.**

Kearns Speed Skating Oval

The fastest ice on earth! That's how speed skaters from all over the world describe the ice at the Kearns Speed Skating Oval. Judging by the performances turned in by the 2002 Winter Olympians on their clap-skates and in their "swift skin" suits, they are right. Nearly every major world speed skating record was set at the oval during the Olympics and in subsequent meets. You can try for your own personal best, or just learn to skate during the public skating times at the indoor oval. Located about 15 miles southwest of downtown Salt Lake City at **4800 W. and 5662 S. 801-966-5555.**

Running, Jogging and In-Line Skating

Jordan River Pkwy.

One of Utah's great recreational treasures is the Jordan River Pkwy. The idea is for an urban parkway that runs the entire course of the Jordan River approximately 40 miles from Utah Lake to the Great Salt Lake. Segments of the trail have already been completed and receive enthusiastic use. Other sections are being acquired and developed as funds and resources permit. A segment of the parkway from the north end of Utah Lake to the Salt Lake/Utah County border is described in the **Provo and Utah Valley** chapter. The best developed stretch in the Salt Lake Valley runs approximately 4 miles between 4800 S. and 7800 S. There are plenty of parking areas along the route, with the 5400 S. trailhead being one of the easiest to reach. You will find walkers, joggers, in-line skaters and bikers making good use of the paved trail. The river and marshlands along the river provide excellent habitat for small wildlife and waterfowl. Other segments closer to the city include an area north along the river from the Utah State Fairgrounds, which you can access off North Temple St. at about 1200 W., and a segment that runs south from 300 and 400 S. at about 1200 W. to the north end of Jordan Park at about 1000 S.

Liberty Park

One of Salt Lake City's largest public parks, this is a favorite with runners and in-line skaters because of the shade from the mature trees, the flat terrain and the lack of automobiles. Joggers can run the inside road, which is about 1.3 miles per lap, or along the outside edge of the park, at about 1.5 miles a lap. The park is located between 900 S. and 1300 S. and 500 E. and 700 E. It is about a 2-mile run to the park from downtown Salt Lake City.

Memory Grove and City Creek Canyon

If you are staying in the downtown area, a great route for running can be found in City Creek Canyon. It is a particularly popular route with lunchtime joggers, especially during the summer when the trees and stream offer relief from the summer heat. The first part of the run is a strenuous uphill stretch, which continues, though not as steeply, up City Creek Canyon. Head north up Main St., circling around the State Capitol, and find Bonneville Rd., which begins just beyond the northeast parking lot of the State Capitol complex. Follow Bonneville Rd. until it makes a U-turn back to the south and return along the east side of City Creek Canyon. Continue up the City Creek Canyon Rd., which is closed to automobile traffic. Follow this road for just over 5 miles to its termination at Rotary Park. On the return, follow the road as it heads back to the city through the canyon to Memory Grove. This nice, easy downhill run is a good place to put yourself on cruise control and experience that runner's high.

Sugarhouse Park

This was the site of the Utah Territorial Prison, but now is one of the city's busiest parks. A favorite for joggers, the gentle rolling hills over the 2.3-mile perimeter lap around the park offer distance, variety and a safe place away from automobiles. You can also run the inner circle of the park, which is a little over a mile in distance. Located at **2100 S. and 1300 E.**

Swimming

There are 18 public pools in the Salt Lake area. For information about the pools located throughout the valley, contact the **Salt Lake County Parks and Recreation Office, 801-468-2529; www.parks-recreation.org.**

Tennis

Liberty Park

Traditionally, Liberty Park has been the place to play tennis in Salt Lake City. There are 16 tennis courts and a pro shop in the west-center area of the public park. Located between 900 and 1300 S. and 500 and 700 E. **801-596-5036.**

Oquirrh Park Tennis Center

Located in the southwestern part of the valley, this is one of the best outdoor tennis facilities in the state. There are eight lighted tennis courts and a pro shop with rental equipment, including a tennis ball machine. Open daily Apr.–Oct. Located across the street from Kearns High School. **5624 S. 4800 W.; 801-966-4229.**

City and County Parks

Most of the city and county parks have tennis courts available on a first-come, first-served basis. One of the six courts just west of Raging Waters are seldom used; on 1700 S. and about 1400 W. **801-972-7800 city parks; 801-468-2560 county parks.**

Seeing and Doing

Children and Families

Children's Museum of Utah

Opened in 1983, the Children's Museum is a wonderful place for children and those who accompany them. It is located in the old Wasatch Springs Plunge swimming facility, which served as a major recreation area for decades. The building has a charm all its own and seems a perfect meeting place for the city's past and future. Favorites include hands-on items, such as an airplane cockpit where children become the pilot; an 18-wheeler cab; a small grocery store, a gas station and a bank; an exhibit where children can experience what it is like to be blind; a healthcare section where children can play doctor on a dummy; and a section where dinosaur bones can be uncovered. Open Mon.–Sat. 10 A.M.–6 P.M. **840 N. 300 W.; 801-328-3383; 801-328-5268; www.childmuseum.org.**

Hogle Zoo

Hogle Zoo is a Salt Lake City and Utah institution. The zoo occupies a 50-acre site at the mouth of Emigration Canyon, just south of the This Is the Place Monument (see the Major Attractions section). With more than 1,000 animals at the zoo, there is plenty to see. Favorites include the sea lions, monkeys, apes, polar bears, elephants, giraffes, rhinoceroses, hippopotamuses, lions and tigers. There is also a children's petting zoo as well as miniature railroad rides. Open daily year-round; 9 A.M.–6 P.M. in the summer, 9 A.M.–5 P.M. in the spring and fall, 9 A.M.–4:30 P.M. in the winter. **2600 Sunnyside Ave.; 801-582-1631; www.hoglezoo.org.**

Lagoon Amusement Park

This popular amusement park was opened in 1886 at a site 4 miles west of present-day Lagoon, on the shores of Great Salt Lake. When the waters of the lake receded, the resort was moved to its present location in 1896 and the name changed from Lakeside to Lagoon. The enterprise was undertaken by Simon Bamberger, a German Jew who became Utah's fourth governor in 1916. Bamberger established the Bamberger Railroad Line between Ogden and Salt Lake City. One of the reasons for building the resort was to encourage riders on the "Bamberger."

Evolving from the original activities of swimming and dancing, Lagoon is perhaps best characterized as four parks within one: an amusement park, a water recreation park, a pioneer village and an entertainment center. Two perennially popular rides are a turn-of-the-century carousel and a wooden roller coaster constructed in 1921. Some rides are geared more to teenagers—or those who think they still are teenagers. There is the Colossus, with its two inverted loops; the Giant Ferris Wheel, a recent attraction, which is now the most visible feature in the park; the Tidal Wave (which marked my crossing from youth to middle age); and dozens of other rides for thrill-seekers. The water park is known as "Lagoon A Beach" and is included in the all-day ticket.

The nucleus of Lagoon's Pioneer Village was moved to the park in 1974, from a private collection of historical buildings and artifacts in Salt Lake City. The historic buildings include an early drugstore, a schoolhouse from Wanship, a railroad station from Kaysville, a post office from Charleston and a rock chapel, moved stone by stone from Coalville. The tool bench and work-bench of John Browning, along with some of the early inventor's guns, are on display. Rides, gun-fight reenactments, a jail where youngsters can be locked up and a log flume ride provide plenty of action in the village. Entertainment is pro-vided by the All-Star Marching Band that parades throughout the park and by the Music USA group. The Victorian opera house is an attractive feature of the park, and musicals and melodramas are staged inside.

Open Sat.–Sun. mid-Apr.–Memorial Day weekend, daily until Labor Day, then Sat.–Sun. for the remainder of Sept. Open 11 A.M.–11 P.M. during the summer months, with earlier closing times in Apr., May and Sept. Visitors can purchase an entrance pass or an all-day ride pass. **P.O. Box N, Farmington, UT 84025; 801-451-8000.**

Raging Waters

On a hot summer day, there are few places more enjoyable than Utah's premier water park, Rag-ing Waters. Opened in 1979 amid some contro-versy about putting ocean waves in the middle of the desert, Raging Waters is visited by more than a quarter million people each year. With 11 pools, including the giant wild wave pool, and 19 slides, Raging Waters is Utah's largest water theme park. There are all kinds of slides—from the most gentle to the world's first H2O Roller Coaster and the 289-foot-long Acapulco Cliff Dive, which has two drops, 40 feet and 20 feet. Other facilities include a popular rope swing, a bilevel kiddy pool and picnic areas. For the young and the young at heart, this is the place to spend a summer day. Open Memorial Day weekend–Labor Day. Located at **1200 W. and 1700 S. 801-972-3300.**

Wheeler Historic Farm

In 1898 Henry J. Wheeler built his farmhouse of brick and adobe on 75 acres. The house, out-buildings, fields, pastures and woods are now operated as a historic farm by Salt Lake County. Glenn Humphries has directed the farm since it opened in the mid-1970s. He has given careful attention to making it a special place for today's urban children to learn about life on a turn-of-the-20th-century farm. **6351 S. 900 East; 801-264-2212; www.wheelerfarm.com.**

Historic Sites

The Utah Heritage Foundation has pulled together an excellent free booklet, *Historic Downtown Salt Lake City Walking Tour Guide,* which outlines four 1-hour walking tours of more than 60 historic architectural gems in the downtown area. There's also a special 1-hour Main St. Kid's Tour. In addition to a Main St. Tour for adults, the other three tours include the Gateway-Railroad District, the Exchange Place and Market St. area and the North Downtown section. The guide is available at most visitor centers or by contacting the **Utah Heritage Foundation; 801-533-0858; www.utahher-itagefoundation.com.** In addition, the fol-lowing historic sites and buildings should not be missed.

Bingham Copper Mine

The world's largest open-cut copper mine is located in Bingham Canyon, in the southwestern corner of Salt Lake Valley near Copperton. The mine is so massive that it is visible from almost anywhere in the valley and looks like a gigantic amphitheater cut from the mountain. Ore was discovered in Bingham Canyon in the 1860s, but it was not until 1906 that the open pit opera-tions began. The excavated hole is more than a half mile deep and 2.5 miles across. The mine itself could seat more than 9 million people, and several Rose Bowl or Cotton Bowl stadiums would fill the pit bottom. In excess of 5 billion tons of material have been removed to produce more than 12 million tons of copper, making the mine the world's largest source of the metal. Copperton was a company town, built by Ken-necott Copper as a home for its managers and workers in the 1920s. It was designed to be a showplace for products made from the mine's copper.

The Copperton Park is a nice place to stop for a picnic lunch. The visitor center includes exhibits and an excellent film on the mining operation. Open early Apr.–Oct. Located 22 miles from downtown Salt Lake City. Take Interstate 15 to 7200 S., then head west to 7800 S., continuing west to the Bingham Hwy. (Hwy. 48). Turn south and follow the highway to Copperton and watch for the signs to the visitor center. **801-252-3234.**

Cathedral of the Madeleine

Constructed in 1909 and completely restored in 1993, the Cathedral of the Madeleine is one of Utah's architectural masterpieces. The Romanesque–style cathedral was built under the direction of Lawrence Scanlan, the first Catholic bishop of Utah, who is buried under the main altar. The interior is in the Gothic Revival style, with beautiful stained glass windows. Free guided tours, which last approximately 1 hour, are available by appointment. Open daily 6 A.M.–6:30 P.M. **331 E. South Temple; 801-328-8641.**

Ft. Douglas

Established 3 miles east of downtown Salt Lake City in 1862 by Civil War volunteers from California under the command of Col. Patrick Edward Connor, Ft. Douglas was named in honor of Illinois Sen. Stephen A. Douglas, Lincoln's opponent in the famous Lincoln Douglas Debates. The military force was sent to Utah to keep the mail and stagecoach line open between the East and California during Indian unrest that threatened to cut off the two sections of the country. It was also said that Connor was to keep an eye on the Mormons and that it was no accident that he had his cannons trained on Brigham Young's home in the valley below. The fort was deactivated in 1991 and turned over to the University of Utah. A drive through it reveals some fine officers' quarters dating from the 1870s, built from red sandstone quarried in nearby Red Butte Canyon. There are also stone barracks buildings and administrative buildings, which date from about 1900 to the 1930s.

One of the most interesting areas is the cemetery, where Patrick Connor is buried, along with some of his soldiers, as well as veterans and dependents who have served in the military since the Civil War. In the southeast corner of the cemetery are the graves of German, Italian and Japanese prisoners of war who died in Utah during or shortly after World War II. In the southwestern corner is the cemetery's largest monument, which commemorates German prisoners of war who died at Ft. Douglas during World War I. The Fort Douglas Military Museum, located on the south side of the parade ground, has exhibits on the history of the fort and the history of the military in Utah. Open Tues.–Sat. 10 A.M.–noon and 1–4 P.M. The entrance to the fort is at the east end of the University of Utah's South Campus Dr., at 400 South and Wasatch Blvd. 32 Potter St.; **801-581-1251.**

Salt Lake City and County Building

Constructed in 1894 to house the offices of Salt Lake City and Salt Lake County, this impressive Richardsonian Romanesque–style building has dominated the Salt Lake City skyline for more than a century. The building was constructed on Washington Square, an early campground for newly arrived immigrants to the Salt Lake Valley. The building served as Utah's first state capitol until the present capitol building was completed in 1915. During the 1980s the county moved its office to a new location, and the city completed an extensive restoration project including seismic stabilization in 1989. It is worth a stop just to walk around the building and admire its grand architecture and the interesting statuary perched high on the building. Inside there is a small exhibit documenting the building's history. You can wander through the building on your own, or join one of the free hour-long tours given by Utah Heritage Foundation volunteers. Call for tour schedules. **801-533-0858.**

Utah State Capitol Building

One of the finest examples of the Renaissance Revival architectural style in the United States, the capitol was designed by German-born architect Richard K. A. Kletting. Most Utahns agree that this is one of the most stately and magnificent public buildings anywhere. The building stands above downtown Salt Lake City and the rest of the valley like a sentinel. The building was completed in 1915 at a cost of $2.75 million. The copper dome and colonnade of Corinthian columns remind visitors of the capitol in Washington, D.C.

Inside, the ceiling of the dome is 165 feet above the floor and is decorated with seagulls, the state bird, and murals depicting events in Utah's history. Many of the paintings throughout the rotunda were made by Utah artists as part of the 1930s New Deal WPA program, which put unemployed artists to work during the Great Depression. Inside the capitol, be sure to see the Gold Room, which is adorned with 23-karat Utah gold leaf. You may view sessions of the Utah State Legislature from the fourth-floor balcony.

In front of the capitol stands a replica of the sculpture of Chief Massasoit, created by Utah-born Cyrus E. Dallin. There is also a monument to the Mormon Battalion, commemorating its 2,000-mile march to California during the Mexican War, and one remembering Utah's Vietnam War veterans. The Vietnam Memorial, located on the west side of the capitol, has become a sacred spot. A more-than-life-size statue of a soldier returning from a patrol stands in front of a wall that lists the names of all Utahns killed in the Vietnam conflict. Located on Capitol Hill, at the head of State St. Just across the street to the south, in the restored Council Hall, is the Utah Travel Council, an excellent source of information about the state.

Museums

Hellenic Cultural Museum

This jewel of a museum is located in the basement of the Holy Trinity Greek Orthodox Church. The church was constructed in 1924 in what was then the heart of Salt Lake City's Greek town. Curators and volunteers have taken great pains to collect and exhibit artifacts from the Greek immigrant experience in Utah. The museum is actually the first in the United States devoted exclusively to Greek immigrants. Many of the items are clothing and artifacts brought to Utah from Greece by the first immigrants who came in the first decade of the 20th century. There are also tools and other items used by the early Greeks in Utah. The museum makes effective use of photographs and documents to illustrate the acculturation process, including aspects of the economic, religious, educational and social life. In 1994 the museum was cited by the American Association for State and Local History as one of the outstanding ethnic museums in the country.

The museum has no paid staff, so hours are quite restricted. If you can't make the scheduled hours, call and ask if special arrangements can be made. Bill Drossos, Jim Kastanis, Andy Katsanevas, Chris Metos and Con Skedros are dedicated volunteers who are often at the church. If you mention how interested you are in seeing the museum, if it is at all possible, one of these gentlemen or another volunteer will likely give you a personal tour. Open Wed. 9 A.M.–noon, Sun. 11:30 A.M.–12:30 P.M. Tours arranged by appointment. **279 S. 300 W., Salt Lake City, UT 84101; 801-359-4163; 801-328-9681.**

Pioneer Memorial Museum

Built by the Daughters of Utah Pioneers in 1950 as a replica of the old 1860s Salt Lake Theater, the Classical Revival–style Pioneer Memorial Museum is located on Capitol Hill, three blocks north of Temple Square and a block west of the state capitol. The museum displays a wonderful collection of pioneer artifacts, original wagons and handcarts, clothing, furniture, photographs and other memorabilia. The Daughters of Utah Pioneers was organized in 1901 and throughout the 20th century has been the leading organization in preserving historic buildings and operating "relic halls" in many of the state's communities. The DUP, as they are affectionately called, were preservationists long before the term became popular, and the Pioneer Memorial Museum is the organization's showpiece. Admission is free. Open Mon.–Sat. 9 A.M.–5 P.M.; in the summer also Sun. 1–5 P.M. **300 N. Main St.; 801-538-1050.**

Salt Lake Art Center

This city art center features outstanding regional and national exhibitions accompanied by stimulating lectures, films and discussions. One recent favorite was a series of exhibitions under the title "History, Memory, and Media: An Examination of the Internment of Japanese Americans During World War II." The exhibition included more than 100 works of art created during the war by more than 30 Japanese-American artists in the internment camps; current photographs from the relocation camps; and a video created from footage commissioned during the internment by the federal government. The accompanying lecture series was held on five evenings over a four-week period. Not all exhibitions reach the level of "History, Memory and Media," but they come close, and the Salt Lake Art Center is a hidden gem still waiting to be discovered by visitors and many locals. Admission is free. Open Tues.–Sat. 10 A.M.–5 P.M., Sun. 1–5 P.M. **20 S. West Temple; 801-328-4201.**

Utah Folk Art Museum

Some of the best folk art research and documentation in the United States is being carried out by the Utah Folk Arts staff. Their office and museum are located in the 1850s Isaac Chase home in Liberty Park. The museum houses Utah's Folk Art collection, which ranges from items by Native Americans and 19th-century pioneers to the more recent art of Southeast Asians and South Sea Island peoples. In addition to collecting art, professionals have undertaken programs to document the music of Hispanics in Utah as well as late 19th- and early 20th-century social dance music. During the summer, a weekly folk arts program is held near the museum in Liberty Park. Open noon–5 P.M. daily Memorial–Labor Day, Sat.–Sun. mid-Apr.–mid-Oct. To reach the Isaac Chase home, drive east on 900 S. to the park entrance at 600 E. Follow the one-way road as it heads west, then south to the designated parking area. **801-533-5760; www.arts.utah.org/folkarts/chase.html.**

Utah Museum of Fine Arts

The Utah Museum of Fine Arts on the University of Utah campus is Utah's oldest and most diverse art museum. Art objects representing all principal artistic styles and periods of civilization may be found here. The museum has a good collection of European and American art, but attention has also been given to art from Egyptian, Southeast Asian, Japanese, Chinese, African, Oceanic, pre-Columbian and Native American cultures. The diversity of art in the museum is a treasure. There are more than 17,000 pieces in the permanent collection covering five millennia of human creativity.

This is a museum for art lovers and for families with children. The African and South Sea Island tribal masks fascinate both the young and old. The museum staff has prepared Family Backpacks that can be checked out, which include activities, games and puzzles for children that focus on a specific collection and are designed to develop a greater understanding of the art on display and to make their visit even more enjoyable.

In 2001 the museum moved into a brand-new 74,000-square-foot, two-story facility, but even so, less than 10 percent of the collection is on display at any given time. Exhibits are located on two floors with space for major traveling exhibits on the first floor. There is also a museum store and cafe near the front entrance. Admission is free. Open Mon.–Fri. 10 A.M.–5 P.M., Sat.–Sun. noon.–5 P.M. Take South Campus Dr. east and follow the signs to the museum parking area. **801-581-7332; www.utah.edu/umfa.**

Utah Museum of Natural History

Located at the southern end of University Circle, in the old University of Utah Library Building, the Utah Museum of Natural History is one of Utah's most popular museums because of its excellent collection of artifacts and fine exhibits. The exhibits feature dinosaur skeletons and prehistoric life in Utah. There are two allosaurus, a camptosaurus and a stegosaurus from the Jurassic Age. Extinct but more recent skeletons include the Huntington Canyon Mammoth, a sabre-toothed cat, a giant beaver, a wolf, a bison and a horse. The museum is the official state depository for prehistoric Native American artifacts, and the collection includes items from most of Utah's important archaeological excavations.

Other exhibits include a minerals and gems area and exhibits of birds, reptiles, amphibians and carnivores of Utah. The Romney Mine on the second floor is a replica of a hard-rock mine from the 19th century. A favorite is the Barrier Canyon Mural that replicates the otherworldly anthropomorphic Fremont Rock Art figures. The mural was painted in 1940 as a WPA project under the direction of local artist Lynn Fausett. There is also a hands-on discovery room for children that includes, among other attractions, a boneyard where children can excavate for dinosaurs. Open Mon.–Sat. 9:30 A.M.–5:30 P.M., Sun. noon–5 P.M. Admission fee charged. Follow 200 S. St. east across 1300 E. St. to University St.; the museum is located across University St. a short distance south of the intersection. **801-581-6927; www.umnh.utah.edu.**

Utah State Historical Society Museum

The Denver and Rio Grande Railroad donated its historic 1910 railroad station to the state of Utah in 1978 to house the Utah State Historical Society. The grand building, which was built in competition with the 1909 Union Pacific Station three blocks to the north, has been a wonderful facility for the state's history agency. The lobby area contains an excellent exhibit covering Utah from prehistory to the present, taking as its theme "Utah at the Crossroads." Exhibit items depict Utah's dinosaurs, earliest peoples, pioneers, agriculture, mining, industry and tourism and recreation. The Utah State Historical Society's library, with its extensive manuscript and photograph collection, has become a second home to Utah historians. The museum is free and open to the public, Mon.–Fri. 8 A.M.–5 P.M., Sat. 10 A.M.–2 P.M. The library operates on a more restricted schedule. **300 S. and 450 W.; 801-533-3500; www.history.utah.org.**

Nightlife

Iggy's Sports Grill

Salt Lake City's most popular sports bar features sports, from the photos, helmets, jerseys and other memorabilia to the dozens of televisions all connected to the major sports' satellite television packages and the huge big-screen TV behind the bar for the really big games. Everybody is welcome, from hard-core sports fans to families. If you are an exile from the football kingdoms of Nebraska, Florida or other sacred places in the sports world, you are likely to find a contingent of fellow citizens gathered at Iggy's for the big games. Open daily. **677 S. 200 W.; 801-532-9999.**

Zephyr Club

Opened in 1983, this private club is considered by many the premier live-entertainment spot in Salt Lake City. With live performances almost nightly, the club features blues, jazz and rock and roll performed by nationally known as well as regional and local groups. The patrons vary greatly according to who is performing, and there are no bad seats in the place, though many regulars prefer the great mezzanine seats. The club has an interesting collection of photos of musicians who have played there. There is no food served at the club, so you can either bring food with you, go without or order food delivered from nearby restaurants using take-out menus that are kept on hand. Open daily 8 P.M.–1 A.M. except New Year's Day and July 4. **301 S. West Temple; 801-355-2582; www.thezephyrclub.com.**

Observatories and Planetariums

Sheila M. Clark Planetarium

From 1965 until 2002, the Hansen Planetarium, a Salt Lake City institution, was located in the stately 1905 Salt Lake Public Library in downtown just off South Temple on State St. The planetarium moved recently to the Gateway Center. With the move came the new name, the Sheila

M. Clark Planetarium. The original founder, George T. Hansen, is memorialized in the facility's major attraction—The George T. Hansen Star Theatre. The new building has state-of-the-art equipment, expanded exhibits, programs, a bookstore and gift shop and the IMAX-style theater. Located on the corner of **100 S. and 400 W. 801-538-2104; www.hansen-planetarium.net.**

Parks and Gardens

International Peace Gardens
Among all of the public parks in Salt Lake City, this is a favorite. The feelings of peace and universal brotherhood make this a special spot. The idea of a peace garden in Salt Lake City was born in 1939, the year World War II broke out in Europe, but it wasn't until after the war that the project was resurrected. In 1947 Salt Lake City's various ethnic groups and nationalities were approached about developing a section of the park that would reflect the diverse cultures and nationalities living in the city. The International Peace Gardens were dedicated on August 15, 1952. As new groups have come to the Salt Lake Valley, they have added their own sections to the gardens. The most recent addition is from Salt Lake's Vietnamese community. Each country has developed a unique way of representing its country with flowers and landscape elements. For example, the Dutch have a model windmill and a 12-foot-long wooden shoe holding tulips; the Germans have a linden tree beside a well and gate to the town as described in an old folk song; the Swiss have a scale model of the Matterhorn; and India has a bronze Buddha. This is a wonderful place to come and reflect on the diversity of people that have come to Salt Lake City from all over the world and to teach children about other countries and their cultures. Open mid-May–Nov. 8 A.M.–dusk, at no charge. Located in Jordan Park. **1000 S. 900 W.**

Liberty Park
One of Utah's oldest and largest urban parks, Liberty Park was established in 1881 on land that was originally settled by Isaac Chase. Brigham Young bought the land and Chase's mill and home from Chase in 1860. In 1881 they were purchased by Salt Lake City from the Brigham Young estate. The park contains a variety of large mature trees and a circular roadway that is popular with joggers and bicyclists. The interior of the park is a joy for walkers. Children enjoy the amusement area and the Tracy Aviary, which was established in 1938 and is home to more than 240 species of birds. The first public tennis courts were built in the park about 1915. Liberty Park has been one of the most popular tennis spots in the city ever since. The park is also the finishing place for the Days of '47 parade, the Salt Lake Classic marathon and the 10-kilometer race, holiday fireworks displays and numerous other summer events. Don't miss the Utah Folklife Museum in the historic Isaac Chase home (see Museums section).

Memory Grove
The closest park to downtown, this is one of Salt Lake City's unappreciated treasures. A good spot for those who seek a quiet, reflective time away from the urban bustle, Memory Grove is located at the mouth of City Creek Canyon just east of Capitol Hill and northeast of the LDS church office building. The park was built by the Salt Lake Chapter of the Service Star Legion as a memorial to the Utah veterans of World War I. It was dedicated in 1924. Within the park is a French railroad boxcar, one of 48 that were filled with mementos and treasures and given to each state by France in gratitude for America's support during World War I. Following World War II, a memorial chapel was built in the park. It is surrounded by memorial stones placed by family members to commemorate veterans who died in service but whose bodies were not returned to Utah. Other artifacts, including cannons, a personnel carrier from the Vietnam era and a memorial to the Utahns killed at Pearl Harbor, are also located in the grove. In August 1999 many of the trees and vegetation were damaged when a tornado, something seldom seen in Utah, struck with unexpected force. **135 E. North Temple.**

Red Butte Garden and Arboretum

Beautiful Red Butte Canyon, just east of the University of Utah and Ft. Douglas, is the setting for one of the real jewels among Salt Lake City's parks and gardens. The canyon was closed to public access for more than 100 years to protect the water supply for Ft. Douglas. Consequently the canyon was largely undeveloped, allowing for the protection of rare species of plants now found only in the canyon. The garden and arboretum are under the direction of the University of Utah, and waterfalls, tranquil ponds, thousands of beautiful flowers and sculpted ornamental grass collections provide an idyllic setting. Outside the gardens are 4 miles of hiking trails in a pristine natural area full of wildflowers, native shrubs and grasses used by native birds and animals. The hiking trails wind through the old stone quarries from which red sandstone was taken to build parts of Ft. Douglas and a number of other buildings in Salt Lake City from the late 1840s until the 1930s. An amphitheater is used for a variety of activities, including concerts, lectures, folk dance performances and classic Greek tragedy productions. A visitor center/arboretum, named for the late Walter Pace Cottam, a distinguished professor of botany at the University of Utah, opened in August 1994. An Orangerie, adjacent to the arboretum, opened December 2001.

Admission fee charged. Open May–Sept. Mon.–Sat. 9 A.M.–8 P.M., Sun. 9 A.M.–5 P.M.; Oct.–Apr. Tues.–Sun. 10 A.M.–5 P.M. Drive east on 500 S. past the University of Utah campus until the street turns south and becomes Foothill Blvd. At approximately 600 S., turn east onto Walkara Way and drive through the University of Utah Research Park uphill (east) until you reach the garden entrance. **801-581-4747; www.redbuttegarden.org.**

Performing Arts

Ballet West

One of America's leading ballet companies, Ballet West has its roots in the University of Utah dance program. Willam F. Christiansen, a pioneer in ballet in the United States and founder of the San Francisco Ballet Company, returned to his native Utah to found the first university department of ballet in the nation. In 1955 the first of the ongoing performances of Tchaikovsky's Nutcracker Suite was given. It has become an annual Christmas tradition, first performed by the University Ballet, then by the Utah Civic Ballet, which was organized in 1963 and renamed Ballet West in 1968. Ballet West also offers a full season of classical, modern and original works at the historic Capitol Theater. **50 W. 200 S.; 801-355-2787; www. balletwest.org.**

Pioneer Theatre Company

Located on the western edge of the University of Utah campus, Pioneer Theatre Company puts on two musicals and five plays a year. Performances run from Sept. to May. This professional theater company operates under the umbrella of the University of Utah's College of Fine Arts; although independent, it has an ongoing relationship with the university's theater department. Located on 300 S. **1350 E. University St.; 801-581-6961; www.ptc.utah.edu.**

Utah Symphony

The Utah Symphony is considered a state treasure. Its origins tie the strong Mormon tradition of music with Franklin D. Roosevelt's 1930s WPA program, which hired unemployed musicians to perform concerts during the Great Depression. The orchestra was so popular that after federal funding decreased, it continued on its own through World War II and, in 1946, was renamed the Utah Symphony. The following year, Maurice Abravanel was chosen as conductor and, under his talented and untiring leadership until his retirement in 1979, the Utah Symphony became one of the nation's best symphony orchestras. Abravanel received much recognition for his work, but short of renaming the symphony after him, the most fitting memorial was to name, in 1993, the newly constructed symphony hall for him. Abravanel Hall, a delightful place to listen to a concert, is located across from Temple Square. The symphony performs year-round, with a full schedule from Sept. to Apr., followed by a summer series in July and Aug. There are usually some ticket returns available for most performances. Located at the corner of **West Temple and South Temple Sts. 801-533-6683; www.utahsymphony.org.**

Shopping

Crossroads Mall and ZCMI Center

These two huge downtown malls are located across the street from one another and, with their combined total of more than 200 stores and shops, you should be able to find anything you are looking for. Both malls have covered parking terraces and are good places to park for touring or attending events on Temple Square, which is across the street to the north. ZCMI, which stands for Zions Cooperative Mercantile Institution, was established in 1868 under the direction of Brigham Young as the hub of a network of Mormon-run cooperatives. The aim of these cooperatives was to keep the economic wealth of the Mormon kingdom circulating among its members, instead of allowing it to slip away to the flood of merchants due to arrive with the coming of the transcontinental railroad in 1869. ZCMI was one of the West's first department stores.

During the 1960s until the 1990s, ZCMI department stores were built at many of Utah's shopping malls. In 1999 the LDS church decided to sell the ZCMI stores, which were purchased by the department store chain of Meier and Frank. All of the former ZCMI stores now bear the Meier and Frank name, although the ZCMI Center with its dozens of other stores still retains the historic name, and the historic store's restored cast iron western facade is a downtown landmark. Both malls are open Mon.–Fri. 10 A.M.–9 P.M., Sat. 10 A.M.–6 P.M.; Crossroads Mall is also open Sun. noon–5 P.M. The Crossroads Mall is on the west side of Main St., between South Temple and 100 S.; the ZCMI Center is on the east side.

Farmers Market

Historic Pioneer Park is the location for one of several farmers markets held throughout the Salt Lake Valley. The Sat. morning farmers market at Pioneer Park includes more than 60 vendors selling everything from fresh vegetables and produce to flowers and art. Open July–mid-Oct. Sat. 8 A.M.–1 P.M. Located at **300 W. and 300 S.**

Gardner Historic Village

The historic mill built by Archibald Gardner in 1853 and replaced in 1877 is the centerpiece for this cluster of old buildings that were moved to this site as well as new structures that were built around ponds, lawns and red brick paths. Within the buildings there is an array of furniture, gift, clothing, candy, art, accessory and craft stores. The historic mill is home to Archibald's Restaurant, which offers a variety of pasta, fish and chicken dishes along with burgers, sandwiches and salads. **1095 W. 7800 S.; 801-566-6940 restaurant; 801-566-8903 village office.**

Gateway

This interesting and somewhat controversial development opened in late 2001 four blocks west of the downtown shopping centers. Using the historic Union Pacific Railroad Station as its anchor, just to the west of which is located the 2002 Olympic fountain and memorial, the center appears at times as a new main street, an outdoor shopping mall and a village center. There are plenty of stores, restaurants and movie theaters, and the downtown Trax line (see the Services section) terminates at the Delta Center right in front of Gateway. Along **400 W. between North Temple and 200 S.**

Mormon Handicraft

Mormon women have a well-deserved reputation as excellent sewers and quilters, and excel at working with anything that involves cloth, needles and thread. One of the best places to acquire these handicraft items is at Mormon Handicraft, located across the street from Temple Square. There are hundreds of items for sale. If you are really serious about learning or improving on such skills yourself, sign up for one of the many classes that are offered in crocheting, tatting, quilting, piecing, doll making, embroidery and other handicrafts. Open Mon.–Fri. 10 A.M.–9 P.M., Sat. 10 A.M.–7 P.M. **15 W. South Temple; 801-355-2141; mormon-handicraft.com.**

Sam Weller's Zion Book Store

Utah's favorite bookstore was opened in 1929 by Sam's father, an immigrant from Germany; Sam has continued the tradition of operating a fine bookstore and is recognized as the foremost authority on Utah and western books in the state. Now his son Tony is following in his father and grandfather's footsteps. This is the place to call for rare and out-of-print books and for the best selection of Utah and western history and literature anywhere. The basement used-book department has thousands of books organized by topic available at bargain prices. Open Mon.–Sat. 10 A.M.–6 P.M. **254 S. Main; 801-328-2586.**

Trolley Square

During the early 1970s the old trolley barns were rehabilitated in one of Salt Lake City's first adaptive reuse projects. They are now a shopping center—an attraction popular with both visitors and longtime residents. A number of specialty shops, restaurants and movie theaters can be found here. Shops are open Mon.–Sat. 10 A.M.–9 P.M., Sun. noon–5 P.M. Located **between 500 S. and 600 S. and 600 E. and 700 E.**

Sports

Salt Lake Stingers

In 1994 Triple A baseball returned to Salt Lake City after having been absent for more than a decade. The Portland franchise moved to Salt Lake City and to a brand-new baseball stadium, Franklin Quest Field, built on the site of the old Derks Field. The inaugural game was played on April 11, 1994. One of the reasons for building the new stadium at the Derks Field location was to preserve what many consider the best stadium backdrop in the world—the towering Wasatch Mountains. The stadium is a modern facility that, coupled with the design and use of traditional green-colored seating, makes it seem historic. The expansive natural green grass of the outfield and the majestic mountains rising in the distance beyond the centerfield fence make this a baseball Shangri-la. Located at 1300 S. and West Temple St. **801-485-3800; www.stingers-baseball.com.**

Utah Grizzlies

Members of the International Hockey League, the Utah Grizzlies' season runs Nov.–Apr. Home games are played in the 118,000–seat West Valley E Arena, completed in 1997 and site of most of the 2002 Winter Olympics hockey games, including the historic (for Canadians, at least) Gold Medal game between the United States and Canada. Located at 2200 W approximately. **3200 S. Decker Lake Dr.; 801-988-8000; www.utahgrizzlies.com.**

Utah Jazz

When the New Orleans Jazz professional basketball team moved to Salt Lake City in 1979, the owners of the team decided to keep the original name, even though most people find Utah and jazz to be quite incongruous. Nevertheless, the Jazz has captured the hearts of Utahns as the state's only major league sports franchise. The 20,000-seat Delta Center was completed in time for the 1991–1992 NBA season, for an increase of nearly 8,000 seats from the previous home in the Salt Palace. The Delta Center is located three blocks west of Temple Square. The changing fortunes of the Jazz and what team they are playing against determine the availability of tickets for home games. Usually you can get tickets, but it is best to get them as early as possible. Located **between South Temple and 100 S. on 300 W. 801-325-2500; www.nba. com/jazz/.**

Where to Stay

Accommodations

There are hundreds of lodging possibilities in the Salt Lake area. Most motel chains are represented at interstate exits throughout the valley, including about 20 clustered around the Salt

Lake International Airport. For online reservations, check out the **Salt Lake Travel and Convention Bureau, www.visitsaltlake. com.** The following bed and breakfast inns and hotels are located in downtown Salt Lake City and adjacent historic neighborhoods.

Bed and Breakfasts and Inns

The Anton Boxrud Bed and Breakfast— $$$ to $$$$

Designed by one of Salt Lake City's best-known architects, Walter E. Ware, this house was built in 1901 for Anton Boxrud and his family, immigrants from Norway who lived in the home until the 1930s. After that it became a boardinghouse until it was renovated as a bed and breakfast in 1985 by Ray and Margaret Fuller, who gave careful attention to preserving the stained glass, woodwork, hardwood floors and pocket doors— doors that disappear into the side walls. When the Fullers retired, Jane Johnson acquired the home and expanded it to seven guest rooms, five with private baths and two with a shared bath. The most romantic is Grandma's Attic with its California king-size bed, sitting area and sloping ceiling. Jane is assisted by her mother, Gladys Allen, whose cinnamon buns and ever-changing full breakfasts bring visitors back year after year. Jane is the president of the Bed and Breakfast Inns of Utah and gives extra attention to make sure that her establishment is a model bed and breakfast. There are no TVs or phones in the rooms, but they are available in common areas. Jane likes to encourage conversation and socializing, and she does so in a gentle way. For those who need to work, there is a small office with a fax, phone and modem just off the living room. All rooms are upstairs and not wheelchair accessible. Located in a quiet neighborhood a half block south of the Governor's Mansion. **57 S. 600 E.; 1-800-524-5511; 801-363-8035; www.antonboxrud.com.**

Armstrong Mansion Bed and Breakfast— $$$$

Francis Armstrong came to Utah by wagon train in 1860 at the age of 21 after he joined the Mormon church. He worked first as a carpenter, then in a lumber and grain mill. Before long, his talents in business came to the fore and ventures in mills, sugar production, banking, ranching, construction, railroads and freighting proved successful. Politics was also an area of interest, and Armstrong was elected in 1886 to the first of two terms as mayor of Salt Lake City. He and his wife, Isabel, traveled to England and made drawings of a Queen Anne–style house, which they brought back to a Salt Lake City architect who drew up plans for the house. Completed in 1893 and listed on the National Register of Historic Places, the house has undergone several renovations, first in 1981 and most recently in 1994, when it became a 14-room bed and breakfast. The beautiful hand-carved woodwork has been preserved throughout the house, and each of the rooms—located on four floors—maintains the Victorian style of the residence. All of the rooms have private baths and all but two have Jacuzzis. Two of the rooms on the third floor—the August Retreat and February Interlude—have Jacuzzis located upstairs from the rooms in what was the attic area. An elevator provides access from the main floor to the two upper floors. Tours are offered for the general public Sun.–Thurs. 1–3 P.M. **667 E. 100 S.; 1-800-708-1333; 801-531-1333; www.armstrong-bb.com.**

The Inn on Capitol Hill—$$$$

This elegant four-story mansion sits midway up Capitol Hill below the State Capitol and Council Hall—home of the Utah Travel Council—and above Temple Square and nearby church buildings and offices. The mansion was built in 1906, a decade before the State Capitol was completed, for Edward D. Woodruff, a Salt Lake City business leader. Renovated as a bed and breakfast in the early 1990s, the inn has 13 rooms, each named for a theme or place in Utah history. The rooms are outfitted with private bathrooms that include jetted tubs, televisions and VCRs. Favorites include the Colonization room—the original master bedroom—which has a fireplace, bay windows and marble and limestone bathroom; the Great Salt Lake room, which occupies part of the original ballroom with a great view from the sunken jetted tub; and the Statehood room, with a balcony that overlooks the Salt Lake Valley. A full breakfast is served in the parlor. **225 N. State St.; 1-888-884-3466; 801-575-1112; www.utahinn.com.**

Saltair Bed and Breakfast—$$$

Jan Bartler and Nancy Saxton are the innkeepers at what is the oldest continuously operated bed and breakfast in Utah. The 1903 two-story house is listed in the National Register of Historic Places because it was the home of Fortunato Anselmo, the Italian vice consul for Utah and Idaho for more than 30 years. It was primarily through Anselmo's efforts in 1919 that Utah became the first state to establish Columbus Day as a state holiday, and the rest of the country followed. Anselmo hosted a number of dignitaries, including Pope Pius XII (before he became pope) and Benito Mussolini's personal secretary and mistress. The main house became a bed and breakfast in 1980 and has five guest rooms—two with private baths, three with a shared bath. The rooms are not overly large, but are very comfortable with down comforters. The Crystal room has a nice, sunny, panoramic view of the Wasatch and Oquirrh Mountains.

Next door, the cottage has three one-bedroom suites with fireplaces, kitchens, cable TV and a hot tub in the back. The cottage started out as a two-room adobe house built probably in the 1860s or 1870s. Jan and Nancy are eager to show the documents and photographs that are all part of the history. Their breakfasts are innovative and memorable. Pumpkin and walnut waffles, raspberry and pecan pancakes, a Saltair McMuffin and that specialty of the house, a breakfast fruit drink whose secret ingredients are known only to those guests who ask for the recipe. No smoking is allowed in the houses. The Saltair is within walking distance of the University of Utah and about 1.5 miles from downtown Salt Lake City. **164 S. 900 E.; 1-800-733-8184; 801-533-8184; www.saltlakebandb.com.**

Wolfe Krest Bed and Breakfast—$$$$

If best-selling author John Grisham ever comes to Utah to do one of his lawyer novels, he would be well advised to consider for his setting this turn-of-the-century Georgian Revival–style mansion situated a short distance southeast of the Utah State Capitol overlooking City Creek Canyon below. Designed by the prominent Salt Lake City architectural firm of Ware and Treganza, the mansion was constructed in 1905 for one of Utah's most prominent attorneys, William H. Dickson. Later the mansion was sold to James H. Wolfe, a constitutional law authority who served for 20 years as a Justice of the Utah Supreme Court. The Wolfe family owned the mansion until 1950. After nearly a half century as a low-rent urban apartment house, among other uses, the mansion was acquired by Kay Malone in 1997 and restored as a 13-suite bed and breakfast. Kay brought the same degree of design talent and care to the mansion that her husband—Utah Jazz immortal Karl Malone—brings to the basketball court. The result is one of the finest bed and breakfast inns to be found anywhere. The suites are located on three floors and all contain fireplaces, private baths with jetted tubs, televisions, VCRs and CD players. A full breakfast is served. **273 N. East Capitol Blvd.; 1-800-669-4525; 801-521-8710; www.wolfekrest.com.**

Hotels

Grand America—$$$$

This 26-story hotel with 775 units opened in 2001 in time to prepare for its role as the Olympic Family Hotel during the 2002 Winter Olympic Games. The Grand America is the younger sibling of the Little America Hotel that is located to the west across Main St. Salt Lake's light rail, Trax, stops in front of both hotels. The Grand America aspires to world-class status by virtue of its architecture, craftsmanship, furnishings, amenities and service. Inside the hotel is the Garden Café. **555 S. Main St.; 800-521-4505; www.grandamerica.com.**

Hotel Monaco—$$$$

This 15-story reinforced concrete, brick and stone-faced building was constructed in 1924 for the Continental Bank and Trust company. During the 1990s it was renovated as the new home of the 225-room Hotel Monaco. The original entrance faced east on Main St.; now guests and visitors enter from what might still be regarded as the back, or west side, of the building. The Bambara Restaurant is located adjacent to the hotel. **15 W. 200 S.; 877-295-9710.**

Inn at Temple Square—$$$ to $$$$

Constructed in 1930 to provide additional lodging across the street from Temple Square, the inn was renovated after the Hotel Utah was closed. While not as luxurious as the old grand hotel, the inn does offer excellent rooms and an other-era ambience not found in the larger hotels that share the same block. There are 90 spacious and nicely decorated rooms. Guests may use the inn's library and the Carriage Court Restaurant. Easy access to Temple Square, Symphony Hall and the Delta Center. **71 W. South Temple; 1-800-843-4668; 801-531-1000.**

Little America Hotel and Towers—$$$ to $$$$

Salt Lake City's largest hotel with 850 units; most of the rooms are located in the 17-story tower. There is a health club, spa, whirlpool, sauna, outdoor/indoor pool, coffee shop and lounge, as well as easy access to the Trax light rail system. The dining room is a Salt Lake tradition for many. **500 S. Main St.; 1-800-453-9450; 801-363-6781; littleamerica.com.**

The Marriott Hotel—$$$ to $$$$

The Marriott forms the eastern side of the popular Gallivan Center with its summer concerts and festivals and winter ice skating in downtown Salt Lake City. There are 370 rooms, an indoor swimming pool and a health club. Located on the corner of **200 S. and State St. 1-800-345-4754; 801-961-8700.**

Peery Hotel—$$$

The Peery Hotel, established in 1910, is Salt Lake City's oldest hotel. Although it fell into dis-repute for a number of years, it was restored in 1985 to an elegance that makes this a favorite stop for visitors who want to combine the best of a hotel and bed and breakfast experience. There are 77 guest rooms, each uniquely appointed with antiques and other furnishings. A continental breakfast is provided, along with daily newspapers, shoe shines and shuttle service to and from the airport. Other amenities include a whirlpool and exercise room, conference rooms, two restaurants and a state liquor store on the premises. **110 W. Broadway (300 S.); 1-800-331-0073; 801-521-4300.**

Salt Lake Hilton—$$$ to $$$$

There are 499 units in this 18-story building located across the street from the Salt Palace Convention Center and one block west of Main St. An exercise room, indoor swimming pool, whirlpool and sauna are on the premises. The popular Spencer's restaurant is located in the hotel. **255 S. West Temple; 1-800-HILTONS; 801-328-2000.**

Hostels

Avenues—$

The Avenues is a member of the American Youth Hostel Association (YHA) and has inexpensive dorm rooms, plus single, double and triple bedrooms. The nondescript, flat-roofed brick 1950s dormitory-style building is a popular lodging place with young travelers to the city. Guests have access to kitchen and laundry facilities and two lounges with fireplaces and color TVs. Located in a large residential area of the same name, just a short walk from downtown. Most of the homes date back to the turn of the 20th century, with a number from the second half of the 19th century. The entire Avenues area has been listed in the National Register of Historic Places. **107 F St.; 801-359-3855.**

Camping

PRIVATE

Salt Lake City KOA/VIP Campground—
This is the closest campground to downtown Salt

Lake City. It's less than 2 miles west of Temple Square, with easy access to downtown via public buses. There are more than 300 RV/tentsites, some with large pull-throughs. Located on 22 acres, the campground also includes cabins, showers, pools, a hot tub, recreation room, laundry, RV wash and store. Open year-round. **1400 W. North Temple; 1-800-226-7752; 801-328-0224; www.camping-vip.com.**

North of Salt Lake City

Cherry Hill Campground—One of the largest and most elaborate private campgrounds in the state, Cherry Hill Campground offers everything from tent camping with no hookups to full hookups with water and electricity. The campground has 250 spaces, including 143 pull-through spaces. Located 20 minutes from both Salt Lake and Ogden, and just 5 minutes from Lagoon Amusement Park, this is a popular campground, so reservations are recommended. The campground is adjacent to Cherry Hill Recreation Park, which includes water slides, miniature golf, theater, swimming pool, baseball batting range, game rooms and an inner-tube river run. The campground is outfitted with a convenience store, laundry, snack bar, service station and gift shop. An added bonus for campers is the invitation to pick and eat cherries and peaches from the orchards as they become ripe. To reach the campground from Salt Lake City, take Exit 326 off Interstate 15, then go 2 miles north on US Hwy. 89 and watch for the campground on the west side of the highway. **1325 S. Main, Kaysville, UT 84037; 801-451-5379.**

Lagoon's Pioneer Village Campground— Located adjacent to the Lagoon Amusement Park, the Pioneer Village Campground offers 204 RV trailer sites, 91 of which have complete hookups and 57 with pull-throughs. Another 58 tentsites are available, and the campground has plenty of shade trees, picnic tables, drinking water, showers and a laundry. Open Apr.–Oct. From I-15 take Exit 325; you will see Lagoon Amusement Park as you exit. Follow the signs to the park and campground. **801-451-8100.**

South of Salt Lake City

Mountain Shadows RV Park—Located in the south end of Salt Lake Valley, just off Interstate 15, Mountain Shadows is a well-maintained campground with 99 full hookup pull-through spaces. The park has a tenting area, swimming pool, spa, exercise room, game room, big-screen TV in the clubhouse, showers, playground, grocery and laundry facilities. Take Exit 294 off Interstate 15 and head east, then take the first road (Minuteman Dr.) south for 2 miles. **13275 S. Minuteman Dr., Draper, UT 84020; 801-571-4024.**

Where to Eat

There are hundreds of eating establishments in Salt Lake City and surrounding communities. New restaurants seem to appear almost daily. Because some restaurants that show great promise do not last, I have highlighted those places with long and well-established reputations that are my personal favorites.

Baba Afghan—$$ to $$$

Located just across the street from the historic Salt Lake City and County Building and the brand-new District Court Building, Baba Afghan is a popular lunchtime place for city and court officials. Kasim, a native of Kandahar in southern Afghanistan, offers a tasty 18-item lunch buffet that includes a good sampling of Afghani soups, salads, rice, vegetable and meat dishes. Vegetarians will find plenty of new selections in the exotic preparations of okra, pumpkin, spinach, cauliflower, tomatoes, onions, rice and eggplant. Among the 15 dinner entrées are a Poushtee Kabab that is a rack of lamb marinated in puree of onion, sun-dried grapes and garlic, then grilled and served on a bed of baked imported basmati rice, caramelized in spices. Open Mon.–Sat. 11:30 A.M.–2:30 P.M.; dinner times vary, but generally Tues.–Fri. 5–9:30 P.M., Sat.–Sun. 5–10:30 P.M. **55 W. 400 S.; 801-596-0786.**

Baci Trattoria—$$ to $$$

Gastronomy, Inc.'s success with fine restaurants

in historic buildings (see the Market Street Grill and Market Street Broiler in this section) led them to expand their endeavors to the historic buildings on Pierpont Ave., where they operate the Baci Trattoria, which features excellent traditional Italian food, and Cafe Pierpont, which specializes in Mexican food. The Baci Trattoria offers European–style individual plate pizzas baked in a wood-burning oven, freshly made pastas and lasagna, and veal, chicken and fish dishes. The interior of the restaurant alone is worth a visit. The huge three-sectioned stained glass pictures behind the bar are magnificent, while the upstairs section has a 50-foot-long mural on the east wall painted by seven Utah artists. Open Mon.–Thurs. 11:30 A.M.–2:30 P.M. and 5–10 P.M.; Fri. 11:30 A.M.–2:30 P.M. and 5–11 P.M.; Sat. 5–11 P.M. **134 W. Pierpont Ave.; 801-328-1500.**

Bombay House—$$ to $$$

Three longtime friends from India—Daniel Shanthakumar, Harpal (Paul) Toor and Ajmer Singh—have joined resources to bring excellent but comparatively inexpensive Indian food to Provo and Salt Lake City. Ajmer, the master chef, divides his time between both restaurants, while Daniel looks after the Provo establishment and Harpal looks to the Salt Lake operation. Located on the east side of Foothill Blvd., the Salt Lake restaurant is plain on the exterior, while inside the simple but elegant touch has a warmth that not all restaurants can offer.

The dinner selections are extensive. Among the most popular are the vindaloos, made from lamb, shrimp or chicken and cooked with potatoes, onions, tomatoes and hot spices. The kurmas are a stewlike dish cooked in cream with onions, raisins, cashews and curry. There is also the traditional flat naan bread baked in the restaurant's tandoor oven, and for desert there is khir, a cardamom-flavored rice pudding with raisins and cashews. All employees are native Indians, most of them attired in attractive dark blue turbans. Their quiet charm and attention add a special dimension to your visit. Open Mon.–Sat. 4–10 P.M. **1615 S. Foothill Dr.; 801-581-0222.**

Café Pierpont—$$ to $$$

Located next door to the Baci Trattoria and also operated by Gastronomy, Inc., the Café Pierpont has the look and feel of an elegant but festive Mexican restaurant. The restaurant is laid out in a long, high-ceiling, two-tiered, hall-like room with large windows and a door that, in summer, leads to the sidewalk dining area. The 15 overhead fans decorated with red, white and green streamers; tile floors; dark brown wainscoting around the walls; and full windows give a festive, palacelike feel that is unique in the Salt Lake area.

A popular place with the lunch crowd and when there is a Jazz game or other special event in the downtown area, Café Pierpont is also known for its excellent Mexican food. In addition to the regular combination plates and fajitas, there is a strong emphasis on seafood dishes. Don't miss the Baja combo, which includes a crab enchilada with salsa verde, a Mexican prawn skewer, grilled halibut served with a wonderful fruit salsa, and Baja rice. Other favorites include the halibut tacos and rock shrimp chile relleno combination and the jumbo Mexican white shrimp Veracruz in which the shrimp is cooked casserole-style with olives, peppers, onions, tomatoes, chiles and mangoes. The fresh vegetable enchilada is popular with vegetarians. Open Mon.–Fri. 11:30 A.M.–10 P.M., Sat. 4–11 P.M., Sun. 4–9:30 P.M. **134 W. Pierpont Ave.; 801-364-1222.**

Cafe Trang—$ to $$

Like other American cities, Salt Lake City has seen the establishment of several Vietnamese restaurants during the past several years, but the most popular with locals is the Cafe Trang. This is a small family restaurant, and there is something heartwarming about watching the young lady working the cash register busy with her homework whenever she has a spare minute. Other family members are congenial waiters and waitresses. The cafe does not look like much either from the outside or the inside, but the Vietnamese food is excellent, as is the Chinese food. The most popular Vietnamese foods with Americans include the rice noodles, served with vegetables and a special fish sauce, or the delicious soups served with bean sprouts and other vegetables. Open Tues.–Thurs. 11 A.M.–9 P.M., Fri.–Sat. 11 A.M.–9:30 P.M. **818 S. Main St.; 801-539-1638.**

Cedars of Lebanon—$$ to $$$

Raffi Daghlian, an Armenian Lebanese, opened this restaurant in 1981, after he came to Salt Lake City to study at the University of Utah Medical School. His Lebanese wife, Marlene, and Moroccan chef and dietitian, Abdule, are instrumental in the restaurant's success. If you are a stranger to Middle Eastern food, be assured that there are plenty of dishes you are guaranteed to like. A good way to experience the variety of foods offered is the reasonably priced luncheon buffet where the meat, vegetable, rice, pasta, soup and salads change daily to ensure a different experience each time you return. While most dishes are Lebanese and Moroccan, the Cedars of Lebanon also offers food from Israel, Armenia, Greece and Turkey. If you are calorie-conscious, Abdule has put together four specials with chicken, beef, lamb and a vegetarian combination plate dinner with less than 600 calories.

On Fri. and Sat. evenings, exotic belly dancers circle around while you eat, making dining at the Cedars of Lebanon a visual as well as a gastronomic delight. For another special experience, ask about dinner in the Moroccan Room, where you sit on the cushioned floor surrounded by handmade carpets from Turkey, Armenia, Iran, Afghanistan and other Middle-Eastern countries—all supplied from Raffi's well-stocked Oriental rug import business in the adjacent building. Open Mon.–Sat. 11 A.M.–3:30 P.M. and 5–10 P.M.; Fri.–Sat. 5–11 P.M. Reservations required on the weekend. **152 E. 200 S.; 801-364-4096.**

La Caille at Quail Run—$$$$

At the turnoff from Wasatch Blvd., a white-and-blue road sign informs you that La Caille is 2 kilometers ahead. This is just one of the small touches that help convince you by the time you leave La Caille that you really have spent the evening at a French country estate rather than at the mouth of Little Cottonwood Canyon. The building is a replica of a French château, and the grounds have a brick road, trees, vineyards, flowers, a creek and a pond. The menu includes some of the most expensive items to be found in all of Utah, but for the connoisseur and the romantic, it is all worth it. Dinner at La Caille is an unforgettable experience. Some friends have a "La Caille savings bank"—they save a couple dollars a week for an annual dinner at La Caille. There is a good variety of French and continental dishes of poultry, seafood, veal, beef and lamb. Favorites include the rack of lamb, broiled and served with marnier glaze, and veal medallions served with portobello mushrooms and champagne cream sauce. For dessert, don't pass up the flaming baked Alaska. Open daily 6–9 P.M., Sun. 10 A.M.–1 P.M. Reservations are required. **9565 S. Wasatch Blvd.; 801-942-1751.**

Lamb's Restaurant—$$ to $$$

One of Salt Lake City's oldest continually operating restaurants, Lamb's was a 20-year-old establishment in Logan before it moved to its present location in Salt Lake City's Herald Building in 1939. The original owner, George P. Lamb, a Greek immigrant, worked his way west, arriving in Utah in 1910. He worked as a waiter until he went into business for himself. In 1941 he took on Ted Speros, born in Bingham Canyon to Greek parents, as a partner, and since his retirement in 1982, Ted's son John Speros has operated Lamb's. The building in which Lamb's is located was constructed in 1905 to house the *Salt Lake Herald* newspaper and is listed in the National Register of Historic Places. Little has changed since 1939, and a visit to Lamb's allows you to step back more than a half-century in time. The booths and table are the same, the menu features most of the traditional items, and the waitresses wear the old-fashioned white uniforms that are seldom seen in Utah anymore. Lamb's is a Salt Lake City favorite for breakfast. The lunch menu features sandwiches and salads, while longtime dinner favorites include large fried oysters, several selections of seafood, grilled pork chops and roast leg of lamb. Open Mon.–Sat. 7 A.M.– 9 P.M. **169 S. Main St.; 801-364-7166.**

The Lion House Pantry—$$

The basement of Brigham Young's 1856 three-story home is the location for this cafeteria-style lunchroom. It is popular with employees at the nearby LDS church offices as well as downtown shoppers. Good, low-priced food and the historic setting make it an excellent choice for lunch. The pantry is located in rooms that were used by the Brigham Young family not only as a pantry and kitchen, fruit cellar and buttery, but for school classes as well. The lunch menu changes daily but features homemade soups, fresh-from-the-oven desserts and traditional main courses of beef, fish and poultry. Vegetarian dishes are also available. Open Mon.–Sat. 11 A.M.– 2 P.M., Thurs.–Sat. 5–8:30 P.M. **63 E. South Temple; 801-363-5466.**

Market Street Grill / Market Street Broiler—$$$

Seafood in Salt Lake City means the Market Street, whether it is the Grill, downtown in the historic 1906 New York Hotel on Post Office Place, or the Broiler, located in old historic Fire Station No. 8 just west of the University of Utah Campus. Both restaurants are operated by Gastronomy, Inc., a restaurant group that prides itself on its national reputation for excellent food, professional service, unique surroundings and an innovative approach to creating and operating good eating establishments. The seafood is flown in daily from both coasts. Other menu items include ribs, steak, chops and chicken, along with a full selection of breakfast items. Both restaurants are open Mon.–Fri. 6:30 A.M.– 10 P.M.; Sat. 7:30 A.M.–11 P.M.: Sun. 4-10 P.M.; the Grill offers brunch Sun. 11:30 A.M.–3:30 P.M. **The Grill: 50 Post Office Pl.; 801-322-4668; the Broiler: 260 S. and 1300 E.; 801-583-8803.**

Metropolitan—$$$$

If you are looking for the very best Utah has to offer in exotic and elegant dining, the Metropolitan is a sure winner. The restaurant has earned a well-deserved reputation for its refined but friendly atmosphere and its ever-changing menu of dishes from all over the world. The food is expensive but well worth it, and you will want to set aside a couple of hours for this dining experience. Reservations recommended. Open Tues.–Sat. 5:30–10:30 P.M. **173 W. Broadway; 801-364-3472.**

The New Yorker—$$$$

Elegant dining is the hallmark of the New Yorker. Located in the basement of the historic New York Hotel, the New Yorker is one of Salt Lake City's most prestigious restaurants. Steaks and the rack of lamb served with a rosemary cream sauce are favorites for meat eaters, while the seafood and pasta selections and specials offer plenty of variety for all tastes. The New Yorker is a private club, and you must purchase a two-week membership for about $5, but at a private club, alcoholic beverages are more accessible than in public restaurants. Open Mon.–Fri. 11:30 A.M.–midnight, Sat. 5:30 P.M.–midnight. Reservations required. **60 Market St.; 801-363-0166.**

Red Iguana—$ to $$

Based on appearance, this is not a place you would think to stop, and if you did, you would have second thoughts about entering. But the Red Iguana likes it that way, and has a loyal following of customers who claim that this is the best spot for authentic Mexican food in all of Utah. Don Ramon, from San Luis Potosi, has put together a menu that includes traditional Mexican dishes, American favorites and new items designed to please the palate of Salt Lakers. Items to consider include the garlic soup and the cheese soup; Ramon's hometown favorite, traditional enchiladas potosinas, which are four small stuffed enchiladas made with thick, fresh masa and filled with cheese, green onions and chiles, served with guacamole; and the vegetarian dish, made up of two deep-fried tortillas folded into a triangle and soaked in black mole then stuffed with beans. Open Mon.–Sat. 11:30 A.M.–9 P.M.,

Fri.–Sat. 11:30 A.M.–10 P.M. **736 W. North Temple; 801-322-1489.**

Rio Grande Cafe—$$ to $$$

This restaurant shares the historic Denver and Rio Grande Railroad Station with the Utah State Historical Society and has a wide-ranging clientele. The food, perhaps best described as Americanized-Mexican, is tasty. A daily special is offered, along with a full menu of salads, combination plates and à la carte plates. Favorites include the tostadas, smothered bean burrito, cheese enchilada or, on a cold winter's day, a bowl of the tasty chili verde. Open Mon.–Sat. 11:30 A.M.–2:30 P.M. and 5–10 P.M. **270 S. Rio Grande St.; 801-364-3302.**

Siegfried's Delicatessen—$ to $$

Siegfried's is a fast-paced, pick-up-your-tray, cafeteria-style German place whose main offerings are sandwiches or the bratwurst dinner, with one of Siegfried's own sausages and a choice of two heaping scoops of sauerkraut, red cabbage, coleslaw, hot or cold potato salad, macaroni salad, green salad or a refreshing cucumber and tomato salad. While you are waiting in line, you will pass a case filled with wonderful German cakes and pastries. Go ahead and order one with your lunch. After all, you only live once. The delicatessen is well stocked with imported items, and Siegfried has his own bakery, which produces delicious German bread, rolls and pretzels. Siegfried Meyer came to Utah from East Germany at the age of 12 and took over the delicatessen from another German family in the 1970s, when he was in his 20s. His food is popular with downtown businesspeople, workers and German-Americans who come to shop. Open Mon.–Sat. 11 A.M.–3 P.M. **69 W. 300 S.; 801-355-3891.**

Tony Caputo's Market and Deli—$ to $$

This authentic Italian deli would fit right in any "Little Italy" in the United States. With an excellent selection of meats, cheeses, oils, vinegars, pastas and sauces, here you'll find all the ingredients for a home-cooked Italian dinner. And if you don't know how to cook it, Tony will teach you. Each week he is the featured chef on a local TV station, and his recipes are collected by hundreds if not thousands of Utahns. A popular place for lunch, with two or three pasta and soup specials each day plus the regular sandwiches, including the Caputo, made with prosciutto, mortadella, salami and cheese. Open Mon.–Fri 9 A.M.–7 P.M.; Sat. 9 A.M.–5 P.M.; Sun. 11 A.M.–3 P.M. **308 W. 300 S.; 801-531-8669.**

Services

Visitor Information

Salt Lake City Visitors and Convention Bureau and Information Center—Open Mon.–Fri. 8 A.M.–7 P.M. (8 A.M.–5:30 P.M. in the winter); Sat. 9 A.M.–4 P.M.; Sun. 10 P.M.–4 P.M. **90 S. West Temple; 1-800-541-4955; 801-521-2822; www.visitsaltlake.com.**

Utah Information Center—Located at **Salt Lake City International Airport.** Also operated by the Salt Lake Convention and Visitors Bureau, the Information Center in **Terminal 2** at the airport has Salt Lake area brochures, visitor information on accommodations and attractions plus information about the national parks and Utah travel regions. Staffed daily 9 A.M.– 5 P.M., with brochures available 24 hours a day. **801-575-2800.**

Utah Travel Council—Located in the historic Council Hall, which was constructed between 1864 and 1866 and moved to its present site in 1962 across the street south of the State Capitol Building, the Travel Council has brochures and information from all over Utah, plus a bookstore with regional books, maps and videotapes. Open year-round Mon.–Fri. 8 A.M.–5 P.M., Sat.–Sun. 9 A.M.–5 P.M. Located on the southeast corner of **State St. and 300 N. 801-538-1900; www.utah.com.**

Transportation

The Utah Transit Authority (UTA) offers light rail service (Trax) from the south end of the Salt Lake Valley (15 miles) and the University of Utah (2 miles) to downtown Salt Lake

City. Bus service is available throughout the Salt Lake Valley and north as far as Ogden and south as far as Provo. Visitors can purchase an inexpensive day pass at all Trax stations and the downtown visitor center **(180 S. West Temple).**

For skiers staying in the Salt Lake area, the UTA system is one of the best and cheapest ways to get to the ski resorts in Big and Little Cottonwood Canyons. The buses are even equipped with special ski racks so you can take your equipment with you. Buses leave every 10–15 minutes starting at 7 A.M. and ending 9 P.M., seven days a week, and make several afternoon departures from the ski areas. **801-262-5626; www.utabus.com.**

While UTA offers bus service to the ski areas only in Big and Little Cottonwood Canyons, two commercial bus companies offer daily morning departures from downtown Salt Lake hotels to Snowbird and Alta as well as to Park West, Park City and Deer Valley. **Le Bus, 801-975-0202; Lewis Brothers Stages, 801-359-8677.**

Taxis—Twenty-four-hour service is available from **Yellow Cab, 801-521-2100; Ute Cab, 801-359-7788;** and **City Cab, 801-363-5550.**

Salt Lake Area Canyons

Salt Lake City could not exist without its canyons. The high mountain snowfields and underground springs of the Wasatch Mountains that form the east rim of the Salt Lake Valley provide much of the water essential to sustain physical life in the metropolitan area. In a less tangible but just as real sense, the mountains are a source of inspiration and rejuvenation that helps sustain the spiritual life of the valley. Gaze upon the mountains for a few moments from just about anywhere in the valley, and your soul will tingle at their beauty and majesty. There is no greater joy to be found than in the spur-of-

the-moment decision to treat yourself to a few hours or even an entire day of downhill or cross-country skiing. No choice seems more right than to head to the mountains for a hike—either in solitude or in the company of family and friends. There is no place where you can be more at one with the world than in the mountains of Salt Lake City. They rise nearly 7,000 feet from the valley floor to elevations of more than 11,000 feet.

There are a dozen or so canyons that rim the Salt Lake Valley, including Emigration Canyon and Parley's Canyon (the route of Interstate 80) in the north, but three—Mill Creek and Big and Little Cottonwood Canyons—are where almost all of the area's recreational activities are centered. Each of the canyons is unique.

Mill Creek Canyon, which takes its name from the pioneer saw- and gristmills that were located along the stream, has no ski resorts, but does have an abundance of hiking trails, some of which connect with adjacent Big Cottonwood Canyon to the south. The narrow, winding road up Mill Creek Canyon is a first choice for a scenic drive because of its beauty and because the only destination in the canyon is the end of the road. Here the pace slows to a more proper speed. You don't have to worry about drivers hell-bent for the ski slopes or other resort activities. Visitors are here for the scenery and the biking and hiking. In winter the road is closed partway up the canyon and becomes a popular cross-country skiing trail. The modest entrance fee into the canyon—much debated at first—has proven to be a boon in controlling traffic and providing much-needed money to help preserve the quality of the canyon and make modest improvements to the trail system.

Big Cottonwood Canyon is where Solitude and Brighton Ski Resorts are located. Popular with local skiers, there have been few overnight accommodations until recently. The road through Big Cottonwood Canyon is Hwy. 152, which goes through Park City and eventually meets US Hwy. 40.

Little Cottonwood Canyon is the home of Alta and Snowbird, where excellent skiing and fine accommodations are available at both resorts. The road into Little Cottonwood Canyon, Hwy. 210, ends at Alta.

Getting There

Directions to reach the canyons, listed from north to south, are given from downtown Salt Lake City. See also Scenic Drives under Seeing and Doing.

To reach Emigration Canyon, take Interstate 15 south to its junction with Hwy. 186; follow Hwy. 186 east to the mouth of the canyon near the University of Utah and Hogle Zoo, then take the canyon road east.

To reach Parley's Canyon, take Interstate 15 south to its junction with Interstate 80. Follow Interstate 80 east through the mountains; it continues to Rockport, then heads north to Wyoming.

To reach Mill Creek Canyon, take Interstate 15 south to Interstate 80, then follow I-80 east to I-215. Turn south onto I-215 and take the 3900 S. exit. Go east under the interstate and turn left (north) onto Wasatch Blvd. After about one block, turn east again onto Millcreek Canyon Rd. and follow it into the canyon.

To reach Big Cottonwood Canyon, take Interstate 15 south to Interstate 80, then follow I-80 east to I-215. Turn south onto I-215 and take the 6200 S. exit (Exit 7); then follow the signs southeast to the mouth of Big Cottonwood Canyon via Hwy. 152.

To reach Little Cottonwood Canyon, take Interstate 15 south to Interstate 80, then follow I-80 east to I-215. Turn south onto I-215 and take the 6200 S. exit (Exit 7), then continue south along Wasatch Blvd., past state Hwy. 152. Hwy. 210 continues south before turning east up the mouth of Little Cottonwood Canyon.

History

The Wasatch Mountains have provided Salt Lake Valley residents with five important resources—water, timber, building stone, precious ores and unsurpassed recreational possibilities. The streams flowing from the canyons were used to irrigate crops, for domestic needs and to power gristmills and other early industrial endeavors.

Sawmills were located in the canyons shortly after the initial settlement, providing building materials for the valley. The first sawmill in Little Cottonwood Canyon was established about 1851, probably near Tanner's Flat.

By 1855 the quarrying of granite rock began at the mouth of Little Cottonwood Canyon. At first teams of four yoke of oxen spent four days transporting granite blocks weighing as much as 5 tons each over the nearly 20 miles to the Salt Lake Temple site. Later, in 1873, a railroad line was completed to the quarry, which provided building stone until the quarry closed in 1899.

Mormon pioneers used the canyons for recreational activities too. In August 1847, several men entered Big Cottonwood Canyon and climbed to the top of Twin Peaks, which they measured at 11,219 feet above sea level. Brigham Young led many of the valley residents to Brighton in Big Cottonwood Canyon in July 1856 and again in 1857 to celebrate the anniversary of their 1847 arrival in the Salt Lake Valley.

However, it was the discovery of silver in July 1864 that brought fame and large numbers of people to Little Cottonwood Canyon. The ore was discovered by soldiers under the command of Col. Patrick Edward Connor, but the difficulty of transporting and smelting the ore postponed extensive mining operations in the canyon until after the completion of the transcontinental railroad to Utah in 1869. The highest production came between 1871 and 1877, when more than $13 million worth of gold and silver ore were taken from the Little Cottonwood Mines. This figure does not include the $5 million that were taken from British investors with the sale of the infamous "Emma" Mine, whose veins of ore disappeared just after the purchase, creating an outcry in Great Britain that the investors had been swindled by unscrupulous Americans.

The town of Alta was established in 1871, and during the summer of 1873 the population was estimated at between 5,000 and 8,000. There were 180 buildings in the town, including three general merchandise stores, four hotels, seven restaurants, and 26 saloons. A snowslide during the winter of 1873–1874 destroyed half the town and killed 60 persons.

A railroad was completed to Alta in 1876 from the granite quarry at the mouth of the canyon. At first cars were pulled up the mountain by mules and the loaded ore cars coasted down the canyon with a brakeman controlling the speed. A few weeks after the railroad opened, a brakeman believed his brake had broken, so he jumped from the car and it flew down the track, stopping only after it crashed into another train and killed the four mules that were pulling the cars up the mountain. Later, motor power was introduced. The railroad operated until the 1920s, and much of the former line is now the location for the highway up Little Cottonwood Canyon.

Brighton in Big Cottonwood Canyon was named for William and Catherine Brighton, who immigrated to the United States from Scotland in 1855 and came to Utah as Mormon handcart pioneers two years later. After working at various jobs in the Salt Lake Valley, Brighton secured employment as a timber hauler and later prospected in the canyon, filing several mining claims in its upper reaches. The Brightons built a cabin, which became a favorite stopping place for local miners, especially when word of Catherine's fine cooking spread across the mountains. The Brightons began construction of a hotel in 1873, which quickly became a popular summer retreat. Cottages were added and by the mid-1890s when the Brightons died, there were two or three dozen cabins at the resort with daily stage service from Salt Lake City in the summer.

Scandinavian miners were the first to pro-

mote the use of skis in the Alta area. The 14-foot-long, 6-inch-wide wooden slats were a far cry from today's skis, but they served their generation well, and in 1884 the first recorded ski race was held in Little Cottonwood Canyon.

As early as 1915 Brighton in Big Cottonwood Canyon became a destination point for skiers from Salt Lake City. Brighton became a favorite place for members of the Wasatch Mountain Club, which was organized in 1920. In the late 1920s, the club began construction of a lodge/cabin, which has been designated a historic site. A rope tow was put in place during the winter of 1938–1939, and in 1947 the first chairlift in Big Cottonwood Canyon—the 4,000-foot-long Millicent lift—was placed in operation.

Meanwhile, across the mountain to the south, George H. Watson, president of the Alta United Mines Company, learned to get around on skis and began to promote the Alta area as a potential ski resort in the 1930s. With the construction of the first ski lifts in Sun Valley in 1936, the concept of the destination ski resort became a reality, and interest increased to duplicate the same plans at Alta. In 1937 mining companies donated land to the federal government for the development of a ski area, and Utah's first ski chairlift (and the second in the entire nation) went into operation during the winter of 1938–1939 in Collins Gulch at Alta. The lift carried skiers a distance of 2,740 feet in 6 minutes. Lift tickets were 25 cents a trip or $1.50 for an all-day pass. The lift was built in part from an abandoned mining aerial tramway that had operated between Tanner's Flat and Grizzly Gulch. Access farther up the mountain came in 1940 with the construction of the Peruvian lift and the Germania lift in 1954. The first ski lodge opened during the winter of 1941–1942 just as America entered World War II.

Early in 1942 paratroopers from Ft. Benning, Georgia, who had never been on skis before were sent to Alta as part of an experiment to determine which would be easier—to make skiers out of soldiers or soldiers out of skiers. The conclusion rested with the latter, and the army turned its attention to the recruitment of skiers for the illustrious 10th Mountain Division. In the postwar years, Alta's reputation grew. New lodges and lifts were constructed, and in 1945 Alf Engen became director of Alta's ski school. A champion ski jumper of the 1930s, Engen helped pioneer powder skiing, for which Alta is without peer.

With the success of the Alta and Brighton ski areas, plans were made to open two other areas. Solitude, in Big Cottonwood Canyon, hosted its first skiers during the winter of 1958–1959, and the much larger Snowbird Resort in Little Cottonwood Canyon opened in 1971.

Construction of the Solitude and Snowbird Resorts brought environmental concerns into the fore, which led to the designation of the Mt. Olympus, Twin Peaks and Lone Peak Wilderness Areas that now take in much of the land included within the three canyons.

Festivals and Events

Snowbird Oktoberfest
weekends, Labor Day–early Oct. First held in 1972, Snowbird's Oktoberfest has become a tradition that draws thousands each weekend. If you like German brass bands, yodeling, dancing, food and beer, there is no better place to be this side of the Atlantic. Entertainers include the Bavarians, a musical group that has performed at every Oktoberfest since the first one; the Salzburger Echo Band; yodeler Kerry Christiansen; and the International Folk Ballet. You can even ride the Snowbird tram to the top of Hidden Peak for a daily performance of the alpenhorns. Most of the activities take place in the huge tent that reminds you of the huge tents set up on the meadows outside Munich for the original Oktoberfest. The dance floor draws enthusiasts of all abilities to polka and waltz, and just about everyone joins in for the bird dance, which has become the traditional dance of Snowbird's Oktoberfest.

A sizable contingent of Salt Lake's German-speaking community—dressed in native costume—act as hosts for the event, leading promenades, teaching the uninitiated how to *shunkel* and sharing the fun and good humor that brings so much *gemutlichkeit* to the event. There is plenty of good food, including sausages, beef and pork cooked on a spit, roasted chicken, sauerkraut, potato salad, red cabbage, potato pancakes and delicious cakes for dessert. Children's activities and booths with crafts and other items surround the tent. With the mountains, the music, the September sun, the changing leaves and everything that goes with this wonderful event, it's not hard to imagine you are in an alpine valley outside Munich, Salzburg or Innsbruck.

Snowbird offers special weekend lodging packages for Oktoberfest that are very reasonable and put you right in the center of the activities. Festivities run Sat.–Sun. noon–6 P.M. Snowbird is on Hwy. 210 in Little Cottonwood Canyon. **1-800-453-3000; 801-933-2222.**

Outdoor Activities

Biking
Some of the trails listed in the Hiking section are also great for mountain biking. For instance, the **Alta Loop** (see under Little Cottonwood Canyon) is a popular mountain bike route, and the road is sufficiently wide that hikers and bikers are quite compatible. Another is **Pipeline Trail** in Mill Creek Canyon, a popular beginning hiking/biking trail because of its easy access and near-level 6-mile length.

Hiking

BIG COTTONWOOD CANYON
Brighton Area Trails
Located at the upper end of Big Cottonwood Canyon, the Brighton area is a popular destination for hikers who want anything from an easy stroll around an alpine lake to a strenuous ascent to the top of one of the Wasatch Range peaks. This is a wonderful place to spend a day hiking. There are two trailheads for the area—the Brighton Store, located 15 miles up Big Cotton-

wood Canyon, and the upper end of the Brighton ski area parking lot on the right side—both reached via Hwy. 152.

Silver Lake Trail—The 1-mile circular route around Silver Lake, at the base of the 10,000-foot Mt. Millicent in Big Cottonwood Canyon, offers no elevation gain, easy access and a unique opportunity to experience an alpine lake and the wildlife that makes its home around the lake. The trail consists of two sections of boardwalk, which cross the marshy meadows, and sections of pathway through wooded areas. The boardwalks also provide wheelchair access to fishing docks at the lake. The trail can be reached in a few hundred yards from the Brighton Store.

Lake Solitude Trail—On the north side of Silver Lake, a trail takes you up 300 feet in elevation to Lake Solitude, about 1.25 miles away.

Twin Lakes Trail—Shortly after you leave Silver Lake, take the left-hand fork onto another 1.25-mile-long trail, which brings you to Twin Lakes at the top of the Evergreen ski lift.

Lake Mary Trail—From Twin Lakes you can take another trail, about 1.25 miles in length, to Lake Mary; from here, you can return the way you came or take the Lake Mary Trail to the trailhead at the Brighton Ski area parking lot, a loop of about 2.5 miles.

Catherine Pass—From Lake Mary, you could also continue up the mountain to Lake Martha, Lake Catherine and Catherine Pass, and from the pass cross into Little Cottonwood Canyon's Albion Basin, a total of 3.5 miles.

Sunset Peak—From Catherine Pass, you also have the option of hiking up to the top of Sunset Peak at an elevation of 10,648 feet.

Donut Falls / Cardiff Fork Trail

Many Salt Lake area youngsters are introduced to hiking in the Wasatch Mountains with the 1.5-mile round trip to Donut Falls, where the water drops through a donut-shaped rock, creating an interesting waterfall. For a much more strenuous hike, where the trail splits to go to Donut Falls, keep to the right and continue toward Cardiff Pass. Much of the trail is an old mining road until

you reach the Cardiff Mine 2.5 miles from the trailhead, where the remains of old buildings and equipment can be seen. From the mine it is 0.75 mile to Cardiff Pass at an elevation of 10,000 feet (2,500 feet above the trailhead), 3.25 miles from the trailhead. From the pass, you can descend another 1.5 miles to Alta in Little Cottonwood Canyon. To reach the Cardiff Fork (also called Mill D South) trailhead, drive up Big Cottonwood Canyon on Hwy. 152 for 9.5 miles, then turn right onto a paved road that becomes gravel and ends at the parking area.

Lake Blanche Trail

The Lake Blanche Trail is a steady and sometimes steep climb, with about 1,000 feet of elevation gain per mile. However, you can hike to three alpine lakes: Lake Blanche, Lake Florence and Lake Lillian, and the view of the lakes and the feeling of going into the heart of the mountains makes this a rewarding hike. The lakes are sometimes called the "Three Sisters Lakes," although the three young ladies for whom the lakes are named were not sisters but the daughters of early hikers into Hidden Valley where the lakes are located. If you don't mind some scrambling over boulders and cliffs, you can continue from the lakes to hike one of the three peaks that loom above the lakes: Sundial Peak at 10,320 feet, Dromedary Peak at 11,107 feet or Mt. Superior at 11,132 feet.

It is about 3 miles to Lake Blanche from the trailhead; it's another 0.5 mile to take in the other lakes. To reach the trailhead, drive up Big Cottonwood Canyon on Hwy. 152 about 5 miles, about a mile beyond the Storm Mountain picnic area. Take the side road located at the base of an S-turn. You can either leave your car along the side of the highway and walk up the service road about a quarter mile to where the trail starts, or you might find a parking spot by driving up to the trailhead.

Mineral Fork Trail

This up-and-back route takes you to two historic mines in the heart of the mountains—the Wasatch Mine, 3 miles up the trail with an elevation gain of nearly 2,000 feet, and the Regulator Johnson Mine, 4.5 miles up the trail at an elevation of 10,220 feet, just over 3,500 feet above the trailhead elevation of 6,710 feet. The trail follows the old mining road and includes a series of 24 switchbacks up the side of the mountain between the two mines. The trailhead is located at a metal gate on the south side of the road about 6 miles up Hwy. 152 in Big Cottonwood Canyon.

EMIGRATION AND EAST CANYONS
Mormon Trail

The most pristine section of the Mormon Pioneer Trail in Utah is also an excellent 10-mile hiking trail that visits Mormon Flat, Big Mountain, and Little Dell Reservoir. You can begin this hike at either end—Little Dell on the west end or Mormon Flat on the east end—or in the middle at the Big Mountain summit. Beginning at the eastern end at Mormon Flat in East Canyon, the hike takes you past stone wall fortifications erected near Mormon Flat in 1857 by Mormon militia men as defenses against the federal army under the command of Col. Albert Sidney Johnston, who was sent to Utah to suppress the alleged "Mormon Rebellion." From Mormon Flat, the trail climbs 1,400 feet in elevation up to the summit of Big Mountain in 4.7 miles. It was from the summit of Big Mountain that Mormon pioneers had their first glimpse of the Salt Lake Valley and the wall of mountains that would guard their new wilderness home. From the summit, a new section of trail that opened in 2001 descends for 5.3 miles to Little Dell Reservoir, site of the Eph Hanks Pony Express Station.

To reach the trailheads at Little Dell and Big Mountain, you can follow the original route up Emigration Canyon—just head east on 800 S. past This Is the Place Heritage Park and Hogle Zoo and keep going into the mountains. After you cross Little Mountain and go down the other side, you will come to the junction of Hwy. 65 and the west trailhead at Little Dell. You can begin your hike here, or turn left (north) and follow the road up the canyon and the switchbacks of Big Mountain. You can also reach Hwy. 65 from Interstate 80 by taking Exit 134 in Parley's Canyon.

To reach the trailhead at Mormon Flat, from Big Mountain continue down Hwy. 65 to between mileposts 13 and 14, and take the dirt road that turns off to the right. The dirt road heads south for 3.4 miles to Mormon Flat. From Interstate 80, you can take Exit 143 (the Jeremy Ranch exit), then go north on the dirt road for 4.2 miles.

LITTLE COTTONWOOD CANYON
Albion Basin Trails

Some of the most popular hiking trails in Little Cottonwood Canyon are located in Albion Basin at the upper end of the canyon about 3 miles above Alta. These trails offer unbelievable views of East Gate and Devil's Gate, Sugarloaf Peak, Wolverine Peak and the other peaks that form the tops of the Wasatch Mountains. To reach Albion Basin, from the end of paved Hwy. 210 in Little Cottonwood Canyon, continue onto the dirt road (passable for two-wheel-drive vehicles). On weekends and holidays, there are volunteers at what looks like a tollbooth just after you leave the pavement. However, there is no toll, at least not yet, and the volunteers give you a map of the area with trail descriptions and remind you of the 15 mph speed limit along the dirt road and 25 mph speed limit through Alta. The dirt road climbs a little less than 3 miles to the Albion Basin Campground at an elevation of about 9,400 feet. About 0.3 mile after you pass the top of the Sunnyside ski lift, you will see a dirt road heading to the left. There is a small parking area about 100 yards up the road at the beginning of the Catherine Pass Trail. If there is no parking here, you can continue another 0.1 mile up the road to the campground parking area, then walk back to the trailhead. If you are going to hike the Secret (often spelled Cecret) Lake Trail, drive on to the campground parking area, where the trail begins on the right, just past the entry station to the campground.

Albion Meadows Trail—If you don't want to drive up the road to the campground from Alta, you can take a 2-mile-long trail that begins just east of the Snow Pine Lodge on the south side of Hwy. 210. For the first part, the trail parallels the left side of the Albion lift, then it turns to the right to cross under the Albion and Sunnyside lifts before reaching the Albion Basin Campground. Combine this hike with the Secret Lake or Catherine Pass Trail if you want to extend the distance.

Catherine Pass Trail—The signpost at the beginning of this trail indicates that it is St. Mary's Lake Trail and that it is 3.4 miles to Brighton, located in Big Cottonwood Canyon. It is easy to spot Catherine Pass, named for Catherine Brighton: just look for the lowest point in the ridgeline to the east. It is a relatively steep climb with an elevation gain of 800 feet along the 1.5-mile trail to the pass. You will walk through some stands of pine and beautiful open meadows as you climb steadily to 10,200-foot Catherine Pass, where you will see below you Catherine Lake and above you Sunset Peak to the east.

From here, you have three options and if you plan properly, you can take all three. You can return to complete your 3-mile hike; you can continue down into Big Cottonwood Canyon past Lake Catherine, Lake Martha and Lake Mary all the way to the Brighton Ski Resort for an out-and-back distance of about 7 miles; or you can follow the right-hand trail up the ridge toward Sunset Peak (see below).

Secret Lake Trail—This trail (often called Cecret) provides relatively easy access to one of the most beautiful spots in all the Wasatch Mountains. Secret Lake lies at the base of the imposing East Gate, Devil's Gate and Sugarloaf Peaks, which stand like sentinels seemingly guarding any exit out of Little Cottonwood Canyon. Be sure to take your camera along to capture the lake and mountains. The trail is about 0.75 mile in length, and the first part is relatively level as it passes under the Supreme and Secret lifts before winding through a meadow strewn with gigantic granite boulders, which were cut away from the mountains high above by glacial action thousands of years ago. Several interpretive signs tell about the mountains, ecology, wildlife and water resources of the area.

The second part of the trail follows a Z course as it climbs steadily up a ridge that is to the right of a huge rock cliff. As you reach the top of the ridge, Secret Lake comes into view. You will want to take time to walk around the lake and search for the best picture angles. This is an extremely popular trail for families with young children and is highly recommended for those who want to see the Wasatch Mountains at their best without the exertion demanded by trails described elsewhere.

Sunset Peak Trail—Unless weather conditions do not permit or you are physically unable to climb another 400 feet in elevation along the 0.6-mile spur trail from the Catherine Pass Trail, you should by all means make the climb to Sunset Peak. The trail is somewhat steep but easy to follow, with a couple of places along the ridgeline where you must exercise caution not to slip or fall. This is one of the easiest peaks in the Wasatch Range to climb, and from the top of the peak you have a 360-degree view that includes the Uinta Mountains in the distance, Mt. Timpanogos, the top of the Snowbird Tram, Wasatch Mountain State Park and the Heber Valley, and an emeraldlike chain of alpine lakes that begin with Catherine Lake at the base of Sunset Peak below. Three canyons—Big Cottonwood, American Fork and Snake Creek Canyons—meet at the top of Sunset Peak, and you have just left the fourth canyon, Little Cottonwood, a few hundred yards back on the trail before you make your final ascent to the top of Sunset Peak. Once you reach the top, you will know you are there and be glad that you made the effort. The view is unforgettable.

Alta Area Trails

Twin Lakes Pass to Brighton—This trail is the best way to hike from Alta to Brighton. En route you pass by many dumps and remnants of Alta's early mining days, including the site of Michigan City. There are two access points in Alta. The easiest is to follow the street across Hwy. 210 from the Alta Lodge as its winds past Our Lady of the Snows Center and around the Alta Police Building. Keep to the right as the old mining road parallels Hwy. 210 up the canyon.

The other trailhead is located just east of the Snow Pine Lodge on the north side of the highway toward the west end of the parking area. From here the trail climbs steadily to intersect with the mining road.

From Alta to Twin Lakes Pass at 9,993 feet is a 1,350-foot elevation gain in just over 2 miles. From the pass, you can look down upon the Twin Lakes, now combined into one large lake much of the year with the construction of a large cement dam. Off to the right is a spectacular view of Wolverine Mountain and the Wolverine Cirque. To continue down into Big Cottonwood Canyon, follow the upper trail that traverses across the slope above the Twin Lakes until it intersects a ski lift maintenance road. The trail then drops down past the cement dam and the top of the Evergreen ski lift. As you follow the road down the mountain, you have a fine view of the Brighton ski area and Silver Lake. From Twin Lakes Pass it is about 2 miles to Brighton. The climb from Brighton back up to Twin Lakes Pass is a 1,250-foot elevation gain. You can also return to Alta via Lake Mary, Lake Martha, Lake Blanche, Catherine Pass and Albion Basin, which is a total distance of about 10 miles.

Alta Loop—This 7-mile loop through Collins Gulch to Germania Pass takes you through most of the Alta ski area, returning via the Sugarloaf Rd. and Albion Basin. It is a favorite trail for viewing wildflowers during the summer. Begin the 2.5-mile uphill hike at the base of Collins lift, opened in 1939 and Utah's oldest ski lift, and follow the ski service road just to the east of the Collins lift as it switchbacks up the north-facing slope. As you make your way uphill, you will want to stop for several views of the Cardiff Pass Trail across the canyon (see Brighton Area Trails under the Big Cottonwood Canyon section) and Mt. Superior to the northwest.

About halfway up the mountain, you reach the base of the Germania lift; the trail continues up the east side of the bowl with Mt. Baldy rising ahead of you to the south. By the time you reach Germania Pass, you will be within 500 feet of the summit of Mt. Baldy at 11,068 feet and, by scrambling, you can continue on to the summit. However, most hikers will opt to continue across Germania Pass and along the road as it passes just below the ridge, making its way for the top of Sugarloaf lift. As you approach Sugarloaf lift, the rounded shape of Sugarloaf Peak lies before you to the east, while to the south you will be able to see Mt. Timpanogos and the top of the Snowbird Tram on Hidden Peak back to the west. You can also make your way to the top of the 11,051-foot Sugarloaf Peak by off-trail hiking across loose rock with some brush.

From the Sugarloaf lift, it is all downhill as you follow the Sugarloaf Rd. down into Albion Basin. As you descend, you have a fine view of the Devil's Gate off to your right and the ridge connecting it with Sugarloaf Peak. Across the valley, you can see the trail up to Catherine Pass, and to the west, part of the trail that heads across Twin Lakes Pass into Big Cottonwood Canyon. In a while, you will come to a fork in the road. The right-hand fork takes you down to Cecret Lake and the Albion Basin Campground. The left fork takes you around a horseshoe turn and past the remains of an old mine before you descend down four lengthy switchbacks to the beginning of Sugarloaf lift. From the lift, climb the hill and continue past the Alpenglow Restaurant building with the Cecret Lake lift in back of it, and in about 50 yards you will come to a road intersecting on your left. Take this road as it turns downhill, with the top of the Sunnyside ski lift on your right. This service road will take you underneath the Sunnyside and Albion ski lifts to an intersection with Hwy. 210.

If you want to take a shortcut, follow the road north just before you pass underneath the ski lift and follow it down to the base of the ski lifts. If you continue on to the highway, the trail turns to the left and follows the road downhill for a short distance before swinging back to the west to intersect with the service road noted above. From the base of the Albion and Sunnyside lifts, follow the towrope back to the Goldminer's Daughter parking area.

This is also a popular mountain bike route, but the road is sufficiently wide that hikers and bikers are quite compatible. You can also make this hike in reverse, if you want a longer, more gradual uphill climb and a steeper but shorter descent from 10,600 feet at Germania Pass to 8,600 feet at the base of Collins lift.

Hidden Peak

There are a couple of trails at Snowbird that lead to the top of Hidden Peak at 10,980 feet. The Gad Valley Trail (a gad is a pointed steel bar used by miners to break up or loosen ore) follows the west side of the mountain and is 4 miles long. The Peruvian Gulch route, along the service road to the top of the tram, is 3.5 miles in length. Both routes climb about 2,900 feet in elevation. The Gad Valley route takes you through more forested areas, while the Peruvian Gulch route allows you to keep the Snowbird Tram in view for most of the route. Many hikers take one trail up and the other back. A popular alternative to the strenuous climb is to ride the tram to the top of Hidden Peak and hike down one of the trails. While this will not tax your lungs, it will work your legs and feet in ways that can be pure torture if you do not have proper hiking boots or shoes.

Snowbird Nature Trail

A barrier-free, half-mile-long nature trail begins at the Snowbird Center in Little Cottonwood Canyon and winds along the base of the mountain, with 10 interpretive signs introducing the natural history along the way. The 8-foot-wide, asphalt-paved trail has no more than a 6 percent grade. The trail takes visitors through meadows filled with wildflowers and frequented by deer, squirrels, porcupines and songbirds, and sometimes elk, moose, coyotes, badgers, hawks and eagles. At the end of the trail, a lookout deck provides a spectacular view of the mountains, as well as down the glaciated Little Cottonwood Canyon to the Salt Lake Valley below.

White Pine Trail

The White Pine Trail offers the most convenient access into the Lone Peak Wilderness Area. White Pine and Red Pine Canyons were the location of two of the earliest timber slides used by pioneer loggers in the canyon in the 1860s and 1870s. White pine was the common name used for Engelmann spruce, and red pine for Douglas fir. At 5.5 miles up Little Cottonwood Canyon and just under a mile down the road from Snowbird Resort, a parking area provides off-road parking in the narrow and heavily traveled canyon.

From the parking area, hikers cross Little Cottonwood Creek over a footbridge and continue along the White Pine Trail for approximately 1.5 miles to where the trail branches. (This portion of the trail—from the parking area to the fork—is an excellent hike for those wanting to spend a couple of hours in the mountains.) Continue up the White Pine Trail as it follows a switchback eastward onto the ridge (the Red Pine Trail crosses the stream over a footbridge about 50 yards upstream from the switchback and continues north and west around the ridge).

As the trail turns to the south, it follows along the ridge through pine forests to an old mine dump, where a bridge crosses the Red Pine Fork and a trail follows westward up a switchback into Maybird Gulch. This route is not marked by signs, and most hikers continue instead up the steep Red Pine Trail approximately another mile to Red Pine Lake, one of the most beautiful sites in the Wasatch Mountains. Surrounded by pine trees, the deep emerald waters reflecting the silhouette of the granite ridge to the west, this is a picture-perfect scene.

But there's more. Upper Red Pine Lake, located above Red Pine Lake to the southeast, can be reached by a steep half-mile trail and scramble across a field of granite boulders. The hike offers a spectacular view of lower Red Pine Lake. The upper route also provides access to the Pfeifferhorn, whose summit at 11,326 feet, with exposed slopes and lingering snow, is an ascent only for well-conditioned and experienced hikers.

MILL CREEK CANYON

Grandeur Peak Trail

This is probably the best hike for a climb to one of the Wasatch Front peaks. Grandeur Peak rises about 4,000 feet from the floor of the Salt Lake

Valley to an elevation of 8,300 feet. From its summit you have a panoramic view of the Salt Lake Valley, Great Salt Lake, Antelope Island and the Oquirrh Mountains to the west; the north face of Mt. Olympus to the south; and Parley's Canyon with Mountain Dell and Little Dell Reservoirs to the north. It is a steady uphill climb of just over 3 miles to the top. The first section follows Church Fork for about a mile along a shady, pleasant route. The next section is a series of switchbacks up the east side of the mountain, then a long uphill climb to the south before you circle around the base of the peak as you climb to the top. All along the route there are spectacular views into Mill Creek Canyon below.

To reach the trailhead, drive up Mill Creek Canyon via Wasatch Blvd. for 3.2 miles to the Church Fork Picnic Area. Drive to the end of the paved road inside the picnic area—about a quarter mile—where there is parking for about 10 cars. At the trailhead, there are a series of cascades as Church Fork tumbles toward Mill Creek.

Mt. Aire Trail

The 2-mile hike to the top of Mt. Aire (8,621 feet) in Mill Creek Canyon offers a spectacular view of the Salt Lake Valley, Parley's Canyon through which Interstate 80 heads east, Mill Creek Canyon, the Wasatch Mountains and the Oquirrh Mountains. Because this is a steep trail, hiking times one way can vary between 1 and 2 hours, depending on one's condition and how much time is spent admiring the scenery.

The trail begins about 6 miles up Mill Creek Canyon, at the Elbow Fork trailhead. Located on the north (left-hand) side of the road going up the canyon, the trail follows straight up Elbow Fork for about 0.5 mile, to where the trail branches; the right-hand trail follows up for about 1.5 miles to Lambs Canyon Pass. Stay to the left on the Mt. Aire Trail as it crosses a stream via a footbridge, then climbs steeply up the canyon to Mt. Aire Pass. En route, the trail passes through dense trees and is especially pretty in the fall.

From Mt. Aire Pass, the trail heads east, zigzagging its way up the southern slope through Gambel oak to the top of Mt. Aire. From here

the sight of quiet, soaring eagles and the breathtaking view is well worth the effort. Particularly impressive is the view from the summit back into Mill Creek Canyon, where the canyon road far below, surrounded by dense pine and aspen trees, appears like a string in a deep hole, giving an impressive perspective to your efforts in climbing to the top.

Pipeline Trail

This is a popular beginning hiking/biking trail because of its easy access and near-level 6-mile length. The original pipeline brought water to a long-gone hydroelectric plant near the mouth of Mill Creek Canyon. The pipeline is gone, but the access remains as a route that parallels Mill Creek and the road up the canyon to the south. Trees and vegetation provide an adequate screen from the road, especially at the upper end of the trail along the 2-mile stretch between Burch Hollow and Elbow Fork. The access points, with mileage up the canyon from Wasatch Blvd., include Rattlesnake Gulch, 1.25 miles; Church Fork, just over 3 miles; Burch Hollow, just over 4.5 miles; and Elbow Fork, 6.5 miles.

Skiing

CROSS COUNTRY
Mill Creek Canyon

Many of the hiking trails described in the Hiking section above are popular cross-country skiing trails. The road up Mill Creek Canyon is closed to vehicle traffic about halfway up, and the road becomes a popular cross-country ski route.

Solitude Nordic Center

With 12 miles of machine-worked trails, the Solitude Nordic Center, located at Silver Lake between the Solitude and Brighton Ski Resorts in Big Cottonwood Canyon, is Utah's oldest cross-country ski area. There are both classic and skating lanes, with two rental shops and a children's trail. Group lessons and private lessons are available. Guided tours are offered, including moonlight tours held for two nights on each of the full moons. **801-272-7613.**

DOWNHILL

Alta Ski Area

Two slogans capture the essence of Alta: "The best powder on earth" and "Alta is for skiers." With a well-deserved worldwide reputation for its dry powder snow, Alta has consciously kept its focus on skiing since the first chairlift—the Collins lift—began operation in 1939. The Alta Lodge was opened for business in 1940. During World War II, Alta continued to develop as a recreational haven from the cares of the war, as well as a training center for ski troops. After the war, Alta continued to cultivate its reputation as the destination for serious skiers. Even today, snowboarding is not permitted at Alta.

Even before it became Utah's ski center, Alta had a colorful history. In 1863 prospectors discovered silver, and claims were located and mines opened. By 1873 Alta boasted a population of 5,000, with 186 buildings, including 26 saloons. A narrow-gauge railroad was constructed up Little Cottonwood Canyon to Alta in 1875. The Panic of 1893 and other economic disasters brought an end to the 19th-century mining town, although a second, smaller mining boom lasted from 1904 to 1927. Today skiers glide across old mine dumps, and in the summer, openings and other evidence of the bygone mining days can be seen.

Alta has one detachable quad, one detachable triple, two fixed triples, four double chairlifts and five rope tows, which service 2,000 acres of ski terrain accessed by more than 40 runs. The terrain is classified as 25 percent beginning, 40 percent intermediate and 35 percent advanced. The longest run is 3.5 miles, with an elevation drop from 10,550 feet to 8,500 feet. If you are an expert skier, you will soon learn about the numerous chutes and powder areas. Beginners might want to stay with the Albion and Sunnyside lifts at the upper or eastern end. In fact, you can purchase a reduced-price ticket if you are just going to ski these areas. Alta usually has some of the best-priced lift tickets around, offering both full-day and half-day passes. The ski season usually runs mid-Nov.–mid-Apr. The average annual snowfall here is more than 500 inches.

The **Alf Engen Ski School** caters to all ages and levels of skiers. They say Alf Engen invented dry powder skiing, so if you want a good introduction to Alta's powder, a lesson might just be the ticket. Reservations for classes are recommended. **801-359-1078.**

Located at the end of the Little Cottonwood Canyon road, 33 miles from the Salt Lake International Airport and a mile beyond the Snowbird Resort. You can now purchase one ticket for both resorts. Take Interstate 215 to the 6200 S. Canyon exit and continue south along Wasatch Blvd., past Hwy. 152, which turns east up Big Cottonwood Canyon. Hwy. 210 continues south before turning east up Little Cottonwood Canyon. **801-572-3939 snow conditions; www.altaskiarea.com.**

Brighton Ski Resort

Brighton has a reputation as Utah's family ski area, and for good reason. With each paying adult, up to two children (10 years and younger) ski for free. A special **Intro-Ski program** is available for both children and adults, which provides a lift pass, ski rentals and lesson all for a price equal to the lift pass at some resorts. A further incentive for families and carpoolers is a discount offered whenever five or more skiers ride together. Not only is this a nice gesture, but it cuts down on traffic and pollution in the canyon.

The skier capacity at Brighton is 11,000 skiers per hour on two high-speed quads, two triple chairlifts and three double chairs. There are more than 60 designated runs and trails, and snowmaking equipment helps Mother Nature along on the lower runs. There are four general areas to the resort: **Mt. Majestic,** the original part of the ski area; **Snake Creek Canyon lift,** which takes you to the summit for a glimpse down the other side of the mountain into Heber Valley; **Clayton Peak,** to which access was provided by construction of the Great Western detachable quad lift in 1992; and on the other side of the parking area, the **Mt. Millicent lift,** first built in 1948, which provides access to skiing on the southern side of the mountain. Night skiing is also offered.

Brighton was named for William Stewart Brighton who, with his wife, Catherine, emigrated to Utah from Scotland in 1857 as handcart pioneers. In 1870 Brighton took out an 80-acre homestead in the Silver Lake area, and in 1874 built a small hotel to accommodate miners traveling back and forth between Alta and Park City. Recreational skiing began as early as 1915, with excursions from Salt Lake City. The Wasatch Mountain Club, organized in 1920, built a cabin at Brighton in 1928, which stands today, hidden in the pine trees not far from the Mt. Majestic lift. The first ski lift, a T-bar tow, was put into operation in 1939.

Located at the top of Big Cottonwood Canyon, 35 miles from downtown Salt Lake City. To reach the canyon, leave Interstate 215 at the 6200 S. exit and follow signs to the Big and Little Cottonwood Canyon recreation areas. At approximately 7000 S., turn east at the light and follow the road to its terminus at the Brighton Ski Resort in 15 miles. **1-800-873-5512; 801-532-4731; www.skibrighton.com.**

Snowbird Ski Resort

Opened in 1971, Snowbird is the Salt Lake City area's largest ski resort. With more than 900 rooms in four facilities, Snowbird is designed to accommodate out-of-town skiers. Snowbird receives an average of 500 inches of snow a year. The ski season usually goes from mid-Nov. to early May. A 120-passenger tram carries skiers from the Snowbird Center, at 8,100 feet elevation, to the top of Hidden Peak, at 11,000 feet. From Hidden Peak, you can ski down through Peruvian Gulch on one of Utah's longest runs— the 3.5-mile Chip's Run, named in honor of the son of a close friend of resort developer Ted Johnson who was killed in the Vietnam War. Six other chairlifts provide access to much of the nearly 2,000 skiable acres along 48 ski trails. The tram and lifts can accommodate up to 9,200 skiers an hour. Skiers can purchase a day or half-day ticket for either the tram and chairlifts or the chairlifts only. Discounts are usually offered for late spring skiing. Skiers age 70 and over ski free. The Snowbird complex is designed for easy

walking access, and the compact layout lets you walk from the upper building, **Cliff Lodge,** to the lower building, **Iron Blosam Lodge,** in about 5 minutes. Cliff Lodge provides ski-out and ski-in access, while the ski lifts are located a short walk away from the other lodges. Half the terrain is for advanced and expert skiers, but beginning skiers have access to plenty of area, including the Chickadee lift, which runs from the base of the tram at the Snowbird Center to just above the Cliff Lodge. The **Snowbird Ski School,** with a full-time staff of 125 qualified instructors, offers private or group lessons for skiers of every ability. Ski rentals are located in the Cliff Lodge and at the Snowbird Center. Snowbird also provides a **Mountain Host Program,** which offers free guided skiing tours daily to acquaint newcomers with the lifts and runs that are best suited to their abilities. Snowbird also sponsors a disabled skier program that provides instructors, guides and equipment to hundreds of individuals who otherwise would never have the chance to ski.

Located in Little Cottonwood Canyon only 29 miles from the Salt Lake City International Airport; skiers from anywhere in the United States can catch an early-morning flight to Salt Lake City and still have a full afternoon of skiing. You can drive to Snowbird, ride the tram and be skiing down the slopes in less than an hour. Take Interstate 215 to the 6200 S. Canyon exit and continue south along Wasatch Blvd., past Hwy. 152, which turns east up Big Cottonwood Canyon. Hwy. 210 continues south before turning east up Little Cottonwood Canyon. **1-800-453-3000; 801-933-2100; www.snowbird. com.**

Solitude Ski Resort

Solitude has a reputation for reasonable lift ticket rates, uncrowded skiing and challenging slopes. It is ranked among the top 40 ski areas in North America. With four double, two triple and one high-speed detachable quad chairlift, Solitude can service more than 10,000 skiers an hour. There are more than 1,200 acres of skiing on 63 runs. For powder skiers, Honeycomb

Canyon offers more than 400 acres of excellent dry powder skiing. Ski lessons are available through the **Solitude Ski School; 801-536-5730.** The Solitude ski season usually runs mid-Nov.–late Apr. Located 12 miles up Big Cottonwood Canyon, 28 miles from the Salt Lake International Airport. To reach the canyon, leave Interstate 215 at the 6200 S. exit and follow the signs that direct you to the Big and Little Cottonwood Canyon recreation areas. At approximately 7000 S., turn east at the light and follow the road up the canyon. **1-800-748-4754; 801-534-1400; www.skisolitude.com.**

Seeing and Doing

Performing Arts

Summer attractions at Snowbird Ski Resort include performances by the **Utah Symphony,** with the traditional program featuring Tchaikovsky's *1812 Overture* with authentic cannons, a perennial favorite. There is also an annual **Utah Jazz and Blues Festival,** mountain biking, wall climbing on the 115-foot climbing wall on the west side of the Cliff Lodge, and five outdoor tennis courts. The **Snowbird Institute** offers a variety of performances, seminars and workshops in dance, music, education and the humanities during the summer. There are a number of special packages available during the winter and summer. Located in Little Cottonwood Canyon (see the Skiing section). **1-800-453-3000; 801-933-2222; www.snowbird. com**

Scenic Drives

Big Cottonwood Canyon Scenic Byway / Hwy. 152

Hwy. 152 is one of Utah's major recreation roads, providing access to the ski resorts of Brighton and Solitude in the winter and a number of hiking trails in the summer. Perhaps the most spectacular point in the canyon is Storm Mountain, located only 4 miles up the canyon. About a mile below Brighton is the **Guardsman's Pass Rd.,** a dirt road that takes you up

over the pass, where you can drop down into Park City, 14 miles away, or head south into Heber Valley, just over 22 miles away.

To reach the canyon, leave Interstate 215 at the 6200 S. exit and follow the signs that direct you to the Big and Little Cottonwood Canyon recreation areas. At approximately 7000 S., turn east at the light and follow the road to its terminus at the Brighton Ski Resort in 15 miles.

Little Cottonwood Canyon Scenic Byway / Hwy. 210

Serving the ski resorts of Snowbird and Alta, this is the most heavily traveled mountain road along the Wasatch Front. Planners have talked for years about developing a public transportation system that would greatly limit the use of private vehicles in the canyon. Such a system would certainly enhance visitation, since it is impossible to take in the canyon's sheer, glaciated granite walls while you are driving. Short of driving up the canyon in an open-top convertible or Jeep, the Utah Transit bus is still the best way to reach the ski resorts and to view the canyon. Alternatively, you may want to join the scores of bicyclists who ascend the nearly 4,000 feet from the canyon's mouth to the highway's end, 7 miles up the road at Alta. In addition to its world-famous skiing, Little Cottonwood Canyon offers plenty of hiking opportunities, such as the White Pine and Red Pine Trails (see the Hiking section).

To reach Little Cottonwood Canyon, take Interstate 215 to the 6200 S. Canyon exit and continue south along Wasatch Blvd., past Hwy. 152, which turns east up Big Cottonwood Canyon. Hwy. 210 continues south before turning east up Little Cottonwood Canyon.

Mill Creek Canyon

This lovely mountain drive is especially pleasant because people who drive up the canyon do so to sightsee and are usually in no big hurry to reach a destination, as is too often the case in other canyons. A modest fee is charged at the entrance to the canyon. There are several picnic areas, some excellent hiking trails (see the Hiking section) and the **Log Haven Restaurant** (see the

Where to Eat section) located in the canyon, which dead-ends after about 12 miles. This drive is especially beautiful in the fall because of the stunning autumn foliage, as well as in the summer.

To reach Mill Creek Canyon, drive to Wasatch Blvd. and 3800 S., then head east toward the mouth of the canyon.

Pioneer Memorial Scenic Backway

This 34-mile-long scenic backway retraces the route of Mormon pioneers into the Salt Lake Valley through Emigration Canyon and heads east up the canyon, over Little Mountain, then swings to the north as Hwy. 65 to ascend Big Mountain. It was from the summit of Big Mountain that the pioneers got their first glimpse of the Salt Lake Valley. The backway continues down Big Mountain, past East Canyon Reservoir and on to the junction with Interstate 84 at Henefer. From Henefer, you can either return along the route you came, take Interstate 84 west toward Ogden or turn right and join Interstate 80 a few miles southeast of Henefer and follow it through Parley's Canyon back to Salt Lake City.

To reach the Pioneer Memorial Scenic Backway, drive east along 800 S., which becomes Sunnyside Ave., and on to the This Is the Place Monument across from Hogle Zoo, then follow the road up the canyon. The backway is impassable during the winter.

Tours

Tram Rides

Snowbird describes itself as a ski and summer resort, and for many visitors, summer and fall are the best times to be at Snowbird. Tram rides continue until the end of Oct., when they stop for a two-week maintenance period before the ski season begins. Take the tram up the mountain and enjoy the breathtaking view of the Wasatch Mountains from Hidden Peak. Some visitors like to ride the tram up and hike back down along the 3.5-mile-long service road to the Snowbird Center (see the Hiking section). You can purchase a "Peaks Picnic" that includes a tram ticket

and a sack lunch at the General Gritts Store on Level 1 of the Snowbird Center. Take Interstate 215 to the 6200 S. Canyon exit and continue south along Wasatch Blvd., past Hwy. 152, which turns east up Big Cottonwood Canyon. Hwy. 210 continues south before turning east up Little Cottonwood Canyon. **1-800-453-3000; 801-933-2100; www.snowbird.com.**

Where to Stay

Accommodations

BIG COTTONWOOD CANYON
Brighton

The **Brighton Lodge** has 20 rooms adjacent to the ski slopes; **1-800-873-5512.** The **Brighton Chalets** are individual private cabins with furnished kitchens; **1-800-748-4824; 801-942-8824. Das Alpen Haus** has four suites, all with private bathrooms, a sauna, a fireplace and gourmet breakfasts prepared by hosts Charles and Nola Hobbs; **435-649-0565. Silver Fork Lodge,** operated by Julie and Dan Knopp, has eight rooms with a homestyle breakfast included and an excellent restaurant; **435-649-9551; 801-533-9977 from Salt Lake City.**

Solitude

Until recently there were no overnight accommodations at the Solitude ski area. However, in the last couple of years three fine facilities have been opened, providing guests with ski-in access to the lifts.

The **Inn at Solitude** is a full-service hotel with 46 rooms, a heated swimming pool, Jacuzzi and health and fitness spa. The **Village** at Solitude offers rooms and condominiums, a heated pool and a hot tub. **Creekside** at Solitude is a four-story building with one-, two- and three-bedroom condominiums, each equipped with a full kitchen, wood-burning fireplace and underground parking. There are also a heated swimming pool and an outdoor hot tub. **1-800-748-4754; 801-536-5700.**

LITTLE COTTONWOOD CANYON
Alta

Accommodations are available in five lodges and a number of privately owned condominiums, townhouses and vacation homes. **The Alta Visitors Information Service (1-888-782-9258; www.utahskilodging.com)** will give you the whole picture as to what is available and at what price. The five lodges, listed below, operate on the American plan, which includes two or three meals a day. Some include lift tickets in the lodging price, and all five lodges are within easy reach of the ski slopes. A variety of rooms are available, from dormitory rooms with shared baths to two-bedroom suites with private bath, sitting room and fireplace. All five lodges face the ski slopes to the south and have tremendous views of the mountains.

Alta Lodge—$$$ to $$$$

Forty rooms, many with beautiful views of the mountains through wall-wide windows, while corner rooms feature two walls of glass. The original lodge building opened in 1939; wings were added later. Heated swimming pool, saunas and sun deck. **Alta, UT 84092; 1-800-707-2582; 801-322-4631; 801-742-3500; www.altalodge.com.**

Alta Peruvian Lodge—$$$ to $$$$

Rooms vary from two-bedroom suites to dormitories. Heated outdoor pool and outdoor therapy pool. **Alta, UT 84092; 1-800-453-8488; 801-742-3000; www.altaperuvian.com.**

Goldminer's Daughter—$$$ to $$$$

Private rooms and dormitory accommodations. Hot tubs, saunas and exercise room. **Alta, UT 84092; 1-800-453-4573; 801-742-2300.**

Rustler Lodge—$$$ to $$$$

First opened in 1947 with one floor of guest rooms, the lodge has been enlarged a couple of times, with the latest expansion in 1997 making a total of 85 guest rooms. Heated outdoor swimming pool, saunas and Jacuzzi. **Alta, UT 84092; 1-888-532-2582; 801-742-2200; www.rustlerlodge.com.**

Snow Pine Lodge—$$$ to $$$$

The smallest of the lodges at Alta, construction on the original stone and timber building began in 1937 by Civilian Conservation Corps workers. After its completion, the building was managed by the U.S. Forest Service until 1987 when it was acquired by Dwight and Mary Janerich, who expanded the building and opened Snow Pine Lodge in 1990. Accommodations include private rooms with private baths, private rooms with shared baths and dormitory rooms. There's an outdoor hot tub and Scandinavian sauna. **Alta, UT 84092; 801-742-2000; www.thesnowpine.com.**

Snowbird

In addition to the listing below, the three other facilities at Snowbird include the **Lodge at Snowbird** with 136 rooms, the **Inn** with 65 rooms and **Iron Blosam Lodge** with 159 rooms. These condominium accommodations include bedrooms only or units that have completely furnished kitchens. Most units face south and offer open-air balconies with a spectacular view of the mountains and ski slopes. **1-800-453-3000; 801-933-2222.**

Cliff Lodge—$$$ to $$$$

A deluxe hotel with 532 rooms and a wide range of amenities, including an open-air, year-round, rooftop pool and giant whirlpool, sauna, steam room, aerobics and weight training rooms, spa, salon, retail shops, game room, children's center and in-room babysitting. Accommodations at the Cliff Lodge during the high ski season range from a dormitory room with four twin beds and a full bath to a two-bedroom suite. **1-800-453-3000; 801-933-2222.**

Where to Eat

BIG COTTONWOOD CANYON
Brighton

Eating facilities at the Brighton Ski Resort include the **Alpine Rose; 435-649-7908.**

Solitude
Creekside at Solitude—$$$ to $$$$

The Creekside Restaurant, located in the Creekside Inn, is a fine addition to the new complex at Solitude. You will find an excellent selection of burgers, sandwiches, wood-oven pizzas, pastas, salmon, sea bass and other fish dishes, along with such meat entrées as dry-rubbed pork chops and herb-stuffed chicken breast. The mountain view from the patio makes this a special dining experience. Open daily 11:30 A.M.–9:30 P.M. during the ski season, closed Mon.–Tues. during the summer. **801-536-5787.**

The Roundhouse at Solitude—$$$$

Many consider this the ultimate in romantic dining in Utah. An open sleigh, pulled by a snowcat, takes you up to the middle of the mountain to a cozy chalet where you are served a wonderful five-course meal. Selections change weekly, so ask for menu items when you call for reservations. The Roundhouse is open only for dinner during the ski season. **801-536-5709.**

Silver Fork Lodge—$$ to $$$

This longtime Big Cottonwood Canyon institution began providing food to hungry skiers and hikers in 1943 and continues to be a favorite of locals who like the friendly, laid-back atmosphere, somewhat rustic decor and spectacular view of the mountains from the deck and huge, south-facing windows in the dining room. The lodge serves breakfast, lunch and dinner. The sourdough pancakes are made from batter that started fermenting about the time the lodge opened. Ribs and beef brisket are smoked on-site, and there are plenty of other choices for just about every taste. **435-649-9551; 801-533-9977 from Salt Lake City.**

LITTLE COTTONWOOD CANYON
Alta

All five lodges listed in the Where to Stay section have excellent restaurants that are usually open to the public, although it is good to make reservations, especially if you are not staying at the lodge. The only nonlodge restaurant is the **Shallow Shaft,** which offers steak, seafood and pizza; **801-742-2177.** Cafeteria-style facilities are open near the lifts for a sandwich, soup or chili lunch.

Snowbird

Most Snowbird restaurants seat on a first-come, first-served basis, but reservations are accepted (and recommended) for the **Aerie, Lodge Bistro** and **Wildflower** by calling between 9 A.M. and 4 P.M.; **801-742-2222, ext. 3663.** After 4 P.M. call the restaurant directly at the number listed below.

On the mountain, the **Mid-Gad** offers a lunch menu of hamburgers, sandwiches, soup, chili and pizza; **801-933-2245.** In the **Cliff Lodge,** there are three eating establishments: the Aerie, the Keyhole Junction and the Atrium. The **Aerie** (American and continental cuisine) has a skiers buffet breakfast that is the place to load up on plenty of carbohydrates before going to the slopes. Located on the top floor of the Cliff Lodge, the Aerie is the place for a special dinner at Snowbird; **801-933-2160.** The **Keyhole Junction** serves Southwestern-style food; **801-933-2025.** The **Atrium** offers a buffet for lunch and après ski daily during the winter; **801-742-2222, ext. 5300.**

The **Wildflower Restaurant,** located on the third level at **Iron Blosam Lodge,** is open during the winter for dinner with pasta, fish and meat dishes; **801-933-2230.** The **Lodge Bistro,** located on the first floor of the **Lodge at Snowbird,** is a good choice for a quiet, intimate dinner with food that is tasty, fresh and often locally grown. Favorites include Utah trout and seasoned tenderloin of elk; **801-933-2145.**

Other eating facilities are located at the **Snowbird Center,** where you can dine in the **Steak Pit** on good-sized steaks or seafood dishes **(801-933-2260),** or eat at the **Forklift,** a family restaurant that serves traditional American breakfasts and lunches **(801-933-2240).** The **Rendezvous** offers cafeteria-style lunches featuring hamburgers, sandwiches, soup, chili and a salad and pasta bar; **801-933-2184.** At **Pier 49 San Francisco Pizza,** order sourdough crust pizza with a variety of sauces and toppings by the slice or pie. Open 10 A.M.– 8 P.M. daily; take-out and delivery service available; **801-742-2222, ext. 4076.** The **Birdfeeder,** on the outdoor plaza, has burgers and fries (no phone).

If you are staying in one of the units with kitchen facilities, it is best to stock up on food and supplies at one of the Salt Lake City supermarkets before you drive up to Snowbird, but if you need a few items, chances are you will find them at the **General Gritts Convenience Store,** located in the Snowbird Center. The store has made-to-order sandwiches, bagels, soup, chili and potato and pasta salads. The **Rocky Mountain Chocolate Factory** is a favorite stop for Snowbird visitors with a sweet tooth. Other shops at the Snowbird Center include a pharmacy and camera, souvenir, ski clothing, wine and liquor stores.

Mill Creek Canyon
Log Haven—$$$ to $$$$

This is my favorite mountain restaurant in Utah. Located up Mill Creek Canyon, just east of Salt Lake City, this twisting and winding road has no ski resorts or large developments at its terminus. There is no greater pleasure than a drive up Mill Creek Canyon, a hike up one of the trails described in the Hiking section, and then a Sun. brunch or dinner at Log Haven. The original log cabin was constructed as a summer home by L. F. Raines, a Utah entrepreneur, in 1920. Across the road, a pond and artificial waterfall offer an added element of charm to Log Haven's setting. The menu includes a variety of American and continental entrées, from pasta to duck, steak to lobster. The Mill Creek Mud Pie is a house specialty. The Sun. brunch is especially popular for the wide selection of excellent food and the chance to enjoy a Sun. outing in the canyon. Open Mon.–Sat. 5:30 P.M.–10 P.M., Sun. 10 A.M.– 2 P.M. Reservations are recommended. Located 4 miles up Mill Creek Canyon (head east on 3800 S. off Wasatch Blvd.). **801-272-8255.**

Services

Visitor Information
Salt Lake City Visitors and Convention Bureau and Information Center—Open Mon.–Fri. 8 A.M.–7 P.M. (8 A.M.–5:30 P.M. in the winter); Sat. 9 A.M.–4 P.M.; Sun. 10 A.M.–4 P.M. **90 S. West Temple; 1-800-541-4955; 801- 521-2822; www.visitsaltlake.com.**

Park City

Park City is the ideal winter destination. Promoters who landed the 2002 Winter Olympics for Utah used the community and its facilities as one of the key arguments in favor of Utah. It has excellent ski slopes, fine restaurants, delightful accommodations and the ambience of a 19th-century mining town that planners have carefully maintained—and all within a few miles drive from Salt Lake City International Airport. It is true that you can leave Salt Lake City, purchase your ski ticket, ride the ski lift and be skiing down the slopes in less time than it takes to watch *60 Minutes* on television.

Park City is actually six areas, if you count the new subdivisions and condominiums to the north of town; the ski jumping and bobsled and luge facilities in Bear Hollow; The Canyons Ski Resort; Park City Mountain Resort; the historic mining town of Park City; and the Deer Valley Resort. During the 2002 Winter Olympics, Park City hosted nearly a third of the winter events, including the slalom, mogul and aerial competitions at Deer Valley; giant slalom and snowboarding events at Park City Mountain Resort; and the bobsled, luge and ski jumping at the Utah Winter Sports Park.

Park City also has a highly developed cultural life, with an arts festival that attracts thousands, the Sundance Film Festival (which draws celebrities from all over the world, and which, under the direction of Robert Redford, is considered one of the top film festivals anywhere) and a number of art galleries, shops and more than 90 restaurants. Park City is much more than a winter resort town; it is also a popular summer resort, with excellent golf courses, summer activities and hiking/biking opportunities.

History

This is a mountain area for which very little is known about prehistoric or American Indian activity. Three more recent interests have developed Park City: pioneering, mining and skiing. The original Mormon Trail winds just to the north of the Park City area and enters the Salt Lake Valley through Emigration Canyon. Parley P. Pratt, a Mormon apostle and member of the first pioneer group to come west with Mormon president Brigham Young, was an explorer by nature. He examined the mountainous area near the trail and found excellent mountain meadows for his livestock in what was soon being called Parley's Park. In 1850 Pratt also built a toll road into Salt Lake City, down the canyon just south of Emigration Canyon. California gold seekers were willing to pay $1,500 in tolls that year to bypass the Emigration Canyon route into Salt Lake City. But Pratt did not stay long before being "called" to other church assignments that took him away from the canyon that continues to

bear his name. In 1853 he sold his interest in what would become the Park City area to Samuel Snyder, who opened a sawmill there. A small settlement known as Snyderville developed around the sawmill. It remains a place name in the area, just a few miles north of Park City.

With Mormons content to cut timber, graze livestock and abide by the admonitions of their leader, Brigham Young, to stay away from gold and silver mining, it was left to prospectors among the California regiment sent to Utah during the Civil War to stake some of the first claims in the Park City area. Their commander, the Irish-born Col. Patrick Connor, encouraged his men, many of whom had plenty of mining experience in California and Nevada, to search the surrounding mountains for precious metals. He maintained that with the development of a strong mining economy, the theocracy of the Mormon church in Utah would dissolve.

The first mining claim was recorded on December 23, 1868, and the first silver ore shipped from the Flagstaff Mine by wagons to the new railroad line in Echo City in 1871. During the July 4 celebration in 1872, George Gideon Snyder announced that the shacks and cabins that had been thrown up near the mine now constituted the new community of Park City. The city grew steadily during the 1870s and by 1880 contained 350 buildings. A newspaper, *The Park Record,* which is still published, was established in 1880. The Utah Eastern Railroad was completed that year between Park City and Salt Lake City. The 1880s were prosperous, as rags-to-riches stories—like those of Thomas Kearns, David Keith, John Judge, Albion Emery and others— spurred hopefuls to strike it rich themselves.

The 1890s brought two major disasters to Park City. The first was a severe economic depression caused by the demonetization of silver and the Panic of 1893. The second occurred on June 18, 1898, when more than 200 wooden buildings and houses, including all of those on Main St., were destroyed by fire. Park City was rebuilt, prosperity returned and the mines continued to operate. Most mines closed during the Great Depression and, although mining was

Getting There

Park City is an easy 35-mile drive from the Salt Lake City airport. Just take Interstate 80 east toward the city. At the junction with Interstate 15, head south on Interstate 15 for about 3 miles and stay to the left to reenter Interstate 80, which heads east up through Parley's Canyon. About 5 miles beyond Parley's Summit, take Exit 145 and head south along Hwy. 224 into the Park City area. In the summer, Park City can also be reached via Hwy. 152 through Big Cottonwood Canyon.

revived to meet the wartime demands of the 1940s, it was all but dead by the 1950s.

History does not record the name of the individual to first tie wooden slats to his feet and slide down the snow-covered slopes around Park City, but among the early miners there were plenty of immigrants from Sweden, Norway and Finland. In all likelihood, they were the ones who introduced skiing to Park City. By 1916 recreational skiing was beginning to develop as members of the Wasatch Mountain Club began to traverse the mountains above Park City. In 1923 the first ski-jumping exhibition was staged and, in 1928, construction of the Ecker Hill ski jump commenced. By the 1930s representatives of Franklin D. Roosevelt's New Deal programs proposed rescuing the economy of Park City by transforming it into "the best winter sports center in America." A combination of factors delayed this reality for 30 years: to the north, in Idaho, the Union Pacific Railroad constructed its famous Sun Valley Resort and, just across the mountains from Park City, the ski areas of Alta and Brighton lured the skiers that Park City had hoped to attract.

In 1962, with mining in rapid decline, real estate prices at rock bottom and few jobs to keep its young people, Park City officials and businesspeople revived the dream of making Park City a skier's mecca. They announced plans to construct a 12,880-foot, 144-car gondola tramway, the Treasure Mountain Resort and two chairlifts as the nucleus of what is now the Park City Mountain Resort. A year later the facilities were opened and, as if by magic, Park City started the transformation from a depressed mining town to a world-class resort. The initial success led to the establishment of a second resort, Park West (now the Canyons), which opened in 1968, and the Deer Valley Resort, which opened in 1981. Park City continues its quest to become America's top ski center. In January 1993 ski-jumping facilities at the Utah Winter Sports Park at Bear Hollow, visible just off the road into Park City from Interstate 80, were dedicated. In January 1997 the Olympic bobsled/luge track opened to world-class athletics and the general public.

All this development has been done with an attempt to preserve the 19th-century mining heritage. Park City Main St. was listed in the National Register of Historic Places in 1978, and Utah's strictest preservation and zoning ordinances have been adopted by the city. Grants and low-interest loans for the preservation of historic buildings are offered to owners by the city, and the city has placed historic markers on many of its historic buildings.

Festivals and Events

Utah Winter Games

Jan. The Utah Winter Games began in 1987 and have become a well-known Utah tradition. Each year participation grows, with more than 4,000 athletes participating in the recent games. Events include ski jumping, free-style jumping, downhill and slalom races, cross-country ski races, snowboarding, hockey, speed skating and figure skating. Clinics are also offered, as well as a host of other winter activities. Most of the events are held at the Park City area ski resorts, but in recent years venues have been expanded to the Salt Lake area resorts and ice rinks and even to the southern Utah ski resorts for some events. **Utah Winter Games, 2175 W. 1700 S., Salt Lake City, UT 84119; 801-973-8824.**

Sundance Film Festival

end of Jan. If the excitement of glamorous movie stars and nervous producers, and the drama of film premiers before discerning audiences, captures your imagination, or if you just like new and innovative films, then the Sundance Film Institute Festival is the place to be. The festival, which includes 10 days of screenings, seminars, tributes and other activities, began in 1981 under the direction of Robert Redford and has become the premier American festival for independent filmmakers. The festival seeks to show films that cover as many diverse points of view as possible. With this philosophy, the festival offers an eclectic mixture of dramas, comedies, documentaries, foreign films, films dealing with important subjects and films produced by a selected group, such as Native Americans. Tickets go quickly, and many showings are sold out in advance as part of package deals, but there is a chance that tickets will be available for some showings, and even if there is a sold-out sign, you can still put your name on the waiting list in hopes that you might get one of the unfilled seats.

The way to work this system is to pick up a copy of the festival program and decide what you want to see. Go to the theater about an hour and a half before the scheduled time and get in line to be put on the waiting list. An hour before the film begins, they will take your ticket money. About 15 minutes before the film starts, if there are any empty seats in the theater, those on the waiting list will be admitted. If you don't get in, your money is refunded. The waiting line experience can be as exciting as watching the film. Until 1993, all screenings were held in Park City, but now that the festival has expanded to Salt Lake City locations, there are more opportunities to view the selected films. **801-328-FILM; www.sundancefilm.com.**

Park City Fourth of July Celebration

July 4. The day begins at 6 A.M. with early-rising enthusiasts setting off loud blasts that can be heard all over Park City. The daylong events are centered around the park and Main St. Breakfast is available at the city park, followed by the traditional not-so-traditional parade down Main St. at 11 A.M., where participants strive for the most unique and bizarre entries. The afternoon activities include children's games at the park; the traditional rugby game, with the local team, the Park City Muckers, taking on challengers, usually from the Salt Lake Valley; food; and musical performers. The day concludes with a spectacular display of fireworks at the Resort Center. **435-649-6100.**

Park City Art Festival

first weekend in Aug. This annual gathering of local and out-of-state artists began in 1979 and now ranks as one of the nation's top fine art events. The festival is held on Main St., which is closed off, and each year the festival sets new attendance records as festival goers jostle elbow to elbow up and down the street to view the works of the 200 artists selected from nearly 1,000 applicants. Artworks include such items as ceramics, drawings, fibers, glass, jewelry, leather, metal, paintings, paper, photography, sculpture and wood. Live music is performed on several stages. In addition to the art, the event is something of a food festival, with more than a dozen Park City and Deer Valley restaurants vying to offer the most upscale and trendy edibles. Held 10 A.M.–6 P.M. Admission fee for those over 12. **Kimball Art Center; 435-649-8882; www.kimball-art.org.**

Miners Day–Labor Day

first Mon. in Sept. Park City is one of the few places in Utah where you can find an old-fashioned Labor Day celebration. Although the labor union locals no longer parade, activities such as drilling and mucking contests help keep alive the area's mining heritage. Other activities include rugby matches, games, music and food. **435-649-6100.**

Outdoor Activities

Biking

When the skiers finally put their skis away in the spring, it is no longer with the same regret as in former years. The two-wheeled mountain bike has become a worthy substitute for a pair of skis or a snowboard. Ski lifts that carry skiers to the tops of the mountains in winter offer an easy way to get your bike to the top of the mountain with no effort. Ski runs that challenge the best of skiers offer the same white-knuckle experience for mountain bikers. But while there are challenging routes for the kamikaze-style rider, there are also miles of wonderful forestland for those who want a relaxing ride. The "Park City Mountain Bike Trails" brochure is available free from the **Park City Visitor Information Center (435-649-6100)** and at other locations in the city. The guide describes 10 rides in the Park City area. The following are a few favorites.

Rails to Trails

If a diversion from the rugged mountain bike trails is in order, the old Union Pacific Railroad grade that connected Park City with the main line of the Union Pacific at Echo Junction is a good bet. The railroad line was opened in 1880, 11 years after the construction of the Union Pacific Railroad through Echo Canyon. The line remained operational for more than 100 years until 1989, when the 26-mile-long line was abandoned and converted, four years later, into Utah's first rails-to-trails recreational trail, the Historic Union Pacific Rail Trail State Park. The trail is open to hikers, horseback riders and other non-motorized recreational users; however, bikers make up the greatest number of users.

The out-and-back trail is 26 miles long one way and rises in elevation from approximately 5,300 feet near Echo Reservoir to about 7,000 feet at the Park City terminus. Most riders leave from Park City so the first half of the ride is downhill and the return trip is uphill. However, since the 1880 track was constructed as a standard gauge line, the uphill grade does not exceed 3 percent. Still, the outride is downhill and the return ride uphill, so pace yourself. The route parallels three highways—Hwy. 248 from Park City to its junction with US Hwy. 40, then Hwy. 40 to its junction with Interstate 80, then I-80 as it passes through Silver Creek Canyon, along the Weber River and by the communities of Wanship, Hoytsville and Coalville before following the east shoreline of Echo Reservoir to Echo Junction.

The Park City trailhead is located on Prospector Dr. just east of Bonanza Dr. Parking is available near the Sun Creek condominiums, just behind the Park City Plaza. Other trailheads, located at 5- to 8-mile intervals, can be found at Silver Summit, Wanship, Coalville and Echo Reservoir. In winter the route is used by cross-country skiers.

Telemark Park

This Park City area favorite has something for all levels of mountain bikers. The total distance of 7 miles is made up by three main routes that take you over dirt roads and double- and single-track trails with fine views of Deer Valley, the Jordanelle Reservoir and the mountains above Park City. The ride begins at the Snow Park Lodge parking lot in Deer Valley. From the northeast corner of the lodge parking area, cross Deer Valley Dr. and start down the service road where, after about 15 yards, you turn left onto a double track that heads north.

The first loop, **Snow Park Loop**, is 1.7 miles and with the switchbacks leading up to Roosevelt Gap, you have a good introduction to the area. This loop also provides access to **McKinley Gap Loop.** The **Spin Cycle Loop** follows a more easterly course off the Snow Park Loop and includes a steep, narrow single track that descends through a tight-laced aspen grove, followed by an uphill climb of nearly 600 feet in elevation along a dirt road.

The trail system is on private land, and local bikers have tirelessly sought to maintain a sympathetic attitude by the landowners. The area is also quite popular with hikers because of its easy access from Snow Park Lodge and the nearby condominiums and homes.

Tour des Suds

When the history of mountain biking is written, the Tour des Suds trail will deserve an important place in that history. Early Park City mountain bikers tested their skills and equipment on the trail and, since 1983, it has been the course for a bike race that is the traditional finale for Park City's mountain biking season. The **Tour des Suds Mountain Bike Race** draws 200 or more riders, usually on the third Sat. in Sept., for a 5-mile uphill race that begins at the city park and ends at Bonanza Flats by the Guardsman Pass road. Because the ride heads in a southerly direction from Park City's Main St., you might guess that the trail takes its name from the German word for south, sud. However, the mountain bike pioneers who developed the trail in the early 1980s had another German word in mind—especially on a hot afternoon at the end of the 1,700-foot-plus ascent.

The ride, one of the most popular in the Park City area, begins at the upper end of town where Main St. ends and Daly Ave. begins. Ride south up Daly Ave. for about 0.6 mile until you come to a gate across the road. A trail sign marks the beginning of the trail, which continues in a generally southwest direction up Daly Canyon (also known as Empire Canyon) until the trail intersects the Guardsman Pass Rd. at about 8,800 feet elevation. Here you can return to Park City by way of the road or retrace the route you have come. The route is also popular with hikers and includes part of the Lower Daly Hiking Trail (see the Hiking section). The Tour des Suds Mountain Bike Race carries with it something of the old rural harvest festival, as mountain bikers meet not only to race, but to offer thanks for the summer of golden biking memories, commemorated with postride festivities, good food and, of course, plenty of suds.

RENTALS AND TOURS

Cole Sport

Two locations offer mountain bike rentals, one at the north end of Park City, **1615 Park Ave.; 435-649-4806;** and the other at Deer Valley's **Silver Lake Village** at the base of the chairlift. Cole Sport also provides bike rentals at the **Sterling Lift at Silver Lake Village; 435-649-4601; www.colesport.com.**

Jans Mountain Outfitters

Jans's has bike rentals and overnight repair service for both mountain and road bikes. **1600 Park Ave.; 1-800-745-1020; 435-649-4949; www.jans.com.**

Mountain Trails Foundation

This private, voluntary, nonprofit organization is committed to keeping trails open for public access. In addition to working on bike trails and representing bikers to private landowners, the foundation sponsors a Tues.-night race series and provides information about mountain biking in the Park City Area. **P.O. Box 754, Park City, UT 84060; 435-649-6839.**

Sport Touring Ventures

If you are looking for an organized tour, led by guides who know the area with support personnel who will look after your equipment and provide you with snacks, meals and drinks, then Sport Touring Ventures might be just your ticket. They offer rentals and half-day, full-day and overnight tours. **4719 Silver Meadows Dr., Ste. 19, Park City, UT 84060; 435-649-1551; www.mtnbiketours.com.**

Golf

Park City Municipal Golf Course

Situated at the base of the Park City Mountain Resort, this course was constructed in 1962 and is quite scenic, a favorite of Utah golfers. Lots of water and trees, as well as condominiums built along some of the fairways, add one more layer of stress for erratic golfers. **1800 Three Kings Rd.; 435-615-5800.**

Park Meadows

Readers of the *Deseret News* voted this golf course the most difficult course in Utah. Designed by golf pro Jack Nicklaus, it is certainly long and difficult, with sand traps sprinkled all over the 6,666-yard course (7,338 yards, if you play the blue tees). While Utah golfers consider it expensive (fees do include a cart), it is a bargain for those accustomed to much higher greens fees. You can cut the price by playing Mon.–Thurs., or if you play after 3 P.M. without a cart. The course is characterized by beautiful scenery, no trees and no crowds. **2000 Meadows Dr.; 435-649-2460.**

Hiking

Deer Valley Resort

Hiking Trail—One of the most pleasant hiking experiences in Utah is at the Deer Valley Resort. Wed.–Sun., mid-June–mid-Sept., the Sterling lift at Silver Lake Lodge will carry you to the top of Bald Mountain, where you can descend the 2-mile-long trail without the exertion of the 1,200-foot climb up the mountain. The Hiking

Trail is reserved for hikers only and offers unsurpassed views south into Heber Valley and Mt. Timpanogos, east to Jordanelle Reservoir and the Uinta Mountains in the distance, and north into the Park City area. The trail begins on top of Bald Mountain just to the left and east of the large white towers, then descends the south slope on a narrow, twisting foot path before it intersects a road that follows east where Jordanelle Reservoir, more than 1,500 feet below, comes into view. Part of the trail is a service road used by resort maintenance vehicles and it is a fairly steep descent, so wear good shoes. A brochure available at the resort includes a brief description and map of the trails.

If you don't want to hike all the way back down the mountain, you can take in the panoramic views from the top and then ride the Sterling lift back down. The lift is especially nice for travelers coming from much lower elevations than the 7,000- to 9,000-foot elevations around Park City. You can begin hiking shortly after your arrival without the added stress on your system of the uphill hikes.

Uphill Route—If you want to hike before the lift opens at 10 A.M. or after it closes at 5:30 P.M., you have several options. You might make the ascent by way of what is called the Uphill Route, another service road that provides mountain bikers with access to the summit without taking the lift. Then you can descend by way of the Hiking Trail.

Naildriver Downhill and Homeward Bound Trail—You can also use both the Hiking Trail and the Uphill Route to hike to the top of Bald Mountain and return by either of two 3-mile-long trails used by mountain bikers—the Naildriver Downhill or the Homeward Bound Trail. Both of these are pleasant hiking trails that cross open meadows and wind through aspen and pine groves to the west of Sterling lift. Because these trails are used by mountain bikers who ride up the Sterling lift, you are likely not to encounter many bikers when the lift is not in operation. In any case, use these two trails only for your descent and listen and watch for mountain bikers.

Lower Daly Trail

This is a favorite Park City trail because it is so easy to imagine that you are a Park City silver miner leaving town and going up into the mountains to stake your own claim. Begin the 5-mile hike anywhere along Park City's Main St. and walk uphill in a southwesterly direction where Main St. ends and becomes Daly Ave. As you pass along Daly Ave., you will see a number of old miners' homes—many are restored but some are not and remind old-timers of what Park City was like before it became a ski destination.

The asphalt road gives way to a gravel road after you pass the last houses, and a little less than a mile from the beginning of Daly Ave. you approach a gate, which blocks motorized traffic. As you cross around the gate, you will see a trail identification for Tour des Suds (see the Biking section) and your route will parallel the lower portion of this popular biking trail. As you follow the road up Daly Canyon, you will pass by tailings piles and other remains of the Daly Mine. After you pass the water tank, follow the road as it climbs up the east side of the canyon. Eventually the trail crosses the ridge and follows the west side of Ontario Canyon south past the old Ontario Mine, now the Park City Silver Mine Adventure. After crossing a large tailings pile, the trail loops back down Daly Canyon, past old mine buildings and the Judge Tunnel, located near the water tank where the loop ends. The mile or so back to the top of Main St. completes the hike.

Park City Mountain Resort Area Trails

The mountains above Park City offer plenty of opportunities to ride and hike on trails that pass under ski lifts and by a mountain lake, old mines and the remains of old mills such as the Silver King and the California Comstock Mines. Picture a series of four connected loops going up the mountain from Park City to near the mountaintop at Scotts Pass, and you have an idea of how the trail system is laid out. The first loop trail is the 3.3-mile **Sweeney Switchback Loop** described below. Pick up a copy of the "Park City Mountain Resort Mountain Biking and Hiking Trail Map" at the resort offices.

The second is the 2.7-mile **Silver King Loop,** which takes off from either side of the Sweeney Switchbacks. The apex of this loop is at the Silver King Mine, where you can continue up the mountain on the 8.2-mile **Thaynes/ Jupiter Loop,** which crosses under the Gondola, Silverlode, Motherlode and Thaynes lifts before it reaches the base of the resort's highest lift, the Jupiter Lift. Here you can take the 0.83-mile **Shadow Lake Loop,** which provides access to the top of the mountains and the Wasatch Crest Trail via the 0.5-mile-long Scotts Pass Trail. You climb nearly 2,400 vertical feet from Park City at 7,100 feet to 9,475 feet at Scotts Pass. Combining the Sweeney Switchback Trail and the Silver King Loop gives you a 6-mile round-trip hike, while it is approximately 16 miles up to Scotts Pass and back.

Sweeney Switchbacks

This trail is popular with Park City visitors and residents alike because of its close proximity to the town. It begins on the western edge of Park City and climbs onto the mountain rising above the city. Part of the trail crosses under the Town lift and by several of the Silver King tramway towers. The trail offers a great variety of experiences—a marvelous view of Park City, meadows of wildflowers and pine and aspen groves. The trail is a 2-mile loop with a 400-foot elevation gain.

There are two ways to begin your hike. Most hikers begin the trail at the Lowell Ave. trailhead. From the Park City Mountain Resort, follow Lowell Ave., which runs right in front of the resort, to the south until the street curves uphill to the right. On the left side of the road is a road with a cable gate. Or, from lower Main St., you can reach the trailhead by heading west on 8th St. just across the street from the Town lift on Park Ave. The road climbs steeply, turns to the right and continues uphill to Lowell Ave. Once on Lowell Ave., head south to the trailhead.

From the trailhead go uphill (south), passing under the Town ski lift. Approximately 300 yards past the lift, you will see a path on your right that climbs in a northerly direction uphill and back toward the Town lift. After you pass under the lift, you will come to an intersection. Take the right-hand trail and continue in the same direction. The trail crosses a wide ski run, then passes through a stand of small quaking aspen before it loops back to the south to pass once again under the Town lift. You will cross two more ski runs (with excellent photo opportunities of the town below) before you descend back into Park City along an old mining road with five switchbacks.

You can hike the trail in the reverse direction from the upper end of Main St. Just climb the 274 steps up the Swede Alley Stairway, which begins at the north end of the Treasure Mountain Inn across Main St. from the Morning Ray Bakery. At the top of the stairs, look to your right for the trailhead located about 30 yards away. Watch for bikers on this trail, as it is popular with advanced bikers who find it a fairly technical ride.

Horseback Riding

Park City Stables

Park City Stables has two locations, one at the Park City Mountain Resort just under the lift that takes you up to the Alpine Slide and the other at the Deer Valley Resort. You can arrange for a 1- or 2-hour trail ride or special breakfast and dinner rides. Open daily late May–mid-Oct. **1-800-303-7256; 435-646-7256; www.rocky-ymtrec.com.**

Skiing

CROSS-COUNTRY
White Pine Touring Center

White Pine has 18 kilometers of set track, plus guided tours, lessons and a full-service ski shop. Open daily 9 A.M.–6 P.M. Located on the Park City Municipal Golf Course, just off Hwy. 224/Park Ave. **435-649-8701.**

DOWNHILL

Park City is home to the U.S. Ski Team and ranks among the top ski areas in the country, if not the world. Park City, The Canyons and Deer Valley all have excellent ski schools, rental shops and lifts that are located within walking distance of accommodations, or a short drive or bus ride from anywhere in the Park City area.

The Canyons

This ski area was first known as Park West, later as Wolf Mountain and, since 1997, as The Canyons. The resort has undergone a radical transformation with the construction of new facilities, including the Sundial Lodge, Grand Summit Resort Hotel and several new lifts, as well as replacement of older ones, giving the resort a total of 16 lifts with access to 140 runs on 3,500 acres spread across eight mountains. The resort has special ski school classes, lower lift prices and an excellent children's ski school, and children 8 and under can ski for free when accompanied by an adult ticket holder. The Little Adventures Child Care caters to infants and children from 6 weeks to 4 years old. Easy access off Interstate 80. **1-888-226-9667; 435-649-5400; www.thecanyons.com.**

Deer Valley

Opened in 1981 and catering to the more affluent skier, Deer Valley is an unbelievable experience compared to every other ski resort in Utah or, for that matter, the United States. *Ski* magazine's readers rate Deer Valley the number one ski area in North America. Deer Valley was also the host for the 2002 Winter Olympics slalom, free-style mogul and aerial events. The number of skiers allowed on the mountain is restricted, lift lines are usually nonexistent, snowboarders are not allowed and skiers are catered to and pampered in ways that are hard to imagine.

When you arrive at the resort, ski valets unload your skis from your car, and complimentary secured ski storage corrals ensure that your skis will be where you left them. Thick, padded chairlifts make the ride up the mountain as comfortable as possible, and if you need to blow your nose or clean your glasses, tissue dispensers are available at each lift. The restaurants and lodging are first class. The resort's six restaurants— **The Mariposa, Silver Lake Restaurant,**

Snow Park Restaurant, McHenry's Seafood Buffet, Bald Mountain Pizza and the **Empire Canyon Grill**—offer some of the best food to be found anywhere.

The 67 ski runs are meticulously groomed and spread out over 1,750 acres. With 19 lifts—including one four-passenger high-speed gondola, six high-speed detachable quads, three fixed-grip quads, seven triple chairs and two double chairlifts—the resort capacity is 4,500 lift passes per day. The runs are spread out over four mountains: Bald Mountain (9,400 feet), Flagstaff Mountain (9,100 feet), Bald Eagle Mountain (8,400 feet) and Empire Mountain (9,570 feet). The ski season usually runs from the first week in Dec. to the first week in Apr.

Actually, for all the amenities, skiing at Deer Valley costs only a few dollars more a day than at the Park City Mountain Resort. Multi-day passes offer some savings. The Deer Valley Children's Center provides supervision and activities for infants and children 2 months to 12 years old. **1-800-558-3337; 435-649-1000; www.deervalley.com.**

Park City Mountain Resort

During Park City's heyday as a mining town, a tram ran from the center of town up the mountain to the mines. Today a triple chairlift follows the old tram route, allowing skiers to stay on historic Main St. and walk to the chairlift for a 13-minute ride. The main resort center is located at what was the northwestern edge of Park City. Park City Mountain Resort was the site of the Alpine Giant Slalom races and all snowboard events during the 2002 Winter Olympics.

The original four-passenger gondola, which served skiers since 1963 with a 22-minute ride to the top of the mountain, was replaced in 1997. The resort now offers four lifts with four high-speed six-passenger lifts, one high-speed quad lift and five triple and four double chairlifts, all of which provide access for more than 27,000 skiers an hour to more than 100 trails (the longest of which is 3.5 miles), plus 650 acres of wide-open skiing in seven bowls at the top of the mountain. The snowfall average for Park City is more than 350 inches a year, with the largest amount usually falling in Mar. The snowfall average is about 60 percent of that at Alta, for example, but the use of snowmaking equipment ensures good skiing, even during infrequent years of little snow. The lifts are located at approximately 6,900 feet elevation and reach 10,000 feet, for a vertical drop of 3,100 feet, with a total ski area of 3,300 acres spread over seven peaks and their slopes.

While the ski schools serve all ages of skiers, a special "It's Never Too Late" program has been developed for older skiers. Some graduates of the school automatically qualify for free lift passes, given to all those 70 and over. Children 12 and under ski for about half price. **1-800-222-7275; 435-649-8111; 435-649-5447 (snow conditions); www.parkcitymountain.com.**

Sledding

Alpine Slide

During the winter, it is the famous PayDay ski run, but in the summer, it is home to a half-mile-long snake of half pipe that twists and turns down the slope, provoking thrills and screams from those who climb aboard the sleds to make the descent to the base of the ski resort. To ride the alpine slide, purchase tickets at the Park City Mountain Resort ticket office, then climb aboard the triple chairlift at the base of the hill for an enjoyable ride up the mountain. At the top of the mountain, you pick up a sled and then climb on one of the two tracks that parallel each other down the mountain. If you plan a slow descent, warn those in back of you to give you plenty of room. Youngsters like to roar down the mountain, threatening to sail out of the pipe at every turn. (Yes, you can go out of the track, so if you are not the daredevil type, exercise caution.) Still, it is a fun activity for all ages. Open daily during the summer 10 A.M.–9 P.M. Located at Park City Mountain Resort. **1-800-222-7275; 435-649-8111.**

Utah Olympic Park

The venue for the 2002 Winter Olympics ski-jumping, bobsled, luge and skeleton competi-

tions, the Utah Winter Sports Park continues to host competitions in all of these events. You can tour the park daily 9 A.M.–5 P.M. A fee is charged, which includes admission to the Alf Engen Ski Museum (see the Museums section under Seeing and Doing). Speed freaks and other thrill seekers should ask about the bobsleds and luge rides that are offered from time to time when the track is open. In the summer you can ride a bobsled on wheels that takes you down the run.

To reach the park, take Exit 134 off I-80 and follow Hwy. 224 for approximately 2 miles to Bear Hollow Dr. Turn west onto Bear Hollow Dr. and follow it up to the top of the mountain and the entry gate. You will then drive down the other side past the bobsled run and down to the Joe Quinney Winter Sports Park and Alf Engen Ski Museum. During competitions, the parking area just off Hwy. 224 is used, so look for directions for public parking. **435-658-4200.**

Tennis

Many of the Park City hotels offer private tennis courts, but there are two free courts at the **City Park,** located at the north end of Park Ave. **Prospector Athletic Club** has two outdoor courts in Prospector Square; **435-649-6670;** and the **Park City Racquet Club, 1200 E. Little Kate Rd.; 435-615-5400,** has seven outdoor and four indoor courts available for a fee.

Seeing and Doing

Art Galleries

The **Gallery Association of Park City** includes more than a dozen members and publishes a *Gallery Guide of Park City,* which lists the names of exhibiting artists and special exhibits throughout the city. Available at the Park City Museum (see the Museums section) and other locations in the city.

Kimball Art Center

Art is an integral part of Park City. While you are there, don't miss the Kimball Art Center, located at the bottom of Main St. You will find exhibited paintings and sculpture of major American artists in the main 3,000-square-foot gallery. The Badami Gallery, on the lower level, features local and regional artists. An extensive gift shop offers a fine selection of ceramics, paintings, prints and posters, stained glass, hand-made jewelry, wood, glass and quilts. A non-profit enterprise, everything that is sold in the gallery, including the gift shop items, is juried and carried on consignment. The art center also sponsors a **Summer Art Institute,** with more than a dozen instructors offering seminars and workshops. During the winter, a variety of weekly classes are offered. The center also sponsors the **Park City Arts Festival** (see the Festivals and Events section). Open Mon.–Sat. 10 A.M.–6 P.M., Sun. noon–6 P.M. **638 Park Ave.; 435-649-8882; www.kimball-art.org.**

Children and Families

Family Tree Center

While you are strolling along Park City's historic Main St., take a few minutes to stop at the Family Tree Center. The center is operated by the Church of Jesus Christ of Latter-day Saints to give visitors a chance to locate ancestors among the hundreds of millions of names collected from around the world and as far back in history as possible. The volunteer missionaries will show you the ropes and offer suggestions for further research. It is amazing how interested older children are in searching the records for their grand-parents and great-grandparents. Admission is free, so you can take a quick glance or stay for a longer intensive research session. Open Mon.–Sat. 10 A.M.–9 P.M., Sun. 1–7 P.M. **531 Main St.; 435-940-9502; www.family-search.org.**

Historic Sites

Historic Main St.

Every visitor to Park City should make the walk up and down the town's historic Main St. With its shops, restaurants, museums, galleries, theater, post office and false-front buildings, Main St.

remains the heart of Park City. The city's Historic Preservation Commission has passed Utah's strictest zoning ordinances to maintain the character and historical accuracy of the 19th-century buildings. Main St. was one of the first historic districts in Utah listed in the National Register of Historic Places. At the Park City Museum, you can purchase an attractive and inexpensive booklet, *Park City Main Street Historic Walking Tour,* published by the Park City Historical Society. Guided walking tours of Main St. are offered during the summer through the Park City Museum. **528 Main St.; 435-645-5135.**

Miners' Hospital

On Christmas Day in 1903, more than 300 members of the Western Federation of Miners Local No. 144 met to consider and adopt plans to construct a miners' hospital and to provide better medical care for the miners. The Park City Hospital is one of 25 miners' hospitals erected by local unions of the Western Federation of Miners in the West between 1897 and 1918. As well as accidents, work in the mines brought a variety of occupational diseases, including lead poisoning, miners' consumption, tuberculosis and silicosis. The hospital was a godsend for families whose fathers and husbands could be treated in Park City rather than in faraway Salt Lake City.

The hospital was closed in the 1950s, and the building became in turn a dentist's office, bar, restaurant and skiers' dormitory. When it was threatened with demolition, the citizens of Park City insisted the building be preserved, and in 1979 it was relocated to the nearby park. The old hospital was renovated and reopened as the Park City Library in 1982. Eight hundred people formed a human chain 3,800 feet long to pass from hand to hand the 5,000 books from the old library to the new. Park City received a commendation by the National Trust for Historic Preservation for the innovative adaptive reuse of the old hospital. In 1993, a new Park City Library was opened and the miners' hospital began its fourth life as a community center.

Museums

Alf Engen Ski Museum

It was no surprise when Alf Engen was named Utah's Athlete of the Century in 1999. Indeed, if Brigham Young is the name most associated with Utah for the 19th century, it is likely that Alf Engen will hold that honor for the 20th century. Engen could do it all—ski, teach, promote and inspire. He set several world records as a ski jumper, and in contests involving all four types of skiing—jumping, downhill, slalom and cross country—he could not be beat. He was picked to represent the United States as a ski jumper for the 1936 Winter Olympics, but the use of his picture in a Wheaties advertisement kept him off the team. Twelve years later, he coached the U.S. Ski Team at the 1948 Winter Olympics in St. Moritz, Switzerland. Also in 1948, he helped establish the Deseret News Ski School, the first school of its kind in the country to provide free or low-cost ski lessons to the public. Still a Utah institution, the school has taught thousands of Utahns to ski. Alf Engen continued to teach skiing into his 80s. He also helped select the Bear Hollow location for the Utah Winter Sports Park, site of the ski jumping events during the 2002 Winter Olympics and now home of the Alf Engen Ski Museum.

Alf Engen's involvement in Utah skiing spanned seven decades, from his arrival in January 1930 as a 21-year-old immigrant from Mjondalen, Norway, until his death at age 88 in 1997. His career followed the evolution of skiing from largely a spectator sport for ski jumping to the development of the country's first ski lifts in the 1930s and the emergence of recreational skiing as a national winter pastime.

Opened in 2002, the Alf Engen Ski Museum could become for skiing what Cooperstown, New York, is for baseball. Among the exhibits are those that explain how Utah's powder snow develops and one with three options for virtual skiing that include powder snow skiing and the 2002 Winter Olympics slalom and downhill courses. An especially impressive exhibit places you in the path of an onrushing avalanche and

demonstrates that your chances of swimming on top of such a force of nature to safety are very slim. An excellent film covers the development of skiing in Utah and the innovations in skiing that have come out of Utah. The museum is part of the Joe Quinney Winter Sports Center at the Utah Olympic Park (see the Tours section). Admission fee charged. Hours vary throughout the year depending on events. Look for the Utah Olympic Park road just south of the intersection of I-80 and Hwy. 224. **435-658-4236 weather conditions; www.engenmuseum.org.**

Park City Museum

The Park City Museum is housed in the 1885 City Hall, the basement of which was used as a jail (locals and children still refer to it as the "dungeon"). Complete with the original jail cells, leg irons and an Industrial Workers of the World inscription that has been preserved in one of the cells, the basement jail depicts what incarceration was like in a 19th-century mining town. While the dungeon is perhaps the most popular part of the museum, it is by no means all there is to it. Excellent exhibits upstairs focus on mining, early skiing, fraternal and community organizations and early community life in Park City. One popular exhibit depicts "China Bridge"—a bridge from the eastern side of Park City down to Main St., which crossed over Park City's Chinatown. A series of videotapes on the history of Park City can be viewed in the museum. Open Mon.–Sat. 10 A.M.–7 P.M., Sun. noon–6 P.M. Admission is free. The **Park City Visitor Information Center,** also located in the museum, is an excellent place to pick up additional brochures, a calendar of events and other information about Park City. **528 Main St.; 435-649-7457; www.parkcityhistory.org.**

Performing Arts

MUSIC

Summers in Park City offer a wonderful diversity of musical concerts and performances. The following summaries describe the major locations and festivals. For a listing of concerts and programs, check *This Week Park City,* a free publication issued twice a month that contains a list of current and upcoming musical events.

The Canyons Concerts

Whereas Deer Valley caters more to those with classical music tastes, concerts at The Canyons resort usually feature well-known country and western, rock, and blues groups and artists performing on a stage at the base of the ski resort. Reserved bench seating is available in front of the stage, or you can sit on the grass on the hill and enjoy more of a picnic atmosphere. Located at the Canyons Resort off Hwy. 224 approximately 3 miles south of I-80 at Kimball's Junction Exit 145 and 3 miles north of Park City. **435-649-5400.**

Concerts in the Park

The bandstand in the Park City Park is the site for a free summer concert series on Wed. evenings 6–8 P.M. Pack a picnic and enjoy music that ranges from classical to folk music to blues to contemporary piano and vocal music. For information on the weekly artists, check the schedule in *This Week Park City.* **1-800-453-1360.**

Deer Valley Concerts

The Boston Pops Orchestra; Peter, Paul and Mary; Pete Fountain; and the Utah Symphony were some of the groups that performed in concert at the Deer Valley Resort during the last few summers. Deer Valley always puts together an excellent series of summer concerts. **801-533-NOTE (6683).**

Park City Folk and Blue Grass Festival

The Deer Valley Resort transforms itself into a small piece of Tennessee the second weekend in Aug. as it hosts an all-day Sun. festival with music from 10 A.M. until after dark. On Sat. there are bluegrass music contests that attract the area's best amateur talent. Sat. evening there are some free outdoor performances followed by jam sessions lasting well into the night. **801-339-7664; 801-532-5218.**

Park City International Music Festival

Since 1984 the International Music Festival has offered Park City residents and visitors six weeks of unsurpassed classical music. Artists from around the world come together from mid-July until the last part of Aug. to perform and offer workshops. Concerts are held at the Kimball Arts Center, Park City Community Church, Sarty Auditorium in the Park City Education Center, and at Deer Valley Resort. For serious music lovers, the Masterclass is an interesting opportunity to observe how a visiting artist works with four or five students, each of whose performance is critiqued and suggestions offered for improving skills. Observers can attend the Masterclasses at no charge. Tickets are required for performances by the festival orchestra and chamber orchestra. Visitors are invited to attend the free open rehearsals, usually held on Thurs., Fri. and Sat. Pick up a schedule of events at the Kimball Arts Center, Park City Visitor Center or area hotels. **PCIMF, P.O. Box 354, Park City, UT 84060; 435-645-8825.**

Park City Jazz Festival

First held in 1997, this event has become the premier jazz festival in Utah, with legends like Ray Charles and Chuck Mangione performing along with exciting new talent at the Deer Valley Amphitheater. Educational workshops and clinics are offered at Park City High School on Fri. and Sat. Held on the last weekend in Aug. **435-655-2651.**

THEATER
Egyptian Theatre Company

This small professional theater company produces several shows each year that include dramas, comedies, musicals and melodramas. The productions are staged in the historic Egyptian Theater, which was built in 1926 as a vaudeville and silent movie theater. The theater opened on December 25, 1926, with a showing of Zane Grey's Man of the Forest. The theater began its modern history in 1981 when local players staged a production of My Fair Lady. The theater is also used for screenings during the Sundance

Film Festival. The theater underwent a major renovation in 1998 to insure its continued use for theatrical performances. In the renovation, care was taken to preserve the elements of the original Egyptian Revival architecture, including false-front columns, a lotus blossom ceiling design and Egyptian hieroglyphic tile motifs. **328 Main St.; 435-649-9371.**

Shopping

The **factory stores** at Park City have become a destination for shoppers from all over the state. Located just off Interstate 80 at Kimball Junction (Exit 145), the famous manufacturer outlets encircle a large parking area, giving the impression that this is a modern-day version of the wagon encirclement or a community fort. There are nearly 70 stores offering reduced prices on quality name-brand items, including Levi's, Eddie Bauer, Bass, Nike, Mikasa, Ashworth, Guess?, Nine West and many more. Open Mon.–Sat. 10 A.M.–9 P.M., Sun. 10 A.M.– 6 P.M. **435-645-7078.**

Park City's Historic Main St. (see Historic Sites section), is also a shopper's delight. Galleries, boutiques and specialty shops, many of which are located in historic buildings, make shopping on Park City's Main St. a special experience.

Tours

Ballooning

Most of us have imagined what it would be like to step into the basket of a hot air balloon and slowly lift off the ground and float high above the houses, fields and mountains below. Park City is Utah's most popular ballooning area, and visitors can take advantage of this strong interest for a never-to-be-forgotten experience. Flights can be arranged throughout the year, depending on wind and weather conditions. **Park City Balloon Adventures; 1-800-396-8787; 435-645-8787; www.pcballoonadventures.com.**

Utah Olympic Park

The site of the 2002 Winter Olympics ski jumping, bobsled, luge and skeleton competitions, the Utah Olympic Park should not be missed when you are in the Park City area. Admission to the park includes an hour-long bus tour up the mountain along the bobsled track to the start of the bobsled and luge runs and to the top of the 120-meter ski jump. Knowledgeable tour guides, some of them competitors in the winter sports, are on hand to provide an overview and answer questions. The Utah Olympic Park is a prime training facility for ski jumpers from around the world. Summer is an especially good time to watch the jumpers who take off and land on synthetic material that replicates winter jumping. Another feature of the park is the 750,000-gallon freestyle training pool. Ski jumpers and aerialists begin on the 10-meter jump to learn how to land in the pool, and then go up from there to the three large jumps where aerialists demonstrate the twists, flips, turns and maneuvers they hope will bring home the gold in the winter competitions. It is quite a sight to see the jumpers fly off the jumps high into the air and come down into the huge pool of water.

Also included in your entrance fee to the park is admission to the Alf Engen Ski Museum (see the Museum section) and Joe Quinney Winter Sports Center. Plan about 2 or 3 hours or longer if you want to watch the ski jumpers. To reach the park, take Exit 134 off I-80 and follow Hwy. 224 for approximately 2 miles to Bear Hollow Dr. Turn west onto Bear Hollow Dr. and follow it up to the top of the mountain and the entry gate. You will then drive down the other side past the bobsled run and down to the Joe Quinney Winter Sports Park and Alf Engen Ski Museum. During competitions, the parking area just off Hwy. 224 is used, so look for directions for public parking. **435-658-4200.**

Where to Stay

Accommodations
Park City and nearby Deer Valley have a good mix of high-quality hotels, condominiums, bed and breakfasts and historic lodges. There are thousands of condominium units and full-

service hotel rooms available in the area. Central reservation service is available through a number of companies, a few of which are listed in the Services section. During the off-season, rooms go for about half the high-season rate. For a complete list of possibilities, contact the **Park City Convention and Visitors Bureau** to request a copy of their winter or summer vacation planner; **1-800-453-1360; www.parkcityinfo. com.** For something out of the ordinary, consider the following possibilities.

Angel House Inn—$$$

Joe and Jan Fisher-Rush are the proprietors of the Angel House Inn. The original Victorian-style building dates from 1889, and the 10 rooms' decor continues the Victorian theme. The eight guest rooms and two one-bedroom suites are each named for different angels, such as: Gabriel & Hope, angelic messengers; Michael & Faith, angels of protection; Chamael & Amora, angels of love; Uriel & Aurora, angels of peace; Victoria & Zadkiel, angels of freedom; Christine, angel of understanding; and Jophiel, angel of wisdom. All rooms have private baths, with some rooms offering claw foot tubs or heated tubs. There's also an outdoor hot tub and cozy living room with a fireplace, TV and VCR plus a great view of Park City's historic Main St. below. A full gourmet breakfast and afternoon hors d'oeuvres are served. No pets, no children under the age of 12 and smoking in designated outside areas only. The inn is centrally located, only a few blocks away from historic Main St., the Town lift, and the Park City Mountain Resort. Angel House Inn has perhaps the only nondenominational minister in the state. Jan has performed a number of marriage ceremonies for guests at the inn, and if you are contemplating such an event, there isn't a nicer person than Jan to handle it. **713 Norfolk Ave., P.O. Box 159, Park City, UT 84060; 1-800-264-3501; 435-647-0338; www. angelhouseinn.com.**

Base Camp Park City—$ to $$

Basic is the operative word here. This hostel-style lodge has 16 rooms that accommodate four persons each with two sets of bunk beds. Pillows, blankets and bed and bath linens are provided. There are 16 private showers in shared bathrooms. There's a lounge with free Internet access, a television room and a full kitchen with vending machines. Private rooms can be rented, but the real bargain is a single bed for $35 a night during ski season and $25 during the off-season. An excellent location. **268 Main St.; 1-888-980-7244; 435-655-7244; www.parkcity-basecamp.com.**

Goldener Hirsch Inn—$$$$

The famous Goldener Hirsch Hotel in Salzburg, Austria, is the model for this Deer Valley inn, which opened in 1990. There are 20 luxurious mini-suites with Austrian furniture and decor, as well as a wonderful collection of Austrian artifacts such as chests, wardrobes and other furniture, along with old-world farm implements such as rakes, pitchforks and sickles. A continental breakfast is provided, and the inn's restaurant is open for breakfast, lunch and dinner (see the Where to Eat section). There are indoor and outdoor hot tubs, a sauna, a fireside lounge and a bar. Closed mid-Oct.–Dec. and mid-Apr.–mid-June. **7570 Royale St. E.; 1-800-252-3373; 435-649-7770; www.goldener hirschinn.com.**

Imperial Hotel—$$$

Known originally as the Bogan Boarding House, the building that now houses the Imperial Hotel was constructed for miners in 1904, after the passage of the 1901 Boarding House Bill by the Utah State Legislature no longer required single miners to stay in company-owned boarding-houses. It has been known as the Imperial Hotel for many years. During the influenza epidemic of 1918, it served as an emergency hospital. It also carries a reputation as a former brothel. The building is listed in the National Register of Historic Places. It was renovated as a bed and breakfast in 1989, and each of the 13 rooms has a private bathroom with a tub large enough for two. An old-fashioned breakfast is served each morning. Located at the top of Main St. **221**

Main St.; 1-800-669-8824; 435-649-1904; www.1904imperial.com.

Old Miners' Lodge—$$$

Even older than the Bogan Boarding House, the Old Miners' Lodge was constructed in 1893 to provide housing for miners working in the nearby silver mines. The original structure was of balloon-style construction and built of inferior-quality lumber. Following several additions, the building was renovated in the 1970s. It is Park City's oldest full-time bed and breakfast inn. Each of the 10 rooms is named for a Park City personality, and each has a private bath. Popular rooms include the Jedediah Grant, the largest room and with a magnificent view of Main St. and the Park City Town ski lift; the Black Jack Murphy, with a mine entrance to the room and named for the only man ever lynched in Park City; and the Mother Urban, named for Park City's infamous 200-pound-plus madame.

Innkeepers Hugh Daniels and Susan Wynne offer a hearty country breakfast and plenty of good conversation around the large living room fireplace. There is a hot tub in back and each room is provided with terrycloth robes and down comforters. The Town ski lift passes just to the north of the lodge. Because of its location on the side of a hill and the 20 steps to climb, access for the physically disabled is difficult. **615 Woodside Ave.; 1-800-648-8068; 435-645-8068; www.oldminerslodge.com.**

Old Town Guest House—$$$ to $$$$

The first time I stopped by the Old Town Guest House, innkeeper Deb Lovci was out training for a triathlon. An active skier and biker, Deb's energetic lifestyle and enthusiasm for the area brings an electricity not found in every bed and breakfast inn. And yet there is a cozy, neighborly, homey feel to the place as well. If the primary reason for your visit to Park City is to ski, hike or bike, then Old Town is just for you. Each room has a queen bed and private bathroom, with two of the rooms sharing a shower across the hall. The two-room McConky's Suite sleeps four, in a queen bed and two bunk beds. It also has a jetted tub, TV and VCR. All rooms are non-smoking. With ski and snowboard storage, a hot tub on the deck, movie library, fireplace, hearty breakfast and afternoon snacks along with Deb's personal attention, extensive knowledge of the area and its location in one of the historic homes in the older section of Park City, what more could you want? **1011 Empire Ave.; 1-800-290-6423, ext. 3710; 435-649-2642; www.oldtownguesthouse.com.**

Stein Ericksen Lodge—$$$$

A legend in skiing, Stein Ericksen has also become a legend in lodging with his elegant 113-unit lodge at Deer Valley, which opened in 1981. The lodge brings the rustic tradition of Norway to Utah with a personal touch that combines the best of old-world tradition with the best of Utah hospitality. It is ranked, for good reason, as one of the top 10 ski lodges in the United States. The lobby contains a trophy case with medals, cups and statues acquired during Stein Ericksen's illustrious skiing career.

Of special interest are Stein's Olympic medals from the 1952 games in Norway—a gold in the giant slalom and a silver in the slalom—which made Ericksen a national hero who was still enthusiastically recognized when he was given the honor of carrying the Norwegian flag in the opening ceremonies of the 1994 Winter Olympics in Lillehammer, Norway. Marius Ericksen, Stein's father and a gymnastics medalist in the 1912 Olympics, taught his son to be a well-rounded athlete through skiing, swimming, running and gymnastics. When Hitler's Germany occupied Norway in 1940 and forbade the young Norwegians to ski, Stein and other teenage friends disobeyed the ban on skiing and retreated deep into the Norwegian woods to train and race. Perhaps it was the combination of gymnastics training and the outlawed skiing that produced a style of skiing that words such as "graceful, smooth, gliding, effortless, poetry in motion" all fail to adequately describe. In 2001 a life-size bronze statue by Utah sculptor Dennis Smith of Stein making one of his gliding turns was placed at the main entrance to Deer Valley.

Stein Ericksen Lodge skiers can ski from the lodge down the mountain and return whenever they are ready via the Viking chairlift. The lodge has two restaurants: the Birkebeiner Cafe and the Glitretind Restaurant (see the Where to Eat section), year-round outdoor pool, hot tub, sauna, exercise room and shuttle service to anywhere in the Park City/Deer Valley area. **7700 Stein Wy., Deer Valley, Park City, UT 84060; 1-800-453-1302; 435-649-3700; www.stein-lodge.com.**

Washington School Inn—$$$ to $$$$

This bed and breakfast, listed in the National Register of Historic Places, is located in the historic 1889 Washington School. Although it was one of Utah's first public schools, Washington School became outdated in the 1930s and was used for a time as a social hall. After remaining vacant for nearly 30 years, it was restored in the 1980s. Even though it contains all modern facilities—including a private bath in each suite—it still has the feel of an old-fashioned schoolhouse. It contains 15 individually decorated suites, each bearing the name of a former schoolteacher. A full complimentary breakfast is served in the formal dining room. Located one block from the Town lift and on a free shuttle route to the three ski areas. **543 Park Ave.; 1-800-824-1672; 435-649-3800; www.washingtonschoolinn.com.**

Where to Eat

You can pick up a free *Park City Menu Guide,* published in winter and summer, at the **Visitor Information Center** on Main St. It lists menus and prices for many of the eating establishments in the Park City/Deer Valley area.

THE CANYONS
The Cabin—$$$$

One of the newest Park City restaurants, the Cabin is located in the Grand Summit Resort Hotel at The Canyons. The menu varies depending on the season, market freshness and "the

chef's creativity." While the emphasis is on "eclectic cuisine of the American West," you will not find any beans and hardtack at this upscale resort restaurant. Rather, venison, halibut, beef, lamb and Utah trout are staples. Open daily. **4000 The Canyons Resort Dr.; 435-615-8060.**

DEER VALLEY
Bistro Toujours—$$$ to $$$$

One of Deer Valley's newest and most popular restaurants, Bistro Toujours opened in 2001 with the slogan "Where the Wasatch Mountains meet the French Alps." It's a fairly accurate slogan, as the decor and charm of a French restaurant are set at mid-mountain in Utah's premier ski resort. The nuances and variety of French cuisine also meet with Western American fare to offer entrées like molasses braised short ribs, boneless rack of pork, New York steak crusted with peppercorns, Opakapaka and Cassoulet Toulousain. Open daily 7:30 A.M.–10:30 A.M., 11:30 A.M.–2:30 P.M., and 5:30–10:30 P.M. Located in the Chateau Lodge at Silver Lake in Deer Valley. **7815 Royal St. E.; 435-940-2200.**

Glitretind—$$$$

The Glitretind describes itself as "a European Mountain Bistro." Lunch entrées include sandwiches, homemade quiche and soup. For dinner, favorites are grilled leg of lamb, Asian duck, baked salmon, grilled buffalo, venison and other wild game dishes. Located in the Stein Ericksen Lodge at Deer Valley. **435-645-6454.**

Goldener Hirsch Inn—$$$$

The Goldener Hirsch has a well-deserved reputation as one of Utah's finest restaurants, located in a near-perfect re-creation of a cheerful but intimate Austrian inn. Depending on the time of year, you will find menu items ranging from buffalo, venison, wild boar, kangaroo, Arctic musk ox, caribou, wild turkey, pheasant, duck, quail and ostrich. If wild game is not your preferred choice, there's pasta, fondue, seafood, rack of lamb, Black Angus tenderloin, salmon and, of course, Wiener schnitzel. For dessert there's the ever-popular apple strudel and chocolate fondue for two. Open for breakfast, lunch, and dinner daily in winter; Wed.–Sat. in summer. Closed mid-Oct.–Dec. and mid-Apr.–mid-June. Reservations recommended for dinner. **7570 Royale St. E.; 435-649-7770.**

HISTORIC MAIN ST.
Bangkok Thai on Main—$$ to $$$
Park City's first Thai restaurant, opened in 1993, is located in the basement of the Park Hotel near the bottom of Main St. and is a sister restaurant to one located in Salt Lake City (1400 Foothill Blvd.). The menu features a good selection of appetizers, soups, salads, entrées and desserts. Each dish can be prepared vegetarian. If you like curry, try the gang keow wan, a homemade, mildly spicy green curry with coconut milk, bamboo shoots and fresh Thai basil. Open year-round daily 5:30–10 P.M., also for lunch during the ski season. **605 Main St.; 435-649-8424.**

Burgies—$ to $$
Even in as gastronomically diverse a place as Park City, you can still suffer a "burger attack." Burgies is the place to go if a burger sounds like the ticket. With more than a dozen different kinds of burgers—garlic, Cajun, turkey, buffalo or lamb, for example—there are plenty of exotic choices. Burgies also offers chicken and veggie sandwiches, chili, soups and salads. The Olympic Onion Rings are a specialty that shouldn't be missed. Upstairs there is a large-screen television, pool and foosball tables, all helping to make Burgies a popular place for young people and families. Open daily 11 A.M.–10 P.M. **570 Main St.; 435-649-0011.**

Chimayo—$$$$
Park City's upscale Southwestern-style restaurant finds the inspiration for its food in a vast geographical area that stretches from southern Utah more than 1,000 miles into southern Mexico. The menu changes regularly and the emphasis is on the unique and unusual, such as buffalo meatloaf with cardamom, coriander and a juniper berry–infused demi glace; honey and chili roasted duck enchiladas; onion encrusted grilled salmon;

pecan and pumpkin seed encrusted trout; and caribou fajitas. Chimayo is located in the old Julius Frankel Clothing Store, which was constructed in 1907. In the 1920s James and Sarah Farrell operated a boardinghouse for miners in the building. Since then, the building has undergone several renovations. Open daily from 5:30 P.M. **368 Main St.; 435-649-6222.**

Cisero's Ristorante—$$$
Cisero's caters to locals, who, in turn, recommend it to inquiring visitors. Open for breakfast, lunch and dinner, it is an excellent choice for Italian food. The lunch menu features salads, sandwiches, pasta and vegetarian casserole. Another favorite is the cioppino, a seafood stew. The dinner menu offers seafood, veal and a great variety of pasta dishes. The historic building has seen a number of uses, including the McPolin Bottle Works and the Vienna Pool Room, which was operated by Mike Yellowvich until city officials closed it in 1920 because it was a hangout for members of the radical Industrial Workers of the World labor organization. Look for the magic card in the ceiling in the front dining room. Reservations are taken. Open daily 8–11 A.M., 11:30 A.M.–3 P.M., 5–10 P.M. **306 Main St.; 435-649-5044.**

The Eating Establishment—$$
The Eating Establishment is another Park City institution, with a casual, fun atmosphere, good sandwiches and burgers, and breakfast served all day. Check out the chalkboard specials if you want something a little more unusual. **317 Main St.; 435-649-8284.**

Grappa—$$$ to $$$$
Opened during summer 1994, Grappa is one of Park City's most popular upscale dinner restaurants. Owner/chef Bill White has taken the old Alpine Prospector Hotel and, with the work of local artisans and craftspeople, turned the old three-story hotel into something that resembles a Park City version of an Italian villa. The building is set into the hill at the top of Main St., above the hustle and bustle farther down the

street, and is surrounded by beautifully tiered gardens with ample seating for outside dining in the summer. Hand-painted ceramic tiles are used on the floors, windows and throughout the restaurant. The menu offers a variety of entrées, each one an adventure in itself. All the food is cooked over a wood-fired grill or in an oven using cherry, apple and oak wood. If you like pizza, the gourmet pizzas are the best you'll find anywhere. Other favorites include cedar-planked sea bass, seasoned with chopped shallots and garlic bread crumbs, then baked in the wood-fired oven on a cedar plank to give it a delicious, slightly smoked flavor. Open daily 5:30–10 P.M. Reservations recommended. **151 Main St.; 435-645-0636.**

Main St. Deli—$

Along with Burgies, the most inexpensive eating establishment on Main St. and a longtime local favorite, the Main St. Deli features omelettes, sourdough bread French toast and whole wheat and honey pancakes for breakfast. Sandwiches, burgers, hot dogs, salads and soups are the main fare for lunch or a light early dinner. Open daily 7:30 A.M.–7:30 P.M. **525 Main St.; 435-649-1110.**

Mercato Mediterraneo di Nonna Maria—$$$ to $$$$

Opened in 1995 and located just off Main St. across from the Kimball Arts Center, the Mercato Mediterraneo is another of Park City's most popular eating places. Eric Debonis, the owner and principal chef, has broadened the culinary map that most Americans associate with Italy to include dishes from most countries whose shores are washed by the waters of the Mediterranean, including Spain, France, Greece, Turkey, Lebanon, Egypt and Morocco. Eric visits the Mediterranean region each year in search of new recipes. A different country is featured on the menu each month. Downstairs, the deli/bazaar offers pizza, salads, soups, specialty breads, espresso and inexpensive samples of some items that are available for lunch or dinner upstairs and, during the summer, on the patio. Eric also

offers regularly scheduled cooking classes, where he passes on his secrets to longtime residents and short-time visitors alike. Reservations are recommended for dinner. Open daily 5–10 P.M., Fri.–Sun. 11:30 A.M.–3 P.M. **628 Park Ave.; 435-647-0030.**

Mileti's—$$$

This is Park City's oldest and favorite place for Italian food. Opened in 1973, the restaurant offers pasta as well as a selection of main courses that includes Italian sausage, chicken, beef, lamb, veal and seafood, with grilled items cooked over Texas mesquite. A favorite is the fettuccine Mileti: fettuccine tossed in heavy cream and three cheeses, plus fresh tomatoes, mushrooms and olives, and a choice of chicken or shrimp. Open nightly for dinner. Reservations are recommended. **412 Main St.; 435-649-8211.**

Riverhorse Cafe—$$$ to $$$$

Housed in the upper floor of one of Park City's most historic buildings, the 1908 wood-framed Masonic Hall, you can dine in the historic hall, the more intimate atrium where live music is performed or, in summer, on the porch overlooking Main St. The menu, which includes pasta, Utah lamb, chicken, steak, salmon, halibut and the Riverhorse vegetable plate, varies during the year. Open daily 5:30–10 P.M. **540 Main St.; 435-649-3536.**

Texas Red's—$$

This is not the place for a quiet, intimate dinner, but it is a fun location for a family or group of friends. "Pit barbecue" and "chili parlor" say it all as far as the menu is concerned, with barbecue dinners of beef, pork, chicken, turkey, ribs and sausage. You can also get chicken-fried steak, T-bone steak or catfish. For homesick Texans, this is about as close to the stereotypical Texas as you can get in Utah. The good food and a chance to rub elbows with a room full of people enjoying themselves make this one of the liveliest spots on Main St. Open daily 11:30 A.M.–10 P.M. **440 Main St.; 435-649-REDS.**

Wahso—$$$ to $$$$

This Asian grill takes its inspiration from several Asian countries to produce dishes like teriyaki salmon, sake steamed mahi mahi, red curry and mint braised lamb shank, jasmine tea leaf smoked duck and soy and ginger glazed sea bass. The interior of Wahso is as interesting and inviting as the food. Open daily from 5:30 P.M. **577 Main St.; 435-615-0300.**

Wasatch Brew Pub—$$

This pub is a delightful place to have lunch or dinner. Seating is available on the patio or indoors. If your interest is a cold mug of beer or ale, the bar is the place to try the varieties of beer made on the premises. The Wasatch Ale, a dark amber ale, was voted one of America's 10 tastiest brews at the Great American Beer Festival. The south windows offer a spectacular view of the surrounding hills, which are especially beautiful in the fall. The lunch menu includes the Milwaukee brat with sauerkraut—it's consistently good. The dinner menu is available after 5 P.M. Open daily from 11 A.M. Located at the top of the hill on Main St. **250 Main St.; 435-649-0900.**

PARK CITY MOUNTAIN RESORT
Baja Cantina—$$ to $$$

A Park City fixture since 1983, the Baja Cantina consistently wins the praise of locals as the best Mexican restaurant in Park City, and there are plenty of supporters who label it the best Mexican restaurant in Utah. There is outside seating during the summer, and the interior offers an unusually effective seating arrangement that combines an intimate dining experience and a communal feeling with other diners. The interior has an eclectic but very interesting collection of artifacts, including an exquisite wooden fireplace, a bull's head with a sombrero and shelves loaded with baskets, snowshoes, old skis, miners' hats and other memorabilia of Park City's early mining and skiing history.

The menu includes a good variety of appetizers, dinner items and even a children's menu. Burritos are a specialty, with the Claimjumper—

pork chili verde and assorted other delicacies rolled in a flour tortilla—the most popular. The Burrito del Mar is a wonderful assortment of black tiger prawns, snow crab and fresh fish. The Carne Asada a la Paz, a tasty New York steak marinated in lime juice and spices served with a cheese enchilada, is worth every penny. Vegetarians will find several burritos, the Baja taco salad and the veggie tostadas to their liking. Drinks are available in a tiny bar in the restaurant. Despite its popularity, the restaurant maintains a strong egalitarian touch, as is apparent in the sign as you enter the restaurant: "If you have reservations, you are in the wrong place." Open daily 11 A.M.–11 P.M. Located at the Park City Mountain Resort Center. **435-649-BAJA (2252).**

Services

Visitor Information

Park City Chamber of Commerce/Convention and Visitors Bureau—Open Mon.–Fri. 8 A.M.–5 P.M. **1910 Prospector Ave., P.O. Box 1630, Park City, UT 84060; 1-800-453-1360; 435-649-6100; parkcityinfo.com.**

Park City Visitor Information Center—Open Mon.–Sat. 10 A.M.–7 P.M.; Sun. noon–6 P.M. **528 Main St.; 435-649-6104.**

Heber Valley

There are more western valleys than you would care to count that claim to be the "Switzerland of America." But if the votes of the Swiss immigrants who settled in Heber Valley in the 1860s count for anything, Heber Valley would win hands down. Swiss families like Probst, Huber, Kohler, Zenger and Abegglen found the towering Wasatch Mountains to the west, the rolling Uinta Mountains to the east and the lush meadows of the valleys to be both a reminder of their homeland and a good place for their dairy and cattle herds. The Provo River flows through the valley, and the deep snows in the mountains and springs in the valley have provided abundant water for residents.

Heber City lies near the center of the valley. Near the western slope of the Wasatch Mountains 3 miles to the west is the town of Midway. The Provo River flows south/southwest between the two towns, with its waters impounded by Deer Creek Reservoir at the southwest end of the valley where the river begins its descent of Provo Canyon to Utah Lake. At the southeast end of Heber Valley is Daniels Canyon, through which Hwy. 40 passes to the Strawberry Valley at the top of the canyon. Here you will find Strawberry Reservoir. Back at the north end of Heber Valley is Jordanelle Reservoir and, in the foothills of the Uinta Mountains, the town of Kamas to the east.

Heber Valley is a popular recreation area with residents along the Wasatch Front. Wasatch Mountain State Park and the Homestead Resort in Midway are especially busy in the summer, but winter activities—primarily cross-country skiing—are drawing more and more winter visitors, especially following the 2002 Winter Olympics, in which the cross-country venue at Soldier Hollow, just south of Midway, captured worldwide attention. The Jordanelle Reservoir, located in the north end of the valley on the Provo River and completed in 1995, draws thousands of anglers and boaters, as has the Deer Valley Reservoir farther downstream in the south end of the valley since it was completed in 1940.

History

Heber Valley was originally called Provo Valley when it was settled in 1858; however, to avoid confusion with the city of Provo on the western side of the mountains and to honor Mormon leader Heber C. Kimball, who was instrumental in converting many of the original English settlers of the valley to the Mormon faith, the name of the town and valley were changed in 1861 to Heber

City and Heber Valley. Settlement of the valley was delayed until a 28-mile road could be constructed through the mountains from Utah Valley.

The first English and American-born Mormons who settled the valley during the 1860s and 1870s were followed by Mormon converts from Switzerland. These early Swiss settlers wrote back to family and friends of the virtues of Mormonism and the beauty of Heber Valley and, as the original converts or their sons returned to Switzerland as missionaries, a small but steady stream of Swiss immigrants made their way to Midway in Heber Valley. The Swiss heritage has been preserved in a number of ways, including the popular Swiss Days held in early September.

Heber City was incorporated as a town in 1889, the same year that the impressive red sandstone tabernacle was completed. A decade later, in 1899, the Rio Grande Western Railroad completed a branch line to Heber City, and the town became a shipping center for agricultural products, especially sheep. A remnant of the railroad has been preserved as Utah's only operating historic railroad: the Heber Valley Historic Railroad. Today Heber Valley has a population of nearly 16,000, contained mostly in Heber City and Midway.

Major Attractions

The Homestead Resort

There is no other place like it in Utah—and probably anywhere, for that matter. The Homestead is many things to many people. It's a 19th-century resort comfortable with the 21st century. It is golf, fine food, a place where guests and the public can share in all the activities. If

---

Getting There
Heber Valley is 50 miles southeast of Salt Lake City, 30 miles northeast of Provo and 20 miles south of Park City.

you want to experience the perfect day that most can only dream about in worlds to come, from the Homestead you can travel to the nearby ski slopes of Park City or Deer Valley, one of the most beautiful sections of Heber Valley, to spend the morning before returning for an afternoon of golf on the challenging 18-hole Homestead Course, followed by a couple of hours scuba diving in the 65-foot-deep thermally heated 90° F-plus waters of Homestead Crater. You would want to start such a day with a hearty breakfast at Fanny's Grill, snatch some lunch at one of the places listed in the Where to Eat section and dine in Simon's Restaurant in the center of the Homestead. Don't worry about sleep. As soon as your head hits the pillow in one of the 150 units located in the 18 buildings at the Homestead, you will be asleep. Guaranteed!

If you don't believe it, just ask any of the more than 300 Olympic athletes from 35 countries who called the Homestead home during the 2002 Winter Olympics. Located only 3 miles from the cross-country skiing venue at Soldier Hollow, the Homestead became a second Olympic village during February 2002.

Simon and Maria Schneitter were converts to the Mormon church in Switzerland and in 1863 came to Utah with John Huber and a group of 60 Swiss converts. They settled in Midway, where Simon, a watchmaker by trade, established a farm on the site of what is now the Homestead Resort. The bathing and therapeutic potential of the huge hot springs on their farm was not lost on the Schneitters, especially when miners from nearby Park City found great relief soaking in the hot springs. Construction on the hotel, known later as the Virginia House, began in 1886, but it was not fully operational until 1891. Horse racing, music and dancing were also popular activities at the resort. Simon died in 1893 at the age of 72, two years after the Virginia House was completed. Maria died seven years later in 1900, also at the age of 72.

Several individuals leased the resort until 1907, when Simon Jr. returned to Midway after a 16-year absence while he chased mining opportunities in Eureka, Utah and Ouray, Colorado.

Simon Jr. and his wife, Fannie, operated the resort until their deaths in 1935 and 1950, respectively. In the early 1950s the resort was acquired by Ferrin W. Whitaker, who changed the name of the resort to "The Homestead," and named the old hotel building the "Virginia House."

The Homestead Crater, or Schneitter's Hot Pot as it was first called, is an interesting geologic phenomenon. The crater, which is 55 feet high with a 400-foot diameter, developed as mineral-rich water overflowed, creating the sloping mound of travertine. Scientists theorize that the source of water, which feeds the crater at about 90 gallons per minute, is from rain and snow high in the Wasatch Mountains that percolates into the ground and through cracks and fractures to a depth of perhaps 2 miles, where it is infused with large amounts of carbon dioxide gas. This allows the water to dissolve substantial amounts of limestone as it returns to the surface, producing the light, lavalike rock called pot rock. Inside the crater, the water reaches a depth of 65 feet and there are between 8 to 14 feet of silt at the bottom. The water temperature is approximately 96° F year-round. In the 1990s a 110-foot-long tunnel was blasted from the north side of the crater to the interior, providing access for swimming, snorkeling and scuba diving in the bluest, clearest, cleanest water to be found anywhere.

The Homestead Golf Course, designed by Bruce Summerhayes and opened in 1990, has cashed in on the popularity of its older neighbor and its association with the historic Homestead Resort. The front 9 are played uphill, west of the resort, while the back 9 open out onto the flatter terrain of the course—obviously a good decision for those who choose to walk.

In addition to the golf and snorkeling, there are plenty of other activities and facilities at the Homestead, including indoor and outdoor swimming pools, tennis courts, horseback riding, buggy rides, bike rentals, lawn games and an activities room. During the winter, snowmobiling, cross-country skiing, snowshoeing and horse-drawn sled rides make the Homestead a special winter wonderland. For those who want to be pampered and rejuvenated in body and mind, the day spa offers a variety of massages, wraps and other treatments.

Part of the fun of being at the Homestead is the grounds. Benches and gazebos are scattered throughout the expanse of lawns and trees. There are goldfish in the ponds near the main building, while ducks, geese, swans and even owls have taken up residence on the grounds. You will want to climb the 78 steps to the top of the crater for a 360-degree view of the Heber Valley and Wasatch Mountains. Pay a visit to the gift shop and stock up on one or more varieties of the cream fudge produced on-site. If you feel guilty, you should be in good company, as the little shop produces and sells more than six tons of fudge each year.

There are plenty of choices for accommodations in the 18 units at the resort. If you want the original 19th-century experience (with the essential modern conveniences!), ask for one of the eight rooms in the Virginia House, the original inn built in 1886. The Bunk House is designed for family reunions: parents can stay in a private room connected to a children's room with bunk beds that, in turn, is connected to an adjoining children's room. The honeymoon suite, located in the Summer House, is ideal for newlyweds and the not so newly wed who want to relive those first magical days of being together. Other personal favorites are the Milk House, the Guest House, and Mountainview, Lakeview and Fairway Cottages. For information on the restaurants at the resort, see the Where to Eat section.

From Hwy. 40 at the intersection just south of the Jordanelle Dam, turn off the highway and follow the signs. From Heber City, head west out of town on 100 S. St., which takes you to Midway, where the way to the Homestead is well marked. **1-800-327-7220; 435-654-1102; www.homesteadresort.com.**

Wasatch Mountain State Park

In 1961 the State of Utah acquired the 22,000 acres that make up Wasatch Mountain State Park. Located on the eastern slope of the Wasatch Mountains 35 miles southeast of Salt Lake City, the park offers year-round recreation. Golfing, picnicking, camping, fishing, horseback riding and sight-seeing are the principal summer activities, while snowmobiling and cross-country skiing are popular during the winter. Soldier Hollow, the venue for the 2002 Winter Olympic Games' cross-country skiing and biathlon competition, is included within the park. While Soldier Hollow will continue to host cross-country skiers during the winter, a new 36-hole golf course is being developed.

Just east of Soldier Hollow is the historic Tate barn. Built at the end of the 19th century, it was used as a dairy barn for decades; plans are underway to restore the barn as a symbol of Heber Valley's farming heritage. Another important historic site is the Huber Farmhouse and Creamery. John Huber was born in Dodtnacht, Switzerland, in 1840 and became a Mormon in 1861, immigrating to Utah in 1863 with 60 other Swiss converts. He married Mary Magdalena Munz, a member of the Swiss immigrant group, shortly after their arrival in Utah. He returned to Switzerland to direct the Mormon church missionary work in Switzerland and German from 1872 to 1874. The wood-frame farmhouse was built in the 1870s after Huber returned from the church mission to his native Switzerland. It was home to John until his death in 1914 and his wife, Mary's, in 1935. Afterward their son lived in the house until 1960. The stone one-and-a-half story creamery was built after the farmhouse. With its steep gable roof and first floor built into the side of a hill, the creamery is, according to architectural historian Roger Roper, the most authentic Swiss building in Heber Valley.

The Huber Farmstead along Snake Creek is on land now occupied by the golf course, about a quarter mile west of the visitor center. The 3-mile Visitors Center Trail hike begins across the road from the visitor center and is popular with day visitors to the park. Another popular hiking trail, the 1.3-mile-long Pine Creek Nature Trail, begins at the northwest corner of the Oak Hollow Campground loop in the Pine Creek Campground. This pleasant walking path has informational signs, and at the northern end of the loop is a glacial wash where great boulders were deposited centuries ago. The Pine Creek Campground has 122 camping sites and is located close to the 27-hole golf course. (See Golf in the Outdoor Activities section). To reach the Wasatch Mountain State Park Visitor Center, follow 200 N. west to Homestead Dr. and then turn north until the road turns to the northwest to start up Snake Creek Canyon. Watch for the visitor center on the right. **435-654-1791; parks.state.ut.us/parks/www1/wasa.htm.**

Festivals and Events

Swiss Days
first Fri. and Sat. in Sept. The Midway Swiss Days is known throughout Utah as one of the state's oldest ethnic festivals. It draws more than 200 craftspeople and artists from all over. The festival includes a parade, musical programs, carnival games for children, a 10-kilometer run and plenty of food. Swiss Days is truly a community event, with Midway residents gathering in midsummer to chop cabbage for the more than 300 gallons of sauerkraut that are served during the two days. Located in the city park in the center of Midway. **435-654-3666.**

Cowboy Poetry Gathering
Early Nov. What does any self-respecting 21st-century cowboy or cowgirl do once the fall roundup is over and before the long winter sets in? In Heber Valley the answer is to attend the Cowboy Poetry Gathering that begins in Midway on a Wed. evening with a Dutch-oven dinner followed by cowboy poetry and music. Thurs. evening a unique cowboy poetry ride on the Heber Valley Railroad gives a special dimension to the gathering and the reciting of this fun and often moving art form. The weekend events move to Wasatch High School in Heber City and include more readings, concerts, a dance and a nondenominational Western gospel service on Sun. **435-654-2353; www.cowboypoetryutah.com.**

Outdoor Activities

Biking
Heber to Midway Trail
A 1.5-mile-long asphalt bike, in-line-skating, jogging and walking path with a wood-covered bridge across the Provo River connects Heber City and Midway. The path begins on about 800 W. and 100 S. on the south side of the park in Heber City and terminates at about 800 W. in Midway.

Fishing
Deer Creek Reservoir
Few Utah communities have an excellent fishing spot in their backyard, but residents of Heber Valley do. Deer Creek Reservoir, constructed between 1938 and 1940 as part of a federal works project, is located on the Provo River, 8 miles southwest of Heber City, on Hwy. 189. The reservoir is about 7 miles long and is a popular spot for boating, windsurfing and year-round fishing.

Jordanelle Reservoir
Completed in 1992, the Jordanelle Dam is located on the Provo River, about 5 miles north of Heber City. One of the interesting places inundated by the reservoir is the town of Keetley. In the aftermath of the Japanese attack on Pearl Harbor, Fred Isama Wada, a prosperous Japanese-American produce dealer in Oakland, California, came to Utah, where he arranged to lease farmland at Keetley for his family and several others from the Oakland area. Wada left California for Utah just four days before the mandatory relocation of West Coast Japanese-Americans was proclaimed. The group remained in Utah until after the war, when most returned to California. Jordanelle Reservoir has become a popular fishing spot with rainbow, brown and cutthroat trout attracting anglers from the Heber, Utah and Salt Lake Valleys. There are two major recreation areas along the lake—**Hailstone** and **Rock Cliff.** Hailstone is the primary

area and is the only location from which boats can be launched. Because of the heavy recreational use on the lake, state park officials have limited the number of watercraft during peak times. There is camping at both locations (see the Where to Stay section). Jordanelle Reservoir is located just east of Hwy. 40 about 7 miles north of Heber City. **1-800-322-3770; 435-649-9540.**

Provo River

The Provo River, along US Hwy. 189 above the Jordanelle Reservoir and below Deer Creek Reservoir, is one of the most popular fly-fishing streams in Utah. There's rainbow, cutthroat and brown trout, and Rocky Mountain whitefish.

Strawberry Reservoir

The original Strawberry Reservoir was constructed in the 1880s by farmers in Heber Valley to secure water from the Upper Strawberry Valley that otherwise would flow in the opposite direction. The reservoir has been enlarged over the years but remains a key element of the Central Utah Project, a massive undertaking by the federal, state and local governments to reclaim and manage the scarce water resources in the state. The reservoir is one of Utah's most popular fishing spots, with Bear River cutthroat trout, kokanee salmon and sterile rainbow trout. The Strawberry Bay Marina offers a store, cafe, boat rentals and fishing supplies. Located off US Hwy. 40, 30 miles southeast of Heber City. **435-548-2500**

Golf

Homestead Golf Course

See The Homestead Resort in the Major Attractions section.

Wasatch Mountain Golf Course

If you were to ask well-traveled Utah golfers to list their half-dozen favorite golf courses, it is a safe bet that Wasatch Mountain Golf Course would be on nearly everyone's list. The 27-hole course is located on the east slope of the Wasatch Mountains, just down off the ridge from the Brighton Ski Resort. The 27 holes are divided into three 9-hole courses—the Lake and Canyon 9s, which were built in 1967, and the Mountain 9, which was completed in 1973. The course designers have made good use of lakes, the mountain and native trees to provide a course that is a real pleasure to play. In addition, while the course is not flat and easy, the spacious greens and large tee areas do offer some advantages to the regular hacker.

Located at an elevation of 5,775 feet, the summer mountain air is much more pleasant than at the Salt Lake and Utah Valley courses, not to mention southern Utah's courses. My favorite time, however, is early fall, just as the leaves are turning. It is simply a golfer's heaven. The course is near Midway. Take US Hwy. 40 south from Interstate 15 and after you pass Jordanelle Reservoir and come down the mountain, watch for the sign to Wasatch Mountain State Park and take the road off Hwy. 40. From Heber City, drive west from the center of town to Midway and follow the road as it winds through Midway to the park, located northwest of Midway. **435-654-0532.**

Hiking

As you head out of the Heber Valley traveling east on US Hwy. 40, you enter **Daniels Canyon,** where there are several nice hiking trails in the Uintah National Forest that are accessible right off the highway. The following are some favorites. See also Wasatch Mountain State Park in the Major Attractions section.

Center Canyon Trail

The 4-mile-long, relatively steep hike up Center Canyon follows along a small stream for most of the way and then climbs onto a ridge for a grand view of the surrounding mountains, including 10,554-foot Currant Creek Peak to the southeast. The trailhead is located 2.5 miles up Forest Road 128 from Hwy. 40.

Clegg Canyon Trail

This 6-mile long trail follows a northeasterly route through a canyon, stands of pine and aspen trees, and mountain meadows. The trail ends at Forest Road 094. You can make a loop hike of the Dry and Clegg Canyon Trails by using Forest Road 094 to connect the two trails and walking the mile along Hwy. 40 back to your vehicle. Both trails offer a wonderful view of the 10,091-foot Bald Knoll. Located off Hwy. 40, in Daniels Canyon, 10 miles from Heber City.

Whiskey Springs Nature Trail

At only 500 feet in length, this does not really qualify as a hiking trail, but the paved and gravel trail with interpretive plant signs along the way offers a nice place to stretch your legs at the Whiskey Springs Picnic Area. Whiskey Springs was so named because this was a good place for early outbound travelers to take their first drink of whiskey after leaving Heber City or for inbound travelers to have their last drink before entering Heber Valley. Located about 8 miles south of Heber City on Hwy. 40 near the mouth of Daniels Canyon.

Seeing and Doing

Historic Sites

Heber Valley Historic Railroad

This railroad, the only operating historic railroad in the state, is a popular attraction in Heber Valley, with more than 60,000 passengers each year. It began operation as Utah Eastern Railway in 1899 and ran from the Rio Grande Western's main line in Provo up Provo Canyon to Heber City. Because of the steep 2 percent grade up the canyon, the trains moved slowly, earning the nickname "the Heber Creeper" from early passengers. Trains stopped running in 1967. The railroad was reestablished in 1993 under the auspices of the Heber Valley Historic Railroad Authority, a nonprofit, state-created organization. The train features two vintage 1907 Baldwin steam locomotives and three vintage diesel electric locomotives.

You can travel from the station in Heber City around the west side of Deer Creek Reservoir and down Provo Canyon to Vivian Park, 32 miles

round trip. The ride takes 3.5 hours, including a half-hour stop at Vivian Park. The railroad runs Mother's Day–end of Oct. and usually makes three trips a day: 10 A.M., 11:30 A.M. and 1:30 P.M. Special runs are made during the winter; during the 2002 Winter Olympics, the train was used to haul passengers from Heber City to the cross-country ski venue at Soldier Hollow. The railroad has been used in numerous movies and TV programs, including *Touched by an Angel.* **Heber Valley Historic Railroad Authority, 450 S. 600 W., P.O. Box 641, Heber City, UT 84032; 1-800-982-3257; 435-654-5601; www.hebervalleyrr.org.**

Midway Historic Homes

One of the most photographed historic homes in Utah is the John Watkins home. Watkins, an architect and builder from England, built the house in 1868. The Gothic Revival–style house has three gables on the front and plenty of wood gingerbread trim. Watkins built several other houses in Midway, which, though not as elaborate as his own home, are easily identifiable. Although none of the homes is open on a regular basis, owners are used to visitors stopping in front to take pictures. Located on the northeast corner of Center and Main Sts.

Wasatch Stake Tabernacle

One of Utah's most beautiful churches, the Wasatch Stake Tabernacle was constructed in 1889 from red sandstone. The tabernacle served as the center of Mormon religious activity in the Heber Valley for many years, until local church authorities decided it was time to build a more up-to-date building. Along with the decision to build a new building, it was decided to demolish the old tabernacle. This led to one of Utah's first historic preservation battles in the early 1960s. Under the leadership of Ruth Witt, wife of Heber City's sheriff, a group of local women and other heritage-conscious individuals successfully challenged the local church leader and won preservation of the building, which was acquired by the local historical society. The building was used as a summer theater and other activities until the late 1980s, when the interior of the building was renovated and converted into Heber City's town hall.

While visiting the tabernacle, take a look at the building in back. The Amusement Hall was built around the turn of the century and originally had a steel-spring dance floor, which old-timers claim was a joy to dance on. The Amusement Hall has been converted into a senior citizen center.

The tabernacle is one of the few remaining 19th-century Mormon tabernacles and stands as a tribute to three generations of Heber Valley residents: the one that built it, the one that preserved it from demolition and the one with the vision to adapt a state treasure to modern needs. Inside the building is a small museum with pioneer artifacts. Located on Main St. on the southwest corner of 100 N.

Scenic Drives

Cascade Springs Backway

This 25-mile-long, well-graded dirt road begins south of Midway, where it leaves Hwy. 113 and heads west, climbing the mountain as it makes its way to Cascade Springs—actually a series of springs that have formed limestone terraces over which 7 million gallons of mountain water cascade each day. Barrier-free walkways provide easy access to the falls; interpretive information along the way describes how springs are formed and rivers are born high in the mountains. One visitor has described the springs as like a Japanese garden with a variety of trees, shrubs, flowers, ferns, vines, pools, bubbling springs and miniature waterfalls. Rainbow trout can be seen in the pools from the boardwalks and bridges. Songbirds, frogs, toads, squirrels and chipmunks are another highlight of a visit here.

Mirror Lake Scenic Byway / US Hwy. 150

With an elevation of 10,687 feet at Bald Mountain Pass near Mirror Lake, Hwy. 150 is the highest of all the state's scenic byways. The highway begins in Kamas, 15 miles northeast of Heber City on US Hwy. 189 at the western edge of the

Uinta Mountains, and follows the Provo River up to its headwaters in the high Uintas. About 24 miles from Kamas are the Upper Provo River Falls. Walkways near the road provide easy access to view the terraced cascades. The distance from Kamas to the Utah-Wyoming border is 56 miles. Travelers can retrace their route or continue on to Evanston, Wyoming, and Interstate 80, which is 23 miles north of the state line. As one of the most popular recreation routes in Utah, the highway provides access to numerous lakes, campgrounds and picnic areas.

Where to Stay

Accommodations

DANIELS CANYON AND STRAWBERRY RESERVOIR

Daniels Summit Lodge—$$$

Eight rooms. Gift shop and restaurant. An excellent location for fishing, hiking, mountain biking and snowmobiling. Located on Hwy. 40, 16 miles southeast of Heber City at the summit of Daniels Canyon as you enter the Strawberry Valley. 1-800-519-9969; 435-548-2230; www.danielssummit.com.

Strawberry Bay Marina and Lodge—$$ to $$$

Twenty-one rooms. Located at Strawberry Reservoir off Hwy. 40. 435-548-2500.

HEBER CITY

If you want inexpensive accommodations in comparison to Midway and Park City, consider one of the following motels in Heber City.

Bear Mountain Chalet Motel—$$

Pool; 22 rooms. 425 S. Main; 435-654-2150.

National 9 High Country Inn—$$

Indoor spa, nonsmoking rooms available; 38 rooms, pool. 1000 S. Main; 1-800-345-9198; 435-654-0201.

Swiss Alps Inn—$$

Heated pool, indoor hot tub and sauna; 14 rooms. **167 S. Main; 435-654-0722.**

Viking Motor Inn—$$

Year-round pool, Jacuzzi spa and sauna, non-smoking rooms available; 34 rooms. **989 S. Main; 1-800-343-2675; 435-654-2202.**

MIDWAY

Blue Boar Inn—$$$$

Located just across the road from the Wasatch Mountain State Park Visitor Center, the Blue Boar Inn is housed in an impressive modern facility that looks like it was plucked right out of Switzerland. All of the 14 rooms, each one named for a prominent author, are uniquely furnished with hand-carved European reproduction furniture, the finest linen and European feather beds with eiderdown comforters. The bright and cheerful dining area has hand-painted wall scenes and designs and sturdy, light wood furniture. Each room is comfortably spacious with a fireplace and jetted tub or therapeutic/aromatic steam shower. All rooms have beautiful views of the nearby mountains to the west or the Heber Valley, which stretches out to the east. There is a common second-story balcony that stretches across the front of the inn. A European-style breakfast is served in the dining room, which is open to the public for lunch and dinner (see the Where to Eat section). **1235 Warm Springs Rd., P.O. Box 1299, Midway, UT 84049; 1-888-650-1400; 435-654-1400; www.the-blueboarinn.com.**

The Homestead Resort

See Major Attractions.

Inn on the Creek—$$$ to $$$$

This charming inn, designed by local architect George Olsen, is located on a rise above the Homestead golf course and a small meandering stream. The structure will make you wonder if you have not just driven up to a rural Swiss château. The inn has eight oversized suites, each with its own fireplace, Jacuzzi and patio deck with spectacular views of the Heber Valley and nearby Wasatch Mountains. There is also an outdoor swimming pool and hot tub. Breakfast is served in the beautiful dining room. In addition to the main bed and breakfast, there are also available one- and two-bedroom chalets with kitchen facilities. **375 Rainbow Ln.; 435-654-0892; www.innoncreek.com.**

Johnson Mill Bed and Breakfast—$$$

Bob and Charlene Johnson are transplants from Los Angeles who renovated this five-story, 8,000-square-foot mill built in the late 1880s as a bed and breakfast inn. The mill was operated by a 40-foot waterfall that still cascades past the mill. The inn is located on 35 acres of natural woodland with a 3.5-acre spring-fed pond and nearly a mile of frontage on the Provo River, providing anglers with a handy and beautiful location to cast a fly. There are five rooms, each with a fireplace and private bath including a jetted tub. A full breakfast is served. **100 Johnson Mill Rd., Midway, UT 84049; 1-888-772-0030; 435-654-4466; www.johnsonmill.com.**

The Kastle Inn—$$$

Appropriately named, the Kastle Inn sits like a European castle with its two towers, on a hill in Midway. Under the care of innkeepers Steve and Jan Clegg, this is a new bed and breakfast with five rooms, all nonsmoking and each with a private bath. There is easy access to Midway's fine golf courses in the summer and fall, and the Park City ski resorts are only 15 minutes away. **1220 Interlaken Ln., P.O. Box 335, Midway, UT 84049; 1-800-561-2291; 435-654-2689; www.kastleinn.com.**

Camping

PRIVATE

Heber Valley RV Park

One hundred sites, 34 with full hookups; tentsites also available. Convenience store, laundry, rest rooms and showers. Weekly and monthly rates can be arranged. Open year-round. Located 6 miles north of Heber City. **7000 N. Hwy. 40; 435-654-4049.**

High Country RV Park

Thirty-six sites with full hookups; laundry and showers, heated pool, indoor spa and adjacent restaurant. Open year-round. **1000 S. Main, Heber City; 1-800-345-9198; 435-654-0201.**

PUBLIC

Hwy. 150 winds from Kamas, 15 miles northeast of Heber City, through the western flank of the Uinta Mountains to the Utah-Wyoming border and on to Evanston. The distance from Kamas to the state line is 56 miles, and, beginning with the Yellow Pine Campground 6.8 miles east of Kamas, and stretching for 50 miles to the State-line Reservoir Campground, there are 33 campgrounds with nearly 700 trailer sites and tentsites located in the Wasatch National Forest. For a list of these campgrounds, see the current issue of *Utah Travel Guide,* published annually by the **Utah Travel Council, 435-538-1030,** and available at most tourist information centers.

Deer Creek State Park

The Deer Creek Campground has 31 RV trailer sites and 10 tentsites, flush toilets, showers, drinking water and wheelchair access. Open Apr.–Nov. Fee charged. Located 7 miles southwest of Heber City on Hwy. 189.

Jordanelle State Park

The Hailstone area has nearly 200 sites in three campgrounds, plus a visitor center, laundry, modern rest rooms and showers. **Keetley Point campground** has 41 tentsites in a scrub-oak draw northwest of the park entrance road. Each of the sites has an earthen tent pad, 8-foot aluminum table, grill and fire pit. Five sites are available to disabled campers. **Henry McHenry campground** has 42 sites similar to those at Keetley Point, but are accessible to recreational vehicles that can get by with no utilities. There are 103 campsites at the RV campground—all with electric and water hookups accessible by a pull-through drive or from a single spur off the campground road. At **Rock Cliff** there are 50 sites in three walk-in campgrounds, with rest rooms and hot showers. Located off Hwy. 40 about 7 miles north of

Heber City. **1-800-322-3770 reservations; 435-649-9540 information.**

Lodgepole Campground

Offers 51 RV trailer sites and tentsites. Equipped with drinking water, toilets and wheelchair-accessible facilities. Open May–Oct. Located in Daniel's Canyon, 16 miles southeast of Heber City off US Hwy. 40.

Soldier Creek Campground

The campground is large, with 166 RV and tentsites. Open late May–late Oct. Fee charged. Located 34 miles southeast of Heber City on US Hwy. 40.

Strawberry Reservoir

One of Utah's most popular fishing spots, Strawberry Reservoir also boasts one of its largest public campgrounds, with 551 RV trailer and tentsites. If you come to fish, you won't mind the size and open setting, but it is probably not the best choice for a getaway. Open late May–late Oct. Fee charged. Located off Hwy. 40, 26 miles southeast of Heber City.

Wasatch Mountain State Park

There are 130 RV sites and tentsites in this state park. Rest rooms and showers are available, plus a children's fishing area and easy access to some of the finest golfing in Utah. Open year-round. Fee charged. Located just north of Midway. **1-800-328-2267; 435-654-1791.**

Where to Eat

HEBER CITY

The Claim Jumper—$$ to $$$

As the most popular eating establishment during the Cowboy Poetry Festival, the Claim Jumper is your traditional western steakhouse. The trademark is the "baseball steak," a nearly round piece of meat that is closer to a softball in size than a baseball. If you want something from the Old West, the buffalo steak is a good choice. There's also Utah trout, salmon, ribs, chicken and other choices. The light-wood-log interior is highlighted with mounted buffalo, elk, deer and longhorn heads, as well as saddles, chaps, cowboy hats and other cowboy artifacts. Open daily 5–10 P.M. **1267 S. Main; 435-654-4661.**

Granny's Drive Inn—$

Voted best milk shakes in Utah, Granny's is located on the east side of Main St. in a turn-of-the-century house covered with red siding. There are more than 60 different flavors of shakes, with the berry shakes the most popular among locals. Other items include a regular fare of hamburgers, sandwiches and soups in the winter. Open Mon.–Sat. 11 A.M.–10 P.M. **511 S. Main; 435-654-3097.**

Snake Creek Grill—$$ to $$$

Housed in a reconstructed western village, the Snake Creek Grill is the enterprise of Barb Hill, who supervised the kitchens of several prestigious Park City restaurants before venturing out on her own. Barb and her husband, Michael, have hit upon a winning combination with fine cuisine at a moderate price. Favorites include the "Belle Isle" Baby Back Ribs with Mopping Sauce and Slaw, the Ten Spice Salmon with Japanese Noodle Stir Fry, and the Zucchini-Tomato Risotto with spiced grilled shrimp or portobello mushrooms. Not to be missed for dessert lovers is the Black Bottom Banana Cream Pie. Open Wed.–Sat. 5:30–9:30 P.M., Sun. 5:30–8:30 P.M. Reservations a must, especially on weekends. **650 W. 100 S.; 435-654-2133.**

MIDWAY

Blue Boar Inn Restaurant—$$ to $$$

It's worth a visit to this restaurant on a cold winter's day just to enjoy the *kachelofen,* which was imported from Austria when the inn was constructed. The *kachelofen,* a traditional tile stove built of firebricks, gives the most pleasant radiant heat you could ever imagine even on the coldest of winter days. The lunch menu includes a soup of the day, salads, pasta, sandwiches, hamburgers and bratwurst. The Emmental cheese fondue for two with bread and apples is offered both at lunch and dinner. House special dinners include Barolo and anise rack of boar or grilled caribou.

Open Tues.–Sat. 11:30 A.M.–2:30 P.M. and 5:30–9:30 P.M., Sun. 9 A.M.–2 P.M. **1235 Warm Springs Rd.; 1-888-650-1400; 435-654-1400.**

Don Pedros Family Mexican Restaurant— $ to $$

With a large menu (more than double the small-capacity, 32-seat dining area), there are plenty of selections—nearly a dozen seafood dishes plus a couple of vegetarian plates and hamburgers, cheese sandwiches and a children's menu. During a late afternoon lunch recently, the restaurant was still nearly full. The only Mexican restaurant in Midway and Heber Valley, its food matches that of any Mexican restaurant in the state. Open daily 11 A.M.–9 P.M. **42 W. Main; 435-654-0805.**

Homestead Resort—$$ to $$$$

At the Homestead there are two fine restaurants, each appropriately given the first names of the Schneitters, who established the resort a short distance north of Midway. **1-800-327-7220; 435-654-1102.**

Fanny's Grill is open daily for breakfast and lunch. There are plenty of choices for breakfast, from the Old-Fashioned Irish Oatmeal and traditional eggs Benedict to omelettes, pancakes, French toast, waffles, steak and eggs, and "The Hot Pot," corned beef hash with eggs and hollandaise sauce served with country potatoes. The lunch fare includes soups, salads, sandwiches, burgers, pasta and fish-and-chips. Open daily 7 A.M.–5 P.M.

Simon's is open evenings for dinner daily with a light menu of salads, navy bean and ham soup or French onion soup, sandwiches, burgers or fish-and-chips along with more traditional dinners featuring steaks, duck, fish and lamb. The warm, light woods of the dining room at Simon's and the good food make it a special dining experience. Open 5:30–10 P.M.

Inn on the Creek Restaurant—$$$

Housed on the main floor of the Swiss château–style inn, the elegant inn's food is excellent. The dinner menu changes with the four seasons to focus on local products and traditional ingredients used in innovative and

always tasteful ways. Open year-round
Mon.–Thurs. 5:30–9 P.M.; Fri.–Sat. 5:30–
9:30 P.M.; Sun. 10:30 A.M.–2:30 P.M.; in summer,
also daily 11:30 A.M.–2:30 P.M. 375 Rainbow Ln.,
Midway; **1-800-654-0892; 435-654-0892.**

Yodels—$ to $$

Great homemade soup, hamburgers, sandwiches, knockwurst, pies and desserts. With
piped Swiss and German music and quaint Gast-
statte decor. Open Mon.–Sat. 11:30 A.M.–9 P.M.
79 E. Main; 435-654-5370.

Services

Visitor Information

Heber Valley Information Center—Located
in the Swiss châlet–style Heritage Building on US
Hwy. 40 at the north end of Heber City, the center offers free maps, brochures and information
about accommodations, restaurants and local
events. Open Mon.– Fri. 8:30 A.M.–4:30 P.M.
475 N. Main; 435-654-3666.

Provo and Utah Valley

Provo lies in the heart of Utah Valley, the first
valley south of the Great Salt Lake Valley.
Located on the east shore of the state's second-
largest natural lake, Utah Lake, the valley and its
lake are connected by the 40-mile-long Jordan
River to the Salt Lake Valley and its lake. Like its
namesake in the Holy Land, the Jordan River
flows out of the freshwater Utah Lake into the
salt waters of the Great Salt Lake, just as the biblical Jordan River flows from the Sea of Galilee
into the Dead Sea, though in opposite directions.

Twelve major communities and an equal
number of smaller settlements were established
along the eastern shore of Utah Lake and
are now home to more than a quarter million

people. From north to south the communities
are Alpine, Lehi, American Fork, Pleasant Grove,
Lindon, Orem, Provo, Springville, Mapleton,
Spanish Fork, Payson and Santaquin. The Wasatch
Mountain Range forms the eastern boundary of
Utah Valley and includes, at the north and south
ends, two peaks that approach 12,000 feet in
elevation—Mt. Timpanogos (11,750 feet) and
Mt. Nebo (11,877 feet). The mountains provide
a variety of recreation possibilities and make
Utah Valley one of the most scenic spots in all the
world. Utah Lake, which takes up much of the
valley between the Wasatch Mountains on the
east and the Lake Mountains along the western
shore, is a feature found only in one other Utah
valley: Bear Lake Valley, far to the north.

Another feature that dominates the area is
Brigham Young University. Students from all
over the world attend this Mormon institution
known for its strict moral and dress codes. Yet
the institution is very much a part of the world,
with its athletic teams, dance companies, law
school and academic programs. The university is
the intellectual center for the LDS church. It is
this institution that brings most visitors to the
Provo and Orem area.

History

When Fathers Francisco Atanasio Dominguez
and Silvestre Velez de Escalante reached Utah
Lake on September 23, 1776, on their journey
from New Mexico, they found villages of Yuta
(Ute) Indians who called themselves the Timpanogotzis, which means "Fish Eaters." Utah Lake
was known as Lake Timpanogos, and while the
mountain that looms above the lake went
unnamed by the Franciscan friars, it and its cave
are the only natural landmark that still bears the
name Timpanogos. The Spanish padres spent only
a few days at Utah Lake, anxious to hurry on
toward California before winter set in, but they
were very impressed with the land and its people.
Escalante recorded that "as many Indian pueblos
can fit inside the valley as there are those in New
Mexico. ... All over it there are good and very

abundant pasturages. ... And the climate here is a good one. ..."The men promised to return the next year and establish a mission among the Timpanogotzis, but were unable to do so.

After Dominguez and Escalante, traders from Santa Fe made infrequent journeys north into Utah and visited the Indians of Utah Valley. By the 1820s the far western fur trade was underway and in 1824, Etienne Provost, a French Canadian fur trapper, trapped as far north as Utah Lake and the Jordan River. Provost was attacked by Snake Indians along the Jordan River in October 1824 and escaped injury, although eight of his men were killed. Provost did not spend much time in Utah, but it is for him that the city of Provo and other landmarks are named.

Provost preceded the first permanent settlers by a quarter century, but when Mormon pioneers moved south from the Salt Lake Valley into Utah Valley in 1849, they became the nucleus of more than a dozen communities established between Alpine on the north and Santaquin on the south.

The valley was not settled without conflict. Isolated Indian battles took place, and in 1853, one of two major Indian wars in Utah—the Walker War, named for the Ute Chief Wakara—began near Springville. The immediate event that touched off the conflict was a fight that arose during a misunderstanding over the trade of three trout for a portion of flour. The war was a series of clashes throughout central Utah between Mormons and Utes, led by Chief Wakara, that lasted more than a year and left 20 Mormons dead. A peace treaty was signed by Chief Wakara in May 1854, eight months before his death.

The lake, good land, a moderate climate and close proximity to Salt Lake City ensured that Utah Valley would be one of the most prosperous areas in the region. Later, with the establish-

ment of Brigham Young Academy, which became Brigham Young University, Provo grew in importance and has been, for much of its history, the state's third-largest city next to Salt Lake City and Ogden.

While originally noted for its agricultural land and especially its orchards, Utah Valley has gone through an industrial revolution with the establishment of steel mills during the 1920s and World War II. In the 1980s, a high-tech revolution brought growth to the area, through such computer software companies as WordPerfect and Novell.

Major Attractions

Brigham Young University

In Utah you can't escape the institution known as the Y or as BYU. Established in 1875, two years before the death of its namesake, BYU has become the largest church-related higher-education institution in the country. BYU plays an important role in the educational, cultural and recreational life of the community: a third of Provo's population is made up of students, and many residents are employed by the university. A perennial football power and "quarterback factory," with such pro stars as Gifford Nielson, Steve Young, Jim McMahon and 1991 Heisman Trophy winner Ty Detmer, BYU football is one of the "tenants" of the Mormon religion for many Utahns. And basketball is not far behind. The Marriott Center, which seats 23,000, is the largest basketball arena in the state and is usually filled.

But BYU is much more than football and basketball. The university provides training for students from all over the world who later return home with professional qualifications and—more often than not—a dedication to serving in the many church positions that make up the Mormon way of life. The university also includes four museums: the Museum of Art; Monte L. Bean Life Science Museum; the Earth Science Museum; and the Museum of Peoples and Cultures (see Museums in the Seeing and Doing section). For first-time visitors and those who

---

Getting There
Provo is located 45 miles south of Salt Lake City on Interstate 15.

have not been on the campus for a while, the free tour offered by the university is recommended. **801-378-4678; www.byu.edu.**

Timpanogos Cave National Monument

Utah's most famous and most often visited cave, Timpanogos Cave is actually three connected limestone caves that were set aside by presidential proclamation in 1922. Located on the steep, northern slope of the 11,750-foot Mt. Timpanogos in American Fork Canyon, the first of the three caves was discovered by Martin Hansen in 1887 and is named **Hansen Cave.** Hansen was cutting timber on the south wall of the canyon when he noticed the tracks of a mountain lion and followed them into an opening. Later that winter he returned with three friends to explore the cave. He placed a wooden door over the natural entrance, and then for several years afterward he led groups through the cave on request.

Timpanogos Cave was discovered in 1914 by two adventuresome teenage boys who began exploring the area while they were waiting outside for a group of relatives who were inside Hansen Cave. The third cave, known as **Middle Cave,** was discovered in 1921 by George Heber Hansen, the son of Martin Hansen, and Wayne E. Hansen, the elder Hansen's grandson. The interior of the cave is decorated with a colorful variety of stalactites, stalagmites, dripstone, flowstone and rimstone formed by calcium carbonate and other minerals in the groundwater that enters the caves. Human-made tunnels connect all three caves.

During the 1890s, Hansen Cave was stripped of most of the onyx and other mineral deposits that lined its walls by crews working for a Chicago onyx company. After the other two caves were discovered, local groups and the Forest Service were determined to preserve the caves. On October 14, 1922, President Warren G. Harding created Timpanogos Cave National Monument in response to recommendations by the U.S. Forest Service and the Timpanogos Outdoor Committee, an organization of local citizens concerned about the preservation and proper maintenance of the caves. The committee had obtained a special use permit from the Forest Service in April 1922 to collect entrance fees, conduct tours and maintain the cave. This agreement continued for 24 years until 1946, when the National Park Service took over all activities in the monument.

Electric lights were installed inside the cave in 1922. They have now been upgraded so that for the half mile or so that you walk inside the cave, you have light. Still, the park ranger does turn off the lights for a few moments so that you can experience the total darkness of the cave. The temperature inside the cave is a cool 43° F, so take a jacket or a sweater. It is located 1.5 miles up the mountain from the visitor center, requiring a strenuous zigzag climb from 5,665 feet to 6,730 feet. Timpanogos Cave is popular with Utahns, and on weekend and holiday afternoons you can expect a long wait before entering the cave. Tickets for specific times can be purchased in advance, and special historic tours and candlelight and flashlight tours can be arranged. The visitor center contains exhibits, a 12-minute slide presentation and a bookstore. Located 2 miles up American Fork Canyon on Hwy. 92. Open mid-May–mid-Sept.; tickets can be purchased 9 A.M.–3:30 P.M. in the visitor center. It's a good idea to call in advance to make reservations. **Superintendent, Timpanogos Cave National Monument, Rte. 3, P.O. Box 200, American Fork, UT 84003; 801-756-5238; www.govtica/index/htm.**

Utah Lake

The principal access to the 150-square-mile Utah Lake is through Utah Lake State Park. Utah Lake is a remnant of Lake Bonneville. Shorelines of old Lake Bonneville can be seen on the Traverse Mountains on the west side of the lake and the Wasatch Range on the east side. It is estimated that 13,000 feet of lake sediment lies beneath the central part of Utah Valley. Fed by streams coming down from the mountains, and with an outlet (the Jordan River) at the north end, Utah Lake has remained a freshwater lake since it was an arm of Lake Bonneville.

As you might expect, the primary activity here is boating. There are 144 boat spaces at the 30-acre marina, four concrete boat launching ramps and boat and trailer storage. Although the average depth of the lake is only 10 feet, Utah Lake is still good for boating, waterskiing, windsurfing and fishing. Carp, catfish and yellow perch are plentiful, while trophy-sized bass and walleye have been taken. The lake has a **visitor center/museum** and 120 camping spaces with picnic tables, modern rest rooms and showers available year-round on a first-come, first-served basis. Located 4 miles east of Provo via Center St. **801-375-0731.**

Festivals and Events

Lehi Round-Up Rodeo
last full week of June. The Lehi Round-Up, one of Utah's oldest continuous rodeos, began in 1938. It runs three nights (Thurs., Fri. and Sat.) and attracts cowboys from all over the country. In addition to the rodeo, other activities include a cowboy poetry gathering, fine arts display, parade, carnival, free museum tours and plenty of food. **801-768-9581.**

Freedom Festival
July 4. Provo goes all out to celebrate the Fourth of July. A month-long celebration that draws politicians from around the state culminates with the state's largest Independence Day parade, down University Ave. The hot-air balloon display includes as many as 40 balloons, one of the largest in the state. Other activities continue throughout the day, with the climax being a huge fireworks extravaganza held in the 65,000-seat Cougar Stadium. **801-370-8019; www.freedomfestival.org.**

Springville World Folkfest
mid-July. This weeklong folkfest runs from the second Sat. through the third Sat. in July and involves nearly a dozen folk dance groups from around the world. This is Utah's largest folkfest and one of the largest in the country. The dancers are accompanied by musicians using native instruments, and each performance is different, as the groups rotate through a large repertory during the six evening performances. There are no performances on Sun., but a free Street Dance is held Wed. evening at the Springville Museum of Art parking lot.

Other highlights include the opening ceremonies, parade of nations and closing ceremonies. All of the performers stay in private homes in the area, and it is especially heartwarming to watch the interaction among visitors and host families who cheer loudly for their guests and otherwise try to make the Utah stay something special. The outdoor stage and setting for the performances is especially beautiful with the Wasatch Mountains rising high above the Spring Acres Arts Park. You can sit on the chairs and benches that are provided or bring your own lawn chair or blanket and claim your spot on the hill above the stage. **620 S. 1350 E., P.O. Box 306, Springville, UT 84663; 801-489-2700.**

Timpanogos Storytelling Festival
end of Aug. One of the state's most unique festivals, the Timpanogos Storytelling Festival began as a modest undertaking in 1990, and now some 2,000 visitors come to the weekend festival to listen to nationally known as well as regional and local storytellers. The tales are gathered from around the world, and the storytellers help remind us that their art is one of our oldest forms of communication and recreation. **801-229-7436; www.timpfest.org.**

Outdoor Activities

Biking

Jordan River Pkwy. Trail
This paved 9-mile trail runs from near the north end of Utah Lake along the Jordan River to the Salt Lake County/Utah County line. To reach the trailhead on Utah Lake, from I-15 take Exit 282 and head west through Lehi on Hwy. 73 for approximately 4 miles to the Jordan River.

Provo Pkwy. Trail

This 15-mile-long trail along the Provo River goes from Utah Lake up Provo Canyon 3.5 miles to Bridal Veil Falls. The western trailhead is located just before the entrance to Utah Lake State Park, 3 miles west of I-15 on Center St./Hwy. 114. **Provo Parks and Recreation Office; 801-379-6600.**

Utah Lake Loop

This 100-mile-long bike ride takes you around Utah Lake over fairly level terrain. A modified route skirts the west side of the lake along Hwy. 68, 34 miles one-way between the junction of Hwys. 68 and 73 (a couple of miles west of Lehi) and the fruit-growing town of Elberta on US Hwy. 6. The west side of the lake offers a unique view of the Wasatch Mountains, with Utah Lake in the foreground. It is a much less traveled road than those on the east side of the lake. If you want to circumnavigate the lake on a bike, pick up a copy of the Utah County map at the Utah Valley Convention and Visitors Bureau office (see the Services section) and ask the helpful staff to show you the alternate routes on the east side of the lake.

Boating

Utah Lake State Park

The 30-acre marina has 144 boat spaces, four concrete boat launching ramps and boat and trailer storage. See Major Attractions section for details. Located 4 miles east of Provo via Center St. **801-375-0731.**

Fishing

American Fork Creek

Although this stream tends to yield smaller German browns and stocked rainbow trout, its clear, pristine water cascading over rocks between the towering Wasatch Peaks makes fishing this stream an aesthetic delight. Access along Hwy. 92.

Provo River

The Provo River offers one of Utah's most popular fly-fishing streams, designated by *Field and Stream* magazine as one of the 10 "blue ribbon" trout streams in the West. You will find rainbow, cutthroat and brown trout, and Rocky Mountain whitefish. Access along US Hwy. 189.

Golf

East Bay Golf Course

If you like the challenge of water, then Provo's East Bay Golf Course is for you. Located near Utah Lake, water is a factor on 13 of the 18 holes, making this the wettest golf course in the state. A number of the holes have water on both sides of the course. The water provides a natural habitat for a variety of waterfowl, including Canada geese, pelicans, blue herons, snowy egrets, ducks and other birds that frequent the marshlands surrounding the golf course. Their soaring and gliding is a pure delight. The course is very flat, in contrast with the towering mountains behind it. Located near the south end of University Ave., just off Interstate 15. Take Exit 266 and turn right at the first light, then follow East Bay Blvd. to the course. **1860 S. East Bay Blvd.; 801-373-6262.**

Hobble Creek Golf Course

You will not find any debate that this is one of the most picturesque golf courses in Utah; readers of the *Deseret News* voted this their favorite golf course to play in Utah. Located in Hobble Creek Canyon, east of Springville, the course is laid out in the narrow bottom of the canyon along the course of Hobble Creek. In the fall the brightly colored leaves on the trees on both sides of the course are breathtaking, while the towering mountains, well-maintained fairways and greens, and bridges across Hobble Creek give this course an unforgettable charm. Take Exit 263 off Interstate 15 and head east for 7 miles along 400 S. as it winds into Hobble Creek Canyon. **801-489-6297.**

Spanish Oaks Course

Located at the mouth of Spanish Fork Canyon, just off US Hwy. 6, the course spreads out beneath the large white cross on top of Dominguez Hill, which marks the spot where

Dominguez and Escalante entered Utah Valley in 1776. The Franciscan fathers followed the Spanish Fork River north toward Utah Lake. The same river cuts through the front 9 of the course, which are characterized by wide fairways and level terrain. The back 9 are played on the slope under Dominguez Hill and are more challenging, as the scrub oak brush seems to attract balls and the uphill-downhill layout adds difficulty to most of the holes. Located about 4 miles off Interstate 15 at Exit 261. **801-798-9816.**

Thanksgiving Point

This privately owned golf course opened in 1997 and was ranked among the top 10 new courses in the country. Designed by Johnny Miller, the demanding course is one of the longest in the state and is laid out on either side of the Jordan River as it meanders from Utah Lake toward the Great Salt Lake. The course hosts the annual Champions Challenge, a father-and-son event that often features golfing greats. The Utah Golf Hall of Fame is housed in the clubhouse. A part of the Thanksgiving Point complex, the 18-hole course is closed Sun. **3003 N. Thanksgiving Way, Lehi; 801-768-7401.**

Tri-City Golf Course

Three towns—American Fork, Pleasant Grove and Lehi—pooled their resources in 1973 to build this challenging golf course. The challenge can be found in two words: distance and trees. The middle tees play a total of 6,710 yards; if you go to the back tees, it's 7,077 yards. This course probably has more cottonwood trees than the rest of Utah's golf courses put together, even though some 300 trees have been removed over the years. Golfers rate this as one of the five most difficult courses in the state. But the trees, the spectacular view of Mt. Timpanogos and isolation from traffic and noise create a beautiful course. **1400 N. 200 E., American Fork; 801-756-3594.**

Hiking

Santaquin Peak and Loafer Mountain

Named for a Ute Indian chief, Santaquin Peak rises to 10,685 feet. Loafer Mountain, just southeast of Santaquin Peak, is 2 feet higher at 10,687 feet. The 12-mile up-and-back hike climbs about 3,000 feet from the trailhead to the ridge just below Loafer Peak. The Loafer Mountain trailhead is located on the north side of the road at the turnoff to the Payson Lakes Campground on the Mt. Nebo Scenic Loop Rd.

Timpanogos Peak

Many Utahns consider this the best hike in the entire state; historically it is one of the most popular. The history books do not record who was the first to climb to the top of the peak, but many family histories record the treks of their ancestors. Starting in 1912, Brigham Young University sponsored an annual Timp Hike, but when the number of hikers grew to more than 7,000 by the late 1960s, the hike was canceled because of the large crowds and their impact on the fragile mountain environment. Today some summer weekends see in excess of 500 hikers on the trail at one time. While the Aspen Grove route is the most popular, there are several other possible routes.

At the Aspen Grove trailhead, the trail starts at an elevation of 6,900 feet. In the first few miles, the trail passes a dozen or so waterfalls. At 6.9 miles you reach Emerald Lake, which some hikers are satisfied to make their goal. The trail climbs another 2.5 miles to the summit at 11,750 feet, 9.4 miles total. If you go all the way to the top, be aware of the rock- and snowfields and the acrophobia-inducing perch on the peak. Keep an eye out for mountain goats, which were reintroduced into the area in 1981.

Most people require 5–6 hours to make the ascent and 3–4 hours for the descent. Strong hikers can make it to the top in 3 hours: the record—90 minutes up and 45 back down—was set in 1967 by Michael R. Kelsey, who has become a prolific author of Utah hiking books, including one on Mt. Timpanogos. Although it is a tradition to slide down the "glacier" above Emerald Lake, Forest Service rangers strongly discourage it because of the jagged rocks, holes and varying hardness of snow. If you are worried about accidents, you might want to hike the trail on weekends, when an emergency response team is on duty with a mission to respond to all injuries within 30 minutes. The Aspen Grove trailhead is located in Provo Canyon, past the Sundance Ski Resort, in the west end of Aspen Grove.

Ice Skating

The Peaks Ice Arena

This state-of-the-art ice rink with a capacity of 6,300 spectators was the site of preliminary round hockey games during the 2002 Olympics. Fans witnessed some of the best men's and women's hockey matches of the 2002 Games. The arena still hosts plenty of hockey matches and also sees good use for open skating. Located on the east side of Provo. You can follow Center St. east to the edge of the mountain, where you will see the arena. **100 N. Seven Peaks Blvd.; 801-377-8777.**

Skiing

CROSS-COUNTRY
Alpine Loop

What better use for a scenic road closed by snow in the winter than to turn it into a cross-country ski trail? The Alpine Loop, famous for its autumn leaves, offers a good outing for about any level of cross-country skier. The ascent is gradual, starting at 6,850 feet at Aspen Grove (the trailhead for the Mt. Timpanogos climb in the Hiking section) and rising to 8,060 feet at the summit of Hwy. 92. As with the scenic drive, you can start either in Provo Canyon, at Aspen Grove or in American Fork Canyon just above Mutual Dell. From Aspen Grove to Mutual Dell is 8 miles. You can either do part of the trail or complete the entire distance and arrange to be shuttled back. Alternatively, if you want a longer jaunt, cross from American Fork Canyon to Aspen Grove, then to Sundance in the morning; enjoy lunch at the Sundance Resort, then return to your car in the afternoon. The Aspen Grove trailhead is located in Provo Canyon in the west end of Aspen Grove.

Sundance

The ski area has 30 kilometers of marked trails for cross-country skiers. See the Downhill section for details.

DOWNHILL
Sundance

Sundance may be the only ski resort named for a western outlaw. When actor Robert Redford acquired what was a small local ski area called Timphaven in 1969, he named it Sundance in honor of the nickname for the bad man Harry Longabaugh whom Redford played in the now classic film *Butch Cassidy and the Sundance Kid*. Yes, in anticipation of your question, you do, on occasion, see Redford at the resort. Despite its big-time name, Sundance still maintains the feel of a small-time resort. Lift tickets are less than the Park City and Little Cottonwood Canyon resorts, and the lift lines ... well, what lift lines? It is easy to understand why Sundance has been named by *Ski Magazine* as one of the best small resorts anywhere. The resort has the feel of a community, with no massive lodges or hotels. Accommodations are in privately owned homes and cottages, which are put into a lodging pool. If you can afford them, these are the places to stay for a quiet, relaxing ski trip. If you can't, the 15-mile drive from Provo takes less than a half hour. The view of the towering, snow-covered peaks of Mt. Timpanogos from the slopes and lifts rivals that of any other ski resort in the world.

There are three lifts, one quad and two triple chairlifts, that provide access to 450 acres of skiing along 41 runs. The elevations range from 6,100 feet at the base to 8,250 feet at the top of the highest lift. A ski school offers full-day programs for children; a learn-to-ski program for beginners that includes lesson, equipment rental and lift ticket; and specialized instruction for skiers at any level. The ski season usually runs late Nov.–mid-Apr. There are two fine restaurants at the resort—**The Tree Room** and **The Foundry Grill**. Located in Provo Canyon, 15 miles north of Provo. Take US Hwy. 189 up Provo Canyon and take Hwy. 92. From Park City it is about 40 minutes via Heber City and Provo Canyon. **1-800-892-1600; 801-225-4107 lodging and general information; 801-225-4100 skiing information; www. sundanceresort.com.**

Swimming

Provo Recreation Center and Swimming Pool

This pool offers lessons, aerobics, lap swimming and open swimming. The complex also has racquetball courts and a weight room. Open during summer Mon.–Fri. 1–8 P.M., Sat. 1–6 P.M.; the rest of the year Mon.–Fri. 5:30 P.M.–8 P.M., Sat. 5:30–6 P.M. Admission fee charged. **1155 N. University Ave., Provo; 801-379-6610.**

Seeing and Doing

Children and Families

Seven Peaks Resort Water Park

Located a few blocks from Brigham Young University, at the foot of Y Mountain, the amusement park is convenient for students and youngsters from the Provo area. The resort also seeks to draw in overnight visitors with special accommodations/golf/water park packages arranged with local hotels. The water park boasts more than 25 heated water attractions, including Utah's largest wave pool, with 5-foot swells and numerous different wave patterns. The park claims among its 12 slides one of the world's longest water slides, 550 feet of which is through darkness punctuated with lights, foggers, misters and sound effects. It also boasts the tallest slides in the world. One, the Lazer's Edge, is a 10-story water roller coaster that delights youngsters, though it may seem to last an eternity for oldsters who dare try it. Another, the Sky Breaker, flushes you down a dark tunnel from which you emerge into a 95-foot waterfall. If you want to enjoy the water without the heart-seizing slides, The Lazy River allows you to lie back in a tube and enjoy an 800-foot-long float ride on the shallow artificial river. There are plenty of picnic tables available on the expansive lawns. The water park is open, weather permitting, mid-May–Labor Day. Follow Provo's Center St. east toward the mountain until you come to the park. **801-373-8777.**

Thanksgiving Point Resort

It is difficult to describe Thanksgiving Point in a few words, especially because it has something for all ages. For golfers, it is one of Utah's premier golf courses (see the Golf section). For photographers and flower lovers, it has one of the most beautiful and extensive gardens in the state. For shoppers, there is a fine collection of shops that offer many local products and works of Utah artisans. For the curious of all ages, the **North American Museum of Ancient Life** is one of Utah's newest and finest museums, boasting that it is the largest dinosaur museum anywhere. There's also a six-story IWERKS Screen theater in the museum. For children and the young at heart, the **Fox Family Farms Animal Park** gives children the hands-on experience of milking cows, gathering eggs and grooming and petting animals. There's also a variety of horse and pony wagon and carriage rides. An interactive children's museum is under construction. For those looking for entertainment, concerts, plays and programs are presented inside the 1,000-seat barn or outdoors at the Waterfall Garden Amphitheater. There are also several restaurants and cafes throughout the resort. At this time there are no lodging facilities, but an RV park is planned.

Located just off Interstate 15 (Exits 287 and 285) at the north end of Utah Valley just across the Point-of-the-Mountain from Salt Lake Valley. **3003 N. Thanksgiving Way, Lehi; 1-800-672-6040; 801-768-4941; www.thanksgivingpoint.com.**

Historic Sites

Brigham Young Academy Building

When it was constructed in 1892, the BY Academy building was the flagship building of the early university and, with a capacity of 1,000 students, one of the largest school buildings in the Intermountain West. Using plans developed by principal and founder Karl G. Maeser, architect Don Carlos Young, a son of Brigham Young, came up with a stately design that used locally made brick trimmed with sandstone. The Academy building served the educational mission of Brigham Young University for more than three-quarters of a century until it was closed in 1968. When the building was scheduled for demolition after years of neglect and deterioration, concerned citizens organized the Brigham Young Academy Foundation to save the building.

Their goal became a possibility when Provo City decided to build a new library. The foundation spearheaded an effort to study the feasibility of using the old Academy building for the new library. A library bond was approved in February 1997 and the foundation was given less than five months to come up with $5.8 million to cover the cost of renovating and bringing the historic building up to code. They did it! The result is a modern new library attached to the renovated historic building. The **children's library** is housed in the basement floor of the old building. The main floor has an **art gallery** and meeting rooms, while the upper floor has several additional meeting rooms and a large ballroom now used for banquets and receptions. Both buildings were dedicated on Sept. 8, 2001. **550 N. University Ave.; 801-852-6650; www.provocitylibrary.com.**

Camp Floyd–Stagecoach Inn State Park

In 1857 President James Buchanan sent 2,500 soldiers—approximately a third of the entire U.S. Army—from Ft. Leavenworth, Kansas, to Utah to put down an alleged Mormon rebellion. After spending the winter near Ft. Bridger, blocked by Mormon militiamen who had set up fortifications east of Salt Lake City, the army, under the command of Albert Sidney Johnston, finally negotiated a truce and was allowed to pass through a deserted Salt Lake City on June 26, 1858. They continued without stopping for another 40 miles southwest of the city, where

they established Camp Floyd. Until the outbreak of the Civil War, in 1861, Camp Floyd was the nation's largest military encampment and Utah's second-largest community. Approximately 400 structures were built, and a large civilian population moved into the adjacent village of Fairfield. In 1858 the Overland Stage route was established through Fairfield, and John Carson built an inn and stagecoach stop that have been preserved as a museum and historic site in this state park. The inn was also a Pony Express station from the time the Pony Express was first established in April 1860 until its demise in October 1861, after the completion of the transcontinental telegraph line. Camp Floyd closed in July 1861, when the last troops were ordered east as soldiers of the North and South moved to their first bloody encounter at Bull Run.

Today you can visit the restored Stagecoach Inn, an old army commissary building, and the Camp Floyd military cemetery, where 84 soldiers are buried. The cemetery is open year-round and the Stagecoach Inn and commissary April 15–Oct. Open daily 11 A.M.–5 P.M. Take Exit 262 off Interstate 15 at Lehi and drive west on Hwy. 73 for 14 miles to the town of Cedar Fort. Continue on the road as it turns south for 5 miles to Fairfield. **18035 W. 1540 N., Fairfield; 801-768-8932.**

John Moyle's Indian Tower

The Black Hawk War raged throughout Utah during the mid-1860s, when John R. Moyle, an 1856 immigrant from England, moved out of the protection of the Mountainville fort at present-day Alpine to build his home. But in case he came under attack by Utes, Moyle built a circular stone tower, approximately 10 feet in diameter and 15 feet tall, in which he and his family could take refuge and protect themselves. A tunnel was to connect the Moyle home with the tower, but the Ute Indians were sent east to the Uintah Reservation before the tunnel could be completed. The Moyle family donated the tower and home to the city of Alpine, which constructed a park at the site, preserved the historic tower and remodeled the Moyle home, and moved in an old timbered house and barn, along with more than two dozen pieces of farm machinery and equipment. Open for free public tours May 1– Sept. Sat. 9 A.M.–1 P.M. Take Grove Dr. to 770 N., turn right and then left on the first street, Moyle Dr. **801-756-1194.**

Lehi Roller Mills

This historic flour mill has been in operation since 1906. While there are no tours of the mills, there is a great little store located on the east side of the original building. You can buy mixes for all kinds of muffins, cookies, brownies, cakes, cobblers, scones and pancakes, plus bread, flour and cereals produced at the mills. Open Mon.–Sat. 9 A.M.–6 P.M. Located just west of I-15 Exit 285 on Main St. in Lehi. **1-800-660-4346; 801-768-4401.**

Peeteetneet Academy

Peeteetneet was a Ute Indian chief who lived in the area when Payson was settled. The school named after him was built in 1901 and is now a community cultural center with a pictorial history gallery, art gallery and academy of arts. Open Mon.–Fri. 10 A.M.–4 P.M. **10 S. Peeteetneet Blvd.; 801-465-9247.**

Provo Historic Buildings

Pick up a free copy of the **Provo Historic Buildings Tour** booklet from the Utah Valley Convention and Visitors Bureau, located in the center of the tour inside the old **Utah County Courthouse (51 S. University St.),** just south of Center St. The 1920s Classical Revival–style courthouse has been restored, so take time to view each of the three floors, where the combinations of marble and polished stone are simply stunning. Most of the 22 buildings can be visited on foot, but you might want to drive to some of the outlying locations. The tour features turn-of-the-century homes, including those of Karl Maeser, founder of Brigham Young University; James E. Talmage, a prominent Mormon apostle; Jesse Knight, a millionaire miner, businessman and philanthropist; and Reed Smoot, a Mormon apostle and U.S. senator

from 1903 to 1933. The historic **Provo Tabernacle,** constructed between 1883 and 1896 to seat 2,000 people, is located across University Ave. from the courthouse. Also included are the downtown commercial buildings, most of which date from the turn of the century. The large red **Knight Block** with its clock tower constructed in 1900 is located on the northeast corner of Center St. and University Ave.

Museums

Brigham Young University Museum of Art

The 100,000-square-foot Brigham Young University Art Museum opened in October 1993, the largest art museum between Denver and San Francisco. The university has more than 14,000 art objects in its collection, and the new museum, with its numerous galleries, offers curators plenty of opportunities to exhibit the collection. The museum opened with a crowd-pleasing exhibit, "The Etruscans: Legacy of a Lost Civilization," from the Gregorian Etruscan Museum of the Vatican Museums. Subsequent exhibits have included "The Imperial Tombs of China," "Masada exhibit from Israel" and "150 Years of American Painting," with paintings by such outstanding artists as Benjamin West, Albert Bierstadt, J. Alden Weir and Maynard Dixon, all taken from the BYU art collection. Admission is free unless there is a special exhibit. Open Mon. and Thurs. 10 A.M.–9 P.M.; Tues., Wed., Fri. 10 A.M.–6 P.M.; Sat. noon–5 P.M. From I-25 take Exit 272 and follow University Pkwy. east to the BYU campus and follow the signs to the visitor parking on the north side of the museum building. **801-378-2787; www.byu.edu/moa.**

Earth Science Museum

Another of Brigham Young University's four museums, this one has some of the largest exhibits, with an allosaurus and camptosaurus dinosaurs. There is also a monstrous fish, crocodile heads and the skull of a diceratops—a close relative of the triceratops—and other items from the university's dinosaur collection. There is a petrified tree trunk, dinosaur footprints, an exhibit explaining a dozen ways in which fossils are formed and a mural depicting the relative size of dinosaurs, including the unbelievably huge ultrasaurus. There is also a viewing area to watch scientists working with the fossil collection. Open Mon. 9 A.M.–9 P.M.; Tues.–Fri. 9 A.M.– 5 P.M.; Sat. noon–4 P.M. Located across the street from the south end of the football stadium, next to the 1912 Page Elementary School. **1683 Canyon Rd.; 801-378-3680; www.byu.edu/esm.**

John Hutchings Museum of Natural History

One of Utah's oldest museums, the John Hutchings Museum of Natural History began in 1913 as a family project to collect artifacts. John Hutchings was born in 1889 and began working in the Eureka silver mines at the age of 12. He later became the postman in Lehi, and this gave him time to pursue his lifelong hobbies of self-education and collecting, which he did with gusto until his death in 1977. With no particular theme, the collection includes items representing the area's Native Americans to the present-day computer industry. You'll be amazed at the range of the collection. The museum is located in a Spanish Revival–style building constructed in 1920 as a Carnegie library and memorial to World War I veterans. Admission fee charged. Open Mon.–Sat. 9 A.M.–5:30 P.M., except holidays. **55 N. Center, Lehi; 801-768-7180.**

Monte L. Bean Life Science Museum

The Monte L. Bean Life Science Museum is a favorite with children and those who like to watch the wonderment of children as they encounter mounted or preserved animals from all over the world. The two floors of this eclectic collection include such animals as caribou, elk, moose, deer, pronghorn antelope, mountain goats, bobcats, timber wolves, mountain lions, bison, five different kinds of bears (Kodiak, polar, grizzly, black and brown), a leopard, a tiger, an emperor penguin and a European boar. In the Monte L. Bean Memorial Room, which displays the mounted heads of large game animals from

Africa, push-button-activated screens show pictures of the animals in their natural habitat. There are displays of shells and snakes. A children's discovery room offers a hands-on experience for everyone. A gift shop offers plenty of opportunities to buy a special gift for all types and ages of animal lovers. A research library is also open to the public. Open Mon. 10 A.M.–9 P.M., Tues.–Sat 10 A.M.–5 P.M. Admission is free. Take I-25 Exit 272 and follow University Pkwy. east to the BYU campus, then follow signs to visitor parking on the north side of the Museum of Arts. Located about 300 yards to the north of the Museum of Arts, across the road on the hill. **801-378-5053; www.byu.edu/mlbean.**

Museum of Peoples and Cultures

This small museum under the direction of Dr. Marti Lu Allen contains more than 40,000 artifacts. Not all are on display at the same time; however, anthropology students work together each year to develop an exhibit. It is well worth a visit to see some of the unique artifacts of prehistoric peoples from Utah and the Southwest. Located on the first floor of Allen Hall on the southwestern fringe of the BYU campus. There is parking across the street to the east. Admission is free. Open Mon.–Fri. 9 A.M.– 5 P.M. Located at the corner of 700 N. and 100 E. **801-378-6112; www.byu.edu/anthro/mopc/main.htm.**

Springville Museum of Art

A visit to Springville, nicknamed "The Art City," is a must for art lovers. Springville was home to two famous Utah artists: John Hafen and Cyrus E. Dallin. In 1903 the two artists donated some of their works to Springville High School. Other Utah artists donated works in 1907. In 1925 the Smart Collection was given to the high school. The white stucco, Spanish Mission–style museum building was constructed with funds from the New Deal Works Progress Administration and completed in 1937. It is now listed in the National Register of Historic Places and is Utah's first and oldest museum of art. The museum's collection includes more than 1,300 works by

250 artists from Utah and throughout the United States, which are exhibited in nine galleries on the second floor. Other educational programs, including lectures, guided tours and films are offered. Open Tues.–Sat. 10 A.M.–5 P.M.; Wed. until 9 P.M.; Sun. 3–6 P.M. Admission is free. **126 E. 400 S., P.O. Box 509, Springville, UT 84663; 801-489-2727; www.shs.edu/museum.**

Performing Arts

Sundance Summer Theatre
You won't find many places with a dramatic setting equal to that offered at the Sundance Resort. Utahns appreciate the magnificent mountain scenery as well as the two or more excellent theater productions that are staged here mid-June–Aug. Both bench seating and lawn seating are available. Performances are held Mon.–Sat. beginning at 8:30 P.M. A Children's Theatre offers two plays in repertory July–Aug., with matinees Thurs.–Sun. at 1 P.M. and evening performances Mon. and Thurs.–Sat. at 6 P.M. If you attend an evening performance, be sure to bring sweaters, jackets and even blankets: the night temperature in the mountains, even during the summer, can be uncomfortable without adequate clothing. **801-225-4100; www.sundanceresort.com.**

Utah Valley Symphony
Concerts of this local symphony orchestra feature a wide range of classical music, held in the historic Provo Tabernacle. **100 S. University Ave.; 801-377-6995.**

Scenic Drives

Alpine Loop / Hwy. 92
When you drive the 24-mile-long Alpine Loop, you have the impression that this road was constructed with only one purpose in mind: to give thousands of motorists an intimate view of spectacular Mt. Timpanogos. The narrow road connects American Fork Canyon with Provo Canyon, twisting and turning as it climbs to just

over 8,000 feet at its summit, making it a slow drive that requires an hour or more. Be sure to allow plenty of time, especially during the autumn, and take lots of film for your camera. Stops at Timpanogos Cave, Sundance Resort and Cascade Springs, along with a picnic lunch, make this a full day's outing. Because of the narrow curves and steep grade, trailers are prohibited. Closed during the winter. The U.S. Forest Service requires a nominal fee for all cars traveling over the Alpine Loop. From Interstate 15, take Exit 287 and head east on Hwy. 92 to American Fork Canyon, where the loop begins. Follow it to the summit, and continue past Sundance to the junction with US Hwy. 189 in Provo Canyon.

Provo Canyon Scenic Byway / US Hwy. 189
Connecting Utah Valley with Heber Valley and providing access to the Sundance Resort, US Hwy. 189 winds around the south side of Mt. Timpanogos and follows up the Provo River, a popular fly-fishing stream. Ten miles up the canyon from Provo is Bridal Veil Falls. At the top of Provo Canyon, the highway skirts around the east side of Deer Creek Reservoir, at the southern end of Heber Valley. Located at the mouth of Provo Canyon is the Olmstead hydroelectric plant. The Olmstead Power Plant was constructed in 1904 by L. L. Nunn and his brother P. N. Nunn for the Telluride Power Company. L. L. Nunn was a pioneer in the development of alternating current high-voltage transmission.

Wildlife Viewing

Provo Bay
The marshlands along the south shore of Provo Bay, on the east side of Utah Lake, provide easy viewing of many wetland bird species Apr.–Nov. Numerous trails you can follow along the dikes give you a close-up view of the birds. Look out for white pelicans, egrets, blue herons and a variety of geese and ducks. Take Exit 263 off Interstate 15 and head west on Hwy. 77 to the Spanish Fork River bridge. There, turn north onto a dirt road and drive to Provo Bay.

Where to Stay

Accommodations

There are numerous motels and accommodation possibilities in Utah Valley. Pick up a complete list from the **Utah Valley Travel and Convention Bureau; 1-800-222-UTAH (8824); 801-370-8393; www.utahvalley.org/cvb.** The following are a few favorites.

Cottontree Inn—$$ to $$$

This Best Western motel has 80 rooms, a heated pool and whirlpool, located three blocks from Brigham Young University in a parklike setting along the Provo River. **2230 N. University Pkwy.; 1-800-528-1234; 801-373-7044.**

Fairfield Inn—$$ to $$$

This modern 72-room motel, part of the Marriott system, is located just off the I-15 University exit (Exit 266) in Provo. Heated indoor pool and hot tub; complimentary continental breakfast. Located in East Bay Business Park. **1504 S. 40 E.; 1-800-228-2800; 801-377-9500.**

Provo Marriott Hotel—$$ to $$$

Considered by many locals to be Provo's best lodging, with 235 guest rooms and suites, the hotel is certainly the area's largest. Smoking and nonsmoking floors are provided, as well as a swimming pool and fitness center. An excellent restaurant, Mingles, and a private club, Seasons, are in the hotel. **101 W. 100 N.; 801-377-4700.**

R. Spencer Hines Mansion
Bed and Breakfast—$$ to $$$$

R. Spencer Hines was a turn-of-the-century iconoclast when he had this lovely two-and-a-half-story Victorian home built in 1895. He was involved in mining and real estate and owned a drug store and a saloon, along with other businesses in the area. He died just three years after the home was completed and his wife, Kitty, remained in the home until 1906, at which point it was rented out.

In its current incarnation, the home is also something of an iconoclastic establishment in its own right. After all, this is probably the only place in all of Utah Valley with a room with a two-person whirlpool tub in the turret where you can soak in privacy while taking in a panoramic view of downtown Provo and sipping a glass of complimentary cider. Gene and Sandi Henderson opened the bed and breakfast in 1996, and it has earned a fine reputation as one of Utah's luxury bed and breakfasts. There are nine theme rooms, each with a private bath and whirlpool tub. The Penthouse in the attic is one of the most popular rooms, along with the library room, which has a secret passageway through a hidden door to the bathroom and a spiral staircase to the whirlpool tub above, where a skylight lets you watch in complete privacy as the moon passes overhead. In addition to the full breakfasts, there are fresh baked cookies and fresh fruit each evening. Even if a stay in this elegant bed and breakfast is not possible, a visit is. Sandi offers free tours of the mansion daily 1–4 P.M. **383 W. 100 S., Provo; 1-800-428-5636; 801-374-8400; www.hinesmansion.com.**

Sundance Cottages—$$$ to $$$$

The accommodations at Sundance Resort range from a standard room to studios, three-bedroom cottages and five-bedroom residences. See the Downhill Skiing section for details. **RR 3, P.O. Box A-1, Sundance, UT 84604; 801-225-4107; www.sundanceresort.com.**

Camping

PRIVATE
American Fork Campground

All 53 RV trailer sites have complete hookups. **418 E. 620 S., American Fork; 801-756-5502.**

East Bay RV Park

Two hundred and ten sites, all with full hookups. Plus a store, clubhouse, swimming pool and fish pond. **1750 W. 1600 N., Springville; 801-491-0700.**

Lakeside Campground

One hundred thirty-five RV sites, all with complete hookups. Drinking water, flush toilets, showers and laundry are available. Adjacent to Utah Lake. **4000 W. Center; 801-373-5267.**

Provo KOA Campground
Ninety sites, 40 with full hookups, plus a small store and clubhouse. **320 N. 2050 W.; 801-375-2994.**

PUBLIC
With the Wasatch Mountains rimming Utah Valley on the east, there are five canyons in which public camping is available mid-May–mid-late Oct. on forest service land.

American Fork Canyon / Hwy. 92 (American Fork and Pleasant Grove)
Echo, Roadhouse, Martin, Warnick and **Mile Rock**—This series of five small campgrounds is located about 12 miles from Pleasant Grove. Each has 6 sites, except for Echo, which has only 4.

    Granite Flat—14.1 miles northeast of Pleasant Grove on Hwy. 144; 32 sites.

    Little Mill—10 miles northeast of Pleasant Grove; 79 RV sites and 35 tentsites.

    Timpooneke—14.1 miles northeast of Pleasant Grove; 32 sites.

Hobble Creek Canyon (Springville, Mapleton and Spanish Fork)
Diamond—18.5 miles east of Spanish Fork off Hwy. 147; 36 RV and tentsites.

    Whiting—6.8 miles east of Springville off US Hwy. 89; 16 RV and tentsites.

Payson Canyon / Nebo Loop Rd.
Blackhawk—16 miles southeast of Payson; 23 RV and tentsites.

    Maple Bench—7.6 miles southeast of Payson; 14 RV and tentsites.

    Payson Lakes—12 miles southeast of Payson; 99 RV and tentsites.

Provo Canyon / US Hwy. 189
Hope—10 miles northeast of Provo; 24 RV and tentsites.

    Mt. Timpanogos—14 miles northeast of Provo off Hwy. 92; 26 RV and tentsites.

Rock Canyon—4.9 miles east of Provo; 7 RV and tentsites.

Santaquin Canyon (off I-15)
Tinney Flat—8 miles southeast of Santaquin; 2 RV sites and 10 tentsites.

Where to Eat

Bombay House—$$ to $$$
Featuring East Indian food prepared by master chef Amjer Singh, the Bombay House offers a fine luncheon buffet and dinners cooked in a tandoori oven—a clay oven shaped like a big jar, insulated with a thick layer of plaster and ceramic tile, and heated by a charcoal fire to 850° F. The full-course dinners include curries, rice, Indian breads (naan), chutney and a variety of chicken and lamb dishes. Don't end your meal without trying one of their unusual desserts such as Kheer, mildly flavored basmati rice, raisins and cashews cooked in milk; or Kulfi, homemade Indian ice cream. This restaurant is a twin to a restaurant of the same name in Salt Lake City, and both have well-deserved reputations for the best Indian food to be found in Utah. Open Mon.–Sat. 4–10 P.M. **463 N. University Ave.; 801-373-6677.**

Brick Oven Pizza—$ to $$
BYU students have been coming here for decades for the excellent pizza. The menu also includes other Italian food such as spaghetti and lasagna. Open Mon.–Thurs. 11 A.M.–11 P.M.; Fri.–Sat. 11 A.M.–12:30 A.M. **150 E. 800 N.; 801-374-8800.**

La Casita Mexican Restaurant—$ to $$
Established in 1978 by Luis and Luz Muzquiz, La Casita is one of the most popular places for Mexican food in Utah Valley. The menu includes five different salsas, traditional combination plates, plus specials like a crab enchilada and machaca—shredded beef cooked with onions, tomatoes and peppers. Open Mon.–Thurs. 11:30 A.M.–10 P.M., Fri.–Sat. 11 A.M.–11 P.M. **333 N. Main St., Springville; 801-489-9543.**

La Dolce Vita—$ to $$

Giovanni Della Corte and his family emigrated from Naples to Coalville, Utah, in 1980 and worked in a restaurant there until they opened their family-style Italian restaurant in Provo on July 4, 1984. The restaurant is a three-generation operation as Giovanni, his wife, Susi, their son Jerry and daughter-in-law Anna Rosa and grandson Jimmy all work to make this a longtime favorite Italian restaurant in the Provo area. The pizza and calzones are popular, but my favorites are the pasta combo, which includes two pastas, one under a white sauce and the other under a red sauce, and the chef's combo, a specially prepared breaded beef cutlet topped with a house sauce and melted cheese served with three different kinds of pasta. On Thurs. the traditional gnocchi (potato and flour dumplings baked with cheeses under a red sauce) is available. Open Mon.–Sat. 11 A.M.–4 P.M. and 5–10 P.M. **61 N. 100 E.; 801-373-8482.**

Ottavio's—$$ to $$$

It's hard to recommend when to eat at Ottavio's. At lunch, in addition to regular menu items, there's a wonderful Sicilian-style lunch buffet with homemade bread, salads, soups, three hot dishes that vary each day, plus four or five different kinds of pizza. If you want great food in a hurry, you can't beat the buffet. But if you want the full Ottavio's experience, come for dinner. There's a nightly special; plus you can't go wrong with the Salmone Alla Ottavio, fresh Alaskan king salmon poached in a creamy basil sauce and served on a bed of fettuccine, or the Rigatoni Fra Diavolo, a pasta served with a sauce made of sausage sautéed with black olives and white onions in a spicy garlic-basil marinara sauce with just a touch of cream. For vegetarians, a favorite is the Eggplant Parmigiana made with ricotta, romano and mozzarella cheeses and baked in a wonderful marinara sauce.

In addition to the fine and large portions of food, you get live Italian music. Most of the evening, it's delightful accordion music, but several times during the evening one of the talented staff launches into an Italian love song or a Puccini aria that will stop your fork in midair. Ottavio's opened in 1998. Two brothers, Ottavio and Lenny Belvedere, and their cousin Vic Balsano, all young immigrants from Palermo, Sicily, had operated restaurants in California in the early 1950s, and with Ottavio's urging decided to open a restaurant in Provo. Vic is in the restaurant nearly every day and oversees the operation with great charm and efficiency. Located across the street from the historic Utah County Courthouse and not far from the historic Provo Tabernacle, Ottavio's is in the heart of downtown Provo. Open Mon.–Sat. 11:30 A.M.–10 P.M. **71 E. Center; 801-377-9555.**

SUNDANCE RESORT

Sundance Resort is located in Provo Canyon on the east slope of Mt. Timpanogos. Take University Ave. (US Hwy. 189) north from Provo to the mouth of Provo Canyon, where it joins Hwy. 52 to go northeast up Provo Canyon to its junction with Hwy. 92. Take Hwy. 92 north for a few miles to Sundance. You can also reach Hwy. 52 by taking the Orem I-15 exit, Exit 275, and continuing east to Provo Canyon.

Owl Bar and Foundry Grill—$$ to $$$

Completed in 1996, the barn-wood building at Sundance is a complex that houses a grocery store, gift shop, offices and the Owl Bar and the Foundry Grill. **1-800-892-1600; 801-223-4220.**

The main attraction at the **Owl Bar,** aside from the variety of liquid refreshments available, is the 18-foot-long counter and 10-foot-high mirrored back bar that has been restored after a long career in Thermopolis, Wyoming. The bar was built in Ireland in the 1890s, sent to England, and then shipped across the Atlantic and west to the frontier town of Thermopolis, where it became a popular stopping point for travelers along the Outlaw Trail, which stretched from Canada to Mexico. The Owl Bar saw generations of patrons until it finally closed in the early 1990s. Robert Redford purchased the bar, moved it to the Sundance Resort and, after a two-year restoration, it was once again ready for public use. Open Mon.–Fri. 2 P.M.–midnight, Sat.–Sun. noon–midnight.

The **Foundry Grill,** adjacent to the Owl Bar, offers panoramic views of the mountains, a wine list with nearly 150 wines—mostly American—and food cooked in a large wood-burning oven. Grilled pork chops, spit-roasted chicken and leg of lamb and smoked red trout are among the dinner entrées. Open Mon.–Sat. 7 A.M.–10 P.M., Sun. 9 A.M.–9 P.M. Dinner reservations especially recommended.

Tree Room—$$$ to $$$$

The premier dining establishment at Sundance, the Tree Room features good food amid Native American art and Western memorabilia collected by Robert Redford. The Tree Room features steaks and fish. My favorite is the pepper tree steak, served with chutney and mango sauce. In addition, the Grill Room is an informal bistro-style restaurant with soups, sandwiches, pizza, pasta and house specialties. Both open 5–10 P.M. **801-223-4220.**

Services

Visitor Information

Utah Valley Convention and Visitors Bureau—100 E. Center St., Ste. 3200, Provo, UT 84606; 1-800-222-8824; 801-370-8390; www.utahvalley.org. The **visitor center** and gift shop are located in Ste. 111 in the historic Utah County Courthouse. Open Mon.–Fri. 9 A.M.–5 P.M. **51 S. University Ave. 1-800-222-8824; 801-370-8394.**

Tooele

Unless you have grown up with the name, most people have a hard time pronouncing Tooele. But it is simple: "too-ILL-ah." The origin of the name for both the city and county located west of the Salt Lake Valley across the Oquirrh Moun-

Getting There

Tooele is located 34 miles southwest of Salt Lake City. Take Interstate 80 west to Lake Point Junction (Exit 99), then follow Hwy. 36 south for 12 miles.

tains is unclear. Some claim that it comes from the Spanish word of Aztec origin, *tule,* which means "bulrush." Rushes and reeds were common in the swampy areas in the valley. Another possible origin is in the name of a Goshute Indian chief named Tuilla. Another possibility is from the Shoshoni word *tuu-weeta,* which means "black bear." One of the six original Utah counties created in 1850, the name was changed from Tuilla to Tooele in 1852.

The three major population areas in Tooele County are the county seat of Tooele, with a population of about 18,000 people, located in the northeastern corner of the county at the western base of the Oquirrh Mountains; Grantsville, the second-largest city in the county, with a population of about 5,000, located about 10 miles northwest of Tooele on the western edge of Tooele Valley near the eastern slope of the Stansbury Mountains; and Wendover (see the **Wendover** chapter), located on the Utah–Nevada border in the northwestern corner of the county more than 100 miles from the county seat. A fourth community, Stansbury Park, was developed in the 1970s and has become a popular residential area where backyards border the popular Stansbury Golf Course or nestle up to a series of waterways fed by springs in the area. Dugway, a military installation about 35 miles southwest of Tooele, was established in 1942.

Most of the western two-thirds of Tooele County is a vast military reserve where no public access is allowed. South of Tooele along the western slope of the Oquirrh Mountains are the mining towns of Stockton, Ophir and Mercur, all of which date from the 19th century. The farming and ranching areas of St. John, Clover and Vernon are located in the valleys south of Tooele. Across the Stansbury Mountains to the west of Tooele is the Skull Valley Indian Reservation, where a few families of Goshute Indians reside. North of the reservation is the abandoned site of Iosepa, where a monument recalls the efforts of Mormon converts from the Hawaiian and other Polynesian islands who struggled from 1889 to 1917 to make a home in the desert.

History

"Hastings Cutoff," the shortcut proposed in 1846 by Lansford B. Hastings for California-bound immigrants, cut through what four years later would become Tooele County. Several groups took the cutoff in the summer of 1846, the last of which was the ill-fated Donner-Reed party. After spending three weeks to travel the 36 miles from the Weber River to the Salt Lake Valley, the Donner-Reed Party finally rounded the southern end of the Great Salt Lake and entered the north end of Tooele Valley. At the western edge of the valley, the group took on water at Twenty-wells—the present site of Grantsville—fed their livestock, cut grass from the meadow to take with them for feed, and did their best to prepare for the difficult 80-mile stretch across the Great Salt Lake Desert to the next water source at Pilot Peak just across the Utah–Nevada border. The desert crossing nearly overwhelmed the group. Animals wandered off or became so weak that they could not continue. Goods and supplies were left behind to lighten the wagons. Some wagons were abandoned, and the immigrants nearly died from thirst when their water supplies ran out. Historians conclude that the difficulties of the desert crossing and the loss of animals, supplies and time were all a prelude to the tragedy that overtook the group a few weeks later in the early snows of the Sierra Nevada.

When Mormons reached the Salt Lake Valley a year later and explorers ventured west into Tooele Valley and then out into the desert, they found ample evidence of the Donner-Reed journey—some of which is now housed in the Donner-Reed Museum in Grantsville.

Just three days after Brigham Young entered the Salt Lake Valley in July 1847, he led an exploring group west into the northern end of Tooele Valley. Five months later, Parley P. Pratt led an expedition from the south end of the Oquirrh Mountains through the entire length of the valley. Although these expeditions indicated that the area could support settlements, it was not until the fall of 1849 that Ezra T. Benson led a small group of settlers into the valley to found the communities of Grantsville and Tooele. Benson also supervised the construction of a gristmill that remains as one of the oldest buildings in Utah.

Mormon settlers concentrated on developing the agricultural potential of the area. However, with the establishment of Ft. Douglas in 1863, Col. Patrick Edward Connor sent his California volunteers out to prospect the nearby Wasatch and Oquirrh Mountains. Ore was found near Tooele. Connor laid out a city—named Stockton for his California hometown—for the 8,000 to 10,000 miners and workers he expected to come.

Rich mines were operated near Stockton—Sunshine, Mercur, West Rip, Ophir and Jacob City. By the fall of 1864 there were eight smelters located in Stockton. With the initial push by Connor and the arrival of the transcontinental railroad in 1869, mining flourished in Tooele County and, though Stockton fell far short of the expected 10,000 residents, the nearby town of Mercur did approach that number until, in 1902, a disastrous fire destroyed the entire business district. By 1917 Mercur was deserted. While Mercur was going through an era of decline, the International Smelting and Refining Company was building a large smelter east of Tooele, which operated from 1910 until 1972.

Mining and smelting transformed Tooele into a diverse ethnic community, as Mormons worked and lived alongside Irish, Italian, Greek and Slavic immigrants. The diversity was accentuated even more with the establishment of the Tooele Ordnance Depot and the Dugway Proving Ground during World War II. The military brought in personnel from all over the United States and even prisoners of war from Italy and Germany.

By the 21st century, mining and the military have been overshadowed economically. Nevertheless, along with a deep pioneer heritage, they remain a vital part of the community's character. Today one of the area's greatest challenges comes from its original inhabitants—the Goshute Indians. With few economic resources available and in the face of strong opposition by Utah's political leaders, tribal leaders have offered to provide sites on their Skull Valley Reservation for nuclear waste

Festivals and Events

Benson Grist Mill Pageant

second week in Aug. Held in the evening at the historic Benson Grist Mill near Stansbury Park, this locally written and produced pageant presents an overview history of early Tooele County, including the difficult period of 1857–1858 when settlers made preparations to abandon their newly established settlements in response to the arrival of federal troops under the command of Albert Sidney Johnston. Other episodes told through music, dance and historical narration include the gold rush, relations with the Goshute Indians, the Pony Express, the development of the mining and smelting industry and the Iosepa Polynesian settlement. **435-882-7678.**

Outdoor Activities

Biking

The Tooele area offers excellent possibilities for all levels of bikers. The Oquirrh Mountains provide uphill routes that will test the stamina of the best riders. Other rides require some elevation gain but are manageable for novice riders. The Tooele County Chamber of Commerce and the Parks and Recreation Department have prepared a free *Mountain Biking Guide*. In addition to these routes, the **Pony Express Trail** and the **Oquirrh–Bingham Mine Scenic Drive and Overlook** routes (see the Scenic Drives

section) are excellent biking routes. The Bingham Mine route climbs nearly 4,000 feet in 9.5 miles from Tooele, while the Pony Express Trail stretches for miles and miles around the southern edge of the Great Salt Lake Desert to Fish Springs National Wildlife Refuge, Callao and Ibapah. The following represent the diversity you will find.

Benson Grist Mill Loop

For a nice ride through rural Tooele County, this 16.8-mile loop is a good choice. The modest elevation gain comes in the first 4 miles; after that, it's a gentle downhill or level ride. The loop begins at the historic Benson Mill north of Tooele and Stansbury Park. Ride east through Stansbury Park to Hwy. 36, the main route into Tooele. Turn right and follow Hwy. 36 south for 3.9 miles, then turn right at Erda Wy. Follow this west for 6 miles as it passes homes, farms and fields. At the intersection of Hwy. 138, turn right for a 7-mile ride back to the Benson Mill.

Soldier Canyon

This 12-mile out-and-back ride for novice and intermediate bikers begins in Stockton at Bryan's Service Store and heads east along Silver Ave. Follow the asphalt road as it turns right after three blocks and then becomes a gravel road after 2.2 miles. Take the left-hand fork into the mouth of Soldier Canyon. Here the road begins a steady uphill climb past the remnants of some of Utah's earliest mining activity. The ride ends at locked gates a mile after you pass the ruins of some charcoal kilns that were used to produce fuel for smelting the gold and silver ore. The elevation gain is 1,740 feet, making it a slow trip out and a fast one back.

Diving

Bonneville Seabase

Utah's most popular scuba diving location is a geothermal pool owned by Linda Nelson and George Sanders. The salt-saturated soil gives the water a salinity content very close to that of the ocean; more than 70 marine species, including groupers, triggerfish, damsel fish, clown fish and nurse sharks (one now more than 8 feet long), have been introduced and now thrive in this "micro-ocean." Fish will eat lettuce from your hand. The geothermally heated water makes scuba diving and snorkeling possible year-round. The pool has a maximum length of 210 yards and width of 150 yards and is 24 feet at its deepest point. An air-filled chamber allows divers to talk and observe below the surface. Scuba and snorkel equipment can be rented at the facility. Located 5 miles west of Grantsville on Hwy. 138. **435-884-3874.**

Golf

Oquirrh Hills Golf Course

This 9-hole public course in Tooele offers plenty of challenges with the 246-yard second hole—considered one of the most difficult par 3 holes in Utah—and the 543-yard par 5 9th hole. It is usually fairly easy to get on this course. **435-882-4220.**

Stansbury Golf Course

When constructed in 1972, Stansbury was a private course for residents of the housing community that surrounds the fairways. A decade later the golf course was acquired by the community and is now leased to a private operator, but open to the public. The course is flat and surrounded by some 20 small lakes formed by the springs in the area. Some of the most difficult holes are the par 3s—especially the 5th and 13th, which have large ponds in front and to the side of the greens. Generally it is no problem to get on the course unless there is a tournament under way. Located in Stansbury Park. **435-882-4820.**

Hiking

Deseret Peak

At 11,031 feet, Deseret Peak is the highest mountain in the Stansbury Range and Tooele County. The magnificent views and variety of terrain that includes meadows, aspen, fir and pine forests, and a high mountain glacial cirque all make for an exciting and inspiring 7.5-mile round-trip hike.

From the summit you have a 360-degree view that takes in the Wasatch Mountains to the east, the Great Salt Lake to the north, Pilot Peak and Nevada to the northwest, the Great Salt Lake Desert to the west, and the accordionlike ridges of a series of desert mountain ranges that seem to stretch forever to the southwest.

The moderately difficult hike takes you up 3,600 feet from the trailhead in Loop Campground, at the end of the road up South Willow Canyon. The loop begins 0.75 mile from the trailhead. Take the left fork and follow Mill Fork in a southerly direction as it ascends for 2 miles to a 10,000-foot ridge. At the top of the ridge, the trail turns in a westerly direction for 0.75 mile to Deseret Peak. The return route heads north for 1.5 miles along the west side of three smaller peaks, then turns east for 0.5 mile into Pockets Fork. When you come to the junction of a trail that connects North and South Willow Canyons, turn right and follow the trail for 1.5 miles to where you took the left fork trail up Mill Canyon, and then return the 0.75 mile to the campground. The Loop Campground is located 10 miles southwest of Grantsville. Take the paved road heading south out of Grantsville (West St.) toward Rush Valley for 5 miles, then take the South Willow Canyon road to the right for another 5 miles to the campground.

Swimming

Tooele City Pool

This indoor public pool is open year-round for adult lap swimming (mornings, noon and evenings) as well as general public swimming. **55 N. 200 W.; 435-882-3247.**

Seeing and Doing

Historic Sites

Benson Grist Mill

E. T. Benson, one of the original 1847 pioneers to Utah, supervised the construction of this gristmill, one of Utah's oldest commercial buildings, in 1854. Timber for the mill was cut in the nearby Oquirrh Mountains; rawhide strips and wooden pegs hold the mortised timbers together. The building was used for nearly a century, but then stood vacant until 1986, when volunteers began renovation and restored much of the original machinery. Open May–Oct. Tues.–Sat. 10 A.M.–4 P.M. Located a block west of the junction of Hwys. 36 and 138 at Mills Junction—4 miles south of Interstate 80 Exit 99, near Stansbury Park. **435-882-7678.**

Iosepa

When Hawaiian members of the Mormon faith joined their fellow saints (members of the Church of the Latter-day Saints refer to themselves and other church members as saints) as part of the 19th-century gathering to Utah, it is hard to conceive that they could have imagined a world so different from their lush island paradise. But Skull Valley and its harsh desert climate became the Utah home to 46 Hawaiian settlers in 1889. They called their community Iosepa, which means "Joseph" in Hawaiian. Two Josephs were recognized in the name of the settlement: Joseph Smith, founder of the Mormon faith, and Joseph F. Smith, who went to the Hawaiian Islands as a missionary in 1854.

The settlers built houses, a schoolhouse and a general store, and irrigated their crops with water from the nearby Stansbury Mountains. When three cases of leprosy were discovered in 1896, the victims were isolated in a house apart from the settlement. By 1915 the population reached 228 and included not only Hawaiians but natives from other Polynesian islands as well. Skull Valley proved a very difficult place economically and, when the Hawaiian Temple was completed in 1917, residents of Iosepa were encouraged to return to their native islands. Today all that remains is the cemetery and a monument to the settlers of Iosepa. Take Exit 77 off Interstate 80 and drive south for approximately 15 miles toward Dugway.

Mercur and Ophir

These two 19th-century-mining areas are not exactly ghost towns. People still live in Ophir,

and though Mercur was destroyed in a fire, mining operations continued until recently. These old mining communities are located on the west slope and at the south end of the Oquirrh Mountains. Mercury was discovered here by a Bavarian prospector in the late 1860s (the name *Mercur* comes from the German word for mercury). Barrick Mercur Gold Mines took over the property in the 1980s and revived mining in the area. However, mining operations ended in March 1997. Ophir, which is a name from the Bible, has a particularly interesting city hall. The false-fronted frame structure, built in 1890, has a bell tower and is an historic remnant from the days of early western mining. Take Hwy. 36 south from Tooele to Hwy. 73 and turn left. Watch for the road to Mercur as it heads back eastward. The road to Ophir, located in the canyon just north of Mercur, is another mile or so farther north off Hwy. 73. The 3.5-mile drive up Ophir Canyon from Hwy. 73 is particularly beautiful in the fall when the trees have their autumn leaves.

Museums

Donner-Reed Museum

The Grantsville adobe schoolhouse was constructed in 1861—only 15 years after the ill-fated Donner-Reed Party replenished their water barrels from the nearby springs and set out for what became a desperate journey across the Salt Lake Desert to the next water source at Pilot Springs some 80 miles away. The party survived the desert, but 40 of the 87 members lost their lives when they became snowbound in the Sierra Nevada a few weeks later. During the desert crossing, wagons and goods were abandoned, some of which (including guns and tools) were recovered and are now on display in the museum. Other items include Grantsville's original iron jail, an early log cabin, a blacksmith shop, old wagons and Indian pottery and artifacts. Across the street from the museum is another early building, the 1866 adobe church. The museum is open Sat. 2–6 P.M. or by appointment. Located on the corner of Cooley and Clark Sts., one block north of Main St.

Grantsville City Office, **435-884-3411; 435-884-3348 during nonoffice hours.**

Tooele County Railroad and Mining Museum

The 1909 Tooele Railroad Station is the home of Tooele's Railroad and Mining Museum and much more. The railroad, mining and smelting were important aspects of Tooele's history, and the museum—through photographs and artifacts—does an excellent job of interpreting this history. One of the largest Utah employers was the International Smelting and Refining Company, whose Tooele Smelter employed more than 3,000 people during World War II. The smelter opened in 1909 to process copper, lead and zinc and did not close until 1972. It is likely that one of the museum volunteers on duty has worked at the smelter, for the railroad or in one of the mines—or at all three. For railroad buffs, there is a steam engine, dining car, cabooses and railroad cars. Among the eclectic collection of artifacts are an iron lung and a dog-powered washing machine. Open Memorial Day–Labor Day Tues.–Sat. 1–4 P.M. Located at the corner of Broadway and Vine Sts. **435-882-2836.**

Tooele Daughters of Utah Pioneers Museum

One of Tooele's oldest buildings, the 1867 stone structure has served many functions—including a courthouse, jailhouse and city office building—before it became a museum. Even older is the 1855 Zachariah Edwards log cabin, which was moved to the east side of the pioneer hall. It is one of the earliest residences in Tooele and one of the oldest log cabins remaining in Utah. Inside the hall are more than 1,000 artifacts, including many pictures from Tooele's pioneer era. Open Memorial Day–Labor Day Thurs.– Sat. 10 A.M.– 4 P.M. or by appointment. **35 East Vine St.; 435-882-8198; 435-882-0982; 435-833-9916.**

Scenic Drives

Oquirrh–Bingham Mine Scenic Drive and Overlook

This drive offers a spectacular view of the Salt Lake Valley, Tooele Valley, the southern end of the Great Salt Lake and the Bingham Canyon Copper Mine. From Tooele the road heads east on Vine St. along a paved road for 7 miles into Middle Canyon and then continues along a steep, winding gravel road that climbs a mile to Butterfield Pass at 8,400 feet. Turn left here and drive another 2.5 miles to the overlook at an elevation of 9,400 feet. Passenger vehicles should be able to handle the road from Tooele to the overlook.

A dirt and gravel road from Butterfield Pass takes you down the east side of the Oquirrh Mountains through Butterfield Canyon into the extreme southwestern end of the Salt Lake Valley; high-clearance vehicles and four-wheel-drive vehicles are recommended for this portion of the road. From the mouth of Butterfield Canyon, you can follow the Bingham-Magna Hwy. (Hwy. 111) along the west side of the Salt Lake Valley to Magna and then back to Tooele all along paved roads, or make an out-and-back ride the way you have come.

Pony Express Trail

For 19 months in 1860–1861, some 80 Pony Express riders pounded along the 1,900-mile-long trail between St. Joseph, Missouri, and Sacramento, California, to deliver letters in 10 days' time—a journey that had previously taken many weeks by wagon or stagecoach. Riding at an average speed of 7 miles an hour, riders weighing no more than 120 pounds and dressed in bright red shirts and blue pants covered between 60 and 120 miles before passing the mail pouches on to the next rider. Horses were exchanged at swing stations approximately 12 miles apart. You can drive the best-preserved portion of the old Pony Express Trail and overland stagecoach route as it heads west for 133 miles from Stage Coach Inn State Park (near Fairfield on Hwy. 73), one of the original Pony Express stations, to Ibapah near the Utah–Nevada border. The federal Bureau of Land Management preserves and interprets the trail.

Watch for visitor information signs at the Faust Station (near Hwy. 36), and plan a stop at the restored Simpson Springs Station, where there is a developed BLM campground with 14 sites just east of the station. Most people take time to visit the isolated Fish Springs National Wildlife Refuge (75 miles west of Hwy. 36 at Fish Springs). The road passes through Callao, site of another station and several ranches that form a small community (see the **Wendover** chapter). Other stops include the Boyd Station ruins and the Canyon Station ruins, where, in July 1863, Indians killed a stagecoach agent and four soldiers before burning the station. You can also take a short detour to the old mining town of Gold Hill. Monuments mark most of the sites of the 16 stations from Camp Floyd to Ibapah, site of the Deep Creek Station.

The road is sand and gravel, and vehicles usually don't have much trouble; wet roads, however, can cause sections of the road to become an impassable quagmire. The route passes just south of the Great Salt Desert, offering an unforgettable view of the desert and mountains. From Ibapah, most travelers head north about 60 miles to Wendover to refuel, eat and visit the casinos before driving back across the Salt Desert 120 miles to Salt Lake City on Interstate 80. There is no gas available for the more than 200 miles between Tooele and Wendover, so start out with a full tank, let people know where you are going and take plenty of water. (Sometimes gas is available at Ibapah, but don't count on it.) You can pick up a BLM brochure that offers a good overview of the trail at the **Tooele County Chamber of Commerce and Tourism Office** (see the Services section) or other visitor information locations in the state.

Wildlife Viewing

Various species of wildlife abound throughout Tooele County, including mule deer, elk, antelope, mountain lions and small game animals. Some exciting opportunities to observe wildlife include the following.

Fish Springs National Wildlife Refuge

The only way to reach the refuge is across the Pony Express Trail (see the Scenic Drives section). The 10,000-acre spring-fed marsh is an almost unbelievable contrast to the desert and barren hills through which most of the trail follows. The refuge is located on the east side of the Fish Springs Range and is formed by the springs that rise from a fault zone along the edge of the mountains. The best time to visit the refuge is during the late fall and early spring, when migrating waterfowl by the thousands can be seen, including swans, Canada geese, blue herons, snowy egrets and many other species. An 11.5-mile-long self-guided auto tour takes you through the refuge. Much of the tour follows along the human-made dikes, which separate the refuge into numerous ponds. **Refuge Manager, Fish Springs National Wildlife Refuge, Dugway, UT 84022.**

Where to Stay

Best Western Tooele Inn—$ to $$
Indoor pool and spa; 32 rooms. **365 N. Main; 1-800-448-5010; 435-882-5010.**

Comfort Inn—$ to $$
Swimming pool and hot tub; 61 rooms. **491 N. Main; 1-800-228-5150; 435-882-6100.**

Where to Eat

Athenas Greek Family Restaurant—$ to $$
Tracy Manousakis opened this establishment in 1983. An orange and olive farmer from the island of Crete, Tracy immigrated to the United States and, after stops in Townsend, Massachusetts, and Pasadena, California, he came to visit his brother in Tooele and decided he wanted to stay. Highly recommended are the Greek dishes including shish kebab, dolmathes, pastistsio and the Greek salad. There is also pizza, spaghetti, oven sandwiches, hamburgers, sandwiches and omelettes. This is a local favorite because of the variety of food that is offered—a good place to bring family or friends who want plenty of choices. Located near the center of town just

west of the Daughters of Utah Pioneers Museum and County Library. Open Mon.–Sat. 9 A.M.– 10 P.M. **21 E. Vine; 435-882-8035.**

Services

Visitor Information

Tooele County Chamber of Commerce and Tourism Office—201 N. Main, P.O. Box 414, Tooele, UT 84074; 1-800-378-0690; 435-807-0690.

Wendover

For Utahns, Wendover and gambling are synonymous. Each week, thousands make the 120-mile drive from Salt Lake City west to Wendover to try their luck at the five casinos located just across the border in Nevada. Technically, there are two towns that share a common boundary along the Utah–Nevada state line and the same Mountain Standard Time zone. In reality, however, there is only one Wendover, and the Wendover Visitor and Convention Bureau has solved the problem of promoting a single town in two states by calling the place "Wendover, USA." Some have proposed that the state boundary be moved east so that Wendover would all be a part of Nevada. Perhaps it will happen, but the odds are against it. For those travelers familiar with Las Vegas and Reno, Wendover is small potatoes, but when you can drive to Wendover in less than 2 hours, it is a much greater attraction than the other Nevada gambling capitals that are 8 to 10 hours away.

Gambling was a latecomer as far as Wendover's fame is concerned. The Bonneville Salt Flats, just outside Wendover, developed international fame in the 1930s as the site where world land speed records were set. In the 1940s archaeologists discovered 10,000-year-old Paleo-Indian artifacts in Danger Cave. The more than 19,000 airmen stationed at Wendover dur-

ing World War II may have had second thoughts about the government's wisdom in sending them to such an isolated spot. They surely appreciated what Bob Hope said when he visited them—that the place should be called "Leftover."

Surrounded by desert on all four sides, Wendover is a neon oasis that you can appreciate only after traveling to it from any direction in the heat of summer or the cold of winter. Wendover lies next to the Toana Mountain Range, which rises 5,000 feet above the desert. Northwest of Wendover, 10,000-foot Pilot Peak was a landmark for early travelers across the desert and the original source of water for Wendover. To the south, the 12,000-foot Deep Creek Mountains are among the highest in the state.

History

Before human beings arrived, and even before there was a Great Salt Lake Desert, a vast area of western Utah and portions of the surrounding states (approximately 9,300 square miles) were covered by the waters of Lake Bonneville. Approximately 12,000 years ago the lake receded, leaving a hard, flat surface of crystalline salt where no vegetation grows. During the winter and spring, the flats resemble a huge lake because the rain and snow falling on the area do not evaporate quickly and the hard salt layer means that percolation beneath the surface is very slow.

The area was not so desolate more than 10,000 years ago when prehistoric humans set foot on the former lake bed. If the State Line Silver Smith Complex accommodates most visitors to Wendover today, for the first 10,000 years of human presence in and around Wendover, it was Danger Cave, located a mile east of town. The cave has yielded more than 2,000 artifacts, including basketry, clothing, netting, cordage, arrows, knives, traps, clay effigies and tools made from bone, horn and stone. Danger Cave was occupied at various times by prehistoric peoples and Native Americans until after U.S. Army Capt. John C. Frémont traversed the area in 1845, stopping at the springs at Pilot Peak, about 23 miles north of Wendover. Travelers on the Hastings Cutoff in 1846 also stopped at the Pilot Peak springs, including the ill-fated Donner–Reed Party, which left several wagons and many of its goods on the salt desert, about 35 miles northeast of Wendover.

Established in 1907 as a watering stop on the just-completed Western Pacific Railroad, Wendover, in comparison with most Utah towns, is relatively new. The origin of the name has been debated for years. Some folks attribute the name to the fact that the town is surrounded by desert on all sides and to get there from anywhere required "wending" over the desert. More likely, though, is that it was named for Charles Wendover, a surveyor employed by the Western Pacific Railroad.

Getting There

Wendover is located along Interstate 80, 120 miles west of Salt Lake City. Heading east along Interstate 80, Wendover is 400 miles east of Reno, Nevada. It's about a 2-hour drive along the interstate from Salt Lake City.

While most Wendover visitors do drive, there are several buses that run daily between Salt Lake City, Ogden and Wendover. There is a charge for riding the bus but, on weekdays, by the time you get cash back, a food discount, free drinks, keno tickets and lucky bets from the casino, they actually pay you to ride the bus. A typical weekday schedule has the bus leaving downtown Salt Lake City about 9 A.M. and returning from Wendover at 5 P.M. Weekend buses depart at 6:30 P.M. on Fri. and return at 2:30 A.M. that night, or leave Sat. evening at 5 P.M. and return at 1 A.M. The following bus lines operate between Salt Lake City and Wendover: **Casino Caravans, 1-800-876-5825; 801-685-9311; Donna's Tours, 1-800-831-0749; 801-280-1434; LeBus, 1-800-366-0288; 801-975-0202.**

Wendover gained a measure of lasting fame in 1914 when the transcontinental telephone line was joined at the Utah–Nevada state line in Wendover. At the time the line was completed, a cross-country call took 23 minutes to place and a 3-minute station-to-station call cost $20.70—a rare case of things having gotten cheaper over the years.

About that time, automobile racers were touting the virtues of the level, hard-packed salt flats east of Wendover. In the 1930s numerous speed records were set on the Bonneville Salt Flats, with Pontiac's Bonneville automobile model taking its name from Utah's salt desert raceway. The salt flats have also been the basis for a potash industry, which began in 1917 and today produces more than 100,000 tons of fertilizer annually.

The two most important dates in Wendover's economic history were 1926, when the Victory Hwy. was completed to Wendover from Salt Lake City, and 1931, when Nevada passed its wide-open gambling law. William and Anna Smith applied for one of the first casino licenses and, at the height of the Great Depression, took their own gamble in opening the State Line Casino. Bill Smith, who, according to tradition, was kicked off the train in Wendover in the 1920s, stayed in the desert town and purchased a gas station, to which he added the casino when the gambling law was passed. The State Line served Utahns and California-bound travelers on US Hwy. 40 until the 1980s, when three other casinos were established in Wendover.

Today Wendover has a population of approximately 4,100, but during the World War II years as many as 19,000 airmen were stationed at Wendover Air Base. High-altitude bombers trained over the salt flats, dropping bombs on full-size salt battleships and cities made of salt. At one of the gunnery ranges, the Tokyo Trolley, which consisted of three machine guns located on a moving railroad car, was used by trainees to shoot at moving targets in an attempt to simulate aerial combat. The isolated location was the site selected by Col. Paul W. Tibbets Jr. for training the 509th Composite Group in preparation for dropping the atomic bombs on Japan. Many of the original World War II–era buildings remain on what was Wendover Air Base. A monument to the 509th Composite Group at the Wendover Welcome Center commemorates the mission's objective, with an August 1945 statement by President Harry Truman: "The atomic bomb is too dangerous to be loose in a lawless world … we pray that [God] may guide us to use it in His ways and for His purposes."

Major Attractions

Wagering

If it is not obvious by now, let me state it clearly: 99 percent of the people who drive to Wendover come for the gambling casinos, which are the closest casinos to Utah's Wasatch Front. While not all of the more than 1 million people who live along the Wasatch Front gamble, enough do to make Wendover a popular weekend destination. There are four casinos, with more planned in the future. You will find the same kinds of games as in most casinos, including poker, craps, blackjack, roulette, sports book and keno, as well as slot and other gaming machines. All have restaurants, accommodations and live entertainment. It is easy to visit all five casinos, either by car or by shuttle bus (see the Services section). Walking is also a possibility, but one that few people seem to take.

Peppermill Casino

With 198 rooms and plans to expand, the Peppermill is trying to keep up with Wendover's gambling boom. It is known as the "Party Place," with top-notch dance and rock bands. The **Peppermill Restaurant** features the only lunchtime prime rib buffet in Wendover. **680 Wendover Blvd.; 1-800-648-9660; 775-664-2255; www.peppermillwendover.com.**

Rainbow Casino

The casino features astrological designs with waterfalls and lots of foliage over the **Rainbow**

Restaurant, open 24 hours. There is also a "moving" sky. There are 298 rooms. **1045 Wendover Blvd.; 1-800-217-0049.**

Red Garter Casino

With 48 rooms, you can usually save a few dollars off the rates and the four other Wendover casinos. The **Garden Court** restaurant has a popular ham-and-egg breakfast, served 24 hours a day, along with other American and Mexican dishes. **1225 Wendover Blvd.; 1-800-982-2111; 775-664-2111.**

State Line Casino and Silver Smith Hotel, Casino and Convention Center

The State Line Casino received one of the first licenses when the Nevada gambling law was passed in 1931. Although the original building has been replaced, the State Line is reportedly the only casino in Nevada still under the ownership of the original licensees. The State Line Casino, located on the south side of Wendover Blvd., and the Silver Smith on the north side, are connected by a skywalk that keeps the gambling traffic flowing between the two casinos. If you make only one stop in Wendover, this is the one you should make. It is the home of the neon sign "Wendover Will" and is the largest casino in Wendover. The two casinos have 950 rooms, with 700 rooms at the State Line and 250 at the Silver Smith. There are also 56 sites at the RV park below the State Line. Weekday rooms are generally available, but weekends usually fill up in advance. Entertainment is offered nightly in the State Line lounge. Well-known stars make appearances from time to time. There are outdoor pools with Jacuzzis at both facilities. The Silver Smith has two tennis courts and an exercise room. Both casinos offer a midweek golf package, which includes 18 holes of golf with a cart for a modest fee.

You won't go hungry, especially if you go for the all-you-can-eat buffet in the **Bonneville Room** at the State Line, open after 5 P.M. **The Pantry** at the Silver Smith and **Anna's Kitchen** at the State Line are open 24 hours a day and offer similar fare for breakfast, lunch and dinner—eggs, omelettes, pancakes, burgers, sandwiches, soups, salads, chicken, beef and seafood. **Lanterns** at the Silver Smith offers an Asian buffet, while **Señor Jones** serves Mexican dishes. A **food court** at the Silver Smith offers several fast-food choices. The **Salt Cellar** at the State Line is the fanciest and highest-priced restaurant in town, offering homemade pasta daily and more elaborate fare, such as lobster, veal, steaks, prime rib and fish. The Salt Cellar is open Tues.–Thurs., Sun. 6–10 P.M., Fri.–Sat. 6–11 P.M. Both casinos are located on Wendover Blvd. at the Utah–Nevada state line. **1-800-848-7300 both casinos; www.statelinenv.com.**

Racing

Bonneville Salt Flats Raceway

At one time, the Bonneville Salt Flats were synonymous with world land speed records; they still attract plenty of racers each year. The salt flats, which range in thickness from less than 1 inch to 6 feet, were formed about 12,000 years ago when prehistoric Lake Bonneville disappeared at the end of the ice age. During the summer months, when water evaporates and the salt is compacted, the flats make a natural speedway. They were first used as early as 1911, when two race car pioneers, W. D. Rishel and Ferg Johnson, began promoting the salt flats as an ideal venue. Three years later, in 1914, Terry Tetzlaff set an unofficial land speed record of 141 mph there, and soon after a 10-mile-long speedway was established, along with an oval track.

Deterioration of the salt flats has been a serious problem for the last couple of decades, and it is doubtful that another world land speed record will ever be set on the Bonneville Salt Flats. Nevertheless, several racing associations continue to sponsor races (one vehicle at a time against the clock), usually between July and Oct. Visitors are permitted in the pit area, on the starting line and at the timing stands down the track. There are no permanent facilities at the raceway, which can be reached by taking Exit 4 off Interstate 80 and following the paved road 1.4 miles north, then 3.7 miles east, to the end of the pavement. **Bureau of Land Management, Salt Lake District, 435-977-4300; Wendover USA Visitor and Convention Bureau; 1-866-299-2489; 775-664-3138.**

Festivals and Events

Cinco de Mayo

May 5. Nearly two-thirds of Wendover's permanent population is Hispanic, and most of them are from Juchipila, Zacatecas, Mexico. They followed family members and friends to Wendover for the employment opportunities in the casinos. In May 1990 the Hispanic community held its first Cinco de Mayo celebration. It has continued to grow since then with a parade, fiesta and Mexican dance. **Wendover Welcome Center, 685 Wendover Blvd.; 1-866-299-2489; 775-664-3138.**

Speed Week

third week of Aug. This is the largest speed event on the Bonneville Salt Flats. It dates from 1948, drawing up to 360 cars and motorcycles. **Southern California Timing Association; 805-526-1805.**

Outdoor Activities

Biking

A nice 12.8-mile circular course begins and ends at the Wendover Welcome Center. The course starts out at an elevation of 4,600 feet and has four ascents, with 5,200 feet the highest point along the course. The climbs can be taxing, but the breakneck downhills are thrilling. The route is a combination of dirt roads, pavement and single track. The scenery is breathtaking, as the seemingly endless desert stretches to the south and east, and 10,600-foot Pilot Peak rises above you to the north. Pick up a map, a course description and information about other mountain bike courses at the **Wendover Welcome Center, 685 Wendover Blvd.; 1-866-299-2489; 775-664-3138.**

Golf

Toana Vista Golf Course

If the brown and white of the Great Salt Lake Desert gets to you, or the lights and noise of the casinos give you a case of "casino fever," you can find your "cure" at the Toana Vista Golf Course. Some insist that this is the only patch of green in the whole 500 miles between Salt Lake City and California. The 18-hole championship course that opened in 1987 is popular with Wendover visitors. This is a challenging links-style course, with narrow fairways and plenty of chances to hit your ball into the desert surrounding the course. Perhaps the most memorable feature of the course is the tremendous view out across the desert and salt flats; you can almost see forever. Open Mar.–Nov. Reservations are taken two weeks in advance and are highly recommended on weekends. Located at the west end of Wendover. Drive down Wendover Blvd. to the street just past the Pizza Hut restaurant, then turn left and follow the road to the golf course. **2319 Pueblo Blvd.; 1-800-852-4330; 775-664-4300.**

Tennis

There are two lighted public tennis courts adjacent to the **Wendover Welcome Center; 1-866-299-2489; 775-664-3138.** The **State Line Hotel, Casino and Convention Center (1-800-848-7300; www.statelinenv.com)** also has two tennis courts available for guests; located on Wendover Blvd. at the Utah–Nevada state line.

Seeing and Doing

Historic Sites

Danger Cave

Archaeologists seem to have a knack for naming sites, and Danger Cave is no exception. Danger Cave received its moniker in 1941, when a large slab of rock fell from the ceiling during an archaeological excavation, narrowly missing one of the workers. Excavation of the 11 feet of deposits in the late 1940s and early 1950s pro-

duced a stratigraphy indicating that the cave had been occupied sequentially by a number of groups from about 10,000 years ago to the present—a much earlier regional occupation than had previously been proven. The cave, and radiocarbon dating of material found in it, helped establish a chronological framework that was a landmark in archaeological studies in Utah. Danger Cave was under the waters of Lake Bonneville until about 12,000 years ago.

The cave remains undeveloped, with no visitor center, exhibits or even signs. Still, it is worth the short drive from Wendover to see the cave and ponder the human story that has been played out inside and around the cave over the millennia. The cave has been closed to the public, so visitors should not attempt to enter the cave and should avoid disturbing anything at the site. Take Exit 4 off Interstate 80, east of Wendover, and drive north to the first paved road to the west (about a half mile) then turn left (west). The paved road becomes a dirt road that parallels I-80 back toward Exit 2. The cave is located a short distance east of the bridge crossing I-80 at Exit 2. The cave entrance is above the dirt road and can be seen from I-80.

Wendover Army Air Field

Long before Wendover became the mecca for Wasatch Front gamblers, it was a temporary home to thousands of members of the Army Air Corps who were stationed there during World War II. The army needed a large, uninhabited, isolated and open area for bombing and gunnery ranges. The deserts around Wendover were a good choice, and in 1941 nearly two million acres of land were set aside as a training ground for high-altitude formation flying, long-range navigation and simulated combat missions. The first detachment of trainees arrived less than four months before the United States entered World War II, following the attack on Pearl Harbor.

The most famous group to train at Wendover was the 509th Composite Group under the command of Col. Paul W. Tibbetts Jr. It was Tibbetts and his crew who, aboard the *Enola Gay*, dropped the atomic bomb on Hiroshima, Japan, which brought the end of World War II eight days later. In preparation for the historic event, the 509th Composite Group made 155 test drops over the Wendover range in 1944 and 1945.

Although the military continues to use the Wendover Bombing and Gunnery Ranges for training, Wendover Field was closed permanently in 1969. You can still see some of the World War II hangars and other buildings if you drive to the southern end of Wendover, on the Utah side. Also look at the rock ledges above Wendover, where some of the World War II airmen spent their free time with what seems to be an overabundance of paint. Pick up a driving tour brochure of the base at the Wendover Welcome Center, on Wendover Blvd. **1-866-299-2489; 775-664-3138.**

Wendover Will

Wendover's symbol and landmark, Wendover Will, was constructed in 1951 and has been welcoming visitors to Wendover for more than half a century. This neon sign that stands more than 70 feet tall is a wonderful example of neon technology from an earlier era. Built for the State Line Casino, the double-sided Will greets visitors coming from both the east and west. One arm waves a hello while the other hand points down to the State Line Casino. Will sports red boots, blue jeans, green shirt, yellow bandanna, white hat and an orange holster slung low on his hip, and he winks at you with one eye and offers an almost audible greeting with a cigarette flapping up and down in his mouth. Located on the Utah side of the state line along Wendover Blvd.

Other Sights

"Tree of Utah"

Along I-80 about 100 miles west of Salt Lake City and 26 miles east of Wendover, you see Karl Momen's "Tree of Utah" looming on the skyline long before you reach it. This somewhat controversial but nevertheless interesting sculpture, completed in 1981, is an 87-foot-tall "tree" built from 255 tons of cement, 1,800 ceramic tiles

and 5 tons of welding rod. There are six spheres on the tree coated with natural rock and minerals found within the state of Utah. The pods below symbolize the changing seasons and natural transformation of trees, while the tree itself came about out of Momen's desire to have a thing of beauty growing out of the seemingly sterile salt.

Scenic Drives

Deep Creek Mountains Backway

The 15-mile road from Callao south to Trout Creek has been designated a Scenic Backway, as it provides spectacular views and access to the east side of the southern end of the Deep Creek Mountains. The mountains seem deceptively low, but Ibapah and Haystack Peaks, the highest points in the range, are actually 12,087 and 12,020 feet in elevation. The Deep Creek Mountains have no developed hiking trails, but the road passes five canyons coming out of the Deep Creeks, which you can explore with a four-wheel-drive vehicle or on foot. The mountains are among Utah's most isolated ranges and are habitat for mule deer, elk, mountain lions and bighorn sheep.

Callao is nearly 100 miles south of Wendover, with about a third of the distance being on a graveled road, much of which was the old Pony Express Trail between Ibapah and Callao. You can combine the drive to Trout Creek with a stop in Callao and Ibapah, where Pony Express stations were located, and which are traditional cattle ranching centers; a visit to the Fish Springs Wildlife Refuge (see the Scenic Drives section under Seeing and Doing in the Tooele chapter); and a tour of the old mining district and town of Gold Hill. The backway is usually closed by snow accumulations late Nov.–Apr. Because of the distance involved, allow the better part of a day for the drive. Travel with a full tank of gas, and let people know of your planned itinerary. To reach Callao, take US Hwy. 93A south from Wendover about 25 miles. Watch for the road to Ibapah, and take it southeast for about 12 miles, then watch for the turnoff onto a dirt road to Gold Hill and Callao. Take this road southeast then south approximately 30 miles to Callao.

Silver Island Mountain Loop

The mountains northeast of Wendover look like islands floating in the distance as the white salt flats appear to give way to water. But it is all illusion: the water seems to recede as you move toward the mountains. The Silver Island Mountain Loop drive covers 54 miles on a graded gravel and dirt road that circles the mountains. The loop takes you near the route taken by the ill-fated Donner–Reed Party, which, in 1846, struggled across an 80-mile, waterless stretch of the salt desert along what was supposed to be a time-saving cutoff to California. The party lost animals, had to abandon wagons and suffered so many delays that early snows in California's Sierra Nevada claimed many of the party. (Survivors were forced to cannibalize the dead to make it through the winter.) The Silver Island Mountains area gives you some perspective of the distance and difficulties that early travelers encountered trying to cross the Great Salt Lake Desert. The road is most passable when it is dry, with summer and fall the best times to make the drive. A four-wheel-drive vehicle is recommended, especially if you plan to do any exploring in the canyons and washes. The loop, which takes a couple of hours to complete, begins 1 mile north of Interstate 80, off Exit 4.

Where to Stay

Accommodations

Accommodations can be difficult to find on weekends, and the Wendover Visitor and Convention Bureau staff reports that on some weekends, hundreds of people are turned away, with every casino and motel being full. If you plan to stay in Wendover, be sure to make reservations in advance. Rates are quite reasonable, with weekday prices about half the price of weekends. Casinos offer special rates and incentives, even on weekends, so inquire about their offerings

when you call. For information on casino accommodations, see Wagering in the Major Attractions section.

Best Western Salt Flat Inn—$$

Heated pool, sauna, whirlpool, steam room and exercise room; 24 rooms. **295 E. Wendover Blvd.; 435-665-7811.**

Bonneville Motel—$$

Heated swimming pool; 87 rooms. **375 Wendover Blvd.; 435-665-2500.**

Days Inn—$$

Heated swimming pool and whirlpool; 80 rooms. **685 E. Wendover Blvd.; 435-665-7811.**

Nevada Crossing—$$

The indoor swimming pool and spa are special attractions; 137 rooms. **1000 Wendover Blvd.; 775-664-2900.**

State Line Inn—$$

This motel in Utah is part of the State Line and Silver Smith enterprise, within walking distance of the parent facility on the Nevada side. Heated pool and whirlpool; 101 rooms. **101 Wendover Blvd.; 435-665-2226.**

Super 8—$$

Adjacent to the Red Garter Casino; 74 rooms. **1325 Wendover Blvd.; 1-800-800-8000; 702-664-2888.**

Camping

PRIVATE
State Line RV Park

Fifty-six sites with full hookups. Showers, complete laundry facilities, tennis courts, Jacuzzi, spa and swimming pool. Located within walking distance of the State Line Casino. **1-800-848-7300; 702-664-2221.**

Wendover KOA Kampground

One hundred sites, 80 pull-throughs with full hookups. Tent spaces. Outdoor heated pool, large store, laundry, playground and a casino shuttle service. Open year-round. Located off Interstate 80 at Exit 410 (on the Nevada side), on Camper Dr. **1-800-KOA-8552; 702-664-3221.**

Where to Eat

Most visitors eat in one of the five casinos described in the Major Attractions section. If you don't want to eat there, it is pretty much fast food at Arby's, Burger King, McDonald's, Subway or Taco Burger.

Services

Visitor Information

Wendover Welcome Center—Located across Wendover Blvd. from the Peppermill Casino, the Welcome Center has an ample supply of brochures and maps about the area and can provide information about events and other things to do and see. The staff are happy to answer questions about the area and to send, upon request, literature about the facilities, activities and events. There are several interesting displays about the Bonneville Salt Flats Speedway, wildlife and travel opportunities in Nevada. The east wall is devoted to the 509th Composite Group and displays a flight jacket and other World War II memorabilia. Outside, near the east end of the parking area, a peace memorial to the 509th was erected in 1990. Open daily 10 A.M.–5 P.M. Mountain Standard Time year-round. **685 Wendover Blvd.; 1-866-299-2489; 775-664-3138; www.wendover.org.**

Transportation

Wendover Casino and Community Shuttle Bus—This community bus service operated by Lewis Brothers Stage has two routes. The **Casino Loop** runs from the Red Garter Casino on the west, down Wendover Blvd., to the State Line and Silver Smith Casino on the east; operates every half hour Sun.–Thurs. 7:30 A.M.–midnight, Fri.–Sat. (and Sun. nights prior to a Mon. holiday) 7:30 A.M.–2 A.M. The **Town Loop** continues east on Wendover Blvd. to all of the motels on the Utah side and, on the Nevada side, as far west as the Toana Vista Golf Course; operates on the hour daily 7:20 A.M.–8 P.M. **West Wendover City Office, 801 Alpine St.; 775-664-3081.**

Northeastern Region

Flaming Gorge
National Recreation Area

High Uintas
Wilderness Area

Ashley
National Forest

191

Dinosaur
National
Monument

N

W   E

S

Uintah and Ouray
Indian Reservation

Vernal

Jensen

40

Roosevelt

88

40

Duchesne

Ouray

Uintah and Ouray
Indian Reservation

191

Ashley
National Forest

Green River

Hill Creek Extension
Uintah and Ouray
Indian Reservation

Roosevelt and Vernal

Utahns call it the Uinta Basin, or simply the Basin. It is not a basin in the strictest sense because the Green River cuts its course southward through the badland cliffs out of the basin into Desolation Canyon, but it does look like a gigantic, elongated dish running west to east. The Uinta Mountains, which form the northern rim of the basin, are the most dominant feature. The rounded summit of Kings Peak at 13,528 feet is the highest point in the state. The towns of Roosevelt and Vernal are at 5,280 feet, making for pleasant summers in the basin and cooler temperatures in the mountains. In winter an inversion layer sometimes sits over the basin, keeping temperatures at or below 0° F for days. Early spring, summer and early fall are the best times to visit, although the area is becoming very popular with winter sports enthusiasts—there are great cross-country skiing and snowmobiling possibilities.

Vernal is the county seat for Uintah County. Roosevelt is located in Duchesne County, whose county seat is at Duchesne 28 miles to the west. Roosevelt's high school is named Union High School because it was built exactly on the county line to allow students from both counties to attend without any complications. Roosevelt, named for Theodore Roosevelt, who was president of the United States when the community was established in 1905–1906, is surrounded by the Ute Indians' Uintah and Ouray Reservation Contention, primarily over water rights and legal jurisdiction, has characterized relations between the Utes and the descendants of the Anglo settlers who arrived in the Uinta Basin after portions of the reservation were opened to settlement in 1905. Ute Tribal Headquarters is located at Ft. Duchesne, about 8 miles east of Roosevelt.

Names in the area can be confusing. Just remember that "Uinta" without the "h" usually refers to a natural geographical area—Uinta Basin, Uinta Mountains, Uinta River, for example—while "Uintah" with the "h" usually refers to a human-created entity such as Uintah and Ouray Indian Reservation, Uintah County or Uintah High School.

History

Millions of years before human arrival in the Uinta Basin, dinosaurs lived in an environment completely different from that of today. The discovery of a rich deposit of dinosaur fossils by Earl Douglass in 1909 led to the establishment of Dinosaur National Monument in 1915. The Fremont people lived in the Uinta Basin from about A.D. 200 to 1300 and left rock art and other remains that have attracted the interest of

Getting There

Roosevelt is 145 miles east of Salt Lake City on US Hwy. 40; Vernal is another 30 miles east of Roosevelt. Driving from Salt Lake, take Interstate 80 east to its junction with US Hwy. 40 as it heads south to Heber City. From Heber City, US Hwy. 40 heads southeast up Daniels Canyon, past Strawberry Reservoir, where it turns back to the east and enters the Uinta Basin at Duchesne. Travelers coming west through Wyoming can exit Interstate 80 just west of Rock Springs onto US Hwy. 191, which heads south, crossing into Utah near Flaming Gorge Reservoir, across the dam, and continues south to Vernal. From Colorado, most travelers enter Utah on US Hwy. 40 heading west.

You can also fly to Vernal from Salt Lake City. **Skywest/Delta** has flights **(1-800-453-9417; 435-789-7263). Avis car rentals (1-800-331-1212; 435-789-7264)** are available at the Vernal Airport.

archaeologists. The Fremont culture seems to have died out around A.D. 1300 just as Ute Indians arrived in the area. The Utes were here when the first Euro-Americans arrived in 1776. The Dominguez-Escalante Expedition crossed the Green River near the southern boundary of present-day Dinosaur National Monument, just north of the town of Jensen, on September 16, 1776. They followed a Ute Indian trail westward through the basin to the Uinta and Duchesne Rivers. Fur trapper William Ashley and company floated down the Green River in 1825 and were glad to escape the adventure with their lives. French-Canadian trapper Etienne Provost, working out of New Mexico, also reached the basin in the mid-1820s, followed by Antoine Robidoux, who established a trading post in the area by 1832.

Perhaps the most important event in the history of the Uinta Basin was the establishment of the Uintah Indian Reservation by President Abraham Lincoln in 1861. The original reservation included more than 2 million acres of land and was to be the home of the Uintah Utes, who already occupied the basin, as well as other Ute tribes throughout the Utah Territory. In 1881 the White River Utes were forced to move from Colorado to the Uintah Reservation. A second reservation of nearly 2 million acres was established in 1882 immediately south of the Uintah Reservation. This Ouray Reservation was to be home to the Uncompahgre Utes who, under their Chief Ouray, were pressured to leave their homeland in Colorado. In time the two reservations merged, to become known as the Uintah and Ouray Indian Reservation. It is now the largest Indian reservation within the state. The population is approximately 3,000.

Anglos began to arrive in Ashley Valley in the early 1870s. By 1880 the settlement of Vernal had been established and Uintah County was formed. During the 1880s and 1890s, and even into the 20th century, the Uinta Basin developed a rough-and-tumble tradition. Vernal lay astride the Outlaw Trail, which connected the Brown's Park area north of the basin and the Robbers Roost region to the south—two isolated places of refuge from

the long arm of the law. Matt Warner, Elza Lay, Butch Cassidy, Harry Longabaugh (alias the Sundance Kid), Harvey Logan (alias Kid Curry) and other members of the Wild Bunch were no strangers to Vernal. The town's Outlaw Trail Festival, held during the summer, commemorates the region's outlaw legacy.

Roosevelt and other communities were established after the Uintah Reservation was opened for settlement in 1905. The Dawes Act of 1887 allowed for each adult Indian married male to be granted homesteads of 160 acres (lesser amounts of land were granted to women, single males and orphaned children) and for the remaining land to be opened for settlement by non-Indians. The opening of the reservation created a land rush in the area, as Anglo settlers poured in from Utah and Colorado to take advantage of the newly available lands.

The agricultural development of the area coincided with the discovery of Gilsonite and other asphaltums. Later, oil was discovered, with commercial production beginning in 1948. The region boomed during the energy crisis of the 1970s, then became depressed during most of the 1980s. Crucial to the present economy and future of the Uinta Basin is the Central Utah Project, which was started in 1959 with the construction of the Steinaker Reservoir, part of the Vernal unit, and followed by Red Fleet Reservoir, part of the Jensen unit of the project. The Central Utah Project, a multimillion-dollar Bureau of Reclamation project that impacts much of the state, including the urbanized Wasatch Front, is still under construction, and the completion of the early projects at Steinaker and Red Fleet have helped sustain the long-term project.

Festivals and Events

Outlaw Trail Festival
mid-June–July. Famous outlaws from the past have been named honorary citizens in the Uinta Basin, where a host of summer activities are sponsored in Vernal as part of the Outlaw Trail Festival. The festival dates from 1985 and has

grown steadily from a weekend activity to one that runs several weeks. It has something for just about everyone: art exhibits and competitions, a multi-day trail ride, a women's .22 shooting competition, a folk arts festival, a rodeo and a musical production based on the legends of Butch Cassidy and the Wild Bunch. **1-800-477-5558; 435-789-6932.**

Northern Ute Pow Wow

early July. This event includes a rodeo; dancing, singing and drumming competitions; and arts and crafts. Held at Ft. Duchesne the weekend closest to the fourth of July, this is an excellent chance to learn more about contemporary and traditional Ute culture. **435-722-5141.**

Dinosaur Roundup Rodeo

second week in July. This rodeo ranks among the top 50 rodeos nationally. **Western Park, 300 E. 200 N., Vernal; 1-800-421-9635; 435-789-1352.**

Outdoor Activities

Biking

The Dinosaurland Travel Board has published a guide, *Dinosaurland Hiking and Mountain Biking Guide,* which describes 13 different routes in the area. For a copy contact **Dinosaurland Travel Board, 25 E. Main, Vernal, UT 84078; 1-800-477-5558; 435-789-6932.**

Asphalt Ridge Loop—The 7-mile loop along graded and paved roads with no major grades is considered an easy ride. From the starting point, the route follows Hwy. 40 for 2 miles to where the power lines cross the highway. Here you turn left onto a dirt road that follows the power lines for 1.7 miles. After you cross a low pass, stay on the dirt road as it turns to the left and heads in a northwesterly direction along the base of Asphalt Ridge for 2.5 miles back to the beginning point. As you ride along Asphalt Ridge, look for outcroppings of natural black asphalt. Vernal residents took advantage of this

resource to become one of the first Utah towns to have paved streets. Begins on US Hwy. 40 at the scenic viewpoint 5 miles southwest of Vernal.

Range Study Loop—The 10-mile loop is suitable for intermediate riders. While it offers an excellent view of Diamond Mountain to the east, the route does violate the natural law of biking: it goes downhill first. The loop makes a gradual descent to the bottom of the draw for the first 4 miles, then turns sharply to the right and begins a steep, but short (0.3 mile) climb, followed by 5 miles of a steady but gradual ascent. Located in Ashley National Forest, 24 miles north of Vernal on US Hwy. 191.

Rentals

Altitude Cycle—Rentals and complete area bike route maps. Open Mon.–Sat. 10 A.M.–6 P.M. **510 E. Main St., Ste. 7, Vernal; 435-781-2595.**

Basin Cycle—Vernal's oldest bike shop, from 1956. Open Mon.–Sat. 8:30 A.M.–6 P.M. **450 N. Vernal Ave., Vernal; 435-781-1226.**

Fishing

Jones Hole Creek

The 4-mile stretch of Jones Hole Creek from the fish hatchery to the Green River is considered one of the most productive sections of trout stream in the state. It is also one of the most popular, and wildlife managers are concerned about its ability to handle more pressure. The paved road begins 4 miles east of Vernal, from 500 N., and travels 80 miles northeast into Dinosaur National Monument. For details, see the Jones Hole Rd. Scenic Backway in the Scenic Drives section.

Moon Lake

There are a thousand or so natural lakes in the High Uinta Mountains, of which Moon Lake is the largest. It was enlarged by the construction of a dam by homesteaders in the Uinta Basin (my grandfather was one of the leaders in the undertaking and, as a young man, my father hauled supplies by pack train from their home in Altonah). Today the lake is 32 miles in length.

Moon Lake is home to eastern brook trout, cut-throat, rainbow trout, splake and kokanee salmon. The edge of the lake also serves as the main trailhead to lakes and streams located within the adjacent wilderness area. **Moon Lake Resort** provides basic accommodations; **435-454-3142.** Located 32 miles north of Duchesne via Hwy. 87, at the southern edge of the High Uintas Wilderness Area. The road to Moon Lake is paved, except for 8 miles of road across the Uintah and Ouray Reservation.

South Slope Streams

The streams coming down the slope of the Uinta Mountains offer some of the best trout fishing in the state. Beginning on the west and moving eastward are the **Duchesne River, Rock Creek, Lake Fork, Yellowstone River, Uinta River** and **Whiterocks River.** They all yield a good number of stocked rainbow and small cutthroat and brook trout. All the streams flow through the Uintah and Ouray Reservation, where fees are charged for fishing; the fewer number of anglers you will encounter might make it worth purchasing a day or seasonal permit, available in Mountain Home, at the Ute Indian Tribe **Bottle Hollow Administration Office**; at **Ft. Duchesne (435-722-3941),** located 8 miles east of Roosevelt off US Hwy. 40; and at sporting goods stores in the Uinta Basin. North of the reservation boundary there is also plenty of good fishing.

The streams are reached by a network of roads north of US Hwy. 40. Hwy. 35, which begins 6 miles north of Duchesne off Hwy. 87, follows the Duchesne River for much of its course. Rock Creek, Yellowstone River and Lake Fork are best reached by taking Hwy. 87 north from Duchesne, then following the road north to Mountain Home. The Uinta and Whiterocks Rivers are located north of Roosevelt. The county road to Whiterocks is located east of Roosevelt off US Hwy. 40.

Starvation Reservoir

The 3,310-acre reservoir completed in 1972 is one of the major components of the Central

Utah Project. The origins of the name "Starvation" are difficult to trace. One version holds that fur trappers caught in the winter snows robbed an Indian food cache and survived while their victims starved. A counter version reports that the fur trappers were victims of Indians who stole food from a cache of provisions hidden in a group of caves along the southwestern shore of what is now the reservoir. Despite its name, the reservoir offers excellent walleye, smallmouth bass and a few brown trout. Administered as a state park, there are fish-cleaning facilities and camping. Located off US Hwy. 40, 4 miles west of Duchesne. **435-738-2326.**

Steinaker Reservoir

Named for a pioneer ranching family in the Vernal area, this reservoir was begun in 1961 as one of the first units of the Central Utah Project. It is filled by waters diverted from Ashley Creek several miles to the west. The reservoir, also a state park, is popular with boaters and anglers, and during the cold Uinta Basin winters, it offers excellent ice fishing. Rainbow trout and largemouth bass have been successfully planted in the reservoir. Located off US Hwy. 191 north of Vernal.

Golf

Dinaland Golf Course

Constructed in the early 1950s, Dinaland Golf Course, with smiling little dinosaurs for its tee markers and 150-yard markers, expanded to 18 holes in 1994. The expansion included new greens for all the holes, new directions for some of the old fairways, new ponds and marshlands, and more effective use of a tributary of Ashley Creek that meanders through the course. Usually open mid-Mar.–mid-Nov. Located east of town. **675 S. 2000 E., Vernal; 435-781-1428.**

Roosevelt Golf Course

Unless you happen to land at the Roosevelt Golf Course on a Wed., when the women's league plays, or during one of the infrequent tournaments, there is usually no waiting to get on the course, and no reservations necessary. The

9-hole course that opened in 1973 has been expanded to 18 holes. One of the most memorable holes is the 16th, with the green located in a box canyon with a human-made waterfall that drops over the wall into four ponds that cut across the front of the green. Located just north of Roosevelt. **1155 Clubhouse Dr., Roosevelt; 435-722-9644.**

Skiing

CROSS-COUNTRY

The **Dinosaurland Travel Board (25 E. Main, Vernal, UT 84078; 1-800-477-5558; 435-789-6932)** publishes a brochure, *Dinosaurland Eastern Uintas Cross-Country Ski Trails,* which describes eight different trails and loops off US Hwy. 191, beginning with the 2.5-mile-long **Little Brush Creek Loop Trail,** 22 miles north of Vernal. The brochure can also be obtained at the **Northeastern Utah Visitor Center, 235 E. Main, Vernal.**

Seeing and Doing

Historic Sites

Parcel Post Bank

Architecturally, it's not exactly a masterpiece— a two-story brick building built in 1916—but the way its materials were obtained shows the kind of ingenuity that was necessary for survival in the isolated Uinta Basin of premotorized vehicle days. Bank President William H. Coltharp wanted to build an impressive building that would reflect the prosperity of the first decade of the 20th century. While "ordinary" red bricks were available from a local brick maker, Coltharp opted for fancy textured bricks that were available only in Salt Lake City, 175 miles away. But the freight cost from Salt Lake City was four times the price of the bricks, so Coltharp hit on the idea of mailing the 80,000 bricks—individually wrapped—from Salt Lake City to Vernal.

At seven cents a brick, the total cost was approximately $5,600 and, since postal regula-

tions prohibited one person from receiving more than 5,000 pounds of parcel, the bricks were sent to several addresses in Vernal. The bricks were sent by the Denver and Rio Grande Railroad to Mack, Colorado, where they were loaded on a narrow gauge railroad and sent to Watson, Utah, and then hauled by wagon to Vernal, a total distance of 407 miles—the last 65 miles by wagon. Shortly after Vernal got its "mail-order" building, postal regulations were changed, limiting the amount of goods that could be shipped by parcel post. The building, constructed in 1916, is still used as a bank. Located on the corner of **Vernal Ave. and Main St.,** Vernal.

Uintah Stake Tabernacle Temple

Constructed from 1900 to 1907 in Vernal, this Mormon tabernacle is one of only a few in Utah to serve as the religious center for cities and outlying areas. The Uintah Stake Tabernacle was used for a number of years as a local arts and culture center; then, in 1994, Mormon church officials announced that the historic building would be renovated for use as a temple. The renovation was completed in 1997, marking the first time in the history of the Mormon church that a building has been renovated to serve as a temple. Located at **500 W. and 200 S.** in Vernal.

Museums

Daughters of Utah Pioneers Museum

Just across the street from the historic Uintah Stake Tabernacle, the DUP Museum is housed in an 1887 stone tithing office. The building once served as a collection and distribution center for the produce and livestock that made up the 10 percent of income tithe that members of the Mormon church are required to donate to the church. Built during the first decade of Mormon settlement in this area, it is one of the oldest surviving structures in eastern Utah. The original tithing office was expanded and the complex now houses an impressive collection of artifacts. Open Memorial Day–Labor Day daily 1–7 P.M., or at other times by special request. Located on the corner of **200 S. and 500 W.** in Vernal.

Utah Field House of Natural History

If you come to Dinosaurland, the name for this travel region, it is almost impossible to escape dinosaurs—whether you find them as tee box markers on the local golf course, on billboards or as life-size replicas at the Utah Field House of Natural History, a state park. Eighteen dinosaurs, including the 8-ton horned triceratops, the 6-ton stegosaurus, the 12-ton, 80-foot-long diplodocus, the ferocious *Tyrannosaurus rex* and the Utah raptor, along with other prehistoric animals, inhabit a garden just west of the Field House and are an irresistible attraction for young and old alike. Inside the Field House, exhibits and paintings introduce the area's geology, natural history, paleontology and anthropology. Open summers daily 8 P.M.—9 P.M.; after Labor Day 9 A.M.– 5 P.M. Also located within the field house is the Northeastern Utah Visitor Center, making this an ideal first stop for visitors to the area. **235 E. Main St., Vernal; 435-789-3799; www. parks.state.ut.us/parks/www1/utaf.htm.**

Western Heritage Museum

This museum is part of the Western Heritage Center operated by Uintah County and features a collection of Fremont and Ute Indian artifacts, including baskets, water jugs, manos and metates, tools, bows and arrows, papoose boards, gloves, beadwork, arrowheads and tools. Leo Thorne was a professional photographer in Vernal for many years who began collecting artifacts in the 1920s in an effort to preserve some of the physical remains of the area's Native American heritage. Among the other artifacts are Thorne's studio camera, plus western carriages, saddles, revolvers and rifles. There is also an old barbershop, a collection of children's toys, the original telephone switchboard for Vernal, blacksmith tools, clothing, farm implements, World War I souvenirs and, outside, a good collection of farm equipment. Open Memorial Day–Labor Day Mon.–Sat. 10 P.M.– 6 A.M.; the rest of the year Mon.–Fri. 10 A.M.– 5 P.M. Located in a huge open-space building next to the amphitheater where the Outlaw Trail Festival Musical Production is performed, a

short distance from the rodeo arena. **300 E. 200 S., Vernal; 435-789-7399.**

Scenic Drives

Uintas Scenic Byway / US Hwy. 191

This section of US Hwy. 191 north of Vernal is also known as the "Drive Through the Ages," a road that climbs through 19 geologic formations during the 30-mile ascent of the Uinta Mountains toward Flaming Gorge Reservoir. Signs indicate the geologic formations for both directions of travel. The Uinta Mountains are a huge anticline that runs east and west. As you drive out of Vernal, the layers read from youngest to oldest, with the gray Mancos shale being the youngest. The oldest rocks, nearly a billion years old, are Precambrian sedimentary rocks of sandstone and siltstone, which make up the core of the Uinta Mountains. A brochure with additional information is available at the **Northeastern Utah Visitor Center.** Located in the eastern end of the Utah Field House of Natural History. **235 E. Main St., Vernal; 435-789-4002.**

Jones Hole Rd. Scenic Backway

This 80-mile-long out-and-back road is paved for its entire length. It begins 4 miles east of Vernal, where it leaves 500 N. and heads in a northeasterly direction to climb out of Ashley Valley, 2,600 feet up Diamond Mountain, before it turns east into Dinosaur National Monument. The paved road is quite narrow, especially as it follows the narrow, rugged canyon into Jones Hole. The road terminates at Jones Hole National Fish Hatchery. Travelers can visit the hatchery, which produces trout for streams, lakes and reservoirs in Utah, Colorado and Wyoming. Open daily 7 A.M.–4 P.M. From the hatchery, visitors can take a 4-mile hike down to the Green River in Dinosaur National Monument.

Diamond Mountain, over which the road passes, was the site of a scandalous swindle in the 1870s, when Phillip Arnold and John Slack salted the area with industrial diamonds, and then sold their claim for a fortune. The well-known geologist Clarence King uncovered the fraud when he found partially cut and polished diamonds on the mountain, which, it was learned, had been smuggled into the United States from South Africa. Arnold and Slack had deceived a group of San Francisco investors that the discovery was genuine by allowing two men to examine the discovery with the condition that they be blindfolded as they entered and left the area. The two swindlers netted $150,000 each; Phil Arnold was caught, but John Slack escaped with his share.

Wildlife Viewing

Ouray National Wildlife Refuge

This refuge, established in 1961, includes 12,467 acres mostly located along 12 miles of the Green River. The refuge is home to a large nesting population of ducks and geese and provides resting and feeding areas to more than 200 species of migratory birds in the spring and fall. Golden eagles are found year-round, and bald eagles gather during early winter. Mule deer are visible year-round. The refuge is owned by the U.S. Fish and Wildlife Service and has an information kiosk and an observation tower. Interpretive brochures are available, including a bird list and an auto tour guide, which covers just over 13 miles on a loop route though the marshlands and feeding areas of Sheppard Bottom, and an out-and-back drive to Leote Butte, which offers a panoramic view of much of the refuge from its 5,072-foot elevation. For a closer look, you might want to hike or bike the 5-mile Sheppard Bottom Loop. Open sunrise to sunset year-round. Take US Hwy. 40 west from Vernal for 14 miles, then turn south onto Hwy. 88. The refuge is located 15 miles to the south. On your way to the refuge you will pass Pelican Lake, which, although outside the refuge area, is also home to a substantial bird population. **Ouray National Wildlife Refuge, 266 W. 100 N., Vernal, UT 84078; 435-789-0351.**

Where to Stay

Bed and Breakfasts and Inns

Falcon's Ledge—$$$$

Jim Bills, co-owner of the Falcon's Ledge, describes it as "a world-class lodge, designed to provide a quality refuge for those seeking personal and private outdoor experiences." Bills, a successful financier, combined his money and dream of an outdoors retreat with the fishing and guide skills of partner Howard Brinkerhoff to undertake a unique enterprise for the Uinta Basin. With only eight units, the personal touch is emphasized at Falcon's Ledge. Even if you don't stay there, you can arrange guided fishing and wilderness trips through the lodge, as well as courses in backpacking, mountain biking and falconry. Located 17 miles north of Duchesne, off Hwy. 87, on the southern slope of the Uinta Mountains. **Stillwater Canyon-Falcon's Ledge, P.O. Box 67, Altamont, UT 84001; 1-877-879-3737; 435-454-3737; www.falcon-ledge.com.**

Landmark Inn—$$$ to $$$$

This pleasant 10-room inn is located in the former Baptist church in Vernal. Baptists began holding meetings in the Episcopal church on Main St. in 1946. Two years later, the basement was completed and church services were held there from 1948 until the ground-level chapel was completed in 1953. By the mid-1990s the Baptist congregation had moved into a new church and brothers Harold and Stephen Henderson, originally from North Carolina, purchased the church; after remodeling the interior, they opened the Landmark Inn in 1998.

All rooms have private baths, telephones and TVs. Three of the rooms are designed as anniversary or honeymoon suites and have Jacuzzis, while the other seven rooms are more for regular business and tourist travelers. All rooms are spacious, quiet, nonsmoking and comfortable. A continental breakfast of cereal, fresh fruit, bagels, English muffins, juice and coffee is included. **288 E. 100 S., Vernal UT 84078;**

1-888-738-1800; 435-781-1800; www.land-mark-inn.com.

Motels

ROOSEVELT
Best Western Inn—$$
Heated pool and adjacent coffee shop; 40 units. Located on US Hwy. 40, 3 miles east of Roosevelt. **1-800-528-1234; 435-722-4644.**

Frontier Motel—$$
Fifty-four rooms. The Frontier Grill is adjacent. **75 S. 200 E.; 1-800-248-1014; 435-722-2201.**

VERNAL
Best Western Antlers Motel—$$
Heated pool, wading pool and playground; 43 rooms. **423 W. Main; 1-800-528-1234; 435-789-1202.**

Best Western Dinosaur Inn—$$
Heated pool, whirlpool and playground; 59 rooms. Coffee shop open daily 6 A.M.–10 P.M. Located adjacent to the Vernal Welcome Center and Utah Field House of Natural History. **251 E. Main; 1-800-528-1234; 435-789-2660.**

Weston Plaza Hotel—$$ to $$$
This is Vernal's largest hotel, with 102 rooms. Indoor heated pool, whirlpool and restaurant. **1684 W. US Hwy. 40; 435-789-9550.**

Camping

PRIVATE
Campground Dina
Dina has 115 trailer sites, 82 of which have full hookups, and 300 tentsites. Toilets, showers, laundry and a dump site are available. Open year-round (winter fees paid on the honor system). **930 N. Vernal Ave., Vernal; 1-800-245-2148; 435-789-2148.**

Fossil Valley RV Park
All 45 trailer sites have complete hookups; plus there are 10 tentsites. The park is equipped with toilets, showers, a laundry and a dump site. Open Apr.–Oct. **999 W. US Hwy. 40, Vernal; 435-789-6450.**

Vernal KOA
All 55 trailer sites have complete hookups, and the campground is equipped to KOA standards. There are also four camping cabins. Open May–Sept. **1800 W. Sheraton Ave., Vernal; 435-789-8935.**

PUBLIC
The Uinta Mountains offer many camping opportunities in the Ashley National Forest. Most campgrounds are open mid- to late May–mid-Sept., and fees are charged at most.

Altamont
North of Altamont, there are five campgrounds within a 5-mile radius, located along the Yellowstone River and Swift Creek: **Yellowstone, Bridge, Reservoir, Riverview** and **Swift Creek.** Riverview is the largest with 19 tentsites. There are no showers or toilets. Yellowstone is located 17.5 miles, and Swift Creek (the farthest north) 22 miles north of Altamont.

Duchesne
Yellow Pine Campground, located 29 miles north of Duchesne, has 29 tentsites, drinking water and toilets. A smaller campground 1 mile to the north is **Miners Gulch** with 5 tentsites.

Hanna
Four campgrounds are located northwest of Hanna off Hwy. 35: **Aspen Grove** (33 sites), **Hades** (17 sites), **Iron Mine** (27 sites) and **South Fork** (5 sites). Aspen Grove is the largest and the closest to Hanna, 8 miles away. The other three are 11, 12.5 and 15.8 miles from Hanna, respectively. There are no toilet or shower facilities in the campgrounds, but all are equipped with drinking water.

Moon Lake
A popular fishing and recreation location, the Moon Lake Campground has 19 trailer sites and

37 tentsites. Drinking water and toilets are available. A group site has 25 RV and tentsites.

Where to Eat

ROOSEVELT
Frontier Grill—$ to $$
Located next to the Frontier Motel, this is Roosevelt's most popular eating establishment. Open daily 6 A.M.–9 P.M. **65 S. 200 E.; 435-722-3669.**

VERNAL
Curry Manor—$$$ to $$$$
The Uinta Basin's best restaurant, the Curry Manor has both good food and a historic location in the Lewis and Sallie Curry House. Listed on the National Register of Historic Places, the house was built of locally produced brick and timber from the nearby Uinta Mountains. Lewis Curry came to the Uinta Basin in 1887 and operated a trading post with his brother on the Uintah Reservation at Ouray. Later he moved to Vernal, where he was cashier for the Uintah State Bank and owner of various businesses including a mill, theater and furniture store. He also served in the Utah State Legislature. Following his death in 1922, the house remained in the Curry family for many years. After several owners, the house was successfully adapted as a restaurant in 1996 by Steve and Holly Jones.

Restaurant guests are seated in one of five rooms, the parlor or library on the ground level or one of three bedrooms upstairs. No room seats more than 18 people and the smallest only eight. Lunch menu items include soup, salads, grilled chicken sandwich, prime rib sandwich and New Zealand red snapper. Dinner entrées range from chicken and pasta to steaks, shrimp and fish. Some of the most popular items include the crab stuffed salmon, filet mignon wrapped in bacon, marinated sirloin topped with mushrooms and leeks, and the pork tenderloin with apricot glaze. For vegetarians, there's a three-cheese tortellini. Open Mon.–Fri. 11:30 A.M.–2 P.M. and 5–10 P.M. (till 9 P.M.

in the winter). Call ahead for reservations. **189 S. Vernal Ave.; 435-789-2289.**

Services

Visitor Information
Ashley National Forest, Roosevelt Ranger District—Provides information and also has maps and publications for sale. Open Mon.–Fri. 8 A.M.–5 P.M. Located on the western edge of town. **244 W. US Hwy. 40, Roosevelt; 435-722-5018.**

Ashley National Forest, Supervisor's Office and Vernal Ranger District—Information about recreation and activities on the national forest, and books and maps for sale. Open Mon.–Fri. 8 A.M.–5 P.M. **355 N. Vernal Ave., Vernal, UT 84078; 435-789-1181.**

Bureau of Land Management, Vernal District—Information about recreation on BLM lands. Open Mon.–Fri. 7:45 A.M.–4:30 P.M. **170 S. 500 E., Vernal; 435-781-4400.**

Dinosaurland Regional Travel Office—Although this office is not set up to handle walk-in visitors, you can obtain tour information and brochures here. **25 E. Main St., Vernal; 1-800-477-5558; 435-789-6932; www.dinoland.com.**

Jensen Welcome Center—A Utah Welcome Center with a rest area and displays on all travel regions in the state. Located approximately 13 miles east of Vernal on US Hwy. 40. **435-789-4002.**

Northeastern Utah Visitors Center—Located in the eastern end of the Utah Field House of Natural History. **235 E. Main St., Vernal; 435-789-4002.**

Vernal Convention and Visitors Bureau—134 W. Main St., Vernal; 435-789-1352; www.utahconvention.org.

Dinosaur National Monument

Dinosaur National Monument spreads out over the mountains, plateaus and deserts in the northeastern corner of Utah and northwestern corner of Colorado, with enough river rafting, hiking, scenic drives and geology to occupy days and days of exploration. Mountains, narrow-cut canyons, raging rapids in the bowels of river gorges, majestic walls of sandstone, broad expanses of benchland and broken vistas of the upper Colorado Plateau are the setting for a treasure house of dinosaur bones nearly 150 million years in age.

The 300-square-mile Dinosaur National Monument is really two parks in one. It started out as just the Dinosaur Quarry in 1915 and was later expanded to include the fabulous scenery and recreation potential of the Green and Yampa Rivers, which merge inside the monument at Echo Park. The national monument is not a 300-square-mile dinosaur graveyard—a number of dinosaur sites are known within the monument, many of which have not been fully evaluated, but these sites constitute only a very small part of the park. The best-known is the Quarry site, and for most visitors, an hour is sufficient time to see it. There are few roads in the monument; see Getting There for an idea of ways to visit the area.

History

Just as Dinosaur National Monument is really two parks, it also has two histories: the geologic history and the history of its evolution as a national monument. Geologically, the area gained its significance 150 million years ago, during more tropical times, when extensive floodplain deposits were laid down over a wide-spread area of what is now Colorado, Wyoming, eastern Utah, northern New Mexico, parts of Montana and South Dakota and the panhandle of Oklahoma. Dinosaurs inhabited the swamps around the shallow river that meandered over this floodplain. As they died, their remains settled into the deposits, and over time were preserved in what is now known in Utah and Colorado as the Morrison Formation. The formation is named for Morrison, Colorado, where the first major discovery of dinosaurs from this formation was made, in 1877.

A "dinosaur rush" developed from the Morrison discoveries, as paleontologists competed to see who could discover the most dinosaurs. By 1900 dinosaur remains had been found in Colorado in Morrison and Cañon City, and in Wyoming in Como Bluff, Bone Cabin Quarry and Howe Quarry. The Utah discovery occurred in August 1909, when Earl Douglass, a paleontologist from the Carnegie Museum in Pittsburgh, Pennsylvania, came upon a hogback, or ridge, that had been formed by the earth tilting steeply upward. In this hogback, Douglass found eight large dinosaur vertebrae weathering out of the sandstone. The bones were from the tails of a sauropod and an apatosaurus, or brontosaurus, and proved to be the most complete skeletons ever discovered. The skeletons had come to rest in a sandbar along an ancient river and were covered over by sand and mud. They were brought near the surface when violent uplifts reshaped

Getting There

Dinosaur National Monument's Quarry Visitor Center is located on Hwy. 149 7 miles north of Jensen, off US Hwy. 40, approximately 200 miles from Salt Lake City and 20 miles southeast of Vernal. From Jensen, it's another 20 miles east on US Hwy. 40 to the Dinosaur National Monument Headquarters, located 2 miles east of Dinosaur, Colorado, at the junction of the highway with Harper's Corner Rd.

Perry's ▶
Egyptian
Theatre,
Ogden

▼ *Ogden Union Station*

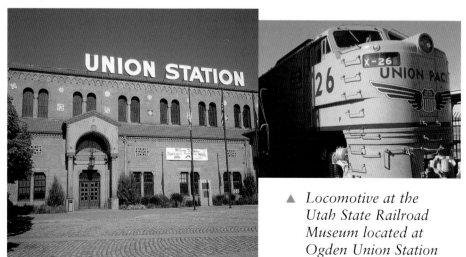

▲ *Locomotive at the*
Utah State Railroad
Museum located at
Ogden Union Station

1

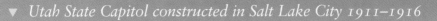

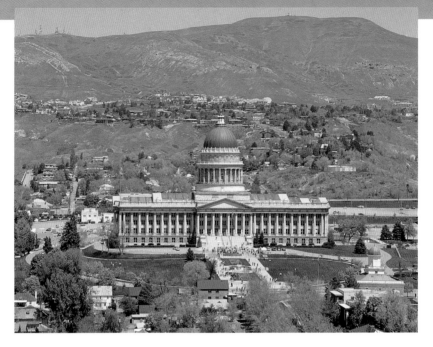

▼ *The Wasatch Mountains make a dramatic backdrop for Salt Lake City's Franklin Quest Stadium*

▲ *The Wasatch Mountains form the east wall of the Salt Lake Valley*

Salt Lake Temple, construction began in 1853 and was not completed until 1893

Saint Patrick's Day in Salt Lake City

Union Pacific Station, now part of Salt Lake City's Gateway Development

Place Monument, constructed to commemorate the 1947 Centennial of the arrival of the Mormon pioneers in the Salt Lake Valley

▼ *Snowbird in winter*

▼ *Snowbird, Oktoberfest*

▲ *Wasatch Mountains near Alta*

▼ Park City Miner's Hospital

▼ Bikes, Park City

▼ Quaking aspens and pines in the mountains east of Park City

▼ *Huber Farmstead at Wasatch Mountain State Park near Midway*

Wasatch Mountains on the east side of Utah Valley ▶

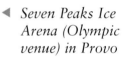

◀ *Seven Peaks Ice Arena (Olympic venue) in Provo*

Lehi Roller Mills ▶

▼ *Donner-Reed Museum, iron jail cage, Grantsville*

◀ *Benson Grist Mill, north of Tooele near Stansbury Park, built in 1854*

▼ *WWII buildings at Wendover Air Force Base*

▼ *Saltwater and mountians east of Wendover*

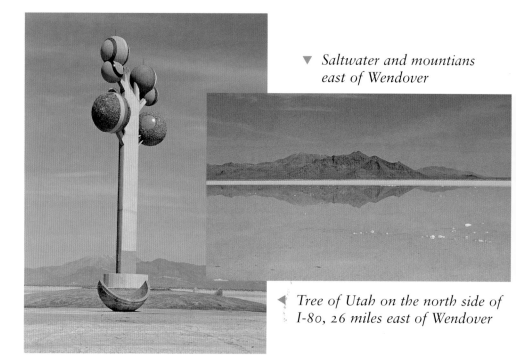

◄ *Tree of Utah on the north side of I-80, 26 miles east of Wendover*

▼ *Mount Nebo at the southern end of the Wasatch Mountain Range near Nephi*

◀ *Topaz Japanese Relocation Camp as it looked during World War II, located northwest of Delta*

Dominguez–Escalante marker in Milford Town Park ▶

▼ *Ute Indian Sign in Gillmore*

▼ *Reminders of the once-thriving sheep industry in Sanpete County*

A violin maker's ▶
shop in Mt. Pleasant,
Main Street

▼ *The Manti Temple overlooks*
Sanpete Valley

◄ *Capitol Gorge–Capitol Reef National Park*

▼ *Chimney Rock–Capitol Reef National Park*

◄ *Bicknell Grist Mill along Hwy. 24 west of Capitol Reef National Park*

*Hole-in-the-Rock Trail ▶
where Mormon pioneers
descended with their
wagons to the Colorado
River in January 1880*

▼ *Kodachrome State Park*

16

the land, creating the Uinta Mountains. Erosion had completed their exposure.

Douglass dug the site for the next 15 years, sending dinosaur bones to the Smithsonian Institution in Washington, D.C., and the University of Utah, and more than 350 tons of fossils to the Carnegie Museum. The quarry proved to be the most prolific dinosaur quarry in the Morrison Formation. In addition to the apatosaurus or brontosaurus, Douglass uncovered a plant-eating camarasaurus, a diplodocus, a barosaurus, a camptosaurus, a dryosaurus and a stegosaurus, as well as meat-eating dinosaurs such as allosaurus, ceratosaurus and torvosaurus. Researchers have found the tracks of more than 200 individual animals in various parts of the monument. Some scientists postulate that the accumulation of dinosaur bones in one place resulted from a terrible drought that hit the area, forcing large numbers of dinosaurs to congregate at ancient river channels to obtain water. As they died, their bodies lay in the dry river channels. Later, flash floods picked up the dinosaur remains and carried them down the river channels, leaving them in a logjam of dinosaur bones that became the quarry.

The 80-acre quarry site was designated a national monument in 1915, while Douglass was still excavating, often using dynamite to blast through the overlying rock layers. During the 1930s a Works Progress Administration project expanded the quarry face, but no new fossils were exposed or excavated.

The park was greatly expanded in 1938, when President Franklin D. Roosevelt recognized the scenic and recreational value of 328 square miles east and northeast of the quarry and added it to the monument. During the 1950s Dinosaur National Monument was embroiled in controversy when the Bureau of Reclamation proposed the construction of a multipurpose dam inside the monument at Echo Park. The proposed dam and reservoir, according to historian Mark W. T. Harvey, "sparked the biggest conservation crusade to date in the 20th century." Led by the Sierra Club, the Wilderness Society and the National Parks Association, a host of groups and individuals pressured Congress into deleting the dam from the Colorado River Storage Project in 1956.

A new visitor center replaced the original sheet-metal building in May 1958. The Quarry Visitor Center proved significant in National Park Service history, as it was the first Park Service facility to employ a modern architectural design instead of the rustic design traditionally favored in national parks.

Major Attractions

Dinosaur Quarry Visitor Center

The 1958 Dinosaur Quarry Visitor Center now encloses the quarry. Until recently, visitors could watch paleontologists pecking away at the rock to expose and extract the dinosaur bones. The exposing of new dinosaur bones is generally completed at this location, and it is no longer possible to watch the scientists at work. Nevertheless, there is plenty to see at the quarry. Interesting displays and knowledgeable park rangers add to the experience, and there is a good selection of books on dinosaurs and natural history for purchase in the bookstore. The quarry is open early June–early Sept. daily 8 A.M.–7 P.M.; 8 A.M.–4:30 P.M. the rest of the year. Memorial Day–Labor Day, you are required to park in the parking lot and take a shuttle bus to the visitor center; the rest of the year you may drive directly to the center. Entrance fee charged. From Jensen on US Hwy. 40, take Hwy. 149 north 7 miles.

Park Headquarters

Park headquarters is located about 30 miles east of the Quarry Visitor Center, at the junction of US Hwy. 40 and the Harper's Corner Rd., 2 miles east of Dinosaur, Colorado. The building is staffed by rangers. Free backcountry camping permits (required for overnight camping) may be obtained at the headquarters office, as well as from other ranger stations. Exhibits, books for sale and other information are available. A 31-mile-long paved scenic drive along Harper's

Corner Rd. heads north from the park headquarters. Open June–Aug. daily 8 A.M.–4:30 P.M.; Mon.–Fri. the rest of the year. **Superintendent, Dinosaur National Monument, 4545 US Hwy. 40, Dinosaur, CO 81610; 970-374-3000.**

Outdoor Activities

Hiking

Box Canyon and Hog Canyon Trails

These are two short, fun hiking trails at the Josie Morris Cabin site. The 0.5-mile **Box Canyon Trail** heads north from the parking area at the end of Cub Creek Rd. An authentic example of a box canyon—steep walls on three sides, and only one way in and out—it was used by Josie Morris, a local rancher, as a corral for her stock. East of the cabin and spring, the 1.5-mile-long **Hog Canyon Trail** takes you farther into a second box canyon—also used by Josie Morris for her livestock. The area is reached via 12-mile-long Cub Creek Rd., which begins at the Utah entrance to Dinosaur National Monument, goes past the Dinosaur Quarry, then on to the Josie Morris Cabin at the foot of Split Mountain.

Desert Voices Trail

This 2-mile-long trail begins at the northwest end of the parking area at the Split Mountain boat ramp, reached by following the main road—the Split Mountain/Green River Campground Rd.—from the park entrance east 3 miles to the turnoff to Split Mountain; the parking area is less than 1 mile from the turnoff. The trail follows up a streambed, then climbs up and over a ridge before looping back to Split Mountain. The climb is moderately strenuous, but this is a trail that invites you to go at an easy pace and is designed as a teaching tool for children. Numerous markers along the trail cover such topics as plants, animals, geology, soil, history, preservation, multiple use, vandalism, chaining, revegetation, cryptogamic soil and cattle. Near the beginning of the trail is a garbage pit; items

were placed there in 1992 to demonstrate how long it takes for them to disintegrate in the desert environment.

Sound of Silence Route

This 2-mile-long trail, located on the north side of the Split Mountain/Green River Campground Rd. 2 miles east of the Dinosaur Quarry, introduces visitors to minimum-impact desert hiking on undeveloped routes. The route is not a trail and is somewhat difficult to follow, as you must estimate the distance in yards from one point to the next. It is also quite steep in some sections. There are 26 markers along the trail that correspond to information about dinosaurs, plants, animals, geology, soil and history provided in a trail guide available for a small charge at the Quarry Visitor Center or park headquarters.

Harper's Corner Trail

The Green River meanders 2,500 feet below around the knifelike point of Harper's Corner. The narrow ridge that leads to the point allows you to look into the channel on both sides. To the right you can see down to Steamboat Rock and Echo Park; to the left, the river heads south through Whirlpool Canyon toward Split Mountain. The 2-mile round-trip trail winds back and forth from one side of the ridge to the other, and at the trail's end, the ridge sweeps up to a point with one of the most dramatic vistas in the monument, where you can look into both sides of the canyon. The trail begins at the terminus of Harper's Corner Rd., 31 miles north of the monument headquarters. An excellent trail guide is available at the headquarters or at the trailhead for a small charge.

Ruple Point Trail

This 8-mile out-and-back trail leads to a spectacular overlook of the Split Mountain Gorge through which the Green River flows. It begins at the Island Park Overlook, just inside the southern boundary of the monument on Harper's Corner Rd., just over 28 miles north of the monument headquarters at the junction with US Hwy. 40.

Jones Hole Trail

This 4-mile-long trail provides foot access to one of the most remote sections of the Green River that otherwise could be seen only by boat or raft. Pick up a brochure about the trail, prepared by the Dinosaur Nature Association, which covers the geology, prehistory and history; provides a sketch of the route; and includes a checklist of flora and fauna you might encounter. The trail heads south through a deep gorge; about 1.5 miles down the trail, a bridge crosses Jones Creek. Steep rock walls with a few petroglyphs occur about 200 yards beyond the bridge. The trail ends at the Green River in Whirlpool Canyon. To reach the trailhead, take the Jones Hole Rd. (see the **Roosevelt and Vernal** chapter), which begins 4 miles east of Vernal from 500 N.; follow it northeast 80 miles.

Two stories account for the naming of the area. The first is that it was named for Stephen Vandiver Jones, the topographer for the 1871 Powell Expedition, which camped at the site. The other comes a decade later: Charley Jones, believing he had killed a man, hid out along the creek during the winter of 1883–1884 and when informed the supposed victim had lived, exclaimed, "You mean I can finally get out of this hole?"

Gates of Lodore Trail

This 1.5-mile round-trip, easy-to-walk nature trail follows the Green River to the Gates of Lodore at the extreme northern end of the monument, at the south end of Brown's Park. The Gates of Lodore was named by Andy Hall, the youngest member of John Wesley Powell's expedition down the Green and Colorado Rivers in 1869. Hall recalled the English poet Robert Southey's poem "The Cataract of Lodore," which includes the words: "All at once and all o'er, with a mighty uproar; And this way the water comes down at Lodore." A trail guide is available at the headquarters and quarry. From US Hwy. 40 at Maybell, Colorado, take Colorado Hwy. 318 north.

River Rafting

Both the Green and Yampa Rivers are popular with river runners, and because the river takes you to places that are otherwise inaccessible, it is one of the best ways to experience Dinosaur National Monument. All trips must have a river permit prior to launching; contact Superintendent, **Dinosaur National Monument, 4545 US Hwy. 40, Dinosaur, CO 81610; 970-374-3000.** Open Mon.–Fri. 9 A.M.–noon.

Green River—A popular trip starts at the north end of the monument, at the **Gates of Lodore,** where the Green River roars through Lodore Canyon for about 20 miles to Echo Park and its junction with the Yampa River. Put-in is reached via Colorado Hwy. 318 from US Hwy. 40 at Maybell, Colorado. Although few rafters use it, **Echo Park** is another good place to put in for the ride through Whirlpool Canyon and Split Mountain to the southern boundary of the monument. Put-in is reached by taking Harper's Corner Rd. 25 miles north to Echo Park Rd., and taking that for 13 miles.

Guides

Adrift Adventures—Although it also offers multi-day river trips, Adrift Adventures specializes in one-day paddle or oar boat trips on the Green River from Split Mountain to Jensen. **P.O. Box 192, Jensen, UT 84035; 1-800-824-0150; 435-789-3600.**

Don and Meg Hatch River Expeditions—This outfit offers one- to five-day rafting trips on the Green River, following the route taken by the 1869 historic John Wesley Powell Expedition through Split Mountain into the Uinta Basin. Hatch Expeditions, which began in the 1920s under Buzz Hatch, is the oldest commercial tour expedition company on the Green and Colorado Rivers. Hatch also offers longer three- to five-day trips on the Yampa River. **P.O. Box 1150, Dept. S, Vernal, UT 84078; 1-800-342-8243; 435-789-4316.**

Seeing and Doing

Scenic Drives

Cub Creek Rd.

This 12-mile-long scenic drive begins at the Utah entrance to the monument on Hwy. 149, 6 miles from its intersection with US Hwy. 40, then goes past the Dinosaur Quarry and continues on to the Josie Morris Cabin at the foot of Split Mountain. One of the region's most colorful characters, Josie Morris built her cabin in 1914 as her ranch headquarters and lived in it for 50 years. The view of Split Mountain is stunning. Ever since Maj. John Wesley Powell named it in 1869, geologists seem to have been at a loss to explain how the Green River could, at least so it appears, split the mountain in two. A road guide is available for a small charge at the park entrance, at park headquarters or at the Quarry Visitor Center. The guide points out such features as the impressive Native American petroglyphs located about 10.5 miles from the entrance to the monument.

Echo Park Rd.

This 13-mile-long dirt road leaves Harper's Corner Rd. 25 miles from the monument headquarters. In dry weather, the road is generally passable for high-clearance passenger vehicles; it is not suitable for trailers, motor homes or other heavy vehicles. The first 8-mile section begins with a steep descent on a series of switchbacks, then descends through Sand Canyon onto the Yampa Bench. At the mouth of Sand Canyon, keep to the left (otherwise you will be on the Yampa Bench Rd.). After 2 miles you reach the James and Rial Chew Ranch, a historic ranch established in 1910 that you may view from the road.

Two miles beyond the ranch, you come to a sign that indicates petroglyphs. Park your vehicle, then follow the short trail, keeping a lookout high up on the sandstone wall where the petroglyphs are located. There has been significant erosion since the ancient inhabitants pecked the figures into the sandstone, so they are much higher up on the cliff than you would expect. From the Chew Ranch, the Echo Park Rd. continues through the narrow Pool Creek Canyon. A half mile down the road is Whispering Cave, a narrow crack in the rock more than 100 feet high that extends back a distance. It's another half mile to Echo Park from Whispering Cave. The road drops down into Echo Park for a close look at Steamboat Rock and the junction of the Yampa and Green Rivers.

During his 1869 trip down the Green River, Maj. John Wesley Powell noted the echoes bouncing off Steamboat Rock. Early in the 1900s, Echo Park was better known as Pat's Hole. Pat Lynch was an Irish-born hermit who lived many years in the caves along the Green River. He died in 1917 at the age of 98. He had a reputation for making pets of wild animals in the area, including a mountain lion that responded from afar when Lynch screeched at it.

Harper's Corner Rd.

This 31-mile-long paved scenic road heads north from US Hwy. 40 and monument headquarters 2 miles east of Dinosaur, Colorado. At the park headquarters, pick up a copy of *Journey Through Time,* a guide that explains that Harper's Corner was actually a natural corral used by a rancher named Harper. The steep walls kept his cattle from climbing out, and all he needed to secure them was a short stretch of fence at the mouth of the box canyon. It is easy to spend an entire day on this road, which measures 62 miles round trip from park head-quarters. At 25 miles from the monument headquarters is the turnoff onto Echo Park Rd. Leave time for the 2-mile round-trip hike to the Echo Park Overlook, 2,500 feet above Echo Park, and the drive down into Echo Park (see Echo Park Rd., above). The Yampa Bench Rd. begins off the Echo Park Rd. 8 miles from the junction of the Echo Park and Harper's Corner Rds.

Where to Stay

Accommodations

There is no lodging within Dinosaur National Monument. The nearest accommodations are in Vernal (see the **Roosevelt and Vernal** chapter).

Camping

PRIVATE

Private campgrounds are located in Vernal (see the Services section; see also the Where to Stay section in the **Roosevelt and Vernal** chapter).

Dinosaur Village

The closest private campground to Dinosaur National Monument, with 50 sites, all with complete hookups. Showers and toilets. Open Apr.–Oct. Located 1.5 miles west of Jensen on US Hwy. 40. **435-789-5552.**

PUBLIC

Green River Campground

This modern campground has 85 sites. Unlike other National Park Service campgrounds, you can usually find a place here. Open Memorial Day–Labor Day. Located 5 miles east of Dinosaur Quarry, on the Split Mountain Green River Campground Rd.

Backcountry camping is permitted in roadless sections of the monument. A permit is required and is available at park headquarters or the Quarry Visitor Center .

Where to Eat

There are no dining facilities within Dinosaur National Monument. For the nearest restaurants, see the Where to Eat section in the **Roosevelt and Vernal** chapter.

Services

See also the Services section in the **Roosevelt and Vernal** chapter.

Visitor Information

Dinosaur National Monument Headquarters—Superintendent, Dinosaur National Monument, 4545 US Hwy. 40, Dinosaur, CO 81610; 970-374-3000; www.nps.gov/dino.

Jensen Welcome Center—Information about Dinosaur National Monument and other attractions in the area. Located at the junction of Hwy. 149, the road to the Dinosaur Quarry, and US Hwy. 40, approximately 13 miles east of Vernal. **435-789-4002.**

Flaming Gorge National Recreation Area

Flaming Gorge is many things. The original name was given by Maj. John Wesley Powell and his men on May 26, 1869, during their epic journey down the Green and Colorado Rivers. As they prepared to pass through the Uinta Mountains, Powell recorded in his diary:

> The river is running to the south; the mountains have an easterly and westerly trend directly athwart its course, yet it glides on a quiet way as if it thought a mountain range no formidable obstruction. It enters the range by a flaring, brilliant red gorge, that may be seen from the north a score of miles away. The great mass of the mountain ridge through which the gorge is cut is composed of bright

vermilion rocks; but they are surmounted by broad bands of mottled buff and gray, and these bands come down with a gentle curve to the water's edge on the nearer slope of the mountain. This is the head of the first of the canyons we are about to explore—an introductory one to a series made by the river through this range. We name it Flaming

---

Getting There

Flaming Gorge is located about 250 miles east of Salt Lake City and can be reached by two major routes. Both routes are approximately the same distance, although the southern route is probably a little longer.

*The **northern route** follows Interstate 80 east into Wyoming, then exits the interstate at Ft. Bridger, located approximately two-thirds of the way between Salt Lake City and the gorge. The route then heads southeast on Wyoming Hwy. 414 across the Utah border onto Hwy. 43, which takes you to Manila, near the western shore of the reservoir. From Manila, Hwy. 43/Wyoming Hwy. 530 winds north along the lake to I-80 at Green River, Wyoming; Hwy. 44 heads south and east to a junction with US Hwy. 191 at Flaming Gorge Dam.*

*The **southern route** follows Interstate 80 east to the junction with US Hwy. 40, which you follow east through Heber City and on to Duchesne, Roosevelt and Vernal. At Vernal, head north on US Hwy. 191, over the eastern portion of the Uinta Mountains, to the junction with Hwy. 44 and through Greendale to Flaming Gorge Dam. The southern route offers the opportunity to do some touring in the Uinta Basin and at Dinosaur National Monument. Just across the dam is the town of Dutch John; US Hwy. 191 continues north along the east side of the reservoir to I-80 near Rock Springs, Wyoming.*

Gorge. The cliffs, or walls, we find on measurement to be about 1,200 feet high.

The name Flaming Gorge was originally applied only to where the Green River cuts into the Uinta Mountains; today, however, when people refer to Flaming Gorge they are talking about both the reservoir and the northeastern corner of Utah where it borders both Wyoming and Colorado. This area includes Brown's Park, a 35-mile-long, 6-mile-wide valley through which the Green River flows.

Flaming Gorge Lake, which covers more than 66 square miles with a shoreline of 375 miles, and the surrounding area are included in the Flaming Gorge National Recreation Area administered by the U.S. Forest Service. The recreation area includes the section of the Green River below the dam, through Red Canyon to the west end of Brown's Park, part of the north slope of the Uinta Mountains on the south, and across the Utah-Wyoming border partway up Blacks Fork and up the main channel of the Green River to a point about 3 miles south of the city of Green River, Wyoming. The visitor centers for the recreation area are located at the Flaming Gorge Dam on US Hwy. 191 and at Red Canyon on Hwy. 44.

History

Flaming Gorge had a colorful history before and after Powell named the area. The first recorded travelers through Flaming Gorge were Gen. William H. Ashley and members of his 1825 fur trapping party. Ashley set out in a 16-by-7-foot bull boat made of buffalo hides on April 22, 1825, to look for beaver. He also hoped to ascertain whether the Green River was the fabled Buenaventura River, which misinformed mapmakers had drawn running southwest from the Rocky Mountains to the Pacific Ocean. Ashley's wild adventure took him through Flaming Gorge and Split Mountain, where his bull boat filled with water and nearly sank before his men rescued the boat and pulled it to land. Ashley recorded in his diary that his men saved his life, for he could not swim.

Ashley continued down the Green River into the Uinta Basin, where he left the Green River at Minnie Maud Creek. After making a circular journey around the Uinta Mountains, he returned to the Flaming Gorge area at the end of June. While floating down the Green River, Ashley designated Henry's Fork as the site of the first Rocky Mountain fur trapper rendezvous. Held 20 miles up Henry's Fork from its junction with the Green River, this first rendezvous established an institution that lasted until the end of the fur trade era in 1840.

As the rendezvous system began to wane and was replaced by trading posts, Philip Thompson and William Craig established a trading post in Brown's Hole, known as Ft. Davy Crockett, in 1837. Nearly a quarter of a century after Ashley's trip down the Green River, the next recorded journey down the Green through Flaming Gorge occurred. Several California-bound '49ers concluded that the Green River offered the easiest route to their goal. Using an abandoned ferryboat, then dugout canoes, they set out down the Green River from near the Sweetwater crossing in Wyoming. They got as far as the mouth of the White River in the Uinta Basin, and then met Wakara, the Ute Indian chief, who convinced them they had better abandon their river route and head west to Salt Lake City if they ever wanted to reach California.

More successful in reaching his objective was Maj. John Wesley Powell and his 1869 voyage down the Green River to its confluence with the Colorado River and on through the Grand Canyon.

In 1870 the first cattle herds were brought to the Brown's Park–Flaming Gorge area. By the 1880s cattlemen, cowboys, rustlers, settlers and outlaws all intermingled in the region. Outlaws like Butch Cassidy, the Sundance Kid (Harry Longabaugh), Matt Warner, Elza Lay, Tom Horn, the Queen of the Cattle Rustlers (Ann Bassett) and many others left their mark on the history of the Brown's Park and Flaming Gorge area. Dirt roads were not completed from Green River,

Wyoming, to the north and Vernal, Utah, to the south until the 1920s and 1930s.

When construction of the Flaming Gorge Dam began in 1958, the northeastern corner of Utah was still very much a primitive area of scattered ranches. Access into the area from the south was made possible by the construction of the Cart Creek dam in 1959; connecting traffic was made possible in 1963 when construction of the dam was completed and the highway built along the crest of the dam. As the lake filled, it became one of the top fishing and boating sites in Utah. The construction of Flaming Gorge Dam led to the establishment of the town of Dutch John—named for John Hanselena, a prospector and horse trader from Prussia who was in the area in the 1860s. Despite his German (Deutsch) origins, Hanselena was called Dutch John, probably for the same reason that the Pennsylvania Germans became known as the Pennsylvania Dutch.

Outdoor Activities

Biking

Dowd Mountain

This 10-mile round-trip ride with moderate grades begins 14 miles south of Manila at the Dowd Mountain road off Hwy. 44. The ride along the dirt road takes you to the Dowd Mountain Overlook for spectacular views of Flaming Gorge and the western portions of Flaming Gorge Lake.

Swett Ranch

This 6-mile round-trip ride begins at the eastern end of the Greendale Rest Area, located on Hwy. 44 a mile north of its junction with US Hwy. 191, and takes you to the historic Swett Ranch (see the Historic Sites section under Seeing and Doing).

Fishing

Flaming Gorge Reservoir

If you want to go for the big ones, Flaming

Gorge Reservoir is the place. As the lake trout, or Mackinaw, matured during the decade of the 1980s, Flaming Gorge yielded more lake trout over 30 pounds than any other spot in the United States—perhaps the world. The Utah record is a 51.5-pound, 46.5-inch lake trout, caught in the Lucerne Bay area by Curt Bilbey of Vernal in July 1988. It goes without saying that Flaming Gorge is one of the most popular fishing spots in Utah.

While catching the really big ones requires a boat, know-how and sophisticated equipment, the lake is also kind to the average angler; rainbow trout can be caught from the shore. Smallmouth bass are numerous and, in the upper end of Flaming Gorge, channel catfish flourish. Kokanee salmon up to 5 pounds are also taken in the open water. In early Sept. and late Oct., the kokanee turn a deep crimson and make their way upstream to spawn. Marinas are located at Cedar Springs near Dutch John and Lucerne Valley, on US Hwy. 191 just north of Flaming Gorge Dam; on the west side of the lake near Manila, at Hwys. 43 and 44; and at Buckboard just below the confluence of the Blacks Fork and Green Rivers in Wyoming, on Wyoming Hwy. 530.

Green River

The Green River just below Flaming Gorge Dam at US Hwy. 191 is famous as one of America's best fly-fishing locations. The river is well stocked with rainbow, brown and cutthroat trout.

Guides

Flaming Gorge Recreation Services— Offers guided fishing trips that include transportation to and from the river, lunch, boat and guide. If you are serious about taking a big lake trout, the use of local guides will increase your chances tremendously. **P.O. Box 367, Dutch John, UT 84023; 435-885-3191.**

Flaming Gorge Lodge—The Collett family can also provide fishing guides for one- to three-day fishing trips. Located on US Hwy. 191 approximately 6 miles south of the Flaming Gorge Dam. **435-889-3773.**

River Rafting

Flaming Gorge Dam to Little Hole

The 7-mile stretch of the Green River from just below Flaming Gorge Dam at US Hwy. 191 not only offers excellent fly-fishing but is a popular river float trip. The high, narrow canyons, wildlife and sections of small rapids make this a memorable but safe trip for families and groups, even those who do not have much experience with the rubber rafts. After the take-out at Little Hole, you can return to Dutch John via a dirt road; from Dutch John it's is only a few miles south on US Hwy. 191 to the dam.

Rentals

Rafts, life jackets, paddles, bail buckets, and guides can be rented at the **Flaming Gorge Lodge (435-889-3773), and Flaming Gorge Recreation Services, P.O. Box 367, Dutch John, UT 84023; 435-885-3191.**

Seeing and Doing

Historic Sites

Flaming Gorge Dam

Although some might argue that a structure that was completed in 1963 is not old enough to be "historic," the Flaming Gorge Dam has certainly had an impact on northeastern Utah. The dam is 502 feet high and required nearly a million cubic yards of concrete. The crest of the dam is approximately 1,200 feet long and carries two lanes of traffic as part of US Hwy. 191. A visitor center is located at the dam, and self-guided tours (daily 8 A.M.–4 P.M. year-round) can be taken inside the dam to view the generators and turbines. There are also exhibits and a small bookstore. The visitor center is open daily 9:30 A.M.–5 P.M. year-round. Located on US Hwy. 191 at the dam. **435-885-3135.**

John Jarvie Historic Property

Obviously, Bureau of Land Management officials had a difficult time coming up with a name to describe what is usually called the John Jarvie

Ranch. More than a cattle ranch, it was the headquarters for Jarvie's prospecting activities; the location of a general merchandise store and post office, which served the Brown's Park area; a cemetery; and a ferry across the Green River. John Jarvie settled in Brown's Park in 1880 and was well liked by the other residents. A native of Scotland, Jarvie could play the organ and concertina and was in high demand at social functions. But his popularity did not prevent his violent death at the hands of two robbers on July 6, 1909. After shooting Jarvie, the murderers placed his body in a boat and sent it down the Green River, where it was discovered eight days later near the Gates of Lodore, in the eastern end of Brown's Park. The two men were never apprehended.

Today the John Jarvie Historic Property includes the original two-room dugout in which Jarvie lived; the reconstructed store, which serves as a museum; a stone house built by Jack Bennett, one of Brown's Park's numerous outlaws (but one who was sent to prison, where he learned enough masonry skills to erect the house); a blacksmith shop; and a corral built from hand-hewn railroad ties that floated down the Green River from the Union Pacific line. Open daily May–Oct. 10 A.M.–5 P.M., with tours available. Take US Hwy. 191 north to the Utah–Wyoming border, then turn east onto the Clay Basin Rd. and follow it as it heads south through Jesse Ewing Canyon to the Green River, then follow the road back to the west. From US Hwy. 191 it is 22 miles, including the 2 miles through Jesse Ewing Canyon, where there are steep grades of up to 17 percent. **435-885-3307.**

Oscar Swett Ranch

The Swett Ranch, owned and operated by the Flaming Gorge Ranger District of the U.S. Forest Service, offers a glimpse of what ranch life was like in the Flaming Gorge area. The Swett family began grazing cattle in the region in the early 1900s. In 1912 Oscar and Emma Swett were married, and their first home was an abandoned log cabin that Oscar disassembled and hauled to their homesite. In 1919 a two-room

log cabin was built, and then in 1929 the five-room frame house was built, using lumber Oscar had cut in the nearby forests and sawed at his own mill.

All three buildings were used by the Swett family, which included seven daughters and two sons. A bathroom was added to the frame house in the 1950s, but after much protest by Oscar, who said, "You're not supposed to have a bathroom in the house." Oscar finally conceded to the bathroom, but he wouldn't let the door open into the house, so to make a visit one had to go out on the porch and then enter the bathroom. Horse-powered equipment was used on the ranch from 1909 until 1970; much of the equipment, including hay mowers, hay rakes, bull rakes, wagons, a bobsled, hay stackers, a hay ram, ditchers, road graders, riding plows and a binder, has been preserved on the ranch.

Oscar died in September 1968, working on the homestead until the day he died. Emma died three years later in May 1971. The ranch is now part of the Flaming Gorge National Recreation Area. Volunteer caretakers live at the ranch during the summer months and act as hosts to visitors. Located 1.5 miles west of the Greendale Campground. For information about access to the ranch, inquire at the U.S. Forest Service office in Dutch John or at the Flaming Gorge Visitor Center on US Hwy. 191 at Flaming Gorge Dam.

Ute Mountain Fire Tower

While fire towers can be found all over the Northwest, there is only one in Utah, and the Forest Service has done an excellent job of preserving this important structure. Constructed by the Civilian Conservation Corps in 1937, the tower rises high above the forest to give a panoramic view of the surrounding area. It was used by Forest Service personnel until 1969 to detect forest fires and provide weather data. For Lee Skabelund, who led the effort to preserve, restore and list the tower in the National Register of Historic Places and open it to visitors, the tower is important for historic and personal reasons. Lee spent his honeymoon at the tower as a brand-new Forest Service employee, and claims that every young couple should start their marriage with such beauty and isolation. Located 10 miles south of Manila via Hwy. 44, off the Sheep Creek Canyon Rd. and west of the Summit Springs Guard Station.

Scenic Drives

Brown's Park Rd. Scenic Backway

The Brown's Park Rd. Scenic Backway leaves US Hwy. 191 5 miles north of Dutch John and in approximately 50 miles reaches the Jones Hole Rd. Throughout your drive, keep an eye out for mule deer, elk and antelope, which are quite common.

The route reaches the junction with Clay Basin Rd. after about 20 miles; to reach the John Jarvie Historic Property, take this as it descends through the narrow, twisting, winding Jessie Ewing Canyon. After visiting the John Jarvie Historic Property (see the Historic Sites section under Seeing and Doing), return to the junction and continue along Brown's Park Rd., following the Green River south and eastward into Colorado. A small suspension bridge, which accommodates just one vehicle at a time, allows you to cross the river. You are now in the heart of Brown's Park with all its outlaw lore and history. The road then loops back into Utah and south into Crouse Canyon as it exits Brown's Park. Continuing south up Crouse Canyon, the road passes through vertical cliffs with pine and juniper forests on the side hills before crossing Diamond Mountain and connecting with the Jones Hole Rd. (see the **Roosevelt and Vernal** chapter). In Brown's Park you have three options: follow the Jones Hole Rd. east to its terminus at Green River; follow the Jones Hole Rd. southwest into Vernal, where you can return to Dutch John via US Hwy. 191; or simply retrace your route back through Brown's Park and on to Dutch John. The road requires a couple of hours both ways.

Flaming Gorge–Uintas Scenic Byway

US Hwy. 191 is one of two paved roads that bisect the Uinta Mountains. The other route, the Mirror Lake Hwy. (see the **Heber Valley** chapter in the Wasatch Front Region), covers the western part of the mountains. About 100 miles to the east, US Hwy. 191 heads north out of Vernal, across the eastern end of the mountains, to reach Flaming Gorge Reservoir, 45 miles away. The steep climb from Vernal passes through rocks laid down more than a billion years ago. A series of 20 interpretive signs point out geological formations along this "Drive Through the Ages." The road also offers magnificent views to the south from the switchbacks up the mountain. Once on top, the drive through pine and aspen forests and mountain meadows is an especially refreshing experience in summer. Continue north on US Hwy. 191 to the Flaming Gorge Dam and visitor center, then retrace your route back to the junction with Hwy. 44.

Take Hwy. 44 west, which skirts Flaming Gorge Reservoir on the east and then continues north to Manila, 67 miles from Vernal. Along Hwy. 44, stop for a stunning view of Flaming Gorge Reservoir from the Red Canyon Overlook, 4 miles from the junction with US Hwy. 191. Eighteen miles from the Red Canyon Overlook is the turnoff to the Sheep Creek Canyon Loop, one of the most scenic canyons of the state (see below).

Sheep Creek Canyon Loop/Spirit Lake Loop Backway

The road through Sheep Creek Canyon and the 17-mile drive to Spirit Lake are a designated Scenic Backway, and the 48-mile round-trip drive offers a unique blend of geology and scenery. The Sheep Creek Canyon Loop is an open book on geology. When volcanic activity along faults beneath the earth's surface created the Uinta Mountains, the northern side of the fault, visible in Sheep Creek Canyon, underwent little vertical movement, but the rock strata were bent up and exposed like ruffled pages of a book. The exposed formations display some primitive marine fossils—trilobites, marine crustaceans, corals, sponges, sea urchins and other life-forms—along with the tracks of crocodilelike reptiles. While the Sheep Creek Canyon Loop is along a paved road for the most part, the Spirit Lake portion of the drive is gravel and can become washboarded with heavy use. Nevertheless, this part of the backway is well worth your time, as the beautiful pine and aspen forest and meadows of wildflowers offer a restful contrast to the dramatic geology and sheer walls of Sheep Creek Canyon. The drive usually takes about 2.5 hours and is located off Hwy. 44, between Manila and the junction with US Hwy. 191.

Wildlife Viewing

Flaming Gorge Lake

Boaters on the reservoir should keep an eye out for a variety of birds, including ospreys and endangered peregrine falcons. Occasionally bighorn sheep can be seen high in the cliffs around the lake and on Kingfisher Island, which lies between Skull Creek and Hideout Canyon on the northern side of the lake. You might also spot pronghorn antelope, elk, black bears, bobcats and mountain lions.

Lucerne Peninsula

The Lucerne Peninsula is located on the northwestern side of Flaming Gorge Reservoir about 8 miles from Manila, where there is a high probability for viewing antelope year-round in and near the Lucerne Valley Campground. The wetlands adjacent to the reservoir are home to ducks, geese, herons, egrets and other waterfowl. Bald eagles can also be seen in the early winter while there is still some open water for them to fish. Take Hwy. 43 east from Manila for 4 miles, then turn southeast onto Forest Rd. 146 at the Lucerne Valley turnoff and follow it 4 miles to the campground.

Where to Stay

Motels

Flaming Gorge Lodge—$$ to $$$

Flaming Gorge Lodge, the largest motel in the area, offers 22 motel rooms and 22 condo units, which are a good bet for families as they offer a queen-size bed, a single bed, a hideaway bed and a full kitchen. There is a restaurant at the lodge. Located on US Hwy. 191 at Greendale, about 3 miles south of the dam. **435-889-3773; www.fglodge.com.**

Red Canyon Lodge—$$ to $$$

The rustic cabins share a central shower house and rest room; deluxe cabins have their own rest-room facilities and either a single or double bedroom; luxury log cabins have two queen beds in a separate bedroom and a pullout couch in the living room. Luxury units also have a kitchenette, vaulted ceilings and full bathrooms. Located 3 miles west of the junction of Hwy. 44 and US Hwy. 191. **435-889-3759; www.redcanyonlodge.com.**

Camping

PRIVATE
Flaming Gorge KOA

With so many public campgrounds, it is not surprising that there is only one private campground in the Flaming Gorge area. Located in Manila, the Flaming Gorge KOA has 40 trailer sites, all with complete hookups, and 25 tentsites. The campground has showers, toilets, a laundry and a dump site. Open mid-April–Nov. Located on **Hwy. 42 and 3 W. Manila; 435-784-3184.**

PUBLIC

Within the Flaming Gorge area there are 22 public campgrounds—including 13 in Ashley National Forest and two maintained by the Bureau of Land Management in Brown's Park—with a total of more than 800 trailer and tentsites. The public campgrounds usually open some time in May and close during Sept. Because of the 6,000-foot elevation, the recreation season is fairly short, and most campgrounds fill up on summer weekends. During the middle of the week, sites are usually available, but if you want to be sure, make reservations. **Ashley National Forest/Flaming Gorge National Recreation Area,** 1-800-280-CAMP.

The largest campground, with 147 trailer and tentsites, is the **Lucerne Valley Campground,** 8.5 miles east of Manila off Hwy. 43. Second in size, with 122 sites, is **Antelope Flat,** 11 miles northeast of Dutch John, off US Hwy. 191. **Firefighters Memorial,** with 94 tentsites and 78 trailer sites, is located near Flaming Gorge Dam and provides good access to fishing and boating on the Green River.

Where to Eat

Flaming Gorge Lodge—$ to $$

Serving traditional American home-style food for breakfast, lunch and dinner. Open Nov.–Feb. daily 8 A.M.–6 P.M.; Mar.–Oct. daily 6:30 A.M.–9:45 P.M. Located 3 miles west of the junction of Hwy. 44 and US Hwy. 191. **435-889-3773.**

Red Canyon Lodge Restaurant—$ to $$

The restaurant is part of the Red Canyon Lodge complex. Breakfasts are traditional, lunches primarily burgers and sandwiches, while dinner offerings include fish, chicken, steaks, prime rib, pasta and more exotic daily specials. Open daily Apr.–Oct. Located off Hwy. 44, 3 miles west of its junction with US Hwy. 191. **435-889-3759.**

Services

Visitor Information

Flaming Gorge Dam Visitor Center— Books about the area can be purchased at the center. Open Memorial Day–Labor Day daily 8 A.M.–6 P.M.; Labor Day–Oct. daily 9 A.M.–5 P.M.; Nov.–Memorial Day daily 10 A.M.–4 P.M.; closed Thanksgiving, Christmas and New Year's. Located on US Hwy. 191 at the dam. **435-885-3135.**

Central Region

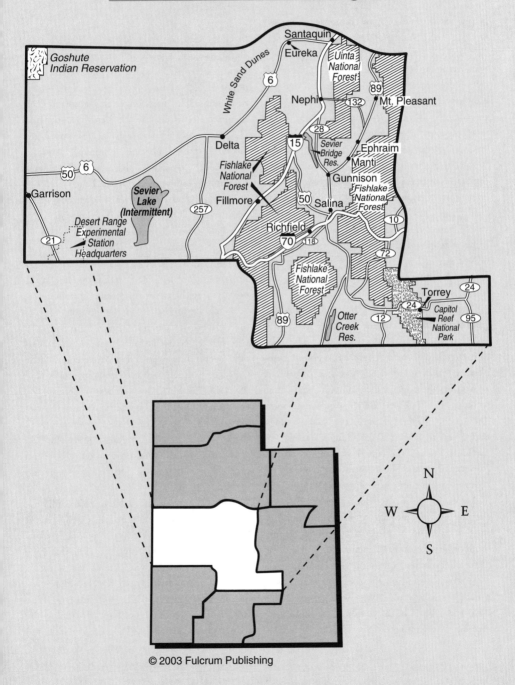

Goshute
Indian Reservation

White Sand Dunes

Santaquin

Eureka

Uinta
National
Forest

6

89

Nephi

132

Mt. Pleasant

Delta

28

15

Sevier
Bridge
Res.

Ephraim

Manti

50 6

Fishlake
National
Forest

Gunnison

Fishlake
National
Forest

Garrison

Sevier
Lake
(Intermittent)

257

Fillmore

50

Salina

10

Desert Range
Experimental
Station
Headquarters

21

70

118

Richfield

72

Fishlake
National
Forest

Torrey

24

24

Capitol
Reef
National
Park

95

89

Otter
Creek
Res.

12

Eureka and Nephi

If two communities ever reflected the diverging forces of 19th-century Utah, it is the towns of Nephi and Eureka. Nephi, established on Salt Creek in 1851, was named by early Mormon settlers for the first of several principal prophets who wrote the Book of Mormon. Nephi is typical of the hundreds of Mormon communities established in Utah by early settlers. Eureka, on the other hand, takes its name from the Greek word meaning "I have found it." What early miners found were rich deposits of silver ore that led to the establishment of a mining town in 1869. Eureka is located high in the Tintic Mountains; its narrow, twisting streets and its mine dumps, head frames and other signs of mining activities visible from about any place in town, are in sharp contrast to the well-ordered grid street system of Nephi, which was laid out according to a plan for communities developed by Mormon founder Joseph Smith.

Nephi sits at the base of the 11,877-foot Mt. Nebo, the southernmost mountain in the Wasatch Range and a landmark that can be seen from much of central Utah. Proceeding westward to the Nevada border, like the folds of an accordion, are a series of mountain ranges that include the East Tintic Range, the West Tintic Range, the Thomas Range, the Fish Springs Range and the Deep Creek Range. Except for the Tintic Range, the rest of the region to the Nevada border and beyond is mostly unoccupied and provides plenty of space for exploring.

Nephi is the Juab County seat and, with about 4,500 people, its largest community. A smaller community, Mona, is north of Nephi; south of Nephi is another small town, Levan. The name of the latter community is the subject of some speculation. Some wags claim that it was named by a practical joker who realized the town was located in the center of the state and, reversing the spelling of "Navel," called it Levan!

History

Fremont Indians occupied the Juab Valley until about A.D. 1300. They left important archaeological sites, such as the Nephi Mounds just north of Nephi along the western slope of the mountains. The Fremont were supplanted by incoming Utes in the eastern part of Juab County, while in western Juab County the Goshute Indians became dominant. Tintic is named for a Goshute Indian chief whose band lived in the valleys west of Utah Lake.

Nephi sits on a historic travel corridor, which was used by Dominguez and Escalante in 1776, Jedediah S. Smith in 1826–1827 and John C. Frémont in 1843–1844. Early Mormon explorers noted the favorable location and, in 1851, a settlement on Salt Creek came into being at the point where the valley reaches the mountains.

Nephi became a farming community and, as the railroad was extended south from Salt Lake City in the 1870s, an important livestock shipping center that acquired the nickname "Little Chicago." The railroad also brought miners, and the Tintic Mining District was organized on December 13, 1869. The Tintic Mining District joined Park City and Bingham Canyon as one of the top three precious metal producers in the state. By 1976, the total production of base and precious metals from the district over a period of more than 100 years was estimated at 16,654,377 tons, with a value of $570 million.

Eureka sits at the center of the district, but it is surrounded by Silver City, Dividend, Mammoth and Knightsville, mining towns that have now become ghost towns. Hundreds of mines operated in the district, but the "big four" producers were Eureka Hill, Bullion-Beck, Blue Rock and Gemini. Much of the early mining history has been documented and preserved by the Tintic Historical Society, which has received national recognition as one of the best local historical societies in the country. Visit their museum in Eureka and inquire about the driving tour of the district and what mining activities are still going on, and purchase a copy of the excellent history *Faith, Hope and Prosperity: The Tintic Mining District* (Tintic Historical Society, 1982), authored by a prominent Utah historian, Philip F. Notarianni.

Major Attractions

Little Sahara Recreation Area

"Little" does not seem quite right for the name of this Bureau of Land Management–administered recreation area, which consists of miles of free-blowing dune sand. The actual recreation area includes 60,000 acres of sand dunes, and in keeping with a multiuse recreation philosophy, there are specific areas for nature study, picnicking and playing in the sand and vehicle recreation. The Dunes, as they are also called, are Utah's most popular area for off-road-vehicle recreation. Dune buggies, four-wheelers, motorbikes and four-wheel-drive vehicles tear across the dunes, and Sand Mountain, with its steep sand slopes, challenges the most skilled drivers. But if you don't have a sand vehicle, the Dunes are still an unforgettable experience. This is a place to build sand castles, to run barefoot through the sand, to jump off sand hills. Even if you are past middle age, you can't help acting like a kid again. Easter is an especially popular time, but fall is also a nice season at Little Sahara. There are four BLM campgrounds at the Dunes (see the Where to Stay section).

To get there, from Eureka go south on US

Hwy. 6 20 miles to Jericho Junction then turn west and follow the paved road until you reach the recreation area. From Nephi, head west on Hwy. 132 for 13 miles, then turn right onto the paved road to Jericho Junction, about 8 miles to the northwest. For information, contact the **Bureau of Land Management, Warm Springs Resource Area, P.O. Box 778, Fillmore, UT 84631; 435-743-6811.**

Festivals and Events

Ute Stampede

second weekend in July. This popular rodeo is held in Nephi. **P.O. Box 404, Nephi, UT 84648; 435-623-0643.**

Outdoor Activities

Golf

Canyon Hills Golf Course

Located at the mouth of Salt Creek Canyon in Nephi, the 9-hole Canyon Hills Course is easily accessible. No reservations are taken, and there is no need. If there are more than a dozen players on the course at any one time, it is considered crowded. Golf junkies traveling up or down Interstate 15 can pull into the golf parking area, pay their fees, play a round in under 2 hours, experience a golfer's high with what should be one of their better scores and be back on the road with time to get wherever they are going.

While the course is quite easy, there are obstacles, notably on the par 4, 412-yard 4th hole. A 50-foot cement silo, left from an earlier era when the course was farmland, looms just to the right, about 20 yards ahead of the white tees. Pay attention here: a misdirected shot can careen off the cement silo into golfers or cars in the parking lot behind the tee. The pockmarked silo looks like it may have been the site of an early western gun battle! But erratic golfers are the culprits, and chances are that if the number of players picks up, it will be only a few decades before they have reduced the proud tower to

---

Getting There

Nephi is 85 miles south of Salt Lake City on Interstate 15 at Exit 228. Eureka, located northwest of Nephi, sits astride US Hwy. 6 and is 21 miles west of the Santaquin exit (Exit 245) off Interstate 15.

rubble. The local rule is that if a ball hits the silo, it can be re-teed without a penalty. Rates are about the lowest in the state. Just off Interstate 15 at Exit 225. E. Canyon Rd., Nephi, UT 84548; **435-623-9930.**

Hiking

Mt. Nebo

At 11,877 feet, Mt. Nebo is the tallest mountain in the Wasatch Range. There are actually three peaks on Mt. Nebo—North, Middle and South Peaks. While North Peak is the tallest, few hikers actually reach it because of the distance, steep climbs and exposed faces that must be crossed to reach the peak. South Peak is only 51 feet lower than North Peak, and that much elevation does not make any difference as far as the breathtaking panoramic view is concerned.

There are four trails that you can take to reach South Peak. All four trails intersect at the saddle 2 miles below South Peak. Whatever trail you choose, plan a full day of hiking and opt for a perfect day for the hike. Lightning storms are especially dangerous from the saddle to the peak. The Forest Service sells a waterproof, tear-resistant *Uinta National Forest Trail Guide* that includes maps of Mt. Nebo, Mt. Timpanogos and Long Peak. It is especially helpful for this hike. **Nephi Office, Uinta National Forest, 740 S. Main; 435-623-2735.**

Andrews Ridge Trail—Sometimes called the South Nebo Bench Trail, this is a 20-mile round-trip hike. Take the Salt Creek Canyon road (Hwy. 132) east from Nephi, then take the Nebo Scenic Loop Rd. north to the second trailhead turnoff.

Nephi Nebo Peak Trail—This is a 16-mile round-trip hike to South Peak that begins at Rees Flat. Take Exit 225 off I-15 at Nephi and head east on Hwy. 132 (Salt Creek Canyon road) for 2.3 miles to a dirt road (Forest Rd. 463), which you follow north for 2 miles to the trailhead.

North Nebo Bench Trail—The longest trail is a 28-mile round-trip hike, but with a basic elevation gain of only 2,624 feet. Take the Salt Creek Canyon road (Hwy. 132) east from Nephi, then take the Nebo Scenic Loop Rd. north; this trail begins from the highest point, at the Monument trailhead.

Willow Creek Trail—If your heart can stand the steep climb, the Willow Creek Trail at 10 miles round trip is the shortest route. The trailhead begins at an elevation of 6,600 feet on the west slope of Mt. Nebo. The average grade is 20 percent as you gain more than a mile in elevation during the 5-mile climb. Two of the other trails also begin at 6,600 feet, but they are longer and hence not as steep as the Willow Creek route. Take the Mona exit off I-15 and head east on a 3-mile-long dirt road to its end.

Seeing and Doing

Museums and Historic Sites

Nephi Daughters of Utah Pioneers Museum and Juab County Jail

There are not many historic jails preserved in Utah, but one of the most interesting is the 1892 Juab County Jail, which remained in use until 1974. As with most jails that have been around for a few years, many stories are told about the old jail, including one about three of the first prisoners who made a hole in the brick wall and escaped, only to be recaptured and returned to the jail. One inmate, incarcerated over the summer for drunkenness, was given a key to the jail by the sheriff, so that he could let himself out during the day and return at night after spending the day doing volunteer work on the city golf course. The jail is not generally open for tours, but with a smile and a little charm you can talk the wonderful ladies inside the Daughters of Utah Pioneers Museum into letting you take the key and unlock the building. The jail is located behind (west of) the museum, which is housed in the old Juab County Courthouse.

The Nephi Daughters of Utah Pioneers have done a fine job of displaying local artifacts and photographs on the three levels of the old courthouse. Be sure to go into the basement, where most of the artifacts are located in several rooms—a bedroom with a patchwork quilt; a parlor; a kitchen with a fireplace, spinning wheel and carding wheel. Hours seem to vary: the permanent sign indicates Mon.–Fri. 9 A.M.–5 P.M.; a more temporary sign on the door indicates 1–5 P.M. **4 S. Main St., Nephi; 435-633-5202.**

Tintic Mining Museum

Operated by the Tintic Historical Society, this is one of the best small-town museums in the state. There are artifacts here from throughout Eureka's history, but the focus is on its heyday as one of the largest mining towns in Utah. One of the most interesting artifacts is a three-dimensional model of the inside of a silver mine. Located on Main St., Eureka. The museum is not open on a regular basis, but you can call the numbers listed on the door and one of the faithful members will be only too glad to come down and give you a personal tour. If you want to make arrangements in advance, call June or Coleen McNulty, **435-433-6842.**

Scenic Drives

Nebo Loop Scenic Byway

Mt. Nebo was named by Mormon pioneers for the highest mountain east of the Jordan River in the Holy Land where Moses died. The pioneers, in recognition of their own Zion, chose to honor the highest mountain in the Wasatch Range, which runs just to the east of Utah's Jordan River, with the name Mt. Nebo. The 38-mile-long Nebo Loop Scenic Byway loops around the 11,877-foot-high Mt. Nebo. The drive leads to the Payson Lakes Recreation Area, 12 miles south of Payson, and takes in breathtaking views of Utah Valley, the Wasatch Mountains and Mt. Nebo from various overlooks.

Magnificent autumn colors makes this one of the top five drives in the state in late Sept. and early Oct. On the north side of Mt. Nebo, chances are good of seeing elk and deer as the herds number an estimated 500 and 5,000, respectively. One site you will want to visit is Devil's Kitchen—a collection of red spires of gravel and silt that have eroded on the steep mountain slope. Devil's Kitchen is about

10 miles from Nephi. The byway can be followed south from its northern terminus at Payson in Utah County, or north from the turnoff off Hwy. 132 about 3 miles east of Nephi in Salt Creek Canyon.

Tintic Mining District Driving Tour

The Tintic Historical Society has prepared a suggested driving tour booklet of the Tintic Mining District, which takes you to some of the historic mining towns and past several of the old mine head frames and buildings. Highlights of the tour include the **Bullion-Beck Headframe** and the sites and ghost towns of **Knightsville, Dividend, Silver City** and **Mammoth.** Located near the junction of US Hwy. 6 and Hwys. 36 and 67 just south of Eureka. For more information see the Tintic Mining Museum, located on Main St. in Eureka, or call June or Coleen McNulty, **435-433-6842.**

Where to Stay

Accommodations

Best Western Paradise Inn—$$

Heated pool; 40 units. **1025 S. Main St., Nephi; 1-800-528-1234; 435-623-0624.**

Budget Host Motor Inn Roberta's Cove—$$

Six of the 43 rooms have private whirlpool baths. Located off Interstate 15 at Exit 222. **2250 S. Main St., Nephi; 1-800-456-6460; 435-623-2629.**

Whitmore Mansion Bed and Breakfast—$$ to $$$

The first time I saw this beautiful mansion in the 1970s it seemed utterly abandoned, hidden behind a used car lot. The cars are gone, the ghosts have been exorcised—at least some of them—and the result is a magnificently restored mansion and a fine bed and breakfast the equal of any in the West. George Whitmore was a Texas cattleman who converted to the Mormon church. He expanded his Utah livestock interests into banking, land and other businesses and by the 1890s was the richest man in Nephi. The beautiful sandstone and brick mansion, with its imposing gables and turret, was a fitting statement of his financial success. Redemption and restoration of the 1898 mansion began in the mid-1970s after its listing on the National Register of Historic Places.

There are nine rooms, all with private baths and some with Jacuzzis. The rooms are located on the second and third floors. If you love the mountains, be sure to ask for one with a breathtaking view of Mt. Nebo. Families might consider the third-story suite with a bedroom, sitting room and play area in the turret where children can roll out sleeping beds. There is also a room with two twin beds—used by the Whitmore children, whose teeth marks are still clearly visible in the wood. On the main floor, there are two parlors, a breakfast room (where a full country breakfast is served) and a formal dining room. **110 S. Main St., Nephi; 435-623-2047.**

Camping

PRIVATE
High Country RV Camp
Located in the south end of Nephi, the campground has 45 sites, most with full hookups; flush toilets, showers, laundry facilities and wheelchair-accessible facilities. Open year-round. **899 S. Main St., Nephi; 435-623-2624.**

Horseshoe Bar Ranch KOA Campground
This KOA campground provides a mountain setting that is only a few miles from Nephi. It has 65 RV sites and 20 tentsites. There are flush toilets, showers and a laundry. Open mid-May–Sept. Located in Salt Creek Canyon along Hwy. 132, near the Mt. Nebo Scenic Loop. **435-623-0811.**

PUBLIC
There are three campgrounds located on national forestlands northeast of Nephi, on the Mt. Nebo Loop Rd. The **Ponderosa Campground,** 11 miles from Nephi, has 22 RV sites and 10 tentsites. The **Bear Canyon Camp-**

ground, 2 miles farther up the road, has 9 RV sites and 20 tentsites; flush toilets. Both campgrounds open late May–Oct. The **Uintah Campground** has 99 tentsites and is open from mid-June–mid-Sept.

The BLM has four campgrounds at its Little Sahara Recreation Area. **Sand Mountain Campground,** with room for 300 trailers, is the largest. **Oasis** has 114 sites and **White Sands,** 99. **Jericho** offers 40 tentsites. All have drinking water and flush toilets, but none have showers. Located west of US Hwy. 6 from Jericho Junction.

Where to Eat

Mickelson's Restaurant—$ to $$
One of only a handful of long-established restaurants in the southern half of the state, Mickelson's was established by Jay Mickelson, a traveling salesman who knew what a good meal away from home should be. After Jay's retirement, his son Jens and daughter-in-law Jacqueline took over the restaurant, keeping the same cooks and same basic menu of American food that made the restaurant so popular among locals and travelers. Open Mon.–Sat. 6:30 A.M.–9:45 P.M. **2100 S. Main; 435-623-0152.**

Services

Visitor Information
Nephi Chamber of Commerce—P.O. Box 71, Nephi, UT 84648; 435-623-5203.

Uinta National Forest—740 S. Main St., Nephi, UT 84648; 435-623-2735.

Sanpete Valley

While many communities claim that they have been saved by being astride the interstate highway system, the fact that the interstate bypasses Sanpete Valley has actually saved what has been described as the best concentration of houses, structures and cultural elements reflecting 19th-century Mormon Utah in the state. Another factor that has helped preserve the character of the valley is the lack of one major city, as is more typical in the rest of rural Utah. The towns of Mt. Pleasant, Moroni, Ephraim, Manti and Gunnison are all located on the US Hwy. 86 corridor, each with about 1,500 to 3,000 people, and all with institutions vital to the valley.

Mt. Pleasant was the sheep capital of Utah around the turn of the 20th century. Those prosperous times are still evident in the well-preserved main street, the magnificent houses and Wasatch Academy, a 125-year-old private institution that draws students from all over the country. Moroni, named for the last prophet in the Book of Mormon, has a turkey-processing plant that employs 200 permanent and 500 seasonal employees. The birds sent to the plant are raised by more than 100 turkey farmers in Sanpete Valley. Ephraim has Snow College, which, with its 3,000 students, is a major cultural and economic institution in the valley. Seven miles south of Ephraim is Manti, the county seat of Sanpete County and the location of one of four pioneer Mormon temples constructed in Utah. Named for a city in the Book of Mormon, Manti, which dates from 1849, was the first Mormon settlement in the Sanpete Valley. To the south lies Gunnison, a small town named for Capt. John W. Gunnison, who was killed by Indians along the Sevier River in 1853. It was established in 1859 and, since the mid-1980s, has been the home of a regional state prison facility.

Sanpete Valley, part of the Great Basin geographical province, lies between the mountains of the Wasatch Plateau on the east and a western range known by four different names—the Sanpete Plateau, Gunnison Plateau, the West Mountains and the Sanpitch Mountains—with lower hills to the north and south. The valley is more than a mile high, with most communities located at around 5,800 feet. The dominant physical feature is Horseshoe Mountain, which rises to more than 11,000 feet east of the valley. The horseshoe shape of the mountain, an ice-cut scallop, is easy to recognize from most locations in the valley. Water flowing down from the mountains to the east forms the Sanpitch River, which flows south through the valley to its junction with the Sevier River near Gunnison. Most of the river is appropriated for culinary and irrigation use within the valley. Although Interstate 15 bypasses Sanpete Valley to the west, about 30 miles on the other side of the Sanpitch Mountains, US Hwy. 89 does pass through the valley, providing good access for travelers. Smaller communities within the valley include Fairview, Fountain Green, Spring City, Wales, Sterling and Mayfield.

There are about 20,000 residents in Sanpete Valley, and ties to the valley run deep. Many are descendants of 19th-century Mormon converts from Denmark and Sweden. As one 10-year resident of the valley observes, "They really are a tough breed of people, to stay and not be enticed to better areas to farm or to the city for jobs. Most were born and raised here and really like it. Professionals would like to come back after college if they could make a living. Some return for retirement, and if they leave they're invariably buried back here."

History

On November 19, 1849, Isaac Morley and 50 families of Mormon settlers completed the 125-mile journey from Salt Lake City into the Sanpete Valley. The group was sent by Brigham Young after Ute Chief Walker (Wakara) invited

Getting There
US Hwy. 89 passes through the valley and is reached from Salt Lake City by taking Interstate 15 south to Spanish Fork (Exit 261), then heading southeast on US Hwy. 6 for 13 miles to its junction with US Hwy. 89. Fairview and Mt. Pleasant, in the north end of Sanpete Valley, are approximately 100 miles south of Salt Lake City on US Hwy. 89.

the Mormon leader to establish a colony alongside Chief Sanpeetch and his people in the Sanpete Valley. The names Sanpitch, for the river, and Sanpete, for the valley and county, come from the undefined Ute name Sanpeetch. The original 220 settlers were later supplemented by others, and during the first decade, communities were established from Gunnison to the south and Fairview to the north.

While relationships with the native Ute people started out with promise, relations deteriorated as settlers took more and more land, drove the deer and elk away from their traditional habitats and were reluctant to understand or accept the Ute practice of helping themselves to the pioneers' cattle, and as the Utes saw their population decimated by disease and starvation. As a consequence the Black Hawk War, which lasted from 1865 to 1872, began in Manti on April 9, 1865, the same day that Robert E. Lee surrendered to Ulysses S. Grant at Appomattox Courthouse to end the Civil War. The altercation between Black Hawk and his companion, Jake Arapeen, with a local interpreter, John Lowry, was followed by several shootings the next day and the theft of the settlers' cattle. During the next three years, dozens of settlers were killed in isolated encounters and a few pitched battles with local militia sent out to retrieve lost livestock and capture the raiders.

Sanpete Valley continued as the center of the conflict, which spread south, east and north and involved Paiutes, Navajos and other Utes who joined with Black Hawk in his daring raids and attacks. Many southern Utah settlements were abandoned and the white population gathered together in places like Manti, Ephraim and Moroni to build forts and provide protection.

Sanpete Valley had a special attraction for Scandinavian converts to the Mormon church. Most were from Denmark, but Sweden and Norway were also well represented. Sanpete Valley became known throughout Utah as Little Scandinavia, and with good reason: of the total population, first- and second-generation Scandinavians comprised 80 percent in 1870 and 70 percent in 1880. In 1870 Ephraim counted

94 percent of its population as Scandinavian. The Jutland region of Denmark was an especially fruitful field for Mormon missionaries in the 1850s. Converts there came mostly from peasants who did not own the land they farmed and felt oppressed by their landlords as well as by clergy of the Lutheran church, who exacted tithes from everyone and charged substantial fees for important sacraments such as marriages and burials. Mormon missionaries, promising free land in America, a new religion in which the people could participate as leaders and the means to reach Utah through the Perpetual Emigration Fund, a travel-now pay-later revolving fund established under Brigham Young's direction, converted hundreds of Danes and sent them off to America aboard ships from Copenhagen, Denmark, and Hamburg, Germany.

But even in Sanpete Valley, the streets were not paved with gold. The Scandinavians worked hard as farmers and helped Sanpete Valley win renown as the "granary of Utah." But limited land and water resources demanded alternatives. Many Sanpeters moved south to settle the Sevier Valley and east into Castle Valley. Those who stayed turned to sheep, sugar beets and, later, turkeys for a livelihood.

Mormons were not the only ones who saw the promise of a new life in Sanpete County. In 1911, 12 Jewish farmers representing 200 immigrant families arrived in Utah and created an agricultural colony 3 miles west of Gunnison, which they named Clarion. Clarion was one of 40 such Jewish settlements in America, established as part of an international back-to-the-soil movement among Jewish people seeking to leave the crowded urban slums and inhuman sweatshops of the East for the countryside.

Human conflict and natural obstacles brought an early end to Clarion, but some Mormons of Sanpete County saw the attempt as part of a grand unfolding strategy that would usher in Christ's second coming. Even more important in this strategy was the completion of the Manti Temple on May 21, 1888. Eleven years in construction, the Manti Temple was the third temple in Utah. Situated roughly halfway between the temples of St. George and Logan, which were 400 miles apart, the Manti Temple was the most centrally located temple for most Utahns until the completion of the Salt Lake Temple in 1893. The temple united and strengthened Sanpete Mormons more than anything save, perhaps, the Atlantic crossing and wagon or handcart trek to Utah. The temple remains the focus of community life in Sanpete Valley. The Mormon Miracle Pageant held at the Manti Temple in June involves hundreds of valley residents and draws hundreds of thousands of spectators.

Festivals and Events

Scandinavian Festival
Fri.–Sat. before Memorial Day. The Scandinavian Festival, held in Ephraim, is an eclectic kind of event that borrows from Sanpete Valley's Scandinavian tradition but includes a healthy dose of American activities. Scandinavian activities include a Little Denmark supper, a Scandinavian breakfast, old-world crafts and an ugly trolls contest. Other activities include historical tours, an art show, craft booths, food booths, a tennis tournament, a fun run, a rodeo, a parade and a selection of festival royalty. **435-283-4747.**

Spring City Heritage Days
Sat. before Memorial Day. You might consider Spring City Heritage Days a part of the Scandinavian Festival since many visitors to Sanpete County take in both events; it helps that Spring City is only 10 miles north of Ephraim. This is one day a year when owners of most of the historic homes in Spring City open them as part of the home tour. The home tour runs 10 A.M.–5 P.M., and you can spend most of the time visiting the houses, especially if you park your car and walk—which gives you glimpses and insights into the community that are missed by just driving around the town. It also helps you work up a good appetite for the turkey barbecue that follows the tour. **435-462-2502.**

Mormon Miracle Pageant
second and third full weeks in June. Every year thousands travel to Manti to witness the Mormon Miracle Pageant held on Temple Hill. The pageant opens with the notes of a trumpet from atop the spires of the Manti Temple, and then, during the next 2 hours, the early history of the Mormon church is presented. While most of the audience are members of the Mormon faith and familiar with the scenes that are portrayed, those not of the Mormon faith are offered a warm welcome and will find the pageantry, if not the story, an unforgettable experience. The first pageant in 1967 attracted 2,000 people for the single performance. Now the audience tops 30,000 each night of the pageant. A third of the audience uses the 10,000 chairs provided, while the rest of the audience views the pageant from blankets and lawn chairs they bring themselves.

Visitors arrive early in Manti to walk around the historic community and to partake of the famous barbecued turkey dinner prepared by local residents. The gates for pageant seating open at 6 P.M., and the performance begins around 9:30 P.M. It's a good idea to arrive at 6 P.M. and take a blanket with you, spreading it across the seats or the spot of ground that you want to claim for the evening; then head downtown for dinner and a tour of the historic sites in the town. Since seats are available on a first-come, first-served basis, this system of saving or reserving seats is a long-standing tradition at the pageant. Be sure to bring jackets and sweaters since the evenings can be cool. Performances are usually Thurs.–Sat. the first week and Tues.–Sat. the second week. A pancake, ham and eggs breakfast is also served 7–10 A.M. There is no cost for the pageant, although there is a modest charge for breakfast and dinner. The dinner is available 5–8 P.M. at the Manti Tabernacle, **1st S. and Main St.,** and at the Manti Stake Center, **300 S. and Main St. 435-835-2401.**

Birch Creek Bluegrass Festival
first weekend in July. This two-day bluegrass music festival attracts more than a dozen

bands to the small town of Fountain Green for concerts and nightly jam sessions. In addition to concerts there are musical workshops, activities for children and a turkey barbecue. 435-445-3378.

Lamb Day Festival

end of July. There is no better place than the small town of Fountain Green for a Lamb Day festival. Usually held the third Sat. in July or the Sat. just before Utah's state holiday, the 24th of July, this festival recalls the days when Sheep County was another way of saying Sanpete County. Thousands of head of sheep brought elusive prosperity to the county, and although you will see more turkeys in Fountain Green than sheep these days, the woolly animals are still an important part of the local economy. The festival features a lamb show, a lamb auction, a lamb barbecue, a parade, children's activities and a dance. 435-462-2502.

Outdoor Activities

Biking

Ephraim Canyon

This is a steep climb to the 10,500-foot summit near the junction with the Skyline Dr. road, a climb of nearly a mile in elevation from downtown Ephraim. It demands caution because of the vehicle traffic up the canyon. But if you want a leg-burning ride into one of Utah's most beautiful canyons, give this 16-mile gravel route a try (see the Scenic Drives section under Seeing and Doing for details). The road begins at 400 S. and Main St. (Hwy. 89) in Ephraim. Turn right at the first stop sign as you head east on 400 S., then follow the road eastward up the canyon.

Sanpete Valley

A series of back roads connect most of the Sanpete Valley communities. It is fun to get on your bike and explore these roads and see where they go. Take time to ride through the communities to see the historic homes and buildings and perhaps spot as many of the Mormon Landscape ele-

ments as you can (see the Historic Sites section under Seeing and Doing). **435-462-2502.**

Spring City / Powerhouse Loop

If you want to test your mountain-climbing abilities, this 22-mile-long loop that circles 10,300-foot Haystack Mountain is a worthy challenge. The ride begins in Spring City and heads east of town onto Forest Rd. 036, which climbs more than 4,000 feet in 9 miles to intersect with the Skyline Dr. road along the crest of the mountains. If you want to avoid this strenuous part of the ride, take a shuttle to Skyline Dr. and begin your ride here. It's a 13-mile-ride back to Spring City along a route that follows the Skyline Dr. road for 3 miles south to the Canal Canyon Trail (Forest Trail No. 58). Turn right onto the trail and follow it south toward Paulson Ridge. After you reach the ridge, the route continues along it for about 2.5 miles before you reach the Canal Canyon Rd. (Forest Rd. 329). From here it is a steep descent down the canyon until you reach the valley floor and the road turns north back to Spring City.

Rentals

Skyline Cycle—Rentals and equipment, as well as directions and advice for other area rides. **71 S. Main, Ephraim; 435-283-5007.**

Fishing

Palisade Lake

Open for year-round fishing, Palisade Lake is the most accessible fishing spot in the Sanpete Valley. Only sailboats, canoes and rafts are allowed on the lake. The northern end of the lake is a popular swimming area, but there is plenty of room for anglers looking for the trout that inhabit the lake. The lake is part of Palisade State Park, located 2 miles east of Sterling off US Hwy. 89. **435-835-7275.**

Golf

Palisade Golf Course

This is an ideal course for those traveling with motor homes and trailers: you can camp at

Palisade State Park and walk to the golf course. The course is fairly easy, with wide fairways, very little water and few sand traps. It has some of the best-maintained greens to be found anywhere. Generally, the course is not too busy, but reservations can be made. Drive south out of Manti along US Hwy. 89 for 5 miles to Sterling and watch for the turnoff to Palisade State Park; the golf course is located about 2 miles off the highway. **435-835-GOLF (4653).**

Hiking

You can pick up a list of hiking trails in the Manti-La Sal National Forest at the **U.S. Forest Service Headquarters** on Main St. in Ephraim; **435-283-4151.** Here are some favorite trails:

Maple Canyon Trails

Two trails can be hiked out of Maple Canyon Campground in a few hours. To reach the trailhead, follow the road west out of Moroni for about 8 miles.

Left Fork Trail—The 2-mile Left Fork Trail is steep and strenuous as it climbs to the top of the plateau for a nice scenic view. Native American petroglyphs are located near the trail.

Maple Canyon Loop Trail—The 1.5-mile Maple Canyon Loop Trail is easier, offers a nice viewpoint and passes a natural arch.

Tennis

In **Manti,** there are six lighted tennis courts behind Manti High School, which is located west of the temple across US Hwy. 89. In **Ephraim,** there are six lighted courts open to the public in the center of the Snow College campus.

Seeing and Doing

Art Galleries

Next door to the Ephraim United Order Cooperative Building (see Historic Houses of Sanpete in the Historic Sites section), the **old mill** has been restored as an art gallery, with work by local artists on display and available for purchase. Open noon–5 P.M. **100 N. Main, Ephraim; 435-283-6654.**

Historic Sites

MORMON LANDSCAPE

Visitors to Utah have long recognized that the human-made landscape that resulted from the Mormon encounter with the western environment has distinctive characteristics; it has produced a recognizable geographical region that writers such as the late Wallace Stegner and geographer Donald Meinig have called "Mormon Country." Another student of the Mormon region, Richard V. Francaviglia, published a book in 1978 entitled *The Mormon Landscape* (AMS Press) that summarizes the characteristics that make up this unique cultural geographical region. Since the publication of Francaviglia's study, others have added to his list. While some of these elements, notably the irrigation ditches, have disappeared since Francaviglia completed his study, Sanpete County remains one of the best locations to view this distinctive landscape heritage.

To view these elements, simply drive the highways, streets and back roads of the county and see how many of them you can identify: rectangular or square fields intensively irrigated, used for hay pasture and separated by unpainted cedar posts and barbed wire fences; erect, spire-like Lombardy poplar trees; cattle and sheep grazing in the same pasture; hay derricks (often called Mormon stackers; the main feature of the hay derrick is the long pole used to stack hay); biblical and Book of Mormon names for communities; the town's initial on a hill; north–south, east–west orientation of streets; ragged, overgrown streets and a rural feeling to the community because open pastures, barns, granaries and haystacks are found right in town; roadside irrigation ditches; unpainted barns; inside-outside granaries (grain storage sheds where the studs are on the outside walls rather than on the inside to allow easier emptying of the granaries and better support of the weight of the grain pushing against the walls); shed rooftops made of loose or baled hay; an LDS ward chapel; cemeteries with Mormon themes on the tombstones and footstones on the older graves made out of the same materials as headstones with the deceased's initials on them; a parallel canal system consisting of the initial ditches, which were diverted low in the creeks to irrigate river bottomland, and the later highline canals constructed to carry water to the benchlands.

The Utah Arts Council, Folk Arts Program and the Sanpete County Heritage Council have combined efforts to produce an excellent audio tour available on both cassette and compact disc with an accompanying booklet that includes maps, photos, illustrations and essays entitled *Utah's Sanpete Valley: The Heart of the Mormon West: A Tour Featuring Local History and Culture.* The audio tour and booklet can be purchased at various locations in Sanpete Valley. **Sanpete County Heritage Council, 115 W. Main St., Mt. Pleasant, UT 84647; 435-462-2502.**

HISTORIC HOUSES OF SANPETE

One of the most obvious and prolific elements of the Mormon Landscape are the stone, adobe and brick houses built to house the early settlers of Sanpete Valley and their children. Sanpete County has the highest concentration of these houses, which were constructed in the second half of the 19th century. The houses demonstrate much about the lifestyle and priorities of the early residents. The early homes were symmetrical structures that characteristically used the Federalist and Greek Revival styles with which pioneers were familiar.

As Scandinavian immigrants arrived, they built in a style similar to that of their homeland. These "pair houses," usually one story, were marked by a central entrance and two rooms of equal size on each side.

Beginning about 1890, a second generation of homes, different from the earlier straight-lined homes of the pioneers, was constructed. The asymmetrical Victorian houses were distin-guished by their gingerbread ornamentation, eyebrow windows, porches that broke up the square facade and a look that suggested the pioneer era was over.

A third generation of houses was built between 1910 and 1930; these reflected the influence of the bungalow style of architecture. These houses can be found in all Sanpete communities, but Spring City, Manti and Ephraim seem to have the greatest number.

Ephraim

Canute Peterson House—There was no individual more important in the early history of Sanpete County than Canute Peterson. Born in Norway in 1824, he immigrated to the United States as a teenager with his parents and joined the Mormon faith at the age of 18. He returned to Scandinavia three times to do missionary work, and many of those he converted followed him to Sanpete County. As husband to three wives, Peterson constructed this surviving rock home in 1869 for his first wife, and had two places of concealment built into the house. Known as "polygamy pits" because they were used to hide from federal marshals seeking to arrest polygamists, one pit was built under the dining room floor as a diversion for a larger one located in a small sitting room next to the kitchen. The home is a private residence. **10 N. Main.**

Ephraim Co-op Building—As you visit this building, look for the inscription "Ephraim U. O. Mercantile Institution" and a beehive encircled by the words "Holiness to the Lord." If it seems strange to apply a religious connotation to mercantile activities, just remember that for 19th-century Mormons, the building of the Kingdom of God included both. In an effort to promote self-sufficiency, Brigham Young directed Mormons to avoid buying all imported goods, especially those sold by non-Mormon merchants. A solution to the problem was seen in cooperative merchandising, a plan where Mormons would establish a wholesale house or parent institution that would purchase all goods imported to Utah. In turn, each Mormon settlement would establish a cooperative retailing store that would deal only with goods delivered by the parent institution from Salt Lake City.

The Ephraim United Order Cooperative Store, constructed of native oolite limestone in 1872, is Utah's best remaining example of one of these stores and one of Utah's best examples of the Greek Revival style. The cooperative was located on the main floor, and the second story was used for dances, theatrical productions, meetings and the first classes of what is now Snow College. After standing vacant for years, the building was restored and opened in 1990 by the Sanpete Trade Association for handicrafts and other locally produced items under the name Sanpete Sampler. Open Mon.–Sat. 10 A.M.– 6 P.M. **96 N. Main.**

Great Basin Experimental Range Station—Now known as the Great Basin Environmental Education Center and operated by Snow College, this historic experimental station was constructed by the U.S. Forest Service between 1912 and 1914 at the base of Haystack Mountain, 10 miles up Ephraim Canyon. The station was the first of its kind in the United States and perhaps the world. For three-quarters of a century, the dozen or so buildings served as a field headquarters for scientists interested in studying ecology and the management of range- and forestlands. The founder and first director of the station, Dr. Arthur W. Sampson, pioneered the science of range management. Snow College took over maintenance and operation of the station in 1992 has preserved the buildings, established a museum, maintained the historic laboratory and uses the facilities for summer school classes and special conferences. The station is one of the stops on the Ephraim Canyon Scenic Dr. From Hwy. 89 in Ephraim, turn right at the first stop sign as you head east on 400 S., then follow the road eastward up the canyon about 7 miles to the Experimental Station.

Manti

John Patten House—Perhaps the oldest remaining residence in the Sanpete Valley, the Patten House was built in the mid-1850s for John Patten, an early convert to Mormonism and one of the first settlers of Manti, in 1850. Built of native limestone using sticky adobe to hold the stone together, the house has an almost medieval style to it. The building has been renovated and houses a museum maintained by the Manti Daughters of Utah Pioneers. The hours vary, and there is usually a telephone number posted on the door to call and arrange a tour. **95 W. 400 N.**

Manti Temple—When Brigham Young visited the infant settlement of Manti in 1850, he pointed to the hill where many of the settlers had spent the first winter and prophesied that a temple would one day be built on the hill. Twenty-five years later, in 1875, Brigham Young dedicated the temple site and construction work began. The temple was completed in 1888 and is one of Utah's most remarkable buildings. Constructed of native oolite limestone quarried at the site, the temple presented its architect, William Folsom, with a special problem. The temple was located on the hill overlooking Manti to the southwest, yet Mormon temples are oriented with their front to the east in anticipation of the resurrected Christ coming from that direction.

The solution was the construction of two different towers. The larger, slightly higher one on the east faces the mountains, while the western tower appears to be level with the eastern tower and gives the appearance that the building faces west. As you travel along US Hwy. 89, the temple looms over the valley like an ancient, strangely designed cathedral or castle. A blending of the Gothic Revival, French Renaissance Revival and French Second Empire styles, according to Mormon architectural historian Paul Anderson, the temple is "perhaps the crowning achievement of 19th-century Mormon architecture."

In the 1980s the interior of the temple was renovated; however, unlike the Logan Temple, which was completely gutted and modernized in the 1970s, great pains were taken to insure that the interior work of the pioneer artisans was preserved. Only faithful members of the LDS faith are permitted inside the temple, but a visitor center just outside the temple a few yards to the north provides information.

Mt. Pleasant

Mt. Pleasant Main St.—The two blocks that make up the northern side of Mt. Pleasant's Main St. are the best-preserved, turn-of-the-20th-century commercial district left in Utah. The prosperous sheep industry stimulated the construction of the two- and three-story buildings that, in recent years, city fathers have seen as a real asset and have encouraged their preservation. Located on the south side of the street is the district's oldest building, the **1875 Liberal Hall.** The hall was built by disaffected Mormons and was the first home for the Wasatch Academy, established by Presbyterians in 1875 to educate and "Christianize" Mormon youth. If you are traveling on US Hwy. 89, it is easy to miss Main St., since it intersects the north–south highway at its western end. Watch for the junction of US Hwy. 89 and Hwy. 116.

Wasatch Academy—Established in 1875 by the Rev. Duncan McMillian, a Presbyterian minister who came west to regain his health and who had been assigned missionary work among the Mormons of Sanpete Valley, Wasatch Academy continues as one of the state's most prestigious private academies. The academy operated in Liberal Hall on Main St. until it outgrew the building and relocated two blocks to the south in 1888. The entire school, with its 20 buildings, has been listed in the National Register of Historic Places. The oldest buildings are the **1893 Lincoln Hall, 1895 President's House** and **1900 Indiana Hall.** Wasatch Academy is located at **200 W. and 200 S. 435-462-9982.**

Snow College

Named for Lorenzo Snow, president of the Mormon church when the institution was founded as a church academy in 1888, and for Erastus Snow, an important southern Utah church leader, Snow College became a state institution in 1932. Students come from all over the state because of the college's reputation and to enjoy the small-town life in Ephraim. The school has excellent theater and music departments. The campus is located two blocks east of Main St. between Center and 100 North Sts. **435-283-7000; www.snow.edu.**

Spring City

The large number of 19th-century buildings in the well-preserved Mormon agrarian village of Spring City led to it being listed in the National Register of Historic Places on Oct. 20, 1980. In any case, a visit to Spring City still should not be missed. Since Spring City was "discovered" by architectural historians in the 1970s, the 850 residents have grown accustomed to visitors driving around town shooting pictures of their homes and buildings. The community has attracted several artists, including Bennion's Horseshoe Pottery.

Museums

Fairview Museum of History and Art

The old Fairview schoolhouse, built in 1900, has been home to the Fairview Museum since 1966. The museum is an eclectic collection of more than 2,000 objects on exhibit that relate to the history of Sanpete Valley and its citizens. A new building was completed in 1995 to house the Huntington Canyon Mammoth, which was uncovered west of Fairview in 1988. There is also a collection of sculptures by noted Utah sculptor Avard Fairbanks, including one entitled "The National Shrine to Love and Devotion of Peter and Celeste Peterson, married 82 years, lived more than 100 years." The museum is free, although donations are accepted. Open in summer Mon.–Sat. 10 A.M.–6 P.M., Sun. 2–6 P.M.; in the winter Mon.–Sat. 10 A.M.–5 P.M., Sun. 2–5 P.M. **85 N. 100 E., Fairview; 435-427-9216.**

Scenic Drives

Eccles Canyon Scenic Byway

If you are traveling in a passenger vehicle that you don't want to subject to the rigors of Skyline Dr., you can see some of the same beautiful scenery by traveling 16 miles through Eccles

Canyon. The high mountain valleys with their pine-forested, steep-sloped mountains could be mistaken for Germany's Black Forest. From Fairview, take Hwy. 31 east to Hwy. 264, then follow it east to its junction with Hwy. 96; take it south a short way to Clearcreek.

Ephraim Canyon

The Forest Service has prepared an excellent 16-mile automobile tour booklet for Ephraim Canyon to the 10,500-foot summit near the junction with the Skyline Dr. road. From downtown Ephraim the road climbs nearly a mile in elevation to the summit and passes through five life zones: Upper Sonoran, characterized by piñon and juniper; Transition, with ponderosa pine; Canadian, where aspen and fir are found; Hudsonian, with spruce and fir; and Alpine tundra, near the summit beyond treeline. Pick up the free *Auto Tour Guide* at the **Forest Service office** in **Ephraim,** or if you are starting the tour from the top of the canyon, a box with guides is located at the summit.

Along the drive, there are nine signs and pullout areas where you can learn much about the human and natural history of the Wasatch Plateau. The road is graveled and easily passable for automobiles, except when wet or blocked by snow. The road begins at 400 S. and Main St. (US Hwy. 89) in Ephraim. Turn right at the first stop sign as you head east on 400 S., then follow the road eastward up the canyon.

Skyline Dr.

One of Utah's most remarkable drives, Skyline Dr. follows the 10,900-foot summit of the Wasatch Plateau, which divides the Great Basin from the Colorado Plateau. There is an abundance of wildlife along the drive. In summer, you can watch eagles soar overhead and deer bound through the trees on either side. Most travelers cover the 30-mile section from Hwy. 31 east of Fairview to the Ephraim-Orangeville Rd., which offers an eagle's view of the Sanpete Valley below and Mt. Nebo and other mountains in the distance. An extension from the heart of the drive takes you farther south approximately

20 miles to the Mayfield-Ferron Rd. An 87-mile northern extension from Hwy. 31 intersects with Hwy. 6 at Tucker, but is only passable with a four-wheel-drive vehicle. The drive is impassable in winter, when it is used by snowmobilers and cross-country skiers.

Shopping

As you drive through Sanpete Valley's towns, you will see a number of small antique and craft shops that are a browser's delight. Keep an eye out for them. Their hours can be somewhat erratic and their longevity unpredictable. For excellent handcrafted items, stop at the **Ephraim Coop Building** (see the Historic Sites section). This is an excellent place in Sanpete Valley to stop for locally made handicrafts and to inquire about other locations in the valley. Open Mon.–Sat. 10 A.M.–6 P.M. **96 N. Main, Ephraim; 435-283-6654.**

Wineries

Bob Sorenson claims to be the last Mormon winemaker, certainly an anachronism in a society that admonishes its members to strict abstinence from alcoholic drink. But that was not always the case, and in the days of Brigham Young, Mormons were "called" or assigned to learn and practice wine-making skills, and even more brought their wine-making skills with them from Europe. "Dixie Wine," made from grapes grown in southern Utah, earned a dubious reputation among 19th-century Utahns.

Bob and his partner, Winnie Wood, have improved the quality and variety of Utah's nascent wine industry, shunning any preservatives, chemicals or filtering processes, and following some pioneer recipes. The wines produced from elderberries, plums, raspberries, apples, rhubarb, figs, cranberries and rose hips appeal to the palate while promising a measure of good health. Wine tastings are held almost every Sat. Located in a 100-plus-year-old building in Mt. Pleasant. **72 S. 500 W.; 435-462-9261.**

Where to Stay

Bed and Breakfasts

Ephraim Homestead Bed and Breakfast—$$$

This unique homestead consists of three buildings: the House, the Barn and the Granary. The former is an 1880s cottage that owners Sherron and McKay Andreasen rescued from certain demise in 1978. They opened their bed and breakfast in the home in 1986. It now serves as their residence and workplace. Two guest rooms are located in an adjacent traditional-style wooden barn built in 1981. The rooms share a bathroom and can be rented separately or as a suite. The third building, known as the Granary, is an 1860s Scandinavian cabin with a bedroom, full bath and kitchen. The bedroom is located upstairs and is outfitted with homemade quilts and a parlor stove. On the ground level is a living area with a fireplace, a small kitchen with a cast-iron stove and a bathroom with a claw-foot tub and corner sink. On the half acre of grounds are lawns, shade trees, benches, a swing and flower and herb gardens. A typical hearty breakfast, served in the dining room or to your room, consists of pancakes with warm apricot syrup made from homegrown apricots. A nighttime treat, such as apple crisp or pie, is also served. All rooms are nonsmoking. **135 W. 100 N., Ephraim, UT 84627; 435-283-6367; www.sanpete.com/Homestead.**

Heritage House—$$$

This Victorian-style, two-story house has five rooms, all with private baths. The family suite sleeps six people. Innkeepers Alvin and Mattie Jean Kilmer built the home and opened the bed and breakfast in 1993. Designed to provide as relaxing an experience as possible, there are no in-room telephones or TVs, although they are available in a common area. Refreshments are served each evening and a full breakfast each morning. French toast with Mattie's unique buttermilk syrup is not to be missed. **489 N. 400 W., Manti, UT 84642; 435-635-5050; www.virtualcities.com.**

Legacy Inn—$$$

Located across from the Manti Temple Hill, this modern Victorian-style house has four rooms, three with private baths. The family suite has two beds and room for additional sleeping bags on the floor. A full breakfast and evening refreshments are served. Proprietors are Jan and Mike Crane. **337 N. 100 E., Manti, UT 84642; 435-835-8352; www.legacyinn.com.**

Manti House Inn—$$$

This historic inn started as a log home built in 1868 that faced south on the corner of 400 N. and Main, and was later expanded using oolite limestone that was left over from the construction of the Manti Temple. The enlarged structure, known as the "Manti Temple Boarding House," had 23 rooms and housed many of the workers on the Manti Temple—especially those who came from throughout central and southern Utah. After completion of the temple, the boardinghouse provided accommodations to those who came from hundreds of miles away to visit the temple, including church authorities from Salt Lake City. In 1896 the building was purchased by John D. T. McAllister, the third president of the Manti Temple, who had nine wives and 32 children scattered from St. George to Salt Lake City. The home remained in the McAllister family until the 1940s. During World War II, it housed workers at the Manti parachute factory.

By the late 1960s the building stood vacant and in disrepair until Jim and Sonja Burnidge and Alan and Taresa Plant completed a three-year restoration in 1987 and opened the Manti House Inn. Jennifer Nicholes became the innkeeper in 2001. Each of the six rooms is named for a president of the Mormon church. Favorites are the Brigham Young Room, with its charming view of the Manti Temple, and the Honeymoon Suite, with its private balcony, private entrance, fireplace and hot tub. All rooms have private baths, televisions and VCRs. Breakfast is served in the dining room. **401 N. Main St., Manti, UT 84642; 1-800-835-7512; 435-835-0161; www.mantihouse.com.**

Yardley Inn—$$ to $$$

Located in a remodeled, turn-of-the-20th-century Victorian home owned by Gill and Marlene Yardley, the inn has four bedrooms, all with a private bath and cable TV. The two suites each have a wood-burning fireplace, private balcony and white marble Jacuzzi with room for two. A full breakfast is served in either the Garden Room or Dining Room. Guests can enjoy the library, the music room and a large living room, and are welcome in the old-fashioned kitchen. **190 S. 200 W., Manti, UT 84642; 1-800-858-6634; 435-835-1861; www.virtual-cities.com.**

Motels

Horseshoe Mountain Lodge—$$$

Swimming pool, hot tub and restaurant; 21 rooms. **850 S. US Hwy. 89, Mt. Pleasant; 1-800-462-9330; 435-462-9330.**

Manti Country Village—$$

Twenty-three units. **145 N. Main, Manti; 435-835-9300.**

Willow Creek Inn—$$

Outdoor hot tub; 58 rooms; continental breakfast. **450 S. Main, Ephraim; 1-800-753-3746; 435-283-4566.**

Camping

PRIVATE

Temple Hill Resort and RV Campground

Located just north of the Manti Temple Hill, this campground has 75 total sites, 20 with full hookup for pull-throughs. There are 20 tent-sites, plus a covered wagon and a yurt tent. Facilities include showers, rest rooms, laundry, pool, hot tub, pavilion and playground. Open year-round. **296 E. 900 N., Manti; 435-835-2267; www.templehillresort.com.**

PUBLIC

Most of the public campgrounds are located east of the Sanpete communities in the mountains of the Wasatch Plateau. Access to these campgrounds is by way of the canyons that open into the Sanpete Valley.

Ephraim Canyon

Lake Hill Campground has 9 sites. Open mid-June–mid-Sept. Located off Hwy. 29, 8.5 miles east of Ephraim.

Fairview Canyon

Gooseberry has 6 trailer sites and **Flat Canyon** has 13 sites. Open mid-June–mid-Sept. Located on forest service land 10 and 12 miles east of Fairview, respectively, off Hwy. 31.

Manti Canyon

Manti Community Campground has 9 campsites. Open mid-June–early Sept. Located 7 miles east of Manti on the Manti Canyon Rd.

Mayfield Canyon

Twelve Mile Flat Campground has 16 sites at an elevation of 9,800 feet. Open July–early Sept. Located 19 miles east of Mayfield.

Palisade State Park

Its 53 camping units are along Palisade Lake, within easy reach of fishing and swimming facilities, the adjacent 9-hole golf course and nearby hiking trails. Modern wheelchair-accessible rest rooms and showers. Located 2 miles east of Sterling.

Where to Eat

In most of the Sanpete towns, you will find fast-food drive-ins that seem to date from the 1950s and 1960s. They offer the old favorites: burgers, hot dogs, fries, shakes, malts and soft drinks. Most have also added other items over time—tacos, corn dogs, a variety of sandwiches, chicken, salads and some even pasta dishes. There's also a McDonald's and Subway in Ephraim. For sit-down meals, the following are worth a visit. Be warned that sometimes the hours listed here may vary for a variety of reasons, so be a little flexible.

Don's Gallery Café—$ to $$
Located next to the Manti Country Village Motel and open daily for breakfast, lunch and dinner. **115 N. Main, Manti, 435-835-3663.**

Sil's Horseshoe Mountain Restaurant— $ to $$
Open Mon.–Sat. 6:30 A.M.–9 P.M., Sun. noon– 6 P.M. **850 S. US Hwy. 89, Mt. Pleasant; 435- 462-9533.**

Services

Visitor Information
Sanpete County Heritage Council—115 W. Main St., Mt. Pleasant; 435-462-2502.

U.S. Forest Service Sanpete Ranger District—150 S. Main St., Ephraim; 435- 283-4151.

Delta and Fillmore

Judging by the number of places in Utah that bear his name, Millard Fillmore, who served as president of the United States (1850–1852) when Franklin Pierce died in office, is the most honored president in Utah. No other county and county seat carry both names of an American president. Millard County is Utah's third-largest county, and Fillmore, the county seat, was once the territorial capital.

The Pavant Mountains to the east of Fillmore and the Pavant Valley, in which are located the towns of Oak City, Delta, Deseret, Hinckley, Scipio, Holden, Fillmore, Meadow and Kanosh, are named for the Indian tribe that occupied the area when the Mormons arrived here in 1851. The small town of Kanosh is named for the Pahvants' leader. Kanosh lived here until 1884 and is buried in the Kanosh town cemetery.

Beyond the string of towns along the moun-

tains and the farms clustered around Delta on the Sevier River, the rest of the area is considered uninhabitable. The West Desert stretches toward the Nevada border and Great Basin National Park; what is left of the Sevier River after providing water to most of the south-central Utah communities sinks into the intermittent Sevier Lake in the Great Basin. Rock hounds enjoy collecting some unique gems in the desert, and outdoor buffs have no shortage of miles in which to roam.

History

Kanosh, the Pahvants' leader who met Mormon settlers when they arrived in 1851, understood that accommodation was the only way that his people could survive. According to historian John Peterson, Kanosh concluded that if one religion—his Native American religious outlook—was good, two or three religions, including Mormonism and perhaps Catholicism, were better. Kanosh was baptized into the Church of Jesus Christ of Latter-day Saints and ordained to the priesthood. His wives included an adopted daughter of Brigham Young, and the Mormon leader was a friend and father.

Fillmore became the territorial capital practically before it was settled in 1851. Pioneer settlers were sent out from Salt Lake City in October of that year; three months later, the new territorial capital was announced. A territorial statehouse was constructed, but the relocation of the capital 150 miles south of Salt Lake City proved impractical after a few years. The region gained national attention when Capt. John W. Gunnison, surveying a route for the transcontinental railroad along the 38th parallel, was killed by Indians west of Fillmore. During the 1860s two forts—Ft. Deseret and Cove Ft.—were constructed as protection from Indian unrest, which grew as more and more Mormon settlers competed for precious resources.

When the Black Hawk War broke out in 1865, Kanosh and his people found themselves between the charismatic Ute leader Black Hawk and Brigham Young. Black Hawk pled with Kanosh to lend his support to the Utes' fight, and while Kanosh never did, many of his tribe, including one wife, did. Brigham Young and other Mormon leaders anxious to halt the raids on livestock and homesteads by Black Hawk and his followers, pressured Kanosh to help locate and punish the warring Utes. Caught in the middle, Kanosh stood his neutral ground and did not help either side. A few years later, in 1872, Kanosh joined in complaints about the government treatment of the Ute people.

But Indians were not the real challenge for settlers, it was the lack of water. The construction of the Yuba Dam and other dams along the Sevier River made possible the extensive agricultural development of western Millard County, and the town of Delta was established in 1907. During World War II, Topaz became the largest city in the area, when about 9,000 Japanese-Americans were relocated from their homes in the San Francisco area to a camp northwest of Delta. The most significant postwar development in the county was the construction of the huge coal-burning Intermountain Power Plant north of Delta in the 1970s.

Getting There

Delta is 133 miles south of Salt Lake City; take Interstate 15 south to Santaquin, Exit 248, and then take US Hwy. 6 west through Eureka and southwest to Delta. Or take I-15 south to Nephi and Hwy. 132 west to its junction with US Hwy. 6 at Lynndyl, then follow US Hwy. 6 into Delta; this route takes you through Leamington with its interesting beehive-shaped pioneer charcoal kilns. South of Leamington is Oak City, on Hwy. 125, which loops west to Delta.
Fillmore is on Interstate 15 about 150 miles south of Salt Lake City and about 40 miles southeast of Delta. Meadow is about 10 miles south of Fillmore on I-15; Kanosh is 7 miles south of Meadow on Hwy. 133.

Major Attractions

Great Basin National Park

Delta is the gateway city to Nevada's Great Basin National Park. Located about 100 miles west of Delta off US Hwy. 6, this newest of the western national parks, created in 1986, is just across the Utah–Nevada border. The 77,000-acre desert park preserves features common to the **Great Basin**—a name explorer John C. Frémont gave to the desert region between Utah's Wasatch Mountains and Plateau on the east and Nevada's Sierra Nevada on the west because it offered no outlet to the ocean. The Great Basin is characterized by a series of mountain ranges with lofty peaks, mountain meadows, alpine lakes, a wide range of plant and animal habitats, broadly sweeping valleys and deserts, and rivers and streams that flow inward to soak into the earth, evaporate or form lakes because they have no access to the sea. The main attractions in the park are the Lehman Caves, 13,063-foot Wheeler Peak and the Lexington Arch.

About 550 million years ago, the area was covered by a shallow inland sea. Sea creatures died and their shells and bones piled up on the seafloor, eventually hardening into limestone thousands of feet thick. **Lehman Caves** were formed by water: part of it was hollowed out by an underground stream. About 20 million years ago, the Snake Range was formed and as water percolated down through the soil, it combined with carbon dioxide gas to form a weak carbonic acid that eroded the limestone even more. In time the caves were emptied of groundwater, leaving smooth, well-scrubbed walls. Then a different chemical process kicked into gear. Calcite deposits, left by the slow-dripping, calcite-laden water, began to form on the roofs and floors of the caves as stalactites and stalagmites, which sometimes grew together to become thick columns. Other deposits left millions of years ago include flowstone, cave popcorn or cave coral, helictites (which resembles dried chow mein noodles), small delicate aragonite crystals, shields and draperies.

Wheeler Peak is named for George Montague Wheeler, who conducted a reconnaissance survey in 1869 to map, collect natural history items and determine anything of potential military value in the Great Basin for the U.S. Army. Wheeler and his party climbed the peak in July 1869 and determined its elevation to be 13,000 feet. The peak was regarded for many years as the tallest mountain in Nevada. (Boundary Peak on the border between Nevada and California is higher at 13,145 feet.) Wheeler spent nine years on his survey of the Great Basin.

Unlike all the other arches described and noted in this guide, which are of sandstone, **Lexington Arch** is a natural limestone arch. On one side, the massive rampart stands like a fortress protecting the arch, while the jagged top of the arch has not yet been worn flat—characteristic of most sandstone arches. Geologists theorize that the arch may have been a passage in a cave system at one time and point to the flowstone at the arch's base in support of their position. Others counter that it is not an arch at all but, rather, a natural bridge carved by an ancient stream.

Getting There / Visitor Information

After crossing into Nevada on US Hwy. 6, take Nevada Hwy. 487 (or the cutoff road) 10 miles south to Baker, then Nevada Hwy. 488 west 5 miles to the main park entrance and Great Basin Visitor Center at the entrance to Lehman Caves. Shortly before reaching the visitor center, the Wheeler Peak Scenic Dr. (see Seeing and Doing, below) heads off to the right, making a circuitous route up to Wheeler Peak.

To reach the park's southern entrances, from Baker drive south on Nevada Hwy. 487; in about 4 miles a dirt road on the right heads west up Snake Creek to primitive campgrounds and hiking rails. Continuing south on Nevada Hwy. 487, you cross into Utah and reach Garrison, where the highway becomes Utah Hwy. 21; continue south for 4.5 miles and watch for a dirt road on your right. Head west on the dirt road, following Lexington Creek and the signs indicating Lexington Arch. It's a 12-mile drive across the desert valley to the road's end at the base of the Snake Creek Range.

Note: The national park is located in the Pacific Time Zone, which is 1 hour earlier than the rest of Utah. The visitor center is open daily in summer 8 A.M.–5 P.M., the rest of the year 8:30 A.M.–5 P.M.; closed Thanksgiving, Christmas and New Year's Day. **775-234-7331; www.nps.gov/grba.**

Outdoor Activities

At the end of the Wheeler Peak Scenic Dr. you can choose from several different **hiking trails** to get a closer look at the country. Maps, trail descriptions and backcountry permits are available at the visitor center.

Alpine Lakes Loop Trail—This pleasant hike begins at the trailhead parking at the end of the Wheeler Peak Scenic Dr. and covers 2.7 miles as it passes two beautiful alpine lakes surrounded by pine and spruce. The elevation gain is only about 600 feet from the trailhead to Stella Lake; after that, it is relatively level and then downhill. This is one of the most beautiful hikes anywhere. Take your time and enjoy it. Stella Lake is the first that you reach and Teresa Lake is about a mile away. Both lakes are quite shallow, no more than 10 feet deep. Plan a period of reflection and meditation at both lakes. Your soul will be refreshed if you let the beauty sink in for a while. This trail also connects with the Wheeler Peak Summit Trail and offers good views of Wheeler Peak.

Glacier and Bristlecone Trail—This trail begins at the end of the Wheeler Peak Scenic Dr. and climbs 3 miles close to the bottom of the Wheeler Peak ice field, often referred to as a glacier—but, unlike active glaciers, it does not move. The hike has an elevation gain of 1,400 feet. Portions of the trail are quite rocky. You pass quartzite boulders that have fallen off the wall of the Wheeler cirque above. Before you reach the end of the trail, you pass through the bristlecone pine forest, where some of the world's oldest living trees—nearly 3,000 years old—can be found. It is approximately 2 miles to the bristlecone pine forest and another mile to the end of the trail near the bottom of the ice field.

Lehman Creek Trail—This 4-mile-long trail connects the Wheeler Peak Campground, located at the end of Wheeler Peak Scenic Dr., with the Upper Lehman Creek Campground located farther down the scenic drive. Look for the trailhead at the eastern end of the Wheeler Peak Campground. Most hikers catch a ride to the Wheeler Peak Campground or arrange for a ride back up the road to pick up their vehicle. The trail follows the north side of Lehman Creek. It is an easy 2,100-foot descent through meadows, aspen groves, spruce and fir forests, mountain mahogany and single leaf piñon.

Lexington Arch—From the end of the southernmost road into the park (see Getting There, above), it's a 1-mile hike to the arch as you climb 1,000 feet up Arch Canyon. As you hike you will see remnants of mining activity, including the remains of an old miner's cabin. The view of Lexington Arch, which stands 75 feet above you with a span of 120 feet, is magnificent.

Wheeler Peak Summit—This is the most strenuous of the several hikes near and at the end of the Wheeler Peak Scenic Dr. The trail climbs 3,000 feet from the trailhead at 10,000 feet to the top of Wheeler Peak at 13,063 feet. The route to the peak is 4.3 miles one way and usually requires an average of 6 hours to make the 8.6-mile round trip. Be prepared for this hike with plenty of water, warm clothing and good hiking boots. The trail up Wheeler Peak is well marked.

During the first mile, the trail is fairly level with only a 200-foot elevation gain until you reach the fork to the left that takes you to Stella Lake. The second mile is also fairly gentle as the trail winds through groves of limber pine and, in summer, hillsides covered with purple-flowering mint. As you reach the second mile, the trail leaves the treeline of stunted spruce and junipers and continues across rock and boulder fields in an ever-steeper climb across the 600-million-year-old quartzite rock, which was laid down during the early Cambrian period when seas covered the area.

Finally, after what seems like a maximum effort, especially given the thin air at 13,000 feet, you reach the summit. The 360-degree panoramic view is well worth the effort. To the west and east, desert valleys with lonely towns and ranches are visible in the distance beyond the sheer drop-off on the west and the 1,500-foot cirque wall formed over millions of years by glaciers atop Wheeler Peak. Also visible to the west are four distinct mountain ranges—the Schell Creek, Egan, Grant and White Pine Mountains. The Snake Range, of which Wheeler Peak is the tallest, stretches to the south with Mt. Washington and Baker and Pyramid Peaks usually visible.

Seeing and Doing

Lehman Caves—Lehman Caves are named for Absalom Lehman, who established a ranch and orchard near the caves about 1870. He discovered the cave system in 1885, and soon hundreds of visitors arrived to explore the caves. Visitors can choose from three ranger-guided tours lasting 30, 60 or 90 minutes. The 90-minute tour visits all of the areas of the cave open to the public. The temperature inside the cave is a cool 50° F, so a jacket or sweater is recommended. Memorial Day–Labor Day the tours begin at 8 A.M.–4:30 P.M.; the rest of the year, tours start at 9 A.M–3:30 P.M. Not all tours are offered at the same time so if you plan to visit the cave, it is best to make the visitor center your first stop to purchase tour tickets and then plan the rest of your day accordingly.

Wheeler Peak Scenic Dr.—This 12-mile scenic drive begins east of the visitor center and climbs the northern slope of Wheeler Peak for nearly 4,000 feet to an elevation of about 10,000 feet. The drive offers breathtaking views of the summit of Wheeler Peak and the beautiful cirque formed under the eastern side of the peak along with the expanse of desert and lower mountain ranges below. The drive is closed when snow makes it impassable. Be sure to stop at both the Wheeler Peak Overlook and the Mather Overlook.

Camping

There are four campgrounds within the park. **Baker Creek Campground,** south of the visitor center, has 32 spaces. Along the Wheeler Peak Scenic Dr., **Lower Lehman Campground** has 11 spaces; **Upper Lehman Creek Campground** has 24 spaces; and the **Wheeler Creek Campground,** at 9,950 feet, has 37 spaces. Only the Lower Lehman Campground is open year-round.

Festivals and Events

Snow Geese Festival

first weekend in Mar. Held in Delta at the peak of the snow geese's migration north. The festival features various local activities—an arts festival, car show and other events. State wildlife officials are also on hand to inform about bird migration and other wildlife habits and activities in the area. See the Wildlife Viewing section for details. **1-800-864-0345; 435-864-4316.**

Outdoor Activities

ATV Riding

Piute ATV Trail

This 200-mile-long trail over public lands loops through four Utah counties and provides ATV riders with a unique opportunity to spend days exploring central Utah. Promoted by tourism officials and ATV dealers, the Piute ATV Trail is actually a series of trails across backcountry roads, mining roads and newly cut tracks. Fillmore is located at the northern end of the trail and provides accommodations, good access, ATV repairs, information and maps. **1-800-441-4ATV (4288); 435-743-5154.**

Golf

Paradise Golf Course

The old pioneer town of Fillmore is the most recent Utah community to be endowed with its own golf course. This 9-hole course opened in 2001. While most of the course has relatively wide and forgiving fairways, the 573-yard-long 5th hole with its dogleg to the right requires a long drive, and the tricky 9th hole with its island green requires an accurate, well-placed shot to avoid the water. Located just east of Interstate 15. **905 N. Main, Fillmore; 435-743-4439.**

Sunset View Golf Course

In 1983 floods covered the original Delta Golf Course, so county officials decided to build a new course above the Sevier River on the sage- and rabbitbrush plain. The course is flat and easy, with fairly wide fairways. The course is an island in a sea of sagebrush, and the horizon is broken only by Pavant Butte and mountain ranges in the distance. Although serious golfers need not go out of their way to play this course, it offers enough challenge to make it fun for most. No reservations are necessary. It is also probably the least expensive public golf course in Utah. Located 2 miles north of Delta on US Hwy. 6. **435-864-2508.**

Hiking

Great Stone Face

Locals claim that a formation in the ancient lava flow south of Delta is the spitting image of Joseph Smith, founder of the Mormon church. A 0.5-mile hike leads up to and around the rock formation. To get to the trailhead, from Deseret drive south on Hwy. 257 for 3 miles and then turn west, just south of Ft. Deseret, onto a dirt road. After a 4-mile drive, you reach the end of the road, where you can park your vehicle.

Pavant Butte

Rising 1,000 feet above the valley floor, this extinct volcano, which erupted about 16,000 years ago under the surface of ancient Lake Bonneville, is one of the area's most interesting geologic features. The ancient waters of Lake Bonneville covered about half of the butte before vanishing at the end of the last ice age, about

10,000 years ago. Remnants of the ancient shore-line can be seen on the butte. Other remnants are human-made. The hike goes up the old road on the south side of the butte. After an elevation gain of about 400 feet in 0.7 mile, you reach the old wind-power plant ruins. Here the road ends, and it is another 0.5 mile to the summit.

To reach the butte from Delta, take US Hwy. 6/50 west 6 miles to Hwy. 257. Follow Hwy. 257 south for 16 miles to Clear Lake, then turn east and drive through the Clear Lake Waterfowl Management Area for 11 miles. Where the road branches, take the left-hand fork and follow it in a northeasterly direction for about 4 miles to Pavant Butte. To get there from Fillmore, head west on Hwy. 100 toward Flowell. After about 4 miles, before you reach Flowell, Hwy. 100 turns north. Continue north for about 10 miles until you reach a dirt road that turns west. Follow the dirt road for about 7 miles to Pavant Butte.

Red Dome

This fascinating geological area is the site of one of the most recent volcanic eruptions in the Lower 48 states. Geologists place the volcanic activity sometime between 1,000 and 4,000 years ago. Currently the site is being mined for its volcanic rock, but you can still see three intact cones and the remnants of eight others. The tallest is Miter Crater, which rises 375 feet above the valley floor. Unlike the dark lava rock that you find in other places in Utah, here you see a rainbow of colors: red, orange, purple, brown and black. The rock is twisted and molded in all kinds of shapes. You are welcome to pick up souvenir rocks and even pick up a brochure about the area at the mine office. Do stay out of the way of mining machinery. To reach Red Dome, in Fillmore turn west at the intersection of 400 N. and Main St. and drive west for 5 miles on Hwy. 100. Continue through the small town of Flowell to the end of the road. Turn south for just less than a mile, then turn west again and it's just over 5 miles to Red Dome—3 miles on paved road and another 2 miles on a dirt road.

Tabernacle Hill

Like Pavant Butte, Tabernacle Hill was formed by volcanic eruptions between 12,000 and 24,000 years ago, while Lake Bonneville was still in existence. Cinder and ash built a circular ring of tuff more than 200 feet high above the waters of Lake Bonneville. The lava hill is said to resemble the Salt Lake Tabernacle, hence its name. From the end of the road, it is a 2.5-mile hike to Tabernacle Hill. There is more than just a hill to see. As you walk across the lava fields, you will see lava tubes, squeeze-ups, pit craters, spatter cones, fissures and lava bubbles that seem frozen in time. For the adventuresome, the lava caves or tubes at Tabernacle Hill offer an intriguing exploration. The tubes are punctuated with skylightlike openings, but still it is wise to take a flashlight and exercise great caution—rattlesnakes have been spotted inside the tubes. Be sure to wear good shoes and gloves and allow yourself plenty of time to explore the miles of lava fields. The easiest way to reach the hill is to take Interstate 15 to Meadow, Exit 158, then follow the gravel road west, then northwest for 8 miles. Look for a dome-shaped hill, more than 0.5 mile across, south of the road.

Seeing and Doing

Historic Sites

Cove Ft.

Modern interstate travelers can appreciate the strategic importance of Cove Ft. when they realize that the 1867 fort was constructed at what would become, more than 100 years later, the intersection of Interstates 15 and 70. The 100-foot-square, 18-foot-high, dark basalt fort, situated about halfway between Fillmore and Beaver, was constructed during the Black Hawk Indian War to provide safety for Anglo travelers from Indian attacks. The 50 miles between the two settlements, across steep hills, was often too far for slow-moving wagons to cover in a day. Other forts were built by early Utah settlers, but none have been preserved or restored. In the late 1980s, the fort was donated to the LDS church. After a thorough renovation, the fort was reopened to visitors in 1992. Tour guides conduct you through the fort, and each of the 12 rooms—six on the north and six on the south side walls—have been outfitted with pioneer-era furnishings. A few years ago a massive barn was built a short distance north of the fort. To reach the fort from the north, take Exit 135 off Interstate 15; from the south, take Exit 132. To reach the fort from the east, head west on Interstate 70 and watch for the road that heads north to Cove Ft., about a mile before the intersection with Interstate 15. Open daily 10 A.M.–dusk. Admission is free. **435-438-5547.**

Ft. Deseret

Constructed in 1866 in response to the Black Hawk War, and located about 60 miles to the north of Cove Ft., Ft. Deseret was built under orders from Brigham Young to "fort up" for protection against the Indians. Unlike the rock-solid Cove Ft., which took seven months to construct, the 10-foot-high, 550-foot-square adobe walls of Ft. Deseret were completed in nine and a half days. Ninety-eight men were divided into two teams competing against each other to see which team could finish its two sides first. After it was completed, the fort was never used for protection against the Indians; in fact, the Indians used the fort themselves. The adobe walls of the abandoned fort are slowly dissolving, but visitors can still see the ruins. Located 2 miles south of Deseret on Hwy. 257.

Gunnison Massacre Site

Near the Gunnison Massacre Site Monument, Capt. John W. Gunnison and seven members of his 12-man group were killed by Indians while the men were carrying out a survey for a transcontinental railroad along the 40th parallel. Head west from Hinckley on US Hwy. 6/50 to milepost 78; turn south on a gravel road and travel 2 miles to the massacre site.

Historic Fillmore

Pick up a copy of the *Historic Homes* brochure at the tourism booth or the Territorial State Capitol. You can use the brochure as either a walking or driving guide to view more than 20 buildings in town.

One building not included in the tour is the **1926 American Legion Hall,** still used as a community center. The octagon-shaped log building was constructed by local veterans of World War I with support from the community, who purchased the logs at $5 each. The hall is located on the south side of the county courthouse on Main St. On the north side of the courthouse is a brand-new **veteran's memorial,** which lists the names of county residents who have served in the military from the days of the territorial militia to the present. Several blank panels remain for future inscriptions. Note the number of Japanese names listed under World War II. These were sons of Japanese-American families interred at the Topaz War Relocation Camp.

Territorial Capitol Building

It is hard to believe that the founder of Salt Lake City, Brigham Young, decided that the capital of Utah should be moved south 150 miles. Yet four years after Salt Lake City was established, Young appointed a commission to select a new, more centrally located site for the capital, and in January 1852, he concurred with their selection of Fillmore. Truman O. Angell, architect for the Salt Lake City Temple, designed an elaborate capitol building with four wings and an imposing dome. Construction on the south wing began during the summer of 1852. It was not until three years later that the south wing was dedicated and used as the location for Legislative sessions from 1856 to 1858. In 1858 Young was replaced as territorial governor by Alfred Cumming, and Salt Lake City became the territorial capital once more.

The Fillmore capitol was used for public meetings, social events, offices, a school, a jail and a theater, but by the turn of the 20th century had fallen into disuse. In the 1920s the Daughters of Utah Pioneers spearheaded its preservation as one of that organization's first projects. Today it is maintained and operated as one of the historic sites in the Utah State Parks system. The original rooms, including the upstairs assembly room, have been preserved. An excellent collection of pioneer artifacts is on display. It is situated in the center of the block behind the Millard County Courthouse; southwest of the building, on the same block, is the 1867 rock schoolhouse. Open daily (except Thanksgiving, Christmas and New Year's Day) Memorial Day–Labor Day 9 A.M.–6 P.M., the rest of the year 9 A.M.–5 P.M. Located Between Main St. and 100 W. and Center St. and 100 N. **435-743-5316;www.parks.state.ut.us/parks/www1/Terr.htm**.

Topaz War Relocation Camp

During World War II 9,000 Japanese-Americans from the San Francisco area were relocated to the Central Utah War Relocation Center as part of a wartime policy that saw the removal of about 100,000 West Coast residents of Japanese ancestry. The Utah camp, named Topaz for the nearby Topaz Mountain, was one of 10 camps located in the western states. Constructed at an estimated cost of $5 million by 800 men, Topaz required another $5 million annually for operation. The camp covered 19,800 acres, but most of the 623 buildings were located within a 42-block, 1-mile-square area. The camp opened on Sept. 11, 1942, and closed in Oct. 1945.

Critics of the relocation camps argue that they were a waste of money and manpower since Japanese-Americans proved their loyalty to the United States time and time again. Defenders point out that relocation was a justifiable precaution in the aftermath of the attack on Pearl Harbor and that the Japanese-Americans could be protected from violence fostered by anti-Japanese sentiment. At Topaz 3,000 students attended school, a newspaper was published and young men volunteered for service in the U.S. Army.

After the war the camp was dismantled; today, only a few foundations and traces of streets can be seen. The Japanese-American Civic League erected a monument at the site in 1976. Many of the Japanese-Americans sent to Topaz chose to remain in Utah after the war, and they and their families return to the site from time to time to remember the dark days of World War II. For all Americans, the camp raises the oft-debated question of whether a nation dedicated to the pursuit of life and liberty can or should arbitrarily restrict the freedoms of its citizens without due process.

There are no telephones, visitor center or facilities at the site. Admission is free; it is open all the time. Located 15 miles northwest of Delta. The easiest way to reach the site is to head west out of Delta on US Hwy. 6 and, after crossing the viaduct, continue west toward Sutherland and Abraham. As you drive north and west, you will see green signs with white lettering pointing toward Topaz Relocation Site. The paved road continues for 10 miles to 7000 W. and 3000 N., where you continue north on a gravel road for 1.5 miles to 4500 N. Turn left (west) onto 4500 N. and follow it for 3.8 miles to the site.

Museums

Great Basin Museum

This museum operated by the local historical society is housed in a building previously used as a maintenance shop for the local telephone company. Exhibits and artifacts focus on the agricultural history of the area, its geology and the World War II–era Japanese relocation camp at Topaz. Work is under way to restore one of the original recreation buildings from the Topaz Camp and to reconstruct an original barracks adjacent to the Great Basin Museum. Open Mon.–Fri. 9 A.M.–5 P.M., Sat.–Sun. 1–5 P.M. Admission is free. **328 W. 100 N., Delta; 435-864-5013.**

Rockhounding

Rock hounds and fossil hunters will think they've arrived in heaven when they reach the Delta area. From land administered by the Bureau of Land Management, a wide variety of rocks and fossils can be taken, including obsidian, topaz, red beryl, bixbyite, sunstones, garnet, muscovite, pyrite, quartz, geodes, agate, trilobite fossils and petrified wood. The local BLM office in Fillmore is a good source of information. **Warm Springs Resource Area, P.O. Box 778, Fillmore, UT 84631; 435-743-6811.**

If you are interested in rockhounding, you should do two things. First, obtain a copy of *The Traveler's Guide to Rocks and Fossils in and around Millard County* (DuWil Publishing, n.d.). This handy guide compiled by Michelle Mazzettia includes an area map to the prime sites along with descriptions of 21 locations and the kinds of rock and minerals you will find there. Many of the sites are accessible only by truck or four-wheel-drive vehicles.

Second, check out the resources in Delta. Stop by the **Harris House Rockshop (442 N. 350 E.)** to see the wonderful display of rocks and fossils from the area that are described in the guide. For more information about rockhounding, contact the **Delta Area Chamber of Commerce (435-864-4316).** You can pick up a trilobite souvenir pin here. Also visit the **West Desert Collectors (298 W. Main; 435-864-2175)** to see what can be found and to ask about directions to a dozen or more locations around Delta. The two most popular areas are Topaz Mountain and Antelope Spring.

Antelope Spring

Here you can find trilobite fossils. These Cambrian Age arthropods were compressed between stratified layers of shale millions of years ago and have become the unofficial symbol for the area. Located west of Delta. Take US Hwy. 6/50 west from Delta for 12 miles to the Antelope Spring dirt road, which begins about 5 miles west of Hinckley. Here you turn right/north and follow it northwest for about 8.5 miles.

Topaz Mountain

As you might guess, Topaz Mountain is a source of topaz crystals. The mountain is mined commercially, but a section has been reserved for amateur collectors. Topaz Mountain, with an elevation of 7,113 feet, is located at the southern end of the Thomas Range about 40 miles northwest of Delta. From US Hwy. 6 about 10 miles

north of Delta, drive northwest on Hwy. 174 past the Intermountain Power Plant and continue to the end of the paved highway, where you will see Topaz Mountain on the right side of the road.

Scenic Drives

Notch Peak Loop Backway

Notch Peak in the House Range mountains is a 9,700-foot peak of exposed sedimentary rock layers said to be the largest limestone formation in Utah. It dominates the surrounding desert, and the Notch Peak Loop road provides access to a little-traveled part of Utah. The 50-mile loop circles the House Range mountains on a maintained gravel road that passenger cars can use except when it's blocked by snow or heavy rains. The loop begins 43 miles west of Delta on US Hwy. 6/50 after passing Sevier Lake and driving through Skull Rock Pass. The dirt road heads north. In about 8 miles you come to an intersection; turn left and follow the road west about 12 miles through Marjum Pass as you cross the House Range mountains. At the next intersection, turn south into Tule Valley for 14 miles. You pass Painter Spring before rejoining US Hwy. 6/50.

Wildlife Viewing

Clear Lake Waterfowl Management Area

This marsh area of the West Desert with its water, cattails and bulrushes provides a good habitat for a variety of wetland species, including ducks, egrets, coots, curlews and other birds. Drive west from Delta on US Hwy. 6/50 for 5 miles, then turn south onto Hwy. 257. Continue for just under 16 miles, then turn east onto a gravel road and continue for 6 miles to the viewing area.

Gunnison Bend Reservoir

Beginning each Feb., thousands of snow geese leave their winter home in California's Imperial Valley for their summer home far to the north in Alaska and Canada. Their route takes them through the Delta area. The magnificent birds begin arriving in mid-Feb. and the last leave by mid-Mar., with the last week of Feb. and first week of Mar. the best time to view the birds. They spend the night on the reservoir, then fly off during the day to feed in the surrounding fields, returning to the reservoir a couple of times during the day. Gunnison Bend Reservoir is one of the few locations on the entire North American continent where you can see and hear the dramatic and spine-tingling flight of thousands of birds as they leave and return in large flocks to the reservoir. Drive west out of Delta on US Hwy. 6/50 across the overpass to 1000 W. Turn north on 1000 W. and proceed about half mile to 1500 N. Turn west on 1500 N. and head west for approximately 2.5 miles to 3000 W., where you turn south and follow the road for 2 miles to the reservoir. **1-800-864-0345; 435-864-4316.**

Where to Stay

Accommodations

DELTA
Best Western Motor Inn—$$
Coin laundry and swimming pool; 83 rooms. Located at the junction of US Hwys. 6 and 50. **527 E. Topaz Blvd.; 435-862-3882.**

FILLMORE
Best Western Paradise Inn—$$
Dining room, coffee shop, heated indoor swimming pool and whirlpool; 80 rooms. Near Exit 167 off Interstate 15. **800 N. Main; 435-743-6895.**

Camping

PRIVATE
Antelope Valley RV Park
Ninety-six sites with full hookups; laundry facilities, rest rooms, showers, a children's play area, a volleyball court and horseshoe pits. Located just west of the overpass. **766 W. Main, Delta; 435-864-1813.**

Fillmore KOA Campground
Forty-nine sites with hookups, 7 large tentsites and five camping cabins; a game room, playground, Laundromat, showers and convenience store. Open Mar.–Nov. Located off Interstate 15 at Exit 163, at the south end of Fillmore. **435-743-4420.**

Wagons West Campground
50 trailer sites, 42 with complete hookups. Showers, laundry facilities, convenience store. Open year-round. **501 N. Main, Fillmore; 435-743-6188.**

PUBLIC
Adelaide Campground
Twenty RV sites and 15 tentsites. Open late May–Oct. Located 6 miles east of Kanosh on Forest Rd. 106.

Oak Creek
In the Fishlake National Forest; 23 trailer sites and 9 tentsites. Open late May–Sept. Located 4.5 miles east of Oak City, off Hwy. 125.

Yuba Lake
A year-round campground with 28 camping spaces. Coming from the south, take Exit 188 off Interstate 15; from the north, Exit 202. Located north of Scipio.

Where to Eat

In addition to fast-food establishments in both Delta and Fillmore, consider the following:

DELTA
Delta Valley Farms Restaurant—$
At this cheese factory, you can purchase fresh curd or any of the 15 varieties of cheese they make. It has a small restaurant that serves homemade soups, burgers, sandwiches and daily specials. Cheese store open Mon.–Sat. 8 A.M.–6 P.M.; restaurant open Mon.–Sat. 10 A.M.–4 P.M. Located 2 miles north of Delta on US Hwy. 6. **435-864-3566.**

Pizza House—$ to $$

Pizza, soup and salad bar, sandwiches and pasta dinners. Open Mon.–Sat. 11 A.M.–10 P.M. **69 S. 300 E.; 435-864-2207.**

FILLMORE

Cowboy Cafe—$ to $$

Traditional Western fare, especially full breakfasts—pancakes, eggs, ham. Open daily 6 A.M.–10 P.M. **30 N. Main; 435-743-4302.**

Paradise Inn Restaurant—$ to $$

Located at the Paradise Inn. Open for breakfast, lunch and dinner. **915 N. Main; 435-743-5414.**

Services

Visitor Information

Bureau of Land Management—Warm Springs Resource Area, P.O. Box 778, Fillmore, UT 84631; 435-743-6811.

Delta Area Chamber of Commerce— 80 N. 200 W., Delta, UT 84624; 1-800-864-0345; 435-864-4316; www.millardcounty. com.

East Millard Travel Council—P.O. Box 848, Fillmore, UT 84631; 435-743-5154; www.millardcounty.com.

Richfield/ Sevier and Piute Counties

Richfield is the major commercial center in central Utah. The city, which lies at an elevation of 5,280 feet and has a population of 5,600, is the county seat for Sevier County and the gateway to Fish Lake.

Richfield sits in a valley bordered by the

Pavant Range on the west and the Wasatch and Fishlake Plateaus on the south. The valley's most dominant feature is 11,227-foot Monroe Mountain southeast of town. Historically the most important feature of the valley has been the Sevier River flowing north out of Marysvale Canyon, which provides irrigation water to the farms along its banks.

While Richfield is the center, Salina, located at the mouth of Salina Canyon, is also an important community because it sits on the historic route out of the Great Basin and into Colorado Plateau country to the east. Other settlements in the Sevier Valley include Redmond, Aurora, Sigurd, Venice, Glenwood, Central, Annabella, Elsinore, Monroe, Joseph and Sevier. In eastern Sevier County, Hwy. 72 runs south from Interstate 70 through the town of Fremont to Hwy. 24 at Loa, gateway to Capitol Reef National Park.

Piute County, with a population of 1,500 and only 754 square miles in size, is one of Utah's smallest counties. Two important reservoirs, Otter Creek and Piute Reservoirs, are found there. Along US Hwy. 89 in Marysvale Canyon are the towns of Marysvale, Junction, Kingston and Circleville. Along Otter Creek/Hwy. 62 are the towns of Koosharem, Greenwich and Angle; just south of Hwy. 62, on Hwy. 22, is the town of Antimony. Piute County was the boyhood home of the famous western outlaw Butch Cassidy.

History

The Richfield area was heavily used by prehistoric peoples. Excavations at Sudden Shelter, east of Salina on Ivie Creek, indicate that this site was occupied for more than 7,000 years. Most of the communities in the area, including Richfield, were established in former Fremont people village sites. Like their neighbors the Anasazi, the Fremont people were farmers but tended to live in pit houses and to rely heavily on hunting and gathering. They made pottery, but are best known for their spectacular rock art. They occupied the Richfield area from about the time of

Christ and reached the height of their civilization about A.D. 1000. Around A.D. 1250, traces of their culture began to disappear, perhaps absorbed into another tribe's. By A.D. 1500 they were completely gone. The culture of this people is documented at Fremont State Park just off Interstate 70 in Clear Creek Canyon near Sevier—and in Capitol Reef National Park (see the Capitol Reef National Park chapter).

During the late 1820s fur trappers, including Jedediah Smith and others, crossed the area. What is now Sevier County lay squarely along the Old Spanish Trail, which ran from Santa Fe to California and was used by travelers between 1830 and 1850. Those using the trail left the Colorado Plateau and entered the Great Basin by way of Salina Canyon. At the mouth of Salina Canyon, they encountered the Sevier River and followed it the length of the valley. Mormons settled near Richfield and other locations beginning in 1864, but during the conflict with the Ute Indians known as the Black Hawk War at least 25 towns, including Salina and Richfield,

were temporarily abandoned in April 1867. Resettled in 1871, Richfield grew rapidly to become a regional center.

By 1891 the Denver and Rio Grande Railroad reached Salina and a decade later was extended through the entire valley to Marysvale. The railroad proved a boon to the agricultural economy of the area and made mining possible at places like Kimberly in the Tushar Mountains. But Kimberly was not like earlier hell-raising, rip-roaring mining camps. As one former resident recalled, "Kimberly was too small and not rich enough to get the drifters ... and the 'boys' were too close to home to 'cut up' much." Although Kimberly was not another Virginia City or even a Park City, the area still has an exciting history.

Major Attractions

Fremont Indian State Park

One of Utah's most exciting state parks and museums, Fremont Indian State Park was established by the state Legislature in 1985 to preserve the archaeological sites and rock art left by the Fremont Indians during their occupation of the area more than 1,000 years ago. The museum was completed in 1987 and houses the material excavated from a large Fremont village site, known as Five Finger Village, that was uncovered in November 1983 during construction of Interstate 70 through Clear Creek Canyon. Working under extreme time pressure, archaeologists collected artifacts from what has been identified as the largest Fremont village in Utah. The village includes 80 residential structures and pit houses and numerous storage granaries. Although the freeway construction led to the destruction of the village, Fremont Indian State Park provides an excellent opportunity to learn more about Fremont culture. More than 500 panels of rock art, both pictographs (painted) and petroglyphs (carved), are located along the north and south sides of Clear Creek Canyon and can be reached by the access road and hiking trails.

Getting There

Richfield is located on US Hwy. 89 and Interstate 70. The 160 miles to Richfield from Salt Lake City may be driven via Interstate 15; four routes lead to US Hwy. 89, which you can follow all the way to Richfield: (1) Take Exit 261 at Spanish Fork and follow US Hwy. 6 east for 13 miles to its junction with US Hwy. 89, then turn south. (2) Take Exit 224 at Nephi and follow Hwy. 132 east to its junction with US Hwy. 89 just north of Ephraim. (3) Take Exit 222 at Nephi and follow Hwy. 28 south through Levan and on to its junction with US Hwy. 89 at Gunnison. (4) Take Exit 188 at Scipio and follow US Hwy. 50 east to its junction with US Hwy. 89 and Interstate 70 at Salina. Coming from southwestern Utah on Interstate 15, take Exit 132 at Cove Ft. onto Interstate 70 and follow it east to Richfield.

Outdoor Activities

A paved, handicapped-accessible, 0.3-mile-long interpretive trail known as **"Parade of the Rocks"** begins at the visitor center (see Visitor Information below). Along the trail you can see some of the best examples of rock art in the state park, including the Spider Woman panel, a hunting scene and a Piute hunting scene. This trail provides access to a 0.5-mile-long **"Court of Ceremonies"** that climbs up a side canyon to disclose more rock art.

You will also want to make the 0.5-mile hike over to the **"Cave of 100 Hands,"** located on the south side of the canyon. While you can see only 26 ancient handprints, archaeologists assure us that there are more buried beneath the cave floor. Cross back to the north side of the canyon for a look at the **Arch of Art,** where a total of 61 panels have been found on the cliff. It takes a sharp eye to spot all of the panels.

For longer hikes, there is the 5-mile **Centennial Trail** that parallels Interstate 70 down and back up Clear Creek Canyon. This trail provides access to the **Indian Blanket Pictograph** on the south side of the canyon, which is one of the largest panels—approximately 12 feet long and 3 feet high—that does look like a woven blanket.

For an orientation to the natural history of the area, the 1.5-mile-long **Alma Christensen Trail,** named for an early homesteader in the canyon, is an excellent way to become more familiar with the area. It is located about 0.25 mile north of the visitor center. Be sure to pick up the *Interpretive Trail Guide* at the visitor center for this hike.

Several of the trails provide spectacular overlook views of the canyon. Don't miss the **"Curse of Spider Woman Rock,"** in the lower part of the canyon. The rock is all that remains of a large white outcropping that was cut away during the interstate construction. A Hopi religious leader visited the site and asked that the ridge be saved because it recorded the Hopi legend of Spider Woman and the creation of the world. When the ridge was destroyed, the religious leader returned and put a curse on the Department of Transportation through Spider Woman's daughter, Salt Woman, who controls all nature phenomena such as weather. After the curse was placed, Utah suffered several unusual weather-related events, including major flooding and a mudslide that blocked US Hwy. 50 for several months.

Not far from the "Curse of Spider Woman Rock" is the **"Dancing Family"** panel, whose six figures may very well be engaged in dancing. Also nearby is **Sheep Shelter,** which has offered protection and shelter to travelers through the canyon for at least seven millennia. Archaeologists postulate that Clear Creek Canyon was a major transportation corridor for ancient peoples en route to the Mineral Mountains to the southwest, which were an important source of obsidian rock for arrowheads and tools. Rock art inside the shelter depicts different animals, including mountain sheep and possibly a scorpion.

Near the west end of the park are more interesting panels, including the largest panel, **"Newspaper Rock,"** which may have been the work of lookouts perched on the outcropping watching for intruders coming from the west. **"Hunkup's Train"** is probably the most recent panel; it is the work of a Piute named Hunkup in the latter part of the 19th century. It depicts two-story houses and two trains running on railroad tracks.

Visitor Information

The visitor center includes exhibits, a replica of a Fremont pit house, a statue of a Fremont woman (which was constructed using a plaster cast from a well-preserved skull uncovered while digging a natural gas pipeline) and an orientation video, "Canyon of Memories: The Fremont of Clear Creek Canyon." You can also pick up maps for the nearby hiking trails.

The park is open daily (except Thanksgiving, Christmas and New Year's) Memorial Day–Labor Day 9 A.M.–6 P.M., the rest of the year 9 A.M.–5 P.M. Admission fee charged. There is a campground (see Where to Stay). Located about 20 miles southwest of Richfield off Interstate 70. Take Exit 23 if you are traveling from Richfield, or Exit 17 if you are coming east from Interstate 15 (17 miles to the west). **11550 West Clear Creek Canyon Rd., Sevier, UT 84766; 435-527-4631; www.parks.state.ut.us/parks/www1/frem.htm.**

Festivals and Events

Independence Day Celebration

July 4. The fourth of July in Richfield features a parade down Main St.; food, races and activities at the park **(300 N. Main);** a dance in the evening; and a fireworks display. The celebration also features performances of a historical pageant, "A Field of Stars," which depicts events from the American Revolution, including the Boston Tea Party, Paul Revere's ride and the Battle of Bunker Hill. **1-800-662-8898; 435-896-5120.**

Outdoor Activities

Biking

The **Sevier County Travel Office** offers a free *Mountain Biking Guide* that provides descriptions and maps for 11 different rides in the Richfield area, ranging from a 3.5-mile loop around Pelican Point near Fish Lake to the nearly 50-mile-long out-and-back ride from Richfield to Fremont Indian State Park. The following is a sampling of the available routes.

Clear Creek Canyon Narrows

This ride follows a combination of asphalt, gravel and dirt trails with an elevation gain of about 1,200 feet. You can ride it as a 14-mile out-and-back or as an 18-mile loop. Begin 2 miles west of Fremont Indian State Park and follow the old highway through the Clear Creek Canyon Narrows for 7 miles to Forest Rd. 114. Here you can either return the way you came or follow the road as it passes beneath Interstate 70, across Shingle Creek and continues for another mile to an old grass airstrip and a fine view of the 12,000-foot Tushar Mountains to the south. The trail heads east across Fish Creek, which you

cross twice, and then runs parallel to Interstate 70 until you come to an underpass; after that it's a 3-mile ride back to the starting point.

Fish Lake Area

The Fish Lake area offers some beautiful summer and fall rides. The 25-mile **Mytoge Mountain Loop** climbs the mountain east of Fish Lake from an elevation of 8,845 feet to nearly 10,000 feet. You can begin the ride from the northwest side of Fish Lake on Hwy. 25 and ride southwest to Forest Rd. 046, which loops over Mytoge Mountain to the east of Fish Lake and then past Crater Lakes onto Forest Rd. 045, which rejoins Hwy. 25 about midway between Fish Lake and the Johnson Valley Reservoir. This is an especially beautiful ride through aspen trees in the fall.

Larry Theivagt, a former recreation officer at the Fishlake National Forest, has written a 24-page booklet, *Mountain Bicycle Trails on the Fishlake National Forest,* describing 21 mountain bike routes in the Fishlake National Forest. **U.S. Forest Service, Richfield Office, 115 E. 900 N., Richfield, UT 84701; 435-896-9233.**

Soldier Canyon

Soldier Canyon takes its name from when the local militia fought Ute Indians during the Black Hawk War, from 1865 to 1869. After two men were killed in Salina Canyon and their cattle taken, a company of 84 men on horseback pursued the Utes up the canyon. A battle left two more Anglos dead and two wounded before the Utes made their escape to the east. This 18-mile loop follows part of the route taken by the militia; it leaves the city park a mile southeast of Salina on US Hwy 89. You ride east on the frontage road for 2 miles to the Soldier Canyon Rd. at the Interstate 70 overpass. Follow the gravel road as it climbs 1,200 feet in about 10 miles before it drops into Gooseberry Valley. Turn onto Gooseberry Rd. (Forest Rd. 640) and follow it as it makes a gradual descent to the Salina Creek Frontage Rd. Follow the frontage road back into Salina.

Boating and Fishing

The U.S. Forest Service and Sevier Travel Council have pooled their resources to produce a handy guide, "Fishing Opportunities in the Fishlake National Forest," which lists more than 40 fishing spots. **Richfield Ranger District, 115 E. 900 N., Richfield, UT 84701; 435-896-9233.** The following are some of the most popular fishing locations in the region.

Fish Lake

One of central and southern Utah's largest natural lakes, Fish Lake covers 2,500 acres, with an average depth of 85 feet. The lake is stocked with lake trout, rainbow trout and splake, while native brown trout are able to sustain their population without being stocked. Most fishing is done from boats, which can be rented at the **Fish Lake Lodge (435-638-1000).** The lake is extremely popular during the summer. Located at an elevation of 8,000 feet, the lake freezes over during the winter and is an excellent location for ice fishing from Dec. to spring. From US Hwy. 89 at Sigurd, take Hwy. 24 south to the junction with Hwy. 25, then take Hwy. 25 northeast 7 miles to Fish Lake.

Gooseberry Area

A number of small reservoirs and ponds in the Gooseberry area are well stocked with trout. Near the Gooseberry Campground, Gooseberry Creek is stocked monthly with small rainbow trout and is one of a few opportunities to try stream fishing. Take Exit 61 off Interstate 70 east of Salina and follow the Gooseberry-Sevenmile Rd. (Forest Rd. 640) south to the Gooseberry Campground.

Otter Creek Reservoir

Constructed on a tributary of the Sevier River in the southern end of Piute County, Otter Creek Reservoir was built by local farmers in the 1890s. It is one of the oldest reservoirs in the south-central part of the state. Otter Creek State Park is located at the southern end of the reservoir. Large rainbow and cutthroat trout have been taken from the reservoir, which is a popu-

lar fishing location in the summer, with ice fishing in the winter. Fly-fishing can be tried in a large pool below the dam. From US Hwy. 89 2 miles south of Junction, turn east on Hwy. 62 and drive 10 miles to the reservoir.

Piute Reservoir

This 2,250-acre reservoir, created in 1908 to impound water for irrigation purposes, is a popular fishing location for cutthroat and rainbow trout. Piute State Park is located at the north end of the lake about 5 miles north of Junction. The reservoir is just east of US Hwy. 89, downstream from the Otter Creek Dam, between the towns of Junction and Marysvale.

Golf

Cove View Golf Course

This is one of the older public courses in the southern half of the state. The most memorable hole is the 343-yard, par 4 7th hole, which requires a tee shot across a lake and in between two groves of trees on either side. Cove View is the only public course along US Hwy. 89 in the nearly 200 miles between Manti and Kanab. Inexpensive, uncrowded, flat, with wide fairways, this course is usually not crowded. Located just east of Exit 37 off Interstate 70, just west of the Richfield Airport. **435-896-9987.**

Hiking

Fish Lake Hightop

This 10-mile out-and-back hike takes you from the Pelican Point trailhead near Fish Lake to 11,633 feet on Fish Lake Hightop. Unlike the typical hike to the top of a mountain peak, the Fish Lake Hightop hike takes you to a high and relatively level plateau. The trail heads across a sagebrush flat before descending into Bowery Canyon. The most strenuous part of the hike is the 1.5-mile ascent to the Hightop, after which the trail levels out as you wind your way through a pine forest with a panoramic view of Fish Lake below. From US Hwy. 89 at Sigurd, take Hwy. 24 south to the junction with Hwy. 25, then take Hwy. 25 northeast 7 miles to Fish Lake and watch for the Pelican Point trailhead near the northern end of the lake.

Seeing and Doing

Historic Sites

Big Rock Candy Mountain

In Marysvale Canyon you can see a wonderfully colored mountain of yellow, pink, brown, tan, green, gray and orange with a "lemonade" spring—colored yellow by calcium and iron rather than lemons. In 1897 "Haywire Mac" McClintock, a brakeman on the railroad that ran through the canyon, wrote a song called "In the Big Rock Candy Mountain." The song was recorded by Burl Ives and Tex Ritter, and its lyrics about chocolate bars, gumdrops and peppermint sticks has reached the stature of a genuine American folk song. A motel and resort operated on the 200-acre site for decades, but was closed for several years. It has recently been renovated (see the Where to Stay section). Drive south on US Hwy. 89 between Sevier and Marysvale; the mountain is to the west.

Maximillian Parker Cabin

Even before Paul Newman and Robert Redford made the hit movie *Butch Cassidy and the Sundance Kid* in 1969, the Utah-born outlaw was a western folk hero. Stories have circulated throughout southern and eastern Utah for more than 100 years of how Cassidy, in true Robin Hood fashion, robbed from the rich to give to the poor. Though many of the stories are apocryphal, it is a fact that Cassidy, born Robert Le Roy Parker in 1866, spent his teenage years on the Parker Ranch, about 2 miles south of Circleville. In 1879 Maximillian Parker purchased the ranch and a two-room cabin from the James family and moved his wife and six children into the homestead. At 13, Robert was the eldest child. Like many rural Utah ranchers, the elder Parker spent much of his time away from the family, earning a livelihood in the mining towns or on the freight roads. He left his eldest son in charge of the ranching operation.

Shortly after his 18th birthday, Robert Parker left the ranch for Telluride, Colorado, where he worked at various jobs for five years. On June 24, 1889, Parker, by then known as Butch Cassidy, along with Matt Warner and Tom McCarty, robbed the Telluride Bank of $31,000. The three men hit the Outlaw Trail in a big way. Between 1889 and 1900, Cassidy committed robberies in Colorado, Utah, Wyoming and Idaho. When an attempt to negotiate an amnesty agreement with Utah officials failed, Cassidy headed east via Texas to New York City where he, Etta Place and the Sundance Kid sailed for South America in 1901. The two outlaws were reportedly killed in a gun battle in 1909, but many people did not believe the story. Lula Parker Betenson, who was born on April 5, 1884, a few days before Cassidy left home for Colorado, claims that her older brother returned to the family ranch and visited with the family at their Circleville home in 1925. In her book, *Butch Cassidy, My Brother* (BYU Press, 1975), Betenson recounts the escapades both here and in South America that her brother related to the family, with the promise that they not talk about them (a promise she kept until after her brother's death). Betenson concludes her account by noting that her brother lived in the Northwest under the alias Bob Parks until his death in 1937, at the age of 71.

The old Parker Cabin is located on private land, but it is visible from the highway. Set off by the towering Lombardy poplars that, according to Lula Betenson, were planted by her mother with the help of her now-famous brother, the ranch is a favorite picture stop for travelers in the area—especially those who know its association with Butch Cassidy. Near US Hwy. 89 about 2 miles south of Circleville.

Piute County Courthouse

A jewel of a public building, the Piute County Courthouse was constructed of red burnt brick made on-site and placed on top of granite slabs hauled by wagon from nearby Kingston. The courthouse, built in 1903, was the center of activity in the county until a new courthouse, post office and school district office building were built on the north end of town a few years ago. Located on the west side of US Hwy. 89 in the center of Junction.

Museums

Charlie's and Lizzie's Working Loom Museum and Factory

When Carl Christensen emigrated from Denmark to Utah in 1894, he found his best prospect for earning a living was to practice his rug-making skills learned in the old country. He traveled around to the various southern Utah communities collecting rags from which to make rugs. In 1929 Carl, who went by Charlie in America, established a small rug-making factory in a wood-frame building in Marysvale that had been built in 1903 as a JC Penny store. Charlie and his wife, Lizzie, continued making rag rugs until their deaths in the late 1940s and early 1950s.

The building remained vacant until Ron and Glenda Bushman moved back to Marysvale. Ron had learned rug-making from his grandfather and began making and selling rugs part-time in the 1960s. Now it is a full-time operation with eight looms producing rugs, both for the public and for special orders, many for historic buildings such as the recently restored Cove Ft. Ron and Glenda are affiliated with the Utah Arts Council and have been recognized for their role in preserving the pioneer-era art of rug-making. They welcome visitors and are pleased to take time to demonstrate the rug-making process. There are hundreds of colorful finished rugs to see, and you can purchase an average-sized (3-by-5-foot) handwoven rug for less than $50. Open Mon.–Sat. 9 A.M.–5 P.M. **210 E. Bullion Ave., Marysvale; 435-326-4213.**

Scenic Drives

Bullion Canyon Driving Tour and Miner's Park

The mountains west of Marysvale have been the location of gold mining activity since at least the 1860s when miners in three camps—Weber City, Virginia City and Bullion City—organized the Ohio Mining District in 1868. By 1880 Bullion City boasted a population of 1,651 and mining continued in the area until the 1950s. You can see the extensive remains of this mining heritage by taking the nearly 7-mile-long drive up Bullion Canyon to the Miner's Park. In the middle of Marysvale, turn west off US Hwy. 89 onto Bullion Ave.

About 4 miles after you leave the highway, you come to a sign that designates the beginning of the "Canyon of Gold" Driving Tour. Along the 2.5-mile-long driving tour, there are nine stops that describe the toll road, mill stables, mines, mill and boardinghouses and an *arrastra* made from a large block of stone about 10 feet long with a 34-inch-diameter circular depression cut into the stone. The *arrastra* is a primitive kind of ore mill that was introduced into the New World by the Spanish—some believe that the *arrastra* in Bullion Canyon is evidence that Spanish miners were in the mountains long before American miners arrived.

The Miner's Park is the last stop on the driving tour. The quarter-mile-long foot trail winds through the trees and includes 15 displays of mining equipment, reconstructed buildings and the refurbished Dalton Cabin, which was built in the 1920s and originally located at 10,500 feet elevation near Mt. Brigham's summit—4 miles from the park. The park includes an interesting collection of mining cars, steam engines, stone boats, drills, winches, muckers, ore crushers and a forge with a drill press, vise and anvil. There is no charge for either the driving tour or the Miners' Park. 'When you've finished exploring, return the way you came.

Fish Lake Scenic Byway

Designated as one of Utah's official Scenic Byways, Hwy. 25 to Fish Lake is a beautiful, high-country drive that winds through aspen forests, providing good opportunities to view autumn leaves, deer, prairie dogs and other small forest animals. If you are lucky, you might spot elk or some of the moose that were introduced into the area a few years ago. The drive begins at the junction of Hwy. 25 with Hwy. 24, the road between Richfield and Capitol Reef National Park. It runs for 13 miles around the eastern and northern ends of Fish Lake as far as Johnson Valley Reservoir, where the paved road ends. At this point, retrace your route back to Hwy. 25; to continue on the unpaved road southeast from Johnson Valley Reservoir, take the Gooseberry/Fremont Rd. Scenic Backway.

Kimberly / Big John Rd. Scenic Backway

From Fremont Indian State Park, take the Kimberly/Big John Rd. Scenic Backway south into the Tushar Mountains. The road to Kimberly is steep and narrow in sections, and can be rough in some areas; high-clearance vehicles are recommended. After 7.5 miles, you reach the old mining town of Kimberly.

Now a ghost town, Kimberly dates from the late 1890s, when the Annie Laurie Consolidated Gold Mining Company established a cyanide leaching mill to extract gold from ore taken from the mountains. At its height, 500 people lived in the two sections—upper and lower—of Kimberly. In 1908, the company went bankrupt and most of the residents moved away. Mining was revived between 1932 and 1938, but today the ruins of the Annie Laurie mill and other structures are a silent monument to another abandoned mining town.

From Kimberly, the road continues south through the Tushar Mountains, reaches an elevation of 11,000 feet, then turns east to drop off the mountain and intersect US Hwy. 89 at Junction. The drive is approximately 40 miles long and takes about 3 hours, with a stop in Kimberly.

From Junction, you can drive back north about 30 miles, through Marysvale, along the Sevier River through scenic Marysvale Canyon, past the multicolored Big Rock Candy Mountain, to the junction of US Hwy. 89 with Interstate 70.

Tours

Richfield Walking Tour

Available at the **Richfield Visitor Center (390 N. Main)** and at a number of locations in Richfield at no cost, the pamphlet *One Mile Walking Tour of Richfield, Utah* identifies 18 sites and buildings along a short route. This walking tour is an excellent way to get acquainted with the town's history.

One of the buildings included on the tour is the **Ralph Ramsay Home (57 E. 200 N.),** a private residence that was built between 1873 and 1874 by my great-grandfather. In 1856, at the age of 32, Ralph Ramsay immigrated to Utah from England as a convert to the Mormon church. That summer, he and his wife, Elizabeth, spent 15 weeks pulling a handcart 1,400 miles from Iowa City to Salt Lake City. During the journey, two of their children died and were buried along the trail. A master woodcarver, Ralph Ramsay carved the famous eagle atop the Eagle Gate in Salt Lake City and left many pieces of fine furniture in the city before moving to Richfield in 1872, at the request of Brigham Young. The upstairs of his home was used as a workshop, and his wife operated a pill and herb remedy dispensary out of a small room on the main floor.

The Ramsays remained in Richfield until 1885 when they moved to the Mormon settlement of Colonial Juarez in Chihuahua, Mexico. They lived there for two years before moving north to Snowflake, Arizona, where Ramsay lived until his death in 1905.

Where to Stay

Bed and Breakfasts, Lodges and Inns

Big Rock Candy Mountain Inn—$$ to $$$

Located at the base of Big Rock Candy Mountain along the Sevier River, the inn was renovated and reopened in 1997. There are two options for accommodations: the motel, in which each of the nine rooms is named after a kind of candy—such as Licorice Stick, Jelly Bean, Lemon Drop and Taffy—or in one of the six cabins located across the road along the river. A couple of the cabins have kitchens and can sleep up to four adults. Amenities include a hot tub, access to fishing, river rafting, biking and ATV rides. A restaurant (see Where to Eat) is also part of the inn. Located on US Hwy. 89 between Sevier and Marysvale. **1-888-560-7625.**

Fish Lake Lodge—$$ to $$$

This is actually the third lodge built at Fish Lake. The first, built in 1911, burned down; the second collapsed into the lake. The present Fish Lake Lodge was constructed between 1928 and 1932. At 360 feet long and 80 feet wide, with a 160-foot-long ballroom, it was considered the largest wooden structure west of the Mississippi at the time of its completion. The rustic lodge includes 25 wooden cabins, some dating from the 1930s and others of recent vintage. During the 1960s and 1970s, the lodge went through difficult times, but since 1983, under the guidance of Gary and Stephanie Moulton, it has been rehabilitated. It is now an attractive location for a peaceful stay at one of Utah's best and most beautiful fishing spots. The dining room is open for weekend dinners early in the season and regular hours during the summer. From the junction of Hwy. 24 with Hwy. 25, take Hwy. 25 northeast 7 miles to Fish Lake. **435-638-1000.**

Moore's Old Pine Inn—$$ to $$$

During its heyday as a mining center and southern terminus for the Denver and Rio Grande Railroad line through central Utah, Marysvale boasted a half dozen hotels, of which the Pines Hotel, built in 1882, was the best. Local tradition holds that the famous outlaw Butch Cassidy stayed in the hotel and that writer Zane Grey penned his famous Western novel *Riders of the Purple Sage* while a guest at the Pines Hotel.

Another significant guest was Grace Hillman, who arrived in Marysvale in 1920 as a young schoolteacher from Pleasant Grove and spent her first night in southern Utah at the Pines Hotel. Grace married and remained in Marysvale and is the paternal grandmother of Randy Moore, who in 1995 moved with his wife, Katie, from Layton to Marysvale and opened their bed and breakfast in the historic Pines Hotel.

Randy and Katie deserve a historic preserva-tion award for their efforts in retaining the layout and fabric of the original hotel while providing up-to-date convenience and comfort for their guests. There are three suites and four rooms in the original hotel, plus two three-room cabins south of the main structure. The three suites all have a private bath. The honeymoon suite is called "Dixon's Hitching Post," and has pictures of Ron's maternal grandparents, Vaughn and Norma Madsen, on their honeymoon in the nearby mountains in the 1920s; other features include a 90-gallon Jacuzzi tub and a separate sitting room with fireplace. The other two suites—the Miner's Suite and the Indian Suite—are located on the first floor. The four rooms upstairs share two large baths with claw-foot tubs that have been in the hotel more than 100 years. Each of the rooms is decorated with antiques and crafts in a distinctive theme—Hunters Lodge, Madsen's Fishing Hole, Zane Grey Room and Betsy Ross Room. A full breakfast, served in the hotel's original dining room, will ensure you won't leave hungry. **60 S. State, P.O. Box 70, Marysvale, UT 84750; 1-800-887-4565; 435-326-4565; www.marys-vale.org/Pine-Inn.html.**

Rockin' R Ranch—$$$$

Would you like to stay at a real working ranch, where they still brand cattle, grow and harvest hay and preserve Old West traditions while still having fun? The Rockin' R Ranch near Antimony, with a 1,000-acre ranch site and 40,000 acres of grazing land in the mountains, is such a place. Guests are provided three meals a day and can participate in a variety of activities, from cattle drives and roundups to hikes, Dutch-oven cook-outs, fishing, horseback riding, riding a bucking bull barrel, western dances, songfests and story-telling. **Rockin' R Ranch and Lodge Office, 9160 S. 300 W., Ste. 20, Sandy, UT 84070; 1-800-767-4386; 435-565-8588; www.rockin-rranch.com.**

Motels

RICHFIELD
Best Western Apple Tree Inn—$$
Heated pool; 63 rooms, five available with two bedrooms. **145 S. Main; 435-896-5481.**

Days Inn—$$
Heated pool, whirlpool, sauna and exercise room, with a coffee shop and restaurant inside the inn; 51 rooms, some nonsmoking. **333 N. Main; 1-800-325-2525; 435-896-6476.**

Quality Inn—$$
Swimming pool, laundry room and some rooms with kitchen facilities; 79 rooms. **540 S. Main; 1-800-228-5151; 435-896-5465.**

SALINA
Shaheens Best Western—$$
Heated pool and restaurant; 40 rooms. Just off Interstate 70 at Exit 54. **1225 S. State; 435-529-7455.**

Camping

PRIVATE
Butch Cassidy Campground
Seventy campsites, most with hookups. Flush toilets, showers and laundry facilities. Open Apr.–Oct. Located in the south end of Salina, just off Exit 54 from Interstate 70. **435-529-7400.**

Fish Lake Area
Bowery Haven (435-638-1040) has 67 sites and a dump site. **Lakeside Resort (435-638-1000)** has 24 sites and 24 indoor units. Flush toilets, showers and laundry facilities available at both campgrounds; all sites have complete hookups. A maximum 14-day stay at both campgrounds. Open late May–end of Oct. From the junction of Hwy. 24 with Hwy. 25, take Hwy. 25 northeast 7 miles to Fish Lake.

Richfield KOA Campground
This KOA has 83 sites, most of which have full hookups. Also 50 tentsites. Flush toilets, showers, laundry facilities and swimming pool.

Open Mar.–Oct. **600 S. 600 W., Richfield; 435-896-6674.**

PUBLIC
Fish Lake and Johnson Valley Reservoir Area
The best and most used public campgrounds are at Fish Lake and Johnson Reservoir about 50 miles southeast of Richfield, via Hwy. 24 and Hwy. 25; **1-800-280-2267.** The **Doctor Creek Campground** is located on the southwestern shore of Fish Lake, 7 miles from Hwy. 24. Twenty-nine RV sites and 29 tentsites are available late May–end of Oct. Two miles north on the eastern side of the lake, **Mackinaw Campground,** the largest campground, has 68 RV sites and 68 tentsites. Situated in an aspen grove overlooking the lake, the campground has drinking water and flush toilets. Five miles up the road near the Johnson Valley Reservoir, the **Frying Pan Campground** has 12 RV sites and 12 tentsites, drinking water and flush toilets. Less than 0.5 mile away, the **Piute Parking Campground** has 16 RV sites. If you are driving a large outfit, this is the public campground for you, since it accommodates RVs up to 48 feet in length, while the other three campgrounds can handle vehicles no longer than 22 feet.

Otter Creek Reservoir Area
Camping facilities include 34 RV sites and 6 tentsites. Modern rest rooms with wheelchair access, showers, picnic tables, drinking water, a sewage disposal station, a fish-cleaning sink, a paved boat ramp and a floating dock adjacent to the campground. From US Hwy. 89, 2 miles south of Junction, turn east on Hwy. 62 and drive 10 miles to the reservoir. **435-624-3268.**

Where to Eat

Big Rock Candy Mountain Restaurant— $$ to $$$
Specialties include barbecued ribs and fresh grilled trout. Patio dining in the summer. Part of the Big Rock Candy Mountain Inn. Open daily for breakfast, lunch and dinner. Located on

US Hwy. 89, 20 miles south of Richfield. **435-326-3200.**

Little Wonder Café—$ to $$

In Sevier County, 1929 was a good year for starting restaurants, with both Mom's and the Little Wonder Café established that year. Both are among Utah's oldest cafes. At the Little Wonder Café, you will find the basics—western breakfasts, chicken, fish, steak, spaghetti, burgers and sandwiches along with home-style soup. Open Mon.–Sat. 7 A.M.–9 P.M. **101 N. Main, Richfield; 435-896-8960.**

Mom's Café—$ to $$

Established in 1929 and still going strong at the corner of Main and State Sts. in Salina, Mom's has been through several generations of moms. Its home-style cooking is known far and wide, especially its homemade soups and pies. Fare includes sandwiches, steaks and a salad bar. Open daily 7 A.M.–10 P.M. **10 E. Main St., Salina; 435-529-3932.**

Pepperbelly's—$ to $$

You walk into Pepperbelly's and it seems as though you have entered a sanitized sheet-metal auto garage out of the 1950s and 1960s. There is even a gas pump that still registers the price of gas at 29.9 cents a gallon. The cash register desk is a piece of automotive sculpture, with three sides made of automobile doors welded together. This is just the beginning—the interior has a fun collection of auto garage memorabilia including license plates; gas, oil and grease cans; and temperature sign gauges, flower pot tires and authentic highway signs with real bullet holes that might just have been made by the group of old-time cowboys in the booth next to you. Owner Jim Holt has spent a lifetime collecting these motor-age artifacts. The Mexican food is surprisingly good, with high marks given for the chunky salsa and spicy chili verde. In addition to other standard Mexican dishes, there are hamburgers and sandwiches. Children and families seem to especially like the laid-back atmosphere. Open Mon.–Fri. 11 A.M.–9 P.M., Fri.–Sat. 11 A.M.–10 P.M. **68 S. Main St., Richfield; 435-896-2097.**

Services

Visitor Information

Sevier Travel Council—Open Mon.–Fri. 9 A.M.–5 P.M. **220 N. 600 W., Richfield, UT 84701; 1-800-662-8898; 435-896-8898; www.sevierutah.net.**

U.S. Forest Service, Richfield Ranger District, Fishlake National Forest—Open Mon.–Fri. 9 A.M.–5 P.M. **115 E. 900 N., Richfield, UT 84701; 435-896-9233.**

Capitol Reef National Park

For many Utah natives, Capitol Reef is their favorite national park. Ward Roylance, who devoted much of his life to Capitol Reef, wrote that the park "features splendid erosive forms—grand cliffs, goblin rocks, carved pinnacles, stone arches, great butte-forms and deep gorges. It combines the fantasy of Bryce and the grandeur of Zion National Parks, with more variety of color than either, and is larger than both combined (378 square miles). It also contains archaeological and historic resources." The park was set aside to protect the bizarre Waterpocket Fold, named by Almon Thompson in the 1870s for the numerous water pockets created by erosion in the sandstone formation of which Capitol Reef is part. The "reef" is an upthrust ridge with a cliff face that rises above its surroundings and stands as a forbidding barrier to travel, hence the name "reef." On top of Capitol Reef itself are white domes of Navajo sandstone that early pioneers thought resembled the dome of the U.S. Capitol in Washington, D.C. The

Capitol Reef is just one of many smooth-domed formations atop the Waterpocket Fold, a long bulge on the earth's surface.

This great hump stretches nearly 100 miles from Thousand Lake Mountain on the north to the southern boundary of the national park where Grand Staircase-Escalante National Monument meets the Glen Canyon National Recreation Area and Lake Powell. The southern reaches of the park along the Waterpocket Fold are relatively narrow—10 or so miles wide. It is accessible by car along the 47-mile-long dirt road that runs down the east side of the fold from Notom on Hwy. 24 to Bullfrog Basin on Lake Powell. The Burr Trail bisects the Waterpocket Fold and the national park as it connects the Bryce Canyon/Escalante/Boulder area on the west with Lake Powell. The remote northern section of the park, Cathedral Valley, can be reached only by four-wheel-drive or high-clearance vehicles.

The area surrounding the park is sparsely populated, but its few services are all the visitor to the national park can rely on. Hanksville, on the east at the junction of Hwys. 24 and 95, is the gateway to southeastern Utah. West of the park, in the 15 miles along Hwy. 24 between Hwys. 12 and 72 are clustered the small towns of Torrey, Caineville, Teasdale, Bicknell and Loa.

The prehistoric Fremont Indians were named for the river that flows through Capitol Reef National Park. There are many sites left by this ancient people within the park, and rangers have given special attention to their preservation and interpretation. The richness and variety of colors, the towering cliffs, the close confinement of the tight and deep gorges, the historic buildings and orchards of Fruita, the prehistoric Indian rock art, the opportunity to hike through canyons cut through the Waterpocket Fold and the lack of crowds—at least during the spring and fall—make a visit to Capitol Reef an inspiring, stimulating and relaxing experience.

History

For millions of years in what is now central Utah, shallow seas, rivers and tidal flats laid down many layers of deposits that eventually hardened into rock formations. In time they were covered by massive sand dunes, which also hardened. About 65 million years ago, the earth began to move beneath the Pacific coast, resulting in a period of intense mountain building, known as the Laramide Orogeny. The sedimentary rock that had been laid down by water and sand dunes was pushed upward in a series of monoclines, or folds, of which the Waterpocket Fold is one of the most spectacular.

Later, volcanic activity began. The deep molten rock pushed up the sedimentary rock and the landscape was reshaped once again. The Henry Mountains were created through this process. To the north of Capitol Reef, lava came to the surface along faults and helped create Thousand Lake Mountain. A third movement of the earth's surface caused the Colorado Plateau to be lifted between 1 and 2 miles above sea level. The forces of erosion began to work the new canvas of the earth's surface, and the result is a masterpiece of cliffs, towers, spires, natural bridges, canyons and valleys that constitute what is now Capitol Reef National Park.

Human ties to Capitol Reef have been tenuous, even though they stretch back more than 1,000 years to the prehistoric Fremont Indians who made the area their home. Archaeologists believe the Fremont occupied the area between A.D. 700 and 1300. The Indians made their home along the Fremont River because of its continual source of water. In the late 1920s, archaeologist Noel Morss identified the prehistoric residents along the Fremont River as a separate and distinct culture from the more widespread and populated Anasazi group to the south and east. Morss named this newly identified people the Fremont culture because he had done most of his research along the Fremont River.

While the scientific origins of the Fremont culture begin within Capitol Reef National

Park, the culture area covers a large part of Utah, extending north to the Uinta Mountains and west to the deserts of southwestern Utah. The Fremont people left a wealth of petroglyphs

> ## Getting There
> *Even though Capitol Reef is the most isolated of Utah's national parks, you can get to this central Utah area from all four directions.*
>
> **From Salt Lake City** *and northern locations, take Interstate 15 south to Nephi, then pick up Hwy. 28 and continue south to US Hwy. 89 and on to Salina. Get on Interstate 70 for a few miles west, then take the Sigurd exit to Hwy. 24, which takes you to Capitol Reef (about 80 miles from I-70). Total distance from Salt Lake City is 225 miles, so plan a 4-hour drive.*
>
> **From the east** *via Interstate 70, take Exit 147, about 12 miles west of Green River, onto Hwy. 24 south. At Hanksville (44 miles south of I-70), the highway turns west and continues for another 40 miles to Capitol Reef.*
>
> **From the southeast** *at Monument Valley, drive US Hwy. 163 north to Hwy. 261, then east on Hwy. 95, the bicentennial highway, past Natural Bridges National Monument northwest to Hanksville, then turn west on Hwy. 24, which continues through Capitol Reef.*
>
> **From the south,** *take US Hwy. 89 to Hwy. 12 east to Bryce Canyon, and continue through Escalante and Boulder, then cross the eastern flank of Boulder Mountain to Torrey and the intersection with Hwy. 24, a few miles west of Capitol Reef. Roads can be snowpacked in the winter, so you might want to take US Hwy. 89 north to Hwy. 62, just south of Junction, then continue east past Otter Creek Reservoir as it heads north to Koosharem and the junction with Hwy. 24, 5 miles north of Koosharem.*

and pictographs. Although similar in many ways, the Fremont are distinguishable from their neighbors, the Anasazi, by their use of leather moccasins fashioned with heels made from the dewclaw of a deer instead of woven fiber sandals; their continued use of pit-house dwellings instead of the large masonry buildings the Anasazi went on to build; the crafting of small unfired clay figurines; and the absence of domesticated dogs and turkeys as could be found among the Anasazi.

Archaeologists speculate that a severe, long-lasting drought and competition for scarce land and resources, or both, account for the demise of these two important prehistoric cultures. By A.D. 1300, both cultures had abandoned the region. While archaeologists trace the movement of the Anasazi to the Rio Grande and Little Colorado River drainages to the south, it is unclear what happened to the Fremont people. They may have been absorbed by other tribes; no one knows. When government explorers, gold prospectors and Mormon settlers penetrated the area in the 1870s, they found abundant evidence of the presence of earlier prehistoric peoples.

Beginning with Nels Johnson in 1878, several families homesteaded along the Fremont River within the present park boundaries. One of the settlers was Eph Hanks, a polygamist, who perhaps sought refuge from arrest in the remote region of the Fremont River. It was Hanks who realized that the heat-absorbing cliffs and the fertile river bottomland would be ideal for growing fruit and planted the first 200 fruit trees at Floral Ranch, 10 miles south of what today is the park's visitor center. Nels Johnson followed Hanks's example and planted fruit trees at what was called Junction. Around the turn of the 20th century, when the residents sought to establish a post office, they were not allowed to use the original name, as there were already too many Junctions in Utah. Instead they chose the name Fruita, to honor their excellent orchards and vineyards.

Although the population of Fruita was never large (the largest population, 46, was recorded in the 1900, 1910 and 1940 census), a sense of community was established in part with the construction of the one-room schoolhouse in 1896, which still stands. As early as 1910, a few local movers and shakers began to promote the area's potential and were successful in getting the Utah State Legislature to set aside 160 acres as a state park. Boosters promoted Wayne Wonderland. Local legislators twisted arms, and along with residents kept their crusade for national recognition before the public. Success came in 1937 when Capitol Reef was set aside as a national monument.

Access to the area was enhanced with the construction of a paved road through the area in 1962. After 1937 the monument was enlarged several times until 1971, when Capitol Reef became a national park. The National Park Service bought out the last residents of Fruita, and now the old town is park headquarters. It is the best base for exploring the park by several hiking trails and as the beginning point for the Scenic Dr. The Fruita Campground offers the only accommodations in the park. Fruit continues to grow and can be picked. As it was undoubtedly in earlier centuries, the Fruita area remains a welcome oasis to visitors.

Outdoor Activities

Biking

Bikes are not allowed to travel off-road or on any of the park trails or backcountry routes but the Cathedral Valley Road and the Scenic Drive described in the ScenicDrive Section are two favorites with bikers.

Hiking

Capitol Reef is for hikers, but hiking here is not like most other places. Experts warn that "rough terrain, scarce water and extreme weather make good physical condition a must. It is unwise to judge your abilities or water needs here based on experience elsewhere." Temperatures rise to almost unbearable levels, and the difficult terrain becomes even harder going in excessive heat. Spring and fall are the best times to enjoy the many hiking opportunities in the park. The hiking map and guide available for sale at the vis-

itor center lists 25 hiking routes ranging from less than a mile to nearly 25 miles in length. Twelve of the trails are maintained and begin close to the visitor center at Fruita.

For those traveling the Notom-Bullfrog Rd., there are several excellent hikes ranging in length from 2.5 miles to the 27-mile round-trip hike from Halls Creek Overlook to Halls Creek Narrows. In the Cathedral Valley area, there are several hikes that are well worth the time to get to. Backcountry hiking may be done throughout the park on rugged, unmarked terrain. Permits are required for backcountry camping. The following are some of the more popular hikes within the park.

FRUITA CAMPGROUND AREA
Cohab Canyon Trail

From the Fruita Campground, about 1 mile south of the visitor center on the Scenic Dr., the 1.75-mile-long Cohab Canyon Trail takes you to the top of Capitol Reef for a breathtaking overview of the center of Capitol Reef National Park. This is one of my favorite trails in the park because of its easy access and the sensation of coming upon a hidden canyon high above the valley floor. According to tradition, the canyon takes its name from Utah's polygamy days when local polygamists hid out in the canyon to avoid federal marshals who sought to arrest them for unlawful cohabitation.

The Cohab Canyon Trail begins across the road from the campground and heads east along steep switchbacks for 0.25 mile. As the trail levels out, you approach the head of Cohab Canyon, which is guarded by a wall of boulders. The trail winds through the rocks and drops into this canyon for a delightful walk along the dry streambed. Just before you reach the junction with the Frying Pan Trail, you can climb a trail up the north side of the canyon for about 0.25 mile onto the mesa high above the canyon for magnificent overviews of Fruita below and the cliffs and terrain to the north and southwest. The main trail continues up the south side of the canyon to the junction with the Frying Pan Trail, then east toward Hwy. 24.

Fremont River Trail

Near the Fruita Campground, about 1 mile south of the visitor center on the Scenic Dr., this 2.5-mile round-trip hike is really two trails in one. The first 0.5 mile is a level, pleasant walk along the river, past orchards and pastures. It is the only trail within the park that offers wheelchair access. The last mile is a strenuous hike up the north face of the cliff for a panoramic view of Fruita below and Capitol Reef to the east. This is a nice morning or evening hike. If you are not staying in the campground, you can park your car in the amphitheater parking in Campground C.

Frying Pan Trail

The Frying Pan Trail heads south off the Cohab Canyon Trail 1.1 miles from the trailhead to connect with the Cassidy Arch Trail and Grand Wash. The trail follows the top of Capitol Reef and is a strenuous 3-mile-long hike because of the many ups and downs; however, it is one that offers unique views of the park, away from the more populated and easier trails.

HWY. 24 AREA

Chimney Rock Loop Trail

If you enter Capitol Reef from the west, the Chimney Rock trailhead is the first you will encounter; it is 3 miles west of the visitor center. You can see the 400-foot-high, multilayered Chimney Rock from the highway. The trailhead is located just to the west of the rock. The first 0.25 mile climbs uphill to the beginning of the 3-mile-long loop.

If you take the trail to the right (south), you will continue a strenuous climb to the north and east of Chimney Rock onto the top of the mesa high above Hwy. 24 and Sulphur Creek. There are a couple of unmarked overlooks—one where you are on the same elevation as the top of Chimney Rock and another where you are high above it.

However, my recommendation for this hike is to take the trail to the left and continue east, following a gradual descent into Chimney Rock Canyon. You will have spectacular views of the red rock cliffs to your left (north). After a mile or so you reach the entrance into the upper portion of Spring Canyon. Watch for the trail signs—the left one points into Spring Canyon; take the right one, which turns to the south and makes a gradual but steady ascent, first to the south and then to the west as it parallels Hwy. 24 and climbs to the top of the mesa for a panoramic view of Capitol Reef and the 12,000-foot Henry Mountains to the east. After you cross the top of the mesa, you begin your descent and Chimney Rock comes into view. From here it is all downhill back to the beginning of the loop, then retracing your steps down the series of switchbacks to the trailhead.

Fremont Culture Walk

About a mile east of the visitor center off Hwy. 24, you can view some of the finest and most accessible Fremont Indian rock art in the park and anywhere in Utah. The petroglyphs are pecked into the south-facing sandstone ledges and include mountain goats, trapezoidal anthropomorphs and other figures. As you take the main trail from the parking area, the largest panel is just in front of you. But don't be content with these easy-to-spot figures. Continue east along the very short trail, perhaps 200–300 yards, as it runs parallel to the cliffs and to Hwy. 24. If you look carefully, you will spot other petroglyphs on the sandstone walls. When you come to a small alcove, go inside to see the initials and date, 1882, left by early travelers through the area.

Grand Wash

You can enter Grand Wash from either the parking area off Hwy. 24, about 4 miles east of the visitor center, or off the Scenic Dr. If you don't want to retrace the 2.2-mile-long hike and have access to two vehicles, you can arrange for a shuttle vehicle at either end. However you do it, this is one hike that you will want to make. An easy hike without any climbing, it takes you through the depths of the Waterpocket Fold into narrows where the cliffs rise hundreds of feet above you in a passage only a few yards wide. Here, you feel the power and majesty of the land, as you are enveloped by the rocks and become part of them rather than just an onlooker. Along the walls, watch for debris and other signs of the flash floods that have roared down the canyon. Do not hike when summer rainstorms are expected: rainwater is quickly funneled down these narrow canyons and destroys everything in its path.

Hickman Bridge Trail

There are few national parks in Utah without a natural bridge or arch. Capitol Reef's Hickman Bridge ranks with any in the state, and the hiking trail to the bridge offers breathtaking views of the Capitol Dome, Fruita and the Fremont River gorge. One of the most popular trails in Capitol Reef—this is not to be missed. Pick up a copy of the trail guide, either at the visitor center or at the trailhead, and use it at each of the 18 numbered posts. The trailhead is located about 2 miles east of the visitor center on the north side of Hwy. 24, where the Fremont River crosses to the north side of the highway.

The 2-mile round-trip trail climbs in a steady but gradual ascent from the trailhead. Along the way, you pass the foundation of a Fremont Indian pit house, a Fremont granary in a ledge just above the trail and a series of potholes (water pockets) and low-lying natural bridges carved by water. Named for Joseph S. Hickman, a local educator who worked to see Capitol Reef established as a national park, the natural bridge is 133 feet wide and 125 feet high. Be sure to continue on the trail around the back side of the bridge, rather than returning along the trail in front of the bridge. Then you can view the Fruita area and the junction of the Fremont River and Sulphur Creek from a high vantage point.

Rim Overlook Trail

About 0.3 mile up the Hickman Bridge Trail, you can head to the right (north) and take the Rim Overlook Trail. From the junction, the trail is 2 miles long as it climbs to the top of the cliffs on the north side of the Fremont River gorge. Part of the trail is across smooth slickrock, where your route is marked by rock cairns. The trail circles above Hickman Bridge as it heads west to the overlook point. From the overlook

you have an unobstructed view of Fruita below and the Scenic Dr. road, as it follows the west side of Waterpocket Fold. Total length of the trail from the Hickman Bridge trailhead to the rim and back is 4.6 miles.

TRAILS OFF SCENIC DR.
Capitol Gorge

This hike is 1.6 miles round trip, unless the 1.5-mile road into the gorge to the trailhead is closed to automobile traffic, as is sometimes the case. Like the Grand Wash hike, the Capitol Gorge route requires no climbing. It winds along narrow canyon bottoms beneath sheer-walled cliffs that offer some shade early in the morning and late in the afternoon. There is nothing quite like the confining walls of a narrow canyon to turn your thoughts inward and find peace within yourself. Within the gorge are the water pockets, or "tanks," that hold water in depressions in the rock, and an inscription rock known as the Pioneer Register. The earliest inscriptions are those of "Wal. Batemen" and "J. A. Call" in 1871. They were probably prospectors passing through looking for gold. The trailhead is located at the end of the Scenic Dr. approximately 12 miles south of the visitor center.

Cassidy Arch Trail

From the Grand Wash parking area on Scenic Dr., you can head downstream about 0.2 mile and watch for the Cassidy Arch Trail as it branches to the left. The 3.5-mile round-trip hike takes you onto the high cliffs above Grand Wash for an excellent view of Cassidy Arch. Unlike the Hickman Bridge, which was formed over a stream, the Cassidy Arch is the result of wind erosion. The arch is named for the outlaw Butch Cassidy, who, according to legend, had one of his hideouts in Grand Wash. The elevation gain to the arch is nearly 1,000 feet in less than 2 miles, so be prepared.

Golden Throne Trail

This is a 4-mile round-trip hike that begins at the Capitol Gorge parking area at the southern end of the Scenic Dr. and travels to the base of the Golden Throne, one of the domes atop the Navajo sandstone formation, nearly 1,000 feet above the gorge.

Horseback Riding

Hondoo Rivers and Trails

Trail rides into Capitol Reef National Park and pack trips into surrounding areas. **90 E. Main St., P.O. Box 750098, Torrey, UT 84775; 435-425-3519.**

Seeing and Doing

Children and Families

A grant from the National Park Foundation provided funds for the development of educational **fun packs** that focus on pioneer history, the Fremont Indian culture, geology, hydrology, plant and animal life and astronomy. The packs include field guides, binoculars, tracing paper, pioneer children's toys and other materials. The packs can be checked out free of charge for up to 24 hours at the park's visitor center.

Historic Sites

Elijah Cutler Behunin Cabin

Constructed in 1882 of red sandstone, this small cabin housed a family of 10 while Behunin attempted to homestead along the Fremont River. All 10 could not sleep in the cabin, so the girls slept in a wagon box and the boys in a dugout. Watch for the cabin along Hwy. 24 near the eastern boundary of the park. There is a parking area and interpretive sign at the cabin.

Historic Fruita

The Capitol Reef Visitor Center sits at the edge of the old Fruita town site. Park Service officials have done a good job of preserving and interpreting the historic Mormon settlement. Historic preservationists employed by the National Park Service have been at work to document the historic orchards (apple, cherry, pear, peach and apricot) and nominate the historic Fruita land-scape to the National Register of Historic Places. At the visitor center, pick up a brochure that describes the historic Fruita area and other sites to visit. Within the radius of less than a mile, you can visit several interesting buildings and sites.

The historic **Pendleton-Gifford Barn** was constructed in 1895 by Calvin Pendleton to store hay. The 2,000-square-foot barn is typical of hay barns constructed throughout Utah and the Intermountain West. The **Merin Smith Shed and Blacksmith Shop,** built in 1925, housed the first tractor in Fruita, which was known as a "power horse." The **Johnson Orchard** has been replanted with varieties of trees from the World War I era, as part of a living history exhibit and demonstration. The **Blue Dugway,** which served as the road between Fruita and Hanksville until 1961, can still be seen along the western exposure of the Waterpocket Fold.

The one-room **Fruita schoolhouse,** built in 1896, was used until 1941, when students were transported by bus over dirt roads to schools in Bicknell and Torrey. Tape-recorded recollections by Merin Smith talking about the blacksmith shop and Mrs. Torgerson, one of the teachers in the one-roomed school, relating her experiences as a teacher are a particularly nice feature of the interpretation provided here.

The Park

One of the most striking features of Capitol Reef is the beautiful park in the Fruita area through which the Fremont River and Sulphur Creek run. The park, part of the old community orchards and farming area, is a refreshing oasis in the otherwise harsh desert and mountains of stone. Take time to walk through the park and across the bridge, if you want a nice place to relax, read a book, stretch out for a nap or enjoy a nice picnic lunch or evening barbecue. The tall cottonwood and walnut trees offer ample shade even on the hottest of days.

Wolverton Mill

The mill was constructed by Edwin Thatcher Wolverton at a remote site on Mt. Pennell in the

Henry Mountains in 1921. Wolverton believed that he had found lost Spanish gold mines in the Henry Mountains and constructed his mill to process the gold from the mines. Reports of lost Spanish mines echo throughout Utah, and the Henry Mountain mines seem to have proven as intangible as the others that enthusiasts claim still exist. The BLM moved the Wolverton mill to Hanksville in 1974 because it was being vandalized. A self-guided tour explains the mill's use and technology. Located behind the BLM office in the southwestern part of Hanksville.

Nature Centers

Entrada Institute

Ask about any lectures or programs sponsored by the Entrada Institute, a nonprofit arts and educational center that works to develop greater understanding and appreciation for the historical, cultural, natural and scientific heritage of Capitol Reef and the Colorado Plateau region. The institute often attracts some of the West's most outstanding writers and scholars. **185 W. Main, Torrey, UT 84775; 435-425-3265.**

Scenic Drives

Cathedral Valley Loop

It is a shame that only a few visitors to Capitol Reef National Park see the Cathedral Valley section of the park. The red Entrada sandstone monoliths are reminiscent of European cathedrals. The tallest rocks reach more than 500 feet skyward from their base—the same height as Germany's world-famous Cologne Cathedral. Cathedral Valley is located in the extreme northern end of the park and laps the flanks of Thousand Lake Mountain. It is accessible only over dirt roads by high-clearance vehicles.

The Capitol Reef Natural History Association has prepared an excellent, inexpensive guide to Cathedral Valley, available at the visitor center. The tour describes the roads into Cathedral Valley and outlines a 59-mile loop that begins at the Fremont River ford off Hwy. 24, 11.5 miles east of the visitor center, and returns

to Hwy. 24 at Caineville, outside the park, 19 miles east of the visitor center. Travelers can purchase a copy of the guide and obtain current information on road conditions into the area at the Capitol Reef National Park visitor center.

The Fremont River ford is just that: there is no bridge, and you must drive your vehicle through the river—usually not much more than a foot deep. But it is advisable to get the river crossing out of the way at the beginning of the trip in case the river level rises. From the Fremont River ford, the dirt road heads northwestward through the South Desert to the Lower Cathedral Valley Overlook, 17.5 miles from the ford. A 1-mile hike to the overlook provides a spectacular view of the Temple of the Sun, the Temple of the Moon and other formations. Ten miles up the road is the Upper Cathedral Valley Overlook, which marks the halfway point of the loop and contains the tallest of the area's formations. It is impossible to describe all of the terrain you will cover in this loop, but it is a drive that you will not soon forget. **435-425-3791.**

Loa to Hanksville Scenic Byway / Hwy. 24

Hwy. 24 through Wayne County and Capitol Reef National Park has been officially designated one of Utah's 27 Scenic Byways. The 70-mile stretch passes through spectacular scenery with the Waterpocket Fold at its center. In Loa, there are two interesting Mormon buildings you can visit: the **Loa Stake Tabernacle** (located at 100 W. and 100 N.), constructed between 1906 and 1909, and the earlier **Loa Tithing Office** (located at 100 W. and Center St.), which dates from 1897.

Continuing eastward, the highway passes through high valley farmlands and by the **Bicknell Gristmill,** located in a beautiful meadow near a poplar-lined stream, about 3 miles east of Bicknell on the north side of the road. The two-story frame gristmill was constructed in 1890 for Hans Peter Nielsen. Nielsen emigrated from Denmark to Utah in 1863. He was a miller in his native country and operated the Bicknell Gristmill until his death in 1909. The mill was operated by various individuals until 1935, when the long arm of the Great Depression ended operations at the mill. Much of the original machinery and equipment remain inside the mill, but it is unfortunately not open to the public.

Past Bicknell, the road continues through Torrey and into **Capitol Reef National Park,** where it follows the Fremont River past the red rock formations, then the blue-colored Mancos shale hills and on to Hanksville.

Notom Rd. Backway

This road is recommended only for high-clearance vehicles. It begins from Hwy. 24 at the eastern boundary of Capitol Reef and heads south to the Burr Trail at the southern end of the park. The road parallels the eastern exposure of the Waterpocket Fold for its entire 29-mile length south of Hwy. 24. As you continue southward, the "breakers" of the fold get deeper and deeper. The road offers fantastic views of the fold and the Henry Mountains in the distance.

Scenic Dr.

Every visitor to Capitol Reef must take the 25-mile Scenic Dr. that follows the old Blue Dugway wagon road and provides access to Grand Wash, Capitol Gorge, Golden Throne and Pleasant Creek. Pick up the free brochure *A Guide to the Scenic Drive* at the visitor center and use it for information on the 11 designated stops along the drive.

The Scenic Dr. leaves the visitor center on Hwy. 24 and winds through part of historic Fruita, then heads south along the western side of the Waterpocket Fold. The road is paved for the 12 or so miles to Sleeping Rainbow Ranch (Sleeping Rainbow was the Paiute name for the Waterpocket Fold because of its many soft colors), but the narrow, twisty road (and National Park Service policy) does not permit speeds of more than 30 miles an hour. Plan to spend at least a half day. This should allow time to stop at each of the designated stops, to hike Capitol Wash and, if you want, to make the strenuous trek up the Golden Throne Trail. (See the Hiking section under Outdoor Activities.)

Wildlife Viewing

The park offers plenty of opportunity to view wildlife. In the morning, mule deer can be seen in the orchards and pastures in Fruita. Drivers must exercise great caution along the roads—to watch out for deer and also for visitors who stop suddenly to photograph the deer that come down to feed and drink. Other "quiet desert" residents of the park include gray foxes, cougars, bobcats, coyotes, many varieties of lizards, water snakes, gopher snakes and two varieties of poisonous rattlesnakes—the prairie rattlesnake and the small, faded midget rattlesnake. You have the best chance of seeing the shy wildlife at twilight along the Fremont River and in the canyon bottoms. Golden eagles, hawks, warblers, grosbeaks and many species of swallows also reside in the park.

Where to Stay

Accommodations

There are no accommodations, other than a campground, within Capitol Reef National Park; however, in the nearby communities of Torrey, Teasdale, Bicknell and Loa to the west and Caineville and Hanksville to the east, you can find a number of motels and the following favorites.

WEST OF THE PARK
Best Western Capitol Reef Resort— $$ to $$$

Swimming pool and hot tub; 50 rooms. **2600 E. Hwy. 24, P.O. Box 750160, Torrey, UT 84775; 1-888-610-9600; 435-425-3761.**

The Lodge at Red River Ranch— $$$ to $$$$

The Old Faithful Lodge at Yellowstone National Park inspired John Alexander to create a modern facility that looked like an old historic lodge. The lodge, located along the Fremont River a few miles west of the park, does fulfill Alexander's dream. Each of the 15 rooms is decorated with impressive artwork, furnishings and Navajo blankets and rugs, which Alexander began collecting several decades ago. Designed to provide a real getaway experience, there are no telephones or televisions in the rooms, but those instruments of modern civilization are close at hand for emergencies. Located a few miles west of Torrey just off Hwy. 24. **P.O. Box 69, Teasdale, UT 84773; 1-800-205-6343; 435-425-3322; www.redriverranch.com.**

Muley Twist Inn—$$$

Named for the Muley Twist Canyon—a place along the Burr Trail that was so wild and difficult that one early traveler declared it would "twist a mule" to get through it—this brand-new bed and breakfast inn sits on 30 acres of land just to the northwest of Teasdale. Each of the five rooms in the two-story inn has a private bath. Several of the rooms have spectacular views, and the large front porch is perfect to sit and relax and enjoy the unbelievable view toward Capitol Reef and Thousand Lakes Mountain. Innkeepers Eric and Penny Kinsman are excellent hosts and provide a delicious full breakfast. **P.O. Box 117, Teasdale, UT 84773; 1-800-530-1038; 435-425-3640; www.rof.net/yp/muley.**

Skyridge Bed and Breakfast—$$$$

Ever since it opened in 1994, the Skyridge Bed and Breakfast has received praise from travelers and travel writers alike. Sunset Magazine named it one of the 24 best inns throughout the West. Appropriately named, Skyridge sits on the top of a ridge surrounded by 75 acres of land with a fantastic view of Capitol Reef, Boulder Mountain and the Torrey area. Capitol Reef National Park is only a few miles away. The five rooms have private baths and TVs with VCRs. Some have a private deck, and the patio, hot tub and living room/library are available. Owners Shauna and Jerry Agnew provide a full breakfast of seasonal fruit and juice, homemade granola and fresh baked muffins for starters, followed by a hot entrée of pecan griddle cakes and sausage, veggie-cheese soufflés or apple-stuffed French toast. Snacks are provided in the evening. Located on Hwy. 24 just east of its intersection with Hwy. 12. **P.O. Box 750220, Torrey, UT 84775; 435-425-3222; www.bbiu.org/skyridge/.**

Wonderland Inn—$$ to $$$

Swimming pool and hot tub; 50 rooms. Open year-round. Located at the junction of Hwy. 12 and Hwy. 24. **P.O. Box 67, Torrey, UT 84775; 1-800-458-0216; 435-425-3775; www.capitolreefwonderland.com.**

EAST OF THE PARK
Caineville Cove Inn—$$

Swimming pool and hot tub; 16 rooms, all with microwaves and refrigerators. **HC-70, P.O. Box 80, Hwy. 24, Caineville, UT 84775; 1-435-456-9133; 435-456-9900.**

Whispering Sands Motel—$$

Twenty-three rooms. **44 S. Hwy. 95, P.O. Box 68, Hanksville, UT 84734; 435-542-3238.**

Camping

PRIVATE
Aquarius Mobile and RV Campground

Twenty-four sites, all with complete hookups. Open year-round. **220 S. 100 E., Bicknell; 435-425-3835.**

Red Rock Campground

Forty-five RV trailer sites, 38 with complete hookups, and 15 tentsites. Toilets, showers and a laundry. Open Apr.–Oct. Located at the junction of Hwys. 95 and 24 in Hanksville. **435-542-3235.**

Sandcreek RV Park and Campground

Fifty RV and tent spaces. Showers, laundry, gift shop and store. **540 Hwy. 24, Torrey; 435-425-357.**

Thousand Lakes RV Park

Forty-four RV sites, 38 with complete hookups, and 50 tentsites. Drinking water, toilets, showers and laundry facilities. Open Apr.–Oct. Located 1 mile west of Torrey on Hwy. 24. **435-425-3288.**

Wonderland Resort RV Park

Thirty-three spaces with full hookups; convenience store across the street. Open Apr.–Oct. Located at the junction of Hwys. 12 and 24 in Torrey. **435-425-3775.**

PUBLIC
In the Park

There are three campgrounds within the national park; however, two are small, primitive and difficult to reach. Most campers in the park stay at the **Fruita Campground,** located along the Scenic Dr. 1 mile from the visitor center. There are 63 RV trailer sites and a large, open tent area; drinking water, toilets and wheelchair-accessible facilities. The two primitive campgrounds are the **Cathedral Campground,** in Cathedral Valley, with 5 tentsites, and in the southern section, **Cedar Mesa Campground,** also with 5 tentsites. No fees are charged at Cathedral and Cedar Mesa, but campers must bring their own water. Fees are charged at Fruita. All three campgrounds are open year-round.

Where to Eat

WEST OF THE PARK
Brinks Burgers—$

If you are in a hurry and the crowd is not too large, Brinks Burgers is a good place for burgers, sandwiches, fries, onion rings, shakes and ice-cream cones. Open 11 A.M.–8 P.M.; closed during the winter. **165 E. Main St., Torrey; 435-425-3710.**

Cafe Diablo—$$ to $$$

Owner and chef Gary Pankow is a graduate of the Culinary Institute of New York who worked in Deer Valley and Salt Lake City restaurants before striking out on his own in Torrey. As you might expect, he offers a variety of dishes with a focus on Southwest cuisine. Some of the most popular items among the 13 regular menu entrées include the Chipotle Fired Ribs—baby back ribs smothered in chipotle sauce; Pumpkin Seed Crusted Fresh Trout; Painted Chicken—

char-grilled chicken breast brushed with lime and honey; and marinated pork tenderloin. Jane Pankow is responsible for a delicious selection of pastries and desserts. Located in a little white house with red trim on the west edge of Torrey. Open mid-Apr.–mid-Oct. daily 4–10 P.M. **599 W. Hwy. 24, Torrey; 435-425-3070.**

Capitol Reef Cafe—$ to $$

Part of the Capitol Reef Inn, the Capitol Reef Cafe is part of a private Shangri-la that Southey Swede has established for himself in the isolated reaches of south-central Utah. Southey gave up a successful psychology career in California and moved to Torrey a number of years ago. His cafe offers a strong vegetarian menu with such dishes as stir-fry vegetables served with brown and wild rice, mushroom lasagna, fettuccine primavera and a vegetarian omelette for breakfast. The Capitol Reef dinner salad is a delicious mixture of 10 fresh vegetables. Other entrées include trout, steak and chicken. Freshly squeezed juices and espresso drinks are a delight. The cafe also has a well-stocked bookstore that features books on local and regional history and the natural history of the Capitol Reef area. Open daily 7–11 A.M. and 5–9 P.M. **360 W. Main St., Torrey; 435-425-3271.**

Red Cliff Restaurant—$ to $$

Located in the Best Western Capitol Reef Resort, between Torrey and the national park, this is a friendly and clean restaurant with a reputation for good food. In the evenings, you can have Dutch-oven-cooked beef and chicken with real mashed potatoes and homemade rolls. For breakfast, the breakfast bar offers all-you-can-eat bacon, sausage, scrambled eggs, pancakes, biscuits and gravy, hash browns and fresh fruit at a reasonable price for adults, and a special price for children under 10. Without any drapes on the windows, you can enjoy a 270-degree panoramic view of the landscape. **2600 E. Hwy. 24, Torrey; 435-425-3761.**

Wonderland Inn Restaurant—$ to $$

A part of the Wonderland Inn Motel located at

the junction of Hwys. 12 and 24 just a few miles west of Capitol Reef National Park, this restaurant serves steaks and trout for dinner, sandwiches for lunch (with sack lunches to go) and hearty breakfasts. A breakfast favorite is the Wonderlands Haystack with melted cheese, diced ham, bell peppers, onions and two eggs (any style) piled high on hash browns. Open Mar.–Oct. daily 7 A.M.–9 P.M.; the rest of the year 7 A.M.–7 P.M. Located off Hwy. 24 a mile east of Torrey. **435-425-3775.**

EAST OF THE PARK
Luna Mesa Cantina—$ to $$
Serves a variety of hamburgers, sandwiches, tacos and burritos along with American and Mexican dinners. Open Apr.–Oct. daily 9 A.M.–9 P.M. Located on Hwy. 24 in Caineville, about halfway between the national park and Hanksville. **435-456-9122.**

Red Rock Restaurant—$ to $$
Breakfast, lunch and dinner. Open May–Sept. daily 7 A.M.–9 P.M.; closed during the winter. Located at the junction of Hwys. 24 and 95 in Hanksville. **435-542-3235.**

Services

Visitor Information
Capitol Reef National Park Visitor Center—Make this your first stop to check on guided hikes and evening programs, obtain backcountry permits, purchase maps and other publications and view the exhibits and large relief map of the park. Open mid-Apr.–Oct. daily 8 A.M.–7 P.M.; during the winter 8 A.M.–4:30 P.M. There is no food or lodging (other than camping) available in the park. The Scenic Dr., which leads to the campground, begins at the visitor center. Visitors register and pay for camping at the campground; the entrance fee for the park is paid beyond the campground at a self-pay station on the Scenic Dr. Located on Hwy. 24 at Fruita, 11 miles east of Torrey. **HC-70, Box 15, Torrey, UT 84775; 435-425-3791; 435-425-3794 visitor center; www.nps.gov/care.**

Wayne County Travel Council—P.O. Box 7, Teasdale, UT 84773; 1-800-858-7951; **www.capitolreef.org.**

Southwestern
Region

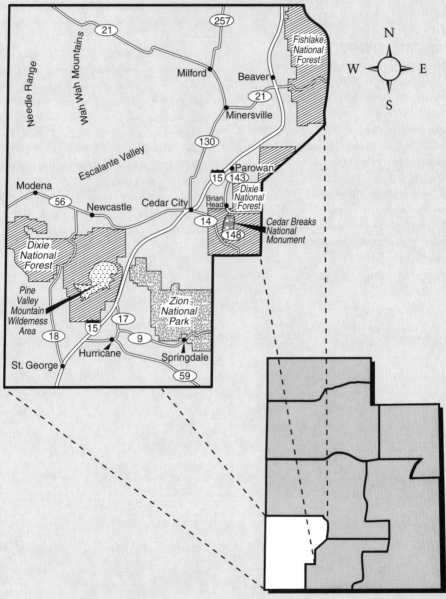

Beaver

Situated halfway between Salt Lake City and Las Vegas, Nevada, Beaver is one of southern Utah's undiscovered treasures. Relatively few skiers have found out about the uncrowded slopes at Elk Meadows. Puffer Lake remains a spot primarily for local anglers. Hiking trails in the Tushar Mountains see little use. The treasure of historic rock and brick pioneer homes in Beaver are seldom noticed, and the ghost towns of Frisco and Newhouse largely unexplored. Rock hounds have only begun to scratch the surface (so to speak) of the treasure house of minerals and gems found throughout the area.

One of the attractions of Beaver is that it does not appear that these resources will soon be overdeveloped. If you're seeking a chance to catch your breath and unwind from the hectic pace of today's world in a place that's full of activities but does not draw the crowds that other southern Utah locations do, Beaver might just be for you.

History

A number of prehistoric sites, dating back to the Archaic and Sevier Fremont periods, have been identified in Beaver County, including obsidian quarry sites in the Mineral Mountains that apparently supplied stone tools for many of central and southern Utah's prehistoric inhabitants. Southern Paiutes met members of the 1776 Dominguez-Escalante Expedition as the Spaniards journeyed from north to south through present-day Milford.

Described by Escalante as "the Bearded Utes," 80 years later the Southern Paiutes encountered Mormon settlers moving into Beaver Valley from Parowan 35 miles to the south. Beaver was initially settled because of its potential for livestock grazing. Raising cattle and sheep has always been an important part of the area's economy. Beaver's economy was enhanced by four factors during the 1870s: an aggressive move to establish woolen mill, tannery and dairy industries; the establishment of Ft. Cameron by the U.S. Army in 1873; a mining boom launched in the 1870s; and the arrival of the Utah Southern Railroad at Milford in 1880.

A local newspaper editor boasted that Beaver would soon be the largest city in the territory, with 20-story skyscrapers pushing upward to rival the mighty Tushar Mountains looming over the city. But by World War I mining was on the wane and Ft. Cameron had long been abandoned by the army. While there are no 20-story skyscrapers in Beaver, an impressive number of 19th-century brick and stone homes and buildings leave a legacy of historic buildings rivaled by few towns in the West.

In 1979 the U.S. Air Force announced plans to establish a new intercontinental ballistic missile system in the desert west of Beaver and Milford. The MX missile system was to be deployed on a circular railroad track that would move more than 200 missiles into 4,600 shelters to be constructed along the track. While many locals saw the MX project as the economic golden calf they had dreamed of for decades, others, who ultimately included Utah's Gov. Scott Matheson and the leaders of the Church of Jesus Christ of Latter-day Saints, spoke out against it. With the election of Ronald Reagan in 1980, enthusiasm for the project began to wane, especially as President Reagan favored his own Strategic Defense Initiative, which would be based in space rather than in the isolated valleys of western Utah. A quarter of

Getting There

Beaver is 200 miles south of Salt Lake City and 100 miles north of St. George on Interstate 15.

a century later, the MX project is a discarded relic of the Cold War that, had it been implemented, would have placed off-limits one of the most interesting and isolated areas of the American West.

Festivals and Events

Pioneer Day

July 24. Horse races at the racetrack, dozens of floats and entries in the parade, a full day of events, a tricycle race and a 5-kilometer race. **435-438-2975.**

Outdoor Activities

Biking

The Tushar Mountains east of Beaver offer a number of good bike routes that allow you to experience the beauty and isolation of the seldom-traveled routes in the area. Maps are available at the **U.S. Forest Service office, Beaver Ranger District, 190 N. 100 E., Beaver; 435-438-2436.**

Beaver Canyon

This 36-mile round-trip route travels Hwy. 153 to Elk Meadows Ski Area. The route starts in the center of Beaver, just north of the high school building on Main St. The first 2 miles take you past the Canyon Breeze Golf Course (see the Golf section), rodeo grounds and racetrack and the site of Ft. Cameron (see the Historic Sites section under Seeing and Doing) before entering Beaver Canyon. The first 10 miles of the route climb gradually from 6,000 feet just east of Beaver to 7,000 feet. The route follows Beaver Creek to Ponderosa Picnic Ground near mile 9 and Mahogany Cove Picnic Ground at mile 11. At Mahogany Cove, the road becomes noticeably steeper as it switches back and forth up the side of the mountain. Merchant Valley Dam is located near the 15-mile mark, and the end of the ride at Elk Meadows Ski Area is at 9,200 feet, 3 miles beyond the dam. If you don't mind a steep climb

and sharing a narrow road with a few automobiles and trucks, this route promises a good workout to the top and exhilarating descent down the mountain on the return leg.

Puffer Lake Loop

For riders looking for a scenic high-country loop road, the 8-mile Puffer Lake Loop is one of Utah's best. The ride begins just beyond the Big Flat Ranger Station, 24 miles east of Beaver. To reach the ranger station, follow Hwy. 153 east from Beaver for 18 miles to where the paved road ends and the gravel road begins near Elk Meadows. Continue along the gravel road past Puffer Lake to Big Flat, then continue for 6 miles to Forest Rd. 581, which begins just south of the Big Flat Ranger Station and heads east. This is the beginning point of the loop.

Follow the road east, then keep to the left as the trail turns north to climb past City Creek Peak 2 miles into the ride. Continuing north another 2 miles, the trail follows the ridge overlooking Piute Reservoir to the east and continues along the Skyline Trail toward Lake Peak and Mt. Holly. At the intersection with Forest Rd. 129, turn left and head west around the north shore of Puffer Lake to the intersection of Hwy. 153 at the northwestern end of the lake. Turn back south and follow Hwy. 153 about 3 miles back to the starting point.

Fishing

Minersville Lake State Recreation Area

The most accessible and most popular boating and fishing spot in the area is Minersville Reservoir. Although Mormon pioneers had constructed dams on the river as early as 1860, a permanent dam on the river was not built until 1914. Named the Rocky Ford Dam, after the boulder-strewn wagon-road crossing of the river just below the dam, the original structure continues to impound the waters of the 1,130-surface-acre Minersville Reservoir. The reservoir is maintained as a state park, and facilities include picnic sites, drinking water, modern rest rooms, showers, sewage disposal, electrical hookups for

29 units and 18 tentsites. Fee is charged. Open for year-round fishing. Located on the Beaver River, about 10 miles west of the town of Beaver along Hwy. 21.

Puffer Lake

Puffer Lake is a natural mountain lake that was discovered by James Puffer in 1865. Located at an elevation of 9,700 feet, the lake is fed by the snowfields of the surrounding 12,000-foot-plus peaks of Mt. Belknap, Baldy Peak and Delano Peak. According to tradition, the lake was not only named in honor of its discoverer but in gratitude by an early group of fishermen who were guided to the lake by James Puffer. Located 22 miles east of Beaver on Hwy. 153.

Golf

Canyon Breeze Golf Course

If it's a nice summer day and the urge for a quick game of golf hits as you are driving along Interstate 15 through southern Utah, you won't do any better than to stop in Beaver to play the Canyon Breeze course. This 9-hole, 2,746-yard, par 34 golf course was laid out in 1965 on part of the site of old Ft. Cameron at the mouth of Beaver Canyon. The trees along the course are mature and add to the beauty of the course, along with a nice one-and-a-half-story pink rock house and well-weathered barn and outbuildings along the right side of the 3rd hole. It's also the only golf course I know that is closed for horse races. The tee box for the par 5, 485-yard 7th hole is located on the infield at the southwestern corner of the racetrack.

But the closure of the course for horse races four times a year is more than offset by the ease of getting on the course. No reservations are needed. Simply show up and expect to be sent out to the first hole. Weather permitting, the course is open Mar.–Nov. **371 N. Hwy. 153; 435-438-2601.**

Hiking

Delano Peak / Mt. Holly

At 12,129 feet, Delano Peak is the highest peak in the Tushar Mountains. It can be reached by a 5-mile hike from Elk Meadows Ski Area. The trailhead begins at an elevation of about 9,700 feet, and the route generally follows a northeasterly course for approximately 4 miles to the saddle between Mt. Holly and Delano Peak. The elevation gain to this point is approximately 2,000 feet. Once you reach the saddle, you can turn right for a half-mile climb to the top of Mt. Holly, or turn left for the mile ascent to Delano Peak. Whichever route you choose, you will have panoramic views of the Tushar Mountains, the Great Basin ranges to the west and Piute Reservoir and the Fishlake Mountains to the east. The round-trip hike of 11 miles (including the side trip up Mt. Holly) is a good daylong hike for most hikers and is best taken in the middle of the summer, when the days are long and the high mountain temperatures cool but pleasant. Drive Hwy. 153 east from Beaver for 18 miles to the ski area at pavement's end.

Skyline National Recreation Trail

This trail takes you along the tops of the Tushar Mountains at an elevation of 10,100 to 11,100 feet. Along the hike you have fine views to the west, and below to the east are Circle Valley and Piute Reservoir. The trail winds through thick stands of spruce, fir and aspen trees and open meadows dotted with wildflowers. Watch for deer and elk in the meadows, mountain goats on the rock slopes of Mt. Holly and Lake Peak, and soaring eagles along much of the trail.

The entire trail is 8.3 miles from the Big Flat trailhead to the Big John Flat trailhead. You can arrange for a shuttle at one trailhead for an 8.3 one-way hike (see Big John Flat/Kimberly Trail in the Biking section for directions to that trailhead); you can hike the entire length out-and-back for a full-day's hike of 16.6 miles; or you can hike just a portion of the trail out-and-back and return to your vehicle at the Big Flat trailhead. To reach the Big Flat trailhead, follow Hwy. 153 east from Beaver for 18 miles to where the pavement ends near Elk Meadows. Continue along the gravel road past Puffer Lake to Big Flat, then continue for 6 miles to the Big

Flat Ranger Station. Watch for a road sign 0.25 mile south of the Big Flat Ranger Station. The trailhead is 200 yards east of Hwy. 153, 24 miles east of Beaver.

Wah Wah Mountains

It's hard to believe that the Indian name for these mountains means "good, clear water." But descriptive names are relative to the local circumstances. Given the surrounding desert and the fact that Wah Wah Springs, located on the east slope of the mountains about 7 miles west of the mining town of Newhouse, was an important water source for travelers, livestock men and the 6,000 residents of Newhouse, no doubt water from these western Utah mountains did seem "good and clear" to early visitors and residents of the area. For information on the area, contact **Beaver River Resource Area, Bureau of Land Management, 444 S. Main, Cedar City, UT 84720; 435-586-2458.**

The hike along the ridge of the mountains is generally cross-country without a well-defined trail. From the trailhead at about 8,100 feet, the route climbs to Wah Peak at 9,383 feet, a distance of 3.5 miles. Bristlecone pines, several thousand years old, can be seen on the ridge to the east of Wah Peak. Plan 4–5 hours to make the round-trip hike. There are few travelers, let alone hikers, in this area, making isolation and solitude attractive features of this hike. The hike also offers spectacular views of Pine Valley and the desert 4,000 feet below.

The trailhead is reached by taking Hwy. 21 west from Beaver through Milford, continuing on about 24 miles beyond Milford, before turning left (south) off the highway onto a gravel road near milepost 54. Follow the road in a southwesterly direction along the eastern slope for 15.5 miles to the highest point on the backbone of the mountains and begin your hike at this point.

Skiing

DOWNHILL

Elk Meadows Ski Area

If you are looking for an out-of-the-way, uncrowded but easily accessible ski area committed to teaching beginning skiers of all ages, Elk Meadows deserves careful consideration. Here, the emphasis is on skiing rather than on fashion, nightlife and other amenities typical of big, expensive resorts. One longtime fan of Elk Meadows wrote, "We've been going there every year since about '79, when it was just called Mt. Holly, and the skiing is great. The lines are almost nonexistent, the people are friendly and the prices are well below average. All this because it's not very close to anywhere big, and that's the way we like it." *Ski* magazine has given the ski school its highest possible ranking for teaching children. The SkiWee half-day and full-day programs for 4 to 12 year olds offer all levels of instruction, lift passes, ski rentals, supervision and lunch at reasonable rates. Lift tickets are usually the lowest in the state. Located 4 hours from Las Vegas or Salt Lake City on Interstate 15, or 9 hours from Los Angeles and Phoenix.

Elk Meadows consists of two areas. The Upper Meadows has two lifts for beginners and those who enjoy their skiing away from the deep powder, steep slopes and people-eating moguls of the more advanced runs. These lifts descend from Tushar Ridge at 10,400 feet to the West Village Base Lodge at 9,200 feet. The second area is located below Tushar Ridge, close to the lodge, and caters to more advanced skiers. The ski season usually runs Thanksgiving–Apr. Open daily 9 A.M.–4 P.M. Lodging is available a short walk from the ski lifts, at prices considerably lower than at other resorts, or at very modest rates 18 miles away in Beaver (see the Where to Stay section). Located 15 miles east of Beaver on Hwy. 153. **1-888-881-7669; 435-438-5433; www. elkmeadows.com.**

Seeing and Doing

Historic Sites

Ft. Cameron

Named for Civil War hero Col. James Cameron, who was killed during the Battle of Bull Run, Ft. Cameron was established in 1873 to control the

"Indian problem" in southern Utah. After more than two decades in the area, Mormons had effectively "handled" the Indians, and it was really the "Mormon problem" that federal troops were sent to southern Utah to keep in check. Despite congressional action outlawing polygamy, Mormons continued to practice it, though they were continually suspected of disloyalty toward the federal government. About 250 soldiers were stationed at Ft. Cameron until 1882, when the fort was abandoned.

The dozen or so buildings and the land were sold to the Mormons for a song. Church leaders established an educational academy, known first as the Beaver Branch of Brigham Young Academy, the forerunner of Brigham Young University, and later as Murdock Academy, which provided high school training until the early 1920s when a public high school was established. During the 1920s, all of the buildings were demolished except one, the laundress quarters, which was last used in 1937 and 1938 to house a branch of the Civilian Conservation Corps. Located 1 mile east of Beaver on Hwy. 153

Frisco Ghost Town

Silver was discovered at Frisco in 1878, and it soon became a booming mining town with a reported 23 saloons and enough boardinghouses and restaurants to serve a population that reached 6,500 by the mid-1880s. Frisco's Horn Silver Mine was both productive and difficult to work. Fred Hewitt, a mining engineer who visited the Horn Silver Mine in 1880, reported that after being lowered in a cage down a shaft to the 900-foot level, they descended another 700 feet by walking down a 31-degree incline.

There is not much left at Frisco, but the charcoal kilns are well worth a visit. They stand today more like ancient religious shrines than the most visible reminder of the once prosperous silver mining area of Frisco. The five beehive kilns were constructed in 1877 by the Frisco Mining and Smelting Company to provide fuel for the smelting of ore from the nearby Horn Silver Mine. Charcoal was produced until about 1884, at which time the smelter was closed and ore from

the mines was shipped to coke-fired smelters in Salt Lake City. Still, the Frisco charcoal kilns are a reminder of a time when mining held the promise of prosperity in an otherwise desolate land.

The former town now has only a few foundations remaining, but once was inhabited by some 6,500 people between 1880 and 1885. Some are buried in the cemetery, which is well worth a visit as the old tombstones give terse testimony of the fate of both children and adults. Drive west of Beaver on Hwy. 21 through Milford, continuing on 15 miles west of Milford. Between mileposts 62 and 63, a dirt road leads off the highway to the right (northwest). The cemetery is located away from the town site; from the Frisco monument along Hwy. 21, take the dirt road to the left for about a half mile.

Newhouse Ghost Town

This ghost town, located 7 miles northwest of Frisco, bears one of the most famous names in Utah mining history. Samuel Newhouse made successful investments in the Bingham Canyon Copper Mine near Salt Lake City and, in 1900, along with investors from England and France, opened the Cactus Mine. Five years later the town of Newhouse was established. Residences of stuccoed adobe, brick, rock and wood were constructed near a business district that included several stores, a livery stable, a hospital, a library, an opera house, a dance hall and a hotel.

About 1910 the Cactus Mine gave out, putting miners out of work and causing the town's sudden demise. It also saw the end of an ambitious plan by Newhouse to set up a non-Mormon business district in Salt Lake City that would rival the older Mormon business district to the north near the temple. Partly with earnings from the Cactus Mine, Newhouse constructed several buildings that still remain Salt Lake City landmarks, including the Boston and Newhouse Buildings, two of Utah's first skyscrapers. Reach Newhouse by driving west of Beaver on Hwy. 21 through Milford, continuing on 19.7 miles west of Milford, then turning north along a dirt road and continuing 2 miles.

BEAVER

If you are looking for a Utah town that is a veritable museum of 19th-century houses, you need search no further than Beaver. There are more than 100 historic buildings, ranging from the early log cabins and one-story adobe houses of the 1860s to beautiful examples of black rock, pink rock and brick homes built during the 1870s and 1880s. Characteristic of Beaver architecture are the black basalt rock houses and pink tuff houses, which were built during the prosperous years of the last quarter of the 19th century by two Scottish stonemasons, Thomas Frazer and Alexander Boyter.

Thomas Frazer, a convert to the Mormon church while living in Scotland, had immigrated to Utah in the 1860s and was asked by church authorities to move to Beaver in 1868 in order to improve the quality of building construction in the town. Unlike Frazer, Alexander Boyter had come to Beaver with the U.S. Army as a non-Mormon. Boyter learned his stonemason skills while serving at Ft. Cameron, just east of Beaver, rather than in "the old country" as had Frazer. Frazer initially worked with black basalt, whereas Boyter made principal use of the pink tuff, which was softer and easier to work than the hard basalt.

While all of these houses are private residences and not open to visitors, a walking or driving tour of the following buildings will give you a good idea of some of the remarkable architectural treasures of Beaver. Each of these buildings has been listed in the National Register of Historic Places. But don't be tied to the following list. A fun exercise, especially with children, is to cover a section of the town and see how many black rock, pink rock, old brick, stuccoed adobe and log homes you can identify.

Alexander Boyter House

Scottish stonemason Alexander "Scotty" Boyter built his own house of pink tuff in 1882. According to local folklore, Boyter quarried the stone for his house three times, but sold it all twice before constructing the one-and-a-half-story house for his family. When he finally began work on his own house, he made sure that it would be a showcase of his skill. The stone was tooled to a smooth finish and the mortar was dyed to match the pink rock. **590 N. 200 W.**

Beaver Carnegie Library

Scottish-born American industrialist Andrew Carnegie believed that the wealthy should use their money to help their fellow human beings. One of the most worthwhile ways he accomplished this was to help construct more than 2,500 public library buildings around the world. This effort began in 1881, when Carnegie built a library for his hometown of Dunfermline, Scotland, and continued for nearly four decades until 1917. One of the last libraries financed by Carnegie was the Beaver Library, built in 1917. The arrangement with Carnegie was that each community furnished the building site, books, interior furnishings and an annual maintenance budget equal to one-tenth the building cost, which was used to pay for the upkeep and operation of the building, the salary of a librarian and the purchase of new books. The building has served the community of Beaver for three-quarters of a century and, with a recent addition to the rear, the library will continue at this location for many years. **50 W. Center St.**

Beaver Historical Park / Philo T. Farnsworth Memorial

There are few individuals who have challenged Brigham Young for equal billing as Utah's most important historic figure, but in 1987, 110 years after the death of the Mormon leader, Beaver-born Philo T. Farnsworth did. That year, following a campaign launched by a Salt Lake City sixth-grade class, Farnsworth was chosen as Utah's second person (Brigham Young being the first) to be honored with a statue in Statuary Hall in the U.S. Capitol in Washington, D.C.

Named for his grandfather, an early Mormon pioneer to Utah and one of the original 1856 founders of Beaver, Philo T. Farnsworth was born Aug. 19, 1906, in his grandfather's log cabin on Indian Creek just north of Beaver. While Brigham Young has been praised as "the Great Colonizer," Philo T. Farnsworth's star shines even brighter as "the Father of Television." In 1927, at the age of 21, Farnsworth demonstrated the first all-electrical television system and, later, successfully defended the patents for his invention. Farnsworth had a natural talent for physics, and his experiments helped in the development of radar, electron microscopes, aircraft guidance systems and incubators for newborn babies. He made millions with his inventions, but died in debt in 1971 at the age of 64. A statue of Farnsworth as a young man has been placed in the Beaver Heritage Park, located just west of the old courthouse. Located at **Center St. and 100 E.**

Beaver Opera House

It is estimated that as many as 30 opera houses were built in Utah before World War I. Most of them have been demolished or severely altered, leaving the Beaver Opera House as the best-preserved opera house in the state. Constructed between 1908 and 1909 at a cost of $20,000, the theater provided seating for 1,000 people and was considered by one commentator to be the "finest playhouse south of Salt Lake." In addition to theatrical performances, the building was used as a dance pavilion, a gymnasium and, in later years, a movie theater. Between 1929 and 1955, the local unit of the National Guard was housed here. It served as storage for another 30 years until it was renovated in 1988. It is now the Beaver Civic Center. **55 E. Center.**

Duckworth Grimshaw House

The crown jewel of Thomas Frazer's work, this one-and-a-half-story black rock house was constructed at a cost of $2,000 between Mar. and Dec. 1877, so that the Duckworth Grimshaw family could move in just in time for Christmas. A Mormon convert from England and local farmer, Grimshaw (who, incidentally, was not pleased that he had been given as a first name the family name of his grandmother) was a polygamist who was eventually convicted and sent to the territorial prison in Salt Lake City for "unlawful cohabitation." The Grimshaw House became the model for other houses constructed by Thomas Frazer in Beaver. **95 N. 400 W.**

Harriet S. Shepherd House

Townspeople considered this home to be Beaver's mansion. Constructed in 1876, it is indeed still one of the largest homes in Beaver and was built by a prominent sheepman and local church leader, Marcus L. Shepherd. Shepherd did not spend much time here, though. Following the counsel of Brigham Young, Shepherd became a polygamist when, in addition to his first wife, Harriet, he took a second, Cedaressa Cartwright, nearly 30 years his junior. Shepherd's two wives did not get along and apparently never shared the same house. Harriet became the owner of this house, while Marcus lived the latter part of his life in another house with the younger second wife. The granary behind the house, which served on occasion as the town jail, was built by Thomas Frazer, but the builder of the Federalist-style house is unknown. One room of the house served as a school, and dances were held upstairs in the early days. **190 N. 200 E.**

Old Beaver County Courthouse

One of Utah's oldest courthouses (begun in 1876 and finished in 1882), the Beaver County Courthouse remains an impressive public building. Built under the direction of William Stokes, the U.S. marshal, the building has a deep basement foundation of black basalt, two stories and an attic. The tower houses a clock facing all four directions, which can be seen from almost anywhere in town. Partially destroyed by fire in 1889, the building was immediately rebuilt and served as the county courthouse until the new building across the street was completed in the 1970s. Today the building houses a museum operated by the Daughters of Utah Pioneers. The second floor courtroom has been preserved and is used on occasion for theatrical performances. **100 E. Center.**

Thomas Frazer House

Built in three stages by the master stonemason, the Frazer House is both unpretentious and very interesting. The oldest section, the middle part, was constructed in 1870 of black basalt, followed by an addition to the east in 1872.

Eighteen years later, the third section was constructed of pink tufa rock. Attached to this addition is a bas-relief portrait in green granite of Frazer and his wife, Annie. **590 N. 300 W.**

Rockhounding

The mountain ranges west of Beaver offer some of the best rockhounding locations in America. The Mineral Mountains and San Francisco Mountains are dotted with old mines and mine dumps. Rock shops in Beaver and Milford make for interesting stops and are a good source for information about locations, access and ownership. Some sites are located on private property, while others are isolated and difficult to find. The following, which represent the diversity of minerals and stones available within the area, have been recommended by the **Beaver County Travel Council, P.O. Box 272, Beaver, UT 84713; 435-438-2975; 435-438-2808.**

Antelope District of the Northern Mineral Mountains

This is a good source for galena, barite, magnetite, malachite and pyrite. Take Hwy. 21 west from Beaver to Milford, then Hwy. 257 north for 11 miles and turn east onto a dirt road that leads to the western slope of the Mineral Mountains.

Mineral Mountains

The Mineral Mountains provide a wide range of minerals and are one of the closest and most accessible areas to Beaver. Follow Hwy. 21 west from Beaver for approximately 5 miles to Pass Rd. Turn north on Pass Rd. and follow it into the Mineral Mountains to the top of the pass. Here you will see a number of old mines and workings.

San Francisco Mountains

Near the site of the Cactus Mine and the old town site of Newhouse, exotic minerals such as chalcopyrite, hematite, azurite, rutile, serpentine, stibnite, tourmaline, galena and even gold can be picked up from the foothills and low ridges on the west side of the San Francisco Mountains. Take Hwy. 21 west from Beaver to Milford and continue about 20 miles west of

Milford, then turn north to Newhouse, where a few foundations remain. Turn east at the town site and follow the road to Copper Gulch.

South Creek

Located 7 miles southeast of Beaver, South Creek is a source of a variety of colored agate, which may be found on the low ridges on both sides of the road. Take Hwy. 160 south from Beaver for 1 mile to the South Creek Rd., then follow it east for 6 miles to the area where the mountains begin.

Wah Wah Mountains

The southeast section of the Wah Wah Mountains is a good source of dendrites, fossils, calcite, magnetite, rhodochrosite and other minerals. From Beaver, take Hwy. 21 west to Hwy. 130 and turn south to Minersville. Head southwest on the road to Lund to reach the eastern slope of the Wah Wah Mountains.

From Cedar City, take Hwy. 56 west and watch for the road to Lund, less than a mile after you cross under Interstate 15, and follow the road northwest to Lund. Then continue another 10 miles on the road that heads north, paralleling the eastern slope of the Wah Wah Mountains.

Scenic Drives

Beaver Canyon Scenic Byway

Hwy. 153 is the main access to most of the recreation spots in the mountains east of Beaver. The route from Beaver to Elk Meadows Ski Area has biking and plentiful hiking opportunities in addition to skiing. The 18-mile route has also been designated as a Scenic Byway within the state. This is another example of the journey, rather than the destination, being of primary importance. Beaver Canyon is a beautiful drive during all seasons of the year, but especially in the fall when the yellow leaves of the aspen glow in contrast to the dark colors of the pine forests. At the ski resort the Scenic Byway ends with the pavement, but the gravel road does continue on to US Hwy. 89 at Junction.

Wildlife Viewing

Big Flat Area
Wildlife can be seen throughout the Tushar Mountains, but one of the most likely areas to spot mule deer is the Big Flat area, which sits on forest service land along the ridge of the mountains. Big Flat, a large meadow surrounded by a conifer forest, extends approximately 4 miles south from the highway to Gunsight Flat. In addition to deer, the area is home to elk, hawks, golden eagles, other mountain birds and coyotes, whose howls can sometimes be heard at night. From Beaver, take Hwy. 153 approximately 23 miles east.

Minersville Reservoir
Minersville Reservoir is a good location for bird-watchers. In the summer you can see white pelicans, great blue herons, killdeer, sandpipers and boat-tailed grackles. During the spring and fall migrations, the reservoir is also a stopping place for double-crested cormorants, western grebes, loons, mergansers and other migratory birds. Located 10 miles west of Beaver on Hwy. 21.

Where to Stay

Accommodations

Best Western Paice Inn—$$
Heated pool, sauna, whirlpool and restaurant; 24 rooms. **161 S. Main; 435-438-2438.**

Best Western Paradise Inn—$$
Fifty-three units. Located at the north end of Beaver near Interstate 15, Exit 112. **435-438-2455.**

Comfort Inn—$$
Fifty-one rooms. **645 N. Main; 435-438-2409.**

Country Inn—$$
Swimming pool; 37 rooms. Located near Interstate 15, Exit 112. **1450 N. 300 W.; 435-438-2484.**

Elk Meadows—$$$ to $$$$
The ski and summer resort at Elk Meadows, high in the mountains, has 40 condominiums available. Located 18 miles east of Beaver on Hwy. 153. **435-438-5433.**

Quality Inn—$$
Heated indoor pool and whirlpool; 52 rooms. Located near Interstate 15, Exit 109. **1540 S. 450 W.; 1-800-228-5151; 435-438-5426.**

Sleepy Lagoon Motel—$ to $$
Located in the southern end of Beaver, this modest 20-room motel, with its delightful small pond and quiet setting, seems like an anachronism among the more modern motels that hug the interstate exits. **882 S. Main; 435-438-5681.**

Camping

PRIVATE
There are three excellent private campgrounds located to the south, east and north of Beaver.

Beaver Canyon Campground
Fifty-seven RV trailer sites and 50 tentsites. Flush toilets, showers, laundry and dump sites. One of the attractions of this campground is Maria's Cocina Mexican restaurant. Located east of Beaver on Canyon Rd. and Hwy. 153. **435-438-5654.**

Beaver KOA
Sixty-six RV sites, 25 of which have complete hookups, plus 10 tentsites. Equipped with all the facilities of a modern campground, including a swimming pool. Located north of Beaver on Manderfield Rd. **435-438-2924.**

United Beaver Campground
This popular campground has 85 RV trailer sites, 80 with complete hookups, plus 30 tentsites, flush toilets, a swimming pool, showers, laundry and other facilities. Its popularity is enhanced by its owners. Several years ago, five women from the Phoenix area decided it was time they became their own bosses and, looking

around for an opportunity, came across the United Beaver Campground, which was for sale. The women delight in making their guests' stay memorable, with activities planned throughout the entire year. Betty Miller, one of the five, is the chairperson of the Beaver County Travel Council and, as one of the movers and shakers in the community, she has made a great difference since her arrival. Located at the southern end of Beaver just off Interstate 15, Exit 109. **435-438-2808.**

PUBLIC

There are five public campgrounds located in the Fishlake National Forest in the Tushar Mountains east of Beaver. All are located off Hwy. 153, have picnic tables and drinking water and charge a fee. **Beaver Ranger District, Fishlake National Forest, 190 N. 100 E., P.O. Box E, Beaver, UT 84713; 435-438-2436.**

Little Cottonwood Campground—Eight RV trailer sites and 14 tentsites; among these campgrounds, the only one with flush toilets. Located at 6,500 feet, it has the longest season, mid-May–mid-Nov. Located 6.7 miles from Beaver.

Little Reservoir Campground—Seven RV trailer sites and 7 tentsites. Usually open early June–Oct. Located 9.7 miles from Beaver.

Mahogany Cove Campground—Seven RV trailer sites and 7 tentsites. Usually open early June–Oct. Located 10.2 miles from Beaver, a half mile beyond Little Reservoir Campground.

Kent's Lake Campground—Seventeen RV sites and tentsites. Located 15.2 miles from Beaver.

Anderson Meadow Campground—Ten RV trailer sites and 10 tentsites. At 9,000 feet elevation, it has the shortest season, June 1–mid-Sept. Located 18.2 miles from Beaver, just beyond Elk Meadows Ski Area.

Where to Eat

Arshel's Cafe—$ to $$

Arshel's has been a Beaver tradition since the 1930s, when Arshel Hollingshead established a gas station and a grill here. The grill expanded to a cafe, and the gas station and cafe were operated by the Hollingsheads until Arshel's death in 1972. At that time, their son Dale returned from military service and took over the cafe. Informed travelers between Salt Lake City and California always stop at Arshel's on their journey. Arshel's is also a favorite of local residents, especially the older set, with whom Dale has a particularly good rapport. Dale is a wonderful storyteller. To get him started, ask him about his uncle learning to fly.

The original name has been retained and a photograph of Dale's parents during their courting days graces the menu. Dale has preserved the original character of the cafe, with such hard-to-find items as "real" French fries and hash browns. He continues to use a number of the old family recipes but supplements the menu with some of his own experiments. Some of the local favorites are the chicken and noodles, which is usually the Wed. special; the honey pecan chicken, which appears from time to time as the Sun. special; and the chicken-fried steak with homemade gravy that is available anytime. Save room for the homemade desserts, which include peach cobbler and a variety of pies. For lemon meringue fans, the meringue on Dale's pie seems to imitate the 12,000-foot Tushar Mountains visible to the east from the cafe windows. Open daily 7 A.M.–9 P.M. **711 N. Main; 435-438-2977.**

Hong Kong Restaurant—$ to $$

The origins of the Hong Kong Restaurant go back several decades, when a Chinese immigrant, whose name has been lost to history, established a restaurant in Milford and secured a contract from the Union Pacific Railroad to provide meals 24 hours a day for railroad workers. Johnny Yee came to Milford in the 1950s to work in the restaurant; in the 1960s, he and a partner purchased it. The partner moved on to Cedar City and opened the China Garden Restaurant there. Johnny turned the Hong Kong Restaurant over to his son, Thomas, and daughter-in-law, Selina, in 1976, and they have continued the tradition of 24-hour service for railroad workers and anyone else who needs breakfast, lunch or dinner anytime of day. **433 S. Main, Milford; 435-387-2251.**

Kan Kun—$$

The large double-poled sign that you see from the interstate on the south end of Beaver reads "Mexican Food." I have driven past it many times, thinking it was another fast-food taco place, but when I finally stopped, I had a very pleasant surprise. Rita and Santiago Amezcua became the proprietors of Kan Kun in January 1992 and have established a local reputation for good Mexican food. This charming young couple are from the town of Jiquilpan, in the state of Michoacan, 2 hours south of Guadalajara. Dishes include carne asada (broiled flank steak with special spices), carnitas (deep-fried pork), authentic fajitas, home-style chili verde and salsa that should please every Mexican food lover. Open Sun.–Thurs. 11 A.M.–9 P.M., Fri.–Sat. 11 A.M.–10 P.M. Located on the west side of Interstate 15 at Exit 109. **435-438-5908.**

Services

Visitor Information

Beaver County Travel Council—P.O. Box 272, Beaver, UT 84713; 435-438-2975; 435-438-2808.

Cedar City

When Cedar City was settled in 1851, the band of settlers who made their way 250 miles south from Salt Lake City envisioned that the "Iron Mission" would become the industrial center of the Mormon empire. Iron ore had been discovered in the mountains to the west and coal in the mountains to the east. While church president Brigham Young had no use for gold and silver mines because they seemed to demand more in resources and labor than they ever produced, the iron and coal mines were another matter.

They could be used to build self-sufficiency and independence from eastern manufacturers. With Mormon converts being recruited to Cedar City from the mines and industrial centers of England, the vital labor force was available.

Brigham Young and others did not intend that Cedar City would become a grimy, soot-choked city, as England's Leeds and Manchester once were; instead, it was understood that Cedar City's new inhabitants would be hardworking, sober followers of the Mormon faith. In light of the city's origins, Cedar City's founders might today be taken aback by the city's promotional slogan, "the festival city," and would wonder why the iron and coal mines and other manifestations of industry are now absent from the city. But recreation, tourism and festivals have come to characterize Cedar City.

One of Utah's oldest and best-known festivals is the Utah Shakespearean Festival, held the last week of June through the middle of Oct. The Shakespearean Festival attracts visitors from all over the world, and the Olympic-caliber Utah Summer Games attract participants from all over the state. These and other nearby attractions, such as Cedar Breaks National Monument and Zion National Park, make Cedar City a tourist destination in the summer. Brian Head Ski Area, about 30 miles east of the city atop the 11,000-foot Markagunt Plateau, serves all of southern Utah and has become a popular destination for Las Vegas and California skiers as well. Cedar City is also the home of Southern Utah University.

History

Human presence in the Cedar City area stretches back into prehistoric times. Rock art in Parowan Gap, just north of Cedar City, covers a long period of time from the Desert Archaic period of several thousand years ago to the Fremont and Anasazi cultures, which matured about 700 years ago. Evidence of prehistoric occupation is found throughout the county, and at least two of the area's pioneer settlements, Paragonah and Summit, were built on extensive Fremont sites that were occupied between A.D. 1000 and 1300.

When the first Europeans, the Dominguez–Escalante Expedition, reached the area in 1776, they met ancestors of the present-day Southern Paiute Indians and learned that they were part of an Indian trading network that extended into southern Arizona and beyond. At a site about 30 miles west of present-day Cedar City, the two Franciscan friars decided to end their quest for an overland route from Santa Fe, New Mexico, to Monterey, California, and to return to Santa Fe. The "casting of the lots" was a dramatic moment in the history of this celebrated expedition, as the two clergymen had concluded they must return to Santa Fe, while others were still set on Monterey.

Fifty years later, another man of deep religious faith, the Bible-packing Methodist fur trapper Jedediah Smith succeeded in making the journey from present-day Utah to California, passing through the Cedar City area in 1826. Both the 1776 Dominguez–Escalante Expedition and the 1826 Jedediah Smith trek contributed to the successful opening of the Old Spanish Trail in 1830, which connected Los Angeles with Santa Fe. The Old Spanish Trail passed near present-day Parowan, Summit and Cedar City. Spanish coins, and crosses and signs carved in rocks, have been reported in the foothills east of these locations.

Getting There

Cedar City is located 250 miles south of Salt Lake City on Interstate 15.

Most travelers get to Cedar City by automobile, but you can also fly into Cedar City from Salt Lake City.

There is air passenger service to the Cedar City Airport with **Delta / Skywest Airlines; 1-800-453-9417.**

Greyhound bus service from Salt Lake City and Las Vegas is also available. **1355 S. Main; 435-586-9465.**

The Spanish Trail was still in use in 1849 when the first Mormon explorers, under the command of Parley P. Pratt, came south from Salt Lake City, with orders from Brigham Young to explore the southern region for colonization. It was this group that named the area the Little Salt Lake Valley, dedicated and marked the future site of the City of the Little Salt Lake with a flagpole and an American flag and discovered the iron deposits on Iron Mountain 9 miles west of Cedar City that were such welcome news to Brigham Young.

Young lost no time in organizing a two-prong colonization of what was called the "Iron Mission." The vanguard group, made up of those with the right skills, was called by Brigham Young to undertake the assignment. The first group, which would provide a good agricultural base for the mission, consisted of 120 men, 30 women and 18 children. They arrived at present-day Parowan on January 13, 1851, a year and five days after Parley P. Pratt raised the liberty pole and dedicated the location for settlement.

With the agricultural needs provided, the second, or industrial, phase of the mission began. Beginning in November 1851, Cedar City was settled. By April 1852 English workers were being recruited from the mines as part of the Deseret Iron Company. The Iron Mission was both a colossal failure and a brilliant success. Little iron was produced, and with disappointment after disappointment, the dream of a self-sufficient iron industry was abandoned, even though the hills still yield abundant iron. Parowan and Cedar City prospered as Mormon settlements, however, and supplied colonists for a host of other later settlements throughout southern Utah, Arizona, Nevada and Colorado.

It is with great pride that Parowan still calls itself the Mother Colony. While Cedar City and Parowan built their 20th-century success on agriculture, mining and tourism, the pioneer past remains a strong element in the mentality and heritage of these communities.

Major Attractions

Cedar Breaks National Monument

The Paiutes are said to have called it "circle-of-painted cliffs," and the name is most appropriate, as Cedar Breaks National Monument is a 3-mile-wide, 2,000-foot-deep amphitheater of eroded and beautifully colored ledges ranging in color from white or orange at the top to deep rose and coral farther down. The colors and shades are constantly changing as sunlight, clouds and shadows play on the cliffs. Visitors often compare Cedar Breaks with Bryce Canyon National Park, and for good reason. Both are cut from the same geological formation and are located close to one another in southern Utah. However, Cedar Breaks, at 10,350 feet, sits 2,000 feet higher than Bryce Canyon National Park and is completely in the subalpine zone.

Both are part of the Claron Formation, which consists of soft pink and white siltstone, sandstone, dolomite and limestone layers. These strata were deposited in a Paleocene lake that filled a series of near-sea-level basins surrounded by lowlands about 50 million years ago. Freshwater creatures lived in the lakes, and when they died, their shells formed deposits that filled the lake bottom. The lake ebbed and flowed over a long period. Eventually the limey skeletons of the marine creatures and other sediments compressed into rock. Violent seismic activity caused the region to lift up and split about 15 million years ago, leaving the former lake bed on top of what are now known as the Markagunt Plateau (Cedar Breaks) and the Paunsaugunt Plateau (Bryce Canyon). Exposed to rain, snow, wind and 200 to 300 freeze-thaw cycles a year, the poorly cemented sedimentary rocks began to erode at an uneven rate, leaving a deep amphitheater that remains pristine compared with Bryce Canyon. The 9.5-square-mile Cedar Breaks National Monument was set aside by Franklin D. Roosevelt in 1933.

Visitor Information

The 5-mile Rim Dr. leads to Point Supreme, where the visitor center and campground are

Getting There

There are two routes to Cedar Breaks National Monument. From Cedar City, take Hwy. 14 (a Scenic Byway) for 20.4 miles east to its intersection with Hwy. 148, then drive north for 3 miles to the monument's south entrance. From the north, exit Interstate 15 at Parowan and follow Hwy. 143 south for 19 miles, past Brian Head Ski Resort, to the national monument's north entrance. From the east, take US Hwy. 89 west 25 miles to its junction with Hwy. 14, then continue north 3 miles to the south entrance.

located; other turnouts are Sunset View, Chessmen Ridge Overlook and North View. The small visitor center has a beautiful "picture window," interpretive displays and a small bookstore. Because the road through the monument is impassible in heavy snowfall, the monument is closed Oct.–late May; hours vary the rest of the year. Located 2 miles north of the south entrance to the monument. **435-586-9451; www.nps/gov/cebr.**

Outdoor Activities

Unlike Bryce Canyon National Park, which offers several hiking trails from the top of the plateau down through the eroded formations to the bottom of the canyon, there is only one rough U.S. Forest Service trail to the bottom of the Cedar Breaks National Park amphitheater. Descent into the steep amphitheater is discouraged by the National Park Service, which tries to keep the Breaks as pristine as possible. However, two rim-level trails provide space to stretch your legs and give you an opportunity to view the exposed rim and forest environments that make up the Breaks.

Alpine Pond Trail—This short 2-mile loop through the forest passes through aspen, fir and spruce forest close to the rim and circles an alpine pond. You will see bluebells, columbines and other glorious woodland flowers in the shady glades and may bump into marmots lazily enjoying the summer bounty. Begins at the Chessmen Ridge Overlook, near the midway point of the scenic drive.

Spectra Point and Wasatch Ramparts Trail—The trail follows the southern rim of the Cedar Breaks amphitheater for 2 miles around the exposed rim, past elkweed and Indian paintbrush, to a stand of ancient bristlecone pines (one specimen is 1,600 years old) on Spectra Point. Beyond Spectra Point, a rugged promontory that sticks out into the Breaks continues into the forest alongside a bubbling stream, past woodland flowers, until you reach the end of the Wasatch Ramparts. The trail is mostly level, with a few ups and downs, and makes an excellent introduction to this unusual park. Allow about 2 hours round trip. Begins at the visitor center.

Seeing and Doing

Historic Sites—Four years after Cedar Breaks was designated a national monument, the Civilian Conservation Corps constructed two buildings in 1937 that, because of their age, architecture and association with Franklin Roosevelt's New Deal program, have been listed in the National Register of Historic Places. The visitor center and the caretaker's cabin are both of log and masonry construction. Their rustic architecture is characteristic of many of the buildings constructed in America's national parks from the turn of the 20th century and into the 1930s. Nearly 60 years after their construction, the two buildings fit the character of Cedar Breaks to a T, and their rustic style enhances the visit to the national monument for many people.

Scenic Drives—The 6-mile road between Hwy. 14 and Hwy. 143 that provides access to Cedar Breaks National Monument, **Cedar Breaks Scenic Byway/Hwy. 148,** is especially beautiful during the summer when many thousands of colorful wildflowers cover the mountain meadows.

The 5-mile **Rim Dr.,** which winds through stands of subalpine fir, Engelmann spruce, quaking aspen and flower-dressed alpine meadows, offer a way to view Cedar Breaks from your car.

Be sure to stop at the four view areas: Point Supreme, at the visitor center near the southern boundary of the monument; Sunset View; Chessmen Ridge Overlook; and North View.

Camping

There is one small campground within Cedar Breaks—Point Supreme. It has 30 RV sites and tentsites and is equipped with drinking water and toilets. A fee is charged. There are no other accommodations or restaurants in the park, so bring a picnic. The campground, like the park, is open only mid-June–mid-Sept. Located 2 miles north of the south entrance next to the visitor center.

Utah Shakespearean Festival

In 1962 Fred C. Adams and his small group of students and volunteers launched the first Utah Shakespearean Festival. Today the festival has grown to be one of Utah's most renowned cultural events. While the focus remains on the presentation of three or four Shakespeare plays (well-known works as well as the obscure), works by other famous playwrights, such as Ben Jonson, George Bernard Shaw and Arthur Miller, are also performed. During the 10-week festival (end of June–Sept.), visitors can spend an entire week and see a different play every day. A good number of Utahns schedule a week's vacation in Cedar City for the festival.

For serious students of the theater, a series of seminars, preperformance lectures and backstage tours provide insight and knowledge that enrich the experience of the plays. The festival spirit is enhanced by jugglers, dancers, musicians, Punch and Judy shows and Renaissance games, as well as entertainment that affords a new appreciation for the people of Shakespeare's England. Tarts, horehound and humbug candies and oranges are sold by strolling maidens who banter with the audience using the authentic language and dialect of the 16th century. For those who want to treat their taste buds to more than tidbits of the period, there is "The Renaissance Feaste," which consists of a seven-course meal served by "winsome wenches" and accompanied by "roguish entertainment and lively humor," under the jocular eye of Henry VIII.

The permanent festival site is located on the campus of Southern Utah University and consists of three theaters, including the 777-seat Adams Memorial Shakespearean Theater, constructed in 1977 as a replica of Shakespeare's Globe Theatre in London. The Randall L. Jones Theatre, named for a man considered to be the father of tourism in southern Utah, was completed in 1989 with an indoor seating capacity of 763. It is best to order tickets well in advance; a few tickets are made available the morning of each performance, and a courtesy booth offers last-minute tickets for resale, if any are available. **Box Office, Utah Shakespearean Festival, Cedar City, UT 84720; 1-800-PLAYTIX (752-9849); 435-586-7878; www.bard.org.**

Southern Utah University

In 1990 this nearly century-old institution attained state university status. The journey to university status was a long one. The institution was established as a branch normal school in 1897, then became a branch agricultural college in 1913. It was recognized as part of the state junior college system in 1953, when the name was changed to College of Southern Utah. In 1965 the school changed from a two-year junior college to a four-year college, and in 1971 was renamed Southern Utah State College. Its new status and name should outlast all the others. Southern Utah University is the center of much of the social, cultural and recreational life of the area, with the famous Shakespeare festival, its popular athletic programs and other activities. The two original buildings, the ivy-covered Old Main and the Braithwaite Liberal Arts Center, date from 1898 and 1899, respectively, and remain at the heart of the campus. **1025 W. 200 S.; 435-586-7700; www.suu.edu.**

Festivals and Events

Parowan's Birthday Celebration

Jan. 13. Parowan was settled on Jan. 13, 1851, and each year the community commemorates its birthday with pioneer dancing by elementary and high school students, a town meeting, a luncheon and a birthday ball. In addition to its pioneer heritage, Parowan likes to remember one of its sons, Alma Richards, who in 1912 during the Olympic Games in Stockholm, Sweden, won the gold medal in the high jump, becoming Utah's first gold medalist in any sport. **435-477-3331.**

Utah Summer Games

June. Who said you have to travel halfway around the world to attend or even participate in the Olympic Games? While Utah's Summer Games do not attract international or even national media coverage, it is still a big event in Utah. It was the brainchild of former university president Gerald R. Sherratt after he witnessed the highly successful 1984 Summer Olympic Games in Los Angeles. The idea was enthusiastically adopted by Cedar City civic leaders, and the first Utah Games were held in 1986. Now, each year nearly 7,000 participants from all over the state compete in regional qualifying meets for the privilege of traveling to Cedar City in June for the finals of the Utah Summer Games. Olympic-style opening and closing ceremonies, dinners, intense coverage by Utah television stations and more than 3,000 volunteers make this a never-to-be-forgotten experience for the athletes and their families. The competition covers 28 sports; activities are held in various locations on and around the SUU campus. **435-586-4484; www.utahsummergames.org.**

Paiute Restoration Gathering

second weekend in June. Held in Cedar City, this Paiute tribal celebration includes a powwow, a parade, a queen and princess contest, a dinner, a talent night and a softball tournament. The Paiutes lost their status as a tribe in the 1950s and were reinstated in June 1980. Cedar City is the tribal headquarters for what is now known as the Paiute Indian Tribe of Utah. **Paiute Indian Tribe Administrative Office, 600 N. 100 E., Cedar City, UT 84720; 435-586-1112.**

Brian Head Bash

first weekend in Aug. The highlight of the mountain biking season, this event was voted Utah's Best Mountain Bike Festival by *Cycling Utah Magazine*. Guided tours, bike clinics, games, live entertainment and a barbecue are among the activities during the three-day event. Lodging packages are offered at reasonable rates. **1-800-27-BRIAN (27426); 435-677-2035.**

Jedediah Smith High Mountain Rendezvous

second weekend in Aug. This is a mountain man's delight and, for that matter, anyone interested in the costumes and activities of the mountain men who roamed the West during the 1820s and 1830s. Activities include black powder competition, games, displays and stories. Held in the mountains above Cedar City. **435-586-5124.**

Cedar City Birthday Celebration

Nov. 11. Cedar City began to be settled on Nov. 11, 1851, 67 years before the rest of the nation would recognize the date as Armistice Day. Every year Cedar City celebrates its founding with activities and events that culminate in a grand birthday ball. **435-586-5124.**

Outdoor Activities

Biking

Brian Head

A popular ski area in the winter, Brian Head has become one of Utah's most popular mountain biking locations in recent years. The area boasts more than 120 miles of single track and hundreds of miles of backcountry dirt roads that beckon riders of all abilities to uncrowded terrain. Brian Head publishes an excellent free *Mountain Bike Guide* that is updated each year and provides good descriptions of rides for all abilities. Round-trip shuttle rides can be arranged at area bike shops; the Brian Head Chairlift 2 at the Giant Steps Base Lodge operates four days a week (Fri.–Mon.), plus holidays, to provide access to mountain biking at its best. Although the biking season is rela-

tively short because of the high elevation (most trails are between 9,000 and 11,000 feet), there are several bike races and festivals throughout the summer. **1-800-27-BRIAN (27426); 435-677-2035.**

The "C"

This 16.5-mile loop begins on Center St. in Cedar City and follows Hwy. 14 for 5 miles up Cedar Canyon. At Milt's Stage Stop, turn south into Right-Hand Canyon. After a mile, the paved road becomes a double-track jeep road as it continues into the canyon. Follow the jeep road for 4.7 miles to where the road splits, then keep to the right as the route follows to the southwest, then turns northwest and heads back into Cedar City. The last third of the ride is downhill and passes through groves of piñons and junipers, then sagebrush and wildflowers as the elevation drops. It offers a grand view of Cedar City and Cedar Valley.

Twisted Forest

Perhaps the most popular ride from Brian Head Ski Resort starts at Upper Bear Flat, at the south end of Brian Head. The 9-mile round-trip route leaves Hwy. 143 and follows Forest Rd. 304, a jeep road that climbs across the downhill ski run before it intersects with Forest Rd. 265. After turning left on Forest Rd. 265, the route heads southwest for 1.5 miles before reaching Forest Rd. 051 to High Mountain. Turn left (south) onto Forest Rd. 051, which passes through Twisted Forest, named for its gnarled forest of ancient bristlecone pines, before reaching a spectacular overlook of Cedar Breaks and the Ashdown Gorge Wilderness Area at the end of the trail. The ride is good for intermediate bikers.

Rentals

Mark Gunderson, owner of **The Bike Route,** has done much to promote biking in the Cedar City area. The shop offers maps, half-day and full-day guided tours of trails in the area, bike rentals, spare parts, repairs and good advice on trails and rides for beginning to advanced riders. **70 W. Center, Cedar City; 435-586-4242.**

Brian Head area full-service bike shops include **Georgs Ski Shop and Bikes, 435-677-2013, and Mt. Bike Park Shop, 435-677-2035.**

Fishing

If you like to fish, then don't forget your fishing gear when traveling to the Cedar City area. Several excellent reservoirs and streams provide a variety of opportunities.

Enterprise Reservoir

One of the most isolated reservoirs in the area, Enterprise Reservoir is situated 10 miles southwest of Enterprise, nearly 50 miles west of Cedar City. Stocked with rainbow, German brown and brook trout, the reservoir has a boat launch and excellent camping facilities. Take Hwy. 56 west from Cedar City to Hwy. 18, then go south to Enterprise; from there, follow the road southwest to the reservoir.

Navajo Lake

All four types of trout—rainbow, German brown, brook and cutthroat—can be found in this natural lake. Boating is permitted, and both improved and unimproved campsites are available. Although Navajo Indians do not and did not inhabit the area, bands of Navajos who had evaded the Long March to New Mexico made their way across the Colorado River and entered Utah from the southeast in the late 1860s. Hungry and angry with whites, the Navajos retaliated by stealing cattle belonging to the settlers in southern Utah. One Navajo raiding party fought a skirmish with Cedar City cattlemen near Navajo Lake, which was named to commemorate the encounter. The Paiute Indians who inhabited the area called the lake Pah-cu-ay, which means "Cloud Lake." Located atop the 10,000–11,000-foot Markagunt Plateau, there is good reason for it to be called Cloud Lake: the road to the lake is closed by snow in the winter. Located off Hwy. 14 about 25 miles east of Cedar City.

Parowan Creek

If you want to test your fly-fishing skills in a rapid, narrow stream, Parowan Creek might be just the ticket. The stream is stocked with brook, rainbow, German brown and cutthroat trout. The fishing area along Hwy. 143 begins 5 miles south of Parowan, at the road to Yankee Meadows, and continues most of the way up to Brian Head Ski Resort.

Golf

Cedar Ridge Golf Course

Expanded to an 18-hole golf course in 1993, Cedar Ridge offers a good variety of holes, easy access from Cedar City's Main St. and no reservations needed. Pro John Evans all but guarantees to have you on the course within a half hour of your arrival. Located in the northeast sector of Cedar City, the course winds around the foothills and uses the natural terrain to good advantage. **900 N. 200 E.; 435-586-2970.**

Hiking

Dominguez–Escalante National Historic Trail

Although California was their objective when they set out from Santa Fe on July 29, 1776, Father Francisco Atanasio Dominguez and Father Silvestre Velez de Escalante and their party faced blizzards by early Oct., a shortage of food and an unknown distance and terrain to complete their journey. Today part of the route they followed, as their course swung from westward to southward near Cedar City, has been designated a hiking trail by the Bureau of Land Management. The expedition's journey through this area (including "the casting of the lots") to Ash Creek, south of Cedar City, took four days, Oct. 10–13, 1776. If you are serious about making this hike, it will be enhanced a thousandfold by taking along a copy of the Dominguez–Escalante journal for these days. The most complete edition is the translation by Fray Angelico Chavez, edited by Ted J. Warner (BYU Press, 1976).

You'll need either a vehicle shuttle or to have someone drop you at the trailhead. To reach the marked 25-mile portion of the trail, head west of Cedar City on Hwy. 56 for 1 mile, then turn right onto Hwy. 19 and drive northwest 30 miles to Lund. At Lund, turn right at the railroad tracks and follow them to the sign indicating Thermo Hot Springs. After leaving Thermo Hot Springs, you hike for about 1 mile, and then reach the site of the Casting of the Lots. Follow the trail as it heads back to intersect Hwy. 56 about 2 miles west of Cedar City.

Rattlesnake Creek and Ashdown Gorge

This steep 10-mile hike along a Forest Service trail descends 3,400 feet via Rattlesnake Creek through the Ashdown Gorge Wilderness Area. About two-thirds of the way down the trail, Rattlesnake Creek joins with Ashdown Creek to form Coal Creek. This is not a hike to be made alone or by inexperienced hikers. In places the footing is very poor, and the trail is exposed and dangerous in the summer when thunderstorms and flash floods occur. You will want to have area maps with you and know how to use them. Always check with a National Park Service or U.S. Forest Service ranger before setting out. The trailhead is located off Hwy. 143, past the Brian Head Ski Resort and just before you reach the northern entrance to Cedar Breaks National Monument. The hike requires a shuttle vehicle or pickup at the dirt road that exits off Hwy. 14 about 7 miles east of Cedar City at Martins Flat.

Skiing

CROSS-COUNTRY

The high-country meadows found in the Brian Head Ski Resort/Cedar Breaks National Monument area are excellent places for cross-country skiing. With more than 30 miles of marked trails and nearly 200 miles of backcountry routes, you can spend an hour or days. One of the most popular trails is the **Town Trail,** which connects most Brian Head businesses and lodging properties, and the 3-mile **Pioneer Cabins Loop.** Several trails into Cedar Breaks National Monument provide a never-to-be-forgotten view of the snow-covered, giant multicolored amphitheater. For information on trails and ski rentals, check at the **Giant Steps Lodge Rental Shop; 1-800-245-3743; 435-677-2012.**

Duck Creek Village

Groomed cross-country skiing trails, rentals and instruction. Located 30 miles east of Cedar City on Hwy. 14. **435-682-2495.**

DOWNHILL

Brian Head Ski Resort

Uncrowded, well-groomed hills, distinguished ski schools, breathtaking scenery and excellent accommodations best describe this fast-growing ski resort located at the top of Parowan Canyon and nestled between Navajo Peak and 11,307-foot Brian Head Peak. With a base elevation of 9,600 feet, this is the highest ski resort in Utah; the town of Brian Head is the highest town. Après skiing is not the emphasis here, making it attractive for families and those for whom a busy nightlife is not essential.

The six lifts—one double-chair and five triple-chairs—provide access to more than 500 acres of mountain terrain over 50 different runs. The lifts are placed at three locations in the canyon, and this adds to the uncrowded feeling. The Riviera lift for first-time skiers offers a nice, gentle hill to learn the basics of skiing. The adjacent Stardust lift, 3,895 feet in length, is one of the longest lifts at the resort, but is primarily for beginning skiers or those who like a gentle slope. The Navajo lift provides access to a good selection of intermediate runs and can be reached via the Stardust lift. The Giant Steps area, serviced by three triple-chair lifts, offers runs for all levels. The resort also caters to snowboarders with a 12-foot half-pipe and snowboard parks. For expert skiers and snowboarders 16 and older willing to sign a release waiver and pay an additional $5, you can catch a ride on a "tricked-out truck with tracks" to the top of 11,307-foot-high Brian Head Peak, where nearly 100 acres of steep, narrow chutes, cliff band drop-offs and powder-filled bowls are all there for the thrill of a lifetime.

Ski and snowboard rentals are available, and an attractive beginners package that includes rentals, a 2-hour lesson and an all-day lift pass is popular. Lift prices compare with most northern Utah resorts. A snow tube park includes a lift and six lanes for this popular winter sport. There are several restaurants and a total of nearly 1,000 rooms. Located on Hwy. 143, 12 miles off the Parowan exit on Interstate 15. **1-800-272-7426; 435-677-2035; www.brianheadutah.com.**

Seeing and Doing

Historic Sites

Old Irontown

There is not much left at Old Irontown, except for a well-preserved charcoal kiln and a brick chimney, but if you are interested in kicking through the sagebrush to discover the stone foundations of houses and other buildings and trying to imagine a town of several hundred inhabitants, the 22-mile drive west from Cedar City to Old Irontown is worth the effort. Old Irontown, or Iron City as it is sometimes called, was the second attempt to establish an iron industry in the region. The initial pioneer attempt, which began with the settlement of Cedar City in 1851 and lasted until about 1858, failed for a number of reasons—mostly problems with the blast furnace and the lack of a suitable source of coke or charcoal. When larger ore deposits were located on Iron Mountain in 1870, a second attempt was launched. More successful than the first attempt at Cedar City, which only produced 25 tons of iron, daily production of iron reached one ton a day in 1870 and climbed to five tons a day for a while after 1874.

The plant operated throughout much of the 1880s, but the lack of coke and the availability of cheaper eastern iron led to the abandonment of the project. By 1890 the plant had been dismantled and the equipment sold, and the former population of Irontown had relocated to Newcastle, Cedar City and other places. Because of its significance in the early industrial history of Utah, the site has been listed in the National Register of Historic Places.

From Cedar City, take Hwy. 56 west approximately 20 miles to the sign for Old Irontown, then follow the road southwest for 2.6 miles. As you travel along Hwy. 56, also of interest is the open-pit iron mine on Iron Mountain, north of the highway before you reach the Irontown turnoff. The iron mine was reopened during the 1920s and greatly expanded during World War II, from a production of 300,000 tons in 1940 to 3,000,000 tons in 1950. Peak production was 4,000,000 tons in 1957, but after that production declined, until today when mining takes place on a limited scale.

CEDAR CITY
Cedar City Railroad Depot

The depot was constructed in 1923, when the Union Pacific Railroad line reached Cedar City. The railroad was a great boon to the agriculture and mining activities of the area and helped to make Cedar City a gateway city to the national parks. Tour buses provided transportation to the parks from Cedar City, and the railroad got into the park concession business, building lodges in Bryce, Cedar Breaks and Zion in the 1920s and 1930s. One of the first passengers on the railroad was President Warren G. Harding, who visited Cedar City and Zion National Park in late June 1923, shortly before his death. The railroad to Cedar City was actually a 30-mile-long spur from Lund and the main line between Salt Lake City and Los Angeles. For the best part of 36 years the "Doodlebug," a one-coach train, carried passengers from Lund to Cedar City. By the 1950s, the automobile had greatly overshadowed the railroad for passenger transportation, and the depot was closed in 1959. Still conspicuous as you drive through town, the depot has since been renovated as a restaurant, convenience store and, in the summer, an antique and craft shop. Located on the northwest corner of **200 N. and Main St.**

Cedar City Rock Church

The Cedar City Rock Church is a monument to latter-day Mormons who, without money for materials and wages during the Great Depression, constructed this church with native materials and donated labor. Red cedar (juniper) from the mountains around Cedar City is used inside, while colorful stones from nearby creek beds were gathered and carefully placed on the exterior walls. Especially stunning is the rock baptismal font in the basement of the church. The church is a very popular landmark. Don't miss it. Open for tours mid-June–Labor Day Mon.–Sat. 11 A.M.–5 P.M. Located on **Center St., between Main and 100 E.**

PARAGONAH

If you want to catch a glimpse of a fading Mormon village that has more pioneer homes and barns than any other remaining town in this area, drive the 4 miles northeast from Parowan. The name Paragonah comes from the Piede Indians, a group of Paiute Indians living in the area, who used the term as the name for the salty springs and marshlands nearby, which Mormons called the Little Salt Lake. Paragonah has a number of early adobe and fired-brick houses as well as log-and-wood barns, which are becoming an increasingly rare sight in rural Utah. One unique style of construction was to build the log barns with spaces between the logs, supposedly to provide better air circulation to the stored hay. Another unique construction technique was mud concrete or poured adobe houses, made possible because of the high lime content of the native clay. A lime mortar mixture was made from lime, sand and animal hair, then poured into forms that were 12 inches high and ran the length of the house. After one level hardened, the forms were removed and placed above for the next 12-inch layer.

It doesn't take long to drive up and down the streets of this hamlet of 300 people and, while all of the buildings that are not vacant are private residences and not open to visitors, there is a museumlike quality to the town. The following buildings are of special interest.

Edward Morgan Edwards House

Constructed in the 1880s, this is probably the best remaining example of the poured-adobe construction technique. After the walls were poured, they were covered with plaster. **19 S. 200 E.**

Helen Bell Robb House

The most elaborate of Paragonah's pioneer houses, this large brick home was built in 1861 for Helen Bell, the first of William Robb's two wives. She immigrated to Utah from Australia with her husband and used money she had earned in a successful Australian business to finance the construction of the house in Paragonah. William Robb arrived in Paragonah in 1858, but in 1861 moved about 50 miles farther south, to Harrisburg, with his second wife, Susannah Drummond. When Susannah died after giving birth to her seventh child, Helen agreed that William could return to Paragonah with Susannah's children, who were raised by Helen. **128 N. Main.**

Marius Ensign / Silas S. Smith House

Constructed about 1862 of locally produced red-clay adobe by Marius Ensign, one of the original settlers of Paragonah, the house was sold to Silas S. Smith in 1872. The older brother of Jesse N. Smith (see Parowan, below), Silas S. Smith, like his younger brother, was one of the stalwarts of western Mormon colonization. The adobe remains in remarkably good condition more than 150 years after its construction. **96 N. Main.**

PAROWAN

Travelers to Parowan will want to take time to visit a few of the historic sites still standing in this historic town.

Jesse N. Smith House

Built of stuccoed adobe, between 1856 and 1858, this early pioneer home stands on the north side of the block just south of the two churches. Jesse N. Smith was the youngest cousin of LDS church founder Joseph Smith. Born in 1834, he lived in all of the eastern gathering places—Kirtland, Ohio; Missouri; and Nauvoo, Illinois—before coming west at the age of 13, during the Mormon exodus. Smith was in his early 20s when he constructed his Parowan house. At the age of 26 he left his two wives and children in Parowan to travel to Denmark as a missionary for the Mormon faith. He was gone for five years! Open May–Aug. Mon.–Sat. 1–5 P.M., or by calling ahead. **Parowan Visitor Center, 75 N. Main; 435-477-8190.**

Parowan Cemetery

The Parowan Cemetery has a number of historic headstones, which make this a worthwhile visit. One of the most famous headstones is that of Ed Dalton, shot and killed by a U.S. marshal on Dec. 16, 1886. The 34-year-old man was one of the first children born in Parowan on Aug. 25, 1852. His crime was marrying two women, in accordance with the Mormon practice of polygamy, and then trying to escape from the marshal, who was trying to arrest him for violating federal laws against cohabitation. Dalton had been in hiding in Arizona, but when marshals in Beaver, 32 miles away, learned that he had returned to his home, they made their way to Parowan under the cover of darkness. In the morning, as Dalton was taking his stock to graze on the range west of town, the fatal shooting occurred. Pick up a copy of the brochure *Parowan Cemetery—A Walking Tour Through Pioneer Folk Art and History* and spend an interesting hour looking at the treasure of folk art to be found on the headstones.

Parowan Gap Rock Art

Parowan Gap is known to rock art scholars throughout the world. Listed in the National Register of Historic Places, it has some of the finest Indian petroglyphs in the state. Unlike much of Utah's rock art, which is painted, the hundreds of Parowan Gap designs have been pecked and cut into the stone; however, like the painted anthropomorphs of eastern and southern Utah, those at the Parowan site have broad shoulders, tapered trunks and headdresses, which are considered characteristic of the Fremont. Other forms and designs are clearly from the older Archaic period.

The 2-mile-long Parowan Gap separates Cedar Valley to the west and Parowan Valley to the east. The petroglyph panels can be found on the northern side of the gap, with the primary panel being near the western end and the other near the eastern end. There is plenty of parking at the western end. The major petroglyphs have been fenced, but spend some time looking along the cliffs on the north and south side of the road,

inside the gap, for petroglyphs that have not been fenced. Located about 15 miles northwest of Cedar City. From Cedar City, take Main St. north to Hwy. 130, where it passes under Interstate 15, and continue north for 13.5 miles. Turn east (right) onto an oiled road, which takes you the 2.5 miles to the rock art. From Parowan, head west at 400 N. under Interstate 15 and continue west for 10.5 miles to the Parowan Gap.

Parowan Rock Church

Parowan's landmark church, located in the center of the block in the town center, is one of the oldest remaining churches in Utah. The rock church was constructed between 1862 and 1866 and, with its separate entries for men and women, reflects the New England origins of many early Parowan residents. According to local tradition, men used the west side and women the east side and sat separated from each other until Brother Watson rebelled, marched up the east steps, and sat by his wife. Within a few weeks, others followed and soon the congregation was sitting together as families. The church is built of an orange-brown sandstone laid in coursed rubble. Since much of the Mormon settlement of southern Utah, northern Arizona and the San Juan River area was under the direction of LDS church authorities in Parowan, this church has special significance, for it was here that many Mormons were "called" to leave and help establish new settlements. The building currently houses a museum operated by the Daughters of Utah Pioneers. Open May–Aug. Mon.–Sat. 1–5 P.M., or by calling ahead. Parowan Visitor Center, **75 N. Main; 435-477-8190.**

Parowan Third Ward Chapel

Standing on the same block as the rock church but facing east on the west side of Main St., the Parowan Third Ward Chapel makes an interesting contrast to the old pioneer church. Designed in 1916 and dedicated in 1918, the building is one of the most impressive examples of the "Prairie School" style of architecture, which was adopted by the Mormon church for several buildings. Salt Lake City architect Miles Miller was familiar with the work of Frank Lloyd Wright, and the new style of architecture served as a physical symbol that the Mormon faith was progressive and forward-looking—a statement that had particular importance shortly after the turn of the 20th century and the long fight over polygamy. An addition was made to the church in 1958, and it is still used for worship services. **50 S. Main St.**

Museums

Iron Mission State Park
Iron Mission State Park is one of a half-dozen history museums operated by the Utah Division of Parks and Recreation. The museum is based on a unique collection of horse-drawn vehicles collected from throughout Utah by Cedar City native Gronway Parry beginning in 1911. Parry ran the first buses to Cedar Breaks. The unique collection includes buggies, surreys, sleighs, a milk wagon, a white hearse—used for children—a replica of a Wells Fargo stagecoach and an authentic bullet-marked stagecoach that operated between Price and San Juan County around the turn of the 20th century. There are hundreds of pieces of horse-drawn farm machinery, freight wagons and other vehicles that were essential to Utah's early economic development.

The museum, as you might expect, also tells the story of the development of the iron industry in the area. It has on display items made from the iron manufactured in Cedar City. These include a bell that was cast in 1854 and an iron cage jail that was last used at Lund. Two early log cabins are exhibited outside on the grounds, one of which is the **George Wood Cabin,** constructed in 1851 and recognized as the oldest remaining residence in southern Utah. The house was actually built in Parowan, then moved to Cedar City later that year shortly after the new settlement was established. Open daily (except major holidays) in summer 9 A.M.– 7 P.M.; in winter 9 A.M.–5 P.M. Admission is charged. **595 N. Main St., Cedar City; 435-586-9290.**

Scenic Drives

Brian Head/Panguitch Lake Scenic Byway
This 55-mile-long Scenic Byway cuts through the Vermillion Cliffs. From Parowan at Interstate 15, follow Hwy. 143 south through Parowan Canyon and on to Brian Head. Take time to drive up to Vista Point, located 1.5 miles east of Brian Head and 0.5 mile before the north entrance to Cedar Breaks; this gravel road is just under 3 miles long and is passable by passenger cars. The steep climb takes you to the top of Brian Head to an elevation of 11,307 feet, one of the highest points in Utah that you can reach by car. At the end of the road is a parking area with a 100-yard walk to a stone shelter, from which you can look down upon the highway, meadows, Brian Head Ski Resort, Cedar Breaks, the Parowan Valley and, in the distance, Bryce Canyon National Park. Four states can also be seen here—Arizona, Colorado, New Mexico and Utah.

If you stop at the Rattlesnake trailhead, at the north entrance to Cedar Breaks, you can look to the northwest and see the shelter on top of Brian Head Peak. Continue on, passing Panguitch Lake, to US Hwy. 89 at Panguitch. If you want to make a day of touring, you can continue south along US Hwy. 89. It's possible also to make a detour on Hwy. 12 east to Bryce Canyon, then return to US Hwy. 89. Head south on US Hwy. 89 to Long Valley Junction and turn west on Hwy. 143. Here you can either head north on Hwys. 148 and 143 back to Parowan, or continue west to Cedar City. Hwy. 148, which intersects with Hwy. 143 at Cedar Breaks, is closed by snow in winter.

Kolob Terrace/Reservoir Rd. Scenic Backway
For a unique view of the western part of Zion National Park, and a memorable 45-mile drive that begins in the piñon forests east of Cedar City, passes by the picturesque Kolob Reservoir and Blue Springs Reservoir, then descends through the red and white sandstone ledges of Zion National Park to the old Mormon pioneer town of Virgin, take the Kolob Terrace/Reservoir Rd. Scenic Backway. It is a drive that you

will not soon forget. From Cedar City head east on Hwy. 14, and at 6 miles the Scenic Backway heads south over a gravel and dirt road for approximately 25 miles to the northern boundary of Zion National Park. From here, the paved road takes you past ranches, in and out of the park, to the junction with Hwy. 9 at Virgin, approximately 20 miles to the south. For details on the southern portion of the drive, see the Scenic Drives section under Seeing and Doing in the **Zion National Park** chapter.

Markagunt Scenic Byway/Hwy. 14

Chances are if you spend any time in the Cedar City area at all, you will travel over this Scenic Byway, which is also known as Hwy. 14, either to Cedar Breaks or to US Hwy. 89 for access to Bryce Canyon. The Markagunt Scenic Byway climbs through Cedar Canyon, east of Cedar City, to the top of the lofty Markagunt Plateau, then descends to intersect US Hwy. 89 at Long Valley Junction. The 40-mile drive can be made in an hour, but travelers will want to plan more time for stops since the twisting road does not offer time to view scenes like Ashdown Gorge Wilderness Area, where sheer cliffs rise above both sides of the canyon, or the Zion Overlook at the top of the canyon, which provides a panoramic view of the Kolob Terrace in the northern part of Zion National Park and the monoliths and canyons in the main park. Navajo Lake, a 3.5-mile-long lake, is visible from the highway.

You can also take a dirt side road that heads south, providing access to Navajo Lake and Cascade Falls, a picturesque waterfall that can be reached by a short hike. Navajo Lake is drained by sinkholes, which carry the water into the north fork of the Virgin River. Like many Utah canyons, this is an especially beautiful drive in the fall, but places like Navajo Lake, Cedar Breaks and Cascade Falls are usually closed by heavy winter snows.

Wildlife Viewing

Wild Horses

There is nothing more symbolic of the Old West or more thrilling to see than a herd of wild horses running free across the open range. Wild horse herds can still be seen west of Cedar City, including horses that display the characteristics of the extinct wild tarpan, which were brought to America in the blood lines of the "Spanish barbs"—the mounts of the early Spanish explorers. According to BLM professionals in charge of managing the horses, "While most wild horses come in a variety of colors [black, bay, sorrel or gray], the descendants of the tarpan are shades of dun and grulla [mouse-dun]. They have a dorsal stripe running from the mane into the tail, and stripes appear on the legs near the hocks and knees and sometimes on the withers. Their manes and tails are multicolored, and they have dark fringed ears." If you are lucky, you might see these horses in the Sulphur Wild Horse Management Area early in the morning or late in the evening. **Cedar City District Office, Bureau of Land Management, 176 E. D. L. Sargent Dr., Cedar City, UT 84720; 435-586-2401**.

Where to Stay

Inns and Resorts

BRIAN HEAD SKI RESORT
Cedar Breaks Lodge—$$$

The largest facility at Brian Head, with 170 rooms—some equipped with refrigerators. Pool, whirlpool, sauna, exercise room, garage, dining room and coffee shop. Bicycles can be rented and guided mountain tours can be arranged. **223 Hunter Ridge Dr.; 1-888-AT CEDAR (282-3327); 435-677-3000.**

Chalet Village—$$$

All 35 units have kitchens and fireplaces; some have two-story loft bedrooms. Sauna and whirlpool. **226 S. Hwy. 143, P.O. Box 143588, Brian Head, UT 84719; 1-800-942-8908; 435-677-2025.**

Lodge at Brian Head—$$$

Sauna and whirlpool; 93 rooms, some with kitchenettes. **314 Hunter Ridge Dr., Brian Head, UT 84719; 435-677-3222.**

Timberbrook Village Condominiums—$$$

Indoor pool, exercise room and covered parking; 65 units, all with kitchens. **424 N. Hwy. 143, P.O. Box 190186, Brian Head, UT 84719; 435-677-2806.**

CEDAR CITY

Abbey Inn—$$

Indoor swimming pool and whirlpool; 81 rooms. Located next door to Shoney's Restaurant. **940 W. 200 N.; 1-800-325-5411; 435-586-9966.**

Best Western El Rey Inn—$$ to $$$

One of Cedar City's oldest motels. Owner Ray Knell was one of two charter members of the Best Western system. New units have been constructed over the years. Today the El Rey has 75 rooms, including family suites that sleep up to six and two suites featuring a hot tub and Jacuzzi. There is a heated pool, Jacuzzi, sauna and game room. Poolside rooms are available, and an elevator provides easy access to the second-floor rooms. Centrally located on Cedar City's Main St., the El Rey is within a couple blocks of the SUU campus and is popular with visitors to the Shakespearean Festival. **80 S. Main; 1-800-688-6518; 435-581-6518.**

Best Western Town and Country Inns— $$ to $$$

The two Best Western inns are located in the center of Cedar City on the south and north sides of 200 N. at Main St. With 161 modern rooms and two heated pools, this is one of the city's most popular lodging facilities. **200 N. Main St.; 1-800-528-1234; 435-586-9900.**

Camping

PRIVATE

There are three excellent private campgrounds in the Cedar City area: two in **Cedar City** and one in **Parowan.**

Cedar City KOA Kampground

One hundred sites, 55 with pull-throughs and 68 with complete hookups. Rest rooms and showers, laundry, heated pool, game room, play-ground and barbecue. **1121 N. Main, Cedar City; 435-586-9872.**

Country Aire RV Park

This Good Sam park has 48 RV sites, all with complete hookups and 28 with pull-throughs, plus 15 tentsites. Rest rooms and showers, laundry facilities, convenience store, playground and pool. Located in the northern end of Cedar City. **1700 N. Main, Cedar City; 435-586-2550.**

Foothills RV Park

This Parowan RV park has 79 sites, all with complete hookups. Laundry facilities, showers and rest rooms with wheelchair-accessible facilities. Situated at Exit 75 off Interstate 15. **1435 W. 200 S., Parowan; 435-477-3535.**

PUBLIC

Most of the public campgrounds in the Cedar City area are located east of town on national forest land just off Hwy. 14. There are five campgrounds along a 17-mile stretch of the highway.

Cedar Canyon—This is the closest campground to Cedar City, at an elevation of 8,100 feet; 19 sites. Open mid-May–end of Oct. Located 13 miles east of Cedar City.

Duck Creek—Seventy-nine RV sites and tentsites. Drinking water, toilets and picnic tables. Open mid-June–mid-Sept. Located 30 miles east of Cedar City.

Navajo Lake and The Spruces Campgrounds—Twenty-eight RV sites and tentsites at each campground. Drinking water, toilets and picnic tables. Open mid-June–mid-Sept. Located 25 miles from Cedar City.

Te-Ah Campground—Forty-two RV sites and tentsites. Drinking water, toilets and picnic tables. Open mid-June–mid-Sept. Located 27 miles from Cedar City.

Vermillion Campground—The only public campground between Parowan and Cedar Breaks National Monument; 16 RV sites and tentsites, with drinking water and toilets. Located on forest service land. Open June–Sept. Located 5.5 miles southeast of Parowan on Hwy. 143.

Where to Eat

Adriana's—$$ to $$$

"Good sister, let us dine and never fret." So spoke Adriana in Shakespeare's *Comedy of Errors,* and that has become the watchword for this fine eating establishment. In keeping with Cedar City's Shakespearean theme, this is a charming bungalow-style house that has been redecorated to resemble an old English inn. Heavy dark woods, a stunning antique fireplace imported from England, an impressive staircase, beautiful buffets in each end of the house, quaint booths, pewter dishes and lace tablecloths all add to the character. Built in 1916 for sheepman Jim Thomas Smith and his wife, Mary, they moved into the house when the last of their 10 children was born. The house was remodeled in 1989. The menu features salads, sandwiches and fish-and-chips for lunch; steaks, fish, chicken and pasta for dinner, with chateaubriand, London broil and tenderloin of pork as the house specialties. Open daily in summer 11 A.M.–3 P.M. and 3:30–10 P.M., in winter 5–9 P.M. Reservations strongly recommended during Utah Shakespeare Festival. **164 S. 100 W., Cedar City; 435-865-1234.**

Market Grill—$ to $$

If you want to rub shoulders with local ranchers and farmers, head out to the Market Grill, which is located adjacent to the Cedar City Stockyards on the west side of town. Out-of-towners are welcome, but relatively few find their way to the stockyards. Bonnie and Larry Beachman started their enterprise cooking hamburgers on a cast-iron grill over two hot plates for the hungry stockmen. The endeavor expanded to include their five children and to be housed in a comfortable ranch-style building that, appropriately enough, has a rutted dirt parking area with plenty of room for pickups pulling horse trailers. Along with all this local flavor, there is plenty of good food, including standard breakfasts and nine different kinds of hamburgers for lunch with side salads and soups.

For dinner, the menu keeps a focus on beef—rib-eye and New York steaks, barbecued ribs, ground sirloin steak and the long-standing local favorite of chicken-fried steak with mashed potatoes and gravy. Open Mon.–Sat. 6 A.M.–9 P.M.; closed most holidays. **2290 W. 400 N., Cedar City; 435-586-9325.**

Milt's Stage Stop—$$$

One of the oldest eating establishments in southern Utah, Milt's Stage Stop opened in 1956 under the direction of Swiss-born and -trained chef Walt Wolfinger. Although Walt passed away several years ago, he established a tradition that the present operators, Rusty and Kim Aiken, consciously seek to maintain. Milt's features steaks, prime rib and seafood with Alaskan king crab, Australian rock lobster and a combination platter of crab, shrimp and cod meeting the needs of both meat and fish lovers. With a beautiful canyon location, this is the place local residents go for special occasions. Reservations are recommended. Open daily 6–10 P.M. Located 5 miles east of Cedar City on Hwy. 14. **435-586-9344.**

Pizza Factory—$ to $$

If pizza is part of your regular diet, you won't find a lot of choices in southern Utah, but the Pizza Factory, patronized by Southern Utah University students and local families, carries the reputation for the best pizza in this part of the state. In addition to the traditional pizzas and calzones, there are specialty pizzas—that is, experimental pizzas for the daring. Check the menu for current offerings. Pasta dishes are also available: you can mix and match the type, toppings and sauces. For dessert there are fresh homemade cookies. **124 S. Main, Cedar City; 435-586-3900.**

Sullivan's—$ to $$

With a complete menu of traditional American breakfasts served all day long, Sullivan's has a large local following. Specialties include rolls, pies and its famous homemade cinnamon rolls, which stand more than 3 inches tall and fill the entire plate. The menu warns you'll never eat all of it, and it's true. Open daily 6 A.M.–10 P.M. **301 S. Main, Cedar City; 435-586-6593.**

BRIAN HEAD SKI RESORT
Columbine Cafe and Summit Dining Room—$$ to $$$

This is the special occasion place at Brian Head, in Cedar Breaks Lodge. The chefs at the Columbine are health conscious and try to offer items that are low in fat and cholesterol. The breakfast buffet is especially appealing with fresh fruits and whole-grain products. For lunch there are a number of sandwiches and pasta dishes, with salmon pasta and smoked chicken pasta being the two favorites. The Summit Dining Room keeps the focus on healthy dishes with such entrées as citrus scalloped pasta and ahi tuna cooked Oriental style in a dark oyster sauce. If you want to splurge, try the rib-eye steak smothered with onions, mushrooms and garlic. The downstairs seating area has a beautiful view of the surrounding mountains, including Brian Head Peak. Columbine Cafe open daily 7 A.M.–2 P.M.; Summit Dining Room open daily 6–10 P.M. **Cedar Breaks Lodge, 223 Hunter Ridge Rd., Brian Head, UT 84719; 435-677-3000.**

The Edge—$$ to $$$

Located at the south end of Brian Head, the Edge's dining room offers a spectacular view of the ski mountain and the Brian Head Valley. Luncheon items include specialty burgers and sandwiches. Dinner items feature steaks, chicken and pasta. The filet mignon is a favorite. Open in summer Mon.–Sat. 11:30 A.M.–4 P.M. and 5–10 P.M., Sun. 10 A.M.–3 P.M. and 5–10 P.M.; during ski season Mon.–Sat. 5–10 P.M., Sun. 8 A.M.– 3 P.M. and 5–10 P.M. **406 S. Hwy. 143; 435-677-3343.**

Services

Visitor Information
Iron County Tourism and Convention Bureau and Cedar City Chamber of Commerce—Open Mon.–Fri. 8 A.M.–5 P.M. **581 N. Main, P.O. Box 1007, Cedar City, UT 84720; 1-800-354-4849; 435-586-5124; www.utah-splayground.org.**

Parowan Visitor Center—75 N. Main St., Parowan, UT 84761; 435-477-8190.

Car Rentals
Car rentals at the Cedar City Airport include **Avis (1-800-831-2847)** and **National (1-800-227-7368; 435-586-7059).**

Zion National Park

There is good reason why this Utah park is so popular. Sheer cliffs of creamy Navajo sandstone rise 2,000 feet above a verdant valley floor; the Virgin River has cut narrow canyons into the rock barely 40 feet wide in places; hand-carved hiking trails, 75 years old, switchback along cliffs with vertical drops of hundreds of feet; scenic drives wind along the canyon floor or take you up the face of the mountain and through a mile-long tunnel carved through a solid sandstone cliff; and mountains of sunset-hued stone with names like the Sentinel, the Watchman, West Temple, Mountain of the Sun, Angel's Landing, the Three Patriarchs and the Great White Throne watch over this sanctuary of living things. Zion is many things to many people.

Within the 229-square-mile park, every spot is a photo opportunity—a place to marvel at the incredible beauty of this location. Zion is a gigantic unroofed cathedral where the sheer size and glory of the mountains demand reverence and awe that cleanse and restore the spirit. Its beauty and inspiration are nature's gift. Long after your visit to Zion, visions of great stone temples appear as reassuring reminders that the world we inhabit is magnificent.

With nearly three million visitors each year, Zion is the eighth most-visited park in the United States. Zion's popularity is also its greatest liability. It is being "loved to death." The area is fragile and, especially during the summer, overcrowded. You can enjoy the park much more in the off-seasons, especially in the early spring and late fall when most of the crowds have disappeared.

Nearby communities of Springdale, Rockville, Virgin and La Verkin, all located on Hwy. 9, provide places for park visitors to rest and refresh themselves, as well as interesting sights in their own right.

History

The Anasazi lived in Zion Canyon and the environs from about A.D. 500 to 1200. Throughout the park, abandoned cliff houses, rock art and chipping sites remain as evidence of their presence. When the Anasazi moved on, the hunter-gatherers moved into the area surrounding the canyon but were reluctant to enter Zion Canyon for fear of retribution from evil spirits living there. Nephi Johnson, a young missionary sent by Brigham Young to the Native Americans along the Virgin River in September 1858, may have been the first Anglo to see the Zion Canyon area. Johnson told family members that his Paiute guide refused to go all the way up the canyon with him, leaving him to make the journey into the depths alone. He reported that he had found places in the canyon where the sun never reached because the canyon walls were so high and narrow. That same year, Johnson helped found the settlement of Virgin.

During the fall and winter of 1862–1863, Springdale, just west of what is now Zion's park headquarters, was settled. One of the settlers, Isaac Behunin, built the first one-room log cabin in Zion Canyon, at a site near the present location of Zion Lodge. It was Behunin who gave the name Zion to the canyon he called home. Behunin had joined the Mormon church shortly after its founding in 1830 and had lived through persecutions in Missouri and Illinois before making the trek to Utah. In Mormon theology, Zion means a resting place where the pure in

Getting There

There are three entrances to Zion National Park. Visitor centers are located at two of those entrances, at the south entrance and at the entrance to the Kolob Canyons.

Most visitors enter through the **south entrance** near the town of Springdale. This entrance is reached by turning off Interstate 15 at Exit 16 onto Hwy. 9. If you are heading north from St. George, drive to La Verkin. From there, it is a scenic drive through the Virgin River Valley to Springdale. From Cedar City, take Exit 27 onto Hwy. 17 and join Hwy. 9 in La Verkin. The park entrance is 43 miles northeast of St. George and 59 miles south of Cedar City.

To reach Zion's **east entrance,** turn off US Hwy. 89 at Mt. Carmel Junction and continue west 24 miles. The east entrance is 41 miles northwest of Kanab and 74 miles southwest of Panguitch. The distance from Salt Lake City, following Interstate 15 south, is 309 miles.

The park's third entrance takes you along a 5.5-mile scenic road to the **Kolob Unit** in the extreme northwestern portion of the park. Access to the Kolob Unit is about 40 miles from the main park entrance, but it is the easiest section to visit for travelers along Interstate 15, as it is located just to the east off Exit 40. There are visitor centers in the main park and at the entrance to the Kolob Canyons.

There is a fourth access point: **Kolob Terrace / Reservoir Rd.,** which heads north from Hwy. 9 at the town of Virgin, taking you past trailheads for backcountry hiking in the middle of the park. The road continues out of the park, passing Kolob Reservoir, and reaches Hwy. 14 just east of Cedar City (see the Scenic Drives section).

heart dwell. When Behunin unhitched his wagon and made his home, he believed that his lifelong journey had brought him to a place of safety and peace.

A few other settlers built cabins within the canyon, but there was little room for farming along the narrow valley floor. In 1872 Maj. John Wesley Powell surveyed the area and gave the canyon its Indian name, Mukun-tuweap, without recording which of several possible meanings or origins was correct. It could mean "Straight Canyon," "Big Canyon," "Red Dirt," "the Place of the Gods" or "God's Land." It also may have been named for Chief Mokun of the Virgin River Indians, with Mukun-tuweap meaning "Land of Mokun." It could also be a derivative of a desert plant called *muk-unk*.

Beginning in 1900, young David Flanigan began experimenting with a cable system that would lower timber from the high mountain forests to the valley floor via what is now Cable Mountain. So successful was his device that, by 1906, he had lowered 200,000 board feet of sawed lumber down the cliff. Four years later, people with nerves of steel started to "ride the cable"—first on a dare, then to avoid the strenuous hike up and down the 1,800-foot-high mountain.

On July 31, 1909, the canyon was designated as the Mukuntuweap National Monument, and eight years later, the first automobile road was constructed into the canyon. Renamed Zion National Monument in 1918, it became a national park in 1919. The original Zion Lodge was built in 1925 by the Utah Parks Company as part of their tourist facilities in Utah. The first entrance fees to the park—50 cents—were levied in 1926.

In 1927 construction began on the Zion–Mt. Carmel Tunnel. The 1.1-mile-long tunnel was designed to shorten the distance to Grand Canyon and Bryce Canyon by providing an east entrance to the park from Long Valley (present-day US Hwy. 89). The tunnel, an engineering marvel, took three years to complete and cost $2 million. In 1937 the scenic Kolob Canyons region (in the northwest corner of the park) was

first designated a new Zion National Monument; it was incorporated into the rest of Zion National Park in 1956. For most of the 1930s, the Civilian Conservation Corps carried out a number of projects, including construction of the entrance stations, the South Campground and the Canyon Overlook and Watchman Trails, among others.

A new era began for the national park with the introduction of a shuttle-bus system (see the sidebar for details) and the opening of the new visitor center in 2000. Both improvements have added significantly to the quality of the Zion National Park experience.

Major Attractions

Kolob Canyons

The Finger Canyons of the Kolob, which, according to Mormon theology, were named for the star (Kolob) at the center of the universe and closest to the throne of God, are a spectacular set of unique sandstone formations and canyons that were added to Zion National Park in 1956. **Kolob Canyons Visitor Center** at the entrance to the Kolob Unit is open year-round daily (except for winter holidays), but has a limited range of services due to its size and location. Friendly rangers here provide information, books, maps and backcountry permits. Open daily 8 A.M.–5 P.M. Located just off I-15 at Exit 40. **435-586-9548.**

Zion Canyon

The North Fork of the Virgin River winds through the heart of Zion Canyon, from the Narrows deep in the midst of the park south to the park's southern boundary at Hwy. 9 (the Zion–Mt. Carmel Hwy.). Along this narrow valley are some of the most spectacular rock formations to be found anywhere. There is something about the majesty of the carved sandstone and domed peaks that seems to bring out the best in people. The size, majesty and beauty of the Great White Throne, for instance, are beyond description—most people photograph it instead. Zion Canyon is the main thing that visitors to the park come to see, and its scale and beauty stagger the imagination. **Zion Canyon Visitor Center,** the largest and perhaps most attractive of any found in the Utah national parks, was opened in 2000. It contains a well-stocked bookstore and gift shop, and offers information and free ranger talks throughout the day. Plan to make this your first stop if you are entering the canyon at the south entrance. Open daily (except Christmas Day) late Mar.–Nov. 8 A.M.–8 P.M.; the rest of the year 8 A.M.–5 P.M. Located on Hwy. 9 just east of Springdale. The visitor center is also Zion National Park headquarters. Open Mon.–Fri. 8 A.M.–4:30 P.M. **Superintendent, Zion National Park, Springdale, UT 84767-1099; 435-772-3256; www.nps.gov/zion.**

Zion–Mt. Carmel Highway / Hwy. 9

This 24-mile drive along Hwy. 9 from the junction with Zion Canyon Scenic Dr. at the park's south entrance to US Hwy. 89 at Mt. Carmel Junction is a must for park visitors. It heads east across the southeastern edge of the park, switch-backing up the spectacular canyon, passing through the impressive tunnel and exiting the park's east entrance. Note that there are restrictions on vehicles using the tunnel. Call the National Park Service **(435-772-3256)** for information if you are driving an RV.

From the turnoff to Zion Canyon Scenic Dr., head east; just beyond, at the bottom of the switchbacks, you cross a beautifully arched stone bridge that, when viewed from one of the turnouts along the switchbacks, blends so well with the natural stone of the canyon that it is almost unnoticeable. Next you loop back and forth 800 feet up the side of the mountain, past the huge "blind" alcove known as the Great Zion Arch.

At the top of the switchbacks you reach the 1.1-mile-long Zion–Mt. Carmel Tunnel, which was blasted through the Navajo sandstone in the 1920s and dedicated in July 1930. Five portals that were opened through the canyon wall were initially used to remove the rock during construction of the tunnel. After the tunnel was opened, visitors could stop their automobiles and gaze out the human-made arches to admire the unbelievable view. The portals are still there, but because of heavy traffic, stopping is no longer allowed inside the tunnel.

On the other side of the tunnel, the landscape looks quite different. Here, the dune-formed nature of the Navajo sandstone is quite obvious. This is particularly true at Checkerboard Mesa, where wind and water have etched dramatic cracks and grooves into the cream-colored rock, creating a "checkerboard" effect.

Festivals and Events

St. Patrick's Day

Mar. 17. Green means a lot in the red rock cliffs of Zion Canyon, and as the trees start to bud and the wildflowers begin to make their appearance, residents of Springdale have taken to celebrating St. Patrick's Day with great vigor. It all started in 1989 when the owners of Flanigan's Inn decided to promote the land of their namesake by celebrating St. Patrick's Day. The rest of the community has joined in, and now a small parade winds its way along Zion Park Blvd., with the music of a bagpipe band echoing off the nearby cliffs. After the parade there is a green Jell-O bake-off and sculpting contest, an Irish concert in the evening and other activities throughout the day. **435-772-3244.**

Outdoor Activities

Biking

Gooseberry Mesa

Off-road biking is prohibited on trails inside Zion National Park, but from Springdale there is an excellent ride west to Gooseberry Mesa on the south side of the Virgin River. The 30-mile out-and-back ride begins in Springdale and follows Hwy. 9 west for 3 miles to Rockville, where you turn south in the middle of town onto Bridge Rd. and cross the Virgin River.

Keep to the right toward Grafton and Hwy. 59 until the paved road becomes dirt and gravel and you reach a cattle guard at a fork in the road, about 1.5 miles south of Rockville. Take the road to the left to Smithsonian Butte Scenic Backway (see the Scenic Drives section) and Hwy. 59. What begins as a gradual climb soon becomes a steep mile-long climb, after which you continue west then south along a fairly level 3.5-mile stretch around the north and west sides of the base of Smithsonian Butte until you come to a junction with a sign point-ing to Gooseberry Mesa to the west. From here it is another 4.5 miles across the top of Gooseberry Mesa to the end of the road. From the top of Gooseberry Mesa, there are spectacular views of Zion Canyon back to the north and east and of the Pine Valley Mountains to the west.

Grafton

This easy ride follows the same route described for the Gooseberry Mesa ride (see above); however, at the fork in the road 1.5 miles south of Rockville (at 4.5 miles from Springdale), take the road to the right. It's about 2 miles along this road to the abandoned ghost town of Grafton, where you will find the old church and a few other buildings (see the Museums and Historic Sites section). You can begin in Rockville for a 7-mile out-and-back ride or ride from Springdale for a 13-mile out-and-back ride.

Upper Zion Canyon

The adoption of the shuttle-bus system for the Upper Zion Canyon area has reduced traffic to the point where the road is now a viable bike route. Many bikers start from Springdale and ride to the end of the road at the Temple of Sinawava, which makes for about a 20-mile round-trip route, depending on where you begin in Springdale.

Rentals

Bikes, a very pleasant way to visit the canyon, can be rented in Springdale: **Bike Zion, 1458 Zion Park Blvd., 435-772-2453,** and **Springdale Cycles, 932 Zion Park Blvd.,**

435-772-0575 can fix you up with one- or multi-day rentals.

Fishing

Kolob Reservoir

This reservoir is stocked with rainbow, German brown, brook and cutthroat trout. A Utah fishing license is required. The road is a designated Scenic Backway (see the Scenic Drives section under Seeing and Doing). Located off the Kolob Terrace/Reservoir Rd., 23 miles north of Virgin and north of the park boundary.

Hiking

Hiking is the best and, in many cases, the only way to see Zion National Park. There are a variety of trails—some that are an easy stroll down a level paved walkway and others that demand stamina and even courage to traverse the exposed cliffs and scale the dizzying heights. The Zion Natural History Association has prepared a handy hiking guide, *Hiking in Zion National Park: The Trails,* which describes 18 trails. Backcountry permits are required for overnight camping within the park and for the Zion Narrows. Some hikes require a shuttle. Shuttle service can be arranged through Zion Lodge; **435-772-3213.**

Most of the hiking trails are located in the Zion Canyon section of the park, but other trails begin near the east entrance, begin near the south entrance, start from the Kolob Terrace/Reservoir Rd. or are located in the Kolob Unit. For the longer hikes, it is strongly recommended that you obtain a topographic map and consult a park ranger to obtain up-to-date trail information. The following are some favorite trails in the four locations.

East Entrance Area Trails

Access to trails in the eastern section of the park is off Hwy. 9. Most hikers spend a couple of days hiking this area of the park.

East Entrance Trail—The trailhead for the East Entrance Trail, which leads to the Deertrap Mountain and Cable Mountain Trails and the

Echo Canyon/Weeping Rock Trail, is located at the east entrance of the park. These trails offer views that are favorites for many hikers in Zion National Park. It is possible to make the 10.6-mile hike from the east entrance to Weeping Rock in Zion Canyon in a day, and even to cover the 20.6 miles of trails to take in Deertrap Mountain and Cable Mountain too, if you are in excellent shape, have good weather, get an early start and arrange a pickup from Zion Canyon Rd. Follow the East Entrance Trail for 5.6 miles to the Stave Spring Junction. The left branch is the Deertrap Mountain Trail, which also leads to the Cable Mountain Trail. The right branch is the Echo Canyon/Weeping Rock Trail.

Deertrap Mountain Trail—At 1.1 miles from the Stave Spring Junction (6.7 miles from the east entrance), the **Cable Mountain Trail** branches from the Deertrap Mountain Trail, leading in 1.8 miles to unforgettable views of the top of the Great White Throne, Angels Landing, Observation Point, the West Rim and David Flanigan's historic cableworks at 8.5 miles from the east entrance. If you stay on the Deertrap Mountain Trail, at 3.2 miles from the Stave Spring Junction you reach the Deertrap Mountain Overlook at 8.8 miles from the east entrance, with its breathtaking view of the Court of the Patriarchs, Twin Brothers and the East Temple in the lower end of Zion Canyon.

Echo Canyon Trail—From Stave Spring Junction, the right-hand trail continues for 5 miles around the head of Echo Canyon, descending along the north side to the Zion Canyon Rd. at Weeping Rock, 10.6 miles from the east entrance.

Canyon Overlook—The trailhead is located about 6 miles west of the east entrance, just beyond the east entrance to the Zion–Mt. Carmel Tunnel and 5 miles east of the Zion Canyon Visitor Center. The trail to the spectacular overlook is only 0.5 mile long and gets plenty of use, but from the overlook you can see into Pine Creek Canyon 1,000 feet below, and into one of the five portals of the Zion–Mt. Carmel Tunnel. There are views of West and East Temples, the Towers of the Virgin and the streaked wall in lower Zion Canyon. Caution is needed on the uneven steps cut into the sandstone at the start of the trail and near the vertical drop-offs (handrails are provided in places). An interpretive leaflet available at the Zion Canyon Visitor Center and usually at the trailhead introduces the natural history of the higher canyon area. Ranger-guided tours are conducted on this trail. Check at the visitor center for schedules.

Kolob Terrace/Reservoir Rd. Trails

This designated Scenic Backway (see the Scenic Drives section) provides access to the least-visited part of Zion National Park, the Kolob Unit, and offers an opportunity to be free of the crowds in other parts of the park during the summer season. The road begins from Hwy. 9 at the eastern end of the town of Virgin 14 miles west of the south entrance to Zion, and runs north through the park and on past Kolob Reservoir to Hwy. 14 just east of Cedar City. Trails from this road link the main part of the park with the remote Finger Canyons of the Kolob. Because the road is steep, some larger vehicles tend to overheat during the summertime, so take your time and watch your heat gauge.

Hop Valley Trail—The trailhead is located about 13 miles north of the junction with Hwy. 9 on the left-hand side of the road. Most hikers usually make this an overnight hike, although strong hikers may be able to cover the 13.8-mile round-trip hike in a day. The trail drops from the trailhead almost 1,000 feet to La Verkin Creek, then winds through the beautiful Hop Valley with its green meadows and 600-foot-high Navajo sandstone cliffs. The trail intersects the La Verkin Creek Trail (see Kolob Unit Trails, below), and Kolob Arch is less than a mile farther north. To reach Kolob Arch, at the junction with the La Verkin Creek Trail at 6.9 miles, turn left and head in a westerly direction for about 0.3 mile, then watch for the 0.6-mile side trail to Kolob Arch. You can either return to the Hop Valley trailhead or continue west, then north, along the La Verkin Creek Trail for 7 miles to its trailhead at Lee Pass. The latter route will require a shuttle.

Wildcat Canyon and Northgate Peaks Trails—Hikers and backpackers have several options from the trailhead located on the south side of the Kolob Terrace Rd. about 16 miles north of the junction with Hwy. 9. A one-way hike along Wildcat Canyon Trail, including the 2.4-mile round-trip spur trail to Northgate Peaks Overlook, is 8.4 miles, ending at the West Rim trailhead. An out-and-back hike returning to the Wildcat Canyon trailhead, including the 2.4-mile side trip to Northgate Peaks Overlook, is 14.4 miles. The elevation gain between the Wildcat Canyon and West Rim trailheads is 450 feet, but in between there is a 500-foot descent into Wildcat Canyon and a 500-foot ascent back out.

Most hikers follow the **Wildcat Canyon Trail** for 5.8 miles in an easterly/northeasterly direction to its junction with the West Rim Trail (see below) and include the 1.2-mile-long side trip to the **Northgate Peaks Overlook** for a view of the Northgate Peaks, North Guardian Angel and the canyons of the left fork of North Creek. The trails pass through ponderosa pine, aspen groves, lush meadows and oak thickets, and offer spectacular views of the mountains and red sandstone cliffs. At the junction with the West Rim Trail, it is only 0.1 mile to the West Rim trailhead, where you can meet a shuttle vehicle.

West Rim Trail—The West Rim trailhead is east of the Lava Point Campground off the Kolob Terrace Rd. Take the Kolob Terrace Rd. for 20 miles north from Hwy. 9, then turn right at the sign for Lava Point and the West Rim Trail. Follow it for 1 mile, then keep to the left to reach the West Rim trailhead 1.3 miles farther on.

The 14.3-mile-long West Rim Trail takes you to the Grotto Picnic Area just north of the Zion Lodge in Zion Canyon. Most hikers make this a two-day hike—it is the most popular overnight hike in the park—but it is possible for well-conditioned hikers to complete it in a day, with a shuttle vehicle on Zion Canyon Rd. From the high country to the depths of Zion Canyon, you lose 3,100 feet in elevation. The scenic vistas

from the West Rim Trail of Red Arch Mountain, Angels Landing, the Great White Throne and East Temple are considered by many to be the finest in the park. The last 5 miles are very steep as the trail descends into Zion Canyon along a rock, pavement and concrete path past the trail to Angels Landing.

Kolob Unit Trails

This section of Zion National Park is often overlooked by visitors because it seems so far from the south entrance's Zion Canyon Visitor Center and Zion Lodge, but the easy access off Interstate 15 makes this a favorite area for informed highway travelers. This is one of the few places in the United States where you can be inside a national park less than a mile from the interstate. The scenery in the Kolob Unit is just as magnificent as anywhere in the park, or in any national park for that matter, and two good hiking trails take you into the heart of the Vermillion Cliffs and deep-cut canyons. Overnight hikes require a backcountry permit that can be obtained from the Kolob Canyons Visitor Center.

La Verkin Creek and Kolob Arch Trails—Lee Pass, located 3.5 miles east of the Kolob Canyons Visitor Center, is the trailhead for the La Verkin Creek Trail. This trail is a popular backpacking trail because of the access to Kolob Arch, which, with a span measuring 310 feet, is one of the largest freestanding arches in the world. To see the arch, hike 6.6 miles to Kolob Arch Trail Junction and another 0.6 mile to Kolob Arch Viewpoint, which is 0.25 mile from the arch. If you push it, you can make the 14.4-mile round-trip hike in a day, but keep in mind that the return leg is an 800-foot climb back up to Lee Pass, and the 1.2-mile round-trip hike on the Kolob Arch Viewpoint Trail is rocky and more primitive than on the main trail. One option that does not require a return hike is to continue down the Hop Valley Trail to its trailhead on the Kolob Terrace/Reservoir Rd. (see above).

Taylor Creek Trail—The trailhead is located 2 miles east of the Kolob Canyons Visitor Center. The Taylor Creek Trail parallels the creek for 2.5 miles to Double Arch Alcove. Along the trail, you pass two historic cabins: the Larsen Cabin, a 1929 homestead cabin built by Gustave C. Larsen of white-fir logs, located just west of the confluence of the middle fork and north fork of Taylor Creek; and farther up the trail, not far from the Double Arch Alcove, the Arthur Fife Cabin built in 1930. The elevation gain is just over 400 feet. One of the best times to make this hike is in the fall, when the autumn leaves against the blue sky and red rock are spectacular.

South Entrance Area Trails

Chinle Trail—The trail begins at a large dirt turnout on the right side of the road between Springdale and Rockville—3.5 miles west of the South Entrance Station. You can begin the hike here or drive your vehicle, if the road is passable, 1.3 miles north to the park boundary. Located in the southern end of the park, this hike is the most popular winter hike because of its lower elevation, level terrain and absence of snow and ice. The one-way length of the trail inside the park is 6.8 miles.

Part of the trail passes the Old Scoggins Stock Trail, built by pioneer cattlemen to move their animals through a break in the cliff. There is also a historic oil well site that dates from 1908 during the pioneer days of oil exploration in Utah. You will see petrified wood scattered throughout the area, and at one time this trail was known as the Petrified Forest Trail. Avoid any temptation to collect petrified wood, as it is against park regulations and diminishes enjoyment for future visitors.

Zion Canyon Trails

The most popular hiking trails within the national park are located within Zion Canyon. Easy access, magnificent scenery and well-developed trails attract thousands of hikers of all levels each year. Unless you hike these trails in the off-season or at daybreak, expect to share the experience with others. But everyone seems ready to share a smile, offer a word of greeting and recount experiences along the trails, so don't avoid these hikes because they are popular; just go out and enjoy the scenery and your fellow visitors.

Watchman Trail—The trailhead is just east of Watchman Campground Information Station. The 3-mile round-trip hike leads to the viewpoint on a plateau near the base of the Watchman. The Watchman guards the south entrance to Zion Canyon and offers a breathtaking view of West Temple, the Towers of the Virgin, the town of Springdale and the Virgin River.

Emerald Pools Trail System—The trail begins across the river bridge west of Zion Lodge. If you are staying at Zion Lodge, this will likely be the first hike you take. Total round-trip distance to the Lower Pool is 1.2 miles, 2.2 miles if you go on to the Upper Pool. The 0.6-mile concrete trail to Lower Emerald Pool can be negotiated by wheelchairs, with some assistance, and by baby strollers. This is a cool, shady hike out of the sizzling summer sun. The "hanging gardens" of monkeyflower, mosses and ferns give an almost tropiclike sensation. The 0.5-mile-long trail to the Upper Pool is unpaved and not maintained. The two small waterfalls and emerald pools, formed by a small perennial spring coming out of Heaps Canyon, and the views of Lady Mountain, Red Arch Mountain, the Great White Throne and other Zion landmarks make this one of the most popular hikes in the park. Because of their small size, these pools are closed to swimming and wading.

Angels Landing—This popular trail begins at the Grotto Picnic Area, about 0.6 mile up the canyon from Zion Lodge. The steep trail is paved, but it is no place for those prone to acrophobia. The 1.9-mile hike to Scout Lookout climbs 1,000 feet, and it's another 0.5 mile and 500 feet of elevation gain to Angels Landing. The trail was cut into the rock in 1926. The most famous part of the trail is the 21 short switchbacks known as "Walters Wiggles"—named for Walter Ruesch, a resident of Springdale and the first custodian and acting superintendent of the park. From Scout Lookout, the 0.5-mile trail to Angels Landing crosses a steep, narrow ridge with support chains anchored into the rock that offer only the illusion of security. If heights bother you, skip this trail. Young children should not be taken on the trail, and anyone who makes the hike should exercise great caution. Avoid the trail when it is wet or icy, or when thunderstorms make such exposure dangerous. Be sure to complete your hike before dark. Despite all these cautions, this amazing trail is thrilling to hike, and the views from Scout Lookout and Angels Landing into Zion Canyon are unforgettable.

Hidden Canyon—The trailhead is at the Weeping Rock parking area. The 1.1-mile paved trail into the canyon was carved out of solid rock in some places by Park Service employees and Civilian Conservation Corps members during the 1920s and 1930s, whereas Hidden Canyon was carved by water cascading between two giants—Cable Mountain and the Great White Throne. The moderately strenuous trail climbs 1,000 feet and features some steep drop-offs.

Observation Point—This trail also begins at the Weeping Rock parking area; it rises 2,200 feet in 3.7 miles—the National Park Service rates this as strenuous. The trail, used by Indians and Mormon pioneers, winds around the base of Cable Mountain before climbing onto the ponderosa pine-covered plateau. From Observation Point you have an unbelievable view of the Great White Throne, Cable Mountain, the West Rim, Angels Landing and Zion Canyon. Plan at least a half day to make the 7.5-mile round trip.

Riverside Walk—The trailhead is at the end of the Zion Canyon Scenic Dr. just beyond the Temple of Sinawava parking area. Apr.–Oct., this parking area is so crowded that finding a parking space can be difficult, but park only in designated parking areas. As you begin the hike from the parking area, note the "Danger Level" sign that is posted: if you wish to hike upriver, you need to know what the water level is. The trail follows the east side of the Virgin River for 1 mile upstream along a paved, mostly level path, making it accessible for wheelchairs and baby strollers. This hike is undertaken by 700,000 visitors a year, making it the most popular trail in the park. The high walls keep the trail in the shade much of the time and ensure a pleasant stroll. It is one hike where the higher the air temperature, the better. At the end of the paved trail, it is decision time. You can either return

from this point for a 2-mile out-and-back, or join the hundreds who plunge into the ankle- to knee-deep water for some river hiking.

Don't be afraid to get a little wet. Wear a pair of hiking boots or sneakers that you don't mind getting soaked. For 21st-century humans, barefoot is no way to go, even with the threat of ruining a pair of shoes; you will remember the hike long after you have forgotten about the shoes. Watch out for submerged rocks that can twist your ankle, and go at your own pace. Many people carry a walking stick to keep their balance. This is especially useful when the water is quite deep. But bring your walking stick with you since park rules prohibit cutting or breaking limbs from living or dead trees for walking sticks. If you are in a group, appoint a designated photographer, or take turns carrying a camera (with a waterproof case or wrapped in a plastic bag) to take pictures that those back home simply will not believe.

If the water level is low, you can wade up the river as far as you want, though few go beyond Orderville Canyon, 1.8 miles from the end of the paved trail. As you proceed up-canyon, the walls become narrower and narrower. The high cliff walls are decorated with "hanging gardens," waterfalls plunge off sheer faces and the ever-beckoning sound of the river keeps you going to see what new wonder is just around the next corner. It is a time to forget about everything else and return to nature's womb.

Gateway to the Narrows Trail—The Riverside Walk may be adventurous enough for 9,999 of the folks who visit the park, but for the one in 10,000 who need more, there is the 17.5-mile stretch of the Virgin River that descends north to south from the Chamberlain Ranch and ends up at the Riverside Walk and the Temple of Sinawava. The hike requires a shuttle to the Chamberlain Ranch, reached via a gravel road from Hwy. 9. Backcountry permits are required for overnight hikes and day hikes through the length of the canyon.

Because of the danger from flash floods in the Narrows—where the canyon walls are no more than 40 feet apart—Park Service rangers exercise great caution and prohibit entrance into the canyon if weather forecasts are unfavorable. While most of the hike is in knee-deep water, there can be deep pools that require swimming. The trek is a strenuous day hike or, with proper equipment and preparation, an overnight hike. Because of the vagaries of weather and water levels, and the need for a backcountry permit, check in at the visitor center to finalize your plans. If you want to make this hike, be prepared physically, have good equipment and supplies—especially rubber-soled hiking boots with good ankle support and a walking stick—go with reliable companions, arrange the necessary logistics and offer an adequate sacrifice so that the weather gods will smile kindly on your venture.

Horseback Riding

Guided horseback rides inside the park are available Mar.–Oct. through Zion Lodge; **801-772-3810.**

Seeing and Doing

Art Galleries

Worthington Gallery

Local artisan Greg Worthington produces his pottery in nearby Rockville and also exhibits pottery and works from nearly two dozen other potters and artisans throughout the West. Worth a visit. Open year-round daily 9 A.M.–8 P.M. **789 Zion Park Blvd., Rockville; 435-772-3446; www.worthingtongallery.com.**

Museums and Historic Sites

Grafton Ghost Town

Initially settled in 1859, the settlement was destroyed by "the Great Flood" of 1861, causing the town to be relocated to a higher location. Succeeding floods continued to batter the little community until unrest during the Black Hawk War caused it to be abandoned until 1868. Today the remains of the church and some pioneer homes, and the use of the town for the 1969 movie *Butch Cassidy and the Sundance Kid,* make

this one of Utah's most popular ghost towns. The Grafton Historic Foundation has undertaken to preserve the community through the acquisition of more than 200 acres that comprise the town site, working to establish easements with other property owners, and the restoration of the 1880s church, the three-room John Woods house and barn and the one-story log home and one-and-a-half-story adobe home occupied by two wives of Lorenzo Russell. The little pioneer cemetery includes a headstone commemorating the massacre of the Berry family by Indians at Short Creek in 1866. The last settlers moved out of the community in 1914. From Rockville, turn south on Bridge Ln. and follow it over the one-way bridge across the Virgin River. Turn right (west) and follow the dirt road as it parallels the river for about 2.5 miles until you reach Grafton.

Zion Park Museum

Opened in the summer of 2002, this museum is the first stop on the shuttle after it leaves the new visitor center. Exhibits and a film interpret the park's cultural history, including the earliest native inhabitants, later settlers and the development of the national park, along with providing an introduction to the natural history of the area. Open daily 9 A.M.–5 P.M. Located in the old visitor center. **1-888-518-7070; www.zion-park.com.**

Nature Centers

Zion Nature Center

June–Aug., daily programs are offered for children ages 6–12. In addition, a variety of ranger-guided walks, evening programs and talks are offered at various locations in the park late Mar.–Nov. Check at the visitor centers for a schedule of activities.

Nightlife

Zion Canyon Theatre

After a long and bitter debate that divided the community of Springdale on the appropriateness of constructing a six-story big-screen theater at the entrance to Zion National Park, the 482-seat theater opened in June 1994. A 37-minute film, Treasure of the Gods, directed by Academy Award winner Keith Merrill, depicts a mythical experience about the Anasazi, Paiutes, Spanish conquistadors and padres, early Mormon settlers and a photographer. Park rangers point out that the story should not be taken too literally. There are no lost Indian or Spanish gold mines, no Indian ruins as featured in the film, no hang gliders are allowed in the park and rock climbing is carefully regulated. The film is worth viewing for the adventure alone—the flash flood and the rock-climbing feats performed by a hand-picked crew from the Yosemite Search and Rescue Team will leave you breathless. Shown daily on a continuous schedule from morning through early evening, Apr.–Oct. 8:30 A.M.–8:30 P.M., Nov.–Mar. 10:30 A.M.–6:30 P.M. Admission fee charged. **Zion Canyon Theatre, 145 Zion Park Blvd., Springdale, UT 84767; 1-888-256-3456; 435-772-2400; www.zioncanyontheatre.com.**

Scenic Drives

Kolob Canyons Rd.

Millions of people bypass this scenic 5.5-mile drive each year as they zoom up and down Interstate 15. What a pity! Even if you have only a half hour, drive to the end of the short road and take in the vista of Kolob Canyons from the viewpoint, then return to the interstate—your soul will be refreshed. A short hike at the turnaround offers glorious views to the south. The road also provides access to the Taylor Creek and La Verkin Creek Trails (see the Hiking section). The Kolob Canyons Visitor Center at the beginning of the drive has a road guide, with numbered stops along the drive, that describes the geology, ecology and history of Kolob. Access is from Exit 40 off Interstate 15 between St. George and Cedar City.

Kolob Terrace/Reservoir Rd. Scenic Backway

This 45-mile scenic drive runs north from the town of Virgin through the middle part of Zion National Park. The road provides access to the Hop Valley, West Rim, Wildcat Canyon and Northgate Peaks Trails (see the Hiking section under Outdoor Activities), as well as to Kolob Reservoir (see the Fishing section under Outdoor Activities). The pavement ends just beyond the northern boundary of the park at 18 miles, and the graded dirt road continues for 25 miles or so to Hwy. 14 at 6 miles east of Cedar City. The road reaches a high elevation and is closed by heavy winter snows, usually until May; however, you can drive part of the way. See the Scenic Drives section under Seeing and Doing in the **Cedar City** chapter for details on the northern section of this road.

Smithsonian Butte Scenic Backway

This 9-mile-long drive between Hwy. 9 and the Arizona Strip offers one of the most spectacular panoramic views of Zion National Park as well as other landmarks, including Canaan Mountain, Smithsonian Butte, the Virgin River Valley, the Eagle Crags and the 2,000-foot headwall at the Pines. To appreciate the varied landscape, plan to drive the route in both directions. Begin in Rockville at the bridge across the Virgin River, then head south, past the turnoff for the ghost town of Grafton (see Museums and Historic Sites), and continue to the junction with Hwy. 59, 8 miles northwest of Hildale and 15 miles southeast of Hurricane.

Zion Canyon Scenic Dr.

This paved road through the heart of Zion Canyon winds along the east side of the North Fork of the Virgin River as it takes you 6.2 miles north from its junction with Hwy. 9—known as the Zion–Mt. Carmel Hwy. inside the park (see the Major Attractions section). The drive dead-ends at the Temple of Sinawava parking area and the trailhead for the Gateway to the Narrows Trail. Unless you make the drive in the off-season (Nov.–Mar.), you will not be permitted to take a private vehicle into upper Zion Canyon unless you have overnight reservations at Zion Lodge. Instead, park visitors during the summer use the shuttle system (see the sidebar), which makes stops along the route.

Highlights include:

Court of the Patriarchs—1.6 miles up the canyon. From the parking area, take the 50-yard-long concrete trail up to the viewpoint, where you can look across the canyon to the massive stone formations that are appropriately named the Three Patriarchs, for the Old Testament prophets Abraham, Isaac and Jacob. You can also see the Streaked Wall, the Sentinel, Mt. Moroni, the Spearhead and Angels Landing. Behind you loom the Mountain of the Sun and the Twin Brothers.

Zion Lodge—2.5 miles up the canyon. The historic Zion Lodge harks back to the days before World War II, when visitors to Zion Canyon often arrived by train and bus and needed a convenient and unobtrusive place to stay. Even if you do not stay at the Zion Lodge (it is usually booked well in advance), it is still fun to walk through and pretend that you are a guest, perhaps even have lunch or dinner at the lodge, and reflect on what it must have been like in the 1920s when the first guests arrived. In 1966 a fire destroyed the original 1925 stone-and-timber building. Because necessity dictated that a new lodge be constructed in three months, Gilbert Stanley Underwood's classic "Rustic Architectural" design for the lodge was sacrificed. Fortunately, during the winter of 1989–1990 the lodge facade was successfully renovated to reflect Underwood's original design.

Weeping Rock—4.5 miles up the canyon. It's a short 0.2-mile hike to the Weeping Rock, where water seeps out of the canyon wall to form a light mist. On a hot summer day, this is a most refreshing stop. Information about the Cable Mountain Draw Works is provided along the trail, and you stand in amazement at how, in pioneer days, the timber could be lowered hundreds of feet over the canyon wall. An Anasazi pueblo was found in the vicinity. Weeping Rock is also the trailhead for hikes to Hidden Canyon and Observation Point (see the Hiking section). This is a popular location in the canyon and, as with other places in the

canyon, parking can be difficult to find, especially in the summer.

Great White Throne View Area—5.1 miles up the canyon. This famous Zion landmark is more than 2,000 feet above the canyon floor, and you do feel that if the Almighty had an earthly throne, this would be it. The view area is far enough from the Throne for you to enjoy the mountain in all its splendor.

Temple of Sinawava—6.2 miles up the canyon. This great natural amphitheater is named for a Paiute spirit who is said to live here, by the Gateway to the Narrows Trail. Take time for a walk up the paved trail (see the Hiking section under Outdoor Activities). Also notice Pulpit Rock just beyond the parking area. If you are lucky enough to visit this area just after a rainstorm, or in late winter and early spring after a good snow year, you will see beautiful waterfalls coming off the tops of the mountains.

Shopping

Springdale Fruit Co. Market

This place exudes good health. You can pick up locally grown, freshly picked organic fruit in season. Also available are hiking and picnic supplies, including trail mixes and freshly made sandwiches. There's also freshly baked carrot cake, banana bread, muffins and coffee cake plus several varieties of European breads, including German rye, whole wheat multigrain and Tuscan white garlic rosemary focaccia. Gourmet coffee, fresh fruit smoothies, natural sodas, ginger ales, root beer and their own chilled apple cider offer plenty of choices for drinks. Open in summer daily 8 A.M.–8 P.M.; closed during the winter. Located in the middle of an apple orchard at the south end of town. **2491 Zion Park Blvd., Springdale; 435-772-3222.**

World of Tribal Arts

If you are looking for authentic Native American art, not factory-made or imported, a visit to World of Tribal Arts should be on your itinerary. Eula Bruce collects Native American art from all over the West and offers it for sale in her Springdale shop. Open in summer daily 10 A.M.–noon and 2–5 P.M.; closed during winter. **291 Zion Park Blvd., Springdale; 435-772-3353; www.tribal-artszion.com.**

Where to Stay

Bed and Breakfasts and Inns

Flanigan's Inn—$$$

This Springdale lodge opened in 1947 under the name "Zion's Rest," when John Drater purchased and moved some barracks from the Japanese War Relocation Camp at Topaz near Delta, Utah, and renovated them for use as tourist cabins. Nine of these original units are still in use, although they have been modernized since the 1940s. Two of the units have been converted into a conference room. The other 25 units are modern rooms located in several beautiful natural wood buildings set among lawns and a pond, with a private walkway to a hilltop vista of Zion Canyon. When Larry McKown purchased the establishment from the Draters several years ago, he changed the name to Flanigan's Inn, in honor of David Flanigan, the local inventor who designed the Cable Mountain Draw Works in Zion Canyon. An excellent restaurant is located at the inn (see the Where to Eat section). **428 Zion Park Blvd., P.O. Box 100, Springdale, UT 84767; 1-800-765-7787; 435-772-3244; www.flanigans.com.**

Harvest House Bed and Breakfast—$$$

Located in a residential area near the entrance to the national park, this B&B has four nonsmoking spacious rooms, each with a private bath and air conditioning. Two rooms have private decks with a magnificent view of the Watchman and Bridge Mountain. Outside, guests enjoy a hot tub and beautifully landscaped yard with a small fountain. A full breakfast is served family–style, which provides a great opportunity to meet and converse with other guests. **29 Canyon View Dr., P.O. Box 125, Springdale, UT 84767; 435-772-3880; www.harvesthouse.net.**

Novel House—$$$

This Springdale bed and breakfast has the world's greatest authors as its theme. Owners Ross and Norma Clay have named each of the 10 rooms for and decorated them in the spirit of such authors as Rudyard Kipling, Mark Twain, Jane Austen, Walt Whitman, Leo Tolstoy, the Brontë Sisters, Robert Louis Stevenson, C. S. Lewis and Charles Dickens. *Deseret News* literary critic Jerry Johnston noted, "Because of the literary angle to the place you find a touch of reverence to the rooms. The presence of desks and books give them the aura of dens of meditation." In addition to the literary character, there is a British flare to the enterprise, with English-style tea time and a good dose of Scottish hospitality, which Norma inherited from her Scottish-born parents. **73 Paradise Rd., P.O. Box 188, Springdale, UT 84767-0188; 1-800-711-8400; 435-772-3650; www.novelhouse.com.**

O'Toole's Under the Eaves Guest House—$$$

Rick and Michelle O'Toole operate this rustic inn in two houses—one a small house and the other a refurbished cabin that was once located in Zion National Park. The original house was constructed in 1929 from red sandstone blocks cut from nearby canyon walls. Two bedrooms are located on the first floor and, while there is a shared bath, each room has its own sink. Upstairs ("under the eaves") is a large honeymoon suite, with a large claw-foot tub in the private bath. Near the main house is the guest house, which has two rooms, each with a private bath. All rooms are nonsmoking. **980 Zion Park Blvd., P.O. Box 29, Springdale, UT 84767; 435-772-3457; www.otooles.com.**

Zion Lodge—$$$

Zion Lodge provides the only accommodations within the park and is, understandably, very popular. It has 80 motel units and 40 renovated historic cabins. Also a restaurant, snack bar and gift shop. You will probably have to book six months to a year in advance. Located at 2.5 miles on Zion Canyon Scenic Dr. **303-29-PARKS(72757)** reservations; 435-772-2001; www.zion-lodge.com.

MOTELS

There are no lodgings of real note in Rockville, Virgin, La Verkin, Toqueville and Pintura; most visitors stay in Springdale. Nice motels with heated swimming pools are located there. These are a few favorites:

Cliffrose Lodge and Gardens—$$

Five acres of lawns, trees and flower gardens; 36 units. **281 Zion Park Blvd.; 1-800-243-8824; 435-772-3234; www.cliffroselodge.com.**

Desert Pearl Inn—$$

A brand-new, well-designed and family-oriented inn; 60 rooms. **707 Zion Park Blvd.; 1-888-828-0898; 435-772-8888; www.desert-pearl.com**.

Driftwood Lodge—$$

Forty-seven units. **1515 Zion Park Blvd.; 1-888-801-8811; 435-772-3262; www.drift-woodlodge.com.**

Zion Park Inn—$$ to $$$

One of Springdale's newest and now largest inns. There are 120 rooms plus meeting and conference rooms. Outdoor swimming pool and hot tub. The Switchback Grille and Trading Company is part of the inn. **1215 Zion Park Blvd.; 1-800-934-7275; 435-772-3200; www.zionparkinn.com.**

Camping

PRIVATE
Zion Canyon Campground

Seventy-five RV sites and tentsites with complete hookups. Facilities include toilets, showers and a laundry. Open year-round. Located just outside the park. **479 Zion Park Blvd., Springdale; 435-772-3237.**

PUBLIC

There are two large campgrounds located inside the south entrance to the national park. **South Campground** has 140 RV and tent spaces; open mid-Apr.–mid-Oct. **Watchman Campground** has 185 RV trailer sites and 229 tentsites; open year-round. Both campgrounds have drinking water, toilets and wheelchair-accessible facilities. No RV hookups. **1-888-518-7070; www.zionpark.com.**

Where to Eat

Bit and Spur Saloon and Mexican Restaurant—$$ to $$$

Before its demise, *Utah Holiday* magazine gave this restaurant its Best Mexican Restaurant in Utah award. While there are plenty of other contenders for the award, the Bit and Spur does offer great Mexican food. House favorites include chili verde, chiles rellenos, pasta Sonora and a Mexican combination plate that is the most popular menu item. There are also special dishes. For a Native American dish, try the Zuni stew made with lamb, corn, sweet potatoes and juniper berries. For vegetarians, there's a curried vegetable burrito made with potatoes, eggplant, squash and peppers wrapped in a whole wheat tortilla. Open daily 5–10 P.M. **1212 Zion Park Blvd., Springdale; 435-772-3498.**

Bumbleberry Restaurant—$ to $$

This time-honored restaurant is known for its Bumbleberry pie. No one is willing to give out the real secret about what a bumbleberry is (most guess that bumbleberries are close relatives to boysenberries and blackberries), but a long-standing definition is this: "Bumbleberries are purple and binkel berries that grow on giggle bushes, so named figure out what it really is." If you want something before the pie, there are hamburgers and sandwiches for lunch or chicken, trout and steak entrées for dinner. Open in summer Mon.–Sat. 7 A.M.–9:30 P.M.; in winter Mon.–Sat. 8 A.M.–8 P.M. **897 Zion Park Blvd., Springdale; 435-772-3224.**

Flanigan's Inn Restaurant—$$ to $$$

Part of Flanigan's Inn just outside the south

entrance to Zion National Park, the restaurant is open daily for breakfast, lunch and dinner during the summer (dinner only during the winter). Specialties include their Southwest game plate, fresh trout, mixed grill, mesquite-roasted chicken and pasta dishes made from original recipes. The dining area offers a delightful view of the cliffs at the entrance to Zion National Park. Open in summer Mon.–Fri. 5–9:30 P.M., Sat.–Sun. 5–10 P.M.; shorter hours in the winter. **428 Zion Park Blvd., Springdale; 435-772-3244.**

Switchback Grille—$$

This attractive restaurant with its spacious high ceilings, American Indian rugs and accessible location is just the place to bring a family with varied tastes. Pizza lovers will find the wood-fired pizzas a real delight. Other favorites include hickory-smoked ribs and the slow-roasted lime-tequila half chicken. There is also a children's menu. **1149 S. Zion Park Blvd., Springdale; 435-772-3700.**

Zion Lodge Restaurant—$$ to $$$

The only restaurant inside the park, the Zion Lodge Restaurant is usually busy, and reservations are a must for dinner during the busy season. The restaurant is open for breakfast, lunch and dinner, and offers sack lunches for hikers. A breakfast buffet is offered. Lunch items include

Shuttle System

Beginning with the summer 2000 season, Zion National Park instituted a shuttle-bus system for visitors into upper Zion Canyon. Traffic congestion in the canyon had become so severe that the quality of the national park experience was diminished as motorists sought for too few parking places at the major scenic points and the steady steam of cars threatened the environment and detracted from the magnificent scenery. At times the number of cars totaled several thousand, with only 450 total parking spaces available. Some people waited hours for parking places, fistfights over parking spots were not unheard of, and some people left the park frustrated with the congestion and lack of any place to park. All that has changed with the efficient and highly effective shuttle system.

The shuttle bus system has two segments. The route that operates inside the park begins at the Zion Canyon Visitor Center near the south entrance and follows the Zion Canyon Scenic Dr. northward into the upper canyon along the North Fork of the Virgin River, making eight stops along the 6.2-mile road: Zion Museum, Canyon Junction, Court of the Patriarchs, Zion Lodge, the Grotto Picnic Area, Weeping Rock, Big Bend and Temple of Sinawava.

There is parking at the visitor center, but during the busy summer months the parking places fill quickly, so your best bet is to park your car in Springdale and catch the Town Shuttle, the second segment in the system, which has six convenient stops. All motels and bed and breakfast inns are within easy walking distance of the shuttle stops. The Springdale shuttle stops at the Zion Canyon Theater, where you walk across a footbridge to the park entrance (an entrance fee is charged), and on a short distance to the visitor center and the Zion Canyon shuttle stop.

Both the Springdale and the Zion Canyon shuttles are free and operate Apr.–Oct. At other times of the year, you can drive your own vehicle into the park. Guests staying at Zion Lodge are permitted to drive their own vehicles into the canyon, and travelers along the Zion–Mt. Carmel Hwy. can drive the route to the turnoff at Canyon Junction.

Shuttles run every 6–10 minutes. Mid-May–first week of Sept. the first bus leaves at 5:30 A.M. from Springdale and 5:45 A.M. from the visitor center, and the last bus leaves the Temple of Sinawava at 11 P.M.; the spring and fall schedule operates 7 A.M.–10 P.M.

burgers, sandwiches, chicken-fried steak and Utah trout. The lodge also features a snack bar with patio seating. Located at 2.5 miles on Zion Canyon Scenic Dr. **435-772-3213.**

Zion Pizza and Noodle Company—$ to $$

Need a pizza or pasta for lunch or dinner? Give the Zion Pizza and Noodle Company a try. Bruce Vander Werff, the owner and chef, is a graduate of LaVarene in Paris, and his salads, calzones and slate stone oven-baked pizzas have won praise from locals as well as travelers from all over the world. Housed in the former Springdale LDS church. Open daily 4–10 P.M. **868 Zion Park Blvd., Springdale; 435-772-3815.**

Services

Visitor Information

Zion Canyon Visitors Bureau—Operated by the local chamber of commerce. Located on Hwy. 9 near the south entrance to Zion National Park. **P.O. Box 331, Springdale, UT 84767; 1-888-518-7070; www.zionpark.com.**

Zion Canyon Field Institute—Working in conjunction with the National Park, this non-profit institute offers a variety of one to three day classes on the ecosystem, environment, and history of the area. For information call **(435) 772-3264 or 1-800-635-3959; www.zion-park.org.**

St. George

"Utah's all-season resort city" is the slogan adopted by the St. George Area Chamber of Commerce to lure visitors to what early Mormon pioneers labeled "Utah's Dixie," for the cotton that grew here. To someone driving in early morning rush-hour traffic on the 14th day of a January inversion that had blocked the sun and turned the Salt Lake Valley into a western version of London fog, these alluring radio spots offering a winter escape 300 miles to the south were almost irresistible. Even if the commitment to duty did triumph and the winter-weary worker continued on to the office, there remains the dream of retirement to St. George, a dream that during the last 20 years has become a reality for thousands.

"Snowbirds" from throughout Utah and all over the Intermountain West begin their migration southward in October and November, returning north in April and May. Some purchase houses or condominiums and, after a few years of maintaining two households, give up their northern home to stay in St. George year-round. Others rent homes or condominiums, often succumbing to the lure of purchase once bitten by the "Dixie" bug. A good number travel in motor homes and trailers to spend the winter months in one of several well-equipped RV parks in the area.

But St. George is not just a retirement center. During spring break in late March, St. George becomes Utah's answer to Daytona Beach, as thousands of high school and college students head south to get a jump on summer. Dixie College, a four-year state college in St. George, is one of the state's most popular destinations for college students. Other visitors come to attend the Vic Braden Tennis College or shed some unwanted pounds at the Red Mountain Spa in Snow Canyon. St. George's location in Utah's far southwestern corner is flanked by mountain ranges to the west and north, Zion National Park to the east and the Arizona Strip to the south, with the Virgin River providing an oasis alongside the interstate.

Although summer high temperatures in this desert location seldom drop below 100° F, St. George is still an excellent summer vacation destination. You can play an early morning round of golf on one of the 10 golf courses that have sprung up here, or walk in Snow Canyon before the heat gets you, then retire to the patio to read or visit one of the four historic sites maintained by the LDS church in the area. There are plenty of places to go for a leisurely lunch. This might be followed by an afternoon swim or a hike up the Virgin Narrows in nearby Zion National Park, or perhaps a drive west to Pine Valley and Mountain Meadows. In the evening, head just 36 miles down Interstate 15 from St. George and visit the casinos at Mesquite, Nevada. Those with a more intellectual bent might consider one of the history lectures or musical programs offered in St. George.

With its close proximity to Zion National Park, Cedar City and Las Vegas, a historical consciousness that still permeates the community despite its rapid development and plenty of activities for residents and visitors of all ages, there is no question why St. George is one of Utah's most popular areas.

History

After the Franciscan Fathers Dominguez and Escalante made the decision to abandon their effort to journey to California and to return to Santa Fe, they reached present-day Washington County on Oct. 13, 1776. They traveled along Ash Creek just east of the present route of Interstate 15 near Zion's western edge, before heading southeast back to New Mexico.

In 1830 another group of travelers from Santa Fe accomplished what the Franciscan friars had been unable to do in opening a route between Santa Fe and Los Angeles. The 1830

Getting There

St. George is located 300 miles south of Salt Lake City and 120 miles northeast of Las Vegas, Nevada, on Interstate 15.

Air transportation is available from Salt Lake City on **Sky West/Delta Connection; 1-800-453-9417.**

Greyhound (435-673-2933) provides bus service to the city. There is also daily shuttle service between St. George, Las Vegas and Salt Lake City.

---

group entered Washington County from the north on the western side of the Pine Valley Mountains, where they rested in the Mountain Meadows—infamous as the site of the massacre of 120 California-bound immigrants in 1857—before continuing on the arduous journey across the Nevada desert. Mormon explorers led by Parley P. Pratt entered the area on a reconnaissance mission from Salt Lake City in 1849 and spent New Year's Day 1850 at the junction of the Santa Clara and Virgin Rivers. The first settlement in Washington County was made at Ft. Harmony in 1852, one year after Parowan was established 35 miles to the north. Communities were later established at Santa Clara (1854), Washington (1857) and St. George (1861).

St. George was named in honor of Mormon apostle George A. Smith, who, although he did not participate in his namesake's settlement, did select most of the 309 original families called to settle near the Virgin River. The term "saints," like "Mormons," was an abbreviated name that members of the Church of Jesus Christ of Latter-day Saints often applied to themselves. The combination of "Saint" with "George" made perfectly good theological sense to 19th-century Mormons.

The settlement of St. George coincided with the outbreak of the Civil War. Settlers already had been experimenting with cotton-growing in Santa Clara and Washington, and Brigham Young wanted to take advantage of this opportunity to further Mormon self-sufficiency by having a locally grown and controlled source of cotton, especially as the war threatened to cut off shipments of the essential material to Utah. Young also saw in St. George the opportunity to establish a larger community for a number of converts to the faith from the southern states. This, and St. George's location in the southern part of the state, quickly led to its designation as "Utah's Dixie." A cotton factory was constructed in Washington, and cotton was grown along Santa Clara Creek and the Rio Virgin until the 1890s, when a depression and competition from other parts of the country led to its demise.

If cotton was not the salvation for St. George, the construction of the Mormon Temple in the community was. Completed in 1877, it was the first Mormon temple in Utah and the only one completed before Brigham Young's death. St. George was, and remains, a religious center for Mormons. In 1911 50 years after St. George was settled, the residents commemorated the event with the establishment of the St. George Academy, a normal school, which became Dixie College in 1933.

The population of St. George remained fairly constant until after World War II, when postwar travel to the West boomed. Beginning in the 1960s, St. George has grown faster than any other part of the state, because of its prominence as a retirement community. Between 1960 and 2000, the population grew from just over 5,000 to nearly 50,000. Since the cotton days, St. George's economy has diversified, and while agriculture is still an important element, recreation, tourism and the town's popularity as a retirement center have led to its unprecedented growth.

Major Attractions

St. George Tabernacle

This is arguably the finest Mormon church building constructed in Utah and is one of the best-preserved pioneer buildings in the entire state. Work began on June 1, 1863, a few months after the settlement of St. George. The tabernacle was dedicated by Brigham Young 13 years later. Designed by pioneer architect Miles Romney, the graceful clock tower rises to a height of 140 feet. Sandstone was quarried nearby, and a close examination of the exterior of the building reveals the chisel marks of the early craftsmen. The glass in the tabernacle is also special. It was transported by ship from the East to the West Coast, and then shipped by wagon to St. George. It is a miracle that any of the 2,244 small panes of glass survived the long trip.

It was perhaps a greater miracle that the St. George Saints were able to come up with the $800 to pay for the windows. According to the long-told story, David H. Cannon was assigned

the task of raising the money for the glass through a public subscription. However, when it came time for the freighters to depart for California to pick up the windows and take the payment with them, only $200 had been raised. Cannon petitioned his God and waited for an answer to his prayers. In the nearby town of Washington, Peter Neilson, a Danish convert to Mormonism, had saved $600 to make a much-needed addition to his two-room adobe house. Under divine promptings, he made his way to St. George the morning the freighters were to leave and presented the full amount needed to pay for the windows.

One of Utah's early examples of religious tolerance occurred in the tabernacle in May 1879 when Catholic Bishop Lawrence Scanlan was invited to celebrate high mass in the tabernacle. Because there was no Catholic choir to help perform the mass, the local Mormon choir learned and sang the sacred Latin music, much to the appreciation of Bishop Scanlan, who complimented the group for singing the Latin as beautifully as he had ever heard. It is still used

Getting There

There are two ways to enter the canyon. From the north, take Hwy. 18 north out of St. George for 8 miles and watch for the Snow Canyon road on your left. From the south, take the old Hwy. 91 road (Sunset Blvd.) west out of St. George through the town of Santa Clara, then watch for the sign indicating a right turn to reach Snow Canyon. Then drive north, passing through the town of Ivins, and turn back to the east to follow as the road curves north to enter the state park. The best way to drive through the park is to head north from St. George on Hwy. 18 to the Snow Canyon turnoff. Start at the top of the canyon and drive down, returning by way of Ivins and Santa Clara, if you don't want to make the drive back up to Hwy. 18.

for special meetings and programs. Open daily 9 A.M.–6 P.M. Located on the corner of **Main St. and Tabernacle Ave.**

St. George Temple

As the first Mormon temple completed after the exodus to Utah, and the oldest temple still in use, the St. George Temple has attracted Mormons from all over the world since its completion in 1877. Historian Nels Anderson explains the significance of the St. George Temple in his book *Desert Saints* (University of Chicago Press, 1942, 1966), noting, "No event in Mormon church history exceeded in spiritual importance the dedication of the St. George Temple. Here was the first sign that God's people had permanently established themselves in the valleys of the mountains. Other temples had been planned or begun, but here was one dedicated eternally. It was a kind of victory monument for 30 years of effort."

The stunningly white building is constructed of native red sandstone covered in white stucco. Only worthy Mormons are allowed inside the temple, where sacred ordinances such as marriages and baptisms are performed. Located on the beautiful temple grounds, which occupy an entire block, is a visitor center where guides explain the purpose of Mormon temples and relate interesting information about the construction of the temple. The visitor center is open daily 9 A.M.–9 P.M. Located between 200 and 300 E. and 400 and 500 S.

Snow Canyon State Park

Despite the fantasies of some Utah ski enthusiasts, Snow Canyon State Park is not the St. George area ski resort. In fact, this red-rock and volcanic desert canyon is a stark contrast to locations like Snowbird and Snowbasin to the north. Named for Erastus Snow, who as the highest-ranking Mormon leader in southern Utah directed the settlement of St. George, Snow Canyon is a 3-mile-long, 1,000-foot-deep gorge cut by water and wind erosion.

Within Snow Canyon, three different kinds of rocks are visible. The oldest rocks are of the Kayenta Formation, which originated about 180 million years ago. Large, slow-moving silt-, mud- and sand-bearing rivers left deposits, which in time hardened into siltstone, mudstone and fine-grained sandstone. After the streams dried up, the area became a vast sand desert. The windblown sands eventually hardened about 183 million to 173 million years ago and the 1,000-foot layer is known today as Navajo sandstone.

About 3 million years ago, a period of volcanic activity began, which saw hot, molten rocks spewed down the canyons, over the streams and across the valleys. As the rocks cooled, they formed thick sheets of basalt. A second period of volcanic activity began sometime between 1,000 and 10,000 years ago and the hot lava rocks once again spread over the landscape from the cinder cones located in the north end of the park. Geologically speaking, these lava flows are very recent, and you have a feeling that the once molten rock cooled just hours ago. The contrast of the black basalt with the red, pink, orange and white sandstone of the Kayenta and Navajo Formations offers a panorama that is a photographer's delight. The swirling Navajo sandstone rock formations, towering cliffs and subtle colors insure that no two pictures will be just the same.

Outdoor Activities

In addition to the designated **hiking** trails listed below, there are other unnamed and undeveloped trails, some marked by the sign of a hiker, throughout the park. These trails follow wash bottoms and are often animal and old cattle trails. If you are in doubt about hiking in a particular area, check with the state park ranger.

Johnson's Arch Trail—For years this 1.5-mile round-trip hike was the most popular in Snow Canyon. Unfortunately, the trail to the arch crosses private land and recently the landowner decided to prevent access to the arch by constructing a barbed wire fence with ominous "no trespassing" signs. The state parks division considers access to the arch a top priority and is working to reopen the trail. At the south entrance to the park, watch for a sign indicating the trailhead. If you don't see it, inquire about the status of the trail at the ranger's hut at the entrance to the campground. The sandstone arch is named for Maude Johnson, a St. George pioneer, and has been a well-known local landmark for more than a century.

Lava Caves and West Canyon Overlook Trail—Located in the northern portion of the park, the Lava Caves Trail is a 1.5-mile out-and-back hike that takes you to caves that have been formed in the lava rock. The caves can be hard to find. As you walk down the trail and leave sight of your vehicle at the trailhead, look for a ridge of lava rock almost straight ahead of you. The most prominent area of the black rock is where the cave is located. Keep your eyes open as you come down the lava ridge and watch for a depression to the right of the trail. The cave looks like an old mining shaft. It is unfenced and open, and can be dangerous if you get too close. As you continue down the trail, you come to another cave located in a ridge of basalt rock perhaps 20 feet thick.

Continue down the trail to the West Canyon Overlook. Here you can look down into West Canyon from the south side of a side canyon of pink and white checkerboarded sandstone from which time has scoured all the lava rock that once covered it.

Three Ponds Trail—This is my personal favorite in Snow Canyon; at 6 miles out-and-back, it is long enough for a couple of hours' hike, and the terrain through which the trail passes is varied and interesting. The trail begins across the road from the entrance to the campground. During the first mile, you cross three low-lying ridges, one of basalt and two of sandstone, before you descend 0.25 mile to the gravel road up West Canyon. The first half of the trail to the gravel road is well marked and easy to follow.

After you cross the road in a westerly direction, the trail becomes less defined as you walk through heavy sand toward a gigantic U-shaped opening between the sandstone walls formed by the intermittent stream that flows down out of the cliffs. After you pass between the sandstone walls as you hike along the bottom of the wash, you enter a broad, circular area. Keep the white dome on top of the sandstone walls ahead of you in sight and follow the wash and trail toward the dome. Don't be tempted to head to the left, but follow the wash as it curves to the right until you come up against the sandstone walls, where you will find the three ponds. They are really three potholes, usually with some water in them, but hardly enough to qualify as ponds. The ponds were a water source used by Indians and later by local pioneers. The ponds are located almost on top of each other—one at the base of the sandstone cliff and the two above in the sandstone rock inside a V-shaped notch cut by the water into the sandstone.

As you return out of the canyon and head back toward the West Canyon Rd., keep your eyes on the ridge straight ahead. This is the ridge over which you just hiked. You will see three windows or small arches along the ridgeline.

Hidden Pinyon Trail—At the entrance to the state park, you can pick up a trail guide at the trailhead to this 1.5-mile trail, which offers an excellent introduction to the plant life of the area. The sandy washes and sand dunes also offer an excellent opportunity to see the tracks of the area's **wildlife.**

Children and adults love the **sand dunes** located in the lower (southern) end of the canyon. You can run barefoot through the sand, write messages in the sand and pretend that you are in the middle of the Sahara.

Visitor Information

Spring and fall are the most popular times to visit the canyon, although an early summer morning excursion when temperatures are still cool makes for a delightful outing. Camping facilities are available in the park. **435-628-2255; www.go-utah.com/snow_canyon_state_park.**

Dixie State College

A four-year state college of more than 5,000 students, Dixie College is at the center of much of the cultural and educational activity in the St. George area. Exhibits, a concert series, lectures, sporting events and other activities are all part of a concerted effort by the administration to integrate the college into the mainstream of community life and to expand the academic experience for its students. Chances are, if you spend any time at all in the area, you will find yourself on the Dixie College campus. It is worth a special trip to view the 15-by-127-foot mosaic mural on the south wall of the Fine Arts Building, which depicts events from Dixie's history. An interpretive marker explains the mural. The college mascot is the "Rebel," and "Dixie Rebel" clothing and souvenirs, available at the bookstore, are popular items for both young and old. Located in the southeastern section of St. George. **225 S. 700 E.; 435-652-7500; www.dixie.edu.**

Gunlock State Park

Built in 1969–1970 to impound waters of the Santa Clara River for irrigation and flood control purposes, Gunlock Reservoir is 2 miles long and 0.5 mile wide, with a maximum depth of 115 feet. Recreation activities include swimming, boating (both powerboats and sailboats) and fishing. The Utah Division of Wildlife Resources stocks the lake with largemouth bass, black crappie, threadfin shad and channel catfish.

The reservoir is located on the Old Spanish Trail a mile south of the hamlet of Gunlock, which was settled by Will Hamblin in 1857. Hamblin was known as "Gunlock" because he reportedly kept in good condition the locks of guns belonging to those in his pioneer company as they journeyed to Utah. Will Hamblin was the brother of Jacob Hamblin, president of southern Utah's Indian Mission and a friend to the Paiutes. Jacob Hamblin's home is located about 20 miles below the reservoir in Santa Clara. It is now a historic site operated by the LDS church (see the Historic Sites section under Seeing and Doing). The little community of Gunlock is nearby, but it is not the original site of the Hamblin/Leavitt settlement.

Gunlock State Park is open year-round.

Camping is available, though amenities are scarce. Drive west from St. George on old Hwy. 91 (Sunset Blvd.) to Santa Clara, then continue another 8 miles to Shivwits, where you turn north for approximately 7 miles until you reach the lake. **435-628-2255; www.go-utah.com/ gunlock_state_park.**

Quail Creek State Park

Quail Creek Reservoir, though one of the state's newest reservoirs, already has a colorful past. Visible from the interstate north of St. George, the reservoir inundates part of the old Harrisburg town site (see the Historic Sites section under Seeing and Doing). Work on the Quail Creek Reservoir Dam was completed in 1985. The 40,000-acre-foot lake impounded water from Quail Creek, but its principal source was water from the Virgin River that was supplied through an 8-mile-long diversion tunnel fed by a pipeline from a concrete dam near the town of Virgin to the east. In the early hours of New Year's Day 1989, the dam gave way, sending a wall of water rushing down the Virgin River and inundating homes downriver in Bloomington, causing millions of dollars of damage. The reconstructed dam was completed in 1991.

Recreation activities include swimming, boating and fishing. Rainbow trout, bluegill, channel catfish, crayfish and a well-deserved reputation as the best largemouth bass hatchery in Utah make this one of the most popular fishing spots in the area. Camping is available at group campsites or in one of the 23 individual sites. The facility is well equipped with modern rest rooms that are wheelchair accessible, as well as drinking water, group pavilions and picnicking facilities. Open year-round. Take Interstate 15 north of St. George 14 miles. **435-879-2378; www.go-utah.com/quail_creek_state_park.**

Festivals and Events

First Night

Dec. 31–Jan. 1. St. George held its premiere First Night Celebration on New Year's Eve 1999.

Since then, the celebration has grown to more than 30,000 people crowding the historic center of St. George near the St. George Tabernacle to welcome in the New Year. Live entertainment, artists and a variety of activities draw residents from all over southern Utah and some from Utah's northern cities who prefer the warmer temperatures of Utah's Dixie to the colder northern climes. Like other First Night celebrations, this one is nonalcoholic and is designed for the entire family. **435-634-5747.**

St. George Art Festival

Easter weekend. Held on the Fri. and Sat. of Easter weekend, the St. George Art Festival began in 1978. It has become southern Utah's largest art celebration, with more than 100 booths, live entertainment, food and activities for all ages. The festival is held along Main St. in front of the tabernacle, library and St. George Arts Center. Sponsored by the St. George City Leisure Services Department. **435-634-5850.**

Lions Dixie Roundup

Sept. A three-day Professional Rodeo Cowboy's Association–approved rodeo is held every year in the Sun Bowl. **435-628-2898.**

Santa Clara Swiss Days

last Fri.–Sat. in Sept. The small town of Santa Clara celebrates its Swiss heritage each fall. Swiss converts to the Mormon church were among the community's early settlers in the 1860s, and people have wondered ever since how the natives of the forested mountains and lush valleys of Switzerland coped with the red rock, sand, scarce water and heat of their new desert home. Presented by the Santa Clara Historical Society, activities include displays, a pageant, a fun run, crafts, food, game booths, entertainment, a parade and a tour of historic homes. **435-673-6712.**

St. George Marathon

first Sat. in Oct. The St. George Marathon, which was first held in 1976, has been named by

Runner's World as one of the 10 most scenic and fastest marathons in the nation. With 6,200 racers, it is the 15th largest marathon in the nation. The course starts in the Pine Valley Mountains north of St. George and descends nearly 2,600 feet along Hwy. 18 through some of Utah's most magnificent scenery on the route to St. George. The long, descending course offers runners the chance to post personal bests. While nearly two-thirds of the competitors are from Utah, there is a heavy demand for accommodations in the area during this weekend. **435-634-5850; www.st-georgemarathon.com.**

Hunstman World Senior Games

mid-Oct. Held throughout the St. George area, this two-week event attracts hundreds of senior athletes (age 50 and over) from all over the world. They participate in a wide range of sporting activities, such as tennis, golf, basketball, cycling, racquetball, softball, swimming, running, horseshoes, bowling, race walking and table tennis. Sponsored by the Huntsman Chemical Corporation, headquartered in Salt Lake City. **82 W. 700 S., St. George; 1-800-562-1268; 435-674-0550; www.seniorgames.net.**

Jubilee of Trees

week before Thanksgiving. This five-day event launches the Christmas season in St. George. Trees sporting original decorations are displayed. There is something for everyone, including booths, fashion shows, gift ideas, live entertainment, food (including a gala dinner), a parade, an auction and activities for the children. **435-628-7003.**

Dixie Rotary Bowl Football Game

first Sat. in Dec. The Dixie Rotary Bowl started in 1986 and has turned into one of the most successful junior college football bowl games in the nation. Bowl festivities include a parade, a marching band competition, a banquet and a tailgate party. **435-634-5747.**

Outdoor Activities

Biking

Pine Valley Loop

Unless you enjoy riding in dry, 100° F-plus desert temperatures, much of the Dixie area does not lend itself to long bike rides in the summer. One exception is the 35-mile-long Pine Valley Loop. In addition to the spectacular views of the west side of the Pine Valley Mountains, the route offers three interesting historic sites to visit during the ride: the Pine Valley Chapel, the remains of the Jacob Hamblin homestead and the Mountain Meadows Massacre Site (see the Historic Sites section under Seeing and Doing). Drive Hwy. 18 north from St. George for 25 miles to Central, then turn east and follow the road (Forest Rd. 035) for 6 miles into Pine Valley. Beginning in Pine Valley, the loop winds north on Forest Rd. 011 through Grass Valley for 12 miles to Pinto. Turn left (west) at Pinto and follow Forest Rd. 009 for about 5 miles to its junction with Hwy. 18. Before you reach the paved road, you pass the Hamblin homestead. From Hwy. 18, turn left and head south, making a stop at the Mountain Meadows site about a mile from the junction. From there it's another 4 miles or so to Central, where you turn left (east) to return to Pine Valley.

Snow Canyon Loop

This is an excellent early morning ride that offers the spectacular scenery of Snow Canyon, the chance to leave directly from your lodging in St. George for a strenuous uphill workout and a thrilling downhill spin at the end of the ride. Begin the 24-mile loop by following old Hwy. 91 (Sunset Blvd.) west to Santa Clara from the junction at Bluff St. Continue west through Santa Clara and, about a mile past the historic Jacob Hamblin house, turn north toward the town of Ivins. At the crossroads in Ivins, turn right (east) and follow the road as it turns northward, to begin the long climb up Snow Canyon. When Snow Canyon Rd. intersects Hwy. 18, turn right (south) for the well-earned coast back to St. George.

Veyo Loop

This is a challenging but popular road ride that covers 48 miles and offers spectacular views of Snow Canyon, the Pine Valley Mountains, extinct volcanoes, hardened lava flows, Gunlock Reservoir and the pioneer towns of Veyo, Gunlock and Santa Clara. The first 19 miles are all uphill as you head north out of St. George on Bluff St./Hwy. 18 to Veyo. In Veyo turn left on Center St. and from here the ride is pretty much downhill all the way back to St. George. It is 8 miles to Gunlock, another 17 miles to Santa Clara, and 4 more miles on to St. George. You can also make this ride in reverse to stretch out the uphill climb. To avoid climbing at all, arrange to be dropped off in Veyo and enjoy the downhill ride without the strain of the uphill climb.

Warner Valley

Ride into history along this 20-mile out-and-back route, which takes you along a portion of the old Honeymoon Trail, to historic Ft. Pearce and to a group of three-toed dinosaur footprints that were left in what was a floodplain about 200 million years ago. This is a nice, fairly level ride, ideal for families, though you can lengthen it to 35 miles if you ride all the way from St. George.

Whether you ride or drive, head east on 700 S. in St. George to River Rd. Follow it south across the Virgin River bridge and turn east onto 1450 S. for 2 miles where the road makes a sharp turn to the right (south). Immediately you will see a fork in the road. Take the left (east) fork and continue on for about 3.5 miles to the end of the paved road and beginning of the dirt and gravel road. Park here if you drove and begin your ride along the gravel road.

After riding a little more than 5 miles, you come to the turnoff to Ft. Pearce, which is about a half mile off to the right. After visiting Ft. Pearce (see the Historic Sites section under Seeing and Doing), continue another 2 miles eastward then take the left fork of the road and continue until it ends. The dinosaur tracks are about 200 yards on and are identified by a sign. After viewing the tracks, return to your vehicle or ride back St. George.

Rentals

Bicycles Unlimited, Inc.—For more information about other biking routes in the St. George area, repairs and rentals, this shop is worth a visit. Open Mon.–Sat. 8 A.M.–7 P.M. **90 S. 100 E.; 435-673-4492.**

Golf

What makes golf special in St. George is that you can golf year-round at reasonable rates, plus there are enough courses to play a different one every day of the week and still have a couple left over for the next week. Winter daytime temperatures average in the 50s and 60s, so any "serious" Utah golfer makes at least one pilgrimage during the winter to play St. George.

During the summer, when the temperatures push past 100° F, there are fewer golfers, but if you are properly prepared—that is, with plenty of cold drinks, light clothing, a suitable hat and, if necessary, a golf cart—2–4 hours perspiring on the golf course can be an enjoyable form of sauna—if your golf game is on—and makes the post-game plunge into the swimming pool all the more wonderful. Here are a few favorite courses:

Coral Canyons Golf Course

One of St. George's newest golf courses, the Coral Canyon Golf Course is laid out in a labyrinth of dry, red washes north of town. There are some long holes on the course, including three that stretch out over 500 yards. This nicely designed course gives special attention to the natural environment. **1925 N. Canyon Greens; 435-688-1700.**

Entrada Golf Course

Located near Snow Canyon, this is a spectacular setting for a golf course, with blue sky, red sandstone, black lava rock and green fairways. Designed by Johnny Miller, his friend and pro-golfer Mike Reid compared the course to a great symphony with three movements. The first movement has the red cliffs as its theme, the second movement the trees and landscape of the wash areas, and the third movement is the holes played through the black rock of an ancient lava flow. Very difficult and one of the most expensive courses in the state, although there are cheaper twilight rates for late afternoons and off-season (May–Sept.). This is a private course open to the public. **2511 W. Entrada Dr.; 435-674-7500.**

Green Spring Golf Course

Owned by the city of Washington, this course is located north of Interstate 15 and is reached from St. George by taking the Washington exit and turning left back under the interstate. The course is rated as one of the most difficult in the state, and most golfers can plan to lose at least one ball trying to play the treacherous 6th hole. The par 4, 400-yard hole has a narrow fairway that runs parallel to a deep ravine for more than 200 yards and requires a second shot that carries nearly 200 yards to a tight green. If you are not a very good golfer and are prone to frustration on challenging courses, you might want to save the greens fees and opt for a course that is a little more forgiving of those who don't shoot straight. **588 Green Spring, Washington; 435-673-7888.**

Red Hills Golf Course

Opened in 1966, this is St. George's first golf course and still a favorite of many golfers. On a couple of the 9 holes, the red cliffs can be either a hazard or a help when errant drives ricochet off the walls and bounce back onto the fairway. **1000 N. 700 W.; 435-634-5852.**

Sunbrook Golf Course

This 27-hole course is particularly sensitive to the natural lay of the land, and the desert, hills and deep ravines coupled with eight lakes and the tree-lined Santa Clara River make this a championship course in every sense of the word. The most unusual hole is the par 3 13th hole, which plays at about 165 yards from the middle tees. The green is situated on an island surrounded by water and is connected by a walkway. *Deseret News* readers voted this the best hole they had played in Utah. Keep in mind that greens fees are about double the price of other public courses within the state. **2240 W. Sunbrook Dr.; 435-634-5866.**

Hiking

There are three popular areas for hiking in the St. George area: Zion National Park (see the **Zion National Park** chapter), the Pine Valley Mountains (see below) and Snow Canyon State Park (see the Major Attractions section).

La Verkin Overlook Trail

You won't see a tree on this 2-mile-long one-way hike, but you will see some of the most scenic and historic country in all of Utah. The trail climbs steadily from the southwest end of La Verkin up the ridge, providing a spectacular view of the towns of La Verkin and Hurricane and then the Virgin River Canyon, where you can trace the Hurricane Canal on the east side of the canyon and the La Verkin Canal on the west side as they seem to literally climb up the canyon walls. You will want to take a good pair of binoculars for a closer look at the tunnels and rock work of the canals, which rank among the most impressive of all pioneer undertakings. Follow along a narrow ridge with unbelievable views into the canyon and Virgin River to the east and the La Verkin–Hurricane area to the west.

To reach the trailhead, from Hurricane on Hwy. 9 east of St. George, head north. After you cross the Virgin River bridge, turn right (east) onto the second road past the bridge (300 S.). Make another right turn onto 100 W. and head south for a block and look for the trailhead on the east side of the road at approximately 400 S.

If you want to avoid the steep climb and can arrange a shuttle, follow Hwy. 9 east toward Zion National Park as it climbs up a steep dugway onto the bench. Just over 2 miles beyond the junction of Hwys. 17 and 9, watch for a sign pointing to the La Verkin Overlook on the right. Follow the dirt and gravel road for 1.5 miles to where it dead-ends at the overlook. The well-maintained trail heads southward down the hill.

Temple Quarry Trail

This interesting historic trail is on Black Hill, west of St. George. The 1-mile round-trip Temple Quarry Trail is part of the old wagon road that was used to haul black rock from the quarry on the west side of Black Hill for use in the foundation of the St. George Temple. The trail is level as it heads south around the hill. At the quarry site, chisel marks, partly worked stones and other evidence remain from pioneer times. To reach the trail, drive up the hill of Bluff St. to Black Hill View Park, then head southwest until you intersect the trail.

Virgin River Pkwy.

This level, paved trail along the west side of the Virgin River is popular with walkers, joggers and in-line skaters. The trail begins just across the Man-of-War bridge in Bloomington, to the southwest of St. George, and follows the Virgin River and then the Santa Clara River for nearly 3 miles to the southwest edge of St. George, where it parallels Bluff St. to the intersection with Hilton Dr.

To reach the trailhead in St. George, it is a short walk from any of the motels near the I-15 Exit 6 off Bluff St. To reach the Bloomington trailhead, take Interstate 15 south to the Bloomington exit (Exit 4). As you exit, keep right, but make a quick left turn onto Pioneer Rd., which parallels Interstate 15. After 0.5 mile turn right (west) onto Man-of-War Dr. and follow it for a mile until you cross the Virgin River. There is parking immediately after the bridge on both sides of the road.

PINE VALLEY MOUNTAINS

The region borders the Pine Valley Wilderness Area (50,000 acres), administered by the U.S. Forest Service. From St. George, take Hwy. 18 north for 25 miles to Central, then turn east and follow the road (Forest Rd. 035) for 6 miles into Pine Valley. To reach trailheads at the end of the road, continue beyond the town 3 miles. **Pine Valley Ranger District, Dixie National Forest, Box 584, St. George, UT 84770; 435-673-3431.**

Forsyth Trail

This 5-mile-long trail begins in the town of Pine Valley and follows Forsyth Creek to its terminus near Burger Peak. The elevation gain is 3,000 feet. The trail is noted for its beautiful mountain scenery and the wildlife—including mule deer, elk, squirrels and chipmunks—that can be observed. Allow 6–7 hours to make the 10-mile out-and-back hike.

Whipple Valley Trail

The 15-mile trail begins east of the Blue Springs Campground at the road terminus in Pine Valley and climbs 2,000 feet in 3.5 miles to Whipple Valley, where it intersects with the Summit Trail. For hardy hikers who don't mind the up and down of following the ridgeline, you can continue on the Summit Trail for 7 miles and then return to Pine Valley along the Brown's Point Trail, which terminates near Lion's Lodge on the road a mile west of the Blue Springs Campground. It is a strenuous hike, with portions of the trail not well marked. The Whipple Valley Trail is a good workout recommended for those who want to experience the beauty and solitude of the Pine Valley Mountains.

Skiing

CROSS-COUNTRY

The Pine Valley Mountains are becoming a popular cross-country location as the U.S. Forest Service now grooms trails and sets about 5 miles of track. Begin from the trailhead located near the Pine Valley Reservoir parking area. Take Hwy. 18 north 36 miles from St. George and turn east at Central to Pine Valley. Maps for groomed and ungroomed trails are available at the **Interagency Information Center, 345 E. Riverside Dr., St. George; 435-628-4491.** For trail and snow conditions call the **Pine Valley Ranger District Office, 435-628-0461.**

Swimming

Public swimming facilities are available at the **St. George City Pool,** an outdoor pool open late May–Sept. **(250 E. 700 S.; 435-634-5867),** and the **Dixie Center Natatorium (425 S. 700 E.; 435-628-7003).** The **Veyo Pool,** located 18 miles north of St. George on Hwy. 18, is a unique pool fed by hot springs **(287 E. Veyo Resort Rd., Veyo; 435-574-2744)**. The **Green Valley Resort** has three pools, including an indoor pool and an outside diving pool **(1515 W. Canyon View Dr.; 1-800-237-1068; 435-628-8060).**

Tennis

Several public tennis courts are located throughout St. George, including six public tennis courts located on the **Dixie College campus,** located at approximately 300 S. and 800 E.

Vic Braden Tennis College

Green Valley Resort, just west across or around the ridge from St. George, is home to the Vic Braden Tennis College, one of the most popular tennis programs in the world. The college includes courts, hitting lanes and practice areas. Group and private lessons are available for players at all levels. Tennis vacation packages attract people from all over the world. **Vic Braden Tennis College, 1515 W. Canyon View Dr., St. George, UT 84770; 435-628-8060; www.tennisresortsonline.com/tro-files/Green_Valley.cfm.**

Seeing and Doing

Children and Families

Fiesta Family Fun Center

This is a nice diversion from all the historic sites, hiking, golf and sight-seeing you will want to do in the St. George area. Designed mostly for children and teenagers, but adults enjoy the miniature golf course and driving range. Other attractions include a go-cart track, bumper boats and batting cages. Inside, there are plenty of arcade games, plus a wonderful soft play area for children 10 and younger where they can work out some of their squirms and wiggles by crawling, climbing, sliding and making their way through a fun-filled obstacle course. Recently a skateboard/in-line skate park was opened as part of the center. Open Mon–Sat. 10 A.M.–10 P.M. **171 E. 1160 S.; 435-628-1818.**

Historic Sites

The St. George area is rich in pioneer historic buildings. Historic homes, public buildings, churches, business buildings, trails and ruins provide the casual visitor as well as the avid history buff with plenty of opportunities to immerse themselves in the history of this unique region. The *Washington County Visitor Guide,* which you can pick up free of charge in the Old Washington County Courthouse, provides a walking guide to 22 St. George buildings within a few blocks. The guide also contains information about historic sites in the area. More detailed information is available in a guide to historic sites published by the Washington County Historical Society. The LDS church maintains five historic buildings within the area—the **St. George Tabernacle** and the **St. George Temple** (see the Major Attractions section), and the **Brigham Young Winter Home,** the **Jacob Hamblin House in Santa Clara** and the **Pine Valley Chapel** (see below)—staffing them with volunteer guides at each location. Because pioneer history still permeates the area so strongly, we like to visit one or two buildings and sites each day we are in the area. The following are not to be missed.

Brigham Young Winter Home

Mormon leader Brigham Young is credited with setting the trend followed by thousands of Utahns—"going to Dixie for the winter." While the warmer weather of southern Utah was indeed good medicine for the aging rheumatic pioneer, the 300-mile annual journey also allowed Young to visit the string of settlements between the two spiritual centers of Salt Lake City and St. George, to supervise work on the St. George Temple and to give support and encouragement to those seeking to establish a foothold on the southern Mormon frontier. Brigham Young, a carpenter and builder himself,

was partial to the use of adobe and chose this material over the native red sandstone or black basalt, although both are used in the foundation of his winter home. The house was started in 1869 and finished in 1873. It is one of the best-restored homes in the state and houses many personal things, such as Young's corncob mattress. Free guided tours begin in the one-room office adjacent to the home, and are offered daily 9 A.M.–dusk. Located on the corner of **200 N. and 100 W.**

Ft. Pearce

During the mid-1860s, Navajo unrest and the threat of raids into southwestern Utah led to the construction of Ft. Pearce for defensive purposes. Although it never came under attack, the small rock-walled fort is an interesting reminder of frontier conditions and has been preserved by the Bureau of Land Management. Located 12 miles southeast of Washington. In Washington, turn south off Main St. onto 400 S. St. and follow it south across the Virgin River toward Warner Valley.

Hurricane Historic Canal and Heritage Park

Located in the center of Hurricane, nicely landscaped Heritage Park has a fine collection of historic artifacts, including wagons, a handcart, a buggy, a plow and other farm machinery. Also in the park is a fine memorial to the heroic struggle that brought the town into existence. In the center of the park is a monumental statue of a family. The monument gives a brief history of the construction of the Hurricane Canal and the founding of the town.

The construction of the Hurricane Canal to bring water up from the Virgin River onto the Hurricane Bench is a story of determination and endurance that spanned two centuries. The possibility of constructing a canal was first investigated by Erastus Snow and several companions in 1863. As they descended the steep hill above the town, a whirlwind blew off the top of their buggy. Snow remarked, "Well, that was a hurricane! We'll call this the Hurricane Hill."

Thirty years after the initial visit by Erastus Snow, a stock company was organized and a survey made that determined that it would take a 7-mile-long canal constructed along the precipitous limestone walls of the Virgin River canyon to bring water to the Hurricane Bench. With picks, shovels, handmade drills, crowbars, wheelbarrows and blasting powder, workers commenced construction. Several tunnels had to be blasted and numerous sections of rock walls erected as the canal was constructed under the most difficult of circumstances. To look at the canal today, it appears that the water had to flow uphill from the diversion dam in the canyon bottom to the bench high above the river. Most of the construction work was done in the winters so that the men and boys could take care of their farmwork the rest of the year. During the first couple of years, there were as many as 300 men at work in the canyon on the canal. The farmers were assisted by unemployed miners who worked for their board during the winter and the promise of a horse and saddle in the spring. The miners' expertise with blasting powder was a great help in building the tunnels through the chert-impregnated limestone.

The success of the canal would allow the establishment of a new community, and in 1896 the builders surveyed the future town and drew lots for homesites. It was not until 10 years later, in 1906, that the first families moved onto their lots and another two years before the first permanent home was built. After working on the canal for nearly a decade, the builders were at the end of their financial rope. Help came when the LDS church bought $5,000 worth of stock in the canal and work pressed forward to completion in 1904. Nevertheless, maintenance of the canal required extraordinary effort as the tunnels filled in, the rock walls broke and wood flumes had to be replaced. The canal was used until 1985 when a piping system was installed. Listed in the National Register of Historic Places, the canal still can be followed out of the river gorge and onto the Hurricane Bench.

Also on the grounds of Heritage Park is the **community museum,** located in the Library-City Hall building that was constructed of local red sandstone between 1938 and 1940 as a New Deal WPA project. The museum includes pioneer and Indian artifacts. Open Mon.–Sat. 10 A.M.–7 P.M. **35 W. State St.; 435-635-3245.**

Jacob Hamblin House

A contemporary of Brigham Young, Jacob Hamblin holds a special place in Mormon history as first president of the Southern Indian Mission. He came to the area in 1854 as one of the first Mormons to undertake missionary work with the Indians. During the next 20 years, Hamblin worked among the Paiute, Navajo and Zuni Indians, explaining Mormon beliefs to them, interceding during disputes and acting as a fair-minded colleague. His travels among the Indians meant exploring much of the Southwest, and Hamblin became the first white man to circumnavigate the Grand Canyon—a barrier to western travelers since the first Spanish travelers in the region. He also assisted Maj. John Wesley Powell with his surveys of the Colorado River area and during negotiations for a peace treaty with the Navajos in 1870.

Hamblin's Santa Clara home was constructed in 1863 of sandstone quarried nearby. He and his two wives, Rachel Judd and Pricilla Leavitt, occupied the home until 1871, when Hamblin was sent by church leaders to the newly established settlement of Kanab. Although polygamy was a complex and multifaceted experience that sometimes produced antagonisms between wives, Rachel and Pricilla seemed to get along very well, and the Santa Clara house is an interesting example of the arrangement for two wives living in the same house. The two rooms on the main floor are nearly identical, with stairs ascending to the second floor from the back of each room. The second floor could also be reached directly from the outside and was something of a community center for religious, civic and social events. Otherwise, the second floor was the work area for the Hamblin household.

Like other LDS church-owned historic sites, free guided tours are offered daily 9 A.M.–dusk. From St. George, head north on Bluff St., then turn left onto Sunset Blvd. and drive west until the road becomes Santa Clara Dr. Watch for the Hamblin House on the right (north) side of the road. **435-673-2167.**

Leeds CCC Camp

The three rock buildings and the stone-terraced hillside make this the best remaining example of a New Deal-era Civilian Conservation Camp in Utah. It was built in 1933 and closed in 1942. Young men between the ages of 18 and 25 were enlisted in the CCC for nine to 12 months and spent their time working in conservation projects throughout the West, living in paramilitary camps like the one at Leeds. Some 250 men were assigned to the Leeds Camp, which has been preserved by the Leeds Historical Society. Located at the south end of Leeds just west of Main St.

Mountain Meadows Massacre Site

A dozen books and hundreds of articles have been written in an attempt to explain the tragic event that occurred at Mountain Meadows north of St. George in early Sept. 1857. In 1990, in an act of reconciliation, descendants of both victims and perpetrators came together to erect a simple granite monument engraved with the names of 120 California-bound emigrants who were killed in the grassy valley by southern Utah militiamen and their Indian allies. Despite a promise of safe conduct through this area of Utah, the victims were executed and their bodies strewn across the rolling hills of this popular rest stop. Eighteen small children were spared and adopted by local Mormon families, with whom they lived for two years before federal officials collected them and returned them to relatives in Arkansas and Missouri.

The Mountain Meadows Massacre is a complex tragedy that grew out of a legacy of persecution of Mormons in Missouri and Illinois before their exodus to Utah. In the summer of 1857 a large force of federal troops was en route to Utah to put down an alleged "Mormon rebellion," a situation that provoked anxiety among Mormons, who felt all too keenly the pressure against their nonconformist lifestyle. Added to this was the Mormons' perceived need to main-

tain their Native American neighbors as allies against the invading "Mericats," as non-Mormon Americans were called by the Indians, and the alleged misconduct of immigrants as they proceeded south from Salt Lake City in the midst of Mormon preparations for war. Last but not least, there were communication difficulties, which left local leaders unsure of what action Brigham Young would have them take. This confusion had tragic consequences.

Men who participated in the atrocity vowed never to talk about it, and until recent years, the massacre was discussed in hushed and secret tones. Only one man, the respected Mormon pioneer John D. Lee, was convicted for participating in the massacre. He was taken to Mountain Meadows in 1877, where he was executed by federal authorities. He is generally acknowledged to have given himself up, knowing he would be tried, found guilty and executed to atone for the sins of his fellow Mormons.

In 1950 a courageous St. George teacher and housewife, the late Juanita Brooks, published what is still regarded as the definitive study of the tragedy: *The Mountain Meadows Massacre.* Despite the storm of protest from those who would rather have ignored and forgotten the event—and a certain amount of criticism from the LDS church—her book began the important process of healing and understanding. For her courage, her scholarship and her commitment to truth, Juanita Brooks has become a Utah heroine. Her other writings include a biography of John D. Lee, several other southern Utah pioneers and her autobiographical *Quicksand and Cactus* (University of Utah Press, 1988).

To reach Mountain Meadows, head north on Hwy. 18 from St. George for approximately 25 miles and watch for the signs to the left (west) of the road. You can go right up to the monument, which, perched high above this vast, lonely valley, has much of the same impact as the Vietnam Memorial in Washington, D.C.

Old Washington County Courthouse

Construction of the impressive courthouse, located in the center of town, began in 1866, three years after the settlement of St. George, and was completed 10 years later. The brick and mortar were manufactured locally. The second-story courtroom has been restored and is used for a weekly history lecture program given by local historian Bart Anderson. As the headquarters for the **St. George Area Chamber of Commerce,** it is recommended as a first stop. The helpful volunteers provide plenty of information about the area, including special events and activities. Open Mon.–Sat. 9 A.M.–5 P.M. **100 E. St. George Blvd.; 435-628-1658.**

Pine Valley Chapel

Perhaps the most photogenic church in all of Utah is the Pine Valley Chapel. The symmetrical, two-story, white-frame building in the picturesque Pine Valley was constructed in 1868, the oldest Mormon chapel still in continuous use. According to tradition, the chapel was designed and built by Ebenezer Bryce, for whom Bryce Canyon National Park is named. Before coming to Utah, Bryce was a shipbuilder in Australia. Using shipbuilding techniques, the wood frame walls were assembled on the ground, raised into position and joined with wooden pegs and rawhide, which can still be seen in the attic. Just east of the chapel is a small, red brick tithing office constructed in the 1880s. The chapel is open for free tours during the summer 9 A.M.–dusk. Head north out of St. George on Bluff St. onto Hwy. 18 for 25 miles, along the western side of the Pine Valley Mountains, then turn right (east) at Central and follow the road for 7 miles.

Silver Reef Ghost Town

In the 1870s and 1880s, Silver Reef was a rip-roaring mining town with a reputation surpassed by few western mining towns. There is enough left of the old town—especially with the restored Wells Fargo Building and the bank building across the street—to give a good indication of what was going on there. In back of the Wells Fargo is the old powder house, which contains a scale model of Silver Reef during its heyday of the 1880s. Old mine tailings, early mining

equipment and Catholic and Protestant cemeteries remain from the glory days.

Silver Reef is unique among western mining towns because it is the only place where silver has been discovered in sandstone. The silver may have originated in volcanic tuffs in the Chinle Formation. Ancient streambeds deposited sand and fragments of petrified trees, bushes and reeds over the silver. Water dissolved the silver and carried it upward. As the silver-bearing water solution reached the decaying vegetation, chemical changes caused the water to precipitate out and become deposited in both the sand and petrified material. Miners kept a close watch for petrified wood, with some petrified logs saturated with silver worth hundreds and even thousands of dollars. There were 37 mines within the Silver Reef district. At its peak, five mills processed the ore from the mines.

During the late 1870s, the mining town grew rapidly. Homes, schools, churches, a newspaper, bakeries, blacksmith and butcher shops and grocery, hardware, furniture, clothing and drug stores sprang up. Saloons, a dance hall, a gambling house, a brothel and a Chinatown made Silver Reef unique among all southern Utah communities.

Silver Reef's glory years did not last long, especially with the Panic of 1893 severely affecting all western silver mining. Around the turn of the 20th century, many of the town's buildings were offered for sale. A rush to purchase the buildings occurred after Peter Anderson bought the old dance hall and found $2,000 in gold coins, apparently left hidden in the building by the original owner, who had been shot in the hall and died of his wounds before he could tell anyone about the money. Other buildings were demolished, but no other hidden treasures were found.

To reach Silver Reef, take the Leeds exit, Exit 23, off I-15, 17 miles north of St. George, and follow the road through pretty little Leeds until, at the north end of town, you see a sign indicating Silver Reef to the west. Follow the road under the freeway, then about 2 miles to the Wells Fargo Building. This impressive stone building constructed in 1877 houses the **Jerry Anderson Studio and Gallery** and the **Silver Reef Museum**. A freestanding safe and a wall safe date from the Wells Fargo days. The photographs, maps and artifacts help make Silver Reef's heyday alive in your mind.

Washington Cotton Mill

St. George was established in 1861 as what was to be the center of a Mormon cotton industry, and the cotton mill, one of Utah's most important industrial buildings, is virtually all that is left of that effort. The mill was constructed of red sandstone in 1866 and expanded in 1870. The old mill now has a new life as a nursery. Take a few minutes to walk through the building to see the flowers and plants that are turning the St. George desert into an oasis, and look at the historic photographs that recall another time and another use for the grand building. Open Mon.–Sat. 9 A.M.–5 P.M. Head north on Interstate 15, take the Washington exit, turn left onto Telegraph and follow the road toward Washington. Look for the building on the right (south) side of the road just before you enter the town. **375 W. Telegraph Rd., Washington; 435-634-1880.**

Museums

Rosenbruch Wildlife Museum

Operating under the philosophy "We did not inherit the earth from our ancestors, we borrowed it from our children," the Rosenbruch Wildlife Museum opened in the spring of 2001 and has quickly become one of the most popular educational attractions in the area. Open Mon. 5–9 P.M., Tues–Sat. 10 A.M.–6 P.M. **1835 Convention Center Dr.; 435-656-0033; www.rosenbruch.org.**

St. George Art Museum

Opened in 1996 as part of the city's Utah Statehood Centennial Project, the art museum houses a fine collection of local and regional artists. There are special exhibits on the main floor and a permanent collection upstairs. It is worth a

visit to see the 12 Legacy paintings that were collected for the centennial, which represent an artistic impression of St. George history. Open Mon. 6–8 P.M., Tues.–Thurs. 10 A.M.–5 P.M., Fri. 10 A.M.–8 P.M., Sat. 10 A.M.–5 P.M. Admission free but donations accepted. **47 E. 200 N.; 435-634-5949; www.sgcity.org/arts/arts museum.asp.**

Performing Arts

Southwest Symphony

The Dixie Center's Cox Performing Arts Center is home to this fine community symphony orchestra that offers Handel's *Messiah* at Christmastime and several concerts throughout the year with major works by well-known composers. **Southwest Symphony, P.O. Box 423, St. George, UT 84771; 435-656-0434; dsc.dixie.edu/music/concert.**

Tuacahn Center for the Performing Arts

The 2,000-seat Tuacahn Amphitheater opened in the summer of 1995 and is one of the most spectacular locations for outdoor productions that you can imagine. You sit encircled by the 1,000-foot-high red sandstone cliffs with the stage blending into the sand, boulders and rocks that lie at the base of Tuacahn, which means "Canyon of the Gods." Located 10 miles northwest of St. George. Take Hwy. 91 west from St. George through Santa Clara and watch for the turnoff about 2 miles west of Santa Clara. Drive north through the town of Ivins to the stop sign, where you turn east for a couple of miles and then just after the road (Hwy. 300) turns to the north, you turn left and follow the road to the Tuacahn parking area. The route is well marked from St. George. **Tuacahn, P.O. Box 1996, St. George, UT 84771; 1-800-746-9882; www.tuacahn.org.**

Scenic Drives

Mojave Desert / Joshua Tree Rd.

One of the most unusual scenic drives in Utah is a gravel and dirt road suitable for passenger cars that goes through the Joshua Tree National Landmark west of St. George. This area in Washington County's extreme southern section marks the northernmost region in which Joshua trees grow, and here you are in a classic Mojave Desert landscape rather than among the red hills, blue mountains and black volcanic ridges characteristic of the rest of Washington County. Wildflowers blooming in the spring make this a particularly good time to travel this 16-mile loop, which can be taken in either direction.

The road begins on old Hwy. 91 2 miles west of the Gunlock turnoff. To reach it, drive west from St. George on old Hwy. 91 (Sunset Blvd.) to Santa Clara, then continue another 8 miles to the Gunlock turnoff at Shivwits and proceed another 2 miles. The road heads toward the south, past the Helca Mining Operation. The first 3 miles pass through the Shivwits Paiute Indian Reservation and climb up Wittwer Canyon (Widow Canyon), its phonetic name probably given for or by one of the 1856 Swiss settlers sent to Santa Clara. The road then skirts the base of Jarvis Peak, paralleling the boundary of the Beaver Dam Mountains Wilderness Area located to the south. About 8 miles from Hwy. 91, the well-maintained mining road ends and you must keep to the left, following a narrow dirt road that climbs to a ridge before reaching the Joshua trees. It then traverses Bulldog Canyon and intersects Hwy. 91 about 4 miles from the Utah–Nevada border. You can return the way you came; you can follow Hwy. 91 north and then east about 30 miles back to St. George; or you can follow Hwy. 91 south into Arizona to Interstate 15 at Littlefield and take the interstate about 20 miles northeast back to St. George.

Virgin River Gorge / I-15

Interstate 15 cuts north-south through Utah for 400 miles, but its most spectacular stretch begins just south of St. George, through the Virgin River Gorge. Flying through the twisting canyon at 65 miles an hour is no way to enjoy a scenic drive, but the 20-mile stretch southwest from St. George to Littlefield, Arizona, following the Virgin River as it cuts through the Beaver Dam Mountains, is one that few drivers will soon forget.

Tours

Historic St. George Live

This fun-filled hour-long tour visits five historic sites and buildings in downtown St. George. The tour takes in the **Orson Pratt home** and **Greene Gate Village, tabernacle, Old Washington County Courthouse, opera house, Brigham Young Winter House** and **Ancestor Square** (see the Where to Stay section for locations and details on these buildings). During the tour you meet local reenactors portraying 19th-century characters associated with each of the stops, such as Brigham and Amelia Young, Jacob Hamblin, Orson Pratt, Erastus Snow and Judge John McFarlane. A modest fee for adults; children under 12 free. May–Aug. one tour a day Tues.-Sat., beginning at 9 A.M.; however, special tours can be arranged year-round. Tour begins at the St. George Art Museum, located at **200 N. and Main St.; 435-634-5942.**

Wildlife Viewing

Two of the best locations for viewing wildlife in the St. George area are **Pine Valley** (see the Biking and Hiking sections under Outdoor Activities) and **Snow Canyon State Park** (see the Major Attractions section), both off Hwy. 18 as it heads north from St. George. Pine Valley offers a high probability for seeing mule deer, along with smaller animals and birds common to Utah's forests. Snow Canyon State Park is more desert than forest and features reptiles like the endangered desert tortoises, Gila monsters, lizards and rattlesnakes. Spring through fall is the best viewing season.

Another good area to see desert wildlife is the **Lytle Ranch Preserve.** Operated by Brigham Young University, Lytle Ranch is open year-round, although the best time to view wildlife is in the spring and late fall. The Lytle Preserve is located along the Beaver Dam Wash drainage where the Mojave Desert of the Basin and Range Province overlaps with the Colorado Plateau. Plant life of the uplands is characterized by Joshua trees, datil yucca, creosote bushes, black brush and cholla cactus. The lowlands along the wash support cottonwoods and black and desert willows. Animals include coyotes, cottontail and jackrabbits, mule deer and beavers in the uplands; along the wash, lizards, Gila monsters, rattlesnakes, roadrunners and the desert tortoise, an endangered species. There is a full-time manager at the preserve, and limited camping facilities are available. Follow Hwy. 91 northwest through Santa Clara on to Shivwits. Approximately 0.5 mile west of the junction of the Gunlock Rd., watch for a sign pointing to the Lytle Ranch. Follow the gravel road in a northwesterly direction approximately 11 miles to the ranch headquarters. **Lytle Preserve, 290 MLBM, Brigham Young University, Provo, UT 84602; 435-378-5052.**

Where to Stay

There are nearly 60 lodging facilities in the St. George area. Although this is a prime travel area, motel rates are generally reasonable, especially during the summer. Unlike other high-travel destinations, such as Moab, Blanding or Monticello, there are usually plenty of vacancy signs out. However, certain events and holiday weekends, such as Presidents' Day and Easter, can make finding a room difficult. St. George was a national leader in providing nonsmoking rooms. Almost all motels offer nonsmoking rooms and some, such as the Claridge Inn, are completely smoke free. **www.utahsdixie.com.**

Bed and Breakfasts

Greene Gate Village Bed and Breakfast Inn—$$ to $$$
St. Georgeites who have watched the evolution of Greene Gate Village are lavish in their praise for Dr. Mark and Barbara Greene, who have transformed several pioneer homes slated for demolition into a unique bed and breakfast.

Their efforts have earned praise from historic preservationists everywhere. Located across the street north of the tabernacle, Greene Gate is a complex of eight historic buildings, some of which have been moved to their present location. Thirteen rooms with private baths are included in the complex. Breakfast is served in the Orson Pratt house, which is also the location for the Bentley Supper House, where dinner is offered by reservation to guests and the public Thurs.–Sat. evenings. **76 W. Tabernacle; 1-800-350-6999; 435-628-6999; www.greene-gate.com.**

An Olde Penny Farthing Inn—$$ to $$$
If you come in Dec., chances are you will be greeted by Mr. and Mrs. Santa Claus; if it's in the summer, expect Brigham Young and Amelia, one of his 27 wives. In addition to running this fine bed and breakfast, Alan and Jacquie Capon are performers who are involved in Christmas activities, "Historic St. George Live" and other community productions that call for their talents. Alan is a native of Coventry, England, and an architectural designer whose touch is evident throughout the house. The Penny Farthing refers to both the English coin and the name for the old-time bicycle, for which the huge front wheel was the penny compared to the much smaller back wheel or farthing.

A full breakfast is served with American and English fare. "Prairie Ploppers," or English scones and fried tomatoes, mushrooms and potatoes are all a part of Alan's English heritage. **278 N. 100 W.; 435-673-7755; www.oldepenny.citysearch.com.**

Seven Wives Inn—$$ to $$$
This early bed and breakfast was opened in St. George in 1981 by Jay and Donna Curtis. The inn is located in two historic houses, the Edwin Woolley House, built ca. 1873, and the adjacent George Whitehead House, built in 1883. The inn draws its name from Donna's great-grandfather, Benjamin Franklin Johnson, a polygamist who really did have seven wives and who found sanctuary from the law in a secret hideout in the

Woolley House. Each of the 13 rooms is decorated with period furnishings, and has its own private bath, although the plumbing has improved considerably since the time George Whitehead ran a pipe from the irrigation ditch outside to a bathroom upstairs to provide running water, albeit cold, for baths. If you want a unique bathing experience, opt for the Sarah Room on the main floor of the Woolley House. This three-room suite includes one room with a whirlpool tub in a 1927 Model "T" Ford car. The inn is now owned by Shellee Taylor, who continues the fine bed and breakfast tradition established by the Curtises. **217 N. 100 W.; 1-800-600-3737; 435-628-3737; www.seven wivesinn.com.**

Hotels and Motels

Best Western Abby Inn—$$$

Opened in 1996; 130 rooms, all with refrigerator and microwave. Indoor spa and outdoor pool. Free continental breakfast. **1129 S. Bluff St.; 1-888-222-3946; 435-652-1234.**

Best Western Coral Hills—$$ to $$$

An excellent downtown location, just across the street from the Old Washington County Courthouse and a block from Ancestor Square and the St. George Tabernacle; 98 units. Indoor and outdoor pools, children's pool, spas, exercise room and game room. A nice, clean, well-run motel. **125 E. St. George Blvd.; 1-800-542-7733; 435-673-4844.**

Best Western Weston's Lamplighter Motel—$$

Pool and Jacuzzi; 63 rooms. Adjacent gift shop and restaurant. **280 W. State St., Hurricane; 1-800-528-1234; 435-635-4647.**

Holiday Inn Resort Hotel and Convention Center—$$$

One hundred and sixty-four units. **850 S. Bluff; 1-800-457-9800; 435-628-4235.**

Motel Park Villa—$$

A clean, charming motel that is considered the best deal in Hurricane and very popular with European travelers; 45 units, 17 with kitchens. **650 W. State St., Hurricane; 1-800-682-6336; 435-635-4010.**

Spas

Red Mountain Spa—$$$$

If you drive through Snow Canyon early in the morning, chances are you will see guests staying at this spa toiling up the steep road. Rated as one of the 10 best fitness resorts in the world, the Red Mountain Spa helps people lose weight using a variety of aerobic activities and a modified diet. Attention is also given to stress reduction and time management. The staff claim to see miracles happening all the time as people learn "that the most enjoyable and satisfying things you can do in life are feats you accomplish with your own strength, your own tenacity, your own body." Most participants spend three days to a week with your choice of standard or deluxe single or double hotel accommodations. **202 N. Snow Canyon Rd., Ivins, UT 84738; 1-800 407-3002; 435-673-4905; www.red-mountainspa.com.**

Campgrounds

PRIVATE

Because the St. George area is a nesting ground for thousands of snowbirds Oct.–May, and many spend the winter in trailers or fifth-wheels, RV parks are of special importance in the area. The RV parks can fill to capacity during the winter, but are practically abandoned during the summer. Most of the parks have elaborate facilities: stores, laundries, clubhouses, swimming pools, hot tubs, saunas, game areas, cable hookups and, in the winter, organized activities. Rates also vary, so if you are planning to spend any length of time in the area in your recreation vehicle or trailer, you will want to get the particulars on prices and amenities. The following list of major RV resorts and parks should provide what you need. **St. George Area Travel Office, 97 E. St. George Blvd.; 435-628-1658.**

Brentwood RV Resort

This is popular with children; 188 full hookups. Water slide, indoor swimming pool, bowling and amusement center. Located 5 miles east of Interstate 15 off Exit 16 along Hwy. 9. **435-635-2320.**

Harrisburg Lakeside RV Resort

Two hundred-plus hookups. Within the resort and just across the interstate are ruins of the 19th-century pioneer stone houses built by the pioneers of Harrisburg (see the Historic Sites section). Located off Interstate 15 near Leeds; northbound, take Exit 22; southbound, take Exit 23; then follow the frontage road 2 miles south from Leeds to the resort. **435-879-2312.**

McArthur's Temple View RV Resort

Clubhouse, laundry and pool; 260 full hookups. **975 S. Main; 1-800-776-6410; 435-673-6400.**

Quail Lake RV Park

Fifty-five full hookups. Located 3 miles east of Interstate 15 off Exit 16 along Hwy. 9. **435-635-9960.**

Redlands RV Park

Two hundred and four sites, 88 with full hookups. Take the Washington exit (Exit 10) off Interstate 15. **650 W. Telegraph, Washington; 1-800-553-8269; 435-673-9700.**

Settlers RV Park

One hundred and fifty-five full hookups. **1333 E. 100 S.; 435-628-1624.**

St. George Campground and RV Park

One hundred full hookups. **2100 E. Middleton Dr.; 435-673-2970.**

PUBLIC

Pine Valley Area

There are three small U.S. Forest Service campgrounds near Pine Valley: **Blue Springs** has 18 RV sites and 3 tentsites; **Juniper Park** has 10 RV sites and 12 tentsites; and **Pines** has 2 RV sites and 6 tentsites. All three have picnic tables, drinking water and flush toilets and charge a fee. Open mid-May–end of Oct. Drive Hwy. 18 north from St. George for 25 miles to Central, then turn east and follow the road (Forest Rd. 035) for 6 miles into Pine Valley; continue 3 miles east of the town to the end of the road.

Red Cliffs Recreation Area

The recreation area operated by the Bureau of Land Management is nestled under the east slope of the Pine Valley Mountains. Ten RV sites and 10 tentsites; drinking water and flush toilets. Open year-round. A fee is charged. From Interstate 15, take Exit 22, turn back to Harrisburg, then follow the road west under the interstate, past Harrisburg for a couple of miles.

Where to Eat

J. J. Hunan—$ to $$

One of St. George's two Chinese restaurants offers 50 different choices on its luncheon menu. There are even more choices for dinner with Canton, Szechwan, Mandarin, Hunan and Shanghai dinners, plus vegetarian entrées. Open Mon.–Fri. 11:30 A.M.–9:45 P.M., Sat. noon–9:45 P.M., Sun. noon–8:45 P.M. Located in Ancestor Square on the second floor of the Tower Building. **435-628-7219.**

Painted Pony Restaurant—$$ to $$$

Located on the second floor of the tower building at Ancestor Square, the Painted Pony offers a variety of salads and sandwiches for lunch. For dinner there's pasta, fish and steak. The Painted Pony is a favorite of locals. Open Mon–Sat. 11:30 A.M.–10 P.M. **2 W. St. George Blvd.; 435-634-1700.**

Panda Garden Chinese Restaurant—$ to $$

Ivan Szu and Dena Chen are the owners of this popular Chinese restaurant. The menu is extensive, with something for everyone: Cantonese-style dishes, spicy selections, family-style dinners and a dozen entrées for vegetarians. Open daily 11 A.M.–10 P.M. **212 N. 900 E.; 435-674-1538.**

The Pasta Factory—$$

What I like best about the Pasta Factory is the

outside seating, where you can enjoy your food outdoors almost year-round. Located in Ancestor Square, the restaurant appears to be an extension of the adjacent Pizza Factory, but they are actually two separate operations. As the name suggests, the focus is on pasta and the menu invites guests "to experiment, to try new zesty flavors and to get over any fear of 'in' food. The pasta we use is full of flavor and body, it's chunky and delicious. The classic pasta flavor, made with hard durum semolina wheat, is a mild, nutty taste that complements any dish." Ask the waiters for recommendations and explanations beyond those that are spelled out with considerable detail on the menu. Open daily 11 A.M.–10 P.M. **2 W. St. George Blvd.; 435-674-3753.**

Paula's Mexican Cazuela—$$

Paula Dominguez brought Mexican food to St. George in the early 1960s when she, her husband, Coronado, and their children arrived from south Texas via Nevada. Looking for work, she was hired by Sue Cannon to cook at the Desert Kitchen Truck Stop and began offering Mexican food to Sue's customers. Later Sue worked for Paula as her cashier and hostess. Paula's Cazuela (or Paula's Clay Cooking Pot) opened nearly 20 years ago and has been at the present location since 1985. After more than 30 years, Paula's Mexican food is still the favorite of St. George locals.

À la carte entrées are available, and while the best-seller is Paula's special deep-fried burrito, my favorite is the enchilada grande, which comes with two beef, chicken or cheese enchiladas topped with sour cream, guacamole, tomatoes, lettuce and olives. Although the food is the main attraction, a close second is the fabulous view of St. George. The restaurant is located on the hill at the west end of St. George and offers a panoramic view of St. George below. Ask for a window seat, even if you have to wait. Open Mon.–Sat. 11 A.M.–10 P.M. Located off Bluff St. **745 W. Ridgecrest Dr.; 435-673-6568.**

Pizza Factory—$ to $$

Locals claim this is the best pizza in town, where they serve pizza made from scratch. We ate there on a Fri. evening in May and found the restaurant busy and full of teenagers and families with children. The waitresses were cheery, and the customers enthused about the weekend and dinner out. We left full of good food and good feelings. In addition to pizza, the menu includes a full range of sandwiches, an excellent salad bar, spaghetti, delicious soups and homemade cheesecake and chocolate chip cookies. Open Mon.–Thurs. 11 A.M.–10 P.M., Fri.–Sat. 11 A.M.–11 P.M. Located in Ancestor Square on **St. George Blvd. and Main St. 435-628-1234.**

Services

Visitor Information

St. George Area Convention and Visitor's Bureau—Open Mon.–Fri. 9 A.M.–5 P.M. **1835 Convention Center Dr., St. George, UT 84790; 1-800-869-6635; 435-634-5747; www.utahsdixie.com.**

St. George Area Chamber of Commerce—Open Mon.–Sat. 9 A.M.–5 P.M. Old Washington County Courthouse, **97 E. St. George Blvd.; 435-628-1658; www.st-george.ut.us.**

Utah Visitor Center—Open daily in summer 8 A.M.–9P.M.; in winter 8 A.M.–5 P.M. Located off Interstate 15 just across the Arizona–Utah border.

South-Central Region

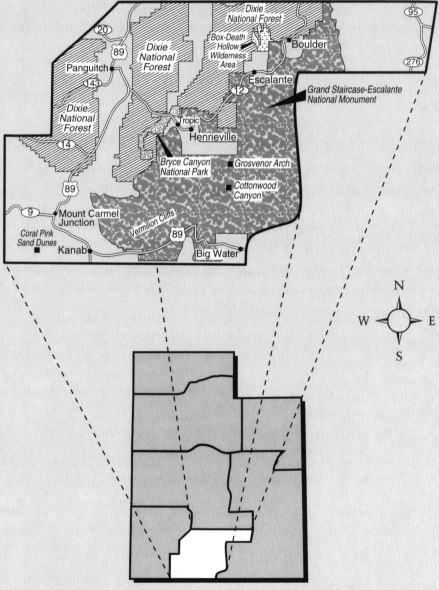

Escalante

The small towns of Escalante and Boulder lie in the heart of some of the most beautiful desert scenery in the Southwest. For most of the 20th century they were isolated, host to only a few hearty visitors. However, with the discovery of the excellent hiking opportunities; the paving of Hwy. 12 from Boulder to Grover in the 1980s, which provides an excellent connection between Bryce Canyon and Capitol Reef National Parks; and better access to Lake Powell via the recently paved Burr Trail, Escalante has come to occupy an important place on the travel map of Utah. Visitors seek solace and rejuvenation backpacking along the Escalante River. Within Boulder, Anasazi State Park has been established to preserve and exhibit the ruins left by the ancient inhabitants of the area.

Escalante and Boulder lie within Garfield County, which is also home to Bryce Canyon National Park and Panguitch. Hwy. 12 connects the three locations, as well as the smaller towns of Henrieville, Cannonville and Tropic. Escalante has 750 people; Boulder, 200. The Aquarius Plateau on the east rim of the Escalante country is an elevated tableland rising to more than 10,000 feet in elevation, on whose surface can be seen deposits from relatively recent volcanic and glacial deposits. As you stand atop the Aquarius Plateau, little has changed since Clarence Dutton penned this description in the 1870s:

It is a sublime panorama. The heart of the inner Plateau Country is spread out before us in a bird's eye view. It is a maze of cliffs and terraces lined off with stratification, of crumbling buttes, red and white domes, rock platforms gashed with profound canyons, burning plains barren even of sage—all glowing with bright color and flooded with blazing sunlight. Everything visible tells of ruin and decay. It is the extreme of desolation, the blankest of solitude, a superlative desert.

As Dutton and other members of the Powell Survey looked over the land, they could see four major landforms all running in something of a southeasterly direction and all quite different in nature.

To the south they could see the Kaiparowits Plateau, sometimes called "Fifty Mile Mountain" for the distance it stretches from south of Escalante to the Colorado River. The historic Hole-in-the-Rock Trail parallels the Plateau on the north.

The middle feature is Escalante Canyon, through which flows the Escalante River carrying water from the Escalante Mountains and the Aquarius Plateau, historically to the Colorado River and now to the waters of Lake Powell.

North of Escalante Canyon are the Circle Cliffs and the Waterpocket Fold, both rock upthrusts that occurred about 85 million years ago. The Waterpocket Fold is included within Capitol Reef National Park.

Flanking the Aquarius Plateau to the northeast is Boulder Mountain, over which passes Hwy. 12 as it heads north to connect with Hwy. 24 near the entrance to Capitol Reef National Park.

History

Throughout the Escalante Canyon are different layers of sandstone, mudstone, siltstone, gypsum and reddish shales. These are the remains of deposits from ancient seas, rivers and sand dunes that have hardened into sedimentary rocks thousands of feet thick, including such formations as the Kayenta, Wingate and Navajo sandstones. Water and wind have worked on these layers to produce an elaborate collection of fins, domes, buttes, cliffs, arches, bridges and deep-cut canyons.

The Escalante/Boulder area was inhabited by the Anasazi, as remains of their village sites testify. The village site at Boulder (see the Anasazi Indian Village State Park entry in the Major Attractions section) was situated on a branch of the Escalante River and, with an estimated population of 200 people, was one of the largest Anasazi settlements in the region. The Indians cultivated beans, corn and squash in fields adjacent to the village. Apparently the village suffered a major fire, either because of war or through natural causes, and was abandoned by about A.D. 1150, less than 100 years after it was established.

During the Black Hawk Indian War of the mid-1860s, the southern Utah militiamen, under the leadership of Capt. James Andrus, passed through the Escalante area on a journey from St. George to Green River. During the journey they found wild potatoes growing here, which they cooked and ate, leaving the name Potato Valley to describe the area just east of the Escalante Mountains. In 1872 a group of Panguitch citizens investigated the valley for potential settlement and met Frederick S. Dellenbaugh and Almon Harris Thompson, members of Maj. John Wesley Powell's expedition. They recommended that any new settlement in the area be called Escalante, in honor of the 1776 Franciscan father who, ironically, was never within 100 miles of his namesake.

Escalante was settled in 1875 and has been one of the most isolated towns in Utah ever since. But even more remote is the town of Boulder, 30 miles north of Escalante. Established as a ranching community in 1889, it has been dubbed the "last frontier in America." Its location is ideal for cattle raising, with the lush summer pastures on Boulder Mountain and the more

---

Getting There

Escalante is located along Hwy. 12 about 300 miles south of Salt Lake City, 40 miles east of Bryce Canyon National Park and 70 miles southwest of Capitol Reef National Park.

---

moderate winter range on the deserts and in the canyons to the east. Boulder was connected to the outside world, if you can call Escalante the outside world, by a treacherous mule and horse trail known as the Boulder Mail Trail, across which mail and small packaged goods were transported three times a week by horse and mule from 1902 until 1940, making Boulder probably the last town in America to receive its mail service in this ancient manner.

Major Attractions

Grand Staircase-Escalante National Monument

The monument is described in the **Kanab** chapter, where its primary access points lie. Information can be obtained at the **Cannonville Visitor Center, 10 Center St., Cannonville; 435-679-8981;** and at the **Escalante Interagency Office, 755 W. Main, Escalante; 435-826-5499.**

Anasazi Indian Village State Park

Like a number of other Utah towns, Boulder is located on the site of an earlier prehistoric village, but, unlike all other Utah towns, the ancient pueblos in only Boulder and Blanding (called Edge of the Cedars State Park) in San Juan County (see the **San Juan County** chapter in the Southeastern Region) have become museums. Anasazi Indian Village State Park was established in 1960, after a two-year excavation by archaeologists from the University of Utah uncovered 87 rooms in the pueblo, which were variously used for storage, living quarters, religious ceremonies and burial chambers. Later excavations were undertaken, beginning in 1978 and continuing to the present. A museum building was constructed in 1970; later a full-scale, six-room replica of a representative Indian dwelling from the period of A.D. 1075 to 1275 was built. Trails wind their way through the stabilized ruins; a self-guided brochure is available in the museum.

An expanded and redesigned museum was

dedicated in April 1997. At the rededication, Wil Numkena, a member of the Rattlesnake Clan of the Hopi Indians, reflected: "I was told that one day the non-Indians would help preserve our history. Our history will be understood here. Our history will be taught to the people who come through here. As I came here, I could feel the presence of my people."

The museum is open year-round (except for major holidays); mid-May–mid-Sept. daily 8 A.M.–6 P.M.; the rest of the year daily 9 A.M.–5 P.M. A modest admission fee is charged. Located in the center of Boulder along Hwy. 12. **435-335-7308.**

Escalante Petrified Forest State Park

There are a number of locations in Utah where you can find petrified wood, but nowhere is there a greater abundance or easier access than at Escalante Petrified Forest State Park. The 1,784-acre reserve was established as a state park in 1963. Tree trunks and stumps have been preserved by volcanic silica that entered the wood through groundwater. One explanation holds that the trees fell during a time of intense volcanic activity. They became buried in mud, which cut off oxygen, thereby preserving them. Silica mixed with groundwater was deposited in the wood from the fine volcanic ash. It is these silicates that led to the mineralization of the interior of the trees and the colorful gems preserved inside them.

You can view a good collection in the petrified wood cove a short distance from the parking lot. The hiking trails within the park cover about 1.75 miles. Just before you enter the petrified wood reserve, there is a trail guide to the 1-mile Petrified Forest Trail that climbs up the hill from the parking lot for a fine view of the ridge of Wide Hollow Reservoir to the west and the town of Escalante to the east. You can see plenty of petrified wood along this trail, but for an even greater concentration of petrified logs, the 0.77-mile-long Trail of Sleeping Rainbows, which loops off the main trail, is well worth the effort. The latter trail requires a steep descent, then ascent. Even though tons of petrified wood

were hauled away from the park before collecting was prohibited, there is still a vast amount of it to be seen.

Within the state park is **Wide Hollow Reservoir,** which was constructed in 1954 for irrigation purposes. A popular local recreation area, there are boating facilities, swimming, open-water fishing and ice fishing at the reservoir. There are picnic facilities, modern rest rooms, showers and 22 camping units within the park. Located 2 miles west of the town of Escalante. **435-826-4466.**

Kodachrome Basin State Park and Grosvenor Arch

You may wonder how Kodak could get a 2,500-acre park named for its most popular brand of film. Known locally as Thorley's Basin, this colorful valley was visited by members of a National Geographic Society expedition in 1948. They named the area Kodachrome Flat, after the color film that appeared on the market in 1935 and was first used in *National Geographic* in 1939. The valley was established as a state park in 1963. Grosvenor Arch was named by members of the 1948 National Geographic Society expedition into the area in honor of Dr. Gilbert Grosvenor, president of the National Geographic Society.

The most distinctive feature within the park are the 67 slender, gray limestone-stratified columns called "chimney rocks," ranging in height from 6 feet to 160 feet. These columns are found nowhere else in the world in such a

---

Getting There

From Cannonville, turn south off Hwy. 12 and follow the scenic Cottonwood Cutoff Rd. for 7 miles to the park/campground. Grosvenor Arch is another 10 miles south on a dirt and gravel road, usually passable for passenger cars, but with some steep climbs and descents that can be very treacherous when wet.

large group. While the chimney rocks look like they might be toppled by a good push or a strong wind, they have stood for thousands of years. Located a few miles east of Bryce Canyon National Park, the limestone chimneys offer an interesting contrast to the sandstone formations at Bryce. Some geologists postulate that the chimney rocks were ancient geyser plugs, vents or tubes that filled with a harder limestone material than the sandstone that encased them. As the sandstone weathered away, the limestone chimney rocks were left. Cowboys had another theory, suggesting to gullible visitors that they were really petrified fence posts!

Outdoor Activities

Seven short **hiking** trails provide access to much of the area.

Angel's Palace Trail—Beginning just east of the campground, this trail makes a scenic loop in less than 1 mile through a narrow canyon onto a plateau where you can look down over the park.

Big Bear Geyser Trail—Named for a spire that looks like a big bear, this 2-mile-loop trail off the Panorama Trail is the newest trail in the park. The trail also takes you to Cool Cave, a spectacular box-canyon cave well worth the hike.

Eagles View Trail—This old cattle trail north to Henrieville is a steep 1-mile climb to the top of the cliffs 1,000 feet above the campground. There are sheer drops along much of the trail so if heights and cliffs bother you, you might want to pass on this one. Still, the trail was used to bring cattle off the mesa for nearly three-quarters of a century until 1977.

Grand Parade Trail—This 1-mile-long trail takes you to the base of several fins and spires that look as if they are lined up in parade formation.

Grosvenor Arch Trail—Located approximately 10 miles southeast of Kodachrome Basin State Park, the paved trail up to the large double arch is approximately 0.2 mile in length and is wheelchair accessible.

Panorama Trail—This easy 3-mile round trip circles among the chimneys and colorful rocks.

Shakespeare Arch Trail—This 0.25-mile-long trail takes you to an arch discovered several years ago by park ranger Tom Shakespeare.

Camping

There are 27 campsites at the park, and rest rooms and showers are available. A modest fee is charged. Open Apr.–Sept.

Outdoor Activities

Biking

See Hell's Backbone Rd. and Hole-in-the-Rock Trail under Scenic Drives.

Fishing

North of the town of Boulder off Hwy. 12, Boulder Mountain is an angler's delight, with many small lakes, reservoirs and streams that attract anglers from all over the state. Usually you will find brook and cutthroat trout in abundance. Pleasant, Raft, Green, Fish Creek, Cook's, Round, Left Hand, Donkey, Blind and Pear are just some of the lakes on Boulder Mountain. Access to most of the lakes is with a four-wheel-drive vehicle over rugged roads. Roads connect off Hwy. 12, but get a Forest Service map that shows access to the various lakes and ask where you can get information on road conditions. **Escalante Ranger District, Dixie National Forest, 270 W. Main St., P.O. Box 246, Escalante, UT 84726; 435-826-4221.**

Hiking

Calf Creek Falls

The Bureau of Land Management's Calf Creek Recreation Area offers access to the 126-foot Lower Calf Creek Falls. The falls are reached along a 2.75-mile trail that is quite sandy, and although it is not too steep, it can be quite strenuous, especially in the heat of the day. Yet the 5.5-mile round-trip hike is well worth the effort, as the falls have created a miniature

▼ *Red Canyon, along scenic Hwy. 12 west of Bryce Canyon National Park*

▼ *Southern Union Equitable Building {SUE}, Panguitch*

▲ *Water wagon, Panguitch*

1

◀ *Bryce Canyon*

▼ *Bryce Canyon Airport constructed of native logs 1936–1937*

▼ Natural bridge with an 85-foot span, Bryce Canyon

▼ Levi Stewart Monument, Kanab

▼ Lake near Alton

▲ Lake and red sandstone, along Hwy. 89 north of Kanab

▼ *Virgin River in
Zion National Park*

▼ *The Three Patriarchs, Zion Canyon*

▼ *Shakespeare Theater at Southern Utah University, Cedar City*

▼ *Canon Memorial on the grounds of St. George Temple*

▲ *Ironton west of Cedar City*

▼ *Black Rock House, Beaver*

Frisco Coke Ovens ▶

◀ *Marcus Shepherd House, Beaver*

7

▼ *Scofield Cemetery with grave markers for some of the 200 coal miners killed on May 1, 1900*

▲ *A scene from the Lynn Fausett Mural in the Price City Municipal Building depicting trappers Caleb Rhodes and Abram Powell in 1877*

▲ *San Rafael River*

▼ *San Rafael Bottle Neck Butte in the Swell area*

▲ *Rock art, the bug-eyed man, located in the Sinbad area of the San Rafael Swell*

◀ *I-70 through the San Rafael Reef west of Green River*

Goblin Valley ▶ *southwest of Green River*

▼ *Robidioux Inscription located in the Book Cliffs north of I-70*

◄ *The Colorado River west of Moab*

Balance Rock, ▶
Arches National Park

▼ *Delicate Arch,*
Arches National Park

◀ *Upheaval Dome area of Canyonlands National Park*

▼ *Monument Valley in the northern end of the Navajo Indian Reservation*

Moon House ▶
ruin once occupied by the Anasazi

▼ *Ranch near Blanding*

▲ *Bluff Cemetery*

14

▼ *Boats on Lake Powell with the Hole-in-the-Rock in the distance*

◀ *Rainbow Bridge*

Shangri-la in this desert region. The refreshing falls; pool; "hanging gardens" of ferns, mosses and colorful wildflowers; and shade are a welcome relief before you make the return trip. The sight of water plunging over the red sandstone cliff is one that you won't soon forget.

Along the hike there are two locations where you can see Fremont–style pictographs on the cliffs. One panel includes three anthropomorphs 6–8 feet high, which are apparently painted on top of older paintings. They are adorned with horns and seem to carry shields, a trademark of Fremont rock art. There is a trail guide that corresponds with 24 markers along the trail. You can pick up the guide at the trailhead. Located off Hwy. 12, 17 miles east of Escalante and 12 miles south of Boulder.

Escalante River Area

The Escalante River, a tributary of the Colorado, provides access to some of the most pristine and glorious backpacking country anywhere in the world. Located within the Grand Staircase–Escalante National Monument and a designated wilderness area, the region is open only to foot travelers. Outdoor recreationists see Escalante Canyon as a great hiking preserve. Spring and fall, when temperatures are cooler and the weather more settled, are the best times to hike the desert. Because of the numerous side canyons and hundreds of miles of hiking possibilities, you generally encounter few people.

Even though the waters of Lake Powell back up into Escalante Canyon, the area still remains as difficult to reach as before the lake was created. Only one road, Hwy. 12, crosses the Escalante along the river's 85-mile-long course between the town of Escalante and Lake Powell. You can reach the canyon from trailheads off two historic trails: the Hole-in-the-Rock Trail, which parallels the canyon to the south, and the Burr Trail, which parallels the canyon to the north.

Backcountry permits are required for more than day hikes. The BLM map that outlines the trails, locates the trailheads and indicates mileage is useful. You can obtain guidebooks, permits and maps at **Escalante Resource Area Office, Bureau of Land Management, Escalante, 755 W. Main, P.O. Box 246, Escalante, UT 84726; 435-826-5499.**

The best place to get supplies, equipment, information and maps about hiking in the area is at **Escalante Outfitters, 310 W. Main St., Escalante; 435-826-4266.** Barry and Celeste Bernards can offer good suggestions for all levels of experience and interest. They have on hand USGS maps and most items that hikers would need.

While most visitors who take the time to reach Escalante usually spend several days backpacking, camping, and exploring in the canyon, a nice **day hike** can be made along the 15-mile stretch of river from Escalante to the Hwy. 12 bridge over the Escalante River. There is no established trail for the entire length, and much of the time you will be hiking in the ankle-deep river. If the river is running higher than ankle deep, you probably won't want to make the hike. Either leave a shuttle vehicle at the Hwy. 12 bridge or arrange for someone to pick you up. The river cuts through the great cliffs of the Escalante Monocline, offering magnificent scenery and a wilderness experience just off Hwy. 12.

Lower Muley Twist Canyon

Muley Twist Canyon is part of the route opened in the early 1880s by Charles Hall as an alternative to the Hole-in-the-Rock Trail, which was used by pioneers into the southeastern part of the state. Hall built a ferry at Hall's Crossing on the Colorado River and laid out a route that passed between 1,000-foot walls of sandstone on either side. The canyon through which much of the new route passed was said to be so crooked that you would "twist a mule" pulling a wagon through it. This area has good possibilities for overnight hikes, but you need a permit from the visitor center at Capitol Reef National Park (see the Central Region).

The Lower Muley Twist Canyon is an excellent 8-mile out-and-back hike that you can combine with a drive across the Burr Trail. Travelers on the Burr Trail (see the Scenic Drives section under Seeing and Doing) pass the Lower Muley

Twist Canyon trailhead about 23 miles east of Boulder. Hiking 4 miles down Muley Twist Canyon takes you to the Post Cutoff, a good turnaround point for an out-and-back hike. Another option is to arrange a shuttle or pickup at the Post trailhead along the Notom-Bullfrog Rd. (see the **Capitol Reef National Park** chapter in the Central Region) and then follow the Post Cutoff for 2.3 miles for a 6.3-mile one-way hike.

Seeing and Doing

Museums

Escalante Tithing Office / Daughters of Utah Pioneers Museum

Constructed in 1894, the Escalante Tithing Office is one of the oldest and best preserved of the tithing offices that were constructed and maintained in every Mormon village to receive and disburse the 10 percent tithes, which until the mid-20th century were usually paid in kind: one out of every 10 eggs, one out of every 10 bushels of wheat, one out of every 10 calves that were born. This rock building has been a museum for more than 50 years, run by the Escalante Daughters of Utah Pioneers since 1938. If the building is not open, look for the telephone number posted there. One of the faithful DUP ladies will be happy to come and give you a personal tour. **40 S. Center St.**

Scenic Drives

Burr Trail

Shortly after the Burr Trail was opened in Oct. 1892, Josephine Catherine Chatterly Wood, a traveler on the trail, wrote, "All well in health but we had the life frightened right out of us all. I don't know what they call this place, but I'll call it the Devil's Twist and that's a Sunday name for it. For all of the roads on earth, I don't think there are any worse than there are here. It is the most God-forsaken and wild looking country that was ever traveled."

The paving of the Burr Trail from Boulder to Lake Powell was one of the most controversial environmental issues of the 1980s in Utah. Local residents fought long and hard—and finally succeeded—in getting the road paved, arguing that the trail forms an essential link for travelers between Lake Powell and Bryce and Zion National Parks. Seventeen miles of this 70-mile-long route is still unpaved: 13 miles through the south of Capitol Reef National Park and 4 miles through Glen Canyon National Recreation Area.

The road begins at Boulder from Hwy. 12, passes across the Waterpocket Fold at the southern end of Capitol Reef National Park, joins the Scenic Backway Notom-Bullfrog Rd. (see the **Capitol Reef National Park** chapter in the Central Region) and intersects Hwy. 276 a few miles north of the Bullfrog Marina on Lake Powell. There are eight designated overlooks along the trail, which offer spectacular views of Long Canyon, the Circle Cliffs, Muley Twist Canyon, the Waterpocket Fold, the Henry Mountains, the southern parts of Capitol Reef National Park, Bullfrog Creek, Clay Canyon and Lake Powell. Plan about 4 hours for this unforgettable drive through the heart of southern Utah.

Cottonwood Canyon Rd.

This 46-mile-long backway connects Hwy. 12 at Cannonville with US Hwy. 89 near the Paria Ranger Station west of Big Water. The Cottonwood Canyon Road heads south past Kodachrome Basin State Park and Grosvenor Arch. As the road follows Cottonwood Creek through Cottonwood Canyon, the prominent monocline (also called a hogback) known locally as the Cockscomb (because of the crest) looms above to the east. At the end of Cottonwood Canyon, the creek joins the Paria River, and the road follows the river some distance before heading southeast to its intersection with US Hwy. 89.

The road requires a couple of hours to travel—in good weather. During wet weather, the road south of Kodachrome Basin State Park is impassable to most vehicles. During dry weather, the road can be dusty and washboarded, but it is heavily used during the summer as a scenic drive and a connecting route between Bryce Canyon National Park and the southern end of Lake Powell.

Hell's Backbone Rd.

Hell's Backbone is a thin ridge with precipitous walls on both sides that drop hundreds of feet. It runs alongside the Box–Death Hollow Wilderness Area to the west and Sand Creek Canyon to the east. On top of the ridge is a deep, narrow crevice first spanned by a bridge constructed by the Civilian Conservation Corps in the late 1930s. While the 30-mile route was first used by horses and mules, until the paved road was completed to Boulder in 1971, this was the only route from Escalante to Boulder, and books could be written about the stories of travel over the dangerous route. This 38-mile-long drive heads north from Hwy. 12 at Escalante along Forest Rd. 153 following the Posey Lake Rd. for 14 miles to the lake, where the road branches. Keep to the right and follow Forest Rd. 153 to its junction with Hwy. 12 just west of Boulder. The road reaches an elevation of 9,200 feet. Passenger cars can usually travel the road in dry weather, which is closed by snow in winter. (It reopens by late May.)

Hole-in-the-Rock Trail Scenic Backway

The 180-mile-long Hole-in-the-Rock Trail between Escalante on Hwy. 12 and Bluff on US Hwy. 191 along the San Juan River was the most difficult of any of America's western pioneer trails. The route was opened during the winter of 1879-1880 by a group of 250 men, women and children who left their homes in Cedar City, Parowan, Paragonah and other southern Utah communities to establish a new settlement on the San Juan River. The route passes Dance Hall Rock, a famous landmark on the trail. It was near Dance Hall Rock that the various groups converged to unite for their journey on to the San Juan River. Dances were held in the amphitheaterlike Dance Hall Rock. Just above the Colorado River at the end of this drive, the pioneers chipped and blasted an unbelievable slit in the sandstone cliffs, down which they drove their loaded wagons.

Today the Hole-in-the-Rock Trail is the best preserved of any of America's western pioneer trails. In some places, evidence of the pioneer trail can still be seen. The nearly 60-mile-long section west of the Colorado River begins 5 miles east of Escalante off Hwy. 12. The road is a good gravel road, suitable for passenger cars for all but the last 5 miles. As the road approaches the Hole-in-the-Rock down to the Colorado River, it goes over hills of slickrock that may not be suitable for passenger cars and that require caution even in high-clearance and four-wheel-drive vehicles. In addition, there are sandy spots that you need to watch for.

Hwy. 12 Scenic Byway: Henrieville to Torrey

As you travel throughout the Escalante region, you will put in a good number of miles on Hwy. 12. The entire route—122 miles from US Hwy. 89 south of Panguitch past Bryce Canyon; through Tropic, Cannonville and Henrieville to Escalante and Boulder; and on to Torrey on Hwy. 24—has been designated a Scenic Byway. From Henrieville east of Bryce Canyon National Park to Torry just west of Capitol Reef National Park, the route is about 90 miles. The 30 miles from Henrieville to Escalante climb to 7,400 feet on the Table Cliff Plateau before dropping to follow the Escalante River. The 29 miles between Escalante and Boulder offer stops at Escalante Petrified Forest State Park, Calf Creek Falls, and Anasazi Indian Village State Park. The route climbs to 9,200 feet on Boulder Mountain before dropping into Grover and Torrey in 32 miles. Allow plenty of time to see everything along this scenic highway.

Smoky Mountain Rd. Scenic Backway

If you want a scenic backway taken by very few people through one of the most isolated parts of the state, the Smoky Mountain Rd. offers such an opportunity. The 78-mile-long road of graded dirt and gravel runs south from Escalante on Hwy. 12 to Big Water City on US Hwy. 89 near the Utah–Arizona border, just west of Glen Canyon Dam and the city of Page, Arizona. The route offers spectacular views of the Kaiparowits

Plateau, Lake Powell, Navajo Mountain and other landmarks. The steep climb up the Kelly Grade (5 miles of switchbacks up the 1,200-foot face of Smoky Mountain) is impassable when wet, as are other portions of the road, and should not be attempted. If it is dry, you are likely to find plenty of dust and rutted roads, and high-clearance vehicles are strongly recommended. Plan several hours for this route, and take extra food and water, just in case.

Tours

Escalante Walking Tour

If you don't think there is anything to see in Escalante besides the magnificent scenery, get a copy of the *Walking Tour of Pioneer Homes and Barns* at one of the several businesses in town and set out to take a look at the nearly 100 homes, buildings and barns identified in the brochure. Most of the buildings date between 1890 and 1920 and several are listed in the National Register of Historic Places. Because Escalante reflects the traditional Mormon town plan with houses located on the four corners of the block, if you walk along the streets running east–west, you will see nearly all but the few buildings constructed in the center of each block. The tour begins in the northwest corner of town and ends on 300 S. and Center St.

Where to Stay

Accommodations

ESCALANTE

Escalante is a small town, so if you are looking for fancy, modern accommodations there, you won't find them. While Escalante is well known to many Utah travelers, camping tends to be more popular than staying in motels. But if you need a place to sleep and take a refreshing shower after a day of hiking, biking or sight-seeing, the following Escalante motels provide the necessities.

Circle D Motel—$ to $$

Some of the 29 rooms have kitchenettes. **475 W. Main St.; 435-826-4297.**

Escalante Outfitters—$

Seven log-cabin bunkhouses, three with double beds and four with bunk beds. These small cabins have heaters and a fan, but no air conditioning. Toilets and showers are located in a common bathhouse. The cabins are situated around a common lawn with barbecues. **310 W. Main St.; 435-826-4266.**

Lott's Legacy Inn—$ to $$

Twenty-three rooms. **75 S. 100 W.; 435-826-4250.**

Moqui Motel—$ to $$

Ten rooms. **480 W. Main St.; 435-826-4210.**

Padre Motel—$ to $$

Twelve rooms. **20 E. Main St.; 435-826-4276.**

Prospector Inn—$$

Opened during the summer of 1994, this 50-room motel is the largest in Escalante. **400 W. Main; 435-826-4653.**

BOULDER

Boulder Mountain Lodge—$$ to $$$

Twelve rooms. **P.O. Box 1397, Boulder UT, 84716; 1-800-556-3446; 435-335-7460.**

Camping

PRIVATE

In Escalante, the **Triple S RV Park** offers 29 spaces with hookups and 19 tent spaces, plus rest rooms and hot showers; **495 W. Main; 435-826-4959.** Across the street, the **Moqui Motel Campground** has 10 RV spaces, all with complete hookups; **480 W. Main; 435-826-4210.**

PUBLIC

About 20 miles north of Escalante, on the Hell's Backbone Rd. (Forest Rd. 153), there are two Forest Service campgrounds open June–mid-Sept. **Posey Lake** has 19 RV sites and 23 camping sites, while the smaller **Blue Spruce** campground has 6 tentsites; however, neither campground has flush toilets or showers. Swimming, boating and fishing are popular at Posey Lake.

Calf Creek Campground

The BLM campground has 5 RV sites and 14 tentsites; flush toilets. Open mid-Apr.–late Nov. Located 15 miles east of Escalante on Hwy. 12. The **Deer Creek Campground,** another BLM facility, has 2 RV sites and 5 tentsites. Located 6 miles southeast of Boulder on the Burr Trail.

Where to Eat

ESCALANTE
Circle D Restaurant—$ to $$
Both American and Mexican food. Breakfast served until 11 A.M. Open in summer daily 6 A.M.–9:30 P.M.; in winter daily 7 A.M.–2 P.M. and 5–8 P.M. Located adjacent to the Circle D Motel. **475 W. Main; 435-826-4282.**

Cowboy Blues Diner—$ to $$
Traditional breakfasts; sandwiches, Navajo tacos, burritos, enchiladas, traditional steaks, roast beef, chicken and trout for lunch or dinner. Try AJ's chili verde, made with a recipe from Mexican sheepherders. Open daily 7 A.M.–9 P.M. **530 W. Main; 435-826-4251.**

Golden Loop Cafe—$ to $$
Big breakfasts, sandwiches for lunch, and American–style food for dinner. Open in summer daily 6:30 A.M.–9 P.M.; in winter 7 A.M.–8 P.M. **39 W. Main; 435-826-4433.**

Prospector Restaurant—$ to $$
Full-menu breakfasts, sandwiches, steaks and Mexican food. Open daily for breakfast, lunch and dinner. Located in back of the Prospector Inn. **400 W. Main; 435-826-4658.**

BOULDER
Boulder Mesa Restaurant—$ to $$$
American food, shrimp, roast beef, New York steaks, Mexican food, homemade soups, vegetable salads and a vegetarian menu. Open daily for breakfast, lunch and dinner. Located just off Hwy. 12. **155 E. Burr Trail; 435-335-7447.**

Burr Trail Grill—$ to $$$
Well known for its huge breakfasts. Pizza, flame-broiled hamburgers, steaks, lemon and garlic chicken and trout, Navajo tacos and Mexican and Italian food. Open daily for breakfast, lunch, and dinner. Located at the junction of the Burr Trail and Hwy. 12. **435-335-7503.**

Hells Backbone Grill—$ to $$$
Emphasis on regional Utah cuisine using organic foods and locally raised meats. Vegetarian selections. Open for breakfast and dinner. Adjacent to the Boulder Mountain Lodge. Located just off Hwy. 12. **435-355-7460.**

Services

Visitor Information
Escalante Ranger District, Dixie National Forest—755 W. Main, P.O. Box 246, Escalante, UT 84726; 435-826-4221.

Interagency Visitor Center—Operated by the Bureau of Land Management, the U.S. Forest Service and the National Park Service. Open mid-Mar.–Oct. daily 7:30 A.M.–5:30 P.M.; Nov.–mid-Mar. Mon.–Fri. 8:30 A.M.–4:30 P.M. Located just off Hwy. 12 at the western end of Escalante. **755 W. Main, P.O. Box 246, Escalante, UT 84726; 435-826-5499.**

Bryce Canyon National Park

Technically, Bryce Canyon is not one canyon in the traditional western sense but, rather, a series of 14 amphitheaters cut into the eastern edge of the Paunsaugunt Plateau and extending approximately 20 miles from north to south. Bryce Canyon is located between an elevation of 6,600 feet and 9,100 feet, which includes three separate life zones. In the Upper Sonor-an Zone (6,600–7,000 feet) in the lower reaches of the

Getting There

Bryce Canyon National Park is located in south-central Utah, just off Hwy. 12 about 24 miles east of Panguitch, 260 miles south of Salt Lake City, and 125 miles northeast of St. George.

To reach the park from the east, take Hwy. 12 south from Torrey on Hwy. 24 just west of Capitol Reef National Park.

canyon, you will find pygmy piñon, juniper trees, Gambel oak and sagebrush. In the 7,000- to 8,500-foot Transition Zone, the stately ponderosa pine dominates, and above 8,500 feet, in the Canadian Zone, the ponderosa pine are replaced by stands of white fir, blue spruce, aspen and bristlecone pine. The high elevation and abundant water produce a wonderful variety of wildflowers, including Indian paintbrush, penstemon, wild iris, yellow evening primrose, dwarf blue columbine and goldenweed that spread across meadows and along the trails.

The fairyland of "hoodoos" spires, temples, turrets and crenelated ridges has been seen as a natural manifestation of western Europe's baroque architecture, compared with the music of Rossini, "all whimsy and delight," and explained "as the graphic representation of a magnificently insane mind." Today Bryce Canyon National Park is one of Utah's top five tourist attractions. Visitors drive the scenic park road and stop to gaze at the fantastic formations that make Bryce Canyon and the surrounding area included in the national park such a unique place. Most come to gaze upon the fairy-castlelike formations of Bryce Canyon National Park. More adventuresome visitors take one of the many hiking trails to mingle with the formations.

History

Like Cedar Breaks atop the Markagunt Plateau to the west, Bryce Canyon is cut into the Claron Formation, which consists of soft pink and white siltstone, sandstone, dolomite and limestone layers that were deposited in a Paleocene lake system. Geologists think that these deposits were laid down about 60 million years ago, when lime-rich sand and mud carried along by streams and rivers for many miles were deposited into shallow lakes. The heavy sand particles were deposited close to the shores of these lakes, while the lighter silt and clay particles settled to the bottom of the lakes farther from shore. Through millions of years, wet and dry cycles changed the size of the lakes and created limestone rock layers of different hardness that are known today as the Claron Formation.

Earth forces began pushing the land upward in this area about 10 million years ago, creating what is now called the Colorado Plateau. The tremendous pressure caused the large plateau to fracture and separate into smaller plateaus, including the Paunsaugunt Plateau, on whose east slope Bryce Canyon is located, and the Aquarius Plateau, which can be seen in the distance east of Bryce Canyon.

After this uplift occurred, the Paria River began to cut through the rock layers as it flowed down off the eastern side of the Paunsaugunt Plateau, acting as a natural shovel to scoop out great bowl-shaped areas called "amphitheaters." The Paria removed the weak rock layers and left the more durable layers in the fantastic formations that make Bryce Canyon so unique.

The erosion of Bryce Canyon continues year-round. In the summer, thundershowers drop heavy rainfall onto the formations, carrying away dirt and gravel and carving gullies in the steep slopes. The rainwater also seeps into cracks in the rock and dissolves the calcium carbonate cement that holds the rock particles together. In the winter, water enters the cracks from melting snow during the day, then freezes and expands during the night, exerting tremendous force and causing large boulders to break off. As the tall ridges, fins and pinnacles emerge, the iron and manganese in the rocks oxidize into colorful hues of red, pink, orange, yellow and purple.

The canyon takes its name from the first

white settler to graze cattle in it: Ebenezer Bryce, a Scottish Mormon who established a homestead in what is now the town of Tropic in the fall of 1875. He used the amphitheaters of what is now called Bryce Canyon to graze his livestock. Like most other pioneers, Bryce was not given to eloquence. He is said to have remarked that the canyon was a hell of a place to lose a cow. In time the canyon became known as Bryce's Canyon. Other cattlemen and people traveling through the area may have seen the wonders of Bryce Canyon before Bryce took up his homestead, but the earliest written description comes from T. C. Bailey, a U.S. deputy surveyor who wrote with unrestrained enthusiasm in 1876:

> There are thousands of red, white, purple and vermilion rocks, of all sizes, resembling sentinels on the Walls of Castles; monks and priests with their robes, attendants, cathedrals and congregations. There are deep caverns and rooms resembling ruins of prisons, Castles, Churches, with their guarded walls, battlements, spires and steeples, niches and recesses, presenting the wildest and most wonderful scene that the eye of man ever beheld, in fact it is one of the wonders of the world.

Glowing descriptions such as these led President Theodore Roosevelt to set aside Bryce Canyon and the surrounding forest as a national forest in 1905. It began to receive more visitors as word spread and a rough road was built to it.

When W. H. Humphrey was transferred in 1915 from Moab, where he held the office of Forest Supervisor for the La Sal National Forest for several years, to a similar assignment in Panguitch, one of his forest rangers insisted that Humphrey go with him to see Bryce Canyon. The forest supervisor was reluctant to take the time for the trip, but the effort was worth it. Humphrey wrote that the canyon was "the most beautiful piece of natural scenery on the face of the earth. You can perhaps imagine my surprise at the indescribable beauty that greeted us. It

was sundown before I could be dragged from the canyon view. ... I went back the next morning to see the canyon once more. ..."

The real pioneer of Bryce Canyon as a scenic resource was Ruben "Ruby" C. Syrett, who took up a homestead at the entrance to the future national park in 1916. Four years later, in 1920, he built a small lodge and cabins, the Tourist Rest, near Sunset Point. Visitation grew, and in 1923 Bryce Canyon was designated a national monument. That same year, the newly formed Utah Parks Company (a division of the Union Pacific Railroad) acquired the Tourist Rest from Syrett and began to construct Bryce Lodge. Syrett returned to his old homestead and built Ruby's Inn, which today is a large hotel complex. The construction of these facilities coincided with the completion of a passable automobile road to the canyon. Bryce Canyon had come to the attention of Horace M. Albright, director of the National Park Service, during a visit to Zion Canyon in 1917; however, it was not until 1928 that Bryce Canyon National Park was established. It was enlarged to its present size in 1931.

It grew in popularity during the 1930s, with the completion of the rim road in 1934 and the construction of lodges by the Union Pacific Railroad, which bused visitors from the railroad station in Cedar City across the high plateau country to Bryce Canyon. One of the most interesting projects of that era is the barnlike Bryce Canyon Airport constructed in 1936 and 1937 (see the Historic Sites section under Seeing and Doing).

Outdoor Activities

Biking

Biking is not recommended in the park because roadways are narrow and congested in the summer months. In keeping with policies in all national parks, no off-pavement biking is permitted. For bike routes just outside the park boundaries, see the **Panguitch** chapter.

Hiking

Walking is, without a doubt, the best way to see Bryce Canyon. There are 60 miles of trails that wind their way among Bryce's pinnacles and hoodoos and along the rim of the canyon, offering an ever-changing perspective on the intricacies of nature's handiwork. The trails begin at the rim and descend along well-maintained paths to the bottom of the amphitheaters. The descents seem easy, but most falls and injuries come on downhill treks, and what seemed an easy stroll on the way down can seem like climbing a 1,000-foot cliff on the way back out! Remember, too, that as you descend the temperature will get warmer, especially as the sun warms the ridges and rocks of this high desert country. In summer watch out for sudden thunderstorms, which can produce lightning strikes and water runoff very rapidly.

Inexperienced or infrequent hikers should note that the elevations of the park range between 6,500 and just over 9,000 feet. At this elevation, there is less oxygen and you will be exerting yourself more than usual. Take it easy, particularly on return hikes out of the canyon, rest often and drink plenty of water.

For extended hikes, bring along rain gear and a warm jacket or sweater. Check at the visitor center for backcountry camping information and backcountry hiking directions and permits. For most visitors, the following trails provide plenty of options to see the canyons in all their glory.

Fairyland Loop Trail

This strenuous, 8-mile-long loop, which takes you through the amphitheater that has a fairyland quality, descends 900 feet into the northern part of the park. During the hike you will see the amphitheaters of Fairyland and Campbell Canyons as you pass by such formations as Boat Mesa, Chinese Wall, Tower Bridge and Seal Castle. Because this is such a long climb back out, you will find the trail much less crowded than other trails in the park. The trail begins at Sunrise Point, near the North Campground.

Navajo Trail

The Navajo Trail drops 520 feet in elevation during the 0.75-mile hike through a narrow canyon to the bottom. Some of the colorful names for the formations along this trail include the Pope, Thor's Hammer, Temple of Osiris and Wall Street—a deep, narrow, 0.5-mile-long canyon entered by a side trail at the bottom of Navajo Trail. Park rangers conduct guided hikes along this trail a couple of times a day; check at the visitor center for times. The trail begins at Sunset Point, near the picnic area.

At the bottom of the Navajo Trail, there are several options. You can retrace your route back to Sunset Point for a 1.5-mile out-and-back; you can make the ascent along a leg of the more gradual Queen's Garden Trail to Sunrise Point and then follow the Peekaboo Loop (a strenuous 3.5-mile hike that goes up and down and has connecting trails to both the Navajo and Queen's Garden Trails) for a 5-mile round trip; or you can head east for 1.5 miles to the town of Tropic—a total of 3 miles one way—where you will need a shuttle (see sidebar on page 304) to return to your vehicle inside the park.

Queen's Garden Trail

The easiest trail into the canyon (if that's possible), the 1.5-mile one-way Queen's Garden Trail descends 320 feet into the Bryce Canyon amphitheater. The amphitheater is full of strange-shaped hoodoos, castles, pillars and balanced rocks, some with fanciful names like Gullivers Castle and Queen Victoria, which does resemble the British monarch who reigned from 1837 to 1901 and was the inspiration for this area's designation as the Queen's Garden. Remember that the return trip is all uphill. Plan an hour or two to make this 3-mile round-trip hike. The trail begins at Sunrise Point, near the North Campground.

Riggs Spring Loop

The most strenuous of all the day hikes within the park, the Riggs Spring Loop begins at Rainbow Point and descends 1,657 feet in 4.4 miles into the southern canyons of the park, then traverses Corral and Mutton Hollows before climbing back up to the rim at 7.7 miles. Plan the entire day for this hike, or check with park rangers about the possibility of an overnight backcountry camp. Drive Bryce Canyon Rd. to its end at Rainbow Point to find the trailhead.

Rim Trail

The best overview of Bryce Canyon is along the 5.5-mile one-way Rim Trail, which follows the rim of the plateau in the northern part of the park. Since it is nearly level and located close to parking facilities, the trail offers the best wheelchair access to the park. There are a number of benches provided for those who need frequent rest stops or who want to sit and contemplate the beauties of the canyon. Beginning from Fairyland Point (the turnoff from Bryce Canyon Rd. is before the entrance station) and heading south, the trail reaches Sunrise Point in 2.8 miles. The most heavily traveled segment of the trail is the 0.5-mile paved portion between Sunrise and Sunset Points. From Sunset Point the Rim Trail continues south to Inspiration Point in 0.7 mile and Bryce Point in 1.5 miles.

Trail to the Hat Shop

Like the Fairyland Loop Trail, this trail also descends 900 feet into the canyon, but it does so in less than 2 miles, making this out-and-back hike from Bryce Point the steepest of the day hikes within the park. If you give license to your imagination, you will find the fanciful forms and shapes to be just like those you would find in an outlandish hat shop. From Bryce Canyon Rd., the turnoff to Bryce Point is just south of Sunset Campground.

Under the Rim Trail

The ultimate hiking experience within the park is the Under the Rim Trail, which begins at various points along the rim between Bryce Point and Rainbow Point. The 22-mile-long trail follows the bottom of the canyon, with many ups and downs. Plan at least two days of strenuous hiking to complete the hike, or if you are going to be in the park for several days, you can cover the entire trail in four segments that descend from Bryce Canyon Rd. Access points are at Bryce Point, just before mile 3 on Bryce Canyon Rd., via Trail to the Hat

Shop; via the Swamp Canyon Trail at mile 6; via the Whiteman Connecting Trail at mile 9; via the Agua Canyon Connecting Trail at Ponderosa Viewpoint, mile 15.5; and from Rainbow Point at the end of the road. If, after 22 miles of hiking, you still want more, you can add more distance by continuing along the Riggs Spring Loop (see above) from Rainbow Point.

Horseback Riding

Two-hour and half-day guided horseback rides along Bryce Canyon trails are offered Apr.–Oct. The rides begin at the corral near Bryce Canyon Lodge. Sign up at the lodge; advance reservations are recommended. **Bryce-Zion Grand Trail Rides, P.O. Box 58, Tropic, UT 84776; 435-679-8665.**

Skiing

CROSS-COUNTRY

Within Bryce Canyon National Park, cross-country skiing offers visitors a unique way to see the park in winter. The beauty of the snow-dusted pinnacles and hoodoos and lack of crowds make this an attractive time to visit the park. Several ski trails are marked out within the park. The 1-mile **Fairyland Point Rd.** and the 1.8-mile **Paria Viewpoint Rd.** are unplowed during the winter so they can be used as cross-country routes. Park rangers strongly discourage skiers from skiing down the trails into the canyon. The steep grades, narrow trails and lack of snow generally make this entirely unsafe. Inquire at the visitor center about which trails are open and about snow conditions.

At Ruby's Inn just outside the park, the **Ruby's Inn Nordic Center (Ruby's Inn, UT 84764; 435-834-5301)** maintains more than 18 miles of groomed and set track, and cross-country ski rentals are available. In addition, there are many miles of backcountry trails, some along the biking trails described in the **Panguitch** chapter.

Snowshoeing

If you have always wanted to try snowshoeing, Bryce Canyon provides an excellent opportunity.

Snowshoes for adults and children are available at the visitor center free of charge, with the deposit of a driver's license, on a first-come, first-served basis. Snowshoers use the same trails as cross-country skiers.

Seeing and Doing

Historic Sites

Bryce Canyon Airport

The Bryce Canyon Airport building is one of the most unique historic buildings in Utah. Built between 1936 and 1937, this was one of the projects of Franklin D. Roosevelt's Works Progress Administration New Deal program. Men who were the children and grandchildren of those who had settled this frontier found themselves without work or income during the Great Depression and were appreciative of the opportunity to earn money from this joint project of Garfield County and the federal government.

With an eye to attracting air service and more tourists to Bryce Canyon, the Ruby Syrett family used tractors to level the 7,586-foot runway. The barnlike airport building was constructed of native ponderosa pine logs infested with the black beetle. Civilian Conservation Corps workers cut down the trees, which were sawed at a nearby sawmill and hauled to the construction site with teams of horses. The corrugated tin used for the gable roof was manufactured outside the area, representing perhaps the largest nonlabor expenditure on the building. The airport is still in use. It is one of the oldest remaining airports in the United States. Hours vary. Located on Hwy. 12 near the junction with Hwy. 63.

Scenic Drives

Bryce Canyon Rd.

No visit to Bryce Canyon National Park is complete without a leisurely drive south on the 18-mile road from the visitor center to its end at Rainbow Point. Many pullouts along the way offer viewpoints and trail access, as well as picnic areas and campgrounds.

Just inside the park boundary, before the entrance station, the 1-mile spur road to Fairyland Point is on the left, with trail access to the Rim Trail and Fairyland Loop Trail.

At the entrance station is the visitor center/ranger station on the right; just beyond it on the left is the loop road that takes you past the North Campground, amphitheater, picnic area, general store, nature center and lodge, with Sunrise Point near the middle of the loop. Shortly after the loop rejoins the main road, the short spur to Sunset Point is on the left, followed by the Sunset Campground to the right.

Just before the 3-mile point, a turnoff on the left leads to Inspiration Point, Bryce Point and picnic area, and Paria Viewpoint. This is the southern end of the most visited area of the park.

As the scenic road winds south, there are picnic areas or trailheads every 2–3 miles. At about 10.5 miles a pullout on the left at Farview Point has a short trail to Piracy Point. An overlook at about 12.5 miles provides a view of a natural bridge. The Agua Canyon overlook is at about 13.5 miles; the Ponderosa Viewpoint is at about 15.5 miles. At the end of the road at 18 miles, Rainbow Point has a picnic area and trailheads as well as incomparable views.

Wildlife Viewing

Mule deer and ground squirrels are plentiful along the roads and hiking trails in the park, and red-tailed hawks ride the air currents overhead. Piñon jays and sparrows are found in the forests; meadowlarks, sage grouse and mountain bluebirds are at home in the meadows. Yellow-bellied marmots, prairie dogs, pocket gophers, chipmunks and skunks are among the animals that live in the meadows, while in the lower reaches of the park, coyotes, bobcats, whip-snakes and lizards can be found.

Where to Stay

Accommodations

Bryce Canyon Lodge—$$

Historic Bryce Canyon Lodge on the canyon rim offers the only accommodations within the park, but you will have to book up to a year in advance. The rustic lodge has 114 units, including 70 rooms, 40 historic cabins—some duplex and some fourplex—with fireplaces now warmed by gas logs, and four suites in the lodge upstairs. The lodge was built between 1923 and 1925 by the Utah Parks Company, and the cabins were built during the 1920s and 1930s. The lodge and cabins have been listed in the National Register of Historic Places. Open Apr.–Oct. Located east off Bryce Canyon Rd. about 2.5 miles south of the park entrance. **TW Services, Box 400, Cedar City, UT 84720; 435-586-7686; www.brycecanyonlodge.com.**

Ruby's Inn—$$ to $$$

Located just outside the park entrance, Ruby's Inn is a landmark in the Bryce Canyon area. The historic lodge was, unfortunately, destroyed by fire, but the new motel has been expanded to 369 units, making it one of the largest motels in Utah. Some rooms have two bedrooms and kitchenettes. Several rooms have whirlpool jet tubs and a few have freestanding whirlpool tubs. The inn has an indoor swimming pool, restaurant, general store and Laundromat. Trail rides, van tours, helicopter flights and mountain bike rentals are available. Open year-round. Located on Hwy. 63 just north of the park entrance. **Ruby's Inn, Bryce, UT 84764; 1-800-468-8660; 435-834-5341; www.rubysinn.com.**

Camping

PRIVATE

Bryce Canyon Pines Country Store and Campground

Of the 50 campsites, 17 are pull-throughs and 25 have full hookups; plus rest rooms, showers, laundry, limited groceries and snacks, RV supplies, playground, game room and indoor pool. Located on Hwy. 12, 5 miles northwest of the park entrance. **Bryce Canyon Pines Campground, Bryce, UT 84764; 435-834-5440.**

Ruby's Inn RV Campground

This RV campground offers 160 sites with RV hookups, and another 40 tentsites. In addition to rest rooms, showers and laundry facilities, it offers plenty of recreation opportunities with an indoor heated swimming pool, recreation hall, arcade and planned activities. There is a shuttle bus into the national park July–Aug. Open Apr.–Oct. Located on Hwy. 63 outside the park entrance. **Ruby's Inn RV Campground, Bryce, UT 84764; 435-834-5301.**

PUBLIC

There are two campgrounds within the park. The **North Campground** and **Sunset Campground** are located within a few miles of each other, a couple miles south of the visitor center. With a total of 206 campsites, the first-come, first-served campgrounds are often unable to accommodate all visitors to the park during summer. Your best bet is to stake out a campsite during midmorning. The North Campground has 55 RV sites and 55 tentsites; Sunset Campground has 50 RV sites and 50 tentsites. Fees are charged; seven-day limit. No hookup facilities, but a fee sewage dump station, located near the North Campground, is available until cold weather sets in. Laundry and showers located at the general store at Sunrise Point are usually in service early May–mid-Oct. If you want a campfire, bring your own firewood since no wood gathering is allowed within the national park. Closed during winter.

Where to Eat

Bryce Canyon Lodge Dining Room—$ to $$

Located in the historic 1924 lodge, the dining room is a long hall that constitutes the middle wing of three parallel sections that form the lodge. There are large stone fireplaces on both sides of the hall, and seven trusses span the hall. Lunch items include sandwiches, mountain red trout and barbecued pork riblets. Dinner includes prime rib, rib-eye steak, halibut, shrimp and roast loin of pork. Vegetarian dishes include wagonwheel pasta with marinara, eggplant parmesan, chef's salad and chili. It is the only dining facility within the park. Reservations advised during the

> ## Shuttle Service
>
> Beginning in 2000, Bryce Canyon National Park implemented a shuttle bus system to ease congestion inside the park. The shuttle boarding and parking area is located just south of Hwy. 12 on the east side of Hwy. 63, which leads to the park.
>
> The shuttle operates mid-May–Sept. and makes stops at the various viewpoints approximately every 10–15 minutes. The shuttle is included with your park admission fee.

peak season, and expect slow service. Open Apr.–Oct. daily 7 A.M.–9 P.M. Located east off Bryce Canyon Rd. about 2.5 miles south of the park entrance. **TW Services, Box 400, Cedar City, UT 84720; 435-586-7686.**

Ruby's Inn Dining Room—$$ to $$$

The dining room at Ruby's Inn serves more Bryce Canyon visitors than any other facility. Most patrons opt for the buffet, offered all day long. The breakfast buffet includes hot cakes, French toast, eggs, hash browns, biscuits and gravy, cereal and fruit. The lunch and dinner buffet offers beef, pork, chicken, pasta, vegetables, fresh fruit and a variety of salads. You can also order sandwiches for lunch and rainbow trout, red snapper, shrimp, prime rib and steaks. For something quick, in the **Canyon Room,** a self-service deli inside the lodge, you can cook your own hamburgers or pick up tacos, chili, pizza, baked potatoes and sandwiches. Open year-round daily 6:30 A.M.–9:30 P.M. Located on Hwy. 63 near the park entrance. **1-800-468-8660; 435-834-5341.**

Services

Visitor Information

Bryce Canyon National Park Visitor Center—Interpretive programs, a bookstore and information. Open year-round with hours that vary seasonally. Located just inside the park entrance. **Superintendent, Bryce Canyon National Park, Bryce Canyon, UT 84717; 435-834-5322; www.nps/gov/brca.**

Garfield County Travel Council—P.O. Box 200, Panguitch, UT 84759; 1-800-444-6689; www.brycecanyoncountry.com.

Wheelchair-Accessible Facilities

The National Park Service has made efforts to accommodate travelers with special needs. Many park buildings, rest rooms and viewpoints in Bryce Canyon National Park meet current accessibility standards in providing wheelchair access. The level, paved Rim Trail between Sunrise and Sunset Points is well adapted for wheelchairs. A few campsites at the North Campground are reserved for mobility-impaired campers. Some of the ranger-led interpretive activities are available to all visitors. Obtain a copy of the *Bryce Canyon Access Guide,* available at the visitor center. **Bryce Canyon National Park, Bryce Canyon, UT 84717; 435-834-5322.**

Panguitch

It is the scenery that brings thousands of visitors to Panguitch each year. Anglers enjoy the beautiful Panguitch Lake. The original settlers named their town Panguitch, the Indian word meaning "big fish." There are few inhabitants in the area. There are about 4,000 people in all of Garfield County, of which Panguitchis the county seat, or one person per square mile, with 1,158 square miles left over. Panguitch has a population of about 1,500 people. The other towns—Hatch, Antimony, Tropic, Cannonville and Henrieville—all have fewer than 200 inhabitants.

Most of the residents still trace their ancestors back to the 1860s and 1870s, when Panguitch,

Escalante and other hamlets were settled. They are fiercely loyal to their homeland, and many have strong opinions about how public lands should be used. Local residents, who have struggled for years to wrest a living from the wilderness, mostly by raising cattle and sheep and doing some timber harvesting, are willing to promote almost any enterprise that will allow them and their children to remain in the area, even when their income (primarily through farming or service jobs) remains half or even a third of Utah's urban residents. This is not to say that locals do not -appreciate the wilderness or have no desire to see it preserved. It is the encounter with the wilderness that has shaped the people of Garfield County and for which they have their own respect and reverence, though not always in ways that are apparent to outsiders.

History

Panguitch was first settled on March 16, 1864, under the direction of Jens Nielsen, a Danish convert to Mormonism who, eight years earlier, had suffered severely in the early winter storms as he pulled a handcart across Wyoming to Salt Lake City. Nielsen led a group of pioneers from Parowan and Beaver eastward across the mountains to establish the settlement near the Sevier River.

The settlers faced difficult times as crops did not mature because of the high elevation. Unstable Indian relations threatened the fledgling community. During the first winter there, seven men left Panguitch for Parowan, 40 miles across the mountains, to try to get flour and food for their starving families. The trek became known as the "Quilt Walk," because according to local lore, the men had to abandon their wagons and oxen and

make their way on foot across the snowfields by laying one quilt down and then another.

In 1867 the newcomers were forced to abandon the settlement during what was known throughout central and southern Utah as the Black Hawk War. Panguitch was officially resettled in 1871 and began to prosper. Houses were built outside the fort, and farmers constructed an irrigation ditch. Other residents built lumber mills, shingle mills and a flour mill. The livestock industry provided a good-enough income that substantial red brick homes could be built during the 1880s and 1890s. After World War I, though, the livestock market dried up and ranchers scraped by until World War II brought better times. Livestock never has regained its earlier preeminence, and tourism has come to play a large role in the local economy.

Outdoor Activities

Biking

Dave's Hollow

This easy 8-mile out-and-back ride through ponderosa forests and meadows along a double-track road begins a mile south of Ruby's Inn at the northern boundary of Bryce Canyon National Park on Hwy. 12. Take the dirt road heading west and, after 0.75 mile, turn right onto the Dave's Hollow Trail. Follow it for approximately 3 miles to its junction with Forest Rd. 087 near Dave's Hollow Forest Service Station. You can either return the way you came or head north along Forest Rd. 087 to its junction with Hwy. 12, and then east to the junction with the Bryce Canyon Rd. and back to Ruby's Inn. The latter route adds another 4 miles (riding in highway traffic may not suit every cyclist), for a total distance of 12 miles.

Indian Hollow

If you are staying in Panguitch and want a good 4- to 6-hour ride, this 18-mile ride takes you through wooded stretches in a relatively untraveled area close to Panguitch. Head west out of Panguitch from the main intersection on Main

Getting There
Panguitch is 236 miles south of Salt Lake City on US Hwy. 89.

St. and follow Forest Rd. 085 through Five Mile Hollow. Turn left onto Forest Rd. 310 and follow it along Five Mile Ridge to its intersection with Forest Rd. 082. Follow Forest Rd. 082 for 1–2 miles in a northwesterly direction, then turn right into Indian Hollow along Forest Rd. 039; the road heads northeast before turning back to the east, where it rejoins Forest Rd. 085 for the return ride through Five Mile Hollow to Panguitch.

Pine Lake Rd.

This 17-mile out-and-back ride winds through pine forests and aspen groves, and the overlook into Henderson Canyon provides a breathtaking view of what has been called a "miniature Bryce Canyon." From the junction of Hwys. 12 and 63 just outside the park, drive north on Hwy. 22 for 11 miles north to a gravel road that heads east. Look for the sign "Pine Lake / Table Cliff Plateau, Campground, Dixie National Forest, Forest Rd. 132." The bike route begins at this point. Climb along Forest Rd. 132 for about 5 miles to Pine Lake. Continue another 3.5 miles along Forest Rd. 282 to the turnaround point at Henderson Canyon Viewpoint.

Rentals

Ruby's Inn—on Hwy. 12 near Bryce Canyon; **435-834-5341.**

Fishing

A number of lakes in the area are stocked with trout and offer the opportunity for peaceful, uncrowded and usually successful fishing trips. Many of the lakes must be hiked into or reached by four-wheel-drive vehicle. **Antimony Lake, Barker Reservoir, Deer Creek Lake** and **Garkane Power Reservoir** are the best-known lakes and reservoirs in the area. Fly-fishing is best done at Antimony Creek, Asay Creek, Mammoth Creek, Panguitch Creek and the East and South Forks of the Sevier River. Additional information is available at the U.S. Forest Service office in Panguitch. **Powell Ranger District, 225 E. Center, P.O. Box 80, Panguitch, UT 84759; 435-676-8815.**

Panguitch Lake

Speak of fishing in southern Utah, and Panguitch Lake comes to mind for most longtime Utah anglers. Located 17 miles southwest of the town of Panguitch, the lake is fed by three streams: Blue Spring, Ipson and Clear Creeks. The natural lake once had a depth of 38 feet, but a dam constructed in the 1890s increased the depth to 61 feet. Chances are you will not snag any of the "big fish" for which Panguitch was named, but the lake's cool water is home to plenty of rainbow, brook, cutthroat and brown trout. The high country location and cold temperatures make this an excellent ice-fishing lake. Boat rentals are available, and there are two public boat launching ramps on the north and south sides of the lake. Lodging is available at four locations near the lake (see the Where to Stay section).

Hiking

There are many hiking trails in Red Canyon, which is on Hwy. 12. Near the Red Canyon Campground adjacent to Hwy. 12, there are a dozen hiking trails from 1 mile round-trip to 14 miles one-way. The main route, the Cassidy Trail, is also a popular horse trail. Off-road vehicles are permitted in Casto Canyon but not on the Cassidy Trail. If you choose to spend more than a day in the area, there are other trails that branch off the Cassidy Trail. No water is available, so carry your own.

Seeing and Doing

Historic Sites

Historic Panguitch Homes

If you want to really see Panguitch, take time to walk or drive around the town. There are nearly two dozen houses of locally produced brick that give the town a distinctive character. Most were built in the 1890s and reflect a period of architecture when Utah builders were just beginning to break away from the symmetrical Federalist style to more asymmetrical Victorian styles.

Panguitch Business District

The economic prosperity of Panguitch a century ago is still visible in the historic commercial buildings that remain on Main St. between Center St. and 1st N. The **Garfield Exchange** (located at **Main and 1st N.**), was established in 1899 as a general mercantile business.

Next to it, the **bank building** saw several locally organized banks attempt to establish an economic foothold in the community, but they succeeded only as long as the national economy was strong, in the first two decades of the 20th century. The Southern Utah Equitable, known throughout southern Utah as SUE, finally closed its doors in the 1980s. This stately building was, according to local tradition, the source of difficulty for one young man who spent the summer in Panguitch. When he returned home to his parents in the northern part of the state, they asked, "Who is this SUE to whom you've been writing all those checks?"

Panguitch Historic Public Buildings

From the number of public buildings constructed in 1907–1908, it seems that those years were the most active construction periods in Panguitch's history. Within two blocks, you can see four buildings that served as the political, social, educational and religious hubs of the community.

In 1907 the **Garfield County Courthouse (55 S. Main)** was constructed. This handsome building of native brick has served as the center of political activity in the county for nearly 100 years.

The **Social Hall** (located on Center St.) was built in 1908, then immediately rebuilt after a fire destroyed the first building. As the social center of the community, it was used mostly for public dances, but it continues to be used for basketball, dancing, gymnastics and summer musicals.

Just south of the Social Hall, the **library** was also built in 1908. Panguitch was one of more than 20 Utah communities that took advantage of start-up money for public libraries offered by Andrew Carnegie.

Panguitch Tithing Office/Bishop's Storehouse / Daughters of Utah Pioneer Museum

If Escalante and Panguitch are representative Mormon villages, it seems that the early settlers of these towns built their tithing offices so that they could be later used by the Daughters of Utah Pioneers as museums. In truth, if it were not for these committed women, the buildings would probably have been demolished long ago. The Panguitch Tithing Office offers an interesting contrast to the Escalante office, reflecting the obvious transition from pioneer times to more modern ones. Built in 1907 of red brick, the Panguitch Tithing Office was designed from one of at least three standard plans that Salt Lake City authorities created for tithing offices around 1905. You can see almost identical buildings in Richmond, Manti, Spring City and Fountain Green.

The building was leased by the local Daughters of Utah Pioneers organization in 1964. They use the building for meetings and as a museum to house artifacts from the pioneer days of Panguitch. Open during summer Mon.–Sat. 1–5 P.M.; the rest of the year by appointment. If you come when the museum is not open, look for a phone number posted on the building; someone will come and open the museum for you. **100 E. Center.**

Museums

Paunsagaunt Wildlife Museum

What better use for the abandoned Panguitch High School than to fulfill one man's dream and to give both travelers and schoolchildren a fascinating opportunity to learn more about western wildlife? At the age of 9, Robert Driedonks immigrated with his parents from their home in Rotterdam, Holland, first to British Columbia and later to Las Vegas, Nevada, where his mother owned a couple of flower shops. As a youngster, Robert developed a passion for hunting and, during his 20 years as a Las Vegas bellman, he spent every opportunity hunting animals to display in the museum he always dreamed of opening. His dream became a reality in 1995 when arrangements were concluded for him and his wife, Teri, to establish a wildlife museum in the 1936 Panguitch High School.

Using lifelike settings to display more than 300 mounted birds and animals, Driedonks offers visitors a chance to see the rich variety of wildlife from the American West. Animals include bobcats, coyotes, peccary, foxes, lynx, deer, elk, antelope, skunks, raccoons, prairie dogs, marmots, mountain lions, beaver, otter, porcupines, mountain goats, black bears and an assortment of rattlesnakes, birds of prey, owls, turkeys and waterfowl. All the animals are real, with one small exception placed in one of the exhibits for schoolchildren to try to locate. There is also an African Room with a mounted lion, baboons, bush pigs, cape buffalo and other African wildlife. It is hard not to be taken with Robert Driedonks's enthusiasm for his museum—a 25-year dream come true to show all animals from the smallest to the largest and teach people about them. The lifelike exhibits and the well-written and thoroughly researched exhibit texts make this museum much more than just a gallery of lifeless animals. Open May 1– Nov. 1 daily 9 A.M.–10 P.M. **205 E. Center St.; 435-675-2500.**

Scenic Drives

Hwy. 12 Scenic Byway: Red Canyon to Henrieville

As you travel throughout the Panguitch/ Escalante region, you will put in a good number of miles on Hwy. 12. The entire route—122 miles from Panguitch through beautiful Red Canyon, past Bryce Canyon, through Tropic, Cannonville, Henrieville, Escalante, and Boulder to Torrey on Hwy. 24 west of Capitol Reef National Park—has been designated a Scenic Byway.

If you are staying at Panguitch and want a full day's outing, you can take Hwy. 12 east to Torrey. Return via Hwy. 24 west through Wayne County, then follow Hwy. 62 south through Koosharem, past Otter Creek Reservoir, onto Hwy. 22 south through Antimony and Widtsoe Junction back to Hwy. 12; or from Otter Creek

Reservoir head west on Hwy. 62 to US Hwy. 89 and back to Panguitch. Plan an early start.

Where to Stay

Accommodations

PANGUITCH

The high tourist season is late spring, summer and early fall. The rest of the year, it can be very quiet in Panguitch, although more and more people are discovering its cross-country skiing potential and that it is easier to reach Brian Head Ski Resort (see the **Cedar City** chapter in the Southwestern Region) from the Panguitch side than the Parowan side. Travelers find that the accommodations in Panguitch meet the basic needs without the frills, and cost, of overdeveloped resort towns.

Best Western New Western Motel—$$

Heated pool and coin laundry; 37 rooms. Open year-round. Located at 200 E. and Center. **435-676-8876.**

The Red Brick Inn—$$$ to $$$$

This Dutch colonial–style red brick home was built in the 1930s for Dr. Welby Bigalow and served as his family residence and the first hospital in the Panguitch area. There are six nonsmoking rooms, all with private bath, TV and VCR. One unit has two bedrooms and sleeps six; the three-bedroom suite has a private kitchen, living room and fireplace and sleeps 10. Hosts Brett and Peggy Egan provide a hearty home-style breakfast. **161 N. 160 W., Panguitch, UT 84759; 1-866-733-2745; 435-676-2141; www. redbrickinnutah.com.**

EAST OF BRYCE CANYON—TROPIC
Bryce Valley Inn—$$ to $$$

In the small town of Tropic 7 miles southeast of Bryce Canyon, the Bryce Valley Inn offers 61 rooms. Open Mar.–Oct. The restaurant is open 6 A.M.–11 P.M. **Bryce Valley Inn, Tropic, UT 84776; 1-800-679-8811; 435-679-8811; www.brycevalleyinn.com.**

Stone Canyon Inn—$$$ to $$$$

This brand-new five-room bed and breakfast is located in Tropic just east of Bryce Canyon, and all the rooms have spectacular views of the national park. All rooms have satellite TV and private baths, and most are equipped with Jacuzzis. The Ivy Room has a double Jacuzzi in the dormer window. The rooms are all non-smoking. To reach the inn, take the Bryce Wy. Rd. in Tropic west for 1 mile to Fairyland Ln. and turn south for 0.5 mile. **1-866-489-4680; 435-679-8611; www.stonecanyoninn.com.**

Camping

PRIVATE

Cannonville–Bryce ValleyKOA Campground and RV Park

This fine campground is owned by John and Marsha Holland, who have become very knowledgeable about the area through Marsha's work as an interviewer for the Southern Utah Oral History Project. Sixty-four RV sites, 16 tentsites and five cabins with showers, flush toilets, laundry, game room, swimming pool and dump station. Located 15 minutes east of the national park in Cannonville off Hwy. 12. **435-679-8988.**

Hitch-N-Post Campground

Facilities include flush toilets, showers, laundry, a dump site, some tentsites and wheelchair-accessible facilities; 34 RV trailer sites, 28 of which have full hookups. Open year-round. **420 N. Main, Panguitch; 435-676-2436.**

Panguitch Big Fish KOA

The usual facilities plus a swimming pool; 70 RV sites, 20 with full hookups, and 20 tentsites. Open Apr.–Oct. **555 S. Main, Panguitch; 435-676-2225.**

Panguitch Lake Resort

Rest rooms, showers, laundry, picnic tables, drinking water and easy access to Panguitch Lake; 72 RV trailer sites with complete hookups. A popular campground during summer. Open early May–Labor Day. **791 S. Resort Rd.; 435-676-2657.**

Riverside Campground

Flush toilets, showers, laundry, swimming and fishing; 124 RV trailer sites, 45 with full hookups. Cactus Cowboy Restaurant located nearby. Open May–Nov. **594 US Hwy. 89, Hatch; 435-735-4223.**

PUBLIC

Not far from Bryce Canyon, two national forest campgrounds provide space for visitors to Bryce Canyon and hikers in Red Canyon. **Red Canyon Campground** has 15 RV spaces and 22 tentsites with flush toilets; open mid-Apr.–mid-Nov. **White Bridge Campground** has 22 RV spaces and 2 tentsites; open June–mid-Sept. Located 10 miles southeast of Panguitch on Hwy. 12.

King's Creek Campground

With 36 tentsites and only 8 RV sites, this is a good campground for tenters. Open June–mid-Sept. Located near Tropic Reservoir. Turn off Hwy. 12 onto Forest Rd. 87 about 4 miles west of the road to Bryce Canyon, and follow it for about 5 miles south.

Where to Eat

Country Corner Cafe—$ to $$

This longtime cafe is a favorite of local residents. **80 N. Main, Panguitch; 435-676-8851.**

Cowboy's Smokehouse—$ to $$

This is one place you will want to write home about. The warm hospitality, excellent food, western music, artifacts and collection of local moose, elk and deer heads on the wall all make this an unforgettable experience. Bill and Edie Collier, transplanted Texans, opened the smokehouse in 1993 in one of the beautiful turn-of-the-20th-century brick commercial buildings on Main St. It has become a favorite with both locals and tourists. The Colliers returned to Texas to be with their grandchildren, selling the restaurant to family members Chris and Marla Gilbert.

Chris grew up on a southern Colorado ranch and started out helping on weekends and singing old cowboy songs to the delight of restaurant patrons. Even with his expanded responsibilities, he still performs on weekend evenings. You can even purchase a CD Chris has cut of traditional western songs. During the summer, live music is provided by local performers almost every evening. Chris smokes the beef, pork, turkey and chicken using mesquite wood. He makes his own barbecue sauce from 15 secret ingredients and serves a bowl of tasty home-cooked pinto beans with each meal. Marla's homemade cobbler with ice cream is a must. Peach is my favorite, but the apricot and cherry are also delicious. Open during summer Mon.–Sat. 11:30 A.M.–10 P.M.; during winter Mon.–Sat. 11:30 A.M.–9 P.M. **95 N. Main, Panguitch; 435-676-8030.**

Flying M Restaurant—$ to $$

Known for its homemade pancakes and huge sweet rolls. **614 N. Main, Panguitch; 435-676-8008.**

Lazy J Steak House—$$ to $$$

Features steak, shrimp, and lobster. Open in summer daily 5–11 P.M.; closed during winter. **523 N. Main, Panguitch; 435-676-8118.**

Services

Visitor Information

Dixie National Forest, Powell Ranger District—225 E. Center, P.O. Box 80, Panguitch, UT 84759; 435-676-8815.

Garfield County Travel Council—P.O. Box 200, Panguitch, UT 84759; 1-800-444-6689.

Kanab

The tourist gods must have inspired the selection of the town site of Kanab in 1870, since it is located in the center of the world's most magnificent landscape. Like spokes connecting with

the hub of a wheel, the roads branch out from Kanab in all four directions to three national parks, three national monuments, one national recreation area, a nationally significant historic ferry crossing on the Colorado River, two nearby Indian reservations, two national forests, two state parks and numerous opportunities to experience the American West as it has existed for thousands of years.

The image of the American West held by millions of movie buffs all over the world is the reality of Kanab. Kanab's sheer vermilion sandstone cliffs, nearby coral sand dunes and unending vistas have brought the movie industry to southern Utah for three-quarters of a century. Beginning in 1922, with the filming of *Deadwood Coach* starring Tom Mix, dozens of westerns have been filmed around Kanab. Movie sets—now historic sites themselves—remain in the canyons around Kanab, waiting for appreciative visitors. Kanab still prides itself on its nickname, Little Hollywood. While you're in Kanab, you will want to search out the "Little Hollywood Walk of Fame" on Main Street, which has mounted monuments to the likes of Tom Mix, Ben Johnson, Romald Reagan and the cast of the TV series *Gunsmoke*.

But even before Hollywood discovered Kanab, it had a long tradition as a western frontier outpost and headquarters for cattle outfits whose herds ranged across the thousands of acres along the Utah–Arizona border. If state makers had followed natural boundaries instead of artificial political boundaries in drawing the line between Arizona and Utah, the extreme northwestern corner of Arizona would have been included in Utah. Known as the Arizona Strip, the area west and north of the Colorado River and the Grand Canyon is isolated from the rest of Arizona, but is a natural extension of southern Utah. The two small settlements in the Arizona Strip, Fredonia and Short Creek (now known as Colorado City), straddle the Utah–Arizona border, with historic, social, economic and religious contacts extending north into Utah.

Travelers from the north approach Kanab along US Hwy. 89 through Long Valley, which begins in the subalpine meadows at the extreme southeastern edge of the Markagunt Plateau at an elevation of 7,500 feet on the rim of the Great Basin. The Markagunt drops off on the west to form the Great Basin Province. The road along the western edge of the Colorado Plateau, through Long Valley, follows the east fork of the Virgin River in its southerly course until, at Mt. Carmel Junction, it flows west through the southern boundary of Zion National Park. The Long Valley drive is one of the most scenic in all of Utah. The historic Mormon villages of Glendale, Orderville and Mt. Carmel suggest a sympathetic, almost reverent, accommodation to the land.

The descent along US Hwy. 89 also takes you down a geological grand staircase of rock formations—the Pink Cliffs, White Cliffs and Vermilion Cliffs—with each formation a step back into the geological past, ending at the Grand Canyon. Kanab Creek, a tributary of the Colorado, originates in the high plateau meadows east of US Hwy. 89 and follows a southerly course through the series of cliffs and into Kanab. From Kanab, it continues on across the state line and through the eastern corner of the Kaibab Paiute Indian Reservation, through the Kanab Creek Wilderness Area and into Grand Canyon National Park, where it flows into the Colorado River. Stretching from just south of Zion National Park on the west to the Paria River on the east, the fiery walls of the Vermilion Cliffs form something of a northern boundary to the Arizona Strip and leave an unforgettable impression, especially where communities like Colorado City and Kanab nestle at their feet.

History

The combination of precipitous cliffs, ancient Indian ruins, vast expanses and isolation have generated a rich tradition of stories and myths about this area that rival the magnificent scenery in color and perhaps unbelievability. The tallest of tales center on reports that the Aztec leader Montezuma dispatched 2,000 warriors to carry much of his treasure to a hiding place in the canyons north of Tenochtitlán, just before the Aztec capital fell to Spaniard Hernán Cortés in 1521.

The Kanab area was first visited by Mormon missionaries under the leadership of Jacob Hamblin, president of the Southern Utah Indian Mission. They made their way from Santa Clara, 90 miles west of Kanab, to the Hopi Indian villages in northern Arizona, where they hoped to convert the Indians to their faith. After Hamblin's visit, Mormon cattlemen moved into the area from Washington and Iron Counties to the west. The cattlemen built dugouts along Kanab Creek (*Kanab* comes from a Paiute Indian name for the willows growing along the creek). Concern about gathering Indian unrest led them to construct a primitive fort during the winter of 1865–1866.

Kanab was the first point of contact with Mormons along the route from the Navajo homeland to the southwest to the older southern Utah settlements. Bands of Navajos, who had evaded capture by Kit Carson and his troops, undertook raids to capture livestock from the Mormons, which sometimes resulted in deadly confrontations between the two peoples.

Late spring of 1870 marked a new milestone in Kanab's history, as a group of settlers arrived from the Salt Lake Valley to homestead. They were joined the following year by Mormon settlers from the Muddy River settlements in Nevada, who left their homes because they were

Getting There

Kanab is located on the Utah–Arizona border 300 miles south of Salt Lake City on US Hwy. 89. Kanab is 75 miles east of St. George via Exit 16, 10 miles north of St. George, and Hwy. 9 to Hurricane. At Hurricane you have two choices: the southern route (the fastest) along Hwy. 59 east across the Arizona Strip, or a route that takes you through the Virgin River Valley and cuts across Zion National Park to Mt. Carmel Junction and US Hwy. 89.

unable to pay back taxes in the hard currency demanded by Nevada state officials. The Mormon settlers wrested a living from the land, growing crops along the east fork of the Virgin River and Kanab Creek and grazing cattle on the mountains, plateaus and deserts surrounding Kanab.

A rich cowboy tradition developed as Kanab became a regional ranching center. Cattle dominated the local economy until after World War II, when tourism and service industries took over. The vanishing cowboy tradition, so much a part of Kanab and the Arizona Strip, has been preserved through the collections of cowboy stories and the restoration and interpretation of Pipe Spring National Monument, just to the west, in the Arizona Strip.

At the same time as the solid cowboy tradition was developing in the Kanab area during the 19th century, two more extreme Mormon practices, polygamy and the United Order Movement, were taking hold. At Orderville, established in 1874 in Long Valley 23 miles north of Kanab, a group of Mormon exiles from the Muddy Mission practiced the purest form of the United Order Movement. Members of the order owned everything in common, took their meals together and undertook a variety of joint economic endeavors that were designed to produce a harmonious communal society in the best tradition of America's pre-Civil War religious utopian settlements.

In some ways the Orderville community resembled the prosperous Shaker communal villages of the East. But at the other end of the spectrum from the celibate Shakers, 19th-century Mormons practiced their belief in polygamy. That practice continued openly in Kanab, Orderville and other Mormon villages until 1890, when LDS church president Wilford Woodruff, under pressure from the U.S. government, issued the "Manifesto," ending more than a half century's practice of what the 1856 Republican election platform labeled, along with slavery, as one of the "twin relics of barbarism." But some committed polygamists were more willing to deny that God had finally spoken through the church prophet on the polygamy issue than to give up the practice.

By the second decade of the 20th century, fundamentalist Mormons (i.e., those who still believed in and practiced polygamy) founded the settlement of Short Creek on the Utah–Arizona border, about 30 miles west of Kanab. The Short Creek Raid of 1953 received national attention as more than 100 Arizona law enforcement officers, accompanied by 25 carloads of newspaper reporters, attempted to carry out a surprise raid on the town. But it was the officers and reporters who were surprised. When they roared into Short Creek, they found the entire town congregated around the flagpole in the town square singing "America."

Still, 107 Short Creek adult males were arrested, then brought to trial in Kingman, Arizona, in a futile attempt to eradicate polygamy. The town name was changed to Colorado City in 1961. But more than a century after polygamy was officially ended by Mormon church authorities, it continues to flourish in remote places such as Colorado City, primarily because of public tolerance for alternative lifestyles. Such communities go about their business quietly and discourage outsiders.

Efforts to promote Kanab as a tourist destination began in the 1880s, when Edwin Wooley and Daniel Seegmiller tried to persuade a group of English aristocrats to visit Kanab and establish a private recreation area there. But the long trip by horseback and wagon only impressed on the aristocrats that Kanab was too inaccessible. The expanded availability of the automobile; the construction of passable roads; the designation of Zion and Bryce as national parks in 1919 and 1920, respectively; the beginning of the movie industry in 1922; and later, the construction of Glen Canyon Dam and gradual filling of Lake Powell in the 1950s and 1960s all contributed immeasurably to Kanab's rise as a tourist center.

Major Attractions

Three of the nation's best-known national parks are within a 1.5-hour drive of Kanab. Closest is

Zion National Park, 40 miles to the northwest via Hwy. 9 (see the **Zion National Park** chapter in the Southwestern Region). **Bryce Canyon National Park** (see the **Bryce Canyon National Park** chapter) is 77 miles up US Hwy. 89 to the north. The **Grand Canyon** is 78 miles to the south in Arizona. In addition to these, Kanab visitors are within reach of two national monuments and a state park.

Grand Staircase-Escalante National Monument

The creation of Utah's newest national monument, the Grand Staircase-Escalante National Monument, in the fall of 1996 was met with an outcry by many rural Utahns against what they considered the unilateral decision of President Bill Clinton. Furthermore, they were incensed that the announcement was made at Grand Canyon National Park across the state line in Arizona.

Like critics of earlier national park and monument designations in Utah, opponents were concerned that the gigantic new monument would put an economic stranglehold on the area, and bring in even greater government impact on what they saw as a traditional way of life. Of particular concern was the tremendous size of the monument, 1.7 million acres. Furthermore, the announcement was viewed as a victory by eastern environmentalists who had unduly influenced a president seeking his second term in office.

Nevertheless, not all Utahns opposed the announcement, and two prominent Utahns— Robert Redford and Norma Matheson, wife of Scott Matheson, a much-revered governor of Utah during the 1970s and early 1980s—were on hand to cheer the announcement. More recent newspaper polls suggest that the majority of Utahns have come to accept and even embrace the decision to create the monument.

The name incorporates two important elements of the area's natural and historic character. The Grand Staircase is used to describe a series of stair-step cliffs spread over a 100-mile stretch that begins on the north side of the Grand Canyon and climbs northward to Bryce

Canyon National Park. The Escalante part of the name is for Silvestre Velez de Escalante, who kept a diary of the Dominguez-Escalante Expedition to Utah in 1776 and for whom the town of Escalante and the Escalante River are named.

The boundaries extend westward from Glen Canyon National Recreation Area and Capitol Reef National Park to Bryce Canyon on the west. The southern boundary is roughly along US Hwy. 89 and the Utah–Arizona border. To the

Getting There

There are only a few roads into the Grand Staircase-Escalante National Monument, including the **Burr Trail** on the north, the **Hole-in-the-Rock Trail** from Escalante to the cliffs above the western side of Lake Powell, and two roads that connect Hwy. 12 on the north with US Hwy. 89 on the south—the **Smoky Mountain Rd.** from Escalante to Big Water and the **Cottonwood Canyon Rd.** from Cannonville through the Cockscomb. Of these roads, only the Burr Trail might be considered passable for regular-drive, regular-clearance vehicles. The Smoky Mountain Rd. takes an average of 4 hours to drive its 60-mile length.

Jerry Meredith, the first manager for the monument, commented, "This is really not developed country. There's virtually no oil on those roads and any road that is not oiled can be a trap. One of my big concerns is that tourists will show up in little rental cars and RVs ... this is not your typical park with a ranger around the corner. You can get yourself in big trouble if you don't have the right equipment, know the weather and know where you are going." If your vehicle breaks down, or a road becomes impassable because of a sudden cloudburst, it could be days before you are rescued. There is simply no excuse for not having enough food, water and gasoline when you venture out into the monument.

north, Hwy. 12 and the Dixie National Forest north and west of the towns of Escalante and Boulder, establish the general boundary.

There are three major sections within the National Monument—the **Escalante Canyons, the Kaiparowits Plateau** and the **Paria River.** Each of these sections has its own personality—in fact, multiple personalities—and individually any of these three areas would be larger than almost any unit within the National Park System.

BLM personnel have come up with four categories of management: the **Monument Front Country,** the parts of the monument that are located adjacent to settlements and paved highways and have no restrictions on visitation; **Passage Zones,** the areas that connect the major access corridors (see Getting There, page 313) and are generally accessible to high-clearance vehicles; the **Outback Zone,** where there are primitive roads and visitors are limited to 25 people per group; and the **Primitive Zone,** which is limited to 12 people per group who hike or travel by horseback without any motorized vehicles.

Visitor Information

There are four visitors centers for the national monument—two on the north side and two on the south side. The center at **Cannonville** on the north, which focuses on the human geography of the area, and the **Big Water** center on the south, which deals primarily with paleontology of the region, opened during the summer of 2002. The **Escalante** visitor center on the north is scheduled to open in 2003, and the **Kanab** visitor center on the south will follow a year or two after the Escalante center is completed. Headquarters for the national monument are located in Kanab: **Old Middle School Building, 190 E. Center St., Kanab, UT 84741; 435-826-5600; www.ut.blm.gov/monument.**

Coral Pink Sand Dunes State Park

If a visit to the West requires hiking and frolicking on Sahara-size sand dunes, then visitors to Kanab are in luck. West of Kanab in the Coral

Pink Sand Dunes State Park, there are 3,700 acres of sand dunes. They have formed in a sheltered depression along the Sevier Fault—a 200-mile-long fault that runs from western Arizona to the mountains north of Panguitch. The depression has filled with dunes of very fine coral-colored sand that has eroded from the surrounding cliffs and hills. The sand dunes rise as high as 20 feet or more. Dawn and sunset are especially attractive to photographers, as the coral sand seems to change color, and accentuated shadows make the landscape even more unbelievable.

While most visitors simply set off walking across the sand dunes, there are three designated **hiking** trails. A 0.5-mile-long nature trail begins at the day-use area and has numbered exhibit signs that point out the vegetation that grows in the sand dunes. Another trail takes you on a fairly strenuous 1.5-mile round-trip hike over the dunes. The third trail begins at the day-use area, follows around the edge of the dunes and then returns by cutting straight across the dunes. This hike is 5.5 miles long and is very strenuous because of the soft sand you are walking on nearly all the way. See also the Biking section under Outdoor Activities.

In an effort to meet different needs, certain areas of the park are designated for **off-road vehicles,** while others are restricted to foot traffic only. Dune buggies, motorcycles and other motorized vehicles are prohibited 10 P.M.–9 A.M.

Camping at 22 sites (no hookups) is available year-round, with modern wheelchair-accessible rest rooms and hot showers. Picnic tables and grills are also available. A fee is charged.

The easiest way of **getting there** is to go north on US Hwy. 89 from Kanab for 7 miles, then west along a paved road for 11 miles. Entrance fee is charged. You can also get to the park from Cane Beds on Hwy. 389 via a 16-mile dirt road. **Coral Pink Sand Dunes State Park, P.O. Box 95, Kanab, UT 84741; 435-648-2800; www.parks.state.ut.us/parks/www1/cora.htm.**

Pipe Springs National Monument

Although Pipe Springs National Monument (located in Arizona) was used by Indians as a rest stop and watering hole for thousands of years, it was named by the 1856 Jacob Hamblin expedition to the Hopi mesas for the purpose of launching missionary work there. Pipe Springs was settled seven years later by St. George resident James Montgomery Whitmore.

At that time the Utah–Arizona boundary had not yet been surveyed by Maj. John Wesley Powell, and Whitmore and the Washington County official who issued the land certificate granting ownership to Whitmore assumed that the spring was in Utah, not 10 miles south of the Utah line. Whitmore had run cattle in Texas before his conversion to Mormonism, and when he and his wife and two small children came west to the Salt Lake Valley in the mid-1850s, he reportedly drove a herd of 500 cattle with them. Whitmore helped found St. George in 1861 and noted then the vast rangelands of what would later be called the Arizona Strip. He recognized its grazing potential for cattle and, after 1863, divided his time between the ranch there and his home and family in St. George.

He constructed a dugout at the ranch site and continued ranching activities in partnership with his brother-in-law Robert McIntire and young son, even though Indian tensions threatened all the fledgling southern Utah Mormon settlements. The concern was justified. In January 1866 a group of Indians stole livestock from the ranch. Whitmore and McIntire were killed 4 miles south of their dugout at Pipe Springs as they pursued the lost livestock through heavy snows. Current opinion is that the perpetrators were Navajos working alongside disgruntled Paiutes.

The unrest continued for the next four years, leading Utah militiamen to erect a small rock fort at Pipe Springs in 1868. A year later Brigham Young purchased Pipe Springs for the LDS church and organized the Canaan Cooperative Stock Company, a quasi-church corporation that took over operations at Pipe Springs. Brigham "called" the bishop of Grafton, Anson Perry Winsor, to run the ranch for a salary of $1,200 a year. It was Winsor who supervised construction of the impressive rock fort/ranch headquarters at Pipe Springs, leading it to be called Winsor's Castle—a play on the good bishop's British heritage. The fort was stocked with beef cattle that were "tithed" to the LDS church by Mormon stockmen. Eventually more than 100 dairy cattle were brought to Pipe Springs to produce beef, butter and cheese for the workers on the new St. George Temple in the 1870s.

In 1923 Pipe Springs National Monument was established "as a memorial of western pioneer life."

Today the monument interprets Pipe Springs' significance to the native people of the area, the early Mormon ranching efforts on the Arizona Strip, the cabin that Major Powell stayed in while staying at Pipe Springs in 1871, domestic ranch life and the everyday life and equipment of late 19th-century and early 20th-century western cowboys. Historic exhibits, longhorn cattle, animals and living history demonstrations of quilting, weaving, spinning, baking, gardening and cattle branding, in addition to the restored ranchhouse and grounds, make Pipe Springs a popular stop for travelers of all ages. Located inside the small Kaibab Paiute Indian Reservation. The Paiute tribe runs a small adjoining campground. A cafeteria in the monument serves western fare. An admission fee is charged. The visitor center, exhibits and gift shop are open during the summer daily 7:30 A.M.–5:30 P.M. (MST); the rest of the year 8 A.M.–4 P.M. (MST). Located about 20 miles southwest of Kanab on Arizona Hwy. 389. **928-643-7105; www.nps.gov/pisp.**

Festivals and Events

Western Legends Celebration

third week in Aug. Want to immerse yourself in the cowboy heritage in a big way? Then the Western Legends Celebration should appeal to you. This four-day event began in 1999 and has quickly become one of the most popular events in southern Utah. Building on its reputation as the cradle of Western movies, Kanab has put together an event with dozens of activities that celebrate the cowboy heritage in music, dance, poetry, storytelling, parades, displays, shows, films, tours and food. Each year a "western legend" such as Dale Robertson is honored. Mountain men and Indians also take part, and there is something for everyone. A Dutch oven cook-off is a popular event, with the winner qualifying for the World Dutch Oven Championship and samples provided after the judging takes place. Every available room is booked during the celebration, so secure reservations early. **Kane County Travel Council; 1-800-7333-5263; www. westernlegendsroundup.com.**

Outdoor Activities

Biking

Johnson Canyon Rd.

In the 1920s Kanab residents searched for Montezuma's treasure in this canyon, but today it offers an excellent opportunity for an undisturbed ride past the vermilion cliffs, ancient Indian pictographs, a ranch house with a windmill, pastures, Eagle Arch and an old movie set where segments of *Gunsmoke* and *Have Gun Will Travel* were filmed. Johnson Canyon is located east of Kanab, about 9 miles off US Hwy. 89. The Johnson Canyon Rd., marked by a road sign, heads north and is paved for about 15 miles. This makes an excellent 20-mile ride for novice bikers and also offers wheelchair access. If you want a longer ride, don't want to transport your bicycle and don't mind highway traffic, you can leave from Kanab and ride the 9 miles east on US Hwy. 89 to the Johnson Canyon turnoff.

You can also make a 65-mile loop from Kanab by continuing north on Johnson Canyon Rd. after the pavement ends and following the road as it heads back west to intersect with US Hwy. 89 at Glendale. From Glendale it's a 25-mile ride into Kanab along US Hwy. 89, or 40 miles back the way you came.

Golf

Coral Cliffs Golf Course

This 9-hole golf course has an excellent design utilizing native junipers. It is also a fun course—challenging enough for most golfers yet not to the point of frustration. The course is generally flat, and the soaring ledges to the west, north and south make this one of Utah's most picturesque courses. Located about 1 mile east of Kanab at 700 E. and US Hwy. 89. **435-644-5005.**

Hiking

Hackberry Canyon Trail

Located in the Grand Staircase-Escalante National Monument, Hackberry Canyon offers perhaps the best route on foot into this rugged and scenic region. The 8-mile round trip takes you through Hackberry Canyon to Sam Pollock Arch. This is a wilderness study area, so there are no features that are marked and no maintained trails. From the trailhead you cross the main wash and make your way up the sandy side canyon into the Navajo sandstone narrows. You will pass the ruins of Watson Cabin on the bench to the west of the creekbed, then turn up the first major side canyon to the west. The arch is approximately 1.5 miles from this point. To reach the trailhead, take Hwy. US 89 east toward Page. Leave the highway past the Paria Ranger Station between mile markers 17 and 18, then follow the dirt road up Cottonwood Wash about 14 miles to an unmarked parking area on the left.

Vermillion Cliffs Trail

A nice, somewhat strenuous, early morning summer hike is the 3-mile up-and-back Vermillion Cliffs Trail (formerly called the Squaw Trail). In the early morning or late afternoon, the trail is in the shade of the surrounding cliffs and hills for most of the hike. There are three overlooks that offer excellent panoramic views of Kanab and the surrounding area and it is well worth packing your camera. For information about the hike, check at the Bureau of Land

Management Office located a couple of blocks south of the trailhead on 100 E.

The trail begins at the north end of 100 E. just past the Kanab city park. There is a trail sign indicating the beginning point. The trail follows up a draw before it swings back to the south to climb in a series of three long switchbacks to the first of three lookout points. The first point is located about a mile up the trail and with a climb of about 400 feet in elevation, this maybe plenty for you.

During the next 0.5 mile there are two other lookout points and another 200 feet in elevation gain as you reach the top of the Vermillion Cliffs that shelter the city of Kanab below. From the top of the mesa, the view south is spectacular, taking in Kanab and the Kaibab Plateau beyond it. Looking north, you get a great view of the rest of the top "steps" of the geological Grand Staircase—the White, Gray and Pink cliffs—as they climb into the distance. From the third overlook, return along the route you have come by.

Seeing and Doing

Museums and Historic Sites

Ghost Towns
The Paria River Valley is the location for the ruins of the historic Mormon farming community of **Pahreah,** which was settled in the early 1870s and abandoned by the mid-1880s. All that remains of the historic community are a small cemetery and some ruins. Nearby is the **movie set** of a pioneer town built in 1963 for the film *Sergeants Three*—it now resembles a ghost town too. To reach the Paria River Valley, head east from Kanab on US Hwy. 89 for 35 miles, then follow the 5-mile-long graded dirt road as it heads north. The road is regularly maintained and usually suitable for passenger cars unless there have been recent rainstorms (usually in summer).

Heritage House Museum
Constructed between 1892 and 1894 for Henry E. Bowman, a prosperous Kanab merchant, the Heritage House is an ambitious (for southern Utah, at least) example of Victorian–Queen Anne architecture. The orange-red brick walls, combination hip-and-gable/wood-shingled roof, sculpted brick chimneys, "gingerbread" porch and tower mark a radical departure from the symmetrical adobe homes of the two previous decades. By 1892 changes in architectural fashion had reached Kanab. The Heritage House, whose restoration was a Kanab City Bicentennial Project in 1976, now serves as a museum and contains furniture and other items from turn-of-the-20th-century Kanab. Usually open in the summer during the day, or can be visited by calling the number posted at the house. Located on the southeast corner of 100 S. Main St.

Mt. Carmel Old Rock Church and School
This stone building with its four-sided roof and bell tower recalls an era when religious, educational, civic and recreational needs were met in one public building in some small American towns. The building was used for church services, school classes, public meetings, dances and other social activities. The original building was constructed in the 1890s and rebuilt between 1923 and 1924 after a 1919 fire. After the fire, school was held for two years in the nearby tithing office, after which students were transported to nearby Orderville. The building was used as a church until 1961 and for other church programs until 1983. Open during the summer with displays of historical artifacts and photos. Located on the west side of US Hwy. 89 in Mt. Carmel.

Scenic Drives

Johnson Canyon Rd. / Alton Amphitheater Backway
The Johnson Canyon Rd. begins 9 miles east of Kanab, off US Hwy. 89, and heads north. The first 15 miles are paved, and the rest of the road is a well-maintained gravel road suitable for passenger cars. (See the Biking section under Outdoor Activities for details.) At the intersection with the road west to Glendale, continue north to the tiny ranching community of Alton. Alton

is especially scenic, as it provides a closer view of the Claron Formation, or Pink Cliffs, in what is called the Alton Amphitheater (on the other side of the plateau from Bryce Canyon) and of volcanic cinder cones. At Alton, turn west to US Hwy. 89, taking the road past several lovely small lakes. From Hwy. 89 it is 38 miles back to Kanab.

Kanab to Junction Scenic Byway/ US Hwy. 89

US Hwy. 89 is the major highway to Kanab from Salt Lake City and the principal road from Kanab north to Zion and Bryce Canyon National Parks. The 60-mile section of US Hwy. 89 through Long Valley, from Kanab to its junction with Hwy. 12, the road to Bryce Canyon, has been given official designation as a Scenic Byway.

The drive north from Kanab is truly spectacular, as the highway ascends part of what Maj. John Wesley Powell dubbed the Grand Staircase—a succession of progressively younger rock formations known as the Vermillion, White and Pink Cliffs, the base rock of southern Utah's canyon country. The road climbs from Kanab's desert setting through Long Valley to the subalpine meadows and headwaters of the Sevier River, passing through the lovely little historic communities of Mt. Carmel, Orderville and Glendale. At Long Valley Junction, Hwy. 14 heads east to Cedar City; a few miles farther north is the town of Hatch (see the **Panguitch** chapter). If you do any traveling north of Kanab, you will certainly follow US Hwy. 89. This stretch of highway is one of the most beautiful in all of Utah, so if you are not driving, sit back and enjoy it.

Tours

Best Friends Animal Sanctuary

Located in Angel Canyon, Best Friends Animal Sanctuary is a home for unwanted animals. At any given time the sanctuary houses more than 1,800 dogs, cats and other abused, abandoned or neglected pets. You can tour the facility, which has dog kennels, catteries with separate areas for cats that prefer the outdoors and those that are indoor cats, and pastures for horses, burros and

goats. Support for the sanctuary comes from well-known and well-to-do supporters, along with the 50,000 members affectionatly called "Guardian Angels." One-hour tours are given a few times during the day. Be sure to call for tour times and a reservation. You can also volunteer for a day or more to help feed and care for the annimals; call for more information. Take US Hwy. 89 north out of Kanab for about 5 miles to the Kanab Canyon Rd. on your right. Turn onto the road and follow it for about 2 miles to the sanctuary. **4100 N. Kanab Canyon Rd., Kanab, UT 84741; 435-644-2001; http://petloss.com/bestfrnd.htm.**

Johnson Canyon Movie Set

When you are alone at this location in Johnson Canyon, it can be hard to remember that this is a movie set and not an old western ghost town. The dozen or so buildings have been used for more than 20 movies and for the perhaps most famous of all western television series, *Gunsmoke*. It may take the tour guide to identify Miss Kitty's saloon, the Dodge House Hotel and Doc Adam's office, but with a little imagination, you can transform yourself back to the western frontier of the 1860s or the television frontier of the 1960s. The red walls of Johnson Canyon and the weathered frame buildings provide plenty of photo opportunities. A favorite time to make the 15-mile drive from Kanab out to Johnson Canyon is in the early evening. The movie set has been open for tours, but as of this writing it is not open to the public. Hopefully that will change in the near future. Check for the current status. **Kane County Travel Council, 78 S. 100 E., Kanab, UT 84741; 1-800-733-5263; 435-644-5033; www.kaneutah.com.**

Moqui Cave

Upon first appearances, Moqui Cave might seem like the quintessential tourist trap—flashy signs, an interior that seems a mystery from the outside and an antiquated name. Undoubtedly some might find such apprehensions to be true, but if you are the kind of traveler who likes poking around eclectic places and visiting with people who have a broad range of interests, Moqui Cave is well worth the modest admission fee.

The history of the cave goes back at least to the Anasazi inhabitants of the area nearly a millennium ago. Pioneers to the area called these ancient dwellers "Moqui," hence the name of the cave. You will find a few old-timers who still refer to the Moqui, but anthropologists and archaeologists have done a good job of educating later generations to using the term "Anasazi."

The cave was undoubtedly used by travelers to the area, but 1951 marks its birth as a recreation site. That year Laura and Garth Chamberlain acquired the cave and in 1952 opened a tavern and dance hall inside the cave. After that use went out of vogue, it became something of a roadside museum and house of curios. You will find the 1952 bar inside, along with authentic dinosaur tracks, minerals, American Indian artifacts and pottery. Of course there is also a gift shop. Open Apr.–mid-Oct. Mon.–Sat. 9 A.M.–7 P.M.; the rest of the year Mon.–Sat. 9 A.M.–6 P.M. Located 5.5 miles north of Kanab. **435-644-2987.**

Where to Stay

Accommodations

GLENDALE / MT. CARMEL
Best Western Thunderbird Resort—$$
Heated pool; 61 rooms. Adjacent restaurant and 9-hole golf course. Located in Mt. Carmel, 17 miles north of Kanab and 24 miles from the east entrance to Zion National Park, at the junction of US Hwy. 89 and Hwy. 9. **435-648-2203.**

Eagle's Nest Bed and Breakfast—$$$ to $$$$
This four-room bed and breakfast is the dream of Shanoan and Dearborn Clark and caters to "adult romance and tranquility." There are no radios or televisions to detract from this wonderful experience; however, you will find plenty of good reading material, comfortable chairs and an antique game table in the living room where you can mingle with other guests. Each room has a private bath; two have fireplaces. There is a small

guest kitchen. Dearborn bakes his special brownies for an evening snack, and Shanoan makes one of the best country gourmet breakfasts you will find anywhere. Located on 13 acres in a side canyon of Lydia's Canyon; drive about 1.5 miles north of Glendale on US Hwy. 89, then go 0.6 mile west on the north side of Lydia's Canyon. **500 W. Lydia's Canyon Rd., P.O. Box 160, Glendale, UT 84729; 1-800-293-6378; 435-648-2200; www.eaglesnestbb.com.**

Smith Hotel—$$
One of the few historic hotels still in operation, the Smith Hotel was built in Glendale in 1927. The hotel has a rural, old-time feel, just perfect for a nice relaxing stay. Its seven nonsmoking rooms are newly decorated, and each has a private bath. A continental breakfast is served in the dining room by innkeeper Shirley Phelan. Open Apr.–Oct. Located off US Hwy. 89 in the north end of Glendale. **1-800-528-3558; 435-648-2156.**

KANAB
Best Western Red Hills—$$ to $$$
Heated pool and whirlpool; 75 rooms. **125 W. Center; 1-800-830-2675; 435-644-2675.**

Parry Lodge—$$ to $$$
Kanab's oldest motel, the Parry Lodge was established in 1929 and has been the home away from home for many Hollywood stars while they were making movies in Kanab. During the 1980s, the marquee at the motel boldly boasted that "Ronald Reagan Slept Here." In fact, he stayed in room 125. The most popular star, at least based on requests for his room, is John Wayne, who had an oversize bathtub installed in his room—room 192. Other stars whose names appear above individual rooms include James Garner, Frank Sinatra, Telly Savalas, Dean Martin, Arlene Dahl, Tyrone Power, Robert Preston, Sammy Davis Jr., Julie Newman, Anne Blythe and Robert Taylor. The lodge has expanded from the original 15 rooms to 89 units, with a nice heated outdoor swimming pool and adjoining restaurant. **89 E. Center; 1-800-748-4104; 435-644-2601.**

Victorian Charm Inn Bed and Breakfast—$$$
This brand-new 20-room inn opened in 2002. All rooms are furnished with 1890s-era reproduction Ethan Allen furniture and have private baths, in-room Jacuzzis and fireplaces. **190 N. US Hwy 89; 1-800-738-9643; 435-644-8660; www.victoriancharminn.com.**

Viola's Garden Bed and Breakfast—$$$
This bed and breakfast began life as a mail-order house from Sears Roebuck purchased in 1912 for $640 by James Swapp, grandfather of Nileen, who with her husband, Von, acquired the home in 1993 and opened the bed and breakfast a few years ago. James Swapp was a sheep rancher and Kanab City marshal and father of 10. All the components of the house were shipped by trail from Chicago, Illinois, to Salt Lake City and then on to Marysvale, Utah, from where it was transported by buckboard wagon another 120 miles to Kanab. Over time, additions were made, but the carpenter gothic–style house retains its early-20th-century character. There are five rooms located upstairs, all of which have private baths, one of which has a private balcony and three of which share a large deck overlooking the backyard. Downstairs are a parlor and formal dining room where a breakfast of juice, coffee, muffins, fruit in season and stuffed French toast or breakfast casserole is served. **250 N. 100 W., Kanab, UT 84741; 435-644-5683; www.violas-garden.com.**

Camping

PRIVATE
Bryce/Zion KOA Campground
Sixty spaces with hookups and 25 tentsites. Toilets, showers, a heated pool, game room and playground. Close to trout fishing in the East Fork of the Virgin River. Open May–mid-Oct. Located 5 miles north of Glendale on US Hwy. 89. **1-800-562-8635; 435-648-2490.**

Crazy Horse Campground
Seventy-four RV sites with full hookups and pull-through locations plus sites for tenters.

Clean rest rooms, showers, a swimming pool, game room, arcade, playground and picnic tables. Coral Cliffs Golf Course is adjacent. Campground open year-round. Located just east of Kanab off US Hwy. 89. **625 E. 300 S., P.O. Box 699, Kanab, UT 84741; 1-800-8300-7316; 435-644-2782.**

Where to Eat

Because Kanab is a tourist destination, there are quite a few eating establishments. However many close during the off-season, and others close for holidays, vacations and other reasons. Mar.–Oct. every place is usually open. For the winter season, schedules can change like the weather.

Houston's Trail's End Restaurant—$ to $$
A family restaurant with a western atmosphere. Waitresses are dressed in cowboy shirts, denim skirts and holstered six-shooters. Fare includes typical western breakfasts, burgers, hot sandwiches, steaks, halibut and trout. Open in summer daily 6 A.M.–11 P.M.; Sept.–June daily 6 A.M.–10 P.M. **32 E. Center, Kanab; 435-644-2488.**

Parry's Lodge Restaurant—$$ to $$$
This charming, houselike restaurant is part of Parry's Lodge (see the Where to Stay section). It carries the lodge's association with movie stars—dozens of photographs, many of them inscribed, are hung on the restaurant walls. You will see pictures of stars that only experienced travelers will remember—Gabby Hayes, Ava Gardner, Walter Brennan, Jane Russell, Robert Taylor, Rhonda Fleming, Frederic Marsh, Anne Bancroft, Roy Rogers and Dale Evans. Breakfast items include omelettes, ham steak, country-fried steak, corned beef and eggs and pancakes. For lunch there are sandwiches, soup and salads, or the hungry man lunches—chicken and dumplings, chicken-fried steak, grilled beef liver or breaded veal. The dinner menu offers prime rib, steaks, fried shrimp, salmon, halibut, trout, veal and pork chops. You can also order a box

lunch to take with you. Open in summer daily 7–10 A.M., 11 A.M.–2 P.M. and 5–10 P.M.; in winter daily 7–10 A.M. and 5–10 P.M. **89 E. Center, Kanab; 435-644-2601.**

Thunderbird Restaurant—$ to $$$

The Thunderbird restaurant began as a service station opened in 1931 by Jack and Fern Morrison. Fern started to bake pies, and truck drivers were given a piece of pie when they stopped to refuel. In 1940 the restaurant was opened and has been serving good foor ever since. The lunch menu includes hot and cold sandwiches, burgers, soup and a salad bar; the dinner menu includes steaks, fish and pasta. Open daily 7 A.M.–10 P.M. Located at the junction of U.S. Hwy. 89 and Hwy. 9 in Mt. Carmel. **435-648-2203.**

The Wok Inn—$ to $$

If you're tired of hamburgers, steaks and Mexican food and want to shift your eating gears toward Chinese, the Wok Inn is a good alternative. You will find Hunan, Szechwan and Chinese food prepared by Chinese chefs. The restaurant is an interesting combination of western ranch house style with Chinese trimmings that include lanterns, screens, parasols, paintings and other artwork. Open Apr.–Oct. Mon.–Fri. 11:30 A.M.–10 P.M., Sat.–Sun. 3–10 P.M.; winter schedule varies. Located a block off Main St. **86 S. 200 W., Kanab; 435-644-5400.**

Services

Visitor Information

Kane County Travel Council—78 S. 100 E., Kanab, UT 84741; 1-800-733-5263; 435-644-5033; www.kaneutah.com.

Southeastern Region

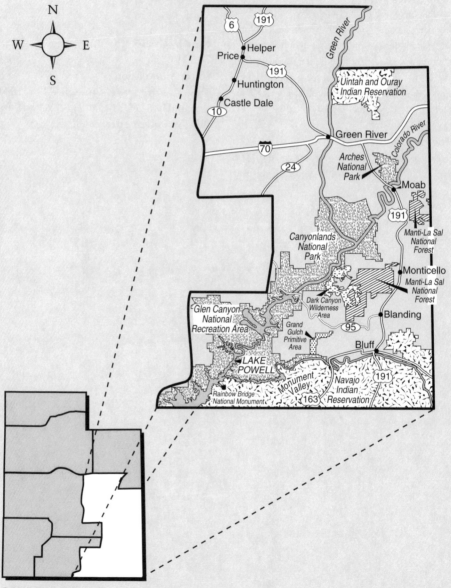

Price

Historian Philip F. Notarianni has described Carbon County as "Eastern Utah's Industrialized Island." It was in fact industrialization that in 1894 led to the creation of the new county of Carbon from part of what was Emery County. The coalfields stretch from the alpine settings of Scofield and Clear Creek in the northwestern corner of the county, high in the mountains of the Wasatch Plateau at an elevation of 7,600 feet, to more desert conditions in the southeast section around Sunnyside.

Price is the county seat of Carbon County, which is often described as the most cosmopolitan county within the state. The reputation is well deserved. The Greeks, Italians, Finns, Slovenians, Croats, Serbs, Austrians, Chinese, Japanese, Mexican-Americans, Armenians and other immigrants from around the world came to Carbon County primarily because of the coal mining that gives the county its name. They have given Carbon County a character much different from surrounding Mormon areas.

Catholic churches in Price and Helper and the historic Greek Orthodox church in Price symbolize the difference, though Mormon ward houses are also found in the communities. Carbonites boast that the interaction among the diverse groups has produced a much higher degree of tolerance and acceptance than in any other part of the state. While this is true today, it was not always so. The conflicts among different nationalities, Mormons, coal operators and miners, and the rivalries between Price and Helper and between Carbon County and Emery County, have left a rich but sometimes violent history.

It has been more than 130 years since the first coal was mined in the area, but the "black gold" still dominates the county. The ever-present coal trains and coal trucks along US Hwy. 6 are constant reminders of this heritage, even though modern mining techniques do not require the large number of coal miners of earlier days. Coal camps and company towns have disappeared as miners and coal haulers commute to the mines from homes around and outside the county.

History

Originally called Castle Valley Junction when the Denver and Rio Grande Railroad first built through the area in 1883, the city's name was later changed to Price. Just why the name was changed is unclear, as are the origins for the name Price. One story holds that it was named for Tom Price, a native of Scotland and the man who surveyed the town site. Another account gives credit to William Price, a Mormon bishop from the town of Goshen across the mountain who explored the area in 1868. The third account comes from trainmen on the Denver and Rio Grande Railroad who purchased produce and other goods from homesteaders when the train stopped at Castle Valley Junction. The goods were expensive, leading the railroad men to refer to the stop as "High Price," which was later shortened to Price.

The origin of Helper's name is much more clear. "Helper" engines were employed to pull

---

Getting There

Located 120 miles south-southeast of Salt Lake City, Price is about a 2-hour drive from Utah's capital. The first half of the trip is along Interstate 15 to Spanish Fork, then along US Hwy. 6 for the last half.
The highway crosses from the Great Basin onto the Colorado Plateau at Soldier Summit, elevation 7,477 feet.

Travelers entering Utah from Colorado along Interstate 70 exit just west of Green River onto US Hwy. 6 and head northwest for about 60 miles to Price.

the Denver and Rio Grande Railroad trains up to the top of the Wasatch Plateau at Soldier Summit to the northwest. Because these "helper" engines were kept at a stop at the north end of the Price River Valley and at the mouth of Price Canyon, the location was soon referred to as "Helper." Pleasant Valley is a most appropriate name for the lush meadowlands around Scofield, where 19th-century cattlemen ranged their herds in the summer. Scofield Reservoir was constructed in the 1940s to impound waters on the upper Price River for irrigation.

Between 1890 and the end of World War II, coal miners were concentrated in the coal camps and in the towns of Price and Helper. Old-timers recall life in the coal camps with fondness. The narrow canyons offered little living space and threw residents together in industrial villages set down in a wilderness. The closeness of the houses, the common fear of death or injury in the mines, the recreation opportunities provided at the company-owned amusement hall, the seemingly schizophrenic coal company—which both offered much-needed jobs but also demanded trade at the company store where prices were often exorbitant—all of it was a new experience, whether residents were from the Mormon farms in the valleys or isolated villages of Italy or Greece.

While community life in the coal camps led to individual friendships among the diverse groups, two events in the 1930s brought the people of the county together in ways that saw the conflict and controversy of the first 50 years give way to harmony, good feelings and pride in diversity. The two events were the establishment of the United Mine Workers of America to represent the area's coal miners in 1933 and, in 1937, the founding of Carbon College as the first institution for higher education in all of eastern Utah.

The union brought miners together in ways that promoted fairness and mutual respect for all miners, regardless of religion or nationality. The college provided the much-needed, inexpensive opportunity for sons and daughters of both foreign and native-born residents to obtain their first two years of education, before moving on to complete four-year and advanced degrees at upstate universities or institutions around the country. Education is both the great equalizer and preserver of heritage. Carbon College, known since the mid-1960s as the College of Eastern Utah, has provided rich opportunities to its students and the entire community.

Festivals and Events

Prehistory and Heritage Week

first week in May. A series of weeklong programs, tours and events celebrate the area's prehistory and heritage. Centered at the College of Eastern Utah Prehistoric Museum. **435-637-5060.**

Greek Festival

second weekend in July. Authentic Greek food, music, dancing and tours of the historic Hellenic Orthodox Church of the Assumption are all a part of the festivities. **61 S. 200 E., Price; 435-637-3009.**

Carbon County International Days

first weekend in Aug. The county celebrates its varied ethnic heritage in this festival with a parade, food, booths and activities in Price. **435-637-3009.**

Helper Electric Light Christmas Parade

second weekend in Dec. First held in 1990, this parade has become one of the most popular Christmastime events in southeastern Utah, with crowds of people lining the street to watch the brightly lit floats. A chili dinner is served beforehand in the Helper Auditorium 4:30–8 P.M. The parade is Fri. and Sat. beginning at 7 P.M. on Main St. in Helper. **435-472-5336.**

Outdoor Activities

Biking

Nine-Mile Canyon Rd.

Nine-Mile Canyon is famous for its prehistoric Indian rock art and ruins (see the Historic Sites section under Seeing and Doing). It can be a fine ride through the canyon or along some of the routes leading off it. See the Scenic Drives section under Seeing and Doing for details. Take US Hwy. 6 east of Price 7.5 miles, just beyond the town of Wellington, and follow Nine-Mile Canyon Rd. north as far as desired. Rock art is found at about 25 miles from the highway. The road leads eventually to US Hwy. 40 near Roosevelt.

Scofield Reservoir to Clear Creek

From the Scofield Reservoir, bikers follow Hwy. 96 south past the reservoir to the old town of Scofield and on to the former company town of Clear Creek, where the houses have been acquired by private individuals for use as summer cabins. This 20-mile round-trip ride takes you through one of the most historic as well as scenic parts of the county.

Fishing

Scofield Reservoir

The cool waters of the reservoir are ideal for trout, and the Utah Division of Wildlife Resources keeps the reservoir well stocked with rainbow trout. Native cutthroat trout also inhabit the reservoir and streams that flow into it. The reservoir is a popular place for anglers during the summer and for ice fishing in the winter. Located on Hwy. 96. Take US Hwy. 6 north to Colton, then Hwy. 96 southwest.

Golf

Carbon Country Club Golf Course

Built just after World War II, this course is the oldest golf course in the eastern half of the state. The course is owned by the Carbon Country Club and Carbon County. In 1994 the course expanded to 18 holes; the new 9 holes, all but 8 of which are located to the south of the old course, offer an interesting contrast between the tree-lined, tight, mature front 9 and spacious open fairways on the back. Located on US Hwy. 6 about halfway between Price and Helper. **435-637-2388.**

Swimming

Desert Wave

Price's excellent swimming facility located in Price Park is an artificial wave pool called Desert Wave; an inflated bubble is used during the winter to cover the outdoor facility. The complex also includes an indoor swimming pool used primarily for lap swimming, water aerobics and swimming team practices. Since few of the motels in the area have swimming pools, travelers with children whose first consideration is a swimming pool might want to make plans for a couple of hours at the Desert Wave. Operated by Price City, rates are quite reasonable for this type of facility. Open year-round. Located on 500 N. between 200 and 300 E. **435-637-7946.**

Tennis

There are three lighted tennis courts in the Price public park. The courts are just west of the College of Eastern Utah and are used by both college and high school students. There is usually a court free. Located at **400 N. and 300 E. 435-637-5092.**

Seeing and Doing

Historic Sites

Castle Gate

It takes little imagination to understand why Castle Gate is such an appropriate name for the massive rock formation on the east side of the highway north of Helper. The top of the formation looks like a castle tower and, before the accompanying tower on the west side of the canyon was blasted away to make room for the present highway, the formation indeed looked like a gigantic castle gate being closed. Near here in 1897, Butch Cassidy made a daring robbery of $8,800 in gold and silver from the Pleasant Valley Coal Company then escaped into the wilderness of the San Rafael Swell. It was also the site of mining history.

Just a few miles below Castle Gate, at the mouth of Price Canyon, a tent colony was set up by United Mine Workers of America strikers in 1904. It was here that the famous labor organizer Mother Jones, who had arrived to assist with the Utah coal strike, was alleged to be planning to lead the strikers back up the canyon to Castle Gate and retake the company homes from which they and their families had been evicted. Coal operators claimed that Mother Jones had been exposed to smallpox before arriving in Utah and would have to be quarantined for 30 days. She was hidden near Castle Gate and avoided capture long enough for strikers to burn down the quarantine house, believing that the charges were part of the strategy to silence the articulate and inflammatory organizer. Before the march could take place, a local posse charged the tent colony and arrested more than 100 strikers. By the end of Apr. 1904, Mother Jones left Utah to continue her fight for America's miners until her death at 100 in 1930. Castle Gate is located on US Hwy. 6 about 4 miles north of Helper.

Hellenic Orthodox Church of the Assumption

One of the buildings depicted in the Fausett Mural inside the Price Municipal Building (see below) is the Hellenic Orthodox Church of the Assumption, located across the street, a block south of the municipal building. Constructed in 1916, the church is the oldest Greek Orthodox church in the state, preceding Salt Lake City's 1925 Holy Trinity Greek Orthodox Church by nearly a decade. Before the church was constructed, few Greek women came to Carbon County, but once the church was built, the few men who were married sent for their wives and families and the majority who were single requested that Greek girls be sent over for them to marry.

The church has been renovated three times—in 1940–1941, after a fire in 1945 and in 1961—but the basic Byzantine architectural style has been maintained. The original stained glass windows and icons had to be replaced after the 1945 fire, but the more recent ones are no less impressive. **61 S. 200 E.; 435-637-0704.**

Millerich Hall

When this building was first presented to the Utah Historic Sites Review Committee for nomination to the National Register of Historic Places, one of the committee members exclaimed, "That's the ugliest building I have ever seen!" Although it lacks architectural distinction, the building has served as a gathering place for Carbon County's Slovenian population since its construction in 1922. Indeed, while Millerich Hall is the historic name for the building, most people know it today as the **Slovenian National Home.**

The present building replaced an older frame structure and was constructed mostly by striking Slovenian coal miners in 1922. In 1933 Millerich Hall became the National Miners Union headquarters for striking miners. Charged with being a communist-dominated union, the union leaders gave some credence to the charge by reportedly displaying a red flag with hammer, sickle and a sheaf of wheat inside Millerich Hall. In the end, the National Miners Union lost its strike, and its members joined the newly recognized United Mine Workers of America. In 1963 the hall was purchased from the Millerich family by members of the local Slovenian community and continues to serve social and recreational activities. Located on Main St. in the small town of Spring Glen, about 2 miles south of Helper on US Hwy. 6.

Nine-Mile Canyon Rock Art

Nine Mile Canyon contains some of the best rock art to be found in the world. The Fremont Indian petroglyph panels scattered throughout the canyon include human figures, birds, snakes, other animals and designs. Both pictographs and petroglyphs can be found along the walls, while higher up on the cliffs, storage granaries and other structures dating back at least 700 years can be spotted.

Binoculars are a must in order to locate many of these structures. Travelers should plan the better part of a day. Pick up a free brochure from the Castle Country Travel Region, which also lists mileages and what to see. Otherwise many of the sites will go unnoticed. The Nine Mile Canyon Rd. is located 7.5 miles east of Price off US Hwy. 6, where it heads north just beyond the town of Wellington. The first major panels of petroglyphs are located about 26 miles from US Hwy. 6. Panels and other ruins are located throughout the canyon for the next 25 miles.

Notre Dame de Lourdes Catholic Church

Another immigrant church depicted in the Fausett Mural inside the Price Municipal Building (see below) is the Notre Dame de Lourdes Catholic Church located two blocks west and two blocks north of the Price Municipal Building. Constructed of brick between 1919 and 1923, the architecture is bungalow style. Although Italian immigrants and their children made up the largest part of the Catholic population in Carbon County, the Price church reflects an attempt to recognize other Catholic groups—specifically French Basques who, by 1920, had become successful in the eastern Utah sheep industry and were major contributors for the construction of the church. Thus, while the Italians were represented in Helper with the naming of St. Anthony's Catholic Church for an Italian patron saint, in Price the name Notre Dame de Lourdes recalled the world-famous pilgrim city of Lourdes at the foot of the Pyrenees in southern France in the center of the French Basque homeland. **200 N. Carbon Ave.**

Price Municipal Building/Fausett Mural

Take a few minutes to go inside the foyer of the Price Municipal Building, constructed in 1938–1939 with local money as well as funds provided under the Works Progress Administration program of Franklin D. Roosevelt's New Deal. In addition to this good example of WPA architecture, the foyer contains a fascinating mural painted by Price-born artist Lynn Fausett as part of the Federal Arts Project of the WPA.

Fausett includes 82 figures in 14 scenes on the 4-by-200-foot surface. The tableaux trace the early history of Carbon County, from the arrival of the first residents Abram Powell (yes, a relative of mine) and Caleb Rhodes, who entered the area as trappers in 1877, through the tremendous expansion of the local coal industry during World War I. On the east wall near the south end, there is a self-portrait of Lynn Fausett as a young boy, leading his blind Swiss immigrant grandfather, Hans Ulrich Bryner. Other scenes depict the construction of the Denver and Rio Grande Western Railroad through the area in 1882–1883 by Chinese and European workers; wagon freighters camped near the rail yards; early commercial establishments; early education efforts; a Fourth of July parade in 1911; and the diverse religious history of the county, with paintings of Catholic Bishop Lawrence Scanlon, the Greek Orthodox Priest Rev. Mark Petrakis, Methodist Rev. R. P. Nichols and Mormon Bishop George Frandsen. A pamphlet available from the travel office explains the history depicted in the mural. Located at **200 E. and Main St.**

Scofield Cemetery

The Scofield Cemetery contains the graves of 149 of the 200 victims of the Winter Quarters Mine Disaster, which occurred on May 1, 1900. The coal dust explosion and carbon monoxide poisoning left few survivors, and the coal camp of Winter Quarters and the town of Scofield were devastated by what, for that time, was the worst coal mining disaster in the history of the United States. The youngest victim was 13 years old; 105 women were left without husbands; and 270 children lost their fathers. Condolences were sent by President William McKinley and foreign heads of state. The dead included 62 immigrant Finnish miners, among whom were seven sons and three grandsons of Abe Louma, the 70-year old patriarch of the family who, with his wife, had recently arrived from Finland to spend their last days with their family.

Trenches for graves were dug, and wooden markers were produced at a local sawmill. Some of the wooden markers remain, while more permanent stone markers were erected later by families of other victims. Other monuments to the disaster victims have also been erected. On the 100th anniversary of the disaster, new wooden markers were placed over the graves. Located on a small rise in the eastern part of Scofield.

Museums

College of Eastern Utah Prehistoric Museum

The College of Eastern Utah Prehistoric Museum was established in 1961 by the college's geology professor, Don Burge, and a group of local rock hounds and rock art enthusiasts who were members of the Carbon County Jeep Posse. They took a geology night class that Burge offered, and in informal discussions after class, the idea of a museum to house local collections emerged. Originally located in an upstairs section of the Price Municipal Building, a newly constructed museum addition dwarfs its former home and provides an excellent facility for one of Utah's best museums.

The western wing houses the dinosaur exhibits and includes seven total skeletons, four of which are from the Cleveland-Lloyd Dinosaur Quarry 30 miles to the south. The replicas include an allosaurus, camptosaurus, camarasaurus and stegosaurus. An extensive collection of dinosaur tracks found in the area's coal mines can be seen. Another skeleton, that of an 11,000-year-old mammoth found in Huntington Canyon in 1988, provides an excellent transition from prehistoric animal life to the story of prehistoric humans, as ancient spear points and atlatl darts were found near the mammoth. Located in the upstairs center section and the east wing of the museum, the exhibits include a magnificent group of large photographs of rock art in the area and a full-size copy of a reproduction of the Barrier Canyon Rock Art Panel, located in Canyonlands National Park.

The most unusual display is a collection of 10 unbaked clay figurines, approximately 4—5 inches long, which are presumed to date from the Fremont era 800–900 years ago. The figurines were discovered by Price resident Clarence Pilling in 1950, on a ranch he owned in the Range Creek area east of Price. Known as the "Pilling Figurines," the pieces are decorated with applied clay ornaments and body parts so that both sexes can be distinguished by their anatomy and dress. Open in summer daily 9 A.M.–6 P.M.; in winter Mon.–Sat. 9 A.M.–5 P.M. **155 E. Main St.; 435-637-5060; www.ceu.edu/museum.**

Western Mining and Railroad Museum

Housed in the old 1913 Helper Hotel located in the Historic Helper District (see the Walking Tours section), this local museum includes artifacts and exhibits on the history of coal mining and railroading in the region. There are four floors of artifacts and two large outdoor displays of mining and railroad artifacts. The museum tells the history of mining from the pick and shovel to the high-tech long wall; of railroading from steam engines to the diesels of today; and of the ethnic lifestyles of the immigrants who came to Carbon County from all over the world to mine coal and work on the railroad.

Railroading and mining history are portrayed with model trains, coal mine diagrams and models and displays on coal camp life, including a company store, the miners union and the major mine disasters of 1900, 1924 and 1984. Community life is also commemorated in exhibit rooms featuring old dentist and doctor offices, a pre-World War II beauty shop, a bootlegger's still from Prohibition days, wine-making equipment used by the area's Italian immigrants, an old iron jail cage from the Helper City jail and the first two steps from the old Wasatch Store in Castle Gate, the site of Butch Cassidy's robbery of the Pleasant Valley Coal Company payroll in 1897.

The artifacts are of special interest to railroad and mining buffs, but one of the most enjoyable aspects of the museum is the volunteers. Men and women from the local Retired Senior Volunteer Program, many of them born and raised in the old company towns, answer questions about the museum and offer spontaneous stories about life in the area. Open May–Sept. Mon.–Sat. 10 A.M.–6 P.M.; Oct.–Apr. Tues.–Sat. noon–5 P.M. **296 S. Main, Helper, UT 84526; 435-472-3009.**

Scenic Drives

Indian Canyon Scenic Byway

This 50-mile mountain drive along US Hwy. 191 leaves US Hwy. 6 about 2 miles north of Helper and heads up Willow Creek past the Castle Gate Power Plant and the old Castle Gate Cemetery, where town residents and victims of the 1924 coal mine explosion are buried. About 7 miles up-canyon, the road is intersected by another road coming in from the west. At this junction is the Bamberger Monument, a sandstone monument that was placed at this location by convicts from the state penitentiary who were sent to Carbon County to work on the road. The monument, according to local lore, was erected in gratitude to Gov. Simon Bamberger for allowing the prisoners to work on the project. A German Jew born in Eberstadt, Germany, Simon Bamberger was Utah's first non-Mormon governor, from 1917 until 1921.

Just north of the monument, the road crosses into Duchesne County and reaches the summit of Indian Creek Pass at 9,100 feet. Passing through the Ashley National Forest, the vegetation ranges from piñon and juniper to aspen and Douglas fir. The road is especially beautiful during autumn. Elk and deer are often visible. From the summit, the road descends the left fork of Indian Canyon until it intersects with the right fork. The route intersects with US Hwy. 40 at Duchesne.

Nine-Mile Canyon

One of the scenic drives not to be missed in eastern Utah is the road through Nine Mile Canyon, which contains some of the best rock art to be found in the world (see Historic Sites). The canyon was named during Maj. John Wesley Powell's first expedition to explore the Green and Colorado Rivers in 1869, when Frank M. Bishop did a 9-mile triangulation along what was named Nine Mile Creek. In the mid-1880s a route was opened through the canyon to transport supplies from the Denver and Rio Grande Railroad at Price to the U.S. Army post at Ft.

Duchesne. By 1889 the canyon had become a two-way transportation route, with returning supply wagons hauling Gilsonite, mined in the vicinity of the fort, back to the railroad at Price. Because of the distances involved, stage stops were established and a telegraph line was erected to improve communications.

The canyon was also used by ranchers beginning in the 1880s. The most famous of the canyon's ranches, the Nutter Ranch, was established by Preston Nutter in 1902. The old homesteads, ranches and stage stops are interesting, but most people visit the canyon to see the Fremont Indian rock art panels scattered throughout the canyon. Travelers should plan the better part of a day for a good introduction to the canyon. Pick up a free brochure from the Castle Country Travel Region that lists mileage and what to see.

The Nine Mile Canyon Rd. is located 7.5 miles east of Price off Hwy. 6. It heads north just beyond the town of Wellington. The paved road becomes gravel after 12 miles, but the road is usually in good condition and easily passable in a passenger car. The first major panels of petroglyphs are located about 26 miles after turning off US Hwy. 6. Panels and other ruins are located throughout the canyon for the next 25 miles. The road eventually reaches US Hwy. 40 south of Roosevelt.

Tours

WALKING TOURS
Historic Helper Main St.

The Helper Western Mining and Railroad Museum has published an informative and nicely illustrated booklet, *Tour of Historic Helper Main Street*, which provides an overview history of Helper and brief histories of nearly 70 buildings and locations along or near Main St. Many of the buildings recall Helper's heyday as a commercial, social and ethnic center for the surrounding coal mining camps during the first half of the 20th century.

Where to Stay

Accommodations

Best Western Carriage House Inn—$$
Swimming pool and hot tub; 41 rooms. **590 E. Main, Price; 1-800-528-1234; 435-637-5660.**

Greenwell Inn—$$
Swimming pool; 125 rooms. Restaurant. **655 E. Main, Price; 1-800-666-3520; 435-637-3520.**

Holiday Inn—$$$
Indoor swimming pool, hot tub and sauna; 148 rooms. Restaurant. Located just off US Hwy. 6 at the West Price exit. **838 Westwood Blvd., Price; 1-800-329-7466; 435-637-8880.**

Camping

PUBLIC

Price Canyon Recreation Area
Maintained by the BLM; 18 RV trailer sites and tentsites. Picnic tables, drinking water and flush toilets. Open June–mid-Oct. Located in Price Canyon, off US Hwy. 6, 18 miles northwest of Price.

Scofield State Park
Two campgrounds at Scofield State Park provide camping opportunities at this popular recreation area. **Madsen Bay** has 100 units; **Mountain View** offers 34 units. Modern rest rooms, showers, wheelchair-accessible area and two boat launching ramps. Open Apr.–Nov. Take US Hwy. 6 north to Colton, then Hwy. 96 southwest to Scofield. **435-448-9449.**

Where to Eat

China City—$ to $$
This is a longtime favorite for inexpensive Chinese and American dishes. Open daily 11 A.M.–10 P.M. **350 E. Main, Price; 435-637-8211.**

Farlaino's—$$ to $$$
The historic Mahleres and Sampinos Building, constructed in 1913 and acquired by Harry Mahleres and Sam Sampinos in 1938, is one of the oldest commercial buildings in Price. Listed in the National Register of Historic Places, since its construction the building has included a restaurant on its main floor. The present restaurant, Farlaino's, has been in the building since 1987. Sam Farlaino's grandparents came from San Giovanni in Fiore, Italy, and some of the recipes Sam prepares, including the homemade sausage, can be traced back to his grandparents' village in Calabria. Sam serves American–style breakfasts, then sandwiches, salads, soups and daily specials at lunch; dinners feature Italian dishes. The evening meal is a special occasion, but Farlaino's is also a place to pick up on the local gossip. Be sure to ask Sam about the Italian marble that was originally used in the restaurant, and what the bell hidden behind the counter is used for. Open Wed.–Sat. 7 A.M.–2 P.M. and 5:30 P.M.–9 P.M. **87 W. Main, Price; 435-637-9217.**

Greek Streak—$ to $$
As the only Greek restaurant in a community with a strong Greek ethnic heritage, this restaurant is patronized by a wide spectrum of Carbon County residents. The original owner, George Gianoulias, came to Price from Crete in 1956, after his uncle, a 1910 immigrant who had never married and had no family, returned to his village to persuade a family member to return with him to America. Twenty-three-year-old George took up the offer, left the village of Kare and its 500 residents and came to Price, where he worked in one of the old Greek coffeehouses owned by his uncle on Carbon Ave. south of Main St. George returned to Crete and married his wife, Katherine. The couple returned to Price and opened the Greek Streak to raise money to put their two children through college. Their son Tony, an athletic scholar in high school, was nicknamed "The Greek Streak," hence the name of the restaurant.

A couple of years ago, after George turned 81, they decided to sell the restaurant to Loretta Trejo, who had worked in the restaurant since she was a high school student and had become just like family. Katherine taught Loretta all the traditional Crete recipes and the menu and specials remain the same—gyros, lamb roast, lamb stew, dolmathes, lentil soup, lemon rice soup, Greek village salads and other items. Katherine still bakes her wonderful Greek pastries, which are considered the best in the state. George still comes every afternoon to enjoy coffee with his Greek friends. Loretta, her husband, Ernesto, and their four children are committed to preserving this part of Carbon County's ethnic heritage. Open Mon.–Sat. 8 A.M.–9 P.M. Located in one of the old Greek coffeehouses. **84 S. Carbon Ave., Price; 435-637-1930.**

Groggs Pinnacle Brewing Co.—$$

Marty and Diann Beckman, natives of Carbon County, opened this establishment in 1995, and its reputation for good food and good beer is spreading throughout the area. Marty, who holds a degree in business administration from Utah State University, loves to experiment with home brewing and cooking. Currently there are four beers—raspberry wheat, pale ale, amber ale and porter. For non–beer drinkers there are homemade lemonade, juices, coffee, milk and soft drinks. The menu has a great variety of foods, with appetizers, burgers, gourmet sandwiches, pizzas and home-style soups being the specialties. Dinner entrées include baked salmon, filet mignon, Cajun roasted chicken, pork loin and barbecued baby back ribs. There are some fine vegetarian offerings, including a garden burger, vegetarian sandwich and pizza. All the food is prepared fresh and the light wood interior and outside seating in the summer make this an especially inviting place.

Open daily 11:30 A.M.–10 P.M. Located in a renovated fast-food store, there is easy access coming from the north by turning off on Carbonville Rd. at the golf course and heading south for 1.5 miles. From the south, take the West Price exit from US Hwy. 6 and turn left onto Carbonville Rd. at the first intersection; it is about 2 miles north. **1653 N. Carbon Ave., Carbonville; 435-637-2924.**

Services

Visitor Information

Castle Country Travel Council—Located on the first floor of the south entrance to a renovated elementary school on the same block and to the northwest of the College of Eastern Utah Prehistoric Museum. Open Mon.–Fri. 9 A.M.–5 P.M. **90 N. 100 E. at 155 E. Main, P.O. Box 1037, Price, UT 84501; 1-800-842-0789; 435-637-3009; www.CastleCountry.com.**

Emery County

There is probably some basic psychological explanation as to why, even though I have lived in the Salt Lake Valley for more than three decades, when I am asked "Where are you from?" I still respond with unbridled loyalty, "Emery County!" This response is not unique; many of my childhood friends still keep a strong lifelong connection with the place where they grew up—for most had to leave.

One old-timer concluded that this seemingly excessive tie to the land was due to a secretly addictive quality of alkali. The area developed an unwanted reputation for being alkaline when excessive irrigation water leached minerals from the hay fields and pastures and left them a white, sometimes yellow-looking crust. This is particularly true along the roads bisecting the thin edge of settlement between the hills and mountains of the Wasatch Plateau to the west and the beautiful but uninhabitable canyons and formations of the mysterious San Rafael Desert to the east. Whether it is alkali in the blood, as my old-time friend claimed, recollections of growing up grounded in a community in which everyone was unique and essential, or a new recognition of the land's inherent beauty, I continue to return to Emery County with unbounded enthusiasm.

There are three major physiographical areas within Emery County: the Wasatch Plateau,

Castle Valley and the San Rafael Swell. The highest area is the Wasatch Plateau, which reaches more than 11,000 feet in some places, stretching from north to south for 70 miles and east to west from about 15 to 25 miles. Four major creeks, fed by numerous springs and smaller streams, flow out of the Wasatch Plateau. The southernmost is the Muddy, which joins with the Fremont River at Hanksville to become the Dirty Devil River, which flows into the Colorado River—now Lake Powell—at Hite Crossing. Huntington, Cottonwood and Ferron Creeks join east of Castle Dale to form the San Rafael River, which flows into the Green River above its confluence with the Colorado River.

The San Rafael Swell is a massive, 75-mile-long, 30-mile-wide anticlinal uplift created about 65 million years ago during the mountain-building period known as the Laramide Orogeny. The San Rafael Swell was created at the same time as the Waterpocket Fold to the south in Capitol Reef National Park. The most dramatic view of the Swell is on the south and east sides—it is known as the San Rafael Reef and looks like the teeth of a gigantic saw thrust upward through the valley floor. A northern extension of the uplift is Cedar Mountain. The forces of erosion have shaped narrow canyons, buttes, pinnacles and cliffs in the San Rafael Swell. The entire area is usually referred to by locals as "the desert," but that term does not do justice to the region. The highest point of the San Rafael Swell is nearly 8,000 feet in elevation. The eroded "castles" of the Swell give the region its name. On the Swell you will find landmarks such as the Little Grand Canyon, Sids Mountain, Buckhorn Draw, Windowblind Butte, the Black Dragon, Sinbad Valley, the Chute and hundreds of other places with colorful names used to identify the nooks and crannies of this remarkable land.

The San Rafael Swell remains unoccupied. Recreation, livestock grazing and limited mining are the principal activities on the Swell. Recently, local and state officials, including Utah's governor, proposed the designation of the area as the San Rafael National Monument. As of now, federal legislative and executive branches are considering the proposal. This chapter looks at the Swell north of Interstate 70; for the area south of the interstate, see the Green River chapter.

Castle Valley, located between the San Rafael Swell on the east and the Wasatch Plateau on the west, is a relatively flat lowland plain interrupted here and there by small hills and benchlands of Mancos shale. It is here that the string of towns and farms along and not far from Hwy. 10 can be found, in the foothills of the Wasatch Plateau.

Today coal mining and energy production are the key industries within Emery County. Third- and fourth-generation residents still farm and ranch, but perhaps more as a hobby than as the primary source of income. Though relatively undeveloped, recreation and tourism become more important each year, and civic leaders are pursuing plans that will preserve, promote, and make more accessible the unique history and resources of this area.

History

The oldest rocks in Emery County are from the Coconino Sandstone Formation and date back 250 million years ago. Cycles of dry and wet periods led to the variety of geological layers that are found within the county. Seas periodically covered the area, leaving deposits of siltstone, limestone and sandstone. Massive sand dunes produced the Wingate and Navajo Sandstone Formations. The Morrison Formation, the source of dinosaur bones found at the Cleveland-Lloyd Quarry, developed about 110 million years ago at a time when large forests of giant trees and shallow lakes covered the land. Seas returned to cover the area for 60 million years about 100 million years ago. The deposits left during this last great period of oceans and seas make up the Mancos Shale Formation, which can be found throughout Castle Valley and the San Rafael Swell area.

Some 25 million or so years after the San Rafael Swell developed, the Wasatch Plateau was also created by an uplift. Later, within the plateau, faults created grabens, or valleys, as the land surface sunk, leaving mountains on either side from 1,500 to 3,000 feet different in elevation on either side.

The beginning of human occupation of what is now Emery County is as mysterious as the painted, tapered human forms and insect people found on the rock walls of canyons in the San Rafael region. What adds to the mystery about these early people is that the rock art they have left, some painted over earlier works, indicates that the pictographs and petroglyphs that attract so much interest today were inscribed over a period of hundreds, if not thousands, of years. Known as the Barrier Canyon style for the 8-foot-tall anthropomorphs in Barrier Canyon, just across the county line in present-day Wayne County, this rock art style found throughout southeastern Utah, Arizona and Colorado finds its northwesternmost expression in Emery County.

In 1984 archaeologists discovered more than 1,000 Folsom artifacts in a location south of Green River. The find indicates that the site was used over a long period of time by members of the Folsom culture and is probably the earliest village site within the state of Utah. Prior to the Green River discovery, only a few isolated Folsom points had been found within the state boundaries. In 1975 excavations by University of Utah archaeologists at Cowboy Cave, in the southeastern corner of Emery County not far from Barrier Canyon, indicate that prehistoric occupation of the region may not have been continuous. Within the cave they discovered three distinct periods of occupation: approximately 5625 B.C. to 4400 B.C.; 1685 B.C. to 1380 B.C.; and A.D. 60 to A.D. 455. The 1988 discovery of the Huntington Reservoir Mammoth with human-made spear points nearby indicates that early humans ranged from the deserts and canyons of the San Rafael Swell to the alpine meadows of the Wasatch Plateau.

As cattlemen and herders in the 1870s pushed into the Castle Valley area from Sanpete Valley and other locations to the west and north, they came across the remnants of these prehis-

toric cultures and undoubtedly wondered about a people whose rock paintings depicted unearthly forms and whose lifeways seemed so alien to their own. Those who eventually settled Emery County did so because of the lack of water and land in the older Mormon settlements that their parents had settled; the opportunities that Castle Valley held for them; and strong encouragement from Mormon church leaders, including Brigham Young. One week before he died, Young wrote to Canute Peterson, leader of the Mormon settlements in Sanpete Valley, on August 22, 1877:

There are number of the brethren in different portions of Sanpete County, who have not an abundant supply of water for their land, who would, no doubt, be happy to remove to a valley where the water is abundant and the soil good. We should like to have at least fifty families locate in Castle Valley this fall. … In making your selection choose good, energetic God fearing young men, whether single or with families, and others who can be spared without interfering with the interests of the settlements in which they now reside.

For a people who see God's hand in almost everything, this last act by Brigham Young has been interpreted two ways. Emery County boosters interpret Brigham's death seven days later, following the August 22 letter, as "The Great Colonizer's" crowning achievement. After

Getting There

Emery County is located in southeastern Utah, approximately 140 miles south-southeast of Salt Lake City. Travelers on Interstate 70 exit at Fremont Junction, Exit 89, and take Hwy. 10 north through the communities of Emery, Ferron, Castle Dale and Huntington. Travelers from the north enter the county via Hwy. 10, after leaving US Hwy. 6 at Price.

his three decades of organizing and promoting the establishment of hundreds of settlements throughout the Intermountain West, the climax of his career was to launch the settlement of Castle Valley. As reward for this accomplishment, Brigham Young was taken directly into heaven. Detractors conclude, however, that with the "call" to settle Castle Valley, it was obvious that Brigham Young was no longer an inspired leader, and in a fit of revenge and out of concern for his Mormon kingdom, God had no other choice but to remove the errant leader permanently.

Between 1880 and 1900, Emery County made a gradual transition from frontier homesteads, where 90 percent of the 453 residents were farmers or ranchers, to a string of communities whose 4,657 residents, while still mostly farmers, also included saloon keepers, musicians, ministers, teachers, a watchmaker and a life insurance salesman. The permanence of the new settlements of Emery, Ferron, Castle Dale, Orangeville and Huntington was reflected in the construction of numerous brick homes at the turn of the 20th century (several of which can still be seen in Castle Dale today) and civic and religious buildings in the communities, of which the Emery church and the Castle Dale school are the best remaining examples. By 1910, the population of the entire county approached 7,000 and remained fairly consistent at that figure until after World War II. By 1970 it had dropped to around 5,000, only to rise dramatically in the energy boom during the 1970s.

Major Attractions

Cleveland-Lloyd Dinosaur Quarry

The Cleveland-Lloyd Dinosaur Quarry has been a source of fossil bones since 1928, when University of Utah scientists conducted the first dig at the site. The bones are scattered in a layer about a yard thick that contains more Jurassic dinosaur bones per square yard than have been found in any other location in the world. Reconstructions of the quarry's most famous dinosaur, the allosaurus, an earlier version of the fearsome

Tyrannosaurus rex, can be seen in the College of Eastern Utah Prehistoric Museum in Price and the Museum of the San Rafael in Castle Dale. At the quarry the visitor center contains a replica of a young allosaur along with replica skulls of a camarasaur, a diplodocus and a stegosaur. Two sheds are placed over the bone bed for protection.

The BLM runs a visitor center, with information and an exhibit. From the quarry visitor center, you can take two **driving tours.** The shorter tour goes 7 miles southeast from the quarry to the rim of Humbug Canyon, where you can follow a 0.5-mile **hiking** trail to the bottom of the canyon. The longer drive, 25 miles long, follows along the rim of Cedar Mountain for breathtaking views of the San Rafael Swell to the south. Keep an eye out for pronghorn antelope. Brochures describing the tours are available at the center. Usually open Memorial Day–Labor Day daily 10 A.M.–5 P.M.; Sept.– Oct. Fri.–Sun. 10 A.M.– 5 P.M. To get there, from Hwy. 10 near Huntington follow signs east to Cleveland, then drive east on a gravel road for 12 miles. **435-636-3600; www.blm.gov/utah/ price/quarry.htm**.

Huntington State Park

Huntington State Park includes the 237-acre Huntington North Reservoir, which was constructed in 1965–1966 by the U.S. Bureau of Reclamation for the Emery County Conservancy District. With a maximum storage capacity of 5,600 acre-feet of water for irrigation use in the northern section of the county, and located just outside of Huntington, the reservoir is an ideal place for locals and travelers to water-ski and fish. A 111-acre area around the lake was developed as a state park in 1969. Twenty-two camping units, a group pavilion area, picnic tables, modern rest rooms, showers and a sewage disposal facility are available. Fee is charged. Located 2 miles north of Huntington. **435-687-2491; www.parks.state.ut.us/parks/ www1/hunt.htm**.

Millsite State Park

The Millsite Reservoir is a 435-acre, multipurpose reservoir constructed between 1969 and

1971. The reservoir provides irrigation water for farms in the southern end of Emery County, domestic water for the city of Ferron, water for the Hunter Power Plant located between Ferron and Castle Dale, flood control and recreation opportunities. The state park includes 20 camping units, two group shelters with 16 picnic tables and smaller picnic areas around the reservoir. In 1989 a 9-hole golf course, the first in Emery County, was constructed adjacent to the state park (see the Golfing section under Outdoor Activities). Located 4 miles west of Ferron. **435-687-2491; www.parks.state.ut.us/parks/www1/mill.htm.**

Festivals and Events

Heritage Days
end of June–beginning of July. As a youth, next to Christmas, July in Huntington was the most exciting time of the year, with celebrations on July 4 and also on July 24, Pioneer Day. Although the two celebrations were wonderful for the children, the effort eventually proved too much for those responsible for all the activities. Today a compromise Heritage Days has been established, with activities extending from the last few days of June to the first weekend in July. Events include a parade, programs, softball tournaments, Little League baseball games, contests and a rodeo. **435-687-2436.**

San Rafael Folk Art Festival
last weekend in July. This is folk art at its grass-roots level. Nearly three dozen local artists participate in this festival held at the Museum of the San Rafael in Castle Dale. You will find artists, painters, wood carvers, wood turners, bronze sculptors, stone carvers, knife makers, rug weavers, quilt makers, crocheters, guitar makers, flute makers, soap makers, potters, leather workers—and my relative, Theron Grange, who, with his wife, Estelle, collects antlers that have been shed by deer in the nearby mountains to make some of the most interesting lamps and other horn creations you will see anywhere. Held at the Museum of the San Rafael in Castle Dale. **435-381-5252.**

Castle Valley Pageant
last week of July–first week in Aug. Surely there is no more dramatic backdrop for a pageant than this one. Located on one of the side hills of East Mountain, the setting offers tremendous views of the towns of Orangeville and Castle Dale below and panoramic vistas of the San Rafael Desert, with landmarks like Buckhorn Draw and Window Blind Peak visible to the east. The pageant depicts the settlement of Castle Valley in the late 1870s and portrays, in dialogue and song, historical incidents that demonstrate the hardship, commitment, community spirit and humor of pioneer life. Before each performance while covered wagons pulled by teams of horses make a half-hour journey northward from the bench below up the ridge to the performance site. That dramatic journey will remain etched in the audience's minds forever as a reminder of the pace of life in an earlier day and how tenuous humans hold on this land has been.

Seating is best on weekdays, with Fri. the most popular evening. Plan to arrive an hour or so early. Attendees are welcome to wander through the pageant site and visit with the performers or view one of several demonstrations such as wagon wheel making, sheep shearing, cow milking or mule outfitting. Before driving up to the pageant site, plan a visit to the Emery County Fairgrounds in Castle Dale where locals serve a traditional mutton dinner, offer historical demonstrations and provide other activities for young and old alike. The performance begins at dusk or about 8:30 P.M. with an impressive mounted horse flag ceremony. **435-381-2311; 435-381-2195.**

Ferron Peach Days
first weekend in Sept. Ferron Peach Days is probably the oldest continuous celebration in Emery County and southeastern Utah. One of several areas of the state known for its peaches, Ferron commemorates the peach harvest with a three-day celebration that includes a queen

pageant, horse races, road races, a golf tournament, a parade, exhibits, a children's carnival, a dance and fireworks. **435-384-2350.**

Outdoor Activities

Biking

Emery County offers two excellent areas for mountain bikers. The San Rafael area is preferable in the spring and fall, while the high Wasatch Plateau attracts riders in the summer. The verdant mountains of the plateau offer an attractive contrast to the sandstone of the San Rafael Desert. Perhaps the best-known route is the Skyline Dr., which, on a hot July or Aug. day in Utah, can be a refreshing ride in 60°–70° F temperatures. (For a description of the Skyline Dr., see the **Sanpete Valley** chapter in the Central Region.) The free *Mountain Bike Trail Guide,* published by the Castle Country Travel Council and available at the **Museum of the San Rafael, 64 N. 100 E., Castle Dale,** describes a number of routes in the area. The following are some favorites.

Huntington Reservoir–Joe's Valley Rd.

A few miles below the Skyline Dr., within the boundaries of Emery County, is the Huntington Reservoir–Joe's Valley Rd. The road leaves Hwy. 31 just east of Huntington Reservoir and traverses about 30 miles south through Scad Valley beneath Bald Mountain and Bald Ridge, to Upper Joe's Valley and Hwy. 29 near Joe's Valley Reservoir. This is a beautiful alpine 60-mile out-and-back ride that climbs from about 7,000 feet to more than 8,500 feet in elevation. This ride can also be made as a loop ride; from Joe's Valley, use the Miller Flat Rd. and Lowry Water Rd. to return to Hwy. 31 for a total of 60 miles. Or arrange for shuttle vehicles to pick up riders at Joe's Valley Reservoir for a 30-mile one-way ride—or get picked up in Orangeville after a 19-mile ride from Joe's Reservoir down Straight Canyon along Hwy. 29, a total of 49 miles one-way.

Mexican Mountain Rd.

The San Rafael Campground makes a good starting point for bikers. From Hwy. 10, 2 miles north of Castle Dale, take Buckhorn Draw Rd. east 13 miles to a fork; stay left to reach the Swinging Bridge and the campground in 11 miles. One popular route is to follow the Mexican Mountain Rd. southeastward for approximately 16 miles, along the north side of the San Rafael River, until you reach Mexican Mountain. Near the end of the road, a short side trail leads to an overlook of the Black Box. The 32-mile out-and-back ride has some short, steep grades, and a 4-mile-long gradual grade off Indian Bench.

Railroad Grade

The old railroad grade across Buckhorn Flat, along the base of Cedar Mountain, was completed in the early 1880s, but never used because the Denver and Rio Grande Railroad decided to head north to Salt Lake City rather than to continue west. The ties and rails were never laid, so you have a relatively smooth and level ride for most of the 22-mile round trip.

From Hwy. 10, 2 miles north of Castle Dale, take Buckhorn Draw Rd. east to the Wedge turnoff at 13 miles. The trail begins near the large power transmission line just north of the Wedge turnoff at Buckhorn Well and heads east. Gravel roads from Cleveland and Huntington also lead to the trailhead. This is both a scenic and a historic ride. Side trails branching off the main route lead to Fremont rock art and rock inscriptions left by railroad workers.

Fishing

Ferron Reservoir

Located high on the Wasatch Plateau above Ferron, this reservoir is well stocked with trout and is popular with both fly and lure anglers. Take the road west from Ferron; the reservoir is a couple of miles before the junction with Skyline Dr.

Huntington Canyon Reservoirs

High in the upper meadows of the Wasatch Plateau in Huntington Canyon, several small reservoirs—Cleveland, Huntington, Boulger, Millers Flat and others—were constructed to

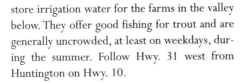

store irrigation water for the farms in the valley below. They offer good fishing for trout and are generally uncrowded, at least on weekdays, during the summer. Follow Hwy. 31 west from Huntington on Hwy. 10.

Huntington River

Located along Hwy. 31, this river was where I had my first experience with fishing. My father and older brother took me on regular trips "up the canyon" to try to teach me the intricacies of fly-fishing. Brown trout are the usual yield from the stream. The left-hand, or south, fork |of the Huntington is a beautiful stream that runs through a narrow canyon away from the highway traffic.

Joe's Valley Reservoir

The largest lake in Emery County and the source for some of the largest trout taken in the area (browns up to 13 pounds and rainbows up to 5 pounds), Joe's Valley is one of the most popular fishing spots in the area. The reservoir was constructed during the mid-1960s in a valley pioneers named for Joe, an Indian who helped them during their trek across the mountain from Sanpete Valley to settle Castle Valley in the 1870s. Take Hwy. 29 west from Orangeville.

Golf

Millsite Golf Course

If, during my growing-up years in Emery County, someone had predicted that within a few decades many of the area's residents would turn in their tractors for golf carts. But since 1989, that is exactly what has happened. That year, the Millsite Golf Course was opened, and it has proved to be one of the state's most distinctive and challenging courses. Set among sand-colored hills, with the 10,000-foot Wasatch Plateau in the background, the 9 holes are all unique. I always plan at least a sleeve or two of extra golf balls just in case I don't clear the wide canyon on the 2nd hole; bounce one into the rocks of the Millsite Dam, which runs along the length of the 592-yard 3rd hole; or lose a few off the rock walls

that form three sides of the 7th hole. From Hwy. 10 in the middle of Ferron, follow the signs that point west. Located on the Canyon Rd., 4 miles west of Ferron. **435-384-2887.**

Hiking

Emery County is a unique area in which to hike. The high ranges of the Wasatch Plateau offer excellent opportunities for alpine hiking, while the San Rafael region offers deserts, beautifully colored canyons and narrow gorges in which the only route is along a channel cut by the San Rafael or Muddy River.

East Mountain Trail

The hike up Horse Canyon to the north point of East Mountain at an elevation of 9,600 feet makes for a good 8-mile out-and-back hike. The trailhead is located in Huntington Canyon off Hwy. 31, approximately 12 miles from Hwy. 10 and 2 miles east of the Stuart Ranger Station. If you want to add more distance and even make a loop hike, you can continue for 4 miles south along the East Mountain Trail as the trail climbs another 800 feet in elevation to the junction with the Mill Fork Canyon Trail. To continue the loop, head east down the Mill Fork Canyon Trail for 4 miles to its intersection with Huntington Canyon Rd./Hwy. 31. This will leave you 6 miles south of your beginning point at the Horse Canyon trailhead. Making arrangements for a shuttle is best, especially because the Mill Fork Canyon Trail is very difficult and the entire 12-mile hike is likely to take most of the day.

Lower Black Box

Utah hikers consider the Lower Black Box of the San Rafael one of the most famous yet least traveled hikes in the state. It is 13.5 miles one-way, 27 miles round trip, so plan on at least two days. Before you make this hike, be sure to check with the BLM about weather and river conditions and any problems that might be expected. **San Rafael Resource Area, Bureau of Land Management, Box AB, Price, UT 84501; 435-637-4584.**

Just getting to the starting point is a difficult

odyssey. From Hwy. 10, 2 miles north of Castle Dale, turn east and follow Buckhorn Draw Rd. 13 miles to a fork; continue on the middle fork through Buckhorn Draw 11 miles to the Swinging Bridge across the San Rafael River, then 13 miles farther to Sink Hole Flat. Or from Green River, take Interstate 70 west to Exit 129 and then follow the road north about 5.5 miles to Sink Hole Flat.

At Sink Hole Flat, a sign indicates the route. Drive southeast just under 2 miles to a water tank, then turn northeast 3 miles until you reach a road that loops for 10 miles around Jackass Bench. Turn right (east) for 3.6 miles until the road turns north, then look for a faint trace headed east. Leave your vehicle here.

You will hike across a pass after 0.5 mile, then begin a drop of several hundred feet over 5 miles to the San Rafael River. After a 3-mile stretch along the east side of the river, you enter the Lower Black Box and walk in the river for most of the 5 miles through the Box. In some places it is necessary to float or swim, so an inner tube is essential. Once in the canyon, you pass under Swasey's or Sid's Leap, a narrow, 14-foot span over the river. Sid Swasey, an early cowboy in the area, bet his brother a herd of 75 cattle that he could jump his saddle horse across the chasm. Sid allegedly made the jump, won the bet and gave the area one of the most dramatic stories behind any place name in the state. Today a wagon box/bridge, used to move sheep over the chasm, looms 60 feet above the river.

South Fork of the Huntington River

One of my favorite summer mountain hikes, this trail takes you along a free-flowing, clear-water mountain stream in an isolated canyon, where the water plays over the rocks and offers trout anglers plenty of opportunities. The trailhead begins at the "Forks," located 18 miles up Huntington Canyon on Hwy. 31. Immediately after you cross the stream, turn west and follow the road along the north side of the creek, until you find a good parking place.

The trail, designated a National Recreation Trail, follows the north side of the south fork of

the Huntington River for 4.5 miles through the canyon to Scad Valley. Simply retrace your route back through the canyon to the forks for an out-and-back hike of about 9 miles. You can also continue along Scad Creek to its intersection with the Miller Flat Rd., where a shuttle can pick you up.

Seeing and Doing

Historic Sites

Some of America's best-preserved rock art is found within Emery County, and in particular in the San Rafael Swell region. Some sites are quite accessible, while others require considerable hiking, and there are undoubtedly some that remain undiscovered even today. Those interested in more than the sampling of rock art sites provided below should inquire at the College of Eastern Utah Prehistoric Museum in Price, the Bureau of Land Management Office in Price (see the **Price** chapter for both of these), or the Museum of the San Rafael in Castle Dale (see the Museums section below) for more information.

Buckhorn Draw Pictographs

This is probably the most visited pictograph site in the county. It is located 22 miles southeast of Castle Dale on the Buckhorn Draw Rd. From Hwy. 10, 2 miles north of Castle Dale, take Buckhorn Draw Rd. east 13 miles to a fork; continue on the middle fork about 9 miles, about 2 miles before the Swinging Bridge across the San Rafael River. The 100-foot-long pictograph panel has been fenced by the BLM, and the Emery County Centennial Commission completed restoration of the pictographs as its state centennial project in 1996. The panel consists of red-painted anthropomorphic figures with elongated forms, small heads, broad shoulders and short arms and legs.

Back up the road 3.3 miles west from the Buckhorn Draw panel, there is a cattle guard. Looking to the north, you can spot a trail going up toward a sand dune under a vertical ledge. Follow the trail to a large panel about 50 feet in length. This panel has stick figures of humans in pairs and one group of five holding hands. Alongside them are deer and sheep forms, arcs, footprints and a set of concentric circles. A smaller 15-foot panel is located about 90 feet from the larger panel. These pictographs have not been vandalized. The forms at both sites are unique, suggesting they were painted at different times and perhaps by different occupants of the area.

Dry Wash Petroglyphs

This popular site is easily reached by driving south out of Ferron along Hwy. 10 for approximately 4 miles, and then turning left off the highway onto a paved road that leads to a couple of farmhouses known as Moore. At the first junction, turn left again, heading east along a road that intersects with Interstate 70, about 15 miles away. After traveling along this road for a couple of miles, look to the left (north) for a number of large boulders upon which can be seen snake-figure petroglyphs, some 6–8 feet long, which have been carved into the rocks. Park your vehicle and search among the boulders for the well-defined outline of a lizard in the stone, a small Kokopelli (hunchbacked flute player) and other figures carved into the stone.

Museums

Emery County Museum

Located in the 1909 Castle Dale School, this museum uses period rooms to depict the early days in Emery County. Among the display rooms are a schoolroom, store, kitchen and coal mining, farming and other artifacts. The museum is operated in conjunction with the Museum of the San Rafael (see below). The county museum is dedicated to the local history of the area and is housed in the county's oldest remaining public building, one that has been listed in the National Register of Historic Sites. Open Mon.–Fri. 10 A.M.– 4 P.M., Sat. noon–4 P.M. No entry fee, but donations are accepted. Located a half block north of the Museum of the San Rafael on the corner of **100 N. and 100 E., Castle Dale. 435-381-5252.**

Museum of the San Rafael

This fine local museum emphasizes the natural and prehistory of the Emery County area. The museum is designed to give an actual orientation to the area, as the plants and animals along the west wall are representative of those found in the high Wasatch Plateau country to the west, while the east side of the museum is typical of the San Rafael area that spreads eastward from the mountains. In the center, between the two walls in a circular kivalike setting, artifacts of prehistoric inhabitants of the region are exhibited. Among these artifacts are a woven rabbit-skin blanket, woven figurines and an Indian toolmaking kit dating from between A.D. 1250 and A.D. 1450 that was found by a local explorer, LaVar Sitterud, 15 miles southeast of Castle Dale in 1968. Archaeologists consider the leather bundle the first of its kind recovered in the region.

In a separate wing is an exhibit of dinosaurs that includes an allosaurus, albertosaurus, chasmosaurus and *Tyrannosaurus rex* skull and foot. Most of the dinosaurs are taken from the nearby Cleveland-Lloyd Dinosaur Quarry (see the Major Attractions section). An eye-catching exhibit is the extensive collection of mounted animals taken in the area. My favorite is the life-like display of a huge mountain lion, paused almost in midair, in pursuit of a mule deer. Most of the background scenes are painted by local artist Clifford Oviatt. Open Mon.–Fri. 10 A.M.– 4 P.M., Sat. noon–4 P.M. No entry fee, but donations are accepted. **64 N. 100 E., Castle Dale; 435-381-5252; www.utahmuseums.org/ sanrafael.**

Scenic Drives

Huntington Canyon Scenic Byway/Hwy. 31

The 48-mile drive from Huntington off Hwy. 31 to Fairview at US Hwy. 89 is one of the most beautiful summer and fall drives in the state, a place of pine trees, quaking aspen and alpine meadows. The ascent to the summit of the Wasatch Plateau from Fairview is a very steep 12-mile climb that takes you from 6,000 to

9,000 feet; the route from Huntington is much more gradual. Both directions provide access to the Skyline Dr., a magnificent four-wheel-drive road and mountain bike route in the summer or cross-country ski trail in the winter. (See Skyline Dr. in the Scenic Drives section under Seeing and Doing in the **Sanpete Valley** chapter in the Central Region.)

Under a joint partnership, the U.S. Forest Service, the Utah Department of Transportation and local government have placed informational kiosks and interpretive panels at major points of interest, including the historic Stuart Ranger Station, along the Scenic Byway. Look for a free guide to this scenic drive at the Museum of the San Rafael in Castle Dale; also available at the College of Eastern Utah Prehistoric Museum or Manti-La Sal National Forest Office in Price (see the **Price** chapter).

Below Skyline Dr., the Upper Joe's Valley Rd. to the south connects Huntington Canyon with Straight Canyon. Although this is a dirt road, it is generally passable for passenger vehicles and is also a delightful bike route.

Orangeville to Joe's Valley Scenic Dr./Hwy. 29

To reach Orangeville, turn off Hwy. 10 onto Hwy. 29, 6 miles south of Huntington, and drive 4 miles, passing Emery County High School. From Orangeville, Hwy. 29 follows Straight Canyon 19 miles to Joe's Valley Reservoir. The mountain valley has been known since pioneer times as Joe's Valley in honor of an Indian who directed Mormon settlers crossing the mountain from Sanpete Valley. In the winter, the Joe's Valley area is especially popular among snowmobilers and cross-country skiers.

En route to Joe's Valley, just over 2 miles from Orangeville, watch for the monument erected by the United Mine Workers of America to commemorate the 26 victims of the tragic Wilberg Mine Disaster on Dec. 19, 1984. During the first 7 miles of the drive, you pass hay fields, pastures and pioneer-era log houses as you gradually enter the mouth of Straight Canyon. Then the aromatic hay fields give way and you enter the narrow confines of the canyon as the road snakes its way

another 8 miles up the north side of the canyon. The sides of the mountain and Cottonwood Creek are strewn with giant boulders around which grow juniper, fir and pine trees. As you reach the head of the canyon, the 195-foot-high, 740-foot-wide Joe's Valley Dam, built between 1963 and 1966, seems to block your way, but the road swings to the north and a beautiful vista unfolds below. The light blue waters of Joe's Valley Reservoir contrast with the dark tree-covered slopes of the surrounding mountains, giving an unforgettable panorama. Although the paved road ends at the Emery-Sanpete county line, a gravel road continues west across the Wasatch Plateau to Ephraim on US Hwy. 89.

The Wedge Overlook/Buckhorn Draw Rd. Scenic Backway

Access to the heart of the San Rafael Desert is by way of the road that heads east off Hwy. 10, 2 miles north of Castle Dale. My favorite time to take this drive is in fall, when the leaves on the cottonwood trees in Buckhorn Wash and along the San Rafael have turned and the deep blue fall sky accentuates the yellow of the leaves and the red of the rocks. Designated as one of Utah's Scenic Backways, this graded road is usually easily passable for passenger cars. In 42.5 miles it reaches Interstate 70 at Exit 129.

At 13 miles from Hwy. 10, the road branches. The right-hand fork heads out to the Wedge Overlook, the middle fork continues to Buckhorn Wash, and the left fork goes east to intersect with US Hwy. 6 north of Green River. If this is your first visit to Emery County, try to make time to drive both the right and middle branches of this road.

To the right, the road takes you up through piñon and juniper for 6 miles until it ends abruptly at the **Wedge Overlook** or, as it is often called by locals, the Little Grand Canyon. The overlook provides a spectacular view of the canyon formed by the San Rafael River, which flows 1,200 feet below.

Back at the intersection, the "main route" (left fork) continues in a southeasterly direction through Buckhorn Draw 11 miles to the San

Rafael River and the historic Swinging Bridge. The drive through Buckhorn Draw is interesting on several counts. Here, you are in the northwestern corner of the magnificent red-rock country for which southeastern Utah is world-famous. The draw contains ancient Indian pictographs (see the Historic Sites section). A dinosaur footprint is also located in the draw. If you happen to be traveling with locals who know where it is, they will usually point it out to you.

Buckhorn Draw was also the scene of a Wild West gun battle, when posses from Castle Dale and Huntington in pursuit of Butch Cassidy met and mistakenly opened fire on each other. No one was killed or even wounded, but Butch Cassidy managed to escape to Robbers Roost. The San Rafael campground is near the Swinging Bridge. Here you have the option of returning the way you came, or continuing another 18.5 miles through open rangelands and piñon-juniper country until you intersect with Interstate 70 at Exit 129.

Where to Stay

Motels

The big draws in Emery County are the scenery, the history and the people—certainly not fine hotels or charming bed and breakfast inns. Expect only basic motel accommodations.

Village Inn—$$
Twenty-one rooms. **375 E. Main, Castle Dale; 435-381-2309.**

Village Inn—$$
Twenty-two rooms. **310 S. Main, Huntington; 435-687-9888.**

Camping

PUBLIC
Ferron Reservoir
Thirty RV sites and tentsites. Open mid-June–mid-Sept. Located 28 miles west of Ferron on Ferron Canyon Rd.

Huntington Canyon / Hwy. 31
Bear Canyon Campground is located approximately 7 miles up the canyon from Huntington. (18 sites) The **Forks Campground** is located 18 miles from Huntington, where the south fork joins Huntington Creek; 6 RV sites and tentsites, available on a first-come, first-served basis, with nonpotable water and toilets. Open June–mid-Sept. Perhaps the oldest campground in the canyon is at **Old Folks Flat,** 21 miles from Huntington, so named because it was the location for one of the annual old folks' gatherings sponsored by the LDS church; 8 RV sites and 30 tentsites, with toilets and nonpotable water. Open June–mid-Sept.

Orangeville / Joe's Valley / Hwy. 29
Joe's Valley Campground at Joe's Valley Reservoir has 46 RV sites and tentsites, drinking water and toilets. Open late May–late Oct. Located about 18 miles west of Orangeville on Hwy. 29. **Indian Creek Campground** has 28 RV sites and tentsites, drinking water and toilets. Open late June–late Sept. Located 2 miles farther west on Hwy. 29.

San Rafael Area
Most camping in the area is done along the hiking trails or in undeveloped locations off the road or in side canyons. The only campground located in the San Rafael area is maintained by the Bureau of Land Management at the Swinging Bridge at the mouth of Buckhorn Draw. The amenities are few: running water, picnic tables, pit toilets and designated camping spots. From Hwy. 10, 2 miles north of Castle Dale, take Buckhorn Draw Rd. east 13 miles to a fork; stay left to reach the campground in 11 miles.

Where to Eat

You won't starve in Emery County, but you might have to look hard for a place to eat. For most residents, eating out is something you do when you travel away from home, for a quick trip to Price or a longer one across the mountains to Provo or Salt Lake City. Because the area is not overrun with travelers, you won't find the usual tourist eating establishments. However, they are likely to come as word of the glories of the San Rafael and the beauties of the Wasatch Plateau gets out. In the meantime, each of the towns along Hwy. 10, from Emery to Huntington, has one or two places that offer food, even if it is a Subway Sandwich Shop located inside a gas station.

Two usually reliable places are **Big Mama's Pizza,** which offers your standard pizza plus well-above-average burgers (located on the east end of Main St./Hwy. 10 in Castle Dale); and the **DeJaVus,** where you can get three square meals a day and it is often the only place in the county open for a breakfast like Mom used to make (located on Hwy. 10 about 1 mile north of Huntington).

Services

Visitor Information

Museum of the San Rafael—The best source of information for travelers in Emery County. Also see the Services section in the **Price** chapter. Open Mon.–Fri. 10 A.M.–4 P.M., Sat. noon–4 P.M. **64 N. 100 E., Castle Dale; 435-381-5252; www.utahmuseums.org/sanrafael.**

Green River

If there is an undiscovered recreation treasure in Utah, it might just be the town of Green River. Located just off Interstate 70 at the edge of the Green River and the scenic San Rafael Swell, the area offers opportunities for river running, hiking and four-wheel driving in a place that most travelers simply pass through on their way south to the better-known Moab area. Here, the Green River flows out of the Gray and Desolation Canyons to the north and enters an open valley before continuing on its southward course into Labyrinth Canyon in Canyonlands National Park.

If you don't have a day or two for a river trip or to explore the canyons of the San Rafael Swell south of Interstate 70 or east of Green River, a visit to the John Wesley Powell Museum, located on the east bank of the Green River, is well worth an hour's stop. If you are lucky and happen to be passing through Green River in late July, August or early September, pick up one of the watermelons or cantaloupes from the fruit stands along the highway running through town. Demand your money back if they are not the best melons you have ever tasted.

History

The town of Green River owes its existence to the simple fact that it is the only location within a 200-mile stretch where the Green River can be crossed. Ute Indians used it as a crossing for centuries, and it was first known as Ute Crossing. It was also on the Old Spanish Trail, opened between Santa Fe, New Mexico, and Los Angeles, California, in 1830. Countless numbers of traders made their way over the trail during the quarter of a century that it was in use. In 1853 Capt. John W. Gunnison, an army explorer, mapped out a transcontinental railroad route along the 38th parallel, which crossed the Green River at what was known for a time as "Gunnison's Crossing"; Gunnison Butte is a prominent landmark north of Green River.

While the 38th parallel route was not followed for the transcontinental railroad, the Denver and Rio Grande Railroad was completed between Denver and Salt Lake City in 1883.

Getting There

Green River is located just off Interstate 70 at Exit 158, on the west side of the river at the junction with US Hwy. 191/6 from Price. Exit 162 on the east side of the river also reaches the town, via a frontage road and river bridge.

Desert Siding, north of Green River, was the location where the rails were joined. The first bridge across the Green River was completed as part of this important railroad project, which led to the founding of the town of Green River.

In addition to supporting the railroad, Green River became a supply point for ranches scattered up the river and to the west in the San Rafael Swell region. During the early 1950s Green River took on the trappings of a boomtown as uranium prospectors used the town as a base for their explorations. The real wealth of Green River, however, is found in those delicious watermelons, which are grown along the river. It must be the combination of plenty of water, cool nights, hot days and alkali in the soil that yields the sweetest-tasting watermelons and cantaloupes to be found on this earth.

Major Attractions

Goblin Valley State Park

This is indeed, a valley inhabited by goblins—petrified goblins; the unusual layered formations of mudstone, sandstone and siltstone have been carved and shaped by wind and rain to resemble goblins and anything else that the imagination can conceive. The long, narrow valley began as a deep deposit of mud at the bottom of a primordial sea that evaporated around 150 million years ago, leaving deep deposits of marine sediments, which solidified into rock. Today, because of the forces of erosion over millions of years, much of the sedimentary rock has been carved away, leaving thousands of odd-shaped pinnacles and formations of all sizes and shapes.

Goblin Valley was noted by cowboys searching for cattle in the area. In the late 1920s, Arthur Chaffin, the owner of Hite Ferry on the Colorado River to the southeast, stumbled upon the valley while traveling between Green River and Caineville on the Fremont River on what is now Hwy. 24. Taken with what he saw, Chaffin returned in 1949 to the area he called Mushroom Valley and spent several days photographing and exploring the area. The ensuing publicity led to

an influx of visitors and concerns about how best to preserve the unique formations. The state of Utah acquired the property and maintained it as a reserve until it was officially designated a state park in Aug. 1964. The valley is an artist's and photographer's delight. There is no other place like it in Utah, or probably in the world.

It is easy to spend a day **hiking** through the valley. The valley encompasses 3,254 acres, or about 5 square miles. There are two maintained hiking trails in the park. The **Curtis Bench Trail** is about 3 miles in length, and the **Henry Mountains Lookout Trail** is a little more than 1 mile in length. Most visitors spend their time wandering around the valley, following their whims to see and explore the fascinating, just larger than human-size formations. Facilities include a covered observation station, a picnic area, an observation overlook and a campground with 21 units, modern rest rooms that are wheelchair accessible, drinking water and showers.

Take Interstate 70 west out of Green River to Exit 147 at its junction with Hwy. 24. Follow Hwy. 24 southwest for approximately 24 miles, and watch for the turnoff to Goblin Valley on the right. Follow the paved road for 5.3 miles, then turn south onto a gravel road for 7 miles to the park entrance. Coming north from Hanksville on Hwy. 24, it is approximately 21 miles to the turnoff. Open year-round. Visitor and camping fees are charged. **Goblin Valley State Park, P.O. Box 93, Green River, UT 84525; 1-800-322-3770 camping reservations; 435-564-8110.**

Green River State Park

Located along the Green River in the town of Green River, this state park serves the many boaters who either leave the river here after a 95-mile journey from the Uinta Basin to the north through Desolation and Gray Canyons or who put in to float the river southward for 120 miles to its confluence with the Colorado River. A 9-hole golf course is part of the park. Interpretive programs are presented during the summer in a small amphitheater; check at the Green River visitor center or at the park entrance for a schedule of programs. In addition to the boating facilities, the park includes 42 developed campsites, piped water and lighted and heated rest rooms with showers. Open year-round. **150 S. Green River Blvd., Green River; 435-564-3633.**

Festivals and Events

Friendship Cruise

end of May/Memorial Day weekend. One of Utah's oldest and most popular motorboat events, the Friendship Cruise follows the course of the Green River south to its confluence with the Colorado River and then up the Colorado River to Moab. The cruise takes participants through some of the most beautiful scenery in the Colorado Plateau. **1-888-564-3600; 435-564-3600; www.ecso.com/friendship/.**

Melon Days

third weekend in Sept. One of Utah's best-kept secrets is the delicious watermelons and cantaloupes grown along the banks of the Green River, as noted above. These are the sweetest, best-tasting melons this side of the Garden of Eden. In season, Green River melons can be purchased from roadside stands in Green River, or from the backs of trucks or trailers at stops along the road and stores within a 125-mile radius of Green River. Green River celebrates Melon Days with a variety of activities, including a parade, city fair, music, races, games, softball tournament, square dancing and free melons. **1-888-564-3600; 435-564-3600.**

Outdoor Activities

Golf

Green River State Park Golf Course

One of Utah's newest golf courses, opened in 1996, this is the third golf course in the state to be operated as part of the state park system. The other two at Wasatch Mountain State Park in Midway and Palisades near Manti are among the most popular outside the Wasatch Front. At present this is a 9-hole course, but there are hopes to expand it to 18 holes in the future. The course does not have the appearance of a barren new course because the designer has incorporated full-grown cottonwood and Russian olive trees in the layout. Because of Green River's usually mild winters, this is a course that is open most of the year. Because there are not enough local golfers, this course was built primarily to attract travelers, and generally reservations are not necessary. **150 S. Green River Blvd., Green River; 435-544-8882.**

Hiking

The following hikes are located just north and west of Goblin Valley State Park (see the Major Attractions section). If you camp at the park for a few days, you could take most of the hikes. Otherwise, if you are in the area for just a day, you might want to combine a visit to the park with one of the shorter hikes.

Chute and Crack Canyons

These two narrow canyons are located on the southeast side of the San Rafael Reef, just north of Goblin Valley State Park. Most hikers go up Chute Canyon and come back down Crack Canyon. The two canyons parallel each other roughly a mile apart. The round-trip distance is approximately 16 miles, making this a good day hike. Inquire at Goblin Valley State Park for specific directions to the canyons; once you are inside the canyons, you can't lose the trail. As Chute Canyon widens, you come to an old mining area and shack. Follow an old trace eastward for about a mile to Crack Canyon, which you can follow back down to your vehicle.

Temple Mountain Loop

Temple Mountain, named by cowboys for the twin-towered Mormon temple in Manti, looms above the desert floor and was once the site of considerable uranium-mining activity, as the remnants of several abandoned miners' shacks and mine portals reveal. A series of abandoned mining roads constitute the 6-mile-long hiking trail around Temple Mountain. Take Exit 147 off Interstate 70 and follow Hwy. 24 southwest for approximately 24 miles, and watch for the turnoff to Goblin Valley on the right. Follow this paved road to its end.

Wild Horse Canyon

From Temple Mountain, you can hike up Wild Horse Creek, surrounded by its sheer Navajo sandstone walls darkly painted with desert varnish. If you search for them, pictographs can be found along the canyon walls. To reach the trail, from the Temple Mountain road, follow an old mining road that runs southwest. After about 2 miles, you come to the first wash. This is Wild Horse Creek; since there is no marked trail, you simply walk down the dry wash bed. The hike is easy, and a couple of short, narrow stretches make it even more interesting. The reformed outlaw Matt Warner left his name on the western wall just north of the junction of Wild Horse and South Temple washes. The trail heads up South Temple Wash to the paved road, which you can follow back to your vehicle. The total round-trip distance is about 9 miles.

River Rafting

The Green River offers several opportunities for all kinds of experiences, from a leisurely calm-water canoe trip to challenging, roaring, heart-stopping rapids in a rubber raft. Depending on how much time you have, trips can be arranged from a day to a week or more in length.

The most popular day trip is the 9-mile section of the river north of town from **Nefertiti Rapid to Swaseys Rapid.** Known as the Green River Daily, the stretch has seven rapids, some of which range in difficulty up to Class III.

Longer runs include **Desolation** and **Gray Canyons,** north of Green River, with 67 rapids in 84 miles. Trips usually take about four days. Desolation Canyon has been designated a National Historic Landmark because it remains essentially the same as when Maj. John Wesley Powell first floated down the Green River in 1869.

From Green River State Park, you can float downriver for 20 miles to **Ruby Ranch,** a pri-

vately owned area with a charge for parking and launching. The next take-out is at **Mineral Bottom,** 68 miles downriver from Green River. This stretch of the river is very calm and slow-moving, popular with canoeists and kayakers.

An extended trip of several days takes you down the Green River to its confluence with the Colorado River, through the infamous **Cataract Canyon,** with its 26 rapids up to Class V in difficulty, and on to Hite, at the north end of Lake Powell and Hwy. 95.

Guides

Professional river guide services are provided by the following companies in Green River:

Holiday River Expeditions—1055 E. Main, Green River, UT 84525; 1-800-624-6323; 435-564-3273.

Moki-Mac River Expeditions—100 Silliman Ln., P.O. Box 116, Green River, UT 84525; 435-564-3361.

Seeing and Doing

Historic Sites

Black Dragon Canyon Pictographs

This rock art takes its name from one of the figures that, upon first glance, resembles a black dragon. On closer examination, though, it looks more like a bird with two legs, a long neck and odd-shaped wings. Other figures include the "praying dog," an animal standing on its hind legs, with its forelegs extending upward and forward as though it is praying, and a group of 7- to 8-foot anthropomorphs. Reach the canyon by leaving Interstate 70 near Milepost 145, approximately 0.5 mile west of the San Rafael River Bridge, and heading west then north through a gate for just over a mile to the head of Black Dragon Canyon. The pictograph panels are located on BLM land on both sides of the canyon about 200 yards up the dry wash.

Sego Canyon Rock Art

Travelers along Interstate 70 east of Green River can see one of Utah's most spectacular rock art sites, in Sego Canyon, where a Fremont-style painted panel includes anthropomorphs with bug eyes, antennae, earrings, snakes in hands and legless torsos. There are also mountain sheep, deer and other animal forms. Another panel appears to be historic Ute art from the 19th century, depicting white bison figures, horses with riders and large human figures with a shield painted in red and white. From Interstate 70, take Exit 185 at Thompson Springs and head north for 3 miles into Sego Canyon.

Temple Mountain Pictographs

Travelers to Temple Mountain will want to take time to view an 8-foot-high, 60-foot-long pictograph panel, located just inside the mouth of South Temple Wash. Here a large Fremont figure has been painted over an earlier Barrier Canyon–style "Bug-eyed Man," providing archaeologists with circumstantial evidence that other Barrier Canyon–style pictographs predate the Fremont-style paintings. Take Exit 147 off Interstate 70 and follow Hwy. 24 southwest for approximately 24 miles, and watch for the turnoff to Goblin Valley on the right. Follow this paved road west until it turns to the south; there you will see a road to Temple Mountain and South Temple Wash on the south side of the mountain.

Museums

John Wesley Powell Museum

One of Utah's newest museums, the John Wesley Powell Museum is located on the east bank of the river in the town of Green River. It serves as both a visitor center and an excellent interpretive museum on the history of Maj. John Wesley Powell and his 1869 and 1871 explorations of the Green and Colorado Rivers. An Illinois schoolmaster and ex-Union Army officer, Powell lost his right arm at the battle of Shiloh early in April 1862 when a half-spent mini-ball shattered his arm. Powell remained in the Union Army until 1865. In 1866 he became a professor of natural sciences at Illinois State Normal University and curator of the Illinois Natural History Museum, which was located on the university campus. With his joint appointments, Powell organized scientific expeditions to Colorado in 1867 and Wyoming in 1868.

On May 24, 1869, Powell and nine other men set out from Green River, Wyoming, in four boats for a three-month journey to explore the unknown Green and Colorado Rivers. With more than a lifetime's worth of adventure packed into the three months, and following the desertion of three of his men (who died under mysterious circumstances), Powell and his group emerged from the Grand Canyon on Aug. 29, 1869, to be greeted by four Mormons, who, under instructions from Brigham Young, were watching for any survivors of the expedition.

In addition to historic boats, other artifacts and well-prepared display panels, the museum's 171-seat auditorium features a 20-minute media presentation, *The River Experience,* that incorporates dramatic slides of the river with narration of extracts from Powell's famous river journal. Anyone who wants to gain a better perspective of the Green River, its history and the man who, according to the late Pulitzer Prize–winning author Wallace Stegner, "by the end of his career … would know the West as few men did, and understand its problems better than any," will not want to miss any opportunity to visit the John Wesley Powell Museum. Open daily 8 A.M.–8 P.M. **885 E. Main St., Green River, UT 84525; 435-564-3427.**

Other Sites

Crystal Geyser

Located on the east bank of the Green River, Crystal Geyser erupts twice a day at irregular intervals. The coldwater geyser sends a powerful and impressive spray of water skyward. If you have the time and patience to wait for the eruption, this is an unforgettable experience. To reach the geyser, drive 1.3 miles east from the Green River Bridge in Green River, then turn left onto the frontage road (located on the south side of Interstate 70). After 2.7 miles, leave the frontage road and turn south onto a dirt road, which you follow for about 9 miles to the geyser.

Scenic Drives

Green River Scenic Dr.
This paved, then dirt, road follows the west bank of the Green River north for about 20 miles into Gray Canyon. This is the road used by day rafters on the Green River for whom the Nefertiti Rapids are the highlight of the run. The rapids are located just below the confluence of the Price River with the Green River.

Interstate 70
Utah Department of Transportation officials could easily justify charging a heavy toll for all vehicles crossing the 100-mile stretch of Interstate 70 from Green River to Salina. This road, through one of the most rugged and difficult sections in the entire nation, was extremely costly to build and it has opened to travelers some fabulous scenery well worth the price of admission. The road passes through deserts, deep canyons and sheer cliffs and around 11,000-foot-high mountains, offering panoramic views of the Colorado Plateau that even lifelong residents of the area stop to admire as they travel along the interstate.

The Grand County Travel Council has published a brochure, *A Guide to I-70 Through Southeastern Utah,* which is available at the John Wesley Powell Museum in Green River or the Thompson Springs Welcome Center at Exit 185. The guide is keyed to the visitor centers, rest areas and view areas along the stretch. There are no services between Green River and Salina, as the interstate passes through what was once a remote, seldom-seen part of the state.

West of Green River, the interstate cuts through the San Rafael Reef, a saw blade-like impregnable wall 800–2,000 feet high that required tons of dynamite to blast the road through in the late 1960s. After negotiating the reef, the interstate crosses the San Rafael Swell, which developed as an uplift of rock 40 to 60 million years ago. Take time to stop at the **Black Dragon, Spotted Wolf, Ghost Rock, Eagle Canyon** and **Devils Canyon** views and rest areas, all well marked.

Where to Stay

Accommodations

Bankurz Hatt Bed and Breakfast—$$ to $$$
Knowing that Hatt was a prominent name in the Green River area and that 19th-century Utahns had given their children some pretty weird names, I asked Ben and Lana Coomer who this guy Bankurz Hatt was. What I heard was an even stranger story about late 20th-century government. In 1897 J. T. Farrer, the local banker and community promoter, had this four-square gambrel-roof home built. During the mid-1930s, the house was acquired by Lana's grandfather, Frank Hatt. After her grandparents passed away, the home sat vacant for several years, much to Lana's distress. She and Ben finally acquired the home and restored it as a bed and breakfast in 1993. When they applied for a business license under the name "Banker's Hatt Bed and Breakfast," they were told that they could not use the word "banker's" in the title. To get over the bureaucratic hurdles, they used the phonetic spelling "Bankurz" to get their desired result.

The master bedroom downstairs has its own bath, while the three upstairs rooms share a bath. All the rooms are furnished with antiques and there is a distinct turn-of-the-20th-century Victorian feel to the house. The tree-shaded grounds, beautiful flower beds and outdoor hot tub are an oasis. A full breakfast is served, with waffles and eggs Benedict the standard fare. All rooms are nonsmoking; no pets or small children. Open Apr.–Dec. **214 Farrer St., Green River, UT 84532; 435-564-3382; www.bankurzhatt.com.**

River Terrace Best Western—$$
A favorite because of its location on the east bank of the Green River across the road from the John Wesley Powell Museum, its swimming pool and the Tamarisk Restaurant adjacent to the motel; 78 rooms. **880 E. Main; 435-564-3401.**

Camping

PRIVATE

Green River KOA

Seventy-seven RV sites, 25 with hookups, plus 50 tentsites. Showers, laundry facilities, store and swimming pool. Open early Apr.–late Oct. **550 S. Green River Blvd.; 435-564-3651.**

Shady Acres RV Park

Ninety-two RV sites and 24 tentsites. Showers, laundry facilities and store. Open year-round. **360 E. Main; 435-564-8290.**

United Campground

Sixty-five RV sites and 15 tentsites. Showers, laundry facilities, store and swimming pool. Open year-round. **910 E. Main; 435-564-8195.**

Where to Eat

Ray's Tavern—$ to $$

It looks like a bar and it is a bar, but Ray's is considered to have the best hamburgers in the state, served with real potato fries and condiments on the side so that you can build the burger the way you want it. Real burger connoisseurs will want to check out Ray's. You can also get char-broiled steaks and a pork chops special, but plan a 45-minute wait for the pork chops.

The original Ray was Ray Sherrill, who bought the bar while he was working for the Civilian Conservation Corps during the 1930s. He sold the establishment to Bob Scott about 25 years ago. Scott made the tavern the unofficial headquarters for river-runners in Green River. Photographs and an amazing display of river running T-shirts along with a couple of pool tables, a long row of 16 bar stools, four wooden tables on the side and two eight-chair tables sandwiched in the center, plus an outdoor patio, all of which has changed little over the years, seem to be the right atmosphere for spinning river-running yarns.

A few years ago Scott sold Ray's to Cathy Gardner and she has maintained the ambience and good food that make this a special place. Open in summer daily 10:30 A.M.–10 P.M.; in winter daily 10:30 A.M.–8 P.M. **280 N. Broadway; 435-564-3511.**

Tamarisk Restaurant—$ to $$

Named for the willowy bush that grows wild along the riverbanks and ponds of the desert region, you can see plenty of tamarisk along the Green River from the large picture windows of the restaurant that overlook the east bank of the river. The restaurant is located just across the highway from the John Wesley Powell Museum. (The Bayles family, who own and operate the restaurant, donated the land for the museum.) Menu items for breakfast include omelettes, pancakes and local watermelon and cantaloupe in season; for lunch there are sandwiches, soups and salads; the dinner menu includes steaks, chicken, turkey, seafood and Utah trout. There are also vegetarian dishes and a daily breakfast, lunch and dinner buffet, which is especially popular with hungry travelers along Interstate 70. Open daily 6 A.M.–10 P.M. **870 E. Main; 435-564-8109.**

Services

Visitor Information

Green River Information Center—Located in the John Wesley Powell Museum on the east side of the Green River. A good selection of pamphlets and books about the region. Open daily 8 A.M.–8 P.M. **885 E. Main St., Green River, UT 84525; 1-800-635-6622; 435-564-3526.**

Thompson Springs Welcome Center— Open Memorial Day–Labor Day daily 8 A.M.–8 P.M.; the rest of the year daily 9 A.M.–5 P.M. Located off Interstate 70 at Exit 185. **435-285-2234.**

Arches National Park

Naturally formed stone arches are a rarity throughout the world, but there is no lack of them in 114-square-mile Arches National Park northwest of Moab. More than 2,000 sandstone arches have been counted within the park boundaries, and more are being discovered all the time or are in the process of forming. The park is a masterpiece created by erosion. You will see not only arches here, but also a panoply of fiery-hued features such as fins of thin sculpted monoliths, balanced rocks, stone chimneys, buttresses and alcoves not yet cut through—all of them laid out underneath a wide, clear azure sky. Spring and fall are the ideal times to visit Arches. Winter days are often beautiful, with surprisingly mild temperatures and usually few people. Summer is the heavy tourist season, so be prepared for crowds and scorching temperatures, especially from mid-morning until after sunset.

History

The first people to make steady use of the area in and around what is now Arches National Park were people of the Desert Archaic culture found throughout the West 3,000 to 8,000 years ago. But the first cultures to leave a tangible trace of their passing were the Anasazi and the Fremont, culturally related peoples who lived on the Colorado Plateau from roughly A.D. 1 to A.D. 1300. These people became culturally distinguished around A.D. 1, when the basketmaker Anasazis progressed to pit houses, then moved into multistory masonry dwellings. They flowered between A.D. 1000 and A.D. 1300. Arches National Park sits just outside the Fremont cultural area, which lies to the west, so the most common vestiges of ancient society are Anasazi.

Within the park are fine examples of rock art (such as those in Lower Courthouse Wash and near the Wolfe Cabin on the trail to Delicate Arch) left in hidden canyons and out-of-the-way places by prehistoric residents. Associated artifacts are also found.

In historic times, the Arches area was used by two different groups of Native Americans: the Ute and the Navajo. The Ute lived and hunted throughout the area, jealously guarding their land and driving out the first white settlers in the area in the 1850s. Arches is north of the Navajo Reservation, and although Navajos passed through the area, there is no evidence that they lived within what is now the park.

The Old Spanish Trail traversed Spanish Valley, where Moab is now located, and crossed the Colorado River just outside the park boundaries. Perhaps travelers on the trail ventured into what is now the park. Juan Maria Antonio de Rivera, a New Mexican trader, passed nearby as early as 1765, when much of the Southwest was under Spanish rule. By the 1840s the trail was a well-used route from New Mexico to California, and functioned as an extension of the Santa Fe Trail between Franklin, Missouri, and Santa Fe, New Mexico. Mountain men frequented the area, but the only one known to have entered the present-day park boundaries was French-Canadian fur trapper Denis Julien, who left an inscription dated 1844 in the park.

The first Mormon explorers, led by William Huntington, entered what is now the Moab area with wagons in 1854 and vowed to return to establish a settlement the next year. Huntington

---

Getting There

One of the most conveniently located national parks, Arches is just 5 miles north of Moab, with a visitor center located adjacent to US Hwy. 191 at the entrance to the park. For travelers on Interstate 70, it is a 26-mile drive south on US Hwy. 191 from Exit 180 at Crescent Junction.

did not return, but Alfred Billings brought back 40 men to found the Elk Mountain Mission in 1855. The mission did not outlast Ute reprisals and quickly folded. Mormons returned to found the town of Moab in 1882.

However, it was not until 1898, when John Wesley Wolfe, a crusty Civil War veteran, and his son Fred settled on Salt Wash near famous Delicate Arch, that the Arches area had its first white inhabitants. In 1906 Wolfe's daughter, her husband, Ed Stanley, and their two children arrived at the ranch and remained there until 1908, when they returned to Ohio. Wolfe continued to live at the ranch until 1910. Now a National Register Historic District, Wolfe Ranch provides a glimpse into the past for today's visitors.

Other Moab residents noted the natural arches and made regular visits to the area. In 1922 a Hungarian-born local miner and prospector named Alexander Ringhoffer was so struck by the unique beauty of the arches that he contacted officials of the Denver and Rio Grande Railroad to try to persuade the railroad company to develop the area as a tourist attraction.

Through a roundabout series of events and coincidences, the National Park Service was informed of the potential of the area for inclusion in the National Park system, and Arches National Monument was created by President Hoover in 1929. A few years later, the new monument was studied in depth and many of its most famous features named and publicized. In 1938 Arches was greatly expanded under a proclamation by President Franklin Roosevelt, from its original 4,500 acres to more than 34,000 acres. Despite increasing tourist interest in the area, the first paved road into Arches was not built until 1958. In 1971 President Richard Nixon signed the law that changed Arches to a national park and set its size at the present 73,379 acres.

Major Attractions

Geology

The three "members" of Entrada sandstone in which this enormous array of arches and win-

dows is located were laid down as sediments in ancient seas and as windblown sand during a time of great aridity. Earlier, about 300 million years ago, the evaporation of inland seas left a thick salt layer (the Paradox Formation), 3,000 feet thick in some places, on top of which the sediment and sand were deposited. Over time, pressure on the lower salt layer caused the salt to push upward in places, bending the upper sediment as well. Arches, which lies on a sloping highland called the Salt Valley Anticline that resulted from this uplift, was also impacted by the faults and joints that developed as part of the uplifting process. Salt domes also developed, while the dissolution of salt along fissures caused fins that eventually weakened into eroded stone features such as arches. The broken layers of Entrada sandstone became very susceptible to erosion because the small, uniform-size quartz grains that make up the sandstone weather easily. Rain, ice, melting water and plant and animal activity caused the sandstone to crack, flake and wash away—a process that continues today.

Writer Edward Abbey, who first arrived in Arches National Park as a seasonal park ranger in 1956, later became one of the most ardent and articulate spokesmen for preservation of the wilderness as a place of refuge and hope. Many of Abbey's books have become basic texts in western environmental literature. In his best-known book, *Desert Solitaire: A Season in the Wilderness* (McGraw-Hill, 1968), Abbey recounts his time at Arches. In that book, laced with humor, sarcasm and love for Utah's canyon country, he offers one of the finest written descriptions of the Arches area that anyone has ever penned.

We drive the dirt roads and walk out some of the trails. Everything is lovely and wild, with a virginal sweetness. The arches themselves, strange, impressive, grotesque, form but a small and inessential part of the general beauty of this country. When we think of rock we usually think of stones, broken rock, buried under soil and plant life, but here all is exposed and naked, dominated by the monolithic formations of sandstone which stand above the surface of the ground and extend for miles, sometimes level, sometimes tilted or warped by pressures from below, carved by erosion and weathering into an intricate maze of glens, grottoes, fissures, passageways, and deep narrow canyons.

At first look it all seems like a geologic chaos, but there is method at work here, method of a fanatic order and perseverance: each groove in the rock leads to a natural channel of some kind, every channel to a ditch and gulch and ravine, each larger waterway to a canyon bottom or broad wash leading in turn to the Colorado River and the sea.

Arches and Bridges

Southeastern Utah has the world's largest collection of natural arches and bridges, and although both terms are sometimes used interchangeably, a bridge is actually formed by the work of a stream upon rock, leaving a "bridge" that spans the streambed. Arches, sometimes called "windows," occur where there is no stream course, but a variety of other erosional factors, including frost, rain and wind, have sculpted them according to the composition of the stone. To be considered an arch, the opening must be at least 3 feet in any one direction. While most of the 2,000 arches here are of the smaller variety, there are a good number of larger arches; Landscape Arch, with its unbelievable 306-foot span more than 100 feet above the ground, is one of the largest arches in the world. A couple of years ago, a large segment fell out of the arch—a reminder that the never-ending process of erosion will destroy this arch even as it creates others.

Visitor Information

Be sure to stop in at the visitor center to view the slide show and exhibits, equip yourself with books and maps, pick up backcountry permits for backpacking and obtain information about weather conditions, guided hikes and special programs. Open 8 A.M.–4:30 P.M., with extended hours during the high season. Located just off US

Hwy. 191 on the park road. **Superintendent, Arches National Park, P.O. Box 907, Moab, UT 84532; 435-259-8161; www.nps.gov/arch.**

Outdoor Activities

Biking

Mountain biking is permitted within Arches National Park only on paved and jeep roads, but most of the potential routes in the park are sandy, washboarded or not as interesting and challenging as other routes outside the boundaries. One ride that can be taken by mountain bikers is into the **Klondike Bluffs area** along the 10.4-mile Willow Flat Rd. and the 10.8-mile Salt Valley four-wheel-drive road. The ride offers the option of a 0.4-mile hike to Tower Arch, and is approximately 21 miles one-way with a shuttle vehicle, or a 29-mile loop with about 8 miles of riding on the main park road. You can also ride the 18-mile paved road from the visitor center out to **Devils Garden** and back, but the usually heavy automobile traffic demands more attention to riding than enjoying the scenery.

Hiking

A booklet available at the visitor center, *Hiking Guide: Arches National Park,* has summaries and outline maps for 13 short hiking trails in the park. The hikes described below are listed in the order they are encountered when driving from the visitor center to the end of the park road.

Park Ave.

After you drive the switchbacks from the park entrance in Moab Canyon, you reach the Park Ave. area, about 2 miles from the visitor center, and the Park Ave. trailhead. Aptly named for New York City's skyscraper-lined Park Ave., the rows of sandstone slabs reaching 150–300 feet offer a southeastern Utah counterpart to human-made towers of steel and concrete. You can view Park Ave. from the viewpoint, about

100 yards from the parking area, or hike along the avenue—an easy downhill stroll just under 1 mile one-way. You will see the evocatively named Egyptian Queen, Sausage Rock, the Organ, the Three Gossips and the Tower of Babel. If you don't want to hike back, you can have someone drive your vehicle down to the other end of the trail at the park road. Don't walk back along the road. The zooming traffic and no shoulder make for potential accidents. Return via the trail.

Balanced Rock Trail

Located 6.3 miles from the Park Avenue trail-head, 9 miles from the visitor center, Balanced Rock is just before the turnoff to the Windows section of the park. It looks as if, at any minute, the 73-foot-high pedestal holding this huge 55-foot-tall boulder will give way and the rock will come crashing down, but this gravity-defying natural formation has stood like this for hundreds of years. You can examine the rock more closely on a short 0.3-mile-long trail that also offers views of the distant La Sal Mountains and the red rock and cliffs within the park.

Windows Section

Just past the turnoff to Balanced Rock, 9.2 miles from the visitor center, the 2.5-mile-long paved road leads to the Windows section. This section of the park offers four magnificent arches—Double Arch, Turret Arch and North and South Windows—grouped together and connected by a network of trails that make a loop a little more than 2.5 miles long. With such easy access, this is one of the most popular sections of the park.

Double Arch's two arches extend outward from each side, like jug handles, a nickname sometimes applied to them. The larger of the two arches spans 144 feet and is 112 feet high, while the smaller one is 61 feet wide and 86 feet high. Turret Arch is unique as one of the few arches that is taller, 65 feet high, than it is wide, 35 feet across. North Window is 48 feet high and 90 feet wide, with breathtaking vistas that capture the attention of photographers who try to frame the magnificent scenery within the window of the arch. Nearby South Window is

56 feet high and 115 feet wide. Plan a couple of hours to visit and examine these arches, and on hot days, carry drinking water with you and protect yourself from the sun.

Delicate Arch Trail

Ask most frequent visitors to Arches what is the one arch everyone should see, and more than 90 percent will probably respond, "Delicate Arch." The arch is famous throughout the world, which led to its being selected as the major design element in Utah's centennial license plate. The best way to view the arch is to make the 3-mile round-trip hike from Wolfe Ranch for a close-up look at the arch, then drive another mile to the viewpoint for a look at the arch in the perspective of the terrain, seen from the south looking north.

The turnoff to the Wolfe Ranch road is 11.7 miles from the visitor center; the trailhead is at 1.2 miles along this road. As you leave Wolfe Ranch, you cross Salt Wash on a suspension bridge—which, if you have children with you, automatically becomes something of a playground attraction. On the east side of Salt Wash, the trail crosses a greasewood flat, then climbs onto the sandstone. As you leave the bridge, keep a lookout for a short trail that branches to the left. Take time to hike this trail to see the Ute pictographs that depict riders on horseback, bighorn sheep and what look like two dogs. Returning to the main trail, you continue to climb toward the arch, making an elevation gain of 580 feet from the trailhead. The trail crosses the slickrock, and as it winds around the north side, the trail narrows as it crosses the steep north face and passes beneath the small Frame Arch.

As you crest the slickrock fin, even if you are forewarned, the view of Delicate Arch is an unforgettable experience. Like the forgotten toy of some ancient giant, the arch stands alone on the lip of slickrock above a canyon with the dark La Sal Mountains in the background. Anyone with a camera will automatically reach for it to try to capture one of the most picturesque sights in all of America's national parks. Compared with other arches in the park, Delicate Arch is not large, as it rises to 46 feet in height with a span of

32 feet between the abutments. But, symbolic of humans in this land, its small, tenuous yet persistent presence in a landscape so vast and rugged speaks sermons of the value of the individual.

Delicate Arch Viewpoint

Even after the 3-mile hike to and from Delicate Arch, you won't want to leave the beautiful site. For another perspective of the arch, take the Wolfe Ranch road, 11.7 miles from the visitor center, and follow the road east 2.2 miles to its end at to the Delicate Arch Viewpoint. The viewpoint also provides access for those who do not have the time or physical ability to hike to the arch. From the parking area, the viewpoint is located 0.4 mile to the north. The trail gains 200 feet in elevation and is mostly across slickrock, with a 200-foot drop into Winter Camp Wash beyond the end of the trail. If you have binoculars, carry them with you. Delicate Arch is about a half mile away.

Fiery Furnace

If you have ever had a nightmare about being trapped in a labyrinth with no way out, the Fiery Furnace is one way to make such a nightmare seem real. This section of the park is full of narrow passageways, blood-red sandstone fins and dead ends. Aptly named, it is easy to imagine that you are among gigantic coals of an enormous furnace. Even if you are an experienced hiker, it is best to join one of the ranger-guided hikes conducted twice daily during the summer. Reservations for these popular walks must be made at the visitor center no more than 48 hours in advance. Groups larger than nine people may request a special walk, but at least two weeks' lead time is required. Anyone entering the Fiery Furnace must have a permit or be on a ranger-led hike. These procedures have been instituted to help preserve the vegetation and cryptobiotic crust and to enhance the quality of experience for all visitors. Remember to stay on the trail. Violators are subject to fines. Check at the visitor center to confirm schedules and for additional information on the guided hikes.

The trailhead is located 3 miles north of the turnoff to Delicate Arch, 14 miles from the visitor center. In places, steps have been cut into the slickrock, just as the Anasazi did to provide access over steep sections. During the hike, you will visit Surprise Arch and Skull Arch, with its empty "eye sockets."

Sand Dune and Broken Arches

The trailhead for Sand Dune and Broken Arches is 2.4 miles north of the Fiery Furnace turnoff, about 16 miles from the visitor center. The trail to both arches is 1.2 miles round trip and is a nice stroll, compared with the slickrock climbing in the Fiery Furnace. The small, 30-foot-long, 8-foot-high Sand Dune Arch is located 200 yards off the trail to Broken Arch. Taking its name from a deep notch in the harder caprock on top of the arch, the 43-foot-high, 59-foot-wide Broken Arch is not really broken.

Skyline Arch

You can see Skyline Arch from Interstate 70, 10 miles to the north, if you know where to look. It is the only arch within the park visible from the highway. Inside the park, though, the arch is visible from the main road as well as the Devils Garden Campground, where the trailhead is located, at the end of the park road, 18 miles from the visitor center. It is only a 0.2-mile walk to the base of the sandstone fin in which the arch is located. The arch is 45 feet high and 69 feet wide. It expanded to its present size in 1940, when a large slab of stone fell from the top of the arch.

Devils Garden Trail

The Devils Garden Trail is the most popular trail in the park. The trailhead is located at the north end of the paved road, 18 miles from the visitor center. Most hikers make only the 1.6-mile round trip to the record-breaking span of Landscape Arch—the largest arch in the park, with a height of more than 100 feet and width of 306 feet. But you can see many other arches in the Devils Garden area, mostly on the way to or near Landscape Arch, including Pine Tree (46 feet high and 48 feet wide), Tunnel (22 feet high by 27 feet wide), Wall (68 feet high by

41 feet wide), Navajo (13 feet high and 41 feet wide), Partition (26 feet high and 28 feet wide) and Double O Arch (with two openings, one 45 feet high and 71 feet wide and the other 9 feet high and 21 feet wide). Double O Arch requires a 4-mile round-trip hike; to push on to the Dark Angel at the end of the trail is a 5.2-mile round-trip jaunt. With a 7-mile round-trip hike, you can visit all the arches and see a good part of the Devils Garden area. Plan most of the day if you undertake this hike and take plenty of water, some food and protection against the sun.

OFF-TRAIL HIKING AND BACKPACKING

While there are plenty of hiking opportunities along the established trails outlined above, if you want to get off the beaten paths for a day's cross-country hike or to backpack and camp in the remote sections of the park, the following are four good possibilities. Remember, backcountry permits, which can be obtained at the visitor center, are required for overnight stays. It is always a good idea to check in at the visitor center for information on trail conditions and weather forecasts. In summer, violent thunderstorms often cause flash floods that are extremely dangerous.

Lower Courthouse Wash

If you can arrange a shuttle, this interesting hike, a little more than 5 miles long, can be completed in a half day. Hikers can be dropped off at the bridge where the paved road crosses Courthouse Wash, 4.5 miles from the visitor center. Arrange a pickup where Courthouse Wash intersects with US Hwy. 191 outside of the park, just west of the bridge across the Colorado River. There is limited parking at the pullout inside the park, if you prefer to leave a vehicle there and start from outside the park. Watch out for flash floods in this section of the wash. The canyon walls grow higher and higher as you descend, and there are a number of side canyons worthy of exploration if you have the time. An excellent rock art panel is located along the northeastern side of the canyon wall, at the mouth of the wash. Unfortu-

nately, the panel was vandalized; attempts to repair it have been partially successful.

Lower Salt Wash to the Colorado River

Two major drainages of the Colorado River bisect Arches National Park: Courthouse Wash and Salt Wash. A hike down the lower portion of Salt Wash from Wolfe Ranch to the Colorado River is 13.4 miles round trip and takes you through one of the most remote sections of the park. There is no trail; hikers simply follow the wash. The canyon walls rise as much as 1,200 feet above the floor of the wash, and a series of salt springs gush from cracks in the rock. The upper section of the hike is through thickets of greasewood, sagebrush and rabbitbrush. Farther down the wash, boulders and rocks are the major obstacles. When you reach the Colorado River, you cannot cross the river to Hwy. 128, so turn around and go back the way you came. This hike can be excruciatingly hot during the summer and is more fatiguing than other hikes. Take plenty of water and plan for a full day to complete the hike.

Seeing and Doing

Historic Sites

Wolfe Ranch National Historic District

Listed in the National Register of Historic Places, the historic district includes the restored 1906 cabin that was the home of John Wesley Wolfe for four years. The cabin, nearby cellar and corrals offer an excellent example of what life was like on the Utah frontier well into the 20th century. The ranch road is located 11.7 miles north of the visitor center; take the road to the right 1.2 miles. The ranch also lies at the trailhead to Delicate Arch (see the Hiking section under Outdoor Activities).

Scenic Drives

At the visitor center you can purchase the booklet *Road Guide: Arches National Park*. This is an excellent guide to the scenic road that winds for 18 miles through the center of Arches National

Park from its entrance to the end of the paved road at Devils Garden. Most of the arches, scenic views and historic sites are readily accessible by auto or by a short hike from convenient parking areas. In addition to the trailheads described in the Hiking section under Outdoor Activities, below are other points of interest and their approximate mileages from the visitor center.

La Sal Mountains Viewpoint, 2.3 miles; Courthouse Towers Viewpoint, 3.4 miles; Petrified Dunes Viewpoint, 5.5 miles; Panorama Point, 10.3 miles; and Salt Valley Overlook, 14 miles.

Wildlife Viewing

There is a rich assortment of wildlife within Arches National Park, although many animals are nocturnal, seeking food and water at night to avoid the searing heat of summer days. The largest mammals are bighorn sheep, deer, coyotes (whose eerie howl can be heard at night) and bobcats. Smaller mammals, such as porcupines, cottontail rabbits, jackrabbits, gray foxes, mice and squirrels, form the diet of coyotes, which range widely throughout the park. Lizards and snakes that have adapted to an arid environment are common, with the midget faded rattlesnake the only poisonous snake found within the park. Bats and a good variety of birds can be seen, both resident and migratory. Some common species include piñon jays, canyon wrens, ravens, eagles, hawks and, along the Colorado River, waterfowl.

Where to Stay

There are no lodging facilities within the park, but you can find plenty of accommodations nearby (see the **Moab** chapter).

Camping

Devils Garden Campground is the only campground in the park. It has 52 sites for RVs and tents. Drinking water and flush toilets in season (water is turned off in winter); wheelchair-accessible facilities. Stays limited to seven days; fee is charged. Campsites fill up quickly, so arrive early at the visitor center to get a space. Open year-round. Located near the north end of the park road, about 18 miles from the visitor center. **Arches National Park, P.O. Box 907, Moab, UT 84532; 435-259-4351 reservations; 435-259-8161.**

Where to Eat

There are no dining facilities within the park, but you can find plenty of restaurants nearby (see the Moab chapter).

Services

Visitor Information

Arches National Park Visitor Center— Open 8 A.M.–4:30 P.M., with extended hours during the high season. Located just off US Hwy. 191 on the park road. **Arches National Park, P.O. Box 907, Moab, UT 84532; 435-259-8161; www.nps.gov/arch.**

Moab

For the traveler who seeks to enter the heaven of Utah's canyon country, Moab is the pearly gates. Although there is no St. Peter to admit or reject aspirants to this eternity of sandstone cliffs, roaring rivers and unbelievable scenery, everyone must pass through the gates of Moab in order to visit Arches and Canyonlands National Parks, to embark on a journey through Cataract Canyon of the Colorado River or to drive to the tops of the La Sal Mountains. It is no coincidence that the first European to enter Utah, Juan Maria Antonio de Rivera, found his way to what would become Moab and noted its strategic location.

Moab is situated on the southeast side of the Colorado River at the only easy crossing of the

Colorado River within the state of Utah. Moab provides access to the river for thousands of adventurers who want to experience the peace and beauty of drifting between enormous red sandstone cliffs and the thrill of shooting giant rapids. During the last two decades, Moab has also become a mecca for thousands of mountain bikers who come for the scenery and to ride over hundreds of miles of Navajo sandstone "slickrock," which poses the ultimate challenge to daredevil bikers.

Moab was named by an early Mormon settler, William Pierce. Just why he chose the name for the Biblical land that "lay beyond the Jordan" where Semitic relatives of the Hebrews dwelled is not clear. Perhaps it was a serious reference to its isolated desert location or perhaps a tongue-in-cheek expression for the region of southeastern Utah that others would refer to as the "backside of the Wasatch"—an area misunderstood, forgotten and not seen by those living along the "Wasatch Front." In any event, the name was not without controversy and in 1890 when Grand County was established and Moab designated the county seat, petitioners called for the hamlet's name to be changed to "Vina" to promote the area's agricultural potential. Moab, on the other hand, was "so unfavorably commemorative of the character of an incestuous and idolatrous community existing 1897 years before the Christian era … we want a name more appropriate, significant or expressive of moral decency and manly dignity, and in har-

mony with the progressive civilization of the present." The progressives did not win out. The name remained Moab and those loyal to the name Moab have perhaps been vindicated by the varied bumper stickers proclaiming the town's stature: "Paris, Rome, Tokyo, New York, Moab."

Moab is the gateway to two outstanding national parks. Accessible Arches National Park, located on a plateau just northwest of the Colorado River, is a wonderland of arches, windows, pinnacles, towers and other formations carved by wind, water and ice. Canyonlands National Park lies at the heart of the scenic Colorado Plateau and is one of the most rugged, isolated and sensational natural landscapes anywhere in the world. You can spend a lifetime exploring its three units, but you will never see it all. Looming above the Moab Valley, the 12,500-foot La Sal Mountains were named by 18th-century Spanish travelers in the region. These craggy, laccolithic giants with their dark interiors stand in sharp contrast to the fiery red sandstone rocks spread across the landscape.

This remarkable place has a radiance and intensity that bring awe, peace and a sense of belonging and oneness to the human spirit. Moab has tried to build a stable economy based on farming, ranching, gold, oil, uranium and potash, but while all of these endeavors have had their day, tourism has now taken over.

History

In 1765, the same year the British were imposing a Stamp Act on colonists on America's East Coast, Juan Maria Antonio de Rivera and his men reached and crossed the Colorado River at present-day Moab. Their expedition north from Abiquiu, New Mexico, made them the first recorded Euro-Americans to enter Utah. Rivera was familiar with the Indians of New Mexico and Arizona (who are descendants of the Anasazi) and was probably not surprised to see the vacant dwellings and rock art left by the Anasazi when they moved south during the 13th century to become part of the Pueblo Indians of New

Getting There

Moab is located 238 miles southeast of Salt Lake City. From Salt Lake City, take Interstate 15 south to Spanish Fork, Exit 256, and head southeast on US Hwy. 6 for 125 miles to its junction with Interstate 70 at Green River. Drive east for 22 miles on Interstate 70, then take Exit 180 at Crescent Junction and continue south on US Hwy. 191 for 30 miles to Moab.

Mexico and Arizona. Rivera encountered members of the Ute tribe, who entered the region from the north and east and may have been one of the factors leading the Anasazi to abandon their centuries-old home.

Rivera's 1765 mission was fivefold: to reconnoiter the land along the Indian trail north to the Colorado River and beyond; to learn more about the Indians who occupied the area; to determine their attitude toward the Spanish; to observe if the French had made contact with the Indians; and to search for precious metals. But the northern Spanish frontier was already overextended, even before the first California missions could be established in San Diego in 1769, and there was little action in the Moab area for the next 50 years.

Decades later, it was California that helped put the Colorado River crossing at Moab on the map, when the Old Spanish Trail was opened between Santa Fe and Los Angeles in 1830. It was necessary to come as far north as Moab and Green River to get around the impassable canyons of the Colorado River. The 1,100-mile trail was used chiefly by hundreds of New Mexican traders who found a ready market for woolen goods—serapes, rugs, blankets, bedspreads, yardage—in the California settlements. The traders returned to New Mexico with herds of as many as 1,000 horses and mules, which were marketed in New Mexico. The Spanish Trail was actually something of a transcontinental extension of the Santa Fe Trail, which opened in the 1820s, when the Southwest became Mexican Territory and trade with the United States was tolerated, if not encouraged.

In 1855 Mormon missionaries attempted to establish the first settlement at the Colorado River crossing. Known as the Elk Mountain Mission, 41 men traveled over a portion of the Spanish Trail from Sanpete Valley and constructed a rock fort, which they abandoned three months after their arrival, when Indian attacks destroyed the crops they planted and left three men dead.

Permanent settlers returned in 1878 to establish farms and ranches. They gave their new community the biblical name of Moab and looked forward to the arrival of the Denver and Rio Grande Railroad in 1881. The railroad link between Denver and Salt Lake City gave Moab access to the railroad 35 miles to the north at Thompson Springs. A ferry across the Colorado River was in operation by 1885, and the first bridge, a three-span steel bridge, was completed in 1912.

As early as 1906, the local newspaper, the Grand Valley Times, began promoting tourism around Moab; the designation of Arches National Monument in 1929 further promised to put Moab on the map. But it was uranium, not scenery, that led to the first invasion of Moab. Spurred on by government bounties, miners flooded into the area and staked claims in the uranium-rich Chinle Formation. Moab's population exploded from 1,275 in 1950 to 4,682 in 1960.

Since 1898, when Marie and Pierre Curie discovered radium in uranium ore, uranium had become one of the world's most sought-after substances. A decade later, medical researchers discovered radium as an effective treatment for cancer, and the race was truly on. For the first two decades of the 20th century, miners who had come to Utah in search of radioactive treasure in the crumbly hills could sell all of the ore they could get out of the ground. One of the first was Howard Balsley, born in Connellsville, Pennsylvania, in 1886, who arrived in Moab on his birthday, December 7, 1908, and pioneered early uranium mining around Moab. In 1922 Madame Curie was presented with a gram of radium that had been extracted from Howard Balsley's mines.

As time wore on, Balsley became the only buyer of uranium ore in southeastern Utah. But with World War II and the creation of the Manhattan Project, which ushered in the atomic era with the dropping of the atomic bombs on Hiroshima and Nagasaki, Japan, the U.S. government established a monopoly for the purchase of uranium ore. In the early 1950s, with the outbreak of the Cold War, the government was again anxious to have a substantial supply of uranium and set the minimum price for uranium ore for a 10-year period, offering a $10,000 bonus to anyone opening up new uranium mines.

One man, Charles A. Steen, emerged as the epitome of the rags-to-riches story on the Colorado Plateau. An unemployed geologist from Texas, living with his wife and four small boys in a small trailer attached to an 8-by-16-foot shack, Steen in July 1952 located the largest deposit of high-grade uranium ore in the United States. His Mi Vida Mine, located south of Moab, made him an instant multimillionaire and brought an even greater number of prospectors and speculators to Moab—each convinced he or she would duplicate, if not surpass, Steen's good fortune.

The aftermath of World War II had a significant impact on tourism in Moab. The surplus rubber rafts proved ideal for running the Colorado River, providing access to the river for thousands, and the uranium boom and oil boom left a network of trails and traces that now serve four-wheel-drive vehicles and mountain bikers. The economic opportunities also introduced many people to the remarkable scenery and convinced them that significant portions of this pristine environment should be preserved. A new environmental ethic and leadership by key individuals led to the creation of Canyonlands National Park in 1964.

While tourism has continued to expand since the 1960s with an ever-increasing number of motels, restaurants and facilities to enhance the visitor's experience, the population of remote Moab has not grown like that of places like Kanab and St. George. The closing of the uranium-processing plant has stressed the local economy. In 1980 Moab's population reached a high of 5,333, but by 1990 it had dropped to 3,971, only to more than double to more than 8,000 by 2000. The future looks bright for Moab. It is a community that appreciates the rich scenic resources that abound and a quality of life that deserves preservation.

Major Attractions

Dead Horse Point State Park

There are a number of places to view the scenery of southeastern Utah and the workings of the Colorado River, but perhaps not even the Grand Canyon surpasses Dead Horse Point in beauty and awe. Far below you, the Colorado River makes a deep hairpin as it cuts its way through 150 million years of geologic history. To the east, the skyscraping La Sal Mountains hulk over the landscape, and the forces of time and divinity seem to come together to inspire the onlooker, reminding us that our lives are but a small part of the grand scheme of things.

Dead Horse Point is a sheer-walled, narrow mesa poised above the hundreds of miles of canyon country that make up Canyonlands National Park. Access to the mesa is by way of a narrow neck only 30 yards wide. According to local legend, in the late 1800s cowboys constructed a fence across this narrow neck of land to corral wild horses. They roped the best of these wild horses and broke them for their own use. The others were left on the mesa, and either because the fence was left up and they could not get out or they simply could not find their way out, those left behind on the waterless mesa died of thirst and exhaustion or in a futile attempt to reach the waters of the Colorado far below. Their bleached bones gave the mesa its name.

Dead Horse Point State Park was established in 1959 and today covers 5,082 acres. Hang-gliders have found the sheer cliffs to be an ideal spot to perform their heart-stopping hobby. If you are lucky, there will be some of these daredevils taking that one step off the solid sandstone to the bench more than 1,000 feet below.

The park has a **visitor center,** a paved 1.5-mile-long walking trail leading to the point, as well as 7 miles of additional **hiking** trails. There is a picnic area for day use. The **campground** has 21 fully developed sites, which can be reserved in advance. The units have electrical hookups, water, grills, tables and benches and tent pads. These are available early Apr.–late Oct.; winter camping is allowed, but water and electricity are turned off, so come prepared.

Located on the way to the Island in the Sky District of Canyonlands National Park. Take US Hwy. 191 north from Moab for 11 miles to its junction with Hwy. 313, then follow the state highway west, then south for 23 miles to the state park. From Crescent Junction (Exit 180) off Interstate 70, it is 21 miles to the junction with Hwy. 313. The Dead Horse Point State Park Visitor Center is open mid-May–mid-Sept. daily 8 A.M.–6 P.M.; the rest of the year daily 8 A.M.–5 P.M. **Dead Horse Point State Park, P.O. Box 609, Moab, UT 84532; 1-800-322-3770 reservations; 435-259-2614; parks. state.ut.us/parks/www1/dead.htm.**

Festivals and Events

Easter Jeep Safari

week of Easter ending Easter Sun. This traditional Easter outing began in 1966 and attracts four-wheel-drive fans from throughout the West. The Red Rock 4-Wheelers, a Moab ORV club, organizes several events and rides. More than 1,500 vehicles and as many as 28 different trails, ranging from relatively easy and safe trails to those reserved for daredevil jeepers who have no fear for their own safety or concern for damage to their vehicles, are used during this weeklong event. **435-259-7625.**

Moab Arts Festival

last weekend in May. More than 100 artists from throughout the West display their crafts, photography, pottery and paintings. There's also live music and plenty of food. Held at the Moab City Park. **435-259-2742.**

Moab Music Festival

mid-Sept. Chamber music under the 500-foot cliffs that rim the Colorado River is the special attraction of this music festival, which began in 1993. Concertgoers are transported to a magical spot on the Colorado River by jet boats, where they enjoy the exquisite music of the old-world masters in a beautifully inspiring new-world wilderness setting. Performances are also held in Star Hall, and there is a family picnic concert in the Moab City Park. The festival is held over a 10-day period. **Moab Music Fes-**

tival, **P.O. Box 698, Moab, UT 84532; 435-259-8431.**

Moab Fat Tire Festival

mid-Oct. Moabites maintain that this is the best-known mountain bike event in the country. The weeklong events include a Halloween bash, guided group rides, hill climbs, time trials and a variety of programs and activities on desert ecology, archaeology and climbing. **435-375-3231.**

Moab Film and Video Festival

early Nov. If you happen to be in Moab during this three-day film festival, which began in 1996, you will find it a unique and memorable activity. The films are mostly short, independent films, and the festival has aspirations to become a small-scale Telluride film festival. Most of the films deal with Western/Southwestern topics and many focus on environmental issues. Films are shown in the evening. Tickets can be purchased at the door—at the historic Star Hall—or in advance at Back of Beyond Books (see the Shopping section under Seeing and Doing). **www.moab-Utah.com/film.**

Outdoor Activities

Biking

The 1950s brought the uranium boom to Moab, but the 1980s brought the "biker boom." Thirty years after Charlie Steen opened his Mi Vida Mine, two brothers, ex-uranium miners, opened their Rim Cyclery bike shop and began promoting off-road bicycling in the nearby slickrock. Their "discovery" of the unusual—and in many ways ideal—biking terrain has made Moab the mecca of the mountain biking world.

Why do they come? The scenery, the camaraderie with other bikers, the free and open spaces, but above all, the miles and miles of smooth slickrock. The huge expanse of rugged, rolling Navajo sandstone, which millions of years ago was laid down when ancient sand dunes hardened into stone, offers excellent traction despite its name.

Because of the isolated nature of the trails and the distances involved, leave word with someone about where you are going and when you expect to return, and carry food and extra water. In hiking, biking and traveling throughout the area, it is essential to be responsible for your own safety and well-being. If you are not familiar with the area, it is easy to become lost, and even if you do know your way around, equipment problems and other factors can affect your ride. The local search and rescue team has had plenty of experience rescuing lost and stranded bikers, especially tourists, and they do charge the rescuee if they are called out. Be sure to wear your helmet at all times when riding.

The Moab Information Center has a free brochure, published by the Moab Area Travel Council, called *Moab Area Mountain Bike Trails*, which describes some of the most popular bike trails within a 15-mile radius of Moab.

Hurrah Pass Trail

This is a convenient daylong loop ride that begins from the junction of Kane Creek Blvd. and US Hwy. 191 in Moab. The round-trip ride is 33 miles, most of it along a paved road and graded dirt trail. If you want to get off the slickrock for a while, or if you want to get acquainted with the terrain and scenery before you tackle the slickrock, this is a good ride. The 600-foot climb up to Hurrah Pass will test your legs and get your heart rate up. The ride offers views of the Colorado River and spectacular scenery in Kane Creek and Hunter Canyons. You won't mind retracing your route later in the day, when the changing light and different perspective offer an entirely new view.

Kane Creek Canyon Rim / Pritchett Canyon Rd.

More difficult and not as convenient as the Hurrah Pass Trail, this trail is a favorite of many riders because it takes you to the magnificent Behind the Rocks area and to several large natural arches. It begins 12.5 miles south of Moab on US Hwy. 191 and heads west before turning northwest to its terminus at Kane Creek Rd. The distance is 20.3 miles, but since the road is much rougher than the Hurrah Pass Trail, the going is slower. You should plan a day for this ride. You can add another 4.5 miles by continuing along the paved Kane Creek Rd. up the Colorado River and back to Moab. This route crosses private land and the landowners have begun to charge a small fee—usually $1—to cross their land.

Kokopelli Trail

For a multi-day ride, consider the 140-mile-long Kokopelli Trail from Moab to Grand Junction, Colorado. The trail, opened in 1989, is named for the humpbacked flute player deity common to the Native Americans of the Colorado Plateau and found depicted in the area's rock art. Perhaps the most challenging part of the trail is the 4,500-vertical-foot climb over the La Sal Mountains. Bikers must carry their own water, and the ride is recommended for only experienced, well-prepared bikers. For more information about the trail, contact the **Bureau of Land Management, Moab Office, 82 E. Dogwood, Moab, UT 84532; 435-259-6111.**

Moab Slickrock Bike Trail

Laid out by motorbikers in 1969, the Moab Slickrock Bike Trail has been taken over by mountain bikers, although motorcycles and motorbikes are still allowed on the trail. The 10.3-mile loop demands good biking skills to handle the ups and downs across the slickrock and the sand, and to stay out of the microbiotic soil or crust, which unfortunately has been highly impacted by bikers. Please be on the lookout for these dark, "sugary" patches of new soil. Once disturbed, they will not recover for decades. If you are not sure about your biking skills, you will want to take the 2.3-mile "practice loop," which, though not as difficult as the main loop, does offer a good introduction as to what to expect. Grand views beckon, but remember you are on top of the cliffs and it is a long fall into Negro Bill Canyon or into the main canyon of the Colorado River. Both loops are outlined on a detailed map available from the Bureau of Land Management, although the trail can be clearly followed by the white dashes painted across the slickrock. Plan 5–6 hours for your first trip over the loop. The trail begins on Sand Flats Rd., 2.3 miles from the BLM office. To reach the trail from Moab, head east on 300 S. to 400 E.. Turn south and continue to Mill Creek Dr., where you turn left and follow the road, staying to the left as you reach Sand Flats Rd. and the Grand Resource Area BLM Office. Continue on Sand Flats Rd. beyond the pavement until you reach the trailhead.

Monitor and Merrimac Trail

For a good introduction to mountain biking, consider this 13.2-mile-long trail through canyons and washes, to buttes and towers, and with an optional short hike to dinosaur fossils. To reach the trailhead, drive north on US Hwy. 191, 14.8 miles from the Moab Visitor Center, and turn left onto a dirt road that crosses the railroad track just before a railroad bridge. Stay on the dirt road for 0.6 mile to an intersection, where the trail begins. It starts with a 2.2-mile ride through open desert, then follows the bottom of a wash for 0.6 mile before climbing out and continuing up Tusher Canyon for another 1.2 miles. Here, the trail follows the left branch of the wash through a gap in the wall dividing the Tusher and Mill Canyon drainages. You reach a jeep road, which you take to Determination Towers.

Just past the towers, cross a large, flat slickrock area, with some sections of sand, for 1.2 miles to the base of Merrimac Butte. Passing to the left of Merrimac, you head south across the slickrock toward the smaller Monitor Butte. From Monitor, the trail returns down Mill Canyon. At the lower end of the canyon you come to a gate. About 0.2 mile from the gate, and less than 2 miles from your vehicle, a spur road leads to the Mill Canyon Dinosaur Trail, where many dinosaur fossils can be seen. Leave your bike at the trailhead and, after you walk the dinosaur trail, you can continue on the road north to the parking area.

Rentals and Guides

For those interested in mountain-biking guided tours, join one of the bicycle tours offered by the companies listed below. They provide all the equipment you need, support vehicles and an experienced guide. These tours range from one to several days. Be sure to make arrangements with the tours well in advance.

Adrift Adventures—378 N. Main, P.O. Box 577, Moab, UT 84532; 1-800-874-4483; 435-259-8594.

Kaibab Tours/Moab Cyclery—391 S. Main, P.O. Box 339, Moab, UT 84532; 1-800-451-1133; 435-259-7432.

Nichols Expeditions—497 N. Main, Moab, UT 84532; 1-800-635-1792; 435-259-7882.

Rim Tours—94 W. 100 N., Moab, UT 84532; 1-800-626-7335; 435-259-5223.

Tag-a-Long Expeditions—452 N. Main, Moab, UT 84532; 1-800-453-3292; 435-259-8946.

Western Spirit Cycling—38 S. 100 W., P.O. Box 411, Moab, UT 84532; 1-800-845-BIKE (2453); 435-259-8732.

Canoeing

Canoeing offers a great opportunity for an inexpensive way to enjoy the calm sections of the Colorado River above and below Moab. Through the section of the Colorado River just south of the Colorado River bridge, and for 30 miles beyond, the river is placid and easy to negotiate even for inexperienced canoeists. The river is administered by either the BLM or the National Park Service. Before embarking on any river trip, visit the **Moab Information Center** (located at Main and Center Sts. in Moab) for information.

You can rent canoes, paddles and life jackets from a number of companies located in Moab. Some companies (see the River Rafting section) provide shuttles to and from your starting point and final destination. Do keep your life jacket on at all times, because if you get into the water, the swift undercurrents can be very dangerous. Do let someone know where you are going and when you plan to return.

Four-Wheel-Drive Trips

There are thousands of miles of jeep trails around Moab, most of which were established by prospectors looking for uranium, gold and oil. Avid local jeepers have devoted years and worn out vehicle after vehicle and still cannot claim to have covered every mile of four-wheel terrain in the area. Although hikers and old-time cowboys might argue, many believe there is no better way to see the canyons, deserts and mountains of southeastern Utah than with a four-wheel-drive outfit.

The jeep made its appearance after World War II, when thousands were sold for surplus. In the Moab area, they proved as essential to the 1950s uranium boom as the Geiger counter and penny uranium stock. Unless you have your own four-wheel-drive vehicle and have some experience driving in sand and across slickrock, your best bet is to sign up for one of the half-day or full-day tours offered by one of the companies listed below. (Longer tours can be arranged.) If you go on your own, it is always best to travel with at least one other vehicle, carry plenty of water, food, topographical maps, shovels and tow rope or cable or preferably a winch and let someone know where you are going. As one old-time jeeper said, "Expect to get stuck or broke down and prepare accordingly."

The Moab Area Travel Council publishes a free brochure, *Moab Area Jeep Trails,* which lists five trails that can be completed in a half day. These are good introductions to the jeeping possibilities in the area and show off some of the region's most beautiful canyons, mesas and vistas. Don't forget to take plenty of film for your camera. Most of the five trails are on public lands and range from 15 to 54 miles in length. They include the Gemini Bridges Trail and the Monitor and Merrimac Trail (see the Biking section for these two trails), the Poison Spider Mesa Trail, the Chicken Corners Trail and the Moab Rim Trail.

Guides

Adrift Adventures—378 N. Main, P.O. Box 577, Moab, UT 84532; 1-800-874-4483; 435-259-8594.

Canyonlands Tours—543-T N. Main, Moab, UT 84532; 1-800-342-5938; 435-259-5865.

Farabee Adventures, Inc.—83 S. Main St., Moab, UT 84532; 1-800-806-5337; 435-259-7494.

Lin Ottinger Tours—600 N. Main, Moab, UT 84532; 435-259-7312.

Tag-A-Long Expeditions—452 N. Main, Moab, UT 84532; 1-800-453-3292; 435-259-8946.

Golf

Moab Golf Course

A few years ago this golf course was expanded from 9 to 18 holes, changing this from a good rural Utah course to one of the most beautiful and fun courses in the state for the average golfer. Expert golfers who play the gold tees will find some challenging holes, but as a rule this course is user-friendly. The fairways, with one or two exceptions, are wide and without any major obstacles. The fairways tend to be hard, giving extra yards with generous bounces. The greens are usually fast and sloping, making putting perhaps the hardest part of the game on this course. Located in Spanish Valley. Follow US Hwy. 191 south out of Moab for about 3 miles to Spanish Trail Rd. Turn left and head east for a mile, passing through a four-way stop and down, then up a gully. At the top of the hill, turn right and follow the road into the golf course parking area. **2705 E. Bench Rd; 435-259-6488.**

Hiking

The Moab Area Travel Council publishes a free brochure, *Moab Area Hiking Trails,* which describes eight short to moderate hikes within a 15-mile radius of Moab.

Millcreek Pkwy.

This recently completed paved parkway that follows Millcreek for about 1.5 miles through Moab is a welcome respite from the red rock and sand of the desert. It is truly an oasis: the small stream provides ample water for the monumental cottonwood trees that grace its banks. The operative words here are "green," "cool" and "shade." It is amazing how much this parkway adds to the charm and appeal of Moab. The Dan O'Laurie Museum has placed old farm and mining machinery at locations along the trail, which passes by some of Moab's historic orchards. There are plans to extend the parkway.

For now, you can reach the trail at several locations, including Main St. where Millcreek flows under US Hwy. 191 at approximately 150 S. between the Greenwell Motel and Ramada Inn; near the Grand County High School at **400 E. Mullberry Ln.** (approximately 550 S.); or at its eastern terminus at Rotary Park located south of the Red Rock Elementary School at approximately **650 E. Millcreek Dr.**

HWY. 279

Hwy. 279 intersects US Hwy. 191 just northwest of the Colorado River bridge and follows the west bank of the Colorado River in a southerly direction.

Corona Arch Trail

Located 10 miles southwest of the junction of Hwy. 279 and US Hwy. 191, the Corona Arch Trail takes you to the 140-by-105-foot opening of the Corona Arch and the adjacent Bow Tie Arch. The 1.5-mile hike begins from the parking lot on the north side of the highway, crosses the railroad tracks and follows an old road through a gap in the rim before it turns onto the slickrock. Rock cairns mark the way across the slickrock to the base of the cliff, where safety cables have been installed, steps cut into the slickrock and a ladder placed to take you up over a short ledge. Corona Arch is visible from this point.

Portal Overlook Trail

This 1.5-mile-long trail, human-made except for the sections across slickrock, follows a series of switchbacks as it climbs above the Colorado River for a breathtaking view of the Moab Valley, the La Sal Mountains and the South Portal. The trail begins 3.7 miles southwest of the junction of Hwy. 279 and US Hwy. 191. Watch for the

parking area on the east side of the road. Since much of the trail is shaded by higher cliffs in the late summer afternoons, this is a good time to make the hike.

HWY. 128

This road follows the east side of the Colorado River from US Hwy. 191 just before the Colorado River bridge north of Moab.

Negro Bill Canyon Trail

Named for William Granstaff, an African-American prospector, Indian trader and cattleman who ran his cattle in the canyon in the late 1870s, Negro Bill Canyon is located 3 miles upriver from the junction of Hwy. 128 and US Hwy. 191. Some efforts have been made to rename this canyon because of a perceived derogatory stigma associated with the name. One proposal is that it be called "Brother Bill Canyon." Others recognize the word "Negro" as antiquated but not derogatory, recalling that it was used in a positive way by Martin Luther King Jr. and other civil rights leaders during the 1950s and 1960s. Ronald Coleman, an African-American professor of history at the University of Utah, argues to keep the name because it is one of the few Utah place names that clearly recognizes the contributions of Utah's African-American pioneers.

Under whatever name, the hiking trail climbs 1.5 miles up the canyon along an old road and the stream bottom. For the last 0.5 mile, the trail crosses the stream and goes along a maintained trail up a side canyon. At the end of the canyon is Morning Glory Natural Bridge, which, unlike the arches in the region, was formed by a stream. The 243-foot-long bridge is the sixth longest natural rock span in the United States. The picturesque setting at the end of a canyon above a spring and small pool makes this a popular hike.

US HWY. 191
Hidden Valley Trail

This is a constructed trail 2 miles long. It follows a series of steep switchbacks as it heads north into Hidden Valley, providing an excellent view of the Moab Valley and the large sandstone fins of the Behind the Rocks area. To reach the trailhead, follow US Hwy. 191 south of Moab for 3 miles and turn right onto Angel Rock Rd. After two blocks, turn right onto Rimrock Rd. and stay on it until you reach the parking area. This is another trail that is shaded by the high cliffs in the late afternoon.

Hunters Canyon

Kane Creek Canyon Rd. also provides access to the Hunters Canyon trailhead, 7.5 miles west of its intersection with US Hwy. 191 in Moab. From the parking area, the trail follows the canyon bottom for 3 miles, past cottonwood trees and along the intermittent spring, and eventually becomes blocked by brush. Just 0.5 mile above the trailhead, on the right is a large arch.

Mill Canyon Dinosaur Trail

This newly developed trail is an exciting experiment in trust. With no guards or rangers looking over their shoulders, visitors have a unique opportunity to view exposed dinosaur bones at several locations along the trail, which heads south down the west side of Mill Canyon. Pick up a free Bureau of Land Management brochure that identifies 15 sites along the trail where you can see the remains of the camarasaurus, the allosaurus and other unidentified dinosaurs, as well as other forms of life that date back millions of years. On the east side of the canyon are the remains of an old copper mill that dates back to the late 1800s. The trailhead is located 15 miles north of Moab off US Hwy. 191. Turn left at an intersection just north of mile marker 141. Cross the railroad tracks and continue on the graded dirt road for 2 miles to the trailhead.

River Rafting

No one should visit Moab without spending some time on the Colorado River. Just knowing that you are floating down one of America's most historic rivers is part of the attraction—and the unbelievable desert scenery is the other. The float on a silt-laden, chocolate-colored river,

with the anticipation of something new around every bend; the omnipresent red-rock cliffs; and blue-and-white La Sal Mountains in the distance offer an experience of a lifetime.

River-running companies operating out of Moab offer everything from a half-day calmwater float above the confluence of the Colorado and Green Rivers to a five-day Cataract Canyon trip that begins calmly in the northern section of Canyonlands National Park, then continues beyond the confluence of the rivers into the funneled white water so aptly named by Maj. John Wesley Powell. Cataract Canyon, which links Canyonlands National Park with Glen Canyon National Recreation Area at Lake Powell, has 26 rapids, some of which are the most thrilling (and dangerous) of any in the United States. Half-day tours are available, as well as three-, four- and five-day trips. Reservations are advised and necessary for the longer trips. Depending on your time, money and desire for thrills, one of the following Moab-based river-running companies can provide boats, guides and all you need for what should be the adventure of a lifetime. (See Guides below.) If you want to put together a do-it-yourself trip with rented equipment and rafts, they are available from those companies indicated with an asterisk (*). Permits are required for many sections of the river, so check with the rental companies, Canyonlands National Park Headquarters or the Moab Information Center about specific areas you plan to float.

Recommended Gear and Clothing for the River—The combination of sun, water and bare rock demands extra precautions. Dress comfortably in clothing that will protect you from the sun and that you can get wet. Everyone going on the river should have a broad-brimmed hat; high-SPF sunscreen; lip balm (preferably an SPF type); good sunglasses that can be secured with a strap; river sandals—or a pair of old tennis or jogging shoes (the older, the better since you may want to throw them away after your trip); a swimsuit; a T-shirt; lightweight nylon shorts; a lightweight, long-sleeved cotton shirt; long pants; and a windbreaker. Waterproof boxes (often called ammo cans) are provided by commercial river-runners for cameras, but if you are any kind of a camera bug, you will want your camera in hand as you make the trip, so bring plenty of film and plan to protect your camera from the water. For anything longer than a day trip, consult with the outfitter for a list of items you should bring or plan to rent.

There are four major areas for river running out of Moab (five if you include the Green River—see the **Green River** chapter). Most rafting companies offer tours for all four areas.

Cataract Canyon

When river-runners think of the Colorado River, they think of two sections: through the Grand Canyon and through Cataract Canyon. John Wesley Powell and his historic 1869 expedition started down Cataract Canyon on July 24, 1869, and he recorded:

> Large rocks have fallen from the walls— great, angular blocks, which have rolled down the talus and are strewn along the channel. ... Among these rocks, in chutes, whirlpools, and great waves, with rushing breakers and foam, the water finds its way, still tumbling down ... a chute of water strikes the foot of a great block of limestone 50 feet high, and the waters pile up against it and roll back. Where there are sunken rocks the water heaps up in mounds, or even in cones. At a point where rocks come very near the surface, the water forms a chute above, strikes, and is shot up 10 or 15 feet, and piles back in gentle curves, as in a fountain; and on the river tumbles and rolls.

Cataract Canyon usually is a three- to five-day outing, as the complete run covers 112 miles down the Colorado from Moab to Hite at the north end of Lake Powell. Cataract Canyon itself stretches about 20 miles below the confluence of the Green and Colorado Rivers, and the canyon contains 28 sets of rapids, some of which reach Class V status. Most commercial tour companies use motorized rafts to plow through the calm waters down to the rapids, and there are companies that offer a one-day Cataract Canyon tour. If you have always wanted to ride one of the most exciting and treacherous sections of the Colorado River, here is your chance.

Dolores River

The Dolores River flows west from Colorado into Utah, and its confluence with the Colorado River is a few miles above Fisher Towers. Often the 30-mile-long run is possible only during the spring runoff, as low water levels in the summer and fall make navigation impossible. When you can ride the Dolores, there are rapids up to Class IV status.

Fisher Towers

This is the closest and easiest section of the Colorado River, so it is the location for most day or half-day trips on the river and is often called the "Colorado River Daily." The 13-mile stretch begins at Hittle Bottom and ends at Takeout Beach, following Hwy. 128 as it winds along the Colorado River northeast of Moab, just east of Arches National Park. There are a few rapids along this stretch of the river, but nothing like those found in Westwater Canyon or Cataract Canyon. This is a section of the river that even the most timid rafters can enjoy.

Westwater Canyon

This 17-mile stretch of the Colorado River begins at Westwater Ranger Station near the Colorado border and ends at the Cisco Landing northeast of Moab, or you can continue downriver to Fisher Towers and on to Takeout Beach. The Westwater run has a number of Class IV rapids that will give you plenty of thrills. The trip can be made in one full day or two days at a more leisurely pace.

Guides

Adrift Adventures—378 N. Main, P.O. Box 577, Moab, UT 84532; 1-800-874-4483; 435-259-8594.*

Canyonlands by Night and Day (calm water only)—**1861 N. US Hwy. 191, P.O. Box 328, Moab, UT 84532; 1-800-394-9978; 435-259-5261.**

Canyon Voyages—352 N. Main, P.O. Box 416, Moab, UT 84532; 1-800-488-5884; 435-259-6007.*

The Moab Rafting Company—P.O. Box 435, Moab, UT 84532; 1-800-RIO-MOAB (6622); 435-259-RAFT.

Navtec Expeditions—321 N. Main, Moab, UT 84532; 1-800-833-1278; 435-259-7983.

Nichols Expeditions—497 N. Main, Moab, UT 84532; 1-800-635-1792; 435-259-7882.

North American River Expeditions—543 N. Main, Moab, UT 84532; 1-800-346-6277; 435-259-5865.

Sheri Griffith River Expeditions—2231 S. US Hwy. 191, P.O. Box 1324, Moab, UT 84532; 1-800-332-2439; 435-259-8229.

Tag-a-Long Expeditions—452 N. Main, Moab, UT 84532; 1-800-453-3292; 435-259-8946.*

Tex's Riverways (calm water only)—P.O. Box 67, Moab, UT 84532; 435-259-5101.

Western River Expeditions—1371 N. Main, Moab, UT 84532; 1-800-453-7450; 435-259-7019.

World Wide River Expeditions—625 Riversands, Moab, UT 84532; 1-800-231-2769; 435-259-7515.

Rock Climbing

I have seen them in person on occasion: rock climbers looking even smaller than ants crawling up a door. Several years ago, all of America saw two climbers in a Coca Cola television commercial standing on a desktop-size area 1,000 feet above the valley floor on top of one of the hundreds of sandstone pinnacles near Moab. Centuries of erosion have created pinnacles, towers and cliffs that lure climbers from all over the world. For expert climbers, there are enough challenges in Castle Valley, the Fisher Towers, along the Colorado River Valley and Indian Creek, and within Arches and Canyonlands National Parks that even the most dedicated of climbers could never master all of them in a lifetime.

In contrast to the hard granite faces that most mountain climbers encounter, the soft sedimentary sandstone presents a unique set of difficulties for the climbers who come to Moab each year to test themselves on Castleton Tower, Sister Superior, Moses, Titan, Lighthouse Tower, Monster Tower, Mystery Towers, Sharks Fin or one of any number of unique formations that the millennia have left scattered throughout southeastern Utah.

If you are interested in climbing or in finding out where people may be climbing, check with the Moab Information Center (see the Services section).

Swimming

Butch Cassidy King World Waterpark

This outdoor park has three giant slides, two kiddie slides, three pools, a lounging area, paddle boats, picnic areas, the famous "King World" rock sculpture and concessions. Open during the summer Mon.–Sat. 10 A.M.–10 P.M., Sun. 12:30–10 P.M. Admission fee charged. **1500 N. US Hwy. 191; 435-259-2837.**

Moab Swim Center

This outdoor swimming pool is open during the summer for lap swimming daily 12:15–1:15 P.M.; open swimming daily 1:30–5:30 P.M.; and for night swimming Mon.–Sat. 6:30–9 P.M. Admission fee charged. **181 W. 400 N.; 435-259-8226.**

Tennis

Public tennis courts are located at the **Grand County High School, 608 S. 400 E.**

Seeing and Doing

Historic Sites

Moab Walking Tour

The Moab Area Travel Council and Dan O'Laurie Museum have prepared a free walking-tour brochure of 23 sites and buildings in the Moab area. The oldest building in town is the **Balsley**

Log Cabin, constructed in 1881 and located next to the Daughters of Utah Pioneers Museum off Center St. Other buildings include the **1888 LDS church; Star Hall,** built as a recreational hall in 1898; the **1892 courthouse and jail;** and several business buildings and homes constructed around the turn of the 20th century. The brochure is available at the **Dan O'Laurie Museum** (see below) and the **Moab Information Center** (see the Services section).

Museums

Dan O'Laurie Canyon Country Museum
Devoted to the prehistory and history of the Moab area, the Dan O'Laurie Canyon Country Museum has exhibits on geology, natural history, prehistory, the historic Old Spanish Trail, ranching, farming, early transportation and the 1950s uranium boom. One of the recent acquisitions was found by three Moab teenagers: a cone-shaped, 2.5-foot-tall Anasazi burden basket that dates from around the time of Christ. Upstairs, an art gallery features exhibits by local artists. The museum is named for an early supporter who came to Moab with the uranium boom of the early 1950s. Since 1989, the museum has published Canyon Legacy, a quarterly journal that contains excellent articles on the history of the area. You can purchase copies of Canyon Legacy and local books in the museum store; you can also obtain a free copy of the *Moab Area Historic Walking Tour* brochure. Open Mon.– Sat. 1–5 P.M. and 7–9 P.M. Admission is free, but donations are accepted. **118 E. Center; 435-259-7985.**

Nightlife

Bar M Chuckwagon
With an emphasis on food and entertainment, the Bar M is a fun-filled and inexpensive way to enjoy the evening. There are no waiters here, but after you go through the line in chuck-wagon fashion, you sit down at picnic tables to enjoy the barbecued chicken or roast beef, baked potato, baked beans, applesauce, buttermilk bis-

cuits with butter and honey and cake, plus coffee, iced tea or lemonade. A vegetarian meal is also available with advance notice.

The grounds open at 6 P.M. and feature a gift shop housed in a 140-year-old cabin, a saloon that offers beer and soft drinks, an Indian tepee, an old covered wagon, old farm implements and games like horseshoes, rope-the-steer and more. The action begins at 7 P.M. with Old West gunfight reenactments. At 7:25 Cookie rings the dinner bell and brings everyone under the "covered wagon" tent top for dinner. Following dinner the tent top opens up to let in the sky, the stage drops down and the Bar M Wrangles begin. Old cowboy songs and ranch-style humor make up the hour-long show, with a Native American dance usually featured. Open Apr.–Sept. with dinner served Mon.–Sat. at 7:30 P.M. Reservations are recommended. Located on US Hwy. 191, 7 miles north of Moab. **435-259-2276.**

Scenic Drives

Colorado River Scenic Byway/Hwy. 128
The Colorado River is known worldwide for its unsurpassed scenery. Hwy. 128 provides the only opportunity for motorists to drive along sections of the Colorado River that have not been tamed by dams. Except for the crossing at Moab and the Dewey Bridge crossing along this Scenic Byway, there are only two other points in Utah where automobiles can cross the main channel of the Colorado River along its more than 200-mile course through Utah. These are at the Hite Crossing Bridge on Hwy. 96 and via Hall's Crossing Ferry on Hwy. 276.

Hwy. 128 begins on the eastern side of the Colorado River, where US Hwy. 191 crosses the river just west of Moab. It continues up the Colorado in a northeasterly direction for about 35 miles, before it crosses next to what was the Dewey Bridge. A new bridge was constructed in 1986. The historic, one-lane suspension bridge that served for 70 years as the only bridge across the river between Moab and Grand Junction, Colorado, has been listed in the

National Register of Historic Places and preserved as a pedestrian bridge. The drive concludes at Cisco, 44 miles from Moab. Unless you need to continue east or west along Interstate 70, follow the same route back to Moab.

The view and vistas are completely different coming back down the river than they are going up. The contrast between the brown-green waters of the Colorado, the red sandstone cliffs and carved formations along the river, the snow-capped La Sal Mountains and the deep blue sky makes this a photographer's dream. Also take a few minutes to watch the rafts coming down the river. There is something to be said for watching boatloads of people floating by, completely relaxed and without a care in the world, except, perhaps, a water bucket attack from friends or strangers on a nearby boat. The drive also provides opportunities to view waterfowl, herons, egrets and, during the winter, bald eagles roosting in the cottonwood trees. Bighorn sheep can occasionally be seen across the river.

La Sal Mountains Scenic Loop
While most visitors to Moab come for the magnificent red-rock scenery, the beauty of the La Sal Mountains is not to be ignored. The La Sal Loop climbs from the desert environment of Spanish Valley up to the alpine meadows and beneath the 12,700-foot peaks. The 62-mile-long road is paved, except for a few sections of gravel. The steep climb, much of it over narrow switchbacks, is slow going and should not be attempted by cars towing trailers or in recreation vehicles. The high-country road is closed by snow in winter, but during the rest of the year, it offers panoramic views of the Colorado Plateau and the Blue and Henry Mountains in the distance.

The loop leaves US Hwy. 191 6 miles south of Moab and climbs the west side of the La Sals. Be sure to stop at the monument erected on the northwestern slope of the mountains to commemorate the Battle at Pinhook Draw. At Pinhook, a band of Paiute Indians who killed two men at an isolated ranch near the Utah–Colorado border in May 1881 ambushed a posse made up of cowboys and led by a brother of one of the dead ranchers. During the battle, 15 to 27 men were killed, including nine members of the posse and seven to 18 Native Americans. This was one of the deadliest battles fought between whites and Native Americans in Utah. The road descends through Castle Valley, where it meets Hwy. 128, which you can follow along the Colorado River back to Moab (see above).

Needles/Anticline Overlook Rd.
This not-to-be-missed drive takes you into the heart of the sandstone formations on the eastern banks of the Colorado River, for views of the Needles District of Canyonlands National Park and the Anticline of the Colorado River. The road to both overlooks begins 35 miles south of Moab and 12 miles south of La Sal Junction off US Hwy. 191. The 21-mile-long road to the Needles Overlook is paved. At the Needles Overlook, you have an excellent view of the Needles District and the Indian Creek Wilderness Study Area to the west and southwest. Looking back to the east, the volcanic La Sal Mountains offer an imposing contrast to the colorful sandstone. Retrace your route from the Needles Overlook 6 miles to the junction with the gravel road that heads north for 17 miles to the Anticline Overlook. The gravel road can be traveled by passenger vehicle and is open year-round except after severe snowstorms. The Anticline Overlook is located on a narrow promontory that offers interesting views of the Colorado River, Dead Horse Point, Hurrah Pass and Kane Creek Canyon. The total distance from the turnoff from US Hwy. 191 to both overlooks is 76 miles. You should plan 3–4 hours for this drive.

Potash Scenic Byway/Hwy. 279
For a shorter trip along the western bank of the Colorado River, turn off US Hwy. 191 3 miles northwest of Moab and follow Hwy. 279 for 17 miles to where the paved road ends at the Moab Salt Plant. Though the plant is important to the local economy, many find it inappropriate and perhaps detrimental to the scenic resources of the area.

Still, there is plenty to be seen along the route, including petroglyph panels identified by two "Indian Writing" signs. A set of dinosaur tracks is indicated by another sign. Jug Handle Arch, 46 feet high and only 3 feet wide, is located above the highway not far from the end of the paved route. If you want to combine a 3-mile round-trip hike with your drive, park your vehicle at the Corona Arch trailhead. The 1.5-mile-long trail takes you to the 140-by-105-foot Corona Arch and nearby Bow Tie Arch (see the Hiking section under Outdoor Activities).

Shopping

There are a number of shops and stores along Moab's main street, including a favorite bookstore and photograph gallery.

Back of Beyond Books

Opened in 1990 by Jose Knighton, who has also written about the area, this bookstore is the best-stocked store in southeastern Utah and something of a memorial to author Edward Abbey, with a shrinelike bookcase that contains first edition books authored by Abbey. You can purchase copies of Abbey's most famous book, *Desert Solitaire*, written while Abbey was a ranger at Arches National Park in the mid-1950s. There is also an extensive collection of regional books and noted western authors. Open during the spring, summer and fall daily 10 A.M.–10 P.M.; during the winter daily 10 A.M.–6 P.M. **83 N. Main St.; 1-800-700-2859; 435-259-5154.**

Tom Till Gallery

Want something to always remind you of your visit to Utah and the red-rock country? Consider a photograph print by one of Utah's best-known scenic photographers—Tom Till, a resident of Moab. Open daily 9 A.M.–10 P.M. **61 N. Main; 1-888-479-9808; 435-259-9808.**

Tours

Canyonlands Field Institute

Established in 1984 to promote understanding and appreciation of the natural environment and the cultural heritage of the Colorado Plateau, the nonprofit Canyonlands Field Institute offers a unique series of outstanding tours and activities to explore and experience the Colorado Plateau. The institute's philosophy is that "all life is sacred. The land and those who have gone before us have much to teach." To promote that understanding, it offers programs that allow participants to experience the Colorado Plateau in a variety of ways: painting, photography, geology, rock art study, ecology, canoeing, hiking and cross-country skiing. **Canyonlands Field Institute, 1320 S. US Hwy. 191, P.O. Box 68, Moab, UT 84532; 435-259-7750.**

Hole 'N the Rock

Some might write off this establishment as simply a tourist trap, and the gigantic lettered signs painted on the sandstone cliff in the bottom of Kane Wash (now offensive to most travelers along US Hwy. 191 despite efforts to remove the letters) indicate how far our environmental consciousness has come since they were first painted in the 1950s. Nevertheless, the Hole 'N the Rock is still an interesting example of how creative humans can be with what they have. Albert Christensen spent 12 years excavating his dwelling within this sandstone monolith. After he died in 1957, his wife, Gladys, worked another eight years to complete the 14-room home, which has 5,000 square feet of living space. She died in 1974 and both are buried in a small alcove underneath the rock about 100 yards east of the gift shop.

More than 50,000 cubic feet of sandstone were excavated from the interior of the huge rock, which is 0.25 mile high and through and 1 mile in circumference. Some of the interesting features include the face of Franklin D. Roosevelt sculpted into the sandstone at the entrance, cabinets built into the rock walls and a bathtub carved out of sandstone. The tourist stop has become so popular that some people confuse this site with the historic pioneer crossing of the Colorado River farther south. Open for tours during the summer daily 8 A.M.–8 P.M.; the rest of the year daily 9 A.M.–5 P.M. Entrance fee charged.

Located on US Hwy. 191, 15 miles south of Moab. **435-686-2250.**

AERIAL TOURS
Moab Skyway Scenic Chairlift

Mountain bikers and sight-seers share this unique chairlift that rises from the Moab Valley floor 1,000 feet to the top of the red cliffs south of Moab. Located across the road from the Matheson Wetlands and opened in 1999, the lift was a lifelong dream of Emmett Mayes, which he has held ever since he pushed his jeep to the top of the rim three decades ago and beheld the unforgettable view of the La Sal Mountains to the east, the Moab Valley below and in the distance to the north the arches and buttes of Arches National Park. Thanks to Emmett, you can see this and more from the top of the lift.

Hikers can wander on a well-marked half-mile loop trail or explore farther afield. Mountain bikers can connect with the Hidden Valley Trail that heads southeast for about 5 miles and is considered difficult to moderate (see the Hiking section under Outdoor Activities). Extreme bikers, those who ride down razor-thin hogsback ridges and jump their bikes down cliffs and boulders, can try their skills on the Moab Trail, which descends the back side of the cliffs to the Colorado River. Extreme bikers can purchase a day pass and ride the trail to the river, follow the river road a couple of miles to the lift and do it all over again. The record is 15 trips in one day.

A special feature, designed by Emmett, is a wheelchair-accessible chair where those confined to wheelchairs can be taken to the top, wheelchair and all. Same day reride tickets can be purchased for a third of the regular price so that you can view the scenery during the day and return for the spectacular evening sunsets. Open Mar.–Thanksgiving daily 9 A.M.–late evening. Located on Kane Creek Blvd., 1.3 miles west of the junction with Main St. **435-259-7799.**

BOAT TOURS
Canyonlands by Night

Canyon country and the Colorado River are a much different experience at night. One of the most memorable ways to spend a couple of evening hours on the Colorado Plateau is to board one of the jet boats that take you upstream about 6–7 miles beyond the Colorado River bridge. During the upstream journey, the host gives an informal talk about the river, points out some of the landmarks and unusual features along the canyon cliffs and answers questions about the river and the area.

When darkness comes, the boat begins the return journey accompanied by a mobile light system onboard a truck that follows along the highway down the river. The spotlights that light up the canyon present an unforgettable view of the 500-foot rock walls, while the narration covers the Indian myths about the Colorado River, geology and history. The narration is interspersed with music specially selected to match the scenery. One of the most memorable segments was the tape of the Sons of the Pioneers singing "Moonlight on the Colorado" as the spotlight threw a gigantic shadow of a huge cottonwood tree across the river onto the far-side canyon wall. As you drift back toward the Colorado River bridge under a brilliant canopy of stars or under a moonlit evening sky, you see another side to Utah's beauty.

Canyonlands by Night has been offered since 1966 and is a popular nighttime activity in the summer. Tours offered May–Sept. daily; usually leave at 8:30 P.M. and return around 10:30 P.M. Reservations are recommended. **Canyonlands by Night Old Mission Gift Shop** is located on the west side of the Colorado River, just south of the bridge. **1-800-394-9978; 435-259-5261.**

DRIVING TOURS
Moab Area Rock Art Auto Tour

This free brochure describes the rock art of the area and the people who produced the rock art, and gives directions to five different sites in the area where you can see some of the best examples of prehistoric rock art to be found anywhere. Pick it up at the Moab Information Center (see the Services section).

MOVIE LOCATIONS TOUR

If you are a movie fan, you already know that the red-rock country around Moab has been the backdrop for numerous full-length motion pictures. While in Moab, pick up a copy of the *Moab Area Movie Locations Auto Tour*. Produced by the Moab Area Travel Council and the Moab Film Commission, the free brochure describes the shooting locations for 16 movies filmed in the Moab area. The movies begin with the 1949 John Ford production *Wagon Master* and include such films as *The Comancheros, Cheyenne Autumn, The Greatest Story Ever Told, Rio Conchos, Indiana Jones and the Last Crusade, Thelma and Louise, Geronimo* and *City Slickers II*. All movie locations are accessible by passenger car, and many motels and bed and breakfasts have videos of some of the movies filmed in and around Moab. If you want a detailed history of movie making in southeastern Utah, pick up a copy of Bette L. Stanton's *Where God Put the West* (Four Corners Publication 1994), a book published in Moab and available in local bookstores.

Wildlife Viewing

Matheson Wetlands

The Matheson Wetlands, named in honor of the late Scott M. Matheson, Utah's distinguished, conservation-minded governor, is a unique spot alongside the Colorado River. Ranchers who grazed cattle in the area called it the Moab Slough. As one of the interpretive signs explains, "Among the sandstone domes, arches, and other jewels of southern Utah lies a small shaded emerald, the Matheson wetlands. Green and fertile, it seems to have emerged as a gift from the dry desert. Here under the shadow of the red rock, the earth is water soaked. The soil, black and rich in decomposing matter, sustains an abundance of wild life."

Early settlers tried to drain the slough and plant orchards and crops. However, when the Colorado River reclaimed the land and reestablished the wetlands with floods during the mid-1980s, the slough returned to its natural condition as the only high-quality wetland along

the length of the Colorado River in Utah. The primary water source is the La Sal Mountains, where snowmelt flows down creeks and seeps through underground channels to leave the area a water-soaked oasis. Home to beavers, river otters, mule deer and many other animals, the wetlands resound with a symphony of bird songs and a spirit of peace that make this a very special place.

In 1990 The Nature Conservancy began to acquire the land and today the 875 acres are owned and jointly managed by the Conservancy and Utah Division of Wildlife Resources. Paths and walkways allow passage through the wetlands. The Nature Conservancy offers free weekly guided nature walks Mar.–Oct. Sat. at 8 A.M. To reach the parking area, take Kane Creek Blvd., which heads in a northwesterly direction off Main St. near the southern end of downtown Moab, and follow it for a couple of miles until you see the parking area on your right. For information contact the **Moab Information Center; 1-800-635-6622; 435-259-8825**.

Wineries

Castle Creek Winery

Self-guided tours give an overview of the process from pressing the grapes to storing the wine in French oak barrels to bottling. Free wine tasting, and wine can be purchased at the winery. Open during the summer Mon.–Thurs. 11 A.M.–7 P.M., Fri.–Sat. 11 A.M.–9 P.M. Located approximately 20 minutes northeast of Moab, at the Red Cliffs Adventure Lodge at milepost 14 along Hwy. 128. **435-259-3332**.

Where to Stay

Bed and Breakfasts

The following inns are a good alternative to the motels, but they fill up fast so reservations are almost always a necessity. On occasion there are no-shows, so don't hesitate to at least call, even on short notice. Unless otherwise noted, all rooms are nonsmoking and no pets are allowed.

Adobe Adobe Bed and Breakfast—
$$$ to $$$$

This rambling, low-profile, brand-new bed and breakfast looks like a 21st-century descendant of a 1,000-year-old pueblo and is definitely Southwest in character, both outside and inside. Owners Lori Bevan and Keith Herrmann were longtime visitors to Moab who, like many, harbored the dream of moving to Moab to live. Their answer to the question, "What do you do when your children grow up and move away?" was to move to Moab, build their dream house and live happily ever after as hosts in their own bed and breakfast. They chose an excellent location with the Scott M. Matheson Wetlands Preserve close by and magnificent views of the red-rock cliffs and azure blue La Sal Mountains. Each of the spacious four rooms has a large private bath, cable TV and private covered patio. **778 W. Kane Creek; 435-259-7716; www. adobeadobemoab.com.**

Cali Cochitta Bed and Breakfast—
$$$ to $$$$

Housed in one of Moab's few remaining 19th-century stone houses, this cozy bed and breakfast offers three rooms and one suite with two beds in the house and an adjacent two-bedroom cottage. Each room has a private bath and cable TV. There's a hot tub, bicycle storage and guest room with a library. Owners David and Kim Boger provide a full breakfast and evening refreshments. **110 S. 200 E.; 1-888-429-8112; 435-259-4961; www.moabdreaminn.com.**

Castle Valley Inn—$$$

With an unbelievable location, about 25 miles northeast of Moab along the Colorado River, and set on 11 acres of fruit orchards, fields and lawn, Castle Valley Inn is a favorite of repeat visitors to Moab. Owners Eric and Lynn Forbes Thomson are mountain bike enthusiasts and willingly share information about mountain biking. They also provide a workspace for bike repairs. There is a hot tub for soaking any stiff biking muscles. The inn has three rooms and three cottages with kitchenettes. Breakfast is included and guest meals can also be arranged. Take Hwy. 128 north along the east side of the Colorado River from the river bridge. **435-259-6012; www.castle-valleyinn.com.**

DreamKeeper Inn—$$$ to $$$$

This inn is located two blocks from Main St. in a spacious ranch-style house surrounded by huge shade trees and pleasant gardens. There are four rooms in the main house and two cottages detached from the main house near the swimming pool. Hosts Jim and Kathy Kempa are enthusiastic hikers with a wealth of information about activities in the area. They keep a well-stocked library with current guidebooks and maps and provide secure bike storage and maintenance facilities. A full breakfast is served in either the sunny dining room or on the patio by the rose garden. **191 S. 200 E.; 1-888-230-3247; 435-259-5998; www.moab.net/dreamkeeper.**

Sunflower Hill—$$$

The guest rooms at Sunflower Hill are in three locations: a two-bedroom upstairs suite with a private bath; three bedrooms downstairs, each with a private bath; and the adjacent Garden Cottage, which has two suites, each with two bedrooms, bath and sitting room. Guests are welcome to wander about the large yard and gardens. Aaron and Kim Robison and their two children, Maxwell and McKay, run the bed and breakfast. In 1996 the original bed and breakfast was expanded into the Cape Cod–style house next door with five additional bedrooms. Guests enjoy a wholesome breakfast of fresh fruit and juice, homemade granola and yogurt, and homemade muffins and bread. **185 N. 300 E.; 435-259-2974; www.sunflowerhill.com.**

Motels

Moab has a good number of motels, and there always seem to be new ones under construction. They remain full much of the year, however, so reservations are highly recommended. If you are traveling in the off-season (late fall and winter), be sure to ask about off-season rates. The following are conventional motels. For a complete list of area accommodations, contact the **Moab Area Travel Council** (see the Services section). For reservations for the Moab–Green River area, call **Central Reservations, 1-800-748-4386.**

Aarchway Inn—$$ to $$$

Heated pool, hot tub and exercise room; 97 rooms. Free continental breakfast. **1551 N. US Hwy. 191; 1-800-341-9359; 435-259-2599.**

Best Western Canyonlands Inn—$$ to $$$

Heated pool, whirlpool, exercise room, video game room and indoor bike storage; 77 rooms. Restaurant. **16 S. Main; 435-259-2300.**

Big Horn Lodge—$$$

Heated pool; 58 rooms. Restaurant nearby. **550 S. Main; 1-800-325-6171; 435-259-6171.**

Castle Rock Inn—$$$ to $$$$

Heated pool; 90 rooms. **815 S. Main; 1-877-581-8700; 435-259-8700.**

Comfort Suites—$$$

Heated indoor pool, exercise room and bike storage; microwaves and refrigerators in all 75 rooms. **800 S. Main; 1-800-228-5150; 435-259-5252.**

Gonzo Inn—$$$$

Several of the 43 rooms have kitchens. Pool and hot tub. **100 W. 200 S.; 1-800-791-4044; 435-259-2515.**

Landmark Motel—$$ to $$$

Heated pool with child's wading pool, hot tub; 36 rooms. **168 N. Main; 1-800-259-6147; 435-259-6147.**

Moab Valley Inn—$$$

Heated pool and hot tub; 127 rooms. Restaurant. **711 S. Main; 1-800-831-6622; 435-259-4419.**

Red Stone Inn—$$ to $$$

Heated pool; 52 rooms. **535 S. Main; 1-800-772-1972; 435-259-3500.**

Hostels

Lazy Lizard Hostel—$

A member of Rucksackers Hostel; guests are mostly young adults, 18 to 30, who come to Moab to bike, although older people are also welcome. There are a number of choices, from basic, single-sex dormitory lodging and tepee accommodations at less than $15 a night, to private rooms and private cabins. The hostel is non-smoking and has laundry and kitchen facilities, along with a hot tub and television. Located about 1 mile south of the center of Moab in a red-and-white house behind the A-1 Storage. **1213 S. US Hwy. 191; 435-259-6057.**

Camping

PRIVATE

Camping places in the Moab area can be as scarce as motel accommodations. There are 15 private campgrounds in and near Moab, with more than 1,000 campsites; below is a representative selection. Because of the relatively low elevation of about 4,000 feet and the consistently warmer temperatures, camping is possible all year for those prepared for it. Unless otherwise noted, all campgrounds listed below are open year-round and charge fees.

Canyonlands Campark

Has 140 RV sites, 70 with full hookups, plus 60 tentsites; all the amenities. **555 S. Main; 1-800-522-6848; 435-259-6848.**

Moab KOA

Has 156 sites, 60 with complete hookups, and the usual KOA amenities. Closed Nov.–Feb. Located 4 miles south of Moab on US Hwy. 191. **435-259-6682.**

Portal R.V. Park and Fishery, Inc.

All 45 sites have full hookups. Tentsites, picnic tables, drinking water, flush toilets, dump sites, showers, laundry and fishing. Located close to Arches National Park. **1261 N. US Hwy. 191; 1-800-574-2028; 435-259-6108.**

Slickrock Campground

One of the closest campgrounds to Arches National Park; 197 sites, 116 with complete hookups, plus 52 tentsites. Amenities include wheelchair access. Located off US Hwy. 191 a mile north of Moab. **1-800-448-8873; 435-259-7660.**

PUBLIC

In the La Sal Mountains, about 22 miles east of Moab, there are two Forest Service campgrounds at an elevation of 8,800 and 9,200 feet. **Oowah Lake** has 6 tentsites and is equipped with toilets but no water. **Warner Lake** has 20 RV sites and tentsites and is equipped with drinking water and toilets. Both are open June–Oct. and available on a first-come, first-served basis. Both can be reached on the loop road either from US Hwy. 191 6 miles south of Moab or from Hwy. 128 at Castle Valley.

For information on BLM campgrounds Hatch Point, on Anticline Overlook Rd., and Wind Whistle, on Needles Overlook Rd., see the **San Juan County** chapter.

Where to Eat

Buck's Grill House—$$ to $$$

The first restaurant at this location opened in 1967 and was called Ft. Moab because of its proximity to the original 1855 Elk Mountain Mission Ft. site just south of the restaurant. Ever since that time, it has been popular with tourists and locals alike. In 1996 Moab native Tim Buckingham opened Buck's Grill House, named for his grandfather, in this building. An award-winning chef, Tim offers an interesting combination of traditional western fare of cowboy steaks, prime rib, burgers, buffalo meat loaf, venison stew, Southwestern dishes and a few of his own specials of fresh fish, zucchini pot pie, vegetable pasta and delicious desserts. Patio and dining room seating available. Open daily 5–10 P.M. **1393 N. US Hwy. 191; 435-259-5201.**

Eddie McStiff's Brew Pub and Restaurant—$$ to $$$

One of only a couple of local breweries in eastern Utah, Eddie McStiff's offers its freshly brewed beers to go with a wide range of food. Choices include New York– and Chicago–style pizza, sandwiches, steaks, char-broiled burgers, pastas, salads and Southwestern dishes. You will find 12 different microbrews, including some that are quite exotic. The most popular is the Raspberry Wheat, which won the People's Choice best beer award at the Southwestern Brewmeisters Festival for 1992–1993. Those who don't want to drink alcohol can enjoy the wonderful homemade root beer, which uses half the sugar of normal soda, and Quillaia, a unique derivative of South American trees, along with herbs, spices and a blend of eight different roots.

There are three parts to McStiff's—the tavern and the patio, where liquor is served with the purchase of food for those 21 or older, and a dining room for families with children, where no alcohol is served. Open daily 3–10 P.M. (dinner), 3 P.M.–midnight (tavern). Located in the Western Plaza. **57 S. Main; 435-259-2337.**

Milt's Stop and Eat—$

This place has been around since the uranium boom and is known for its good traditional pancake-and-egg breakfasts. It also has burgers, real fries, shakes and malts. Open daily 6 A.M.–8 P.M. **356 Millcreek; 435-259-7424.**

Moab Brewery—$$ to $$$

One of the liveliest and largest gathering spots in Moab since it opened in 1996, the Moab Brewery has an extensive lunch and dinner menu to go with its selection of microbrewed beers. The most popular brew is the Dead Horse Ale, a traditional English mild ale named for the famous overlook of the Colorado River—Dead Horse Point. The menu includes a good selection of vegetarian dishes—pasta, burritos, enchiladas and ravioli. There are also six different kinds of hamburgers, several chicken entrées and the ever-popular fish-and-chips. Other fish items include a tuna steak sandwich, mahi mahi burger and fresh salmon fillet. Meat eaters have plenty of choices with a mixed sausage grill, ribs, steaks and prime rib. For light eaters there are salads and soups—the beer cheese and the black bean soups are well worth a try. There's also a children's menu.

Outside there's a nice patio dining area that is especially pleasant in the late afternoon when it is shaded by the building. Open daily from 11:30 A.M. **686 S. Main St.; 435-259-6333.**

Pasta Jay's—$$ to $$$

Located in the center of town on the southwest corner of the intersection of Main and Center Sts. just across from the Moab Visitors Center, it's hard to miss Pasta Jay's. As the name indicates, this place is about pasta, and there are plenty of choices plus other Italian dishes, salads and a children's menu. There is a large outside patio dining area with both shaded and sunny sections. Open daily from 11:30 A.M. **4 S. Main; 435-259-2900.**

Poplar Place Pub and Eatery—$$ to $$$

Named for the poplar trees that used to line the streets of Moab, specialties at this favorite of locals include gourmet pizza, deli sandwiches on fresh-baked breads, homemade soups and fresh salads. Carryout and deliveries available. Open 11 A.M.–1 A.M. **100 N. Main St.; 435-259-6018.**

Slick Rock Cafe—$$ to $$$

No one has done more to promote mountain biking in Utah than Jan Wilking. He has put together a series of nine regional biking guidebooks that have introduced hundreds of bikers to the varied terrain from the slickrock of southern Utah to the mountains of northern Utah. In 1994 he and two partners opened the Slick Rock Cafe in the historic 1906 two-story brick business building located across from the Moab Visitor Center. The interior is a bright, cheerful, happy place.

Breakfast items include omelettes, pancakes, French toast and "slickrock" granola. Lunch and dinner items are a good mix of Italian, Mexican, Cajun and vegetarian dishes. For lunch, burger lovers might try the "Uranium Burger," made with a half pound of beef with fresh garlic and chunks of blue cheese mixed throughout. There is a grilled fish of the day, New York strip steak, pasta and Utah trout. The grilled vegetables are

also very popular with the younger set that frequents this establishment. Open Mon.–Sat. 7 A.M.–10 P.M. Located on the northwest corner of **Main St. and Center St. 435-259-8004.**

Sunset Grill—$$ to $$$

Also located in a historic home, Sunset Grill was formerly known as the Mi Vida Restaurant. Mi Vida was the name of the uranium mine that lifted Charles Steen from the depths of poverty to multimillionaire status. A modern-day legend, Charlie Steen discovered the first commercial uranium deposits in the Colorado Plateau region. He built the uranium mill on the west side of the Colorado River, where uranium from the many mines all over southeastern Utah was processed. He spent his millions lavishly, and his mansion, built in 1955 atop a hill overlooking Moab, was visited by guests from all over the world. Steen's good fortune did not last, as questionable investments left him bankrupt. His hilltop mansion is now the Sunset Grill, which features mesquite-broiled steaks, seafoods and specialty menu items. Open daily 11 A.M.–2 P.M. and 5–10:30 P.M. **900 N. US Hwy. 191; 435-259-7146.**

Services

Visitor Information

Bureau of Land Management Grand Resource Area—82 E. Dogwood Ave., Moab, UT 84532; 435-259-2196.

Canyonlands National Park Headquarters—Open Mon.–Fri. 8 A.M.–4:30 P.M. 125 W. 200 S., Moab, UT 84532; 435-259-7164.

Moab Area Travel Council—P.O. Box 550, Moab, UT 84532; 435-259-1370; www.discovermoab.com.

Moab Information Center—Located at Center and Main Sts., Moab, UT 84532; 1-800-635-6622; 435-259-8825.

U.S. Forest Service, Manti-La Sal National Forest—125 W. 200 S., Moab, UT 84532; 435-259-7155.

Canyonlands National Park

In Canyonlands lies the heart and soul of the Colorado Plateau. A vast, rugged land of remarkable beauty, the expanses of rocks under an even more expansive sky, this is a land of paradox. There is something quite eternal about this land, yet it continues to change in response to the ongoing but seldom-seen forces of erosion. The delicateness of the wind-sculpted pinnacles stands against a backdrop of monumental buttes and mesas. Majesty, durability and fragility are all linked in a panorama of beauty. The landscape is a three-dimensional divine work of art. A multitude of elements are perfectly placed and masterfully combined in this tapestry of the gods.

Canyonlands National Park is known for its canyons, mesas, pillars, standing rocks, grabens, arches and two of the West's most important rivers: the Colorado and the Green, whose confluence takes place in the heart of the park. The best way to approach Canyonlands is to consider it three national parks combined under one administrative jurisdiction. The three sections of Canyonlands—Island in the Sky, the Maze and the Needles—are distinct units, separated by natural boundaries formed by the Green and Colorado Rivers and their canyons. Each requires a separate access, and it is impossible to see more than one section in a day. Much of the park remains undeveloped, and the best way to really see it is by hiking. Located northeast of the park, Moab is the gateway city, although as you will learn, there is really no "gateway" to the Maze District. Monticello provides good access to the Needles District.

The largest of Utah's five national parks, with 337,570 acres, Canyonlands is nearly 10 times larger than Bryce Canyon, five times larger than Arches, three times as large as Zion and half again as large as Capitol Reef. Even so, it receives far fewer visitors than most of the other national parks in Utah. The newest of Utah's national parks, Canyonlands was created on September 12, 1964, when President Lyndon Johnson signed the act making Canyonlands the 32nd national park.

History

The history of Canyonlands is nearly as complex as the geography and geology that make up the park. Prehistoric use dates back more than 11,000 years ago, as evidenced by the discovery of a Clovis projectile point near Canyonlands. These Paleo-Indians lived in the region from about 11,000 B.C. to around 5000 B.C. As the culture of the Paleo-Indians changed from a reliance on big game such as giant bison, elk and

Getting There

Canyonlands National Park is located 304 miles southeast of Salt Lake City. To get to the area from Salt Lake City, take Interstate 15 south to Spanish Fork at Exit 256 and take US Hwy. 6 southeast to Interstate 70 at Green River. From here, your destination within the park will determine which route to take.

Hwy. 24, at Exit 147 on Interstate 70, heads south relatively near the park's western border, providing access to the Maze District. At Hanksville, the highway joins Hwy. 96, which heads south then east to its junction with US Hwy. 191 near Blanding, circling far to the south of the park's southern edges. US Hwy. 191, from Exit 180 on Interstate 70, heads south relatively near the park's eastern edge, through Moab and Monticello, providing access to the Island in the Sky District and the Needles District. This is just an overview of this complex region; for access to the three districts, see Getting There for each section, below.

possibly mammoths to one that emphasized using plants as well as animals and a greater variety of methods and weapons, such as nets, snares and atlatls, to hunt animals, the early inhabitants became known as the Archaic culture. The Archaic people lived in the area until about 500 B.C. and left outstanding examples of rock art known as the Barrier Canyon style, characterized by large, trapezoidal, ghostlike anthropomorphic figures.

While the Paleo-Indians and their descendants, the Archaic people, were nomadic, the next groups of people were basically sedentary. As the Archaic people turned more and more to planting and farming instead of hunting, they developed into two related but somewhat different cultures, known today as the Fremont and the Anasazi. While the Fremont tended to occupy the region to the west and north, and the Anasazi lands to the south and east, the Canyonlands area became an important point of contact between the two groups.

Both peoples seem to have left a rich treasure of millions of artifacts, dwellings, kivas, pit houses, granaries and rock art. Archaeologists continue to research and debate the extent of both cultures in the Canyonlands area, and current scholarship holds that the Anasazi presence was greater than that of the Fremont. Both cultures flourished from about the time of Christ until around A.D. 1250, at which time a particularly long drought and the invasion of other peoples—notably the Utes and Navajos from the north—may have caused them to flee. The Anasazi moved to the south and east and intermingled with the Pueblo Indians of Arizona and New Mexico; no one is sure what happened to the Fremont.

Fur trapper Denis Julien was probably the first Euro-American to see what is now Canyonlands National Park, although it is possible that Spanish traders, including members of the 1765 Juan Maria Antonio de Rivera expedition, visited the area before Julien left his engraved signature in the canyons in 1836. But it was not until 1859 that an organized expedition, under Capt. John N. Macomb, was sent out to locate the confluence of the Green and Colorado Rivers. This was the first systematic exploration of Canyonlands. Macomb was not impressed with what he found, penning in his final report, "I cannot conceive of a more worthless and impracticable region than the one we now found ourselves in." But another member of the expedition, Dr. John S. Newberry, offered a dissenting opinion, describing the towers of the Needles District as a "forest of Gothic spires," without parallel in nature or art.

Ten years later, Maj. John Wesley Powell passed through the heart of Canyonlands as he floated down the Green River, through its confluence with the Colorado and into the fury of Cataract Canyon. At the end of the next decade, cattlemen began to move into southeastern Utah, and they too began to note many of the formations and sites in Canyonlands. These cowboys were joined by lonely prospectors and gold miners who ventured into Canyonlands but did not tap any significant sources of wealth. During the 1950s, uranium miners scoured the region for radioactive "gold," blazing jeep trails across this convoluted canyon landscape. They, along with an ever-increasing number of river-runners, stirred a dormant interest in the area by outsiders.

In 1936 Harold Ickes, Secretary of the Interior under Franklin D. Roosevelt, proposed the creation of a 7,000-square-mile Escalante National Monument that would encompass nearly all of southeastern Utah west of US Hwy. 160, between Bluff and Moab, and a large chunk of real estate west of the Colorado River. World War II and the opposition from state commercial interests doomed the Escalante proposal. But in 1961, Utah's U.S. Sen. Frank E. "Ted" Moss introduced legislation to establish Canyonlands National Park. This proposal met with resistance, delays, counterproposals and indifference, if not hostility, from many of his constituents, and criticism from environmentalists when he offered compromise in their behalf.

Nevertheless, Canyonlands was given a huge boost by the support of then–Secretary of the Interior Stewart Udall. He flew over the area and decided then and there that such a place must be a national park. Superintendent Bates Wilson of Arches National Park was also very involved in having the park established. Senator Moss persisted in spearheading the initiative and on September 12, 1964, Canyonlands National Park was created. Senator Moss took unrestrained pride in being labeled the "Father of Canyonlands National Park."

Major Attractions

Geology

Canyonlands is geology, and the sculpted rocks and mile-deep canyons trace their history back 300 million years when movements along ancient faults formed the Uncompahgre Uplift—a range of lofty mountains to the northwest. At the same time the mountains were being formed, the area that encompasses Canyonlands, known as the Paradox Basin, dropped. Over millions of years the Paradox Basin was covered by ancient seas, which left salt deposits that are thousands of feet thick. Added to the salt deposits were layers of dark shale, which washed down from the 15,000-foot mountains formed by the Uncompahgre Uplift. On top of these deposits were added layers of silt, sand, mud and lime from the shells of dying marine creatures. The seas receded and were replaced by vast sand dunes covering thousands of square miles over almost all of the Colorado Plateau.

This happened several times, the result being a multilayered geology thousands of feet thick. These layers hardened into stone and caused the salt layers underneath to flow away. As the salt layers flowed and shifted, forces inside the earth began pushing upward, intensifying the cracking and fracturing and leaving a broken landscape that was intensified through the forces of erosion acting on layers of differing hardness and thickness. These layers range from the Navajo sandstone on top to the Honeker Trail and Paradox Formations, the latter visible only in the depths of the canyon of the Colorado River.

As you travel Utah's Canyonlands, you will see black streaks formed on the canyon walls.

They come mostly from windblown soil. The clay particles in the soil adhere to moist rock surfaces to which very small amounts of iron and manganese are attracted. Over time, a thin veneer of minerals builds up, creating what is called desert varnish.

Plant and Animal Life

Rock and sky dominate the view throughout Canyonlands, but the varied plant and animal life should not go unnoticed. The way plants have adapted to a nearly waterless environment and the way wildlife survives in the seemingly hostile desert are an exciting part of the Canyonlands story. Part of the story is the elevation of Canyonlands, which ranges from 4,000 feet along the Colorado River to nearly 7,000 feet atop Cedar Mesa in the Needles District. Cottonwood trees, willows and tamarisk are found along the rivers and some canyon bottoms. Hanging gardens of maidenhair fern and columbine are clustered around seeps in the rocks. Indian ricegrass, cactus, narrow-leafed yucca, sagebrush, rabbitbrush, blackbrush, Mormon tea and piñon-juniper woodlands are found in the broad valleys and on top of the mesas that are the backdrop for the canyons and stone formations.

Animal life ranges from tiny biting midges that can be very bothersome to visitors, to the curious inhabitants of potholes—tadpoles, toads and horsehair worms—to countless lizards, kangaroo rats, piñon mice, chipmunks, ground squirrels, sage sparrows, scrub jays, cliff swallows (which build their nests of mud and plant materials under the protection of overhanging ledges), ravens, hawks, peregrine falcons, turkey vultures, golden eagles, beavers, bobcats, deer, coyotes, foxes and bighorn sheep.

Visitor Information

Canyonlands National Park Headquarters is located in Moab: **2282 SW Resource Blvd., Moab, UT 84532; 435-259-7164.** However, unless you have business with park officials, visitors are urged to use the **Moab Information Center,** located at **Main St. and Center St., Moab, UT 84532; 1-800-635-**

6622; 435-259-8825. This interagency information center is staffed by national park employees and representatives of other agencies as well. The **Multi-Agency Visitor Center** in **Monticello** is located in the San Juan County Courthouse, **117 S. Main; 1-800-574-4386; 435-587-3235.** These three locations are all outside the national park boundaries.

Because a visit to the three sections of the park requires three trips, each district is discussed separately below. The Needles District has a visitor center, as does the Island in the Sky District; the Maze District does not. However, about 46 miles east of Hwy. 24, the Hans Flat Ranger Station serves both Canyonlands National Park and the northern end of Glen Canyon National Recreation Area, whose eastern boundary is the western boundary of Canyonlands. Park entrance fees collected at one Canyonlands district are good for the other districts of the park.

Island in the Sky District

The northernmost district within Canyonlands, the Island in the Sky District is a 6,000-foot-high mesa wedged between the Colorado River on the east and the Green River on the west, with its southern tip towering above the confluence of the two rivers. Located about 35 miles west of Moab, it is the most accessible of all the park's units. However, no water is available anywhere in the Island in the Sky District—bring all the water you will need.

Visitors to Island in the Sky generally spend the day driving the scenic park road, stopping at the overlooks and perhaps hiking some of the shorter trails. Most visitors also combine a visit to Island in the Sky with a stop at Dead Horse Point State Park, located just before the park boundary (see the **Moab** chapter). The Island in the Sky road is paved and, unlike many other sections of the park, is user-friendly for automobiles. If you have only a day to see Canyonlands National Park, this is the best unit of the park to visit.

Upheaval Dome, an intriguing feature of the Island in the Sky District, is described by geologists as among the most peculiar geological features in the world. The dome is thought by many geologists to be either a collapsed salt dome or a meteorite impact crater. The salt dome theory is based on the fact that a salt layer thousands of feet thick underlies the entire area. Because the salt is less dense than the sandstone covering it, the salt moved upward into the sandstone at this location, forming a "salt bubble"; when the overlying sandstone eroded away, the salt was exposed. It also eroded away, leaving the sandstone, which separated the bubble from the rest of the salt layer. The meteor theory, a more recent theory proposed by some geologists, holds that this was the site of impact for a meteor approximately 0.33 mile in diameter that struck around 60 million years ago. Erosion has washed away any evidence of meteorite debris.

Visitor Information

Island in the Sky Visitor Center provides information, books, maps, a schedule of interpretive activities and backcountry permits. Open in winter daily 8 A.M.–4:30 P.M.; rest of the year 8 A.M.–6 P.M. Located on Hwy. 313 about 25 miles southwest of US Hwy. 191. **435-259-4712.**

> ### Getting There
>
> *From Moab drive northwest on US Hwy. 191 for 10 miles to Hwy. 313, then turn west onto Hwy. 313 and follow it southwest. In about 25 miles the highway ends at the visitor center; beyond here, the park road continues south. About 6 miles southwest of the visitor center, the road branches. The southern branch continues on for 6 miles to its terminus at **Grand View Point,** the breathtaking climax to the drive. The western branch heads about 6 miles to Upheaval Dome Overlook for a look at the park's geological origins.*

Outdoor Activities

BIKING

White Rim Trail

One of the most unforgettable mountain biking experiences Utah has to offer is the White Rim Trail, a 100-mile road that loops around the Island in the Sky District in Canyonlands National Park. Most riders take three or four days to make the ride; overnight campers on the trail must obtain a permit at the Island in the Sky Visitor Center. Because there is no water available on the ride, a four-wheel-drive support vehicle is almost a necessity. The ever-changing vistas and the quiet solitude make this a truly remarkable ride. However, all bikers and four-wheel units must remain on established roads.

FOUR-WHEEL-DRIVE TRIPS

Shafer Trail Rd.

This road is not recommended for everybody, but if your heart and mind can take it, you are in for a never-to-be-forgotten ride. The road climbs via a series of switchbacks with no guard rails and clifflike exposures some 1,200 feet from the end of the Potash Road (Hwy. 279) to the top of the Island in the Sky Mesa inside the national park boundaries. The road is best suited to high-clearance four-wheel-drive vehicles and can be driven in either direction. Before setting out on the road, it is good to check conditions with a park ranger at the Moab Information Center, or call park headquarters, **435-259-7164.** From Moab, follow the Potash Scenic Byway/Hwy. 279 to its end in 17 miles (see the Scenic Drives section under Seeing and Doing in the **Moab** chapter), then follow the unpaved road another 20 miles to the park road Hwy. 313. The Shafer Trail Rd. junction with the park road is about a mile north of the visitor center.

HIKING

The park road south of the end of Hwy. 313 provides access to a dozen or more trailheads that lead to walks and hikes over smooth slickrock of less than a mile to 20 miles in length. Here are some favorite and easy-to-hike trails.

Grand View Trail

One of the most popular trails in Canyonlands, the Grand View Trail provides a stunning view over at least 100 miles of canyons, mesas, rivers and distant mountains. After studying the display at the Grand View Overlook to become familiar with the landmarks in the distance, hike the 2-mile round-trip trail and drink in this remarkable desert landscape. Located at the southern end of the park road.

Murphy Point Overlook Trail

The Murphy Point Overlook Trail offers superb views of the Green River below and a panorama that takes in the Needles District and Blue Mountains to the southeast, the Maze District and Henry Mountains to the southwest, and the San Rafael Swell to the west. The 2.4-mile round-trip hike is mostly across unmarked slickrock, but it is not difficult to negotiate or to keep your orientation. Located 3 miles beyond the Mesa Arch Loop trailhead, on the park road about 8.5 miles south of the visitor center.

Neck Spring Loop Trail

The 5-mile-long Neck Spring Loop Trail offers magnificent views of Canyonlands and a more intimate perspective on the early cattle-ranching activities in the region. The remains of an old corral, water trough and drift fence are visible. The trail follows paths used by animals to reach the springs. On occasion mule deer, bobcats and bighorn sheep have been spotted; more likely you will see the ground squirrels and chipmunks. Located 0.5 mile south of the visitor center on the park road, it's the same trailhead for the Shafer Canyon Overlook Trail, but start west instead of east.

Syncline Loop Trail

If you want to hike into the crater of Upheaval Dome, take the Syncline Loop Trail, which descends 1,300 feet below the Upheaval Dome

Overlook Trail. It is a strenuous 10-mile hike through Syncline Valley and into Upheaval Canyon. One section along the western side is across a loose talus slope and another traverses a high cliff along which the Park Service has built iron railings as a safety measure. It is a good idea to check at the park headquarters if you are serious about this hike. Be sure to take plenty of water and avoid the trail during the hot summer season. Located at the end of the Upheaval Dome Rd., the western branch of the park road.

Upheaval Dome Overlook Trail

This 2-mile round-trip hike offers sensational close-up views of 1,500-foot Upheaval Dome. The Upheaval Dome viewpoint offers a panorama of the western Canyonlands stretching from the Henry Mountains north to Thousand Lake Mountain, the San Rafael Swell and the Book Cliffs. The trail is a geology enthusiast's dream. The "Upheaval Dome View Trail Guide," available at the trailhead, describes the theories of crater origin. Located at the end of the Upheaval Dome Rd., the western branch of the park road.

White Rim Overlook Trail

For the best view in the Island in the Sky District of the 2,000-foot-deep canyon of the Colorado River, you will want to take the 1.5-mile round-trip White Rim Overlook Trail. About 11 miles south of the visitor center, turn off the park road into a picnic area where the trailhead is located.

Where to Stay

CAMPING

At Island in the Sky, camping is allowed only in the Willow Flat Campground or at backcountry vehicle sites by permit only.

Willow Flat Campground

Twelve sites available on a first-come, first-served basis. No water available at the campground—bring all the water you will need. Arrive very early to secure a site. No fee.

Located on the Island in the Sky Mesa just off the Upheaval Dome Rd. near its junction with the road to Grand View Point.

Maze District

Even though the Maze District is visible from both the Island in the Sky and the Needles Districts, you have to really want to go into it to get there. But the pure experience that the Maze District offers, the desert and the rocks at their finest, make the effort to get there all the more worthwhile. Located west of the Green and Colorado Rivers, it is accessible only by four-wheel-drive roads and hiking trails, and it is the intent of the National Park Service to keep it this way. This primitive area has no facilities. Its primary users are hikers wishing to see the spectacular

Getting There

From Interstate 70, take Hwy. 24 south about 25 miles, to 21 miles north of Hanksville, where the road into the Maze District leaves Hwy. 24 and heads east. Take the unpaved road 46 miles to Hans Flat Ranger Station, which is usually passable to two-wheel-drive vehicles, but from the ranger station you must hike or use a high-clearance four-wheel-drive vehicle. During the drive into Hans Flat, at about 30 miles east of Hwy. 24, is **Horseshoe Canyon,** a separate unit of Canyonlands National Park in which impressive 2,000-year-old pictographs have been left by the Archaic people.

From Hans Flat Ranger Station, the four-wheel road continues 14 miles south to the top of the **Flint Jeep Trail.** Carefully driving down the narrow switchbacks, the road intersects several jeep trails that eventually make their way to the **Maze Overlook.** Because of the difficult switchbacks, this road is a high-clearance four-wheel-drive vehicle trail.

Barrier Canyon–style rock art in Horseshoe Canyon and backpackers who spend several days hiking and exploring the deep canyons and strange rock landmarks that begin west of the rivers' confluence.

Visitor Information

Before venturing into the Maze District, it is best to get outfitted with proper maps and reliable information at the **Moab Information Center,** at the **Needles Visitor Center** or at the **Island in the Sky Visitor Center** (see the Services section). Carry at least 1 gallon of water per person per day (if not more), a towrope (or, better yet, a winch), a shovel, tire chains and survival gear. Be prepared in case you get stuck or your vehicle breaks down. The road is rough and slow-going in most sections.

    Hans Flat Ranger Station serves both Canyonlands National Park and the northern end of Glen Canyon National Recreation Area, whose eastern boundary is the western boundary of Canyonlands. Hours vary. Located about 46 miles east of Hwy. 24 (no telephone). **www. nps.gov/cany.**

Outdoor Activities

HIKING

The hiking route into the Maze begins at the Maze Overlook. It is steep and difficult, requiring the use of rope in some places to lower your pack. However, once you enter the Maze, the hiking is along sandy wash bottoms. The trails are marked with rock cairns, but all hikers should carry a compass and topographical maps and know how to use them.

Doll House Trails

Southeast of the Land of Standing Rocks is the Doll House, where there are two established trails. The **Spanish Bottoms Trail** is a steep, shadeless, 1.2-mile descent to the Colorado River just above Cataract Canyon. The **Colorado/Green River Overlook Trail** is 5 miles one way and winds up and down over the slickrock, offering wonderful views. The trailhead is located at the end of the Flint Jeep Trail.

Horseshoe Canyon

The 6.5-mile round-trip hike through Horseshoe Canyon can take the good part of a day, especially if you count the drive time from Moab, Green River or Hanksville. The panels of rock art in Horseshoe are arguably the most fascinating and best executed in Utah. They include Archaic and possibly Fremont pictographs, with, in some cases, the more recent red paintings superimposed over the older Archaic panels. The stillness of the canyon, its isolation and the realization that little has changed in the 2,000 years since the first paintings were sketched on the canyon walls are an experience not soon forgotten. Located on the road to Hans Flat Ranger Station, 30 miles east of Hwy. 24.

Land of Standing Rocks

The Land of Standing Rocks is an 8-mile stretch of high plateaus and spires. There are no established trails here, but there are a wide variety of routes that you can follow to **Lizard Rock, the Plug, Chimney Rock** and **the Wall,** as well as past hundreds of unnamed formations. Located off the Flint Jeep Trail.

Where to Stay

CAMPING

At the Maze, camping is by backcountry permit only.

The Needles District

In the southeastern district of Canyonlands, the Needles, four-wheel-drive trails take you to overlooks, Anasazi ruins and rock art. The **Salt Creek Archaeological District** is a 55,000-acre district along Salt Creek and its tributaries that includes Anasazi sites where arrowheads and other points were made, storage granaries, pictograph and petroglyph panels and habitation sites ranging from temporary locations to open habitation sites and houses built in alcoves.

    Much more recent inhabitants of the Needles District included cowboys, who lived in temporary "line camps" to watch over herds of cattle. Because the cattle herds were spread over a vast area, cowboys were required to live away from the ranch to tend the animals. Cowboys often spent six weeks at a time in isolation at the line camps, where they cooked over an open fire and spent their days keeping track of the cattle—an idyllic and adventuresome life that many have envied. Hikes in the Needles District visit some of these sites.

One of the most interesting features of the Canyonlands region are potholes that have formed in the slickrock. They range in size from a foot or less in diameter to deep depressions that are more like caves turned on their side. Sometimes called "tanks" because they serve as natural reservoirs to store rainwater, they have become the source of legend and folklore in southeastern Utah.

Visitor Information

The Needles Visitor Center is located on Hwy. 211, 35 miles west of US Hwy. 191.

Outdoor Activities

BIKING

Within the Needles District, there are two excellent mountain bike trails, which are also used by backpackers and four-wheel-drivers.

Colorado River Overlook Rd.

This 14-mile round-trip, moderately difficult road offers beautiful scenery all along the route. The view from the Colorado River Overlook, more than 1,000 feet down, is one not soon to

be forgotten. Bikers in good shape can make the ride in a couple of hours, but with so much scenery on this ride, it is best to take your time. The trail begins from the southwestern end of the visitor center parking area, off Hwy. 211, 35 miles west of US Hwy. 191, and heads north along a signed dirt road.

Elephant Hill Rd.

The Elephant Hill Rd. is more difficult because of the sandy and rocky sections that bikers will need to walk, but it is a good ride of 9.6 miles over a semiloop, which can be expanded to 28.5 miles by taking a couple of side trips. The trail begins at the Elephant Hill trailhead, about 5.5 miles past the visitor center, at the end of the south branch of the park road toward Campground B. Instead of entering the campground, continue straight ahead onto the dirt road after the pavement ends. It is about 2.5 miles from the end of the pavement to the trailhead.

FOUR-WHEEL-DRIVE TRIPS

Long before the hikers and mountain bikers discovered the Needles District, and while cowboys from Dugout Ranch were still herding cattle in the region on horseback, the jeepsters, as the early four-wheel-drivers were often called, discovered the unlimited opportunities to test their machines and driving skills over the slickrock, around the pinnacles and ledges and through the sand of the Needles. Four-wheel-drive vehicles are considered a part of the basic transportation requirements for most residents of southeastern Utah, and four-wheel-drive trips are a popular form of recreation. Rentals and tours can be arranged at the **Needles Outpost**, located on a spur road near the Hwy. 211 entrance to Canyonlands, or in several of the surrounding communities (see the **Moab** and **San Juan County** chapters). In addition to the Colorado River Overlook Rd. and the Elephant Hill Rd. noted in the Biking section above, other four-wheel-drive trips include the following.

Davis Canyon

Davis Canyon parallels Lavender Canyon to the northwest and heads in a southwesterly direction. Watch for the small "Davis Canyon" sign on the left or west side of Hwy. 211 about 24 miles from the junction of Hwy. 211 and US Hwy. 191. The round-trip distance is 24 miles and offers plenty of opportunities to explore the side canyons into Davis Canyon at the end of the road.

Lavender Canyon

If you are inexperienced, this 35-mile round-trip drive is a good choice. The road access is the same as for Davis Canyon, off Hwy. 211 about 24 miles from its junction with US Hwy. 191, and heads up Lavender Creek in a southwesterly direction from Hwy. 211. It does not enter Canyonlands National Park until the last couple of miles, near the Cedar Mesa area. Several arches and a labyrinth of narrow canyons make this an interesting area to explore on foot once you get there.

HIKING

Always bring water with you no matter what the season. You'll need 1 gallon per person per day, more for summer hiking or extended trips. Wear lightweight hiking boots and protect yourself from the sun, especially your head! Carry a map and know how to use it.

Cave Spring Trail

This 0.6-mile loop walk is a great trail for families. Pick up a trail guide for this hike at the trailhead. The leaflet interprets the vegetation along the trail, which winds past a pictograph panel with ancient handprints and a well-preserved cowboy line camp near Cave Spring that was used from the late 1800s until the 1950s. Here you can touch many of the items left by the cowboys, but be sure to leave everything for others to enjoy. The walk requires the use of two ladders to negotiate the steep Cedar Mesa sandstone sections, but is still a fairly easy walk. You start out walking along and underneath the cliff, then climb on top of the mesa using the ladders. The trailhead is located on Hwy. 211 2.5 miles west of the visitor center.

Confluence Overlook

This moderate hike of 11 miles round trip takes the better part of a day, but the view of the confluence of the Green and Colorado Rivers is well worth the effort and the time. The confluence comes into view suddenly and is one of the most impressive sights in all of southeastern Utah. The trail begins at the end of the north branch of the paved road, 5.5 miles past the visitor center.

Elephant Hill Trailhead

This trailhead offers three excellent day hikes of 10 to 11 miles round trip each. The trailhead is located about 5.5 miles past the visitor center, at the end of the south branch of the park road toward Campground B. Instead of entering the campground, continue straight ahead onto the dirt road after the pavement ends. It is about 2.5 miles from the end of the pavement to the trailhead, but the dirt road is passable for passenger cars. Watch for rocks and sand and pay attention to the sharp curves and narrow stretches.

Druid Arch—The most popular hike is the 10.8-mile round-trip Druid Arch Trail. One of the most impressive arches anywhere, Druid Arch appears to be southeastern Utah's version of England's Stonehenge.

Chesler Park Trail—The 10.7-mile semi-loop Chesler Park Trail takes you into Chesler Park—a grassy, broad, relatively level area with a cluster of spires jutting up in the middle—and to the east edge of the Grabens, an area of narrow, shallow, grassy valleys that lies between two elevated faults. It is a popular backpacking destination, with three designated camping zones (backcountry permit and fee required) in Chesler Park. The hike also includes the Joint Trail section, one of the most exciting trails within Canyonlands, and one that claustrophobic hikers will not enjoy because of the narrow squeeze (only about 2 feet wide in some sections) between the rocks.

Devil's Pocket Trail—The Devil's Pocket Trail is a 10.5-mile semiloop hike that takes you around the most impressive 500-foot-high pinnacles in the Needles District, through the Graben valley known as Devil's Pocket, to the edge of Chesler Park. Many regard this as the most scenic hike in the Needles District because of the magnificent vistas, balanced rocks and the 500-foot-high slender needles of stone that you pass. Nevertheless, it is one of the least-used trails in the district.

Roadside Ruin Trail

This 0.3-mile walk leads to a well-preserved Anasazi granary. A leaflet keyed to numbered posts along the trail, available at the trailhead, describes native plants, many of them used by the Anasazi, such as the Utah juniper, the soft bark of which was used as diapers and cradle-board padding for babies. The seeds of Indian ricegrass were gathered, cooked and ground into meal. Prickly pear cactus was used as a food and for compresses for wounds. The spines of the narrow-leaf yucca were used as needles and the leaf fibers were made into cord and rope, and woven for sandals and mats. The trail begins 0.4 mile west of the visitor center.

Slickrock Foot Trail

This 3-mile walk is quite easy and offers panoramic views all along its length, plus a good introduction to the slickrock trails marked by rock cairns (small stacks of rocks that mark the way) on the "petrified" sand dunes. A trail guide with a map and brief description interprets the trail. The trailhead is roughly 5 miles past the visitor center, just a short distance before the end of the paved road.

Squaw Flat Trailhead

Squaw Flat Trailhead offers access to four day-hikes, ranging in length from 7.4 miles to 10.7 miles. These trails take you into the heart of the red spires and pinnacles of the Needles themselves and are part of the reason that most campers in the Needles area are hikers. You can spend up to a maximum 14 days in the campground and take a different hike each day. These hikes are best taken in the spring and early summer or late Sept.–Nov. to avoid the extreme summer heat.

The four trails from Squaw Flat Trailhead are

the **Squaw Canyon Loop Trail** (7.4 miles); **Lost Canyon Trail** (8.7 miles over a semiloop); **Peekaboo Arch Trail** (9.4 miles round trip); and **Elephant and Big Spring Canyons Trail** (10.7 miles over a semiloop). The trailhead is at the end of the middle branch of the paved road, about 3 miles from the visitor center.

Where to Stay

CAMPING
Squaw Flat Campground
Campground A has 16 sites; **Campground B** has 10 sites. Chemical toilets are provided in each campground. Water is available Apr.–Oct.; the rest of the year, it must be either brought in or obtained in other locations within the park. Fees are charged; stays limited to seven days. The adjacent campgrounds are located about 5.5 miles past the visitor center.

Where to Eat

There are no dining facilities located within Canyonlands National Park, but there are restaurants available in the surrounding communities. See the **Moab** and **San Juan County** chapters.

Services

Visitor Information
Canyonlands National Park Headquarters—Open Mon.–Fri. 8 A.M.–4:30 P.M. **125 W. 200 S., Moab, UT 84532; 435-259-7164.**

Hans Flat Ranger Station—Hours vary. Located about 46 miles east of Hwy. 24 (no telephone). **www.nps.gov/cany.**

Island in the Sky Visitor Center—Information, books, maps, a schedule of interpretive activities and backcountry permits. Open in winter daily 8 A.M.–4:30 P.M.; spring through fall 8 A.M.–6 P.M. Located on Hwy. 313 about 25 miles southwest of US Hwy. 191. **435-259-4712.**

Moab Information Center—Open daily 8 A.M.–8 P.M.; in winter 9 A.M.–5 P.M. Located at

Center and Main Sts., Moab, UT 84532; 1-800-635-6622; 435-259-8825.

Multi-Agency Visitor Center—Open Mon.–Fri. 8 A.M.–5 P.M.; Apr.–Oct. Sat.–Sun. 10 A.M.–5 P.M. Located in the San Juan County Courthouse. **117 S. Main, Monticello; 1-800-574-4386; 435-587-3235.**

The Needles Visitor Center—Open daily 8 A.M.–6 P.M.; in winter 8 A.M.–4:30 P.M. Located on Hwy. 211, 35 miles west of US Hwy. 191. **435-259-4711.**

San Juan County

Utah archaeologists half joke that the entire southeastern corner of Utah should be declared one large archaeological area and that the number of archaeological sites in San Juan County should be counted by the square mile, if not the acre. Only a handful of the thousands of sites have been excavated, and even fewer have been restored; others have been preserved because of their isolation and a growing awareness of their beauty and value. Ancient Puebloan ruins are one of the big draws in this area. Hovenweep National Monument, Edge of the Cedars State Park and Grand Gulch Primitive Area offer just three of the best-known sites to study the legacy of these people.

The modern Ute and Navajo tribes are also an important part of the region. The enormous Navajo Reservation begins 23 miles south of Blanding and stretches across the Utah–Arizona border, taking in a large chunk of northeastern Arizona and part of northwestern New Mexico. More than 150,000 members of the Navajo Nation, or Diné as they call themselves, live on the reservation.

The center for Utah Navajos is Monument Valley, a remarkably beautiful valley full of eroded red sandstone monoliths, pinnacles and towers that make up one of the most famous backdrops in the world. The Monument Valley scenery is reason enough to visit southeastern Utah, but there's so much more. The small but lovely Natural Bridges National Monument, the sinuous San Juan River that cuts through the area, the Blue Mountains and nearby Canyonlands National Park are a few of the attractions that lure travelers.

The area described in this chapter, San Juan County, is the largest of Utah's 29 counties. With an area of 8,103 square miles, it is larger than the states of Connecticut, Rhode Island, New Jersey, Delaware and Hawaii. Visitors will find services along US Hwys. 191 and 163 in six towns, located approximately 20 miles from each other, starting with La Sal Junction in the north, then Monticello, Blanding, Bluff, Mexican Hat and Monument Valley on the Utah-Arizona border.

History

Human presence in southeastern Utah for the last 12,000 years is a dramatic story of survival in a land that most of the world would regard as desolate and unappealing. No area of Utah has received greater attention by archaeologists than San Juan County. Their research indicates that the earliest inhabitants, the Paleo-Indians, hunted big game in the area during the ice age, leaving spear points as the only trace of their presence.

By 5000 B.C. the Paleo-Indian cultures had left the area, their destiny tied to the large herds of big game that had moved eastward onto the Great Plains. These hunters were replaced by Desert Archaic hunter-gatherers who did not establish permanent residences but moved from place to place in search of small game and wild

---

Getting There
Monticello is located on US Hwy. 191, 291 miles southeast of Salt Lake City; Blanding is another 25 miles farther south.

foods. They were extremely well adapted to this desert region and pursued their practical lifestyle for at least 5,000 years.

Around A.D. 200 corn was introduced from Mesoamerica, and the Archaic peoples began to cultivate small crops as a supplement to their wild food. To remain close to their crops, they began to establish permanent residences and to pursue a more settled lifestyle. In time, the Archaic peoples made the transition to the people we call the Anasazi—a Navajo word meaning "enemy ancestor." Because of the resentment of the Anasazi's descendants—the Hopi and Zuni—to the term "Anasazi," some now refer to the early inhabitants as Puebloans.

Over the next millennium, the people occupied what is now called the Four Corners region of Utah, Colorado, New Mexico and Arizona, progressing from small farming hamlets to large-scale villages, or pueblos. They made exquisite baskets but soon began developing fired pottery, which was both practical and increasingly artistic. Irrigation techniques improved, and new crops, such as beans and squash, were added. As interactions with other cultures brought new ideas, between A.D. 1100 and A.D. 1200, clans began to coalesce into very large villages, of which the best known are Mesa Verde in nearby Colorado and Chaco Canyon in New Mexico. Numerous examples of these pueblos also remain in San Juan County, in such places as Westwater Canyon, Montezuma Canyon and Chinle Wash.

About A.D. 1250 the Anasazi began to move away from the San Juan area to better farmlands along the Rio Grande and the Little Colorado River. Archaeologists speculate that the move was caused by several factors: a particularly long drought that tipped the balance in this marginal land, not enough land to support the growing number of occupants, and perhaps attacks by invading nomadic Indians from the north, such as the Utes and Navajos. Pueblo Indian traditions indicate that internal strife and the need to purify people through a religious pilgrimage to a new land were the primary reason they abandoned their homes and moved south.

Navajo traditions relate that the Navajo and Anasazi lived together in peace and cooperation, as the Anasazi introduced the Navajo to corn. Disputes arose, however, and the friction left the Navajos impoverished and often enslaved by the Anasazi. Because of their wrongdoing, their unwillingness to live in harmony and their abuse of supernatural powers given them by the gods, the Anasazi were punished in a variety of ways. Various Navajo legends recount the Anasazi were turned to fish in the San Juan River, beset with lockjaw and paralysis, had the air sucked out of their lungs by a strong wind, were burned in a great fire, were crushed by an ice storm or were drowned in a flood that destroyed everything in its path.

While the Navajo, or Diné, are the largest group of Indians living in southeastern Utah today, they are relative latecomers to the area. Anthropologists indicate that they migrated from northwestern Canada with other Athapascan peoples, such as the Apache, and reached the Southwest sometime between A.D. 1300 and A.D. 1500. The Navajo may have pushed up to the San Juan River about the time that the Pilgrims were founding Plymouth Colony in 1620 and were as far north as Elk Ridge by the late 1700s. Navajo oral tradition says nothing of a migration from the north but does describe their arrival in this region as a journey through three worlds beneath this one.

Originally hunter-gatherers, in historic times the Navajo have depended on crops such as corn, beans and squash, which their pueblo neighbors taught them to grow, and raising livestock, especially sheep, goats and horses, which they later obtained from Spanish settlers. The early Navajo seemed to have alternately lived alongside their neighbors peaceably and at times raided them. This was a tactic they used against Anglo settlers in Utah, New Mexico and Arizona, after the settlers arrived in the Southwest in the 1850s and 1860s. The U.S. government back East sent military expeditions to protect American, Pueblo and Mexican settlers when much of the Southwest was ceded to the United States in 1848.

In 1864 U.S. Army Capt. Kit Carson succeeded in rounding up approximately two-thirds of the Navajo Nation, using intimidation tactics that led many of the people to surrender. They were forced to make what has come to be called the Long Walk to Ft. Sumner on the dry southeastern New Mexico plain, where they were incarcerated at Bosque Redondo and forced to submit to reservation living in an area that could not support them. They were finally allowed to return to their home in 1868, after many Navajo had died and the government conceded that the experiment had failed miserably. A number of the 4,000 Navajo who eluded capture and refused to surrender took refuge in the isolated reaches of Navajo Mountain and Elk Ridge in Utah's San Juan County.

Today the Navajo have successfully preserved many of their old traditions, while accommodating the economic and political realities of today. As well as being a sovereign nation within the United States and in charge of their own affairs, the Navajo also hold elected county offices and work in all areas of the economy. They are no longer required to send their children to government-run boarding schools. Instead the children attend high schools at Montezuma Creek and Monument Valley, built and administered by the San Juan School District. Nevertheless, because the Navajo have not traditionally lived in a cash economy, the poverty level is high and living conditions are substandard compared to Anglo-America. Many Native Americans still feel an undercurrent of discrimination—even racism—in their relations with white neighbors.

Mormon pioneers did not establish a foothold in southeastern Utah until 1880, three years after the death of the Great Colonizer Brigham Young and 33 years after the arrival of the first Mormon pioneers into the Salt Lake Valley 330 miles to the north. Two hundred and fifty Mormon settlers arrived on the San Juan River on April 6, 1880, after an arduous six-month, 180-mile journey across the canyons of southeastern Utah from older Mormon settlements in southwestern Utah. Known as the Hole-in-the-Rockers, because of the narrow slit through which they had taken their wagons and livestock to cross the Colorado River, these Mormon pioneers established the towns of Bluff in 1880, Monticello in 1887, Blanding in 1905 and other Mormon outposts in Colorado and New Mexico. The Mormons succeeded economically by first working in the silver mines in nearby Colorado, and then by developing cattle and sheep herds that competed with already established non-Mormon outfits from Colorado and Texas. Economic and social tensions marked relations between Mormons and non-Mormons, but around the turn of the 20th century, the non-Mormon outfits were bought out.

In the 1950s uranium and oil booms brought in non-Mormons and gave a strong boost to a stagnating economy. Over the last five decades the boom-bust cycles of uranium and oil have been a challenge. The tourism industry, which traces its origins to the turn of the 20th century when national articles about the region led to the designation of Natural Bridges National Monument in 1908, has grown steadily, through the popularity of Monument Valley as a setting for John Ford–directed Western movies and with the designation of Canyonlands as a national park in 1964.

Major Attractions

Natural Bridges National Monument

Two hundred and sixty million years ago, this area was a white sandy beach along a receding shallow sea. The sand hardened into a 1,000-foot-thick layer known today as the Cedar Mesa Sandstone Formation of the Permian geologic period. The formation is older than the more familiar Navajo, Kayenta, Wingate, Chinle and Moenkopi Formations of the Triassic period. Over time, water began to cut through the siltstone and sandstone, forming entrenched meanders or large goosenecks like those seen nearby on the San Juan River. Eventually water, rocks, sand and silt pushed down the canyons at terrific speeds by flash floods cut through the narrow necks, leaving a natural bridge above. The bridges were originally thick and massive, but through gradual erosion by precipitation, percolation and wind, they eventually become more delicate until they collapse.

Natural Bridges is one of the nation's earliest national monuments. It was established by presidential proclamation in 1908, following the publication of a *National Geographic* article describing the three large natural bridges in White and Armstrong Canyons. The natural bridges were formed by tributaries of the Colorado River, which eroded the soft Cedar Mesa sandstone through deep bends in the river, leaving behind the bridges. The buttresses and spans that you see today have been formed by the harder caprock that tops the softer sedimentary layers.

One of the bridges—Sipapu—is second in size only to Rainbow Bridge in Glen Canyon National Recreation Area, which is the largest known natural bridge in the world. **Sipapu Bridge** measures 220 feet in height with a span of 268 feet. The span is 31 feet wide and 53 feet thick. Sipapu is a Hopi word to describe the hole or passageway by which the ancestors of the Hopi entered this world from another world.

Only slightly smaller than Sipapu, the **Kachina Bridge** is 210 feet high with a span of 204 feet but is the most massive of the three bridges, with a width of 44 feet and thickness of 93 feet. The name Kachina was given because of the Indian pictographs on the bridge abutment, which resemble the Kachina masks of the Hopi.

The smallest, oldest and most fragile of the three bridges, **Owachomo Bridge** has a height of 106 feet and a span of 180 feet, but it is only 27 feet wide and 9 feet thick. Owachomo is also a Hopi word that means "flat-rock mound," for a protrusion on the bridge.

Outdoor Activities

The **hiking** trail to Sipapu Bridge descends 600 feet to the bottom of White Canyon, for a total round-trip distance of about 1.2 miles; Sipapu is 2 miles from the visitor center. Kachina Bridge is reached via a 1.5-mile round-trip hike to the bottom of the canyon and back; located 5 miles from the visitor center. Owachomo Bridge can be reached by an easy 0.8-mile round-trip hike that descends 300 feet; located 7 miles from the visitor center. To shorten the hike to all three bridges by 2.5 miles, you may want to use a shuttle between the Sipapu and Owachomo trailheads, or start midway at the Kachina Bridge trailhead, hike down to Sipapu, retrace your route to Kachina and continue up to Owachomo, then return to Kachina.

The hike between Sipapu and Kachina Bridges takes you past the 1,000-year-old **Horse Collar Ruin,** abandoned by the ancient Puebloans in the 1200s. The ruin complex includes two adjacent ruins, several dwellings, two large granaries, smaller storage bins and two nicely preserved kivas. Inside the kivas are shelves and benches along the circular walls, a plastered fire pit with an accompanying stone windbreak and a ventilation shaft.

Seeing and Doing

For nonhikers, there are overlooks of each bridge within easy walks of the **scenic drive.** The Horse Collar Ruin can be viewed from an overlook located on the driving loop 3 miles from the visitor center.

Visitor Information

Natural Bridges National Monument Visitor Center—Exhibits, a slide show, area books and maps and rangers provide information about current conditions and answer questions about the monument. A booklet entitled

---

Getting There

Natural Bridges is located 48 miles west of Blanding, just off Hwy. 95. An 8-mile, one-way loop road connects the visitor center with trailheads to the Sipapu, Kachina and Owachomo Bridges. If you want to hike to all of the bridges and explore some of the surrounding attractions, plan to spend the entire day.

Of Wind, Water and Sand: The Natural Bridges Story offers an excellent introduction to the monument. Open during winter daily (except for holidays) 8 A.M.–4:30 P.M.; May–Aug. hours are extended. **435-692-1234; www.nps. gov/nabr.**

There is a **campground** within the monument with 13 campsites and rest rooms, located 0.3 mile from the visitor center; the closest motel accommodations are in Blanding on US Hwy. 191 or west on Hwy. 95 at Fry Canyon.

Hovenweep National Monument

The Ute Indians called this remote area on the Utah-Colorado border Hovenweep, meaning "deserted valley," and the six unusual villages left behind by the Pueblo people in the late 1200s still convey a here-one-day, gone-the-next feeling. The original inhabitants may have migrated westward from nearby Mesa Verde or perhaps were outcasts from that major center.

Whatever their origin, they cultivated corn, beans and squash in the scattered villages located between Montezuma and McElmo Creeks. Archaeologists postulate that many acres that have now returned to sagebrush were cultivated fields. Corn was the first domesticated crop and may have been planted as early as 2,000 years ago as the inhabitants began the transition from big game hunting to agriculture. By about A.D. 1270, villages like the Square Tower community were populated by several hundred individuals with houses, granaries, fields, gardens, reservoirs and dams to regulate the flow of water.

Getting There

To reach the monument, head south from Blanding on US Hwy. 191 for 15 miles, then turn east on Hwy. 262 to Hatch Trading Post and then continue eastward for 16 miles. All but 2 miles of the road to the Hovenweep Visitor Center and Square Tower Ruins are paved, and the graveled 2 miles are easily negotiated by passenger vehicles.

When a major drought struck the region about A.D. 1200, the outlying villages were abandoned as inhabitants relocated to canyons with permanent springs.

One of the most interesting aspects of the ruins is the variety of shapes employed for these dwellings. Oval, circular, square and D shapes were used. The towers here may possibly have been built as defensive fortifications against attack from other clans or perhaps Shoshone Indians coming from the north. Some towers, such as the northwest end of Hovenweep Castle, may have been used to track the summer and winter solstices and the autumnal and vernal equinoxes. Certain windows within the towers are placed in such a way that sunlight strikes particular points on the interior walls at those times of year. The towers may also have been used for signal fires between this area and Mesa Verde.

The oral traditions of the present-day Pueblo Indians of Arizona and New Mexico tell of their ancestors coming from the area known today as the Four Corners region. Here they lived for hundreds of years and developed a high level of civilization before the Great Spirit directed them to abandon their homes and move to other places with better food sources and a better environment—a place where they might attain the perfection of their society. By the last quarter of the 13th century, large communities were being established to the south, perhaps with new and more elaborate religious ceremonies, which, with the push of a severe drought, drew the Hovenweep community to a new homeland. It is likely that the former residents of the Hovenweep area moved southwest to the Hopi villages, south to the Zuni villages and southeast to the Pueblo villages at Acoma and along the Rio Grande.

The Hovenweep ruins were probably known to the early settlers on Montezuma and McElmo Creeks, including Mormon frontiersman Peter Shirts, who was at the mouth of Montezuma Creek in 1879. Over the next four decades, the ruins became better known and in 1917–1918 J. Walter Fewkes, chief of the Bureau of American Ethnology, made an archaeological survey and recommended they be designated a national monument. Hovenweep was designated a national monument in 1923 and is administered by the National Park Service at Southeast Utah Group in Moab.

Outdoor Activities

A number of loop **hiking** trails will take you to the most significant ruins. Visitors are urged to stay on existing trails and not to disturb the ruins in any way or to pick up any artifacts. Hovenweep is a treasure house for archaeologists, who hope to learn more about the culture and life of the Anasazi. Its sites and ruins are also sacred places for the Pueblo Indians. Plan a full day to visit Hovenweep, but you can see the major ruins at Square Tower in a few hours. An especially beautiful time to view the ruins is at sunset or sunrise. If you stay overnight in the campground you can expect to enjoy a brilliant starlit night.

The Square Tower group includes the famous **Square Tower, Hovenweep Castle, Hovenweep House, Twin Towers, Stronghold House** and **Tower** (entrance to which was gained by climbing up the still visible hand- and toeholds chiseled into the rock) and **Eroded Boulder House** (which was built inside the overhang of a large boulder, incorporating the boulder into the walls and roof). In addition to Square Tower Ruins, the **Holly, Horseshoe** and **Hackberry** ruins may be visited along a 9-mile round-trip hiking trail.

Seeing and Doing

If you find you have a little extra time, head south from the visitor center on Hwy. 262 to Aneth, on the San Juan River, then follow the river as it flows westward past Montezuma Creek, where you take Hwy. 163 to Bluff. There are other ruins along this **scenic drive.**

Visitor Information

Hovenweep National Monument Visitor Center—A trail guide is available here. For a well-written, beautifully illustrated introduction to Hovenweep, pick up a copy of Ian Thompson's *The Towers of Hovenweep* (Mesa Verde Museum Association, 1993), which is also available at other centers in the area. Open year-round daily (except for December 25) 8 A.M.– 5 P.M. Located near the Square Tower Ruins. **970-562-4282; www.nps.gov/hove.**

Gas and supplies can be purchased at Hatch Trading Post or in the nearby communities of Montezuma Creek and Bluff. The closest accommodations are at Bluff and Blanding; within the monument, a small **campground** designed for tent camping and RVs 25 feet or less in length is located 1 mile from the visitor center. It has water and rest rooms. Open Apr.–Oct.

Monument Valley Navajo Tribal Park

Monument Valley's eroded sandstone buttes and pinnacles fit almost everyone's notion of what the Southwest should look like. But before it became a valley of beauty to serve the imagination of thousands of visitors, the area was a solid 1,000-foot layer of sandstone. As the early Rocky Mountains deposited sediments in a vast lowland basin, they cemented into rock. About 50 million years ago, pressure from inside the earth slowly lifted the deposits to an elevation of 1–2 miles above sea level. Since that time, the forces of wind and water have slowly chiseled away at the layers of sandstone, shaping and reshaping the rock until the last vestiges of the immense sandstone plateau remain as the pinnacles, towers and buttes of Monument Valley. As you look at the rocks, you will see on some of them the younger and harder Shinarump Formation, which serves as a cap over the De Chelly Formation, which makes up the cliffs. At the base of the cliffs, the softer Organ Rock Shale or Claystone forms a kind of pedestal for the monuments. Beneath the Claystone, the Cedar Mesa sandstone serves as a broad foundation for the entire valley.

Monument Valley was home to the ancient Puebloan Indians for nearly 1,000 years until they abandoned their homes here and elsewhere in the Four Corners region around A.D. 1270. By the 1500s the Navajo Indians had entered the Four Corners region and by the 1800s had established homes in Monument Valley. As westward expansion brought contact and conflict with the Anglos from the east, the Navajo were forced to leave their traditional lands and 8,500 made the Long Walk to Bosque Redondo in eastern New Mexico in 1864. Some escaped the ordeal by hiding out in Monument Valley and in places north of the San Juan River. One of the groups, led by Hoskaninni, escaped capture by the soldiers and crossed the San Juan River with only one horse, one rifle and a band of 20 sheep, then journeyed several days on foot to the south slope of Navajo Mountain. The Navajo at Bosque Redondo were allowed to return to their homeland at Navajo Mountain after a four-year exile. Hoskaninni returned to Monument Valley to live until his death in 1912.

When the Navajo Reservation was established in 1868, Monument Valley was the northwest corner of the original reservation. Later, in 1884, the reservation was expanded to its approximate present boundaries, with the annexation of areas north and west of Monument Valley. The expansion came after four miners were killed—James Merrick and Ernest Mitchell in 1880 and Samuel Walcott and James McNally in 1884—when they went into Monument Valley looking for silver mines.

Anglo miners were not permitted on the reservation, but Anglo traders were. In 1906 John and Louisa Wetherill from Mancos, Colorado, started a trading post at Oljato ("Moonlight Water"). The Wetherills established friendly relations with the Navajo and thus were allowed to stay. Seventeen years later, another young Colorado couple, Harry and Leone "Mike" Goulding, arrived to establish their trading post under the Big Rock Door Mesa.

It was Harry Goulding who in 1938 brought Hollywood director John Ford to Monument Valley, where he filmed Stagecoach. Since then Monument Valley has served as the location for hundreds of commercials and dozens of movies.

In 1959 Monument Valley was designated a Navajo Tribal Park and a year later, a visitor center was constructed just across the state line in Arizona.

Seeing and Doing

A 17-mile self-guided **scenic drive** over a dirt road begins at the visitor center and provides access to the heart of Monument Valley. The road is native surface and can be somewhat rough, but it is passable by regular automobiles. Overlooks along the drive provide plenty of photo opportunities. After you descend the switchbacks to begin the driving tour, you pass an old abandoned gas station that will catch the eye of any photo bug. But save plenty of film for the natural wonders.

The first viewpoint is of the **Mittens, East and West,** and **Merrick Butte.** It was near this butte that James Merrick was found scalped and covered with rocks and brush in 1880 when he and his partner, Ernest Mitchell, entered the valley looking for a secret Navajo silver mine. The Navajo blamed the murder on local Paiutes, who maintained their innocence. The Mittens are probably the most famous and most often photographed formations in Monument Valley, and their namesake is easily recognized in the sandstone formation. Navajo myth holds that the formations are two hands left behind by the gods as a promise that someday they would return and rule with power from Monument Valley.

As the drive continues, you pass other unusual formations: **Elephant Butte; Three Sisters** (three holy people who were turned to

Getting There

Monument Valley is on US Hwy. 163 at the Utah–Arizona border about 40 miles southwest of Bluff. It is wholly within the Navajo Reservation, whose northern boundary is the San Juan River. Keep in mind that permission to photograph the Navajo residents and their property is required and a gratuity is expected. In order to better preserve the valley and because people live in Monument Valley, hiking and off-road travel are prohibited.

stone); **Thunder Bird Mesa; Rain God Mesa;** and **Totem Pole,** an important site for Navajo rain-producing ceremonies. The drive provides ever-changing perspectives of the sandstone formations, while clouds and different times of day color and shade the stone with unrestrained variety.

This is a drive not to be hurried. Take your time. Drive slowly and stop often and contemplate the beauty with a singleness of mind. If you do, the rocks and the land will begin to speak to you in ways you may never have heard before. Even for the uninitiated, Monument Valley can be a very sacred place.

While you are in Monument Valley, a stop at Goulding's Trading Post and Lodge is worthwhile. Harry and Mike Goulding established their trading post in 1923 and constructed the two-story red sandstone building in 1928. The building now serves as a **museum** depicting how the trading post looked during many of the 40 years it was operated by the Gouldings. Open year-round daily 7:30 A.M.–9 P.M. A few steps in back of the museum is the movie set reproduction of Capt. Nathan Brittle's Quarters, which was constructed in Oct. 1949 during the filming of *She Wore a Yellow Ribbon.* Goulding's also provides the closest motel **accommodations** to Monument Valley as well as a variety of **tours.**

Guides

You can also arrange for **guided tours** with Navajo tour guides. A group of tour operators are located in front of the visitor center, and they offer a 1.5-hour tour over the scenic drive route, or a 2.5-hour tour that takes you into the restricted area where you can see natural bridges, Anasazi ruins and rock art, and a Navajo weaver at work inside a hogan. Half-day, all-day and other specialized tours, including horseback tours, can also be arranged. When you arrive at the visitor center, you are likely to be approached by several individuals about a guided tour, so it is good to decide beforehand if that is what you want, and, if so, inquire about the details of the tours being offered. Depending on the demand, prices are sometimes negotiable.

Visitor Information

Monument Valley Navajo Tribal Park Visitor Center—Exhibits, an Indian crafts shop and an information desk are all part of the center. Open mid-Apr.–mid-Oct. daily 7 A.M.–8 P.M.; rest of the year daily (except Christmas and New Year's; closes at noon on Thanksgiving) 8 A.M.–5 P.M. Admission fee is charged. Located at the Utah–Arizona border 3.5 miles off US Hwy. 163. **435-727-3353.**

Edge of the Cedars State Park and Museum

Settled in 1905, Blanding was built, in part, on an ancient Pueblo village, part of which has been excavated and is now included in the Edge of the Cedars State Park. The state park includes six clusters of ruins, of which only one group has been excavated. An underground kiva, or ceremonial room, has been partly restored so that visitors can now enter it using a ladder that descends through the roof. Museum exhibits include pottery, jewelry, stone tools, baskets, sandals and clothing as well as artifacts from the Hispanic and Anglo settlers. A gift shop sells contemporary Navajo and Ute crafts. A variety of exhibits are presented throughout the year. Open during the summer daily 9 A.M.–6 P.M.; rest of the year daily (except for official holidays) 9 A.M.–5 P.M. Located on the northwestern edge of Blanding, where signs from Center St. direct you to the site. **660 W. 400 N., Blanding, UT 84511; 435-678-2238; parks.state.ut.us/ www1/edge.htm.**

Four Corners Monument

The only place in the United States where you can be in four states at the same time is at the meeting point of Utah, Arizona, New Mexico and Colorado, known as the Four Corners. An inlaid concrete slab marks the point where the four states meet, and a visit to the monument makes a good geography lesson for both young and old. Since there is not much at the monument—except the chance to spread-eagle yourself across four states and have your photo taken—people usually stay less than a half hour.

You will probably want to combine a stop at the monument with a visit to Hovenweep National Monument, Monument Valley or both. There are Indian craft booths encircling the marker that sell pottery and jewelry.

Located on US Hwy. 160. To reach the Four Corners Monument from Utah, take US Hwy. 191 south from Bluff across the Utah–Arizona border until you reach US Hwy. 160. Head east on US Hwy. 160 for approximately 35 miles until you reach the monument. If you want to return along an alternate route, continue east on US Hwy. 160 for about 5 miles to Colorado Hwy. 41, which turns to the north. Follow it back into Utah, where it becomes Utah Hwy. 262, which you can follow through Aneth and Montezuma Creek, where it becomes Hwy. 163, to its junction with US Hwy. 191 in Bluff, 15 miles south of Blanding.

Goosenecks of the San Juan State Park

The Goosenecks of the San Juan River are a textbook example of an "incised meander" as the mighty San Juan River winds back and forth for 6.5 miles yet covers only 1 mile of actual distance. Millions of years ago, the once flat land was lifted up by powerful subterranean forces. As the land rose, the San Juan River cut deeper and deeper, eventually reaching older layers of rock of the Pennsylvanian Hermosa Formation. Now the river flows 1,000 feet below the overlook. This is another one of those spots that suggests the timelessness of the region, yet erosion continues, especially when wind scours the grains of sand from the canyon walls and violent thunderstorms seem to melt away the earth, adding tons of silt and sand to the sediment-laden waters of the river.

The powerful, magnificent view of the Goosenecks is not to be missed, but a half hour or so is all that most visitors spend at the state park. There are no restraints in areas of the park and caution is advised, especially with children. From here, the hairpin curves of the Goosenecks of the San Juan River are most dramatic, and you can wave at the river rats far, far below you.

While there are a dozen primitive campsites at the overlook, there are probably better places to camp with water available. Located on Hwy. 361 5 miles north of Mexican Hat. To reach the Goosenecks, head northwest from Mexican Hat on US Hwy. 163 for 3 miles, then turn west onto Hwy. 261 for 1 mile until you reach the paved park road, Hwy. 316, which heads west for 4 miles to the overlook.

Festivals and Events

Folk Fair Festival

July 4. This celebration in Blanding offers performances, folk singers, ethnic dancers, demonstrations, exhibits, booths and Dutch-oven meals. Local craftspeople, including members of the Ute and Navajo tribes, usually participate. **Blanding City Office, 50 W. 100 S., Blanding, UT 84511; 435-678-2791.**

Four Corners Indian Art Festival

end of Aug. This unique festival is held in Blanding at the Edge of the Cedars State Park Museum and highlights Indian arts and crafts. The two-day event features some of the region's most outstanding Native American artists displaying their paintings, sculpture, jewelry, pottery, weaving and other works. Native American dancers, demonstrations, educational programs and Native American food offer something for everyone. **435-678-2238.**

Outdoor Activities

Biking

Valley of the Gods Scenic Loop

The Valley of the Gods offers a wonder-filled route for cyclists. An 18-mile scenic loop road winds through the valley, which is inhabited by fanciful rock formations. From US Hwy. 163 approximately 10 miles southwest of Bluff, turn right (north) to enter the valley on the native-surface road; the road exits at Hwy. 261 6 miles northwest of the intersection of Hwy. 261 with US Hwy. 163.

Four-Wheel-Drive Trips

The carefree days of going wherever you could take a jeep are gone, as federal land management policies have now brought restrictions. Still, there are hundreds of miles of four-wheel roads and trails open for travel in San Juan County. For information about self-guided, four-wheel-drive trips, contact the **Bureau of Land Management, San Juan Field Office, 435 N. Main St., P.O. Box 7, Monticello, UT 84535; 435-587-1500.**

Guides

For guided tours of the area, contact **Tours of the Big Country, P.O. Box 309, Bluff, UT 84512, 435-672-2281,** and **Far Out Expeditions,** also in Bluff; **435-672-2294.** Other tour companies are headquartered in Moab (see the **Moab** chapter).

Golf

Blue Mountain Meadows Golf Course

Operated by the city of Monticello, and expanded to 18 holes in 2002, the course is generally not crowded, and greens fees are very reasonable. Unlike most Utah courses, the course is located in an arroyo, or wash, and the course plays over wooded and rocky hillsides contrasted with grassy meadows and a pleasant stream in the bottom of the arroyo. Generally open Apr.–Oct. Located on the southern end of town, just west of US Hwy. 191 in Monticello. **435-587-2468.**

Hiking

Blue Mountain and Elk Ridge Trails

The excellent hiking trails in the Manti-La Sal National Forest, which encompass the Abajo Mountains and Elk Ridge, are often overlooked in favor of the lower trails. The following seven trails are highly recommended by forest rangers and the San Juan County Visitor Series.

Loyd's Lake—Developed by the City of Monticello, Loyd's Lake provides a picnic area and a 2-mile hiking trail that is very easy.

Located about 2 miles west of Monticello. From Main St. (US Hwy. 191), turn west onto 200 S. Follow this through the S-turn at the high school and continue west until you cross the cattle guard. Turn left on the first road on the left and proceed to the lake.

Camp Jackson Trail—From US Hwy. 191 about 4 miles north of Blanding, drive west on the north side of Recapture Reservoir on Forest Rd. 084 approximately 14 miles to the southern trailhead of Camp Jackson Trail. The trail climbs northwest for 3.5 miles to the Marvin Tunnel and the intersection with Forest Rd. 079. Going this direction, the trail climbs out of Recapture Canyon, makes its way up the ridge and ends on the side of the mountain. It may be easier to walk it in the opposite direction. In that case, leave Blanding on 100 E. and travel north into the national forest, where the road becomes Forest Rd. 095. Follow this road to the intersection with Forest Rd. 079 and turn northeast onto Forest Rd. 079. Follow this road to the northern trailhead for the Camp Jackson Trail. From here the trail goes 3.5 miles south and east to Forest Rd. 084.

Butler Wash Interpretive Trail

This 1-mile-long loop was developed by the BLM to provide access to the Butler Wash Indian ruins and to interpret the geology and native plants of the area. A free interpretive trail brochure about the site is available at a number of locations in the area, including Edge of the Cedars State Park near Blanding and the Multi Agency Visitor Center in Monticello. There are 20 markers along the trail that identify such plants as prickly pear, yucca, sagebrush, cliffrose, rabbitbrush and Mormon tea. A 20-room, multistory dwelling is the main structure in the Pueblo ruin, which was occupied approximately 700 years ago. These are some of the most interesting and accessible stabilized ruins in the area. To reach the trail, drive south from Blanding on US Hwy. 191 for 3 miles, then turn west onto Hwy. 95 and follow it for 10 miles to the parking area on the north side of the road marked with an "Indian Ruins" rest area sign.

Grand Gulch

Superlatives do not do justice to Grand Gulch. Designated a primitive area by the BLM in 1970, the canyon has no motorized traffic and livestock grazing is no longer allowed. Sitting just below Elk Ridge at an elevation of 6,400 feet, it consists of a main canyon and numerous side canyons that drop 2,700 feet through miles of carved sandstone to meet the beautiful San Juan River far below. Grand Gulch is essentially a 50-mile-long Puebloan museum in one of the most superb outdoor settings anywhere. Secreted away in the canyons are pictographs that decorate south-facing alcoves and other warm exposures. A hiker can spend anywhere from a couple of days to a month or more exploring Grand Gulch, some of the most silent and awe-inspiring places in the Southwest. Most visitors hike in for a day or two, set up camp, explore the surrounding area and return the way they went in. Another option is to hike the entire length of the canyon and arrange for a boat to pick you up at the junction of Grand Gulch with the San Juan River. The latter option is recommended for only the hardiest and best prepared of hikers who can secure an ironclad commitment from friends to make the rendezvous.

One of the largest ruins in the canyon, **Junction Ruins,** is located 4.5 miles from the Kane Gulch trailhead at the junction of the Kane and Grand Gulches and can be visited in a day. There are good camping spots at Junction Ruins, and most hikers plan to stay overnight there or farther down the canyon. Because of the increased use of the canyon, the BLM limits the number of hikers in the canyon. A backcountry permit is required and can be obtained at the **Kane Gulch Ranger Station,** open Mar.–mid-Nov., or at the **Bureau of Land Management, San Juan Resource Area Office, 435 N. Main, Monticello; 435-587-1500.** These locations are very helpful with additional information about conditions. There is a fee for overnight stays and day use. All hikers must sign in at the ranger station, where trail maps—an essential purchase—are available. To reach the Kane Gulch Ranger Station, take Hwy. 95 toward Natural Bridges National Monument and turn south on Hwy. 261. Drive about 4 miles south, then turn left (east) at the sign "Kane Gulch Ranger Station."

Owl Creek and Fish Creek Loop

On the 15.5-mile Fish Creek and Owl Creek Loop, there are many ruins to see and plenty of side canyons to explore. During the 6.5 miles from the trailhead to the junction with Fish Creek, you drop 1,400 feet in elevation, but regain the altitude on the 9-mile hike back up Fish Creek. From the trailhead, follow the rock cairns for 0.25 mile to the edge of Owl Canyon. Climb down over the creamy Cedar Mesa sandstone into the canyon and watch for rock cairns that mark the trail. In Owl Creek about halfway between the trailhead and the junction with Fish Creek is a special feature, **Nevills' Arch.** In Fish Creek, 6 miles up from the junction with Owl Creek, follow the left fork for 0.5 mile to a spring, a good campsite. At the spring, the trail begins a steep climb along the south side of the canyon, with an elevation gain of 600 feet to the top. Once you are on top of the canyon, follow the well-worn trail back to the south for 1.5 miles to the trailhead.

The trailhead is located about 6 miles from the Kane Gulch Ranger Station. Take Hwy. 95 toward Natural Bridges National Monument and turn south on Hwy. 261. In about 4 miles, on the left (east) is the sign "Kane Gulch Ranger Station"; go 1.5 miles past the Kane Gulch Ranger Station, then turn left (east) onto a graded road, which you follow for about 5 miles to the trailhead. Since this area is also administered by the BLM, you can pick up information at the **Kane Gulch Ranger Station,** open Mar.–mid-Nov., or at the **Bureau of Land Management, San Juan Resource Area Office, 435 N. Main, Monticello; 435-587-1500.**

River Rafting

If you would like a river trip that can be made in one or two days, offers some of the most spectacular scenery anywhere and has enough gentle rapids to make the run interesting but not dangerous (unless you happen to be on the river when a flash flood comes through), a float on the San Juan River between Bluff and Mexican Hat is highly recommended. The stretch can be run in a day, but if you have the time, the two-day trip is unforgettable. The extra time allows for stops at Indian rock art, a Puebloan ruin and the ruins of the Barton Trading Post where Amasa M. Barton was murdered in 1887, shortly after the trading post was established at the Rincon Crossing of the San Juan River. Near the Barton Trading Post is the last stretch of the historic Hole-in-the-Rock Trail, the route up San Juan Hill. You can camp across the river from the mouth of Chinle Wash, where you might be treated to an incredibly beautiful and powerful lightning display off to the south on the Navajo Reservation.

For an extended trip, you can continue down the San Juan from Mexican Hat to the Clay Hill Crossing take-out just above Lake Powell. The extended trip (three or four days) takes you through the famous Goosenecks of the San Juan, beneath soaring cliffs and past the mouths of Grand Gulch and other side canyons to the eastern tip of Lake Powell.

Guides

Wild Rivers Expeditions, Inc.—This Bluff outfitter offers a variety of river-running trips on the San Juan and Colorado Rivers. This company has been in the business a long time and offers a thrilling and comfortable river trip. The river guides make a concerted effort to provide insights into the archaeology, history, geology and natural history of the area. **P.O. Box 118, Bluff, UT 84512; 1-800-422-7654; 435-672-2244; www.riversandruins.com.**

Seeing and Doing

Historic Sites

Historic Bluff Houses

As you travel through Bluff, take a few minutes to drive around the town (it really does take only a few minutes!) and note the fine red sandstone houses. You can pick up a free brochure,

Historic Bluff City by Bicycle and on Foot, for a more detailed introduction to the town. The historic Bluff houses were constructed after the original Bluff settlers turned from farming to cattle. The vast rangeland and juniper-clad mesas of southeastern Utah provided excellent grazing for cattle, and lucrative markets in the Colorado mining camps and farther east brought wealth to several Bluff families. The most prominent were the Redds and the Scorups.

Good luck and hard work by the nonprofit Historic Bluff organization have preserved **two log cabins,** which date from the original settlement of Bluff in 1880. The cabins are located across the street west of the Jens Nielson House, and have been stabilized and protected with a separate roof structure. The cabins are, for the most part, constructed of cottonwood logs, which the pioneers found along the San Juan River.

Al Scorup's House—Scorup was a relative latecomer to Bluff, arriving as a 19 year old in 1891, 11 years after the Hole-in-the-Rock pioneers founded the town. Scorup worked as a cowboy for different cattle owners until 1897, when he contracted with several cattle owners to round up missing cattle that were roaming wild in the piñon-juniper forests near Bluff. The young cowboy and his brother collected 2,000 head, for which they were paid $5 each. With their $10,000 they were able to purchase their own herd of cattle and develop one of the most successful cattle operations in southeastern Utah. In 1903 construction began on the Bluff house, located on the eastern side of Bluff facing west.

Jens Nielson House—One of the first red sandstone homes constructed in Bluff, about 1890. It is located in the center of town. Jens Nielson was the quintessential Mormon pioneer. Born in Denmark in 1820, Nielson and his wife joined the Mormon church and immigrated to Utah in 1856, pulling a handcart loaded with supplies for more than 1,100 miles from Iowa to Utah. At age 60, he was the oldest of the Hole-in-the-Rock pioneers and was the bishop of the LDS church in Bluff for 26 years until his death in 1906. He was, in the words of historian Charles S. Peterson, "the glue that held Bluff together in its early years." Located on the corner of **1st N. and 2nd W.**

Lemuel H. Redd Jr. House—Located northwest of the Jens Nielson House on the south side of the street. At 24, Lemuel H. Redd was a much younger member of the 1880 Hole-in-the-Rock group than Jens Nielson. Redd was the most prominent livestock man, religious leader and politician in southeastern Utah until his death in 1923. Redd was a polygamist, and his Bluff house was occupied by his first wife, Eliza Ann Westover and her family. His second wife, Lucy Zina Lyman, lived in a log house across the street until a new house was constructed in 1909. The house is now a private residence. Located near the corner of **1st N. and 2nd W.**

James Bean Decker House—This is the fourth surviving house from Bluff's heyday as a livestock center. Unlike the other sandstone houses, Decker's home was constructed from brick in 1898 and later stuccoed. Decker was also a Hole-in-the-Rock pioneer. He lived in this house until 1900, when a diphtheria epidemic struck the town, killing Decker and four of his seven children. The house has been renovated as a guest house, known as "Pioneer House." **300 E. Mulberry St.**

The Nations of the Four Corners Cultural Center

This center, now run by Utah State University, focuses on four cultures that coexist in southeastern Utah. These include the Ute, Navajo, Hispanic and Anglo cultures, all of which were brought to the area during the last 800 years. The center includes a 0.5-mile trail that takes you to a Navajo hogan, a Ute tepee, a Mexican hacienda, a pioneer log cabin outfitted with wagons and farm implements and an observation tower that offers a spectacular view of the Four Corners area. Call to get information about tours, meals, entertainment and workshops. **707 W. 500 S., Blanding; 435-678-2322.**

Newspaper Rock State Park

Located on the road to the Needles District of Canyonlands National Park, the southwest-facing panel of petroglyphs is one of the best displays of rock art to be found in Utah or anywhere else. Newspaper Rock is worth spending some time to study the more than 350 distinctive inscriptions that were left by the ancient people 800 years ago, as well as other Indians, including the Utes in the 19th century. Hundreds of figures and designs have been "pecked" into the dark desert varnish on the sandstone face over a period of hundreds of years. Some figures are depicted on horseback shooting arrows, an apparent portrayal by Ute Indians, who obtained the horse in the 1600s. Others are more symbolic and stimulate enthusiastic speculation as to their meaning. Remarkably, the rock art has survived with a minimum of vandalism. A small **campground** with 8 campsites is situated across the highway from the rock. Located on Hwy. 211, 12 miles west of US Hwy. 191.

St. Christopher's Episcopal Mission

Father Harold Lieber established St. Christopher's Mission in 1943, and the school and chapel have become an important institution for Utah Navajos. Before bus transportation became the norm for Navajo students, they crossed the San Juan River on a swinging footbridge east of the mission. Visitors are welcome to the mission; located 2 miles east of Bluff on US Hwy. 163. You can still visit the footbridge, which is reached by continuing east past the mission for 1.3 miles, then turning right onto a dirt road for 0.5 mile to the bridge. The Navajo Nation is on the opposite side of the river.

Westwater Ruins

These ruins, which date from the 1200s, are located in Westwater Canyon, along with those known as the Edge of the Cedars Ruins. The Westwater Ruins are southwest of Blanding and can be reached by heading south out of Blanding on US Hwy. 191 for about 1 mile. Take the road on the right that heads west for about 2 miles. At the end of the road, it is a short hike over to the ruins, which are on BLM land.

Museums

Dinosaur Museum

For dinosaur lovers, and that includes almost all children, this nonprofit museum is not to be missed. The museum seeks to stay on the cutting edge of dinosaur research and to offer exhibits and material found nowhere else. At the entrance to the museum are three huge petrified Permian logs that are 275 million years old—predating the dinosaur era by 50 to 100 million years. The logs, found near Canyonlands National Park, are three of only six known logs to exist in North America. The dinosaur track exhibition is a fascinating study of the footprints left by all kinds and sizes of dinosaurs. A unique exhibit is the Hall of Feathered Dinosaurs with reproductions of feathered animals that is an eye-opening introduction into a whole other world of these prehistoric creatures. You will find a nice souvenir for yourself, your children or your grandchildren in the small but tasteful gift shop. Open Apr. 15– Oct. 15. Mon–Sat. 9 A.M.–5 P.M. **745 S. 200 W., Blanding; 435-678-3454; www.moab-utah.com/dinosaur/museum.html.**

Scenic Drives

Abajo Loop Scenic Backway

This 22-mile drive offers beautiful alpine scenery and spectacular views of Sleeping Ute Mountain and the La Plata Mountains to the east in Colorado. The La Sal Mountains near Moab to the north are also visible. The high-country, single-lane, dirt-and-gravel road reaches nearly 9,000 feet in elevation as it approaches the heights of the 11,000-foot Abajos, the Blue Mountains. High-clearance vehicles are recommended. The road is impassable in winter and after heavy rains. The road loops between Monticello and Blanding west of US Hwy. 191. From Monticello, head west into the mountains and turn left (south) on Forest Rd. 079, which climbs over the mountains and then descends to Blanding.

Bluff through Monument Valley Scenic Byway/US Hwy. 163

This drive takes you literally through the heart of the West. From the time you cross the San Juan River at Mexican Hat, you are on the Navajo Reservation. The 45-mile stretch of US Hwy. 163 from Bluff to the Arizona border is designated a Utah Scenic Byway; however, you will want to continue another 25 miles into Arizona and go as far as Kayenta, so that you can see all of Monument Valley and spend a little time in one of the major towns on the Navajo Reservation (see the Major Attractions section).

The Moki Dugway Scenic Backway

From Hwy. 361 north of the turnoff for Goosenecks of the San Juan State Park, 5 miles north of Mexican Hat, continue north on Hwy. 261 for the 37-mile drive over the Moki Dugway Scenic Backway. Early white settlers referred to the Hopi and prehistoric Indians as "Moki," and this road, like others in the region, follows an ancient Indian trail. The 3 miles of steep gravel switchbacks of the Dugway climb 1,000 feet to the top of Cedar Mesa for a breathtaking view of Monument Valley to the south and the Valley of the Gods to the northeast. This can be a white-knuckle ride for some, but the view is worth it. Hwy. 261 connects with Hwy. 95 a couple of miles east of Natural Bridges National Monument; Blanding is 42 miles to the east.

Squaw Flats Rd. Scenic Byway/Hwy. 211

The Squaw Flats Rd. provides access to Newspaper Rock and the Needles District of Canyonlands National Park. The 35-mile-long road passes through sheer red sandstone walls along Indian Creek. This is a favorite area for rock climbers. The Scenic Byway begins 14 miles north of Monticello from US Hwy. 191 and heads southwest. In 12 miles the road reaches Newspaper Rock (see the Historic Sites section), then turns north.

Eight miles from Newspaper Rock is the privately owned Dugout Ranch, one of the oldest cattle ranches in the region. It was headquarters for the Indian Creek Cattle Company and is still a working ranch. In 1919 Al Scorup purchased the ranch as part of his cattle enterprise. Later the ranch was acquired by another Bluff rancher, Charles Redd. Current owner Heidi Redd has provided for the preservation of the ranch through a conservation easement. The road continues another 15 miles to the northwest, past South Six Shooter Peak and North Six Shooter Peak, which rise more than 1,000 feet above their bases, to the entrance to Canyonlands National Park (see the **Canyonlands National Park** chapter).

Trail of the Ancients Scenic Byway / Hwy. 95

If you spend any time at all in southeastern Utah, there is a good chance that you will travel over portions, if not all, of Hwy. 95 between Hanksville on the west at Hwy. 24 and Blanding at the eastern end at US Hwy. 191. When the last segment of this road was completed in 1976, it was named the Bicentennial Highway to commemorate the 200th anniversary of American independence. The road connects Capitol Reef National Park and Natural Bridges National Monument, and leads to Canyonlands National Park, Hovenweep National Monument and three of Lake Powell's four major marinas: Hite, Halls Crossing and Bullfrog. The volcanic Henry Mountains, the last mountain range to be named in the United States, rise to the right of the highway. While the entire 125-mile drive from Hanksville to Blanding can take more than a day, with stops at all the possible places, it can also be made in 3–4 hours with one or two brief stops.

About 30 miles south of Hanksville, you reach the junction with Hwy. 276, which leads to Bullfrog Marina at Lake Powell, 45 miles away (see the **Lake Powell** chapter). Continuing east on Hwy. 95, you pass Hog Springs Campground, which offers picnic facilities, before you reach Lake Powell and the beautiful Hite Bridge, about 20 miles from the northern junction with Hwy. 276. For many people, this is the first glimpse of Lake Powell, and it is unforgettable. Stop at the Lake Powell Overlook to take pictures and enjoy the contrast of the red sandstone with the blue waters of the lake.

After crossing the bridge, you reach Hite Marina, and then follow White Canyon to Natural Bridges National Monument. Between Hite Marina and Natural Bridges on Hwy. 95 is Fry Canyon Lodge where a good, plain outpost meal is available as well as lodging and camping (see the Where to Stay section). As you continue east to Blanding, look to the left to see the Bears Ears on the mountain, an important and highly visible landmark to early travelers in the area.

At about 35 miles from Hite Crossing, you reach the second junction with Hwy. 276, which leads to Hall's Crossing at Lake Powell, 40 miles away. In about 8 miles, you reach the turnoff to Natural Bridges National Monument, Hwy. 275, to the left. In 2 miles you reach the junction with Hwy. 261, which heads to the south 33 miles to US Hwy. 163 at Mexican Hat. A few miles east of the entrance to Natural Bridges National Monument, Hwy. 95 becomes the northern segment of the multistate driving tour called Trail of the Ancients Loop, and along this 30-mile stretch travelers can visit prehistoric Indian ruins at Mule Canyon and Butler Wash (see the Hiking section under Outdoor Activities).

Valley of the Gods Scenic Loop

The Valley of the Gods is inhabited by fanciful rock formations. An 18-mile scenic loop road winds through the valley and is passable by highway vehicles if the weather is clement and if the driver is comfortable with native-surface roads. From US Hwy. 163 approximately 10 miles southwest of Bluff, turn right (north) to enter the valley; the road exits at Hwy. 261 6 miles northwest of the intersection of Hwy. 261 with US Hwy. 163.

Where to Stay

Accommodations

Motel and bed and breakfast accommodations can be found in Monticello, Blanding, Bluff, Montezuma Creek, Mexican Hat and Monument Valley. Rooms can be difficult to find during the heavy tourist season—late spring to early fall—

so it is a good idea to make reservations beforehand.

BLANDING

Best Western Gateway Motel—$$

One of the oldest motels in southeastern Utah, it was built in at least three stages. Older rooms are usually available at a lower price. Outdoor heated pool and playground. Located on the south side of US Hwy. 191 as it winds through Blanding. **88 E. Center; 1-800-528-1234; 435-678-2278.**

Comfort Inn—$$ to $$$

Some of the 52 rooms have suites or kitchenettes. Indoor pool, hot tub and exercise room. Complimentary continental breakfast available next door at the Old Tymer Restaurant. **711 S. Main; 1-800-622-3250; 435-678-3271.**

Four Corners Inn—$$$

Thirty-two rooms. Homestead Restaurant is next door. **131 E. Center; 1-800-574-3150; 435-678-3257.**

Rogers House Bed and Breakfast—$$ to $$$

Pete and Charlotte Black have turned a 1915 stucco house into a bright and cheerful four-room inn. **412 S. Main St.; 1-800-355-3932; 435-678-3932; www.rogershouse.com.**

BLUFF

Desert Rose Inn—$$ to $$$

Some of the 40 units are individual cabins. **701 W. US Hwy. 191, P.O. Box 148, Bluff, UT 84512; 1-888-475-7673; 435-672-2217; www.desertrose.com.**

Pioneer House Inn—$$$

Located in the 1898 James B. Decker House (see the Historic Sites section under Seeing and Doing), this inn has five suites with one to three bedrooms. There are private entrances, private baths and kitchenettes. A hearty breakfast is provided by hosts Thomas Rice and Kelly McAndrews, who are also excellent guides to the surrounding area. **300 E. Mulberry St., P.O. Box 219, Bluff, UT 84512; 1-888-637-2582; 435-672-2446; www.pioneerhouseinn. com.**

Recapture Lodge—$$

Bluff's oldest lodge/motel; 28 rooms; heated pool. **P.O. Box 309, Bluff, UT 84512; 435-672-2281; www.llamapack/com/recap_ld.htm.**

FRY CANYON/HWY. 95

Fry Canyon Lodge—$$ to $$$

This place started out as an oasis for uranium miners in the 1950s; now the cafe serves mostly travelers along the Bicentennial Highway and is the only building along the 125-mile stretch between Hanksville and Blanding. The cafe still maintains much of the character of its beginnings as a 1950s desert outpost. If you want to spend a few days away from just about everything but magnificent scenery, book one of the six rooms available at the lodge. Also on-site are a general store, gas, campsites and showers. Located on Hwy. 95 about 55 miles west of Bluff. **435-259-5334; www.frycanyon.com.**

LA SAL

La Sal Mountain Guest Ranch—$$ to $$$$

The heart of this guest ranch is the original La Sal Mountain Ranch founded in 1914 by Charles Redd, one of Utah and the West's most famous cattlemen. Charles Redd was born in Bluff in 1889, nine years after the Hole-in-the-Rock expedition arrived to settle on the San Juan River. His father, Lemuel H. Redd, was one of the leaders of the expedition and the early Bluff settlement (see the Historic Sites section under Seeing and Doing). Charles Redd died in 1976; however, his family continues to operate the historic ranch as both a guest and working cattle ranch. The complex has seven homes and cabins. A full breakfast is provided. Located in the center of La Sal on Hwy. 46. **1-888-870-1088; 435-686-2223; www.moab-canyonlands.com/mtranch.**

MEXICAN HAT

All of the motels in Mexican Hat are located along Hwy. 163. It is a very small place with no street addresses.

Burch's Trading Co. and Motel—$$

Forty-one rooms. 435-683-2221.

Canyonlands Motel—$$

A small but serviceable motel; 10 rooms. 435-683-2230.

Mexican Hat Lodge—$$

Ten rooms and one tepee. Evening steak fry. 435-683-2222.

San Juan Inn—$$

Thirty-six units. Located along a cliff above the north side of the San Juan River. The adjacent Olde Bridge Bar and Grille is part of the complex (see the Where to Eat section). **P.O. Box 535, Mexican Hat, UT 84531; 1-800-447-2022; 435-683-2220.**

Valley of the Gods Bed and Breakfast—$$$

If you want to get away from it all, the Valley of the Gods Bed and Breakfast at the Lee Ranch is an ideal place. Located between Monument Valley, the San Juan River, Grand Gulch and Natural Bridges National Monument, there are plenty of activities and tours that can be arranged. The rustic old stone ranch house has been renovated to function on a solar-powered system. The broad front porch provides a panoramic view of the Valley of the Gods. The original structure was built about 1935 and was renovated by Claire and Gary Dorgan as a bed and breakfast several years ago. There are four rooms, including the root-cellar suite. All have private baths. Open year-round. Located just off Hwy. 261. **P.O. Box 310307, Mexican Hat, UT 84531; 970-749-1164; www.zippitydodah.com/vog/default.htm.**

MONTICELLO

Best Western Wayside Inn—$$$

Some of the 38 rooms are nonsmoking. Heated pool and whirlpool. **195 E. US Hwy. 666, P.O. Box 669, Monticello, UT 84535; 1-800-528-1234; 435-587-2261.**

Canyonlands Motor Inn—$$ to $$$

Thirty-two rooms. **197 N. Main, P.O. Box 1142, Monticello, UT 84535; 435-587-2266.**

Days Inn—$$ to $$$

Largest motel in Monticello; 43 rooms. Heated indoor pool and whirlpool. **549 N. Main, P.O. Box 759, Monticello, UT 84535; 1-800-325-2525; 435-587-2458.**

The Grist Mill Inn Bed and Breakfast— $$ to $$$

Nine guest rooms, all nonsmoking and with private bathrooms, in the old Monticello Flour Mill. The mill was constructed in 1933 after a fire destroyed Monticello's original flour mill. Six of the rooms are located in the mill and three in the mill's granary. There is a Jacuzzi, an outside deck, a main-floor sitting room with a fireplace, a second-floor TV room and a third-floor library. Operated by Glen and Phyllis Swank. **64 S. 300 E., P.O. Box 156, Monticello, UT 84535; 1-800-645-3762; 435-587-2597; www.bnblist.com/ut/grist-mill/.**

MONUMENT VALLEY
Firetree Bed and Breakfast—$$$

A unique lodging experience in an authentic one-room Navajo hogan built of juniper logs and earth. There's a modern bed inside and a modern bathroom located a short distance from the hogan. A continental breakfast is provided. Call for directions. **435-727-3228; www.natureworksbooks.com/hogan/html.**

Goulding's Trading Post and Lodge— $$ to $$$

Some of the 62 rooms offer a panoramic view of Monument Valley; most rooms have a refrigerator. The original trading post was established by Harry Goulding and his wife, Mike, in 1923 and remained under their ownership for 40 years. The original trading post, a flat-roofed structure of locally quarried sandstone blocks, is now a museum and has been listed in the National Register of Historic Places. Heated indoor pool. Slide show and tours of Monument Valley available for a fee. This is a popular stop for international tour groups, so don't be surprised if they are booked full. Located just inside the Utah–Arizona border 2 miles west of US Hwy. 163.

P.O. Box 1, Monument Valley, UT 84536; 1-800-874-0902; 435-727-3231; www.gould-ings.com.

Camping

PRIVATE
Blanding
Blue Mountain RV Park—Twenty-six sites with complete hookups, and 15 tentsites. Drinking water, toilets, showers and dump site. Open year-round. Located south of Blanding. **1888 S. US Hwy. 191; 435-678-2570.**

Kampark—Fifty-three sites with complete hookups, and 16 tentsites. Drinking water, toilets, showers and a laundry. Open year-round. Located south of Blanding on US Hwy. 191. **861 S. Main; 435-678-2770.**

Bluff
Cadillac Ranch RV Park—Twenty sites, 15 with complete hookups, plus 15 tentsites. Toilets, showers and laundry. Open year-round. Located on US Hwy. 191. **435-672-2262.**

Cottonwood RV Park—Forty-two RV sites, all with complete hookups, and 14 tentsites. Drinking water, flush toilets and dump site. Open year-round. Located on US Hwy. 191. **435-672-2287.**

Mexican Hat/Monument Valley
Goulding's Good Sam Park—Offers 66 RV sites, all with complete hookups, and 50 tentsites. Toilets, showers, laundry, dump sites and wheelchair-accessible facilities. Open mid-Mar.–Nov. Located near Goulding's Trading Post in Monument Valley. 435-727-3280.

The Navajo Tribal Park—Offers 100 trailer sites, but no hookups; toilets and showers. Open year-round. Located in Monument Valley in Arizona. **602-727-3287.**

Monticello
Bar 'TN RV Campground—Sixteen RV sites with complete hookups, 6 tentsites and a few camping cabins. Drinking water, flush toilets, showers and dump site. Open Mar.–Oct. **348 S. Main; 435-587-1005.**

Mountain View RV Park—Has 29 RV sites with complete hookups, and 6 grassy tentsites, 8 of which have partial hookups. Dump site, toilets, showers and laundry. Open year-round. Located on the north end of Monticello. **632 N. Main; 435-587-2974.**

Westerner RV/Trailer Park—Twenty-eight RV sites with complete hookups; toilets, showers and laundry. Open year-round. **516 S. Main; 435-587-2762.**

PUBLIC
West of Monticello on Blue Mountain are two U.S. Forest Service campgrounds. **Dalton Springs** has 16 RV sites and tentsites; located 5 miles west of Monticello. **Buck Board Campground** has 10 sites; located 6.5 miles west of Monticello. Fee area. Both are open late May–end of Oct.

Devil's Canyon, is the largest public campground in the area, with 33 RV trailer sites and tentsites. Fee area. Open mid-May–Oct. Located approximately halfway between Blanding and Monticello on US Hwy. 191.

Sand Island Campground, operated by the BLM, has 25 sites, used primarily by rafters on the San Juan River. Fee area. Located at Bluff.

The BLM also maintains two campgrounds on the Anticline/Needles Overlook road off US Hwy. 191 about 15 miles northwest of Monticello. **Windwhistle** has 30 sites; located 27.5 miles northwest of US Hwy. 191. **Hatch Point** has 14 sites; 45 miles off US Hwy. 191. Water is provided. Both require fees.

At **Newspaper Rock State Park,** there are 8 tentsites. No fee. Located on Hwy. 211, about 15 miles northwest of Monticello and 12 miles west on Hwy. 211.

Where to Eat

BLANDING

The Homestead Steakhouse—$$ to $$$
Owned and operated by Sharon and Gary Guymon. Offers steaks, fish, soups and a salad bar and tasty desserts. Gary is a lifelong resident of

Blanding and a retired school teacher with a special interest in the history of the area. Open for breakfast, lunch and dinner. **121 E. Center; 435-678-3456.**

The Old Tymer Restaurant—$$ to $$$

Has an interesting collection of local artifacts and photographs as an added bonus to the hearty breakfasts, burgers and sandwiches, steak, prime rib and Mexican dinners. Located just south of the Comfort Inn. **733 S. Main; 435-678-2122.**

BLUFF
Cottonwood Steakhouse—$$ to $$$

Offers steak, barbecued chicken and ribs; both inside and outside dining available. Located on US Hwy. 191. **435-672-2282.**

Cow Canyon Trading Post Restaurant—$$

The Cow Canyon Trading Post Restaurant is an unpretentious building that is home to one of the best eating establishments in southeastern Utah. Operated by Liza Doran since 1987, she combines her understanding of what makes a good restaurant with the culinary skills of local Navajo cooks. A variety of home-cooked dishes are available—squash blossom stew, lamb kebabs, lemon ginger garlic chicken, chicken teriyaki, lasagna, Navajo–style quiche, ash bread, minted cucumber and bell pepper buttermilk soup, gazpacho and special desserts like peach dumplings. Menus change weekly. Open Apr.–Oct. Thurs.–Mon. 6–9 P.M. Located in an old trading post on the northeast edge of town. **435-672-2208.**

FRY CANYON/HWY. 95
Fry Canyon Lodge—$$ to $$$

In the 1950s, this was the only place within a 10-hour jeep drive where miners, cowboys and travelers could buy a sandwich, a cup of coffee or a cold soda pop. When 3,000 uranium miners and prospectors invaded the area in the 1950s, the establishment is reported to have sold more beer during a two-year period than any other place in Utah. Now the cafe, the only building along the 125-mile stretch between Hanksville and Blanding, serves homemade style dinners. Also on-site are a general store, gas, campsites and showers.

Located on Hwy. 95 about 55 miles west of Bluff. **435-259-5334; www.frycanyon.com.**

MEXICAN HAT
Burch's Trading Company Restaurant— $ to $$

A part of Burch's Motel, this restaurant offers large Western-style breakfasts, steaks and Mexican and Navajo specialties. It operates with a liquor license. Open daily 7 A.M.–10 P.M. Located on US Hwy. 163. **435-683-2221.**

The Olde Bridge Bar and Grille—$ to $$

Mark and Julie Sword came to Mexican Hat in 1975 as Vista volunteers and spent their first year of marriage living in a one-room tent in the nearby Valley of the Gods. They fell in love with the area and acquired the trading post established by Jim Hunt. The original red sandstone trading post functions as a store, while motel rooms and a cafe and bar have been constructed nearby along the north bank of the San Juan River. A sign on a door on the south side of the Old Bridge Bar and Grille reads "Parachute or raft required beyond this point." It was on this part of the San Juan River where Bill Weidman, driving a truck heavily loaded with uranium ore, tried to cross the old cable bridge on June 5, 1953. Bill got halfway across the bridge before it gave way, sending the truck into the San Juan River 50 feet below. Badly shaken, Weidman managed to swim away from the truck; his adventure underscored the need for a new bridge across the San Juan River.

Native American cooks make Navajo tacos and *Haani Gai,* a lamb and hominy stew. There is also beef stew, a vegetarian taco, sandwiches and burgers, steaks and omelettes, pancakes and eggs for breakfast. Open May–Oct. daily 6 A.M.– 9 P.M.; Nov.–Apr. daily 7 A.M.–8 P.M. Located on US Hwy. 163. **435-683-2220.**

MONUMENT VALLEY
The Stagecoach Restaurant—$$

Located as part of the Goulding's Trading Post and Lodge in Monument Valley, the Stagecoach Restaurant offers a dramatic view of the northern end of Monument Valley through large picture windows. The restaurant was clearly constructed with the magnificent view in mind. Offerings at the Stagecoach include omelettes, huevos rancheros, granola, hot oatmeal and two favorites: Mike Goulding's croissant breakfast sandwich (ham and cheese with a fried egg on a warm, buttered croissant roll with breakfast potatoes) and the Duke, named for John Wayne (corned beef hash and eggs with toast or biscuits). Lunch items include burgers, hot beef and turkey sandwiches, beef stew with Navajo fry bread and the Monument Valley specialty, a Navajo taco made with fry bread, a mild beef chili con carne, diced onions, grated cheese, shredded lettuce and ripe tomatoes. Dinner items include steaks, a pasta of the day, fresh stir-fried vegetables and other traditional Anglo-American dishes. Open daily 7 A.M.–10 P.M. Located just north of the Utah-Arizona border, 2 miles west of Hwy. 163. **P.O. Box 1, Monument Valley, UT 84536; 1-800-874-0902; 435-727-3231; www.gouldings.com.**

MONTICELLO

Monticello offers a little variety, with **Burger Barn and Grandma's Kitchen; Los Tachos** east on US Hwy. 666 should handle any cravings for Mexican food that arise. If you want pizza, the **Wagon Wheel Pizza (164 S. Main),** while the only choice, is still a good one with pizza made from scratch.

Lamp Light Restaurant—$$ to $$$

For steak and fish dinners served with home-baked bread, this is a local favorite with an excellent salad bar in addition to soup and sandwiches, plus prime rib, filet mignon, sirloin, rib-eye, New York and T-bone steaks. Open Wed.–Sat. 4–11 P.M. **655 E. Central; 435-587-2170.**

MD Ranch Cookhouse—$$ to $$$

Hearty breakfasts, burgers and sandwiches for lunch, and steaks, chicken and trout for dinner. The 8-ounce buffalo steak is the highest-priced item on the menu. Live music on Fri.–Sat. nights. **380 S. Main; 435-587-3299.**

Services

Visitor Information

Edge of the Cedars State Park—640 W. 400 N., P.O. Box 788, Blanding, UT 84511; 435-678-2238; parks.state.ut.us/www1/edge. htm.

Monument Valley Visitor Center—At the southern end of the county, the Navajo Nation provides information about accommodations, tours and events on the Navajo Reservation. Located just south of the Utah-Arizona border a few miles east of US Hwy. 163. **602-727-3287.**

Multi-Agency Visitor Center—Operated jointly by the U.S. Forest Service, the Bureau of Land Management, the National Park Service, Canyonlands Natural History Association and San Juan County Visitor Services. The center carries brochures, maps and publications for sale, and provides information about southern Utah and the Four Corners region. Open year-round Mon.–Fri. 8 A.M.–5 P.M.; Apr.–Oct. Mon.–Fri. 8 A.M.–5 P.M., Sat.–Sun. and holidays 10 A.M.–5 P.M. Located in the San Juan County Courthouse. **117 S. Main, Monticello; 1-800-574-4386; 435-587-3235.**

San Juan County Visitor Services—P.O. Box 490, Monticello, UT 84535; 1-800-574-4386; 435-587-3235; www.southeastutah-com.

Lake Powell

Lake Powell, named for 19th-century explorer and scientist Maj. John Wesley Powell, was conceived on October 15, 1956, in Washington, D.C., when President Dwight D. Eisenhower pushed a button on his desk in the White House, setting off the first blast in the construction of the Glen Canyon Dam. By March 13, 1963, the new dam had begun to impound the waters that would eventually lead to the 1,960 miles of shoreline that form Lake Powell. Glen Canyon

Dam is located 8 miles into Arizona. The 710-foot-high dam has created a lake of 250 square miles that extends 186 miles up the former channel of the Colorado River and 72 miles up the San Juan River, a tributary of the Colorado, while filling more than 100 side canyons of both rivers.

The lake provides access to hundreds of miles of previously inaccessible canyons and scenery that only Native American inhabitants, a few river-runners and cowboys had been able to reach. Now 3 to 4 million visitors a year enjoy the many recreational opportunities offered by the lake, with more than a half million visitors at the lake on Labor Day weekend alone. "Powell" is the most popular water recreation destination for Utahns. Annual family outings and reunions have become a recent tradition and, during the summer, each weekend sees long convoys of trucks and trailers headed toward the lake from all over the state. The magnificent scenery is the primary attraction, but for water-sports enthusiasts, Lake Powell warms up faster and reaches a higher summer water surface temperature, around 80° F, than any other lake in the state.

Even before its construction, critics argued that the lake was a mistake because the silt-laden waters of the Colorado and San Juan Rivers would be deposited into it, creating a gigantic sandbox within a few decades. Scientists recognize that thousands of tons of sediment are being deposited into the lake each year, but hedge their bets as to just how long it will take for the lake to fill up. The "best" educated guess is somewhere between 400 and 700 years. Opponents still call for the dam to be demolished, the lake drained and the land restored to its previous character and beauty. The Glen Canyon Dam was built to meet five objectives: to store water, to control floods, for irrigation, to generate hydroelectric power and to regulate the Colorado River.

Highway access to the lake is possible at only three locations on the river: on Hwy. 95 at Hite Marina; on Hwy. 276—at Bullfrog Marina on the west side and at Hall's Crossing Marina on the east; and on US Hwy. 89 at Wahweap Marina just across the Utah–Arizona border. Lake Powell is located within the Glen Canyon National Recreation Area, a 1.2-million-acre reserve established by Congress on October 27, 1972, to manage the recreational, historical, cultural and scenic resources of the area. The recreation area includes Rainbow Bridge National Monument, which was established by President William H. Taft in 1910. Both the recreation area and the national monument are administered by the National Park Service.

Private boats are used by most visitors to the lake, but boat rentals, including houseboats, are available at the four marinas, and tour boats operate daily from Wahweap and Bullfrog Marinas. At the southern end of the lake, visitors will not want to miss a tour of the Glen Canyon Dam or a visit to Historic Lee's Ferry, located on the Colorado River just below the dam.

History

One of the great tradeoffs in the construction of Lake Powell is that while hundreds of miles of scenic landscape and recreation potential were opened to easy access, thousands of prehistoric and historic sites were inundated by the lake's waters. During construction of the dam, the Bureau of Reclamation contracted with University of Utah archaeology professor Jesse Jennings and history professors Gregory Crampton and David Miller to document the innumerable archaeological and historical sites that would disappear as the lake filled.

Two places sacred to the Navajo were also victims of the new lake. One, the confluence of the San Juan and Colorado Rivers, is where "the water children of the cloud" and "the rain people" were created by two Navajo deities. The other, Rainbow Bridge, the largest natural bridge in the world, is sacred as symbolic of male and female holy beings who created clouds, rainbows and moisture. The lake has caused both sites to be desecrated and they are no longer used for worship.

But long before these sites became sacred to the Navajo, the canyons of the Colorado and San Juan Rivers were occupied by prehistoric peoples dating back to about 9,000 years ago. Like the rest of southeastern Utah, the primary occupants were the Anasazi, who were here for 2,000 years but reached the apex of their culture between A.D. 900 and A.D. 1300. The Anasazi left numerous cliff dwellings, storage granaries and rock art panels in the canyons of the Colorado, many of which were inundated by the lake, but some can still be seen in the side canyons off the main channel of the lake.

The Spanish padres Francisco Atanasio Dominguez and Silvestre Velez de Escalante also left their mark on history as reflected in these canyon walls. In 1776 they made their way back to Santa Fe via the Crossing of the Fathers, just north of the present Utah–Arizona border, after their unsuccessful attempt to reach California. Padre Bay, Dominguez Butte, the Escalante River and the Crossing of the Fathers all commemorate this important expedition.

The Crossing of the Fathers was used by other travelers from New Mexico, including Antonio Armijo and the 31 men of his trading party en route to California in Dec. 1829. To the north, in Cataract Canyon, the fur trapper Denis Julien was one of the first Anglos to leave his inscription on the canyon walls, in 1836.

With the arrival of the Mormons in Utah in 1847, the settlement of the southern Utah communities in the 1850s and the beginning of missionary work among the Hopi Indians by Jacob Hamblin and others in the late 1850s and 1860s, the area around Lee's Ferry and the Crossing of the Fathers became known to early Mormon explorers. As Mormon settlers pushed into northern Arizona in the 1870s, the need for a ferry across the Colorado River led to the establishment of Lee's Ferry in Dec. 1871.

John D. Lee's first ferry trip across the Colorado River was on Jan. 18, 1872, when he took a group of Navajo across the river in a boat belonging to Maj. John Wesley Powell. Powell first traveled the length of what would become Lake Powell during his epic 1869 trip from Green River, Wyoming, through the Grand Canyon. He returned for his second expedition in 1871. Mutual respect and high-level coopera-

tion marked relations between Powell and Mormon frontiersmen like John D. Lee and Jacob Hamblin. Powell's surveys and scientific study of the Colorado River brought national attention to the scenic wonders of southeastern Utah and explained the importance of water and irrigation in the arid West.

Eight years later, 80 miles upriver from Lee's Ferry, Mormon settlers bound for the San Juan River in the corner of southeastern Utah blasted and chiseled their way through a 40-foot cliff and down a treacherous descent known ever since as the Hole-in-the-Rock to establish another crossing of the Colorado River. By the time they moved on to settle Bluff, then Monticello and Blanding, these "Hole-in-the-Rockers" had grown to heroic stature in Mormon and Utah history for their exploits in building a seemingly impossible 180-mile-long wagon road from the town of Escalante to Bluff.

Charles Hall, who had built the ferryboat at the Hole-in-the-Rock, located another crossing of the Colorado River in 1881, upstream from the original crossing. Hall's Crossing is now the middle crossing of Lake Powell.

By the mid-1880s, cattlemen were expanding into the canyons of the Colorado River from both the east and west sides. From the west, small cattle outfits from Kanab, Escalante and Hanksville pushed their livestock into the canyons and onto the mesas. On the east, larger cattle companies like the Bluff Pool, the Elk Mountain Cattle Company, the Scorup Brothers and later the Scorup and Somerville Cattle Company used what rangeland was available east of the Colorado River and north of the San Juan River.

Contemporary with the livestock frontier in southeastern Utah was a gold rush that started in 1883, when prospector Cass Hite arrived on the Colorado River. Some gold was found, and Hite located Dandy's Crossing of the Colorado, now covered by the lake waters. A post office operated at Hite from 1889 to 1914, and during the three decades between 1883 and 1913, hundreds of prospectors hunted for gold along the Colorado and San Juan Rivers. Gold was found, but for the most part it proved too expensive to mine and too powdery to be of great value.

As the gold rush began to subside, tourists began to come to enjoy the magnificent scenery that Powell and colleagues such as Frederick S. Dellenbaugh had written about. The first recreational river trip was in 1909, when Julius Stone and Nathaniel Galloway traveled from Green River, Wyoming, to Needles, California. But river-running was slow to catch on, and it was not until after World War II and the availability of surplus army rubber rafts and a public anxious to ride the river and see the scenery that recreational rafting on the Colorado became big business.

The postwar period saw America refocus on domestic issues, and in the West, no issue continued to be of greater importance than water. A series of agreements between states through which the Colorado River flows led to the completion of a master plan by the Bureau of Reclamation in 1952, which called for the construction of four large dams above Lee's Ferry. Congressional approval for the plan did not come until the spring of 1956; that fall, preliminary work began on Glen Canyon Dam. Diversion tunnels were blasted through the sides of the canyon, and the Colorado River was diverted on Feb. 11, 1959. The pouring of concrete for the dam took more than three years, with the first bucket poured on June 17, 1960, and the last on September 13, 1963. Lake Powell started to form on March 13, 1963, but it took until June 22,

Getting There

There are three major highways that reach Lake Powell; however, the three roads are a long way apart. It is about 100 miles between US Hwy. 89 at the southern end of the lake and Hwy. 276, to Bullfrog and Hall's Crossing; it is nearly 50 miles between Hwy. 276 and Hwy. 95 at Hite. **US Hwy. 89 heads east** from Kanab for 65 miles before it crosses the Colorado River via the Glen Canyon Dam, then heads south out of Page through the Navajo Reservation in Arizona. **The middle route,** Hwy. 276 loops south from Hwy. 95 about 30 miles south of Hanksville and rejoins Hwy. 95 to the east about 35 miles west of Blanding; there is no bridge across the river on Hwy. 276, which requires a ferry crossing. **The northern route,** the Bicentennial Highway/Hwy. 95, crosses the lake on the beautiful Hite Crossing Bridge.

The crossing between Bullfrog and Hall's Crossing is on the ferryboat John Atlantic Burr, which can hold a maximum of eight cars, two buses and 150 passengers. The crossing takes about a half hour, and there is a charge. The ferry normally operates year-round, with departures beginning at 8 A.M. from Hall's Crossing and returning from Bullfrog at 9 A.M., then continuing on the hour. The last departure from Bullfrog is at 7 P.M. during the summer season (mid-May–mid-Oct.) and 3 P.M. during the winter months. Today the ferry is the only commercially operating ferry in the state. Be prepared for some delays, especially during the heavy travel season.

Most visitors traveling from Salt Lake City and the Wasatch Front take Interstate 15 to Spanish Fork, then join US Hwy. 6 from Exit 261 and follow that highway to its junction with Interstate 70, just west of Green River. After just 8 miles west on Interstate 70, exit onto Hwy. 24 (Exit 147) and take it south to Hanksville, then continue south out of Hanksville on Hwy. 95. About 30 miles south of Hanksville, you reach the junction with Hwy. 276, which most Lake Powell-bound travelers take to reach the larger Bullfrog Marina. If you stay on Hwy. 95, you will reach the bridge and marina at Hite, on the east side of the lake. The distance from Salt Lake City to Bullfrog is about 300 miles; to Hite about 280 miles. The drive from Salt Lake City to the southern end of the lake, via Interstate 15 and US Hwy. 89, is nearly 400 miles.

1980, to first reach the high-water mark of 3,700 feet.

Beginning in 1996, authorities experimented with releasing large volumes of water from Lake Powell in the spring to re-create the natural spring runoff cycle. Indications are that this is very good for the environment downriver as it helps reestablish beaches and has other positive effects. As an explorer, reclamationist and conservationist, Powell is one of Utah's heroes, and the naming of Lake Powell in his honor has only added to his stature.

Major Attractions

Lee's Ferry

If John D. Lee had not won fame as the scapegoat for the tragic 1857 Mountain Meadows Massacre, he would have become famous for establishing a ferry across the Colorado River just below Glen Canyon. Strangely enough, though the one event led to the other, if it hadn't been for the Mountain Meadows Massacre and the threat of arrest, it is doubtful that Lee would have ever left his prosperous farms and ranches in southwestern Utah to establish a ferry at what his 17th wife, Emma, would call "Lonely Dell."

The request for Lee to establish the ferry came from his old friend Brigham Young, as he began preparations for a series of Mormon settlements in northern Arizona. The settlements became a reality in 1873 and, until the Navajo Bridge was completed across the Colorado River 5 miles downstream in 1929, Lee's Ferry linked hundreds of Arizona Mormons with the St. George Temple and the Mormon capital of Salt Lake City. Lee's Ferry was so remote that Lee was safe as long as he remained there; but when he returned to the Mormon settlements, he was apprehended while visiting his family in Panguitch. After Lee's arrest, the Mormon church continued to operate the ferry until 1909. In 1910 it was acquired by Coconino County to ensure its continued operation.

The ferry site, two log buildings reportedly built by John D. Lee, a cemetery dating from 1874, segments of the pioneer road and other historic artifacts, now comprise the Lee's Ferry Historic Site, which is administered by the National Park Service as part of the Glen Canyon National Recreation Area. Lee's Ferry is also the starting point for river trips through Marble Canyon and the Grand Canyon.

To reach Lee's Ferry, drive south from Page, Arizona, on US Hwy. 89 for 23 miles to its junction with US Hwy. 89A, then turn right and follow US Hwy. 89A north for 13 miles to Navajo Bridge. On the western side of the bridge, watch for the road that heads north to Lee's Ferry. There are a couple of motels, restaurants and gas stations just beyond the turnoff.

Rainbow Bridge National Monument

You have not really been to Lake Powell until you have left the main channel to wind your way through Forbidding Canyon into Rainbow Bridge Canyon and have stood in awe before the largest, most symmetrical and most beautiful natural bridge in the world. The bridge rises 290 feet above Bridge Creek and spans 270 feet. The narrowest section of the bridge is 32 feet thick. The beautiful salmon-colored Navajo sandstone contrasts vividly with the dark bulk of 10,000-foot-high Navajo Mountain. This sacred mountain watches over the bridge like a colossal sentinel, while the 1,000-foot-high walls of the canyon envelop the bridge like an oyster shell sheltering a precious pearl.

Rumors of a massive natural bridge that resembled a petrified rainbow and that was sacred to the Navajo and Paiutes were whispered for years, but it was not until 1909 that the first white men viewed Rainbow Bridge. Two expeditions led by Byron Cummings of the University of Utah and William B. Douglass of the U.S. General Land Office joined forces and reached the bridge on Aug. 14, 1909, thanks to explorer John Wetherill and their two Paiute guides, Nasja Begay and Jim Mike. Less than a year later, President William H. Taft established the 160-acre Rainbow Bridge National Monument on May 30, 1910. Former president Theodore Roosevelt visited the bridge in 1913 and recorded that, during the moonlit night, he awoke several times to gaze in awe at the natural wonder. Until the 1960s, all visitors wishing to view the bridge had to make a tortuous overland pack trip around Navajo Mountain or a dangerous raft trip down the Colorado River through Cataract Canyon, and then an exhausting hike several miles up the canyon.

But the waters of Lake Powell, which extend under the bridge when the lake is at or near capacity, allow boaters to come within a few hundred yards of the bridge. You can now tie your boat to a floating dock and follow the well-worn 0.25-mile path to the bridge. If you don't have your own boat, you can still visit Rainbow Bridge on one of the tour boats that leave regularly from Wahweap Marina.

Until recently, visitors to the bridge could walk up under and through the landmark. In 1995 the National Park Service erected a 2-foot rock wall along the trail approaching the bridge and revised its brochure, suggesting that visitors "approach and visit Rainbow Bridge as you would a church." On the 2-foot rock wall across the trail, a sign notifies visitors that "American Indians consider Rainbow Bridge a sacred religious site. Please respect their long-standing beliefs. Please do not approach or walk under Rainbow Bridge." These measures were taken in response to complaints from area Indian tribes that visitors walking under the beautiful bridge were desecrating an ancient place of worship. At present only 200 visitors are permitted at the bridge at one time.

The decision by Park Services officials was a compromise. Some Native Americans wanted boats and visitors kept away from Rainbow Bridge altogether. Others argued for a 750-foot boundary and some urged the National Park Service to prohibit alcohol and require visitors to be properly clad. Non-Indians who have visited the site for years claim going under the bridge is a "spiritual experience" that they should not be denied. Other argued that the action put the National Park Service in the position of managing a religious shrine—something that was never envisioned for the National Park Service. The policies, however, are an attempt to follow the guidelines of a 1994 executive order to conduct activities in a "knowledgeable, sensitive manner respectful of tribal rights and sovereignty."

There is no dispute that Rainbow Bridge is a sacred Native American site. When the first Anglos visited the site there was evidence of a religious altar or shrine, and when Theodore Roosevelt visited Rainbow Bridge in 1913 he recorded: "I noticed that the Navajo rode around the outside. His creed bade him never pass under an arch, for the arch is the sign of the rainbow, the sign of the sun's course over the Earth, and to the Navajo is sacred." Some speculate that the natural bridges represent the doorway between life and death.

Rainbow Bridge is located on the south shore about halfway between Glen Canyon Dam and Hall's Crossing. The best way to visit Rainbow Bridge is by boat, either private boat or one of the 5-hour tour boats that operates out of Wahweap Marina. A few hardy souls still make the overland trek from Navajo Mountain, via a hiking trail. **www.nps.gov/rabr.**

Glen Canyon Dam

The **Carl Hayden Visitor Center** at Glen Canyon Dam has a variety of audiovisual exhibits and films on the construction of the dam and the history of the area. A large-scale relief map of the Colorado Plateau helps orient visitors, as well as longtime residents of the Colorado Plateau, to the unusual geography of this unique region. From the visitor center, you can take a 30- to 45-minute self-guided tour of the dam, or during the summer months join one of the guided tours. The visitor center is administered by the National Park Service. Open daily (except Christmas and New Year's Day) 8 A.M.–5 P.M.; extended hours in summer. Located 2 miles north of Page, Arizona, on the western side of the dam. **P.O. Box 1507, Page, AZ 86040; 520-608-6404.**

Outdoor Activities

Though there are land-based activities to be found surrounding Lake Powell, they are described elsewhere (see the **San Juan County** chapter; see also the **Escalante** and **Kanab** chapters in the South-Central Region). Here, on the lake and its shoreline, it's all about the water.

Boating

Most overnight visitors to Lake Powell either camp along the beaches or sleep on their boats. However, another popular way to experience Lake Powell is onboard a houseboat. Houseboats are slow and difficult to maneuver, and guzzle gas almost as fast as a commercial passenger plane. Yet they provide a kitchen large enough to feed an army, a place to get in out of the relentless sun, sleeping accommodations for a whole tribe and a dock for a motorboat that can be used for waterskiing or exploring the narrow canyons of the lake.

Rentals

Lake Powell Resorts and Marinas—Houseboats can be rented at all four sites of this marina—a subsidiary of ARAMARK and concessionaire under arrangement with the National Park Service: Wahweap, Hall's Crossing, Bullfrog and Hite. However, to avoid disappointment, be sure to make your reservations well in advance. Most rentals are for a week, but three-day rentals are possible. Instructions and training films are available for those with no experience but who want to try their hand at navigating the floating houses. The boats range in size from 36-footers that sleep six to 59-footers that sleep 12. **1-800-528-6154 reservations and information; 602-645-2433 Wahweap Marina; 435-684-3000 Bullfrog Marina; www.visitlakepowell.com.**

River Rafting

Guides

Wilderness River Adventures—Offers half-day float trips on the 15-mile stretch of the Colorado River from just below the Glen Canyon Dam to Lee's Ferry, and multi-day rafting tours through the Grand Canyon. **P.O. Box 717, Page, AZ 86040; 520-645-3296; 1-800-992-8022; www.riveradentures.com.**

Seeing and Doing

Historic Sites

Lake Powell has so many access points to historic sites on its shores—including Crossing of the Fathers, Hole-in-the-Rock and Red Canyon—that it is beyond the scope of this book to mention them all.

Museums

John Wesley Powell Museum

This fine regional history museum has exhibits on the area's Native American culture, geology, the Colorado River and Maj. John Wesley Powell and his contributions as a river explorer, scientist and reclamationist. The museum includes a gift shop, and videos on the geography, geology and history of the area are shown upon request. Modest admission fee. Open May–Oct. Mon.–Sat. 8 A.M.–6 P.M., Sun. 10 A.M.–6 P.M.; Nov. and Mar.–Apr. Mon.–Fri. 9 A.M.–5 P.M. Located in Page, Arizona, at Lake Powell Blvd. and N. Navajo Dr. **602-645-9496; www.powellmuseum.org.**

Tours

Boat Tours

Lake Powell Resorts and Marinas—This subsidiary of ARAMARK and concessionaire under arrangement with the National Park Service offers a number of boat tours of Lake Powell from the Wahweap and Bullfrog Marinas. They are an excellent way to see the lake and a good opportunity to rub shoulders with visitors from all over the world. The lower, enclosed section of the boat, with its large windows, offers protection from the wind and sun, while the upper deck puts you in the center of the Lake Powell universe, surrounded by deep-blue skies, blue-green water and red rock. Most tours are a half day or a full day. **1-800-528-6154 reservations and information; 602-645-2433 Wahweap Marina; 435-684-3000 Bullfrog Marina; www.visitlakepowell.com.**

Where to Stay

The Wahweap-Page area at the south end of the lake offers the most accommodations, though lodging is also available at Hite, Hall's Crossing, Bullfrog and Ticaboo, which is on Hwy. 276 11 miles north of Bullfrog Marina.

Accommodations

Summer is the high season at Lake Powell and it is always best to make reservations in advance. The shoulder seasons—Mar.–May in the spring and Sept.–Oct. in the fall—are excellent times to visit Lake Powell because of the more moderate temperatures, fewer people and lower lodging costs.

BULLFROG AND TICABOO
Defiance House—$$$

Situated on a bluff overlooking Lake Powell at the Bullfrog Marina; 48 rooms. The Anasazi Restaurant is located at the lodge. Located at the south end of Hwy. 276. **1-800-528-6154; 435-684-3000.**

Ticaboo Lodge—$$$

Swimming pool; 70 rooms. Restaurant and lounge. Open Apr.–Oct. Located at Ticaboo about 11 miles north of Bullfrog Marina on Hwy. 276. **1-800-987-5253; 435-788-2110.**

HALL'S CROSSING
Hall's Crossing Family Units—$$$ to $$$$

Twenty units. Located at Hall's Crossing Marina at the northern end of Hwy. 276. **1-800-528-6154; 435-684-7000.**

HITE
Hite Family Units—$$$ to $$$$

Five units. Located on Hwy. 95 east of Hite at mile marker 49. **1-800-528-6154; 435-684-2278.**

PAGE, ARIZONA

Of any location adjacent to Lake Powell, Page, Arizona, has the largest number of motels, including those of such national chains as Comfort Inn, Days Inn, Econo Lodge, Holiday Inn, Motel 6, Ramada and Super 8. Here are a couple of favorites:

Best Western at Lake Powell—$$$

Heated pool, whirlpool and exercise room; 132 rooms. Restaurants close by. **208 N. Lake Powell Blvd.; 520-645-5988.**

Courtyard by Marriott—$$$ to $$$$

Heated outdoor pool, whirlpool, workout room, gift shop and restaurant; 153 rooms. **600 Clubhouse Dr.; 1-800-851-3855; 520-645-5000.**

WAHWEAP
Wahweap Lodge—$$$

Excellent accommodations in 350 rooms; a number have balconies and patios facing the lake. Two heated pools. The Rainbow Room, a fine restaurant, offers a breathtaking view of the lake through its panoramic semicircular windows. Located at Wahweap Marina, just across the Utah–Arizona state line a few miles west of Page, Arizona. **1-800-528-6154; 602-645-2433.**

Camping

PRIVATE

Concessionaire-operated RV parks **(1-800-528-6154)** with lights, electricity, water, sewer hookups, rest rooms, showers and a coin-operated laundry are located at **Wahweap Marina** (178 sites), **Bullfrog Marina** (86 sites) and **Hall's Crossing Marina** (65 sites). Cost for full hookups varies, depending on the season, with an additional charge for air-conditioning and heater hookups.

The **Ticaboo RV Park (435-788-2212)** has 22 hookups with water, toilets and showers. Open year-round. Located 11 miles north of Bullfrog.

PUBLIC

Most visitors to Lake Powell stay on the lake in houseboats or at shoreline campsites accessible by boat. See the Rentals listing in the Boating section under Outdoor Activities.

Where to Eat

Anasazi Restaurant—$$$

Located in Defiance Lodge. Open daily for breakfast, lunch and dinner. Located at Bullfrog Basin. **435-684-3000.**

Rainbow Room/Wahweap Lodge—
$$ to $$$

With its 270-degree panoramic view of Lake Powell, the Rainbow Room has one of the most spectacular views anywhere. It is worth a visit to the Rainbow Room just for the view. Dinner is an especially nice time with the ever-changing colors on the lake as the sun sets and evening unfolds. If you are going to spend only one day on the lake, dinner at the Rainbow Room seems to enhance the anticipation of the next day's activities. You will find everything from typical western breakfasts to sandwiches, steaks and seafood.

Open in the summer daily 6 A.M.–10 P.M.; the rest of the year daily 7 A.M.–9 P.M. Located at Wahweap Marina. **602-645-2433.**

Services

Visitor Information

Carl Hayden Visitor Center—Provides good advice about hiking, camping and other recreational activities. Includes a bookstore that is operated by the Natural History Association has maps, hiking guides and area history books. Open during the summer daily 7 A.M.–7 P.M.; other months daily 8 A.M.–5 P.M. Located at the south end of the lake at Glen Canyon Dam. **Glen Canyon National Recreation Area, P.O. Box 1507, Page, AZ 86040; 520-608-6404.**

Index